te Gargano
ele

Trani
Invenatium
vino   Bari

A   Monopoli

P U L I A

ntepiloso
R. Bradano   Matera
Brindisi

Tarentum

Otranto

Marcangelo

Gallipoli

40°

Rossano

A

enza

Cotrone

R I A

eto
a

race

38°

18°

SOUTHERN ITALY
and
SICILY
in the
IXth., Xth. & XIth. Centuries.

English Miles
0   10   20   40   60   80   100

18°

Walker & Boutall sc.

THE DECLINE AND FALL OF THE ROMAN EMPIRE

VOLUME VI

AMS PRESS · NEW YORK

"PALACE OF THE PORPHYROGENITUS," CONSTANTINOPLE; BYZANTINE BUILDING OF THE 13TH CENTURY

THE HISTORY
OF THE
DECLINE AND FALL OF THE
ROMAN EMPIRE

BY

EDWARD GIBBON

EDITED

WITH INTRODUCTION, NOTES, AND APPENDICES

BY

J. B. BURY, D.Litt., LL.D.

CORRESPONDING MEMBER OF THE IMPERIAL ACADEMY OF SCIENCES, ST. PETERSBURG
FELLOW OF KING'S COLLEGE AND REGIUS PROFESSOR OF MODERN HISTORY
IN THE UNIVERSITY OF CAMBRIDGE

IN SEVEN VOLUMES

VOLUME VI

WITH TWENTY ILLUSTRATIONS AND TWO MAPS

METHUEN & CO. LTD.
36 ESSEX STREET W.C.
LONDON
1912

Library of Congress Cataloging in Publication Data
Gibbon, Edward, 1737-1794.
The history of the decline and fall of the Roman Empire.
Reprint of the 1909-14 ed.
1. Rome—History—Empire, 30 B.C.-476 A.D.
2. Byzantine Empire—History.
I. Bury, John Bagnell, 1861-1927, ed.
II. Title.
DG311.G5   1974   937'.06   78-168113
ISBN 0-404-02820-9 (set)

Reprinted by arrangement with Methuen & Company Ltd., London, England
From the edition of 1912, London
First AMS edition published in 1974
Manufactured in the United States of America
International Standard Book Number: Complete set: 0-404-02820-9
Volume VI: 0-404-02826-8
AMS PRESS INC.
NEW YORK, N.Y. 10003

CONTENTS OF THE SIXTH VOLUME

CHAPTER LII

The Two Sieges of Constantinople by the Arabs—Their Invasion of France, and Defeat by Charles Martel—Civil War of the Ommiades and Abbassides—Learning of the Arabs—Luxury of the Caliphs—Naval Enterprises on Crete, Sicily, and Rome—Decay and Division of the Empire of the Caliphs—Defeats and Victories of the Greek Emperors

CHAPTER LIII

State of the Eastern Empire in the Tenth Century—Extent and Division—Wealth and Revenue—Palace of Constantinople—Titles and Offices—Pride and Power of the Emperors—Tactics of the Greeks, Arabs, and Franks—Loss of the Latin Tongue—Studies and Solitude of the Greeks

CONTENTS OF THE SIXTH VOLUME vii

CHAPTER LIV

Origin and Doctrine of the Paulicians—Their Persecution by the Greek Emperors —Revolt in Armenia, &c.—Transplantation into Thrace—Propagation in the West—The Seeds, Character, and Consequences of the Reformation

CHAPTER LV

The Bulgarians—Origin, Migrations and Settlement of the Hungarians—Their Inroads in the East and West—The Monarchy of Russia—Geography and Trade—Wars of the Russians against the Greek Empire—Conversion of the Barbarians

CHAPTER LVI

The Saracens, Franks, and Greeks, in Italy—First Adventures and Settlement of the Normans—Character and Conquest of Robert Guiscard, Duke of Apulia—Deliverance of Sicily by his Brother Roger—Victories of Robert over the Emperors of the East and West—Roger, King of Sicily, Invades Africa and Greece—The Emperor Manuel Comnenus—Wars of the Greeks and Normans—Extinction of the Normans

CONTENTS OF THE SIXTH VOLUME ix

CHAPTER LVII

The Turks of the House of Seljuk—Their Revolt against Mahmud, Conqueror of Hindostan—Togrul subdues Persia, and protects the Caliphs—Defeat and Captivity of the Emperor Romanus Diogenes by Alp Arslan—Power and Magnificence of Malek Shah—Conquest of Asia Minor and Syria—State and Oppression of Jerusalem—Pilgrimages to the Holy Sepulchre

CHAPTER LVIII

*Origin and Numbers of the First Crusade—Characters of the Latin Princes—
Their March to Constantinople—Policy of the Greek Emperor Alexius—
Conquest of Nice, Antioch, and Jerusalem, by the Franks—Deliverance of the
Holy Sepulchre—Godfrey of Bouillon, first King of Jerusalem—Institutions of
the French or Latin Kingdom*

CHAPTER LIX

Preservation of the Greek Empire—Numbers, Passage, and Event, of the Second and Third Crusades—St. Bernard—Reign of Saladin in Egypt and Syria—His Conquest of Jerusalem—Naval Crusades—Richard the First of England—Pope Innocent the Third; and Fourth and Fifth Crusades—The Emperor Frederic the Second—Louis the Ninth of France; and the two last Crusades—Expulsion of the Latins or Franks by the Mamalukes

CHAPTER LX

Schism of the Greeks and Latins—State of Constantinople—Revolt of the Bulgarians—Isaac Angelus dethroned by his Brother Alexius—Origin of the Fourth Crusade—Alliance of the French and Venetians with the Son of Isaac —Their Naval Expedition to Constantinople—The Two Sieges and final Conquest of the City by the Latins

CHAPTER LXI

Partition of the Empire by the French and Venetians—Five Latin Emperors of the Houses of Flanders and Courtenay—Their Wars against the Bulgarians and Greeks—Weakness and Poverty of the Latin Empire—Recovery of Constantinople by the Greeks—General Consequences of the Crusades

CHAPTER LXII

The Greek Emperors of Nice and Constantinople—Elevation and Reign of Michael Palæologus—His false Union with the Pope and the Latin Church—Hostile Designs of Charles of Anjou—Revolt of Sicily—War of the Catalans in Asia and Greece—Revolutions and Present State of Athens

CHAPTER LXIII

Civil Wars, and Ruin of the Greek Empire—Reigns of Andronicus, the Elder and Younger, and John Palæologus—Regency, Revolt, Reign, and Abdication of John Cantacuzene—Establishment of a Genoese Colony at Pera or Galata— Their Wars with the Empire and City of Constantinople

APPENDIX

(By Editor)

MAPS

ILLUSTRATIONS

(SELECTED BY O. M. DALTON, M.A., F.S.A.)

ILLUSTRATIONS

THE DECLINE AND FALL OF THE ROMAN EMPIRE

VOLUME VI

THE HISTORY

OF THE

DECLINE AND FALL OF THE ROMAN EMPIRE

CHAPTER LII

The two Sieges of Constantinople by the Arabs—Their Invasion of France, and defeat by Charles Martel—Civil War of the Ommiades and Abbassides—Learning of the Arabs —Luxury of the Caliphs—Naval Enterprises on Crete, Sicily, and Rome—Decay and Division of the Empire of the Caliphs—Defeats and Victories of the Greek Emperors

W HEN the Arabs first issued from the desert, they must have been surprised at the ease and rapidity of their own success. But, when they advanced in the career of victory to the banks of the Indus and the summit of the Pyrenees, when they had repeatedly tried the edge of their scymetars and the energy of their faith, they might be equally astonished that any nation could resist their invincible arms, that any boundary should confine the dominion of the successor of the prophet. The confidence of soldiers and fanatics may indeed be excused, since the calm historian of the present hour, who strives to follow the rapid course of the Saracens, must study to explain by what means the church and state were saved from this impending and, as it should seem, from this inevitable danger. The deserts of Scythia and Sarmatia might be guarded by their extent, their climate, their poverty, and the courage of the northern shepherds; China was remote and inaccessible; but the greatest part of the temperate

The limits of the Arabian conquest

zone was subject to the Mahometan conquerors, the Greeks were exhausted by the calamities of war and the loss of their fairest provinces, and the barbarians of Europe might justly tremble at the precipitate fall of the Gothic monarchy. In this inquiry I shall unfold the events that rescued our ancestors of Britain, and our neighbours of Gaul, from the civil and religious yoke of the Koran; that protected the majesty of Rome, and delayed the servitude of Constantinople; that invigorated the defence of the Christians, and scattered among their enemies the seeds of division and decay.

First siege of Constantinople by the Arabs. A.D. 668-675

Forty-six years after the flight of Mahomet from Mecca, his disciples appeared in arms under the walls of Constantinople.[1] They were animated by a genuine or fictitious saying of the prophet, that, to the first army which besieged the city of the Cæsars, their sins were forgiven; the long series of Roman triumphs would be meritoriously transferred to the conquerors of New Rome; and the wealth of nations was deposited in this well-chosen seat of royalty and commerce. No sooner had the caliph Moawiyah suppressed his rivals and established his throne than he aspired to expiate the guilt of civil blood by the success and glory of his holy expedition;[2] his preparations by sea and land were adequate to the importance of the object; his standard

[1] Theophanes places the *seven* years of the siege of Constantinople in the year of *our* Christian æra 673 (of the Alexandrian 665, September 1), and the peace of the Saracens, *four* years afterwards: a glaring inconsistency! which Petavius, Goar, and Pagi (Critica, tom. iv. p. 63, 64) have struggled to remove. Of the Arabians, the Hegira 52 (A.D. 672, January 8) is assigned by Elmacin, the year 48 (A.D. 668, February 20) by Abulfeda, whose testimony I esteem the most convenient and creditable. [Theophanes gives 672-3 as the year of Moāwiya's preparation of the expedition, 673-4 as that of his investment of Constantinople. It seems safest to follow Theophanes here; the Arabic authors say little or nothing of an event which was disgraceful in Mohammadan history. But we cannot accept his statement that the siege lasted seven years; in fact he contradicts it himself, since he places the peace in the fifth year after the beginning of the siege. We have no means of determining with certainty the true duration. Nicephorus (p. 32, ed. de Boor) states that the *war* lasted seven years, and, though he evidently identifies the war with the siege, we may perhaps find here the clue to the solution. The war seems to have begun soon after the accession of Constantine (εὐθύς, Niceph. *ib.*); and perhaps its beginning was dated from the occupation of Cyzicus by Phadalas in 670-1 (Theoph. A.M. 6162), and peace was made in 677-8. Thus we get *seven* years for the duration of the war (671-7), and perhaps three for the siege (674-6).]

[2] For this first siege of Constantinople, see Nicephorus (Breviar. p. 21, 22 [p. 32 ed. de Boor]), Theophanes (Chronograph. p. 294 [A.M. 6165]), Cedrenus (Compend. p. 437 [i. 764, ed. Bonn]), Zonaras (Hist. tom. ii. l. xiv. p. 89 [c. 20]), Elmacin (Hist. Saracen. p. 56, 57), Abulfeda (Annal. Moslem. p. 107, 108, vers. Reiske), d'Herbelot (Bibliot. Orient. Constantin.), Ockley's Hist. of the Saracens, vol. ii. p. 127, 128.

was entrusted to Sophian,[3] a veteran warrior, but the troops were encouraged by the example and presence of Yezid, the son and presumptive heir of the commander of the faithful. The Greeks had little to hope, nor had their enemies any reasons of fear, from the courage and vigilance of the reigning emperor, who [Constantine IV.] disgraced the name of Constantine, and imitated only the inglorious years of his grandfather Heraclius. Without delay or opposition, the naval forces of the Saracens passed through the unguarded channel of the Hellespont, which even now, under the feeble and disorderly government of the Turks, is maintained as the natural bulwark of the capital.[4] The Arabian fleet cast anchor, and the troops were disembarked near the palace of Hebdomon, seven miles from the city. During many days, from the dawn of light to the evening, the line of assault was extended from the golden gate to the eastern promontory, and the foremost warriors were impelled by the weight and effort of the succeeding columns. But the besiegers had formed an insufficient estimate of the strength and resources of Constantinople. The solid and lofty walls were guarded by numbers and discipline; the spirit of the Romans was rekindled by the last danger of their religion and empire; the fugitives from the conquered provinces more successfully renewed the defence of Damascus and Alexandria; and the Saracens were dismayed by the strange and prodigious effects of artificial fire. This firm and effectual resistance diverted their arms to the more easy attempts of plundering the European and Asiatic coasts of the Propontis; and, after keeping the sea from the month of April to that of September, on the approach of winter they retreated fourscore miles from the capital, to the isle of Cyzicus, in which they had established their magazine of spoil and provisions. So patient was their perseverance, or so languid were their operations, that they repeated in the six following summers the same attack and retreat, with a gradual abatement of hope and vigour,

---

[3] [The expedition was first entrusted to Abd ar-Rahmān, but he was killed, and was succeeded by Sofyān.]

[4] The state and defence of the Dardanelles is exposed in the Mémoires of the Baron de Tott (tom. iii. p. 39-97), who was sent to fortify them against the Russians. From a principal actor, I should have expected more accurate details; but he seems to write for the amusement, rather than the instruction, of his reader. Perhaps, on the approach of the enemy, the minister of Constantine was occupied, like that of Mustapha, in finding two Canary birds who should sing precisely the same note.

till the mischances of shipwreck and disease, of the sword and of fire, compelled them to relinquish the fruitless enterprise. They might bewail the loss or commemorate the martyrdom of thirty thousand Moslems, who fell in the siege of Constantinople ; and the solemn funeral of Abu Ayub, or Job, excited the curiosity of the Christians themselves.   That venerable Arab, one of the last of the companions of Mahomet, was numbered among the *ansars*, or auxiliaries, of Medina, who sheltered the head of the flying prophet.   In his youth he fought, at Bedar and Ohud, under the holy standard; in his mature age he was the friend and follower of Ali; and the last remnant of his strength and life was consumed in a distant and dangerous war against the enemies of the Koran.   His memory was revered; but the place of his burial was neglected and unknown, during a period of seven hundred and eighty years, till the conquest of Constantinople by Mahomet the Second.   A seasonable vision (for such are the manufacture of every religion) revealed the holy spot at the foot of the walls and the bottom of the harbour; and the mosque of Ayub has been deservedly chosen for the simple and martial inauguration of the Turkish sultans.[5]

Peace and tribute, A.D. 677   The event of the siege revived, both in the East and West, the reputation of the Roman arms, and cast a momentary shade over the glories of the Saracens.   The Greek ambassador was favourably received at Damascus, in a general council of the emirs or Koreish ; a peace, or truce, of thirty years was ratified between the two empires; and the stipulation of an annual tribute, fifty horses of a noble breed, fifty slaves, and three thousand pieces of gold, degraded the majesty of the commander of the faithful.[6]   The aged caliph was desirous of possessing his dominions, and ending his days, in tranquillity and repose; while the Moors and Indians trembled at his name, his palace and city of Damascus was insulted by the Mardaites, or Maronites, of mount Libanus, the firmest barrier of the empire, till they were disarmed and transplanted by the suspicious policy of the

[5] Demetrius Cantemir's Hist. of the Othman Empire, p. 105, 106.   Rycaut's State of the Ottoman Empire, p. 10, 11.   Voyages de Thévenot, part i. 189.   The Christians who suppose that the martyr Abu Ayub is vulgarly confounded with the patriarch Job, betray their own ignorance rather than that of the Turks.

[6] Theophanes, though a Greek, deserved credit for these tributes (Chronograph. p. 295, 296, 300, 301 [A.M. 6169, 6176]), which are confirmed, with some variation, by the Arabic history of Abulpharagius (Dynast. p. 128, vers. Pocock).

Greeks.[7]   After the revolt of Arabia and Persia, the house of Ommiyah [8] was reduced to the kingdoms of Syria and Egypt; their distress and fear enforced their compliance with the pressing demands of the Christians; and the tribute was increased to a slave, an horse, and a thousand pieces of gold, for each of the three hundred and sixty-five days of the solar year. But as soon as the empire was again united by the arms and policy of Abdalmalek, he disclaimed a badge of servitude not [Abd al-less injurious to his conscience than to his pride; he discontinued Malik. A.D. 685-705] the payment of the tribute; and the resentment of the Greeks was disabled from action by the mad tyranny of the second Justinian, the just rebellion of his subjects, and the frequent change of his antagonists and successors.   Till the reign of Abdalmalek, the Saracens had been content with the free possession of the Persian and Roman treasures, in the coin of Chosroes and Cæsar.   By the command of that caliph, a national mint was established, both of silver and gold, and the inscription of the Dinar, though it might be censured by some timorous casuists, proclaimed the unity of the God of Mahomet.[9] Under the reign of the Caliph Waled, the Greek language and [Walid I. characters were excluded from the accounts of the public revenue.[10] A.D. 705-715] If this change was productive of the invention or familiar use of

---

[7] The censure of Theophanes is just and pointed, τὴν 'Ρωμαικὴν δυναστείαν ἀκρωτηριάσας . . . πάνδεινα κακὰ πέπονθεν ἡ 'Ρωμανια ὑπὸ τῶν Ἀράβων μέχρι τοῦ νῦν (Chronograph. p. 302, 303 [A.M. 6178]).   The series of these events may be traced in the Annals of Theophanes, and in the Abridgment of the Patriarch Nicephorus, p. 22, 24.

[8] These domestic revolutions are related in a clear and natural style, in the second volume of Ockley's history of the Saracens, p. 253-370.   Besides our printed authors, he draws his materials from the Arabic Mss. of Oxford, which he would have more deeply searched, had he been confined to the Bodleian library instead of the [Cambridge] city jail: a fate how unworthy of the man and of his country!

[9] Elmacin, who dates the first coinage A.H. 76, A.D. 695, five or six years later than the Greek historians, has compared the weight of the best or common gold dinar, to the drachm or dirhem of Egypt (p. 77), which may be equal to two pennies (48 grains) of our Troy weight (Hooper's Enquiry into Ancient Measures, p. 24-36) and equivalent to *eight shillings* of our sterling money.   From the same Elmacin and the Arabian physicians, some dinars as high as two dirhems, as low as half a dirhem, may be deduced.   The piece of silver was the dirhem, both in value and weight; but an old though fair coin, struck at Waset, A.H. 88, and preserved in the Bodleian library, wants four grains of the Cairo standard (see the Modern Universal History, tom i. p. 548 of the French translation).   [But see Appendix 2.]

[10] Καὶ ἐκώλυσε γράφεσθαι ἑλληνιστὶ τοὺς δημοσίους τῶν λογοθεσίων κώδικας ἀλλ' [ἐν] 'Αραβίοις αὐτὰ παρασημαινεσθαι χωρὶς τῶν ψήφων, ἐπειδὴ ἀδύνατον τῇ ἐκείνων γλώσσῃ μοναδα, ἢ δυάδα, ἢ τριάδα, ἢ ὀκτὼ ἥμισυ ἢ τρια γράφεσθαι. Theophan. Chronograph. p. 314 [A.M. 6199].   This defect, if it really existed, must have stimulated the ingenuity of the Arabs to invent or borrow.

our present numerals, the Arabic or Indian *cyphers*, as they are commonly styled, a regulation of office has promoted the most important discoveries of arithmetic, algebra, and the mathematical sciences.[11]

Second siege of Constantinople. A.D. 716-718

Whilst the caliph Waled sat idle on the throne of Damascus, while his lieutenants achieved the conquest of Transoxiana and Spain, a third army of Saracens overspread the provinces of Asia Minor, and approached the borders of the Byzantine capital. But the attempt and disgrace of the second siege was reserved

[Sulaiman. A.D. 715-7]

for his brother Soliman, whose ambition appears to have been quickened by a more active and martial spirit. In the revolutions of the Greek empire, after the tyrant Justinian had been punished and avenged, an humble secretary, Anastasius or Artemius, was promoted by chance or merit to the vacant purple. He was alarmed by the sound of war; and his ambassador returned from Damascus with the tremendous news that the Saracens were preparing an armament by sea and land, such as would transcend the experience of the past, or the belief of the present, age. The precautions of Anastasius were not unworthy of his station or of the impending danger. He issued a peremptory mandate that all persons who were not provided with the means of subsistence for a three years' siege should evacuate the city; the public granaries and arsenals were abundantly replenished; the walls were restored and strengthened; and the engines for casting stones, or darts, or fire, were stationed along the ramparts, or in the brigantines of war, of which an additional number was hastily constructed. To prevent is safer, as well as more honourable, than to repel an attack; and a design was meditated, above the usual spirit of the Greeks, of burning the naval stores of the enemy, the cypress timber that had been hewn in mount Libanus, and was piled along the sea-shore of Phœnicia, for the service of the Egyptian fleet. This generous enterprise was defeated by the cowardice or treachery of the troops who, in the

---

[11] According to a new though probable notion, maintained by M. de Villoison (Anecdota Græca, tom. ii. p. 152-157), our cyphers are not of Indian or Arabic invention. They were used by the Greek and Latin arithmeticians long before the age of Boethius. After the extinction of science in the West, they were adopted by the Arabic versions from the original Mss. and *restored* to the Latins about the eleventh century. [There is no doubt that our numerals are of Indian origin (5th or 6th cent.?); adopted by the Arabians about 9th cent. The circumstances of their first introduction to the West are uncertain, but we find them used in Italy in the 13th cent.]

new language of the empire, were styled of the *Obsequian Theme*.[12]
They murdered their chief, deserted their standard in the isle
of Rhodes, dispersed themselves over the adjacent continent,
and deserved pardon or reward by investing with the purple a
simple officer of the revenue. The name of Theodosius might
recommend him to the senate and people; but, after some
months, he sunk into a cloister, and resigned, to the firmer hand
of Leo the Isaurian, the urgent defence of the capital and empire.
The most formidable of the Saracens, Moslemah the brother of [Maslama]
the caliph, was advancing at the head of one hundred and twenty
thousand Arabs and Persians, the greater part mounted on horses
or camels; and the successful sieges of Tyana, Amorium, and
Pergamus were of sufficient duration to exercise their skill and
to elevate their hopes. At the well-known passage of Abydus,
on the Hellespont, the Mahometan arms were transported, for
the first time,[13] from Asia to Europe. From thence, wheeling
round the Thracian cities of the Propontis, Moslemah invested
Constantinople on the land side, surrounded his camp with a
ditch and rampart, prepared and planted his engines of assault,
and declared, by words and actions, a patient resolution of expecting the return of seed-time and harvest, should the obstinacy
of the besieged prove equal to his own. The Greeks would
gladly have ransomed their religion and empire, by a fine or
assessment of a piece of gold on the head of each inhabitant of
the city; but the liberal offer was rejected with disdain, and
the presumption of Moslemah was exalted by the speedy approach and invincible force of the navies of Egypt and Syria.
They are said to have amounted to eighteen hundred ships;
the number betrays their inconsiderable size; and of the twenty
stout and capacious vessels, whose magnitude impeded their pro-

---

[12] In the division of the *Themes*, or provinces described by Constantine Porphyrogenitus (de Thematibus, l. i. p. 9, 10 [p. 24-26, ed. Bonn]), the *Obsequium*, a
Latin appellation of the army and palace, was the fourth in the public order.
Nice was the metropolis, and its jurisdiction extended from the Hellespont over the
adjacent parts of Bithynia and Phrygia (see the two maps prefixed by Delisle to
the Imperium Orientale of Banduri). [Gibbon omits to mention the most remarkable
incident in this episode. The Opsician troops proceeded to Constantinople and
besieged Anastasius. The fleet and the engines, which had been prepared by the
Emperor to defend the city against the Saracens, had to be used against the rebels.
When Theodosius ultimately effected his entry, the Opsicians pillaged the city.
For the Themes see Appendix 3.]

[13] [At the previous siege, Saracens had also landed on European soil; see above,
p. 3.]

gress, each was manned with no more than one hundred heavy armed soldiers. This huge armada proceeded on a smooth sea and with a gentle gale, towards the mouth of the Bosphorus; the surface of the strait was overshadowed, in the language of the Greeks, with a moving forest, and the same fatal night had been fixed by the Saracen chief for a general assault by sea and land. To allure the confidence of the enemy, the emperor had thrown aside the chain that usually guarded the entrance of the harbour; but, while they hesitated whether they should seize the opportunity or apprehend the snare, the ministers of destruction were at hand. The fireships of the Greeks were launched against them; the Arabs, their arms, and vessels, were involved in the same flames, the disorderly fugitives were dashed against each other or overwhelmed in the waves; and I no longer find a vestige of the fleet that had threatened to extirpate the Roman name. A still more fatal and irreparable loss was that of the caliph Soliman, who died of an indigestion [14] in his camp near Kinnisrin, or Chalcis in Syria, as he was preparing to lead against Constantinople the remaining forces of the East. The brother of Moslemah was succeeded by a kinsman and an enemy; and the throne of an active and able prince was degraded by the useless and pernicious virtues of a bigot. While he started and satisfied the scruples of a blind conscience, the siege was continued through the winter by the neglect rather than by the resolution of the caliph Omar. [15] The winter proved uncommonly rigorous; above an hundred days the ground was covered

[Omar II.
A.D. 717-20]

[14] The caliph had emptied two baskets of eggs and of figs, which he swallowed alternately, and the repast was concluded with marrow and sugar. In one of his pilgrimages to Mecca, Soliman ate, at a single meal, seventy pomegranates, a kid, six fowls, and a huge quantity of the grapes of Tayef. If the bill of fare be correct, we must admire the appetite rather than the luxury of the sovereign of Asia (Abulfeda, Annal. Moslem. p. 126). [Though the manner of Sulaiman's death is uncertain, it is agreed that he was a voluptuary. Tabari says that cooking and gallantry were the only subjects of conversation at his court.]

[15] See the article of Omar Ben Abdalaziz [Ibn Abd al Azīz], in the Bibliothèque Orientale (p. 689, 690), præferens, says Elmacin (p. 91), religionem suam rebus suis mundanis. He was so desirous of being with God that he would not have anointed his ear (his own saying) to obtain a perfect cure of his last malady. The caliph had only one shirt, and in an age of luxury his annual expense was no more than two drachms (Abulpharagius, p. 131). Haud diu gavisus eo principe fuit orbis Moslemus (Abulfeda, p. 127). [Weil takes another view of the virtues of the bigot, and writes: " The pious Omar was greater than all his predecessors, not excepting Omar I., in one respect; he sought less to increase or enrich Islam at the cost of the unbeliever than to augment the number of Musulmans without making forced conversions." Geschichte der Chalifen, i. p. 582.]

with deep snow, and the natives of the sultry climes of Egypt and Arabia lay torpid and almost lifeless in their frozen camp. They revived on the return of spring; a second effort had been made in their favour; and their distress was relieved by the arrival of two numerous fleets, laden with corn, and arms, and soldiers; the first from Alexandria, of four hundred transports and galleys; the second of three hundred and sixty vessels from the ports of Africa. But the Greek fires were again kindled, and, if the destruction was less complete, it was owing to the experience which had taught the Moslems to remain at a safe distance, or to the perfidy of the Egyptian mariners, who deserted with their ships to the emperor of the Christians. The trade and navigation of the capital were restored; and the produce of the fisheries supplied the wants, and even the luxury, of the inhabitants. But the calamities of famine and disease were soon felt by the troops of Moslemah, and, as the former was miserably assuaged, so the latter was dreadfully propagated, by the pernicious nutriment which hunger compelled them to extract from the most unclean or unnatural food. The spirit of conquest, and even of enthusiasm, was extinct: the Saracens could no longer straggle beyond their lines, either single or in small parties, without exposing themselves to the merciless retaliation of the Thracian peasants. An army of Bulgarians was attracted from the Danube by the gifts and promises of Leo; and these savage auxiliaries made some atonement for the evils which they had inflicted on the empire, by the defeat and slaughter of twenty-two thousand Asiatics. A report was dexterously scattered that the Franks, the unknown nations of the Latin world, were arming by sea and land in the defence of the Christian cause, and their formidable aid was expected with far different sensations in the camp and city. At length, after a siege of thirteen months,[16] the hopeless Moslemah received from the caliph the welcome permission to retreat. The march of the Arabian cavalry over the Hellespont and through the provinces of Asia was executed without delay or molestation; *Failure and retreat of the Saracens*

[16] Both Nicephorus and Theophanes agree that the siege of Constantinople was raised the 15th of August (A.D. 718); but, as the former, our best witness, affirms that it continued thirteen months, the latter must be mistaken in supposing that it began on the same day of the preceding year. I do not find that Pagi has remarked this inconsistency. [Tabari places the beginning of the siege in A.H. 98 = A.D. 716-17, but does not mention the month; and he makes Omar II. recall Maslama in A.H. 99 (Aug. 25, 717—Aug. 2, 718). See Tabari, ed. de Goeje, ii. 1342.]

but an army of their brethren had been cut to pieces on the
side of Bithynia, and the remains of the fleet was so repeatedly
damaged by tempest and fire that only five galleys entered the
port of Alexandria to relate the tale of their various and almost
incredible disasters.[17]

Invention
and use of
the Greek
fire

In the two sieges, the deliverance of Constantinople may be
chiefly ascribed to the novelty, the terrors, and the real efficacy
of the *Greek fire*.[18] The important secret of compounding and
directing this artificial flame was imparted by Callinicus, a
native of Heliopolis in Syria, who deserted from the service of
the caliph to that of the emperor.[19] The skill of a chymist and
engineer was equivalent to the succour of fleets and armies;
and this discovery or improvement of the military art was
fortunately reserved for the distressful period, when the degenerate Romans of the East were incapable of contending with the
warlike enthusiasm and youthful vigour of the Saracens. The
historian who presumes to analyse this extraordinary composition
should suspect his own ignorance and that of his Byzantine
guides, so prone to the marvellous, so careless, and in this instance so jealous, of the truth. From their obscure and perhaps
fallacious hints, it should seem that the principal ingredient of
the Greek fire was the *naptha*,[20] or liquid bitumen, a light, tenacious, and inflammable oil,[21] which springs from the earth and

[17] In the second siege of Constantinople, I have followed Nicephorus (Brev. p.
33-36 [pp. 53-4, ed. de Boor]), Theophanes (Chronograph. p. 324-334 [A.M. 6209,
6210]), Cedrenus (Compend. p. 449-452 [i. 787, ed. Bonn]), Zonaras (tom. ii. p 98-
102 [xv. c. 1.]), Elmacin (Hist. Saracen. p. 88), Abulfeda (Annal. Moslem. p. 126),
and Abulpharagius (Dynast. p. 130), the most satisfactory of the Arabs.

[18] Our sure and indefatigable guide in the middle ages and Byzantine history,
Charles du Fresne du Cange, has treated in several places of the Greek fire, and his
collections leave few gleanings behind. See particularly Glossar. Med. et Infim.
Græcitat. p. 1275, sub voce Πῦρ θαλάσσιον ὑγρόν. Glossar. Med. et Infim. Latinitat.
Ignis Græcus. Observations sur Villehardouin, p. 305, 306. Observations sur Join-
ville, p. 71, 72. [See below, note 22.]

[19] Theophanes styles him ἀρχιτέκτων (p. 295 [A.M. 6165]). Cedrenus (p. 437 [i.
p. 765]) brings this artist from (the ruins of) Heliopolis in Egypt; and chemistry
was indeed the peculiar science of the Egyptians.

[20] The naptha, the oleum incendiarium of the history of Jerusalem (Gest. Dei
per Francos, p. 1167), the Oriental fountain of James de Vitry (l. iii. c. 84), is introduced on slight evidence and strong probability. Cinnamus (l. vi. p. 165 [c. 10]) calls
the Greek fire πῦρ Μηδικόν; and the naptha is known to abound between the Tigris
and the Caspian Sea. According to Pliny (Hist. Natur. ii. 109) it was subservient
to the revenge of Medea, and in either etymology the ἔλαιον Μηδίας, Μηδείας
(Procop. de Bell. Gothic. l. iv. c. 11) may fairly signify this liquid bitumen.

[21] On the different sorts of oils and bitumens, see Dr. Watson's (the present
bishop of Llandaff's) Chemical Essays, vol. iii. essay i., a classic book, the best
adapted to infuse the taste and knowledge of chemistry. The less perfect ideas of

A NAVAL BATTLE: USE OF GREEK FIRE. FROM THE MS. OF SKYLITZES AT MADRID

catches fire as soon as it comes in contact with the air. The naptha was mingled, I know not by what methods or in what proportions, with sulphur and with the pitch that is extracted from evergreen firs.[22] From this mixture, which produced a thick smoke and a loud explosion, proceeded a fierce and obstinate flame, which not only rose in perpendicular ascent, but likewise burnt with equal vehemence in descent or lateral progress; instead of being extinguished, it was nourished and quickened, by the element of water; and sand, urine, or vinegar were the only remedies that could damp the fury of this powerful agent, which was justly denominated by the Greeks the *liquid* or the *maritime* fire. For the annoyance of the enemy it was employed with equal effect, by sea and land, in battles or in sieges. It was either poured from the rampart in large boilers, or launched in red-hot balls of stone and iron, or darted in arrows and javelins, twisted round with flax and tow, which had deeply imbibed the inflammable oil: sometimes it was deposited in fire-ships, the victims and instruments of a more ample revenge, and was most commonly blown through long tubes of copper, which were planted on the prow of a galley, and fancifully shaped into the mouths of savage monsters, that seemed to vomit a stream of liquid and consuming fire. This important art was preserved at Constantinople, as the palladium of the state; the galleys and *artillery* might occasionally be lent to the allies of Rome; but the composition of the Greek fire was concealed with the most jealous scruple, and the terror of the enemies was increased and prolonged by their ignorance and surprise. In the treatise of the Administration of the Empire

the ancients may be found in Strabo (Geograph. l. xvi. p. 1078 [1315]), and Pliny (Hist. Natur. ii. 108, 109) : Huic (*Napthae*) magna cognatio est ignium, transiliuntque protinus in eam undecunque visam. Of our travellers I am best pleased with Otter (tom. i. p. 153, 158).

[22] Anna Comnena has partly drawn aside the curtain. 'Από της πεύκης καὶ ἄλλων τινῶν τοιούτων δένδρων ἀειθαλῶν συνάγεται δάκρυον εὔκαυστον· Τοῦτο μετὰ θείου τριβόμενον ἐμβάλλεται εἰς αὐλίσκους καλάμων καὶ ἐμφυσᾶται παρὰ τοῦ παίζοντος λάβρῳ καὶ συνεχεῖ πνεύματι (Alexiad. l. xiii. p. 383 [c. 3]). Elsewhere (l. xi. p. 336 [c. 4]) she mentions the property of burning, κατὰ τὸ πρανὲς καὶ εφ' ἑκάτερα. Leo, in the nineteenth chapter [§ 51, p. 1008, ed. Migne] of his Tactics (Opera Meursii, tom. vi. p. 843, edit. Lami, Florent. 1745), speaks of the new invention of πῦρ μετὰ βροντῆς καὶ καπνοῦ. These are genuine and *Imperial* testimonies. [It is certain that one kind of " Greek " or " marine " fire was gunpowder. The receipt is preserved in a treatise of the ninth century, entitled Liber ignium ad comburendos hostes, by Marcus Graecus, preserved only in a Latin translation (edited by F. Höfer in Histoire de la chimie, vol. 1, 1842). But other inflammable compounds, containing pitch, naphtha, &c., must be distinguished. See further, Appendix 5.]

the royal author[23] suggests the answers and excuses that might best elude the indiscreet curiosity and importunate demands of the barbarians.   They should be told that the mystery of the Greek fire had been revealed by an angel to the first and greatest of the Constantines, with a sacred injunction that this gift of heaven, this peculiar blessing of the Romans, should never be communicated to any foreign nation; that the prince and subject were alike bound to religious silence under the temporal and spiritual penalties of treason and sacrilege; and that the impious attempt would provoke the sudden and supernatural vengeance of the God of the Christians.   By these precautions, the secret was confined, above four hundred years, to the Romans of the East; and, at the end of the eleventh century, the Pisans, to whom every sea and every art were familiar, suffered the effects, without understanding the composition, of the Greek fire.   It was at length either discovered or stolen by the Mahometans; and, in the holy wars of Syria and Egypt, they retorted an invention, contrived against themselves, on the heads of the Christians.   A knight, who despised the swords and lances of the Saracens, relates, with heartfelt sincerity, his own fears, and those of his companions, at the sight and sound of the mischievous engine that discharged a torrent of the Greek fire, the *feu Gregeois*, as it is styled by the more early of the French writers.   It came flying through the air, says Joinville,[24] like a winged long-tailed dragon, about the thickness of an hogshead, with the report of thunder and the velocity of lightning; and the darkness of the night was dispelled by this deadly illumination.   The use of the Greek or, as it might now be called, of the Saracen fire was continued to the middle of the fourteenth century,[25] when the scientific or casual compound of nitre, sul-

---

[23] Constantin. Porphyrogenit. de Administrat. Imperii, c. xiii. p. 64, 65 [vol. iii. p. 84-5, ed. Bonn].

[24] Histoire de St. Louis, p. 39, Paris, 1668 ; p. 44, Paris, de l'imprimerie Royale, 1761 [xliii., § 203 *sqq*. in the text of N. de Wailly].   The former of these editions is precious for the observations of Ducange ; the latter, for the pure and original text of Joinville.   We must have recourse to the text to discover that the feu Gregeois was shot with a pile or javelin, from an engine that acted like a sling.

[25] The vanity, or envy, of shaking the established property of Fame has tempted some moderns to carry gunpowder above the fourteenth (see Sir William Temple, Dutens, &c.), and the Greek fire above the seventh, century (see the Saluste du Président des Brosses, tom. ii. p. 381) ; but their evidence, which precedes the vulgar æra of the invention, is seldom clear or satisfactory, and subsequent writers may be suspected of fraud or credulity.   In the earliest sieges some combustibles of oil and sulphur have been used, and the Greek fire has *some* affinities with gun-

phur, and charcoal effected a new revolution in the art of war and the history of mankind.[26]

Constantinople and the Greek fire might exclude the Arabs from the Eastern entrance of Europe; but in the West, on the side of the Pyrenees, the provinces of Gaul were threatened and invaded by the conquerors of Spain.[27] The decline of the French monarchy invited the attack of these insatiate fanatics. The descendants of Clovis had lost the inheritance of his martial and ferocious spirit; and their misfortune or demerit has affixed the epithet of *lazy* to the last kings of the Merovingian race.[28] They ascended the throne without power, and sunk into the grave without a name. A country palace, in the neighbourhood of Compiègne,[29] was allotted for their residence or prison; but each year, in the month of March or May, they were conducted in a waggon drawn by oxen to the assembly of the Franks, to give audience to foreign ambassadors, and to ratify the acts of the mayor of the palace. That domestic officer was become the minister of the nation, and the master of the prince. A public employment was converted into the

Invasion of France by the Arabs. A.D. 721, &c.

---

powder both in nature and effects : for the antiquity of the first, a passage of Procopius (de Bell. Goth. l. iv. c. 11), for that of the second, some facts in the Arabic history of Spain (A.D. 1249, 1312, 1332, Bibliot. Arab. Hisp. tom. ii. p. 6, 7, 8), are the most difficult to elude.

[26] That extraordinary man, Friar Bacon, reveals two of the ingredients, saltpetre and sulphur, and conceals the third in a sentence of mysterious gibberish, as if he dreaded the consequences of his own discovery (Biographia Britannica, vol. i. p. 430, new edition).

[27] For the invasion of France, and the defeat of the Arabs by Charles Martel, see the Historia Arabum (c. 11, 12, 13, 14) of Roderic *Ximenes*, archbishop of Toledo, who had before him the Christian chronicle of Isidore Pacensis, and the Mahometan history of *Novairi*. [And Chron. Moissiac. ad ann. 732 (in Pertz, Mon. Germ. Hist. vol. i.).] The Moslems are silent or concise in the account of their losses; but M. Cardonne (tom. i. p. 129, 130, 131) has given a *pure* and simple account of all that he could collect from Ibn Halikan, Hidjasi, and an anonymous writer. The texts of the chronicles of France, and lives of saints, are inserted in the Collection of Bouquet (tom. iii.) and the Annals of Pagi, who (tom. iii. under the proper years) has restored the chronology, which is anticipated six years in the Annals of Baronius. The Dictionary of Bayle (*Abderame* and *Munuza*) has more merit for lively reflection than original research.

[28] Eginhart. de Vitâ Caroli Magni, c. ii. p. 13-18, edit. Schmink, Utrecht, 1711. Some modern critics accuse the minister of Charlemagne of exaggerating the weakness of the Merovingians; but the general outline is just, and the French reader will for ever repeat the beautiful lines of Boileau's Lutrin.

[29] *Mamaccae* on the Oise, between Compiègne and Noyon, which Eginhart calls perparvi reditus villam (see the notes, and the map of ancient France for Dom. Bouquet's Collection). Compendium, or Compiègne, was a palace of more dignity (Hadrian. Valesii Notitia Galliarum, p. 152), and that laughing philosopher, the Abbé Galliani (Dialogues sur le Commerce des Bleds), may truly affirm that it was the residence of the rois très Chrétiens et très chevelus.

patrimony of a private family; the elder Pepin left a king of
mature years under the guardianship of his own widow and her
child; and these feeble regents were forcibly dispossessed by
the most active of his bastards.   A government, half savage and
half corrupt, was almost dissolved; and the tributary dukes, the
provincial counts, and the territorial lords were tempted to
despise the weakness of the monarch and to imitate the ambition of the mayor.   Among these independent chiefs, one of the
boldest and most successful was Eudes, duke of Aquitain, who,
in the southern provinces of Gaul, usurped the authority and
even the title of king.   The Goths, the Gascons, and the
Franks assembled under the standard of this Christian hero; he
repelled the first invasion of the Saracens; and Zama, lieutenant
of the caliph, lost his army and his life under the walls of
Toulouse.[30]   The ambition of his successors was stimulated by
revenge; they repassed the Pyrenees with the means and the
resolution of conquest.   The advantageous situation which had
recommended Narbonne[31] as the first Roman colony was again
chosen by the Moslems: they claimed the province of Septimania, or Languedoc, as a just dependence of the Spanish
monarchy: the vineyards of Gascony and the city of Bordeaux were possessed by the sovereign of Damascus and
Samarcand; and the south of France, from the mouth of the
Garonne to that of the Rhone, assumed the manners and religion
of Arabia.

[A.D. 721,
June 9]

Expedition
and vic-
tories of
Abderame.
A.D. 731
But these narrow limits were scorned by the spirit of
Abdalrahman, or Abderame, who had been restored by the
caliph Hashem[32] to the wishes of the soldiers and people of
Spain.   That veteran and daring commander adjudged to the
obedience of the prophet whatever yet remained of France or
of Europe; and prepared to execute the sentence, at the head

---

[30] [The first invasion of Gaul was probably that of Al-Hurr in A.D. 718, but it
is not quite clear whether the invasion had any abiding results.   It is a question
whether the capture of Narbonne was the work of Al-Hurr (as Arabic authors state),
or of Al-Samā (as Weil inclines to think : Geschichte der Chalifen, i. p. 610, note).
The governor Anbasa crossed the Pyrenees in 725 to avenge the defeat of Toulouse,
and captured Carcassonne and reduced Nemausus.   Gibbon's " successors " refers
to him and Abd ar-Rahmān.]
[31] Even before that colony, A.U.C. 630 (Velleius Patercul. i. 15), in the time of
Polybius (Hist. l. iii. p. 265, edit. Gronov. [B. 34, c. 6, § 3]), Narbonne was a Celtic
town of the first eminence, and one of the most northern places of the known world
(d'Anville, Notice de l'Ancienne Gaule, p. 473).
[32] [Hishām, A.D. 724, Jan.—743, Feb.]

of a formidable host, in the full confidence of surmounting all opposition, either of nature or of man. His first care was to suppress a domestic rebel, who commanded the most important passes of the Pyrenees : Munuza, a Moorish chief, had accepted [Abu-Nesa] the alliance of the duke of Aquitain; and Eudes, from a motive of private or public interest, devoted his beauteous daughter to the embraces of the African misbeliever. But the strongest fortresses of Cerdagne were invested by a superior force; the rebel was overtaken and slain in the mountains; and his widow was sent a captive to Damascus, to gratify the desires, or more probably the vanity, of the commander of the faithful. From the Pyrenees Abderame proceeded without delay to the passage of the Rhone and the siege of Arles. An army of Christians attempted the relief of the city; the tombs of their leaders were yet visible in the thirteenth century; and many thousands of their dead bodies were carried down the rapid stream into the Mediterranean sea. The arms of Abderame were not less successful on the side of the ocean. He passed without opposition the Garonne and Dordogne, which unite their waters in the gulf of Bordeaux; but he found, beyond those rivers, the camp of the intrepid Eudes, who had formed a second army, and sustained a second defeat, so fatal to the Christians that, according to their sad confession, God alone could reckon the number of the slain. The victorious Saracen overran the provinces of Aquitain, whose Gallic names are disguised, rather than lost, in the modern appellations of Périgord, Saintonge, and Poitou : his standards were planted on the walls, or at least before the gates, of Tours and of Sens; and his detachments overspread the kingdom of Burgundy, as far as the well-known cities of Lyons and Besançon. The memory of these devastations, for Abderame did not spare the country or the people, was long preserved by tradition; and the invasion of France by the Moors or Mahometans affords the groundwork of those fables which have been so wildly disfigured in the romances of chivalry and so elegantly adorned by the Italian muse. In the decline of society and art, the deserted cities could supply a slender booty to the Saracens; their richest spoil was found in the churches and monasteries, which they stripped of their ornaments and delivered to the flames; and the tutelar saints, both Hilary of Poitiers and Martin of Tours, forgot their miraculous powers in the defence of their own sepulchres.[33]   A victorious line of march had been prolonged above a thousand miles from the rock of Gibraltar to the banks of the Loire; the repetition of an equal space would have carried the Saracens to the confines of Poland and the High-lands of Scotland : the Rhine is not more impassable than the Nile or Euphrates, and the Arabian fleet might have sailed without a naval combat into the mouth of the Thames.   Perhaps the interpretation of the Koran would now be taught in the schools of Oxford, and her pulpits might demonstrate to a circumcised people the sanctity and truth of the revelation of Mahomet.[34]

Defeat of the Sara- cens by Charles Martel. A.D. 732

From such calamities was Christendom delivered by the genius and fortune of one man.   Charles, the illegitimate son of the elder Pepin, was content with the titles of mayor or duke of the Franks, but he deserved to become the father of a line of kings.[35]   In a laborious administration of twenty-four years, he restored and supported the dignity of the throne, and the rebels of Germany and Gaul were successively crushed by the activity of a warrior, who, in the same campaign, could display his banner on the Elbe, the Rhone, and the shores of the ocean. In the public danger, he was summoned by the voice of his country ; and his rival, the duke of Aquitain, was reduced to appear among the fugitives and suppliants.   " Alas ! " exclaimed the Franks, " what a misfortune ! what an indignity !   We have long heard of the name and conquests of the Arabs : we were apprehensive of their attack from the East ; they have now con-quered Spain, and invade our country on the side of the West. Yet their numbers, and (since they have no buckler) their arms,

[33] With regard to the sanctuary of St. Martin of Tours, Roderic Ximenes accuses the Saracens of the *deed*. Turonis civitatem, ecclesiam et palatia vastatione et incendio simili diruit et consumpsit.   The continuator of Fredegarius imputes to them no more than the *intention*.   Ad domum beatissimi Martini evertendam destinant.   At Carolus, &c.   The French annalist was more jealous of the honour of the saint.

[34] Yet I sincerely doubt whether the Oxford mosque would have produced a volume of controversy so elegant and ingenious as the sermons lately preached by Mr. White, the Arabic professor, at Mr. Bampton's lecture.   His observations on the character and religion of Mahomet are always adapted to his argument, and generally founded in truth and reason.   He sustains the part of a lively and eloquent advocate ; and sometimes rises to the merit of an historian and philo-sopher.

[35] [For the life and acts of Charles see Th. Breysig's monograph, Die Zeit Karl Martells, in the series of the Jahrbücher des fränkischen Reiches, 1869.]

are inferior to our own." "If you follow my advice," replied the prudent mayor of the palace, "you will not interrupt their march, nor precipitate your attack. They are like a torrent, which it is dangerous to stem in its career. The thirst of riches, and the consciousness of success, redouble their valour, and valour is of more avail than arms or numbers. Be patient till they have loaded themselves with the encumbrance of wealth. The possession of wealth will divide their counsels and assure your victory." This subtle policy is perhaps a refinement of the Arabian writers; and the situation of Charles will suggest a more narrow and selfish motive of procrastination: the secret desire of humbling the pride, and wasting the provinces, of the rebel duke of Aquitain. It is yet more probable that the delays of Charles were inevitable and reluctant. A standing army was unknown under the first and second race; more than half the kingdom was now in the hands of the Saracens; according to their respective situation, the Franks of Neustria and Austrasia were too conscious or too careless of the impending danger; and the voluntary aids of the Gepidæ and Germans were separated by a long interval from the standard of the Christian general. No sooner had he collected his forces than he sought and found the enemy in the centre of France, between Tours and Poitiers. His well-conducted march was covered by a range of hills, and Abderame appears to have been surprised by his unexpected presence. The nations of Asia, Africa, and Europe advanced [October] with equal ardour to an encounter which would change the history of the whole world. In the six first days of desultory combat, the horsemen and archers of the East maintained their advantage; but in the closer onset of the seventh day the Orientals were oppressed by the strength and stature of the Germans, who, with stout hearts and *iron* hands,[36] asserted the civil and religious freedom of their posterity. The epithet of *Martel*, the *Hammer*, which has been added to the name of Charles, is expressive of his weighty and irresistible strokes: the valour of Eudes was excited by resentment and emulation; and their companions, in the eye of history, are the true Peers and Paladins of French chivalry. After a bloody field, in which

---

[36] Gens Austriæ membrorum pre-eminentiâ valida, et gens Germana corde et corpore præstantissima, quasi in ictu oculi manu ferreâ et pectore arduo Arabes extinxerunt (Roderic. Toletan. c. xiv.).

Abderame was slain, the Saracens, in the close of the evening, retired to their camp. In the disorder and despair of the night, the various tribes of Yemen and Damascus, of Africa and Spain, were provoked to turn their arms against each other; the remains of their host was suddenly dissolved, and each *emir* consulted his safety by an hasty and separate retreat. At the dawn of day, the stillness of an hostile camp was suspected by the victorious Christians : on the report of their spies, they ventured to explore the riches of the vacant tents ; but, if we except some celebrated relics, a small portion of the spoil was restored to the innocent and lawful owners. The joyful tidings were soon diffused over the Catholic world, and the monks of Italy could affirm and believe that three hundred and fifty, or three hundred and seventy-five, thousand of the Mahometans had been crushed by the hammer of Charles ; [37] while no more than fifteen hundred Christians were slain in the field of Tours. But this incredible tale is sufficiently disproved by the caution of the French general, who apprehended the snares and accidents of a pursuit, and dismissed his German allies to their native forests. The inactivity of a conqueror betrays the loss of strength and blood, and the most cruel execution is inflicted, not in the ranks of battle, but on the backs of a flying enemy. Yet the victory of the Franks was complete and final ; Aquitain was recovered by the arms of Eudes ; the Arabs never resumed the conquest of Gaul,[38] and they were soon driven beyond the Pyrenees by Charles Martel and his valiant race.[39] It might have been expected that the

They retreat before the Franks

[37] These numbers are stated by Paul Warnefrid, the deacon of Aquileia (de Gestis Langobard. l. vi. p. 921, edit. Grot. [c. 46]), and Anastasius, the librarian of the Roman church (in Vit. Gregorii II.), who tells a miraculous story of three consecrated spunges, which rendered invulnerable the French soldiers among whom they had been shared. It should seem that in his letters to the pope Eudes usurped the honour of the victory, for which he is chastised by the French annalists, who, with equal falsehood, accuse him of inviting the Saracens.

[38] [This is not quite accurate. Maurontius, the duke of Marseilles, preferred the alliance of the misbelievers to that of the Frank warrior, and handed over Arles, Avignon, and other towns to the lords of Narbonne, who also obtained possession of Lyons and Valence. They were smitten back to Narbonne by Charles the Hammer in A.D. 737, and yet again in 739. Cp. Weil, *op. cit.*, p. 647. Okba was at this time governor of Spain. For the expedition of Charles in 737, see Contin. Fredegar. 109.]

[39] Narbonne, and the rest of Septimania, was recovered by Pepin, the son of Charles Martel, A.D. 755 (Pagi, Critica, tom. iii. p. 300). Thirty-seven years afterwards it was pillaged by a sudden inroad of the Arabs, who employed the captives in the construction of the mosque of Cordova (de Guignes, Hist. des Huns, tom. i. p. 354).

saviour of Christendom would have been canonized, or at least applauded, by the gratitude of the clergy, who are indebted to his sword for their present existence. But in the public distress the mayor of the palace had been compelled to apply the riches, or at least the revenues, of the bishops and abbots to the relief of the state and the reward of the soldiers. His merits were forgotten, his sacrilege alone was remembered, and, in an epistle to a Carlovingian prince, a Gallic synod presumes to declare that his ancestor was damned ; that on the opening of his tomb the spectators were affrighted by a smell of fire and the aspect of a horrid dragon; and that a saint of the times was indulged with a pleasant vision of the soul and body of Charles Martel burning, to all eternity, in the abyss of hell.[40]

The loss of an army, or a province, in the Western world was less painful to the court of Damascus than the rise and progress of a domestic competitor. Except among the Syrians, the caliphs of the house of Ommiyah had never been the objects of the public favour. The life of Mahomet recorded their perseverance in idolatry and rebellion; their conversion had been reluctant, their elevation irregular and factious, and their throne was cemented with the most holy and noble blood of Arabia. The best of their race, the pious Omar, was dissatisfied with his own title ; their personal virtues were insufficient to justify a departure from the order of succession ; and the eyes and wishes of the faithful were turned towards the line of Hashem and the kindred of the apostle of God. Of these the Fatimites were either rash or pusillanimous ; but the descendants of Abbas cherished, with courage and discretion, the hopes of their rising fortunes. From an obscure residence in Syria, they secretly dispatched their agents and missionaries, who preached in the Eastern provinces their hereditary indefeasible right; and Mohammed, the son of Ali, the son of Abdallah, the son of Abbas, the uncle of the prophet, gave audience to the deputies of Chorasan, and accepted their free gift of four hundred thousand

Elevation of the Abbassides. A.D. 746-750

---

[40] This pastoral letter, addressed to Lewis the Germanic, the grandson of Charlemagne, and most probably composed by the pen of the artful Hincmar, is dated in the year 858, and signed by the bishops of the provinces of Rheims and Rouen (Baronius, Annal. Eccles. A.D. 741 ; Fleury, Hist. Ecclés. tom. x. p. 514-516). Yet Baronius himself, and the French critics, reject with contempt this episcopal fiction.

pieces of gold. After the death of Mohammed, the oath of allegiance was administered in the name of his son Ibrahim to a numerous band of votaries, who expected only a signal and a leader; and the governor of Chorasan continued to deplore his fruitless admonitions and the deadly slumber of the caliphs of Damascus, till he himself, with all his adherents, was driven from the city and palace of Meru, by the rebellious arms of Abu Moslem.[41] That maker of kings, the author, as he is named, of the *call* of the Abbassides, was at length rewarded for his presumption of merit with the usual gratitude of courts. A mean, perhaps a foreign, extraction could not repress the aspiring energy of Abu Moslem. Jealous of his wives, liberal of his wealth, prodigal of his own blood, and of that of others, he could boast with pleasure, and possibly with truth, that he had destroyed six hundred thousand of his enemies; and such was the intrepid gravity of his mind and countenance that he was never seen to smile except on a day of battle. In the visible separation of parties, the *green* was consecrated to the Fatimites; the Ommiades were distinguished by the *white*; and the *black*, as the most adverse, was naturally adopted by the Abbassides. Their turbans and garments were stained with that gloomy colour; two black standards, on pike-staves nine cubits long, were born aloft in the van of Abu Moslem; and their allegorical names of the *night* and the *shadow* obscurely represented the indissoluble union and perpetual succession of the line of Hashem. From the Indus to the Euphrates, the East was convulsed by the quarrel of the white and the black factions; the Abbassides were most frequently victorious; but their public success was clouded by the personal misfortune of their chief. The court of Damascus, awakening from a long slumber, resolved to prevent the pilgrimage of Mecca, which Ibrahim had undertaken with a splendid retinue, to recommend himself at once to the favour of the prophet and of the people. A detachment of [A.D. 744] cavalry intercepted his march and arrested his person; and the unhappy Ibrahim, snatched away from the promise of untasted royalty, expired in iron fetters in the dungeons of Haran. His

---

[41] The steed and the saddle which had carried any of his wives were instantly killed or burnt, lest they should be afterwards mounted by a male. Twelve hundred mules or camels were required for his kitchen furniture; and the daily consumption amounted to three thousand cakes, an hundred sheep, besides oxen, poultry, &c. (Abulpharagius, Hist. Dynast. p. 140).

two younger brothers, Saffah [42] and Almansor,[43] eluded the search of the tyrant, and lay concealed at Cufa, till the zeal of the people and the approach of his eastern friends allowed them to expose their persons to the impatient public. On Friday, in the dress of a caliph, in the colours of the sect, Saffah proceeded with religious and military pomp to the mosque; ascending the pulpit, he prayed and preached as the lawful successor of Mahomet; and, after his departure, his kinsmen bound a willing people by an oath of fidelity. But it was on the banks of the Zab, and not in the mosque of Cufa, that this important controversy was determined. Every advantage appeared to be on the side of the white faction: the authority of established government; an army of an hundred and twenty thousand soldiers, against a sixth part of that number;[43a] and the presence and merit of the caliph Mervan, the fourteenth and last of the house [Marwan II. A.D. 744-50] of Ommiyah. Before his accession to the throne, he had deserved, by his Georgian warfare, the honourable epithet of the ass of Mesopotamia;[44] and he might have been ranked among the greatest princes, had not, says Abulfeda, the eternal order decreed that moment for the ruin of his family: a decree against which all human prudence and fortitude must struggle in vain. The orders of Mervan were mistaken or disobeyed; the return of his horse, from which he had dismounted on a necessary occasion,[45] impressed the belief of his death; and the enthusiasm of the black squadrons was ably conducted by Abdallah, the uncle of his competitor. After an irretrieveable defeat, the caliph escaped to Mosul; but the colours of the Abbassides were displayed from the rampart; he suddenly repassed the Tigris, cast a melancholy look on his palace of Haran, crossed the Euphrates, abandoned the fortifications of Damascus, and, without halting in

---

[42] [Abd Allāh Abū-l-Abbās al-Saffāh (the bloody), caliph 750-754.]

[43] [Abū-Jafar Mansūr, caliph 754-775.]

[43a] [So Tabari, ed. de Goeje, iii. 45.]

[44] *Al Hamar.* He had been governor of Mesopotamia, and the Arabic proverb praises the courage of that warlike breed of asses who never fly from an enemy. The surname of Mervan may justify the comparison of Homer (Iliad, v. 557, &c.), and both will silence the moderns, who consider the ass as a stupid and ignoble emblem (d'Herbelot, Bibliot. Orient. p. 558).

[45] [This motive seems to have been drawn from Persian sources—Gibbon took it from Herbelot. We must rather follow Tabari's account. Marwān sent his son with some troops back to the camp to rescue his money. This back movement was taken by the rest of the army as a retreat and they all took to flight. See Weil, *op. cit.*, i. p. 701; Tabari, ed. de Goeje, iii. 38 *sqq.*]

Palestine, pitched his last and fatal camp at Busir on the banks
Fall of the
Ommiades.
A.D. 750,
Feb. 10 of the Nile.[46] His speed was urged by the incessant diligence
of Abdallah, who in every step of the pursuit acquired strength
and reputation ; the remains of the white faction were finally
vanquished in Egypt ; and the lance, which terminated the life
and anxiety of Mervan, was not less welcome perhaps to the unfortunate than to the victorious chief.   The merciless inquisition
of the conqueror eradicated the most distant branches of the
hostile race : their bones were scattered, their memory was
accursed, and the martyrdom of Hossein was abundantly revenged on the posterity of his tyrants.   Fourscore of the Ommiades, who had yielded to the faith or clemency of their foes,
were invited to a banquet at Damascus.   The laws of hospitality
were violated by a promiscuous massacre ; the board was spread
over their fallen bodies ; and the festivity of the guests was
enlivened by the music of their dying groans.   By the event of
the civil war the dynasty of the Abbassides was firmly established ;
but the Christians only could triumph in the mutual hatred and
common loss of the disciples of Mahomet.[47]

Revolt of
Spain.
A.D. 755   Yet the thousands who were swept away by the sword of war
might have been speedily retrieved in the succeeding generation,
if the consequences of the revolution had not tended to dissolve
the power and unity of the empire of the Saracens.   In the
proscription of the Ommiades, a royal youth of the name of
Abdalrahman alone escaped the rage of his enemies, who hunted
the wandering exile from the banks of the Euphrates to the

----

[46] Four several places, all in Egypt, bore the name of Busir, or Busiris, so
famous in Greek fable.   The first, where Mervan was slain, was to the west of the
Nile, in the province of Fium, or Arsinoe ; the second in the Delta, in the Sebenny-
tic nome ; the third, near the pyramids ; the fourth, which was destroyed by
Diocletian (see above, vol. i. p. 474), in the Thebais.   I shall here transcribe a note
of the learned and orthodox Michaelis : Videntur in pluribus Ægypti superioris
urbibus Busiri Coptoque arma sumpsisse Christiani, libertatemque de religione
sentiendi defendisse, sed succubuisse quo in bello Coptos et Busuris diruta, et circa
Esnam magna strages edita.   Bellum narrant sed causam belli ignorant scriptores
Byzantini, alioqui Coptum et Busirim non rebellasse dicturi, sed causam Christian-
orum suscepturi (Not. 211, p. 100).   For the geography of the four Busirs, see
Abulfeda (Descript. Ægypt. p. 9, vers. Michaelis.   Gottingæ, 1776, in 4to), Michaelis
(Not. 122-127, p. 58-63), and d'Anville (Mémoire sur l'Egypte, p. 85, 147, 205).

[47] See Abulfeda (Annal. Moslem. p. 136-145), Eutychius (Annal. tom. ii. p.
392, vers. Pocock), Elmacin (Hist. Saracen. p. 109-121), Abulpharagius (Hist.
Dynast. p. 134-140), Roderic of Toledo (Hist. Arabum, c. 18, p. 33), Theophanes
(Chronograph. p. 356, 357 [A.M. 6240, 6241], who speaks of the Abbassides under
the names of Χωρασανῖται and Μαυροφόροι), and the Bibliothèque of d'Herbelot, in
the articles of *Ommiades, Abbassides, Mærvan, Ibrahim, Saffah, Abou Moslem.*
[Tabari, vol. iii. 44-51.]

valleys of mount Atlas. His presence in the neighbourhood of Spain revived the zeal of the white faction. The name and cause of the Abbassides had been first vindicated by the Persians; the West had been pure from civil arms; and the servants of the abdicated family still held, by a precarious tenure, the inheritance of their lands and the offices of government. Strongly prompted by gratitude, indignation, and fear, they invited the grandson of the caliph Hashem to ascend the throne of his ancestors; and, in his desperate condition, the extremes of rashness and prudence were almost the same. The acclamations of the people saluted his landing on the coast of Andalusia; and, after a successful struggle, Abdalrahman established the throne [A.D. 756] of Cordova, and was the father of the Ommiades of Spain, who reigned above two hundred and fifty years from the Atlantic to the Pyrenees.[48] He slew in battle a lieutenant of the Abbassides, who had invaded his dominions with a fleet and army: the head of Ala, in salt and camphire, was suspended by a [A.D. 763] daring messenger before the palace of Mecca;[49] and the caliph Almansor rejoiced in his safety, that he was removed by seas and lands from such a formidable adversary. Their mutual designs or declarations of offensive war evaporated without effect; but, instead of opening a door to the conquest of Europe, Spain was dissevered from the trunk of the monarchy, engaged in perpetual hostility with the East, and inclined to peace and friendship with the Christian sovereigns of Constantinople and France. The example of the Ommiades was imitated by the real or fictitious progeny of Ali, the Edrissites of Mauritania, and the more powerful Fatimites of Africa and Egypt. In the tenth century, the chair of Mahomet was disputed by three caliphs or commanders of the faithful, who reigned at Bagdad, Cairoan, and Cordova, excommunicated each other, and agreed only in a principle of discord, that a sectary is more odious and criminal than an unbeliever.[50]

Triple division of the caliphate

[48] For the revolution of Spain, consult Roderic of Toledo (c. xviii. p. 34, &c.), the Bibliotheca Arabico-Hispana (tom. ii. p. 30, 198), and Cardonne (Hist. de l'Afrique et de l'Espagne, tom. i. p. 180-197, 205, 272, 323, &c.).

[49] [Others say the head was exposed at Kairawān; Dozy, Histoire des Musulmans d'Espagne, i. 367.]

[50] I shall not stop to refute the strange errors and fancies of Sir William Temple (his works, vol. iii. p. 371-374, octavo edition) and Voltaire (Histoire Générale, c. xxviii. tom. ii. p. 124, 125, édition de Lausanne), concerning the division of the Saracen empire. The mistakes of Voltaire proceeded from the want of knowledge

Magnifi-
cence of
the caliphs.
A.D. 750-960 Mecca was the patrimony of the line of Hashem, yet the Abbassides were never tempted to reside either in the birthplace or the city of the prophet. Damascus was disgraced by the choice, and polluted with the blood, of the Ommiades; and, after some hesitation, Almansor, the brother and successor of Saffah, laid the foundations of Bagdad,[51] the Imperial seat of his posterity during a reign of five hundred years.[52] The chosen spot is on the eastern bank of the Tigris, about fifteen miles above the ruins of Modain; the double wall was of a circular form; and such was the rapid increase of a capital, now dwindled to a provincial town, that the funeral of a popular saint might be attended by eight hundred thousand men and sixty thousand women of Bagdad and the adjacent villages.   In this *city of peace,*[53] amidst the riches of the East, the Abbassides

or reflection; but Sir William was deceived by a Spanish impostor, who has framed an apocryphal history of the conquest of Spain by the Arabs.   [The Omayyad rulers of Spain called themselves emirs (Amīr) for a century and three-quarters. Abd ar-Rahmān III. (912-961) first assumed the higher title of caliph in 929.   Thus it is incorrect to speak of two Caliphates, or a western Caliphate, until 929; the Emirate of Cordova is the correct designation.]

[51] The geographer d'Anville (l'Euphrate et le Tigre, p. 121-123), and the Orientalist d'Herbelot (Bibliothèque, p. 167, 168), may suffice for the knowledge of Bagdad.   Our travellers, Pietro della Valle (tom. i. p. 688-698), Tavernier (tom. i. p. 230-238), Thévenot (part ii. p. 209-212), Otter (tom. i. p. 162-168), and Niebuhr (Voyage en Arabie, tom. ii. p. 239-271), have seen only its decay; and the Nubian geographer (p. 204), and the travelling Jew, Benjamin of Tudela (Itinerarium, p. 112-123, à Const. l'Empereur, apud Elzevir, 1633), are the only writers of my acquaintance, who have known Bagdad under the reign of the Abbassides.   [See Ibn Serapion's description of the canals of Baghdād, translated and annotated by G. Le Strange, in the Journal of the Asiatic Society, N.S. vol. 27 (1895), p. 285 *sqq.,* and the sketch plan of the city (*ib.* opposite p. 33); and the same scholar's full history and description of the city in his Baghdad during the Abbasid Caliphate, 1900.]

[52] The foundations of Bagdad were laid A.H. 145, A.D. 762; Mostasem [Mustasim, 1242-1258], the last of the Abbassides, was taken and put to death by the Tartars, A.H. 656, A.D. 1258, the 20th of February.

[53] Medinat al Salem, Dar al Salem [Dār al-Salām].   Urbs pacis, or, as is more neatly compounded by the Byzantine writers, Εἰρηνόπολις (Irenopolis).   There is some dispute concerning the etymology of Bagdad, but the first syllable is allowed to signify a garden, in the Persian tongue; the garden of Dad, a Christian hermit, whose cell had been the only habitation on the spot.   [" The original city as founded by the Caliph Al-Mansūr was circular, being surrounded by a double wall and ditch, with four equidistant gates.   From gate to gate measured an Arab mile (about one English mile and a quarter).   This circular city stood on the western side of the Tigris, immediately above the point where the Sarāt Canal, coming from the Nahr 'Isā, joined the Tigris, and the Sarāt flowed round the southern side of the city."   " In the century and a half which had elapsed, counting from the date of the foundation of the city down to the epoch at which Ibn Serapion wrote, Baghdād had undergone many changes.   It had never recovered the destructive effects of the great siege, when Al-Amīn had defended himself, to the death, against the troops of his brother Al-Mamūn; and again it had suffered semi-depopulation by the removal of the seat of government to Samarrā (A.D. 836-892).   The original

soon disdained the abstinence and frugality of the first caliphs, and aspired to emulate the magnificence of the Persian kings. After his wars and buildings, Almansor left behind him in gold and silver about thirty millions sterling;[54] and this treasure was exhausted in a few years by the vices or virtues of his children. His son Mahadi, in a single pilgrimage to Mecca, expended six [Al-Mahdi] millions of dinars of gold.   A pious and charitable motive may sanctify the foundation of cisterns and caravanseras, which he distributed along a measured road of seven hundred miles; but his train of camels, laden with snow, could serve only to astonish the natives of Arabia, and to refresh the fruits and liquors of the royal banquet.[55]   The courtiers would surely praise the liberality of his grandson Almamon, who gave away four-fifths of the income of a province, a sum of two millions four hundred thousand gold dinars, before he drew his foot from the stirrup.   At the nuptials of the same prince, a thousand pearls of the largest size were showered on the head of the bride,[56] and a lottery of lands and houses displayed the capricious bounty of fortune.   The glories of the court were brightened rather than impaired in the decline of the empire; and a Greek ambassador might admire or pity the magnificence of the feeble Moctader.   "The [Al Muktadir] caliph's whole army," says the historian Abulfeda, "both horse and foot, was under arms, which together made a body of one hundred and sixty thousand men.   His state-officers, the favourite slaves, stood near him in splendid apparel, their belts

round city of Al-Mansūr had long ago been absorbed into the great capital, which covered ground measuring about five miles across in every direction, and the circular walls must, at an early date, have been levelled. The four gates, however, had remained, and had given their names to the first suburbs which in time had been absorbed into the Western town and become one half of the great City of Peace." Le Strange, Journal As. Soc., cit. supra, pp. 288, 289-290.]

[54] Reliquit in ærario sexcenties millies mille stateres, et quater et vicies millies mille aureos aureos. Elmacin, Hist. Saracen. p. 126. I have reckoned the gold pieces at eight shillings, and the proportion to the silver as twelve to one. [But see Appendix 2.]   But I will never answer for the numbers of Erpenius ; and the Latins are scarcely above the savages in the language of arithmetic.

[55] D'Herbelot, p. 530. Abulfeda, p. 154. Nivem Meccam apportavit, rem ibi aut nunquam aut rarissime visam.

[56] Abulfeda, p. 184, 189, describes the splendour and liberality of Almamon. Milton has alluded to this Oriental custom :—
    —Or where the gorgeous East, with richest hand,
    Showers on her kings Barbaric pearls and gold.
I have used the modern word *lottery* to express the *Missilia* of the Roman emperors, which entitled to some prize the person who caught them, as they were thrown among the crowd.

glittering with gold and gems. Near them were seven thousand eunuchs, four thousand of them white, the remainder black. The porters or door-keepers were in number seven hundred. Barges and boats, with the most superb decorations, were seen swimming upon the Tigris. Nor was the palace itself less splendid, in which were hung up thirty-eight thousand pieces of tapestry, twelve thousand five hundred of which were of silk embroidered with gold. The carpets on the floor were twenty-two thousand. An hundred lions were brought out, with a keeper to each lion.[57] Among the other spectacles of rare and stupendous luxury, was a tree of gold and silver spreading into eighteen large branches, on which, and on the lesser boughs, sat a variety of birds made of the same precious metals, as well as the leaves of the tree. While the machinery affected spontaneous motions, the several birds warbled their natural harmony. Through this scene of magnificence, the Greek ambassador was led by the visir to the foot of the caliph's throne."[58] In the West, the Ommiades of Spain supported, with equal pomp, the title of commander of the faithful. Three miles from Cordova, in honour of his favourite sultana, the third and greatest of the Abdalrahmans constructed the city, palace and gardens of Zehra. Twenty-five years, and above three millions sterling, were employed by the founder : his liberal taste invited the artists of Constantinople, the most skilful sculptors and architects of the age; and the buildings were sustained or adorned by twelve hundred columns of Spanish and African, of Greek and Italian marble. The hall of audience was encrusted with gold and pearls, and a great bason in the centre was surrounded with the curious and costly figures of birds and quadrupeds. In a lofty pavillion of the gardens, one of these basons and fountains, so delightful in a sultry climate, was replenished not with water, but with the purest quicksilver. The seraglio of Abdalrahman, his wives, concubines, and black eunuchs, amounted to six thousand three hundred persons; and he was

---

[57] When Bell of Antermony (Travels, vol. i. p. 99) accompanied the Russian ambassador to the audience of the unfortunate Shah Hussein of Persia, *two* lions were introduced, to denote the power of the king over the fiercest animals.

[58] Abulfeda, p. 237 ; d'Herbelot, p. 590. This embassy was received at Bagdad A.H. 305, A.D. 917. In the passage of Abulfeda, I have used, with some variations, the English translation of the learned and amiable Mr. Harris of Salisbury (Philological Enquiries, p. 363, 364).

attended to the field by a guard of twelve thousand horse, whose belts and scymetars were studded with gold.[59]

In a private condition, our desires are perpetually repressed by poverty and subordination; but the lives and labours of millions are devoted to the service of a despotic prince, whose laws are blindly obeyed, and whose wishes are instantly gratified. Our imagination is dazzled by the splendid picture; and, whatever may be the cool dictates of reason, there are few among us who would obstinately refuse a trial of the comforts and the cares of royalty. It may therefore be of some use to borrow the experience of the same Abdalrahman, whose magnificence has perhaps excited our admiration and envy, and to transcribe an authentic memorial which was found in the closet of the deceased caliph. "I have now reigned about fifty years in victory or peace; beloved by my subjects, dreaded by my enemies, and respected by my allies. Riches and honours, power and pleasure, have waited on my call, nor does any earthly blessing appear to have been wanting to my felicity. In this situation I have diligently numbered the days of pure and genuine happiness which have fallen to my lot: they amount to FOURTEEN:— O man! place not thy confidence in this present world!"[60] The luxury of the caliphs, so useless to their private happiness, relaxed the nerves, and terminated the progress, of the Arabian empire. Temporal and spiritual conquest had been the sole occupation of the first successors of Mahomet; and, after supplying themselves with the necessaries of life, the whole revenue was scrupulously devoted to that salutary work. The Abbas-

(margin note: Its consequences on private and public happiness)

[59] Cardonne, Histoire de l'Afrique et de l'Espagne, tom. i. p. 330-336. A just idea of the taste and architecture of the Arabians of Spain may be conceived from the description and plates of the Alhambra of Grenada (Swinburne's Travels, p. 171-188). [Owen Jones, Plans, elevations, sections and details of the Alhambra, 2 vols., 1842-5. On Saracen architecture and art in general, see E. S. Poole's Appendix to 5th ed. of Lane's Modern Egyptians, 1860. Architecture in Spain may be studied in the colossal Monumentos Architectonicos de España (in double elephant folio). For a brief account of Saracenic architecture in Spain, see Burke's History of Spain, vol. ii. p. 15 *sqq.*]

[60] Cardonne, tom. i. p. 329, 330. This confession, the complaints of Solomon of the vanity of this world (read Prior's verbose but eloquent poem), and the happy ten days of the emperor Seghed (Rambler, No. 204, 205), will be triumphantly quoted by the detractors of human life. Their expectations are commonly immoderate, their estimates are seldom impartial. If I may speak of myself (the only person of whom I can speak with certainty), *my* happy hours have far exceeded, and far exceed, the scanty numbers of the caliph of Spain; and I shall not scruple to add that many of them are due to the pleasing labour of the present composition.

sides were impoverished by the multitude of their wants and
their contempt of œconomy.   Instead of pursuing the great
object of ambition, their leisure, their affections, the powers of
their mind, were diverted by pomp and pleasure ; the rewards
of valour were embezzled by women and eunuchs, and the royal
camp was encumbered by the luxury of the palace.   A similar
temper was diffused among the subjects of the caliph.   Their
stern enthusiasm was softened by time and prosperity : they
sought riches in the occupations of industry, fame in the pursuits
of literature, and happiness in the tranquillity of domestic life.
War was no longer the passion of the Saracens ; and the increase of pay, the repetition of donatives, were insufficient to
allure the posterity of those voluntary champions who had
crowded to the standard of Abubeker and Omar for the hopes
of spoil and of paradise.

Introduc-
tion of
learning
among the
Arabians.
A.D. 754, &c.
813, &c.   Under the reign of the Ommiades, the studies of the Moslems were confined to the interpretation of the Koran, and the
eloquence and poetry of their native tongue.   A people continually exposed to the dangers of the field must esteem the healing powers of medicine or rather of surgery ; but the starving
physicians of Arabia murmured a complaint that exercise and
temperance deprived them of the greatest part of their practice.[61]
After their civil and domestic wars, the subjects of the Abbassides, awakening from this mental lethargy, found leisure and
felt curiosity for the acquisition of profane science.   This spirit
was first encouraged by the caliph Almansor, who, besides his
knowledge of the Mahometan law, had applied himself with
success to the study of astronomy.   But, when the sceptre devolved to Almamon, the seventh of the Abbassides, he completed
the designs of his grandfather, and invited the muses from their
ancient seats.   His ambassadors at Constantinople, his agents
in Armenia, Syria, and Egypt, collected the volumes of Grecian
science ; at his command they were translated by the most
skilful interpreters into the Arabic language ; his subjects were
exhorted assiduously to peruse these instructive writings ; and
the successor of Mahomet assisted with pleasure and modesty

---

[61] The Gulistan (p. 239) relates the conversation of Mahomet and a physician
(Epistol. Renaudot. in Fabricius, Bibliot. Græc. tom. i. p. 814).   The prophet
himself was skilled in the art of medicine ; and Gagnier (Vie de Mahomet, tom.
iii. p. 394-405) has given an extract of the aphorisms which are extant under his
name.

at the assemblies and disputations of the learned. "He was not ignorant," says Abulpharagius, "that *they* are the elect of God, his best and most useful servants, whose lives are devoted to the improvement of their rational faculties. The mean ambition of the Chinese or the Turks may glory in the industry of their hands or the indulgence of their brutal appetites. Yet these dexterous artists must view, with hopeless emulation, the hexagons and pyramids of the cells of a bee-hive : [62] these fortitudinous heroes are awed by the superior fierceness of the lions and tigers ; and in their amorous enjoyments they are much inferior to the vigour of the grossest and most sordid quadrupeds. The teachers of wisdom are the true luminaries and legislators of a world which, without their aid, would again sink in ignorance and barbarism." [63]   The zeal and curiosity of Almamon were imitated by succeeding princes of the line of Abbas ; their rivals, the Fatimites of Africa and the Ommiades of Spain, were the patrons of the learned, as well as the commanders of the faithful ; the same royal prerogative was claimed by their independent emirs of the provinces ; and their emulation diffused the taste and the rewards of science from Samarcand and Bochara to Fez and Cordova. The visir of a sultan consecrated a sum of two hundred thousand pieces of gold to the foundation of a college at Bagdad, which he endowed with an annual revenue of fifteen thousand dinars. The fruits of instruction were communicated, perhaps at different times, to six thousand disciples of every degree, from the son . of the noble to that of the mechanic ; a sufficient allowance was provided for the indigent scholars ; and the merit or industry of the professors was repaid with adequate stipends. In every

[62] See their curious architecture in Réaumur (Hist. des Insectes, tom. v. Mémoire viii.). These hexagons are closed by a pyramid ; the angles of the three sides of a similar pyramid, such as would accomplish the given end with the smallest quantity possible of materials, were determined by a mathematician, at 109 degrees 26 minutes for the larger, 70 degrees 34 minutes for the smaller. The actual measure is 109 degrees 28 minutes, 70 degrees 32 minutes. Yet this perfect harmony raises the work at the expense of the artist : the bees are not masters of transcendent geometry. [An attempt has recently been made to show that there is no discrepancy between the actual dimensions of the cells and the measures which would require the minimum of material.]

[63] Said Ebn Ahmed, cadhi of Toledo, who died a.h. 462, a.d. 1069, has furnished Abulpharagius (Dynast. p. 160) with this curious passage as well as with the text of Pocock's Specimen Historiæ Arabum. A number of literary anecdotes of philosophers, physicians, &c., who have flourished under each caliph, form the principal merit of the Dynasties of Abulpharagius.

city the productions of Arabic literature were copied and collected by the curiosity of the studious and the vanity of the rich. A private doctor refused the invitation of the sultan of Bochara, because the carriage of his books would have required four hundred camels. The royal library of the Fatimites consisted of one hundred thousand manuscripts, elegantly transcribed and splendidly bound, which were lent, with jealousy or avarice, to the students of Cairo. Yet this collection must appear moderate, if we can believe that the Ommiades of Spain had formed a library of six hundred thousand volumes, forty-four of which were employed in the mere catalogue. Their capital, Cordova, with the adjacent towns of Malaga, Almeria, and Murcia, had given birth to more than three hundred writers, and above seventy public libraries were opened in the cities of the Andalusian kingdom. The age of Arabian learning continued about five hundred years, till the great irruption of the Moguls, and was coeval with the darkest and most slothful period of European annals; but, since the sun of science has arisen in the West, it should seem that the Oriental studies have languished and declined.[64]

Their real progress in the sciences   In the libraries of the Arabians, as in those of Europe, the far greater part of the innumerable volumes were possessed only of local value or imaginary merit.[65] The shelves were crowded with orators and poets, whose style was adapted to the taste and manners of their countrymen; with general and partial histories, which each revolving generation supplied with a new harvest of persons and events; with codes and commentaries of jurisprudence, which derived their authority from the law of the prophet; with the interpreters of the Koran and orthodox tradition; and with the whole theological tribe, polemics, mystics, scholastics, and moralists, the first or the last of writers, according to the different estimate of sceptics or believers. The works of speculation or science may be reduced to the four

[64] These literary anecdotes are borrowed from the Bibliotheca Arabico-Hispana (tom. ii. p. 38, 71, 201, 202), Leo Africanus (de Arab. Medicis et Philosophis, in Fabric. Bibliot. Græc. tom. xiii. p. 259-298, particularly p. 274), and Renaudot (Hist. Patriarch. Alex. p. 274, 275, 536, 537), besides the chronological remarks of Abulpharagius.

[65] The Arabic catalogue of the Escurial will give a just idea of the proportion of the classes. In the library of Cairo, the Mss. of astronomy and medicine amounted to 6500, with two fair globes, the one of brass, the other of silver (Bibliot. Arab. Hisp. tom i. p. 417).

classes of philosophy, mathematics, astronomy, and physic. The sages of Greece were translated and illustrated in the Arabic language, and some treatises, now lost in the original, have been recovered in the versions of the East,[66] which possessed and studied the writings of Aristotle and Plato, of Euclid and Apollonius, of Ptolemy, Hippocrates, and Galen.[67] Among the ideal systems, which have varied with the fashion of the times, the Arabians adopted the philosophy of the Stagirite, alike intelligible or alike obscure for the readers of every age. Plato wrote for the Athenians, and his allegorical genius is too closely blended with the language and religion of Greece. After the fall of that religion, the Peripatetics, emerging from their obscurity, prevailed in the controversies of the Oriental sects, and their founder was long afterwards restored by the Mahometans of Spain to the Latin schools.[68] The physics both of the Academy and the Lyceum, as they are built, not on observation, but on argument, have retarded the progress of real knowledge. The metaphysics of infinite or finite spirit have too often been enlisted in the service of superstition. But the human faculties are fortified by the art and practice of dialectics; the ten predicaments of Aristotle collect and methodize our ideas,[69] and his

[66] As, for instance, the fifth, sixth, and seventh books (the eighth is still wanting) of the Conic Sections of Apollonius Pergæus [flor. circa, 200 B.C.], which were printed from the Florence Ms. 1661 (Fabric. Bibliot. Græc. tom. ii. p. 559). Yet the fifth book had been previously restored by the mathematical divination of Viviani (see his Eloge in Fontenelle, tom. v. p. 59, &c.). [The first 4 books of the κωνικὰ στοιχεῖα are preserved in Greek. Editions by Halley, 1710; Heiberg, 1888.]

[67] The merit of these Arabic versions is freely discussed by Renaudot (Fabric. Bibliot. Græc. tom. i. p. 812-816), and piously defended by Casiri (Bibliot. Arab. Hispana, tom. i. p. 238-240). Most of the versions of Plato, Aristotle, Hippocrates, Galen, &c., are ascribed to Honain [Ibn Ishāk, a native of Hira], a physician of the Nestorian sect, who flourished at Bagdad in the court of the caliphs, and died A.D. 876 [874]. He was at the head of a school or manufacture of translations, and the works of his sons and disciples were published under his name. See Abulpharagius (Dynast. p. 88, 115, 171-174, and apud Asseman. Bibliot. Orient. tom. ii. p. 438), d'Herbelot (Bibliot. Orientale, p. 456), Asseman (Bibliot. Orient. tom. iii. p. 164), and Casiri, Bibliot. Arab. Hispana, tom. i. p. 238, &c., 251, 286-290, 302, 304, &c. [See also Wenrich, de auctorum Græcorum versionibus et commentariis Syriacis, 1842; J. Lippert, Studien auf dem Gebiete der griechischarabischen Uebersetzungs-Litteratur, pt. 1, 1894; Brockelmann, Geschichte der arabischen Litteratur, i. 201 sqq. On Arabic versions from Latin, see Wüstenfeld, Die Uebersetzungen arabischer Werke in das Lateinische seit dem xi. Jahrh., in Abh. d. k. Ges. d. Wiss. zu Göttingen, vol. 22, 1877.]

[68] See Mosheim, Institut. Hist. Eccles. p. 181, 214, 236, 257, 315, 338, 396, 438, &c.

[69] The most elegant commentary on the Categories or Predicaments of Aristotle may be found in the Philosophical Arrangements of Mr. James Harris (London,

syllogism is the keenest weapon of dispute. It was dexterously wielded in the schools of the Saracens, but, as it is more effectual for the detection of error than for the investigation of truth, it is not surprising that new generations of masters and disciples should still revolve in the same circle of logical argument. The mathematics are distinguished by a peculiar privilege that, in the course of ages, they may always advance and can never recede. But the ancient geometry, if I am not misinformed, was resumed in the same state by the Italians of the fifteenth century; and, whatever may be the origin of the name, the science of algebra is ascribed to the Grecian Diophantus by the modest testimony of the Arabs themselves.[70] They cultivated with more success the sublime science of astronomy, which elevates the mind of man to disdain his diminutive planet and momentary existence. The costly instruments of observation were supplied by the caliph Almamon, and the land of the Chaldeans still afforded the same spacious level, the same un-

[Sinjar] clouded horizon. In the plains of Sinaar, and a second time in those of Cufa, his mathematicians accurately measured a degree of the great circle of the earth, and determined at twenty-four thousand miles the entire circumference of our globe.[71] From the reign of the Abbassides to that of the grandchildren of Tamerlane, the stars, without the aid of glasses, were diligently observed; and the astronomical tables of Bagdad, Spain, and Samarcand,[72] correct some minute errors, without daring to

1775, in octavo), who laboured to revive the studies of Grecian literature and philosophy.

[70] Abulpharagius, Dynast. p. 81, 222. Bibliot. Arab. Hist. tom. i. p. 370, 371. In quem (says the primate of the Jacobites) si immiserit se lector, oceanum hoc in genere (*algebrae*) inveniet. The time of Diophantus of Alexandria is un-known [probably 4th century A.D.], but his six books are still extant, and have been illustrated by the Greek Planudes and the Frenchman Meziriac (Fabric. Bibliot. Græc. tom. iv. p. 12-15). [His work entitled 'Αριθμητικά originally consisted of 13 books; only 6 are extant. Meziriac's ed. appeared in 1621, and Fermat's text in 1670; but these have been superseded by P. Tannery's recent edition.]

[71] Abulfeda (Annal. Moslem. p. 210, 211, vers. Reiske) describes this operation according to Ibn Challecan and the best historians. This degree most accurately contains 200,000 royal or Hashemite cubits, which Arabia had derived from the sacred and legal practice both of Palestine and Egypt. This ancient cubit is re-peated 400 times in each basis of the great pyramid, and seems to indicate the primitive and universal measures of the East. See the Métrologie of the laborious M. Paucton, p. 101-195. [See Al-Masūdī, Prairies d'or, i. 182-3; and cp. Sedillot, Hist. Générale des Arabes, ii. Appendice 256-7. There seems to be no mention of the degree in Tabari. There is a mistake in Gibbon's reference to Abulfeda, which the editor is unable to correct.]

[72] See the Astronomical Tables of Ulegh Begh, with the preface of Dr. Hyde in the first volume of his Syntagma Dissertationum, Oxon., 1767.

renounce the hypothesis of Ptolemy, without advancing a step towards the discovery of the solar system. In the eastern courts, the truths of science could be recommended only by ignorance and folly, and the astronomer would have been disregarded, had he not abased his wisdom or honesty by the vain predictions of astrology.[73]   But in the science of medicine, the Arabians have been deservedly applauded.[74]   The names of Mesua and Geber, of Razis and Avicenna, are ranked with the Grecian masters; in the city of Bagdad, eight hundred and sixty physicians were licensed to exercise their lucrative profession;[75] in Spain, the life of the Catholic princes was entrusted to the skill of the Saracens,[76] and the school of Salerno, their legitimate offspring, revived in Italy and Europe the precepts of the healing art.[77]   The success of each professor must have been influenced by personal and accidental causes; but we may form a less fanciful estimate of their general knowledge of anatomy,[78] botany,[79] and chemistry,[80] the threefold basis of their theory and practice.   A superstitious reverence for the dead confined both the Greeks and the Arabians to the dissection of apes and quadrupeds; the more solid and visible parts were known in the time

[73] The truth of astrology was allowed by Albumazar, and the best of the Arabian astronomers, who drew their most certain predictions, not from Venus and Mercury, but from Jupiter and the sun (Abulpharag. Dynast. p. 161-163). For the state and science of the Persian astronomers, see Chardin (Voyages en Perse, tom. iii. p. 162-203).

[74] [Wüstenfeld, Geschichte der arabischen Aerzte.]

[75] Bibliot. Arabico-Hispana, tom. i. p. 438. The original relates a pleasant tale, of an ignorant but harmless practitioner.

[76] In the year 956, Sancho the fat, king of Leon, was cured by the physicians of Cordova (Mariana, l. viii. c. 7, tom. i. p. 318).

[77] The school of Salerno, and the introduction of the Arabian sciences into Italy, are discussed with learning and judgment by Muratori (Antiquitat. Italiæ Medii Ævi, tom. iii. p. 932-940) and Giannone (Istoria Civile de Napoli, tom. ii. p. 119-127). [The school of Salerno was *not* under the influence of Arabic medicine. See below, p. 197.]

[78] See a good view of the progress of anatomy in Wotton (Reflections on ancient and modern Learning, p. 208-256). His reputation has been unworthily depreciated by the wits in the controversy of Boyle and Bentley.

[79] Bibliot. Arab. Hispana, tom. i. p. 275. Al Beithar [Abd Allāh al-Baitar] of Malaga, their greatest botanist, had travelled into Africa, Persia, and India.

[80] Dr. Watson (Elements of Chemistry, vol. i. p. 17, &c.) allows the *original* merit of the Arabians. Yet he quotes the modest confession of the famous Geber of the ninth century (d'Herbelot, p. 387), that he had drawn most of his science, perhaps of the transmutation of metals, from the ancient sages. Whatever might be the origin or extent of their knowledge, the arts of chemistry and alchymy appeared to have been known in Egypt at least three hundred years before Mahomet (Wotton's Reflections, p. 121-133. Pauw, Recherches sur les Egyptiens et les Chinois, tom. i. p. 376-429). [The names alcali, alcohol, alembic, *al*chymy, &c., show the influence of the Arabians on the study of chemistry in the West.]

of Galen, and the finer scrutiny of the human frame was reserved
for the microscope and the injections of modern artists. Botany
is an active science, and the discoveries of the torrid zone might
enrich the herbal of Dioscorides with two thousand plants.
Some traditionary knowledge might be secreted in the temples
and monasteries of Egypt; much useful experience had been
acquired in the practice of arts and manufactures; but the *science*
of chemistry owes its origin and improvement to the industry
of the Saracens. They first invented and named the alembic
for the purpose of distillation, analysed the substances of the
three kingdoms of nature, tried the distinction and affinities of
alcalis and acids, and converted the poisonous minerals into soft
and salutary medicines. But the most eager search of Arabian
chemistry was the transmutation of metals and the elixir of
immortal health; the reason and the fortunes of thousands were
evaporated in the crucibles of alchymy, and the consummation
of the great work was promoted by the worthy aid of mystery,
fable, and superstition.

Want of
erudition,
taste, and
freedom But the Moslems deprived themselves of the principal benefits
of a familiar intercourse with Greece and Rome, the knowledge
of antiquity, the purity of taste, and the freedom of thought.
Confident in the riches of their native tongue, the Arabians disdained the study of any foreign idiom. The Greek interpreters
were chosen among their Christian subjects; they formed their
translations, sometimes on the original text, more frequently
perhaps on a Syriac version; and in the crowd of astronomers
and physicians there is no example of a poet, an orator, or even
an historian being taught to speak the language of the Saracens.[81]
The mythology of Homer would have provoked the abhorrence
of those stern fanatics; they possessed in lazy ignorance the
colonies of the Macedonians, and the provinces of Carthage and
Rome: the heroes of Plutarch and Livy were buried in oblivion;
and the history of the world before Mahomet was reduced to a
short legend of the patriarchs, the prophets, and the Persian
kings. Our education in the Greek and Latin schools may have
fixed in our minds a standard of exclusive taste; and I am not

---

[81] Abulpharagius (Dynast. p. 26, 148) mentions a *Syriac* version of Homer's
two poems, by Theophilus, a Christian Maronite of Mount Libanus, who professed
astronomy at Roha or Edessa towards the end of the eighth century. His work
would be a literary curiosity. I have read somewhere, but I do not believe, that
Plutarch's Lives were translated into Turkish for the use of Mahomet the Second.

MOHAMMEDAN ART: THE MOSQUE OF OMAR, OR DOME OF THE ROCK (KUBBET ES SAKKRA) JERUSALEM; END OF THE 7TH CENTURY A.D.

forward to condemn the literature and judgment of nations of whose language I am ignorant. Yet I *know* that the classics have much to teach and I *believe* that the Orientals have much to learn; the temperate dignity of style, the graceful proportions of art, the forms of visible and intellectual beauty, the just delineation of character and passion, the rhetoric of narrative and argument, the regular fabric of epic and dramatic poetry.[82]   The influence of truth and reason is of a less ambiguous complexion. The philosophers of Athens and Rome enjoyed the blessings, and asserted the rights, of civil and religious freedom.   Their moral and political writings might have gradually unlocked the fetters of Eastern despotism, diffused a liberal spirit of enquiry and toleration, and encouraged the Arabian sages to suspect that their caliph was a tyrant and their prophet an impostor.[83]   The instinct of superstition was alarmed by the introduction even of the abstract sciences; and the more rigid doctors of the law condemn the rash and pernicious curiosity of Almamon.[84]   To the thirst of martyrdom, the vision of paradise, and the belief of predestination, we must ascribe the invincible enthusiasm of the prince and people.   And the sword of the Saracens became less formidable, when their youth was drawn away from the camp to the college, when the armies of the faithful presumed to read and to reflect.   Yet the foolish vanity of the Greeks was jealous of their studies, and reluctantly imparted the sacred fire to the barbarians of the East.[85]

In the bloody conflict of the Ommiades and Abbassides, the Greeks had stolen the opportunity of avenging their wrongs and

Wars of Harun al Rashid against the Romans.
A.D. 781-805 [806]

[82] I have perused with much pleasure Sir William Jones's Latin Commentary on Asiatic Poetry (London, 1774, in octavo), which was composed in the youth of that wonderful linguist. At present, in the maturity of his taste and judgment, he would perhaps abate of the fervent, and even partial, praise which he has bestowed on the Orientals.

[83] Among the Arabian philosophers, Averroes has been accused of despising the religion of the Jews, the Christians, and the Mahometans (see his article in Bayle's Dictionary). Each of these sects would agree that in two instances out of three his contempt was reasonable.

[84] D'Herbelot, Bibliothèque Orientale, p. 546. [Abd Allāh al-Mamūn (813-833 A.D.).]

[85] Θεόφιλος ἄτοπον κρίνας εἰ τὴν τῶν ὄντων γνῶσιν, δι' ἣν τὸ 'Ρωμαίων γένος θαυμά-ζεται, ἔκδοτον ποιήσει τοῖς ἔθνεσι, &c. ; Cedrenus, p. 548 [ii. p. 169, ed. Bonn], who relates how manfully the emperor refused a mathematician to the instances and offers of the caliph Almamon. This absurd scruple is expressed almost in the same words by the continuator of Theophanes (Scriptores post Theophanem, p. 118 [p. 190, ed. Bonn]). [The continuation of Theophanes is the source of Scylitzes, who was transcribed by Cedrenus.]

enlarging their limits.   But a severe retribution was exacted by
Mohadi,[86] the third caliph of the new dynasty, who seized in his
turn the favourable opportunity, while a woman and a child, Irene
and Constantine, were seated on the Byzantine throne.   An army
of ninety-five thousand Persians and Arabs was sent from the
Tigris to the Thracian Bosphorus, under the command of Harun,[87]
or Aaron, the second son of the commander of the faithful.   His
encampment on the opposite heights of Chrysopolis, or Scutari,
informed Irene, in her palace of Constantinople, of the loss of
her troops and provinces.   With the consent or connivance of
their sovereign, her ministers subscribed an ignominious peace ;
and the exchange of some royal gifts could not disguise the
annual tribute of seventy thousand dinars of gold, which was
imposed on the Roman empire.   The Saracens had too rashly
advanced into the midst of a distant and hostile land ; their retreat was solicited by the promise of faithful guides and plentiful
markets ; and not a Greek had courage to whisper that their
weary forces might be surrounded and destroyed in their necessary passage between a slippery mountain and the river San-
[A.D. 786]   garius.   Five years after this expedition, Harun ascended the
throne of his father and his elder brother:[88] the most powerful
and vigorous monarch of his race, illustrious in the West as the
ally of Charlemagne, and familiar to the most childish readers
as the perpetual hero of the Arabian tales.   His title to the
name of *Al Rashid* (the *Just*) is sullied by the extirpation of the
generous, perhaps the innocent, Barmecides ; yet he could listen
to the complaint of a poor widow who had been pillaged by his
troops, and who dared, in a passage of the Koran, to threaten
the inattentive despot with the judgment of God and posterity.
[A.D. 786-   His court was adorned with luxury and science ; but, in a reign
807]   of three-and-twenty years, Harun repeatedly visited his provinces
from Chorasan to Egypt ; nine times he performed the pilgrimage of Mecca ; eight times he invaded the territories of the
Romans ; and, as often as they declined the payment of the
tribute, they were taught to feel that a month of depredation

[86] [Al-Mahdī Mohammad ibn Mansūr, A.D. 775-785.]
[87] See the reign and character of Harun al Rashid [Hārūn ar-Rashīd, caliph
786-809 A.D.], in the Bibliothèque Orientale, p. 431-433, under his proper title ; and
in the relative articles to which M. d'Herbelot refers.   That learned collector has
shewn much taste in stripping the Oriental chronicles of their instructive and
amusing anecdotes.
[88] [Abū Mohammad Mūsā al-Hādī, A.D. 785-6.]

was more costly than a year of submission. But, when the [A.D. 802] unnatural mother of Constantine was deposed and banished, her successor Nicephorus resolved to obliterate this badge of servitude and disgrace. The epistle of the emperor to the caliph was pointed with an allusion to the game of chess, which had already spread from Persia to Greece. " The queen (he spoke of Irene) considered you as a rook and herself as a pawn. That pusillanimous female submitted to pay a tribute, the double of which she ought to have exacted from the barbarians. Restore therefore the fruits of your injustice, or abide the determination of the sword." At these words the ambassadors cast a bundle of swords before the foot of the throne. The caliph smiled at the menace, and drawing his scymetar, *samsamah*, a weapon of historic or fabulous renown,[88a] he cut asunder the feeble arms of the Greeks, without turning the edge or endangering the temper of his blade. He then dictated an epistle of tremendous brevity: " In the name of the most merciful God, Harun al Rashid, commander of the faithful, to Nicephorus, the Roman dog. I have read thy letter, O thou son of an unbelieving mother. Thou shalt not hear, thou shalt behold, my reply." It was written in characters of blood and fire on the plains of Phrygia; and the warlike celerity of the Arabs could only be checked by the arts of deceit and the show of repentance. The triumphant caliph retired, after the fatigues of the campaign, to his favourite palace of Racca, on the Euphrates;[89] but the distance of five hundred miles, and the inclemency of the season, encouraged his adversary to violate the peace. Nicephorus was astonished by the bold and rapid march of the commander of the faithful, who repassed, in [A.D. 803] the depth of winter, the snows of mount Taurus: his stratagems of policy and war were exhausted; and the perfidious Greek escaped with three wounds from a field of battle overspread with forty thousand of his subjects.[90] Yet the emperor was ashamed

---

[88a] [Samsāma, = " inflexible sword," was particularly the name of the sword of the Arab hero Amr ibn Madi Kerib.]

[89] For the situation of Racca, the old Nicephorium, consult d'Anville (l'Euphrate et le Tigre, p. 24-27). The Arabian Nights represent Harun al Rashid as almost stationary in Bagdad. He respected the royal seat of the Abbassides, but the vices of the inhabitants had driven him from the city (Abulfed. Annal. p. 167). [" The extirpation of the Barmecides made such a bad impression in Bagdad, where the family was held in high respect, that Harun was probably induced thereby to transfer his residence to Rakka." Weil, *op. cit.*, vol. ii. p. 144.]

[90] [According to Arabic authorities Hārūn himself invaded Asia Minor twice in A.D. 803. The first time he appeared before Heraclea and the promise of tribute

of submission, and the caliph was resolved on victory.   One hundred and thirty-five thousand regular soldiers received pay, and were inscribed in the military roll; and above three hundred thousand persons of every denomination marched under the black standard of the Abbassides.   They swept the surface of Asia Minor far beyond Tyana and Ancyra, and invested the Pontic Heraclea,[91] once a flourishing state, now a paltry town; at that time capable of sustaining in her antique walls a month's

[A.D. 806]   siege against the forces of the East.   The ruin was complete, the spoil was ample; but, if Harun had been conversant with Grecian story, he would have regretted the statue of Hercules, whose attributes, the club, the bow, the quiver, and the lion's hide, were sculptured in massy gold.   The progress of desolation by sea and land, from the Euxine to the isle of Cyprus, compelled the emperor Nicephorus to retract his haughty defiance.   In the new treaty, the ruins of Heraclea were left for ever as a lesson and a trophy; and the coin of the tribute was marked with the image and superscription of Harun and his three sons.[92]   Yet this plurality of lords might contribute to remove the dishonour of the Roman name.   After the death of their father, the heirs of the caliph were involved in civil discord, and the conqueror, the liberal Almamon, was sufficiently engaged in the restoration of domestic peace and the introduction of foreign science.

The Arabs subdue the isle of Crete, A.D. 823   Under the reign of Almamon at Bagdad, of Michael the Stammerer at Constantinople, the islands of Crete[93] and Sicily

induced him to retreat; but the tribute was not paid and he repassed the Taurus at the end of the year to exact it.   The battle in which 40,000 Greeks are said to have fallen was fought in the following year, A.D. 804, but Hārūn's general, Jabril, led the invaders.   Heraclea was not taken till a subsequent campaign, A.D. 806.   Cp. Weil, *op. cit.*, ii. p. 159-60.   Tabari, ed. de Goeje, iii. 695-8.]

[91] M. de Tournefort, in his coasting voyage from Constantinople to Trebizond, passed a night at Heraclea or Eregri.   His eye surveyed the present state, his reading collected the antiquities of the city (Voyage du Levant, tom. iii. lettre xvi. p. 23-35).   We have a separate history of Heraclea in the fragments of Memnon, which are preserved by Photius.   [The Heraclea which Harun took is not the Pontic city, but Eregli, west of Tyana.]

[92] The wars of Harun al Rashid against the Roman empire are related by Theophanes (p. 384, 385, 391, 396, 407, 408 [sub A.M. 6274, 6281, 6287, 6298, 6300]), Zonaras (tom. ii. l. xv. p. 115, 124 [c. 10 and c. 15]), Cedrenus (p. 477, 478 [ii. p. 34, ed. Bonn]), Eutychius (Annal. tom. ii. p. 407), Elmacin (Hist. Saracen. p. 136, 151, 152), Abulpharagius (Dynast. p. 147, 151), and Abulfeda (p. 156, 166-168). [An English translation of extracts from the most important Arabic sources (Tabari, Baladhuri, &c.) is given by E. W. Brooks, Byzantines and Arabs in the Time of the Early Abbasids, English Historical Review, Oct. 1900 and Jan. 1901.   See Weil, *op. cit.*, ii. p. 155 *sqq.*]

[93] The authors from whom I have learned the most of the ancient and modern state of Crete are Belon (Observations, &c., c. 3-20, Paris, 1555), Tournefort

were subdued by the Arabs.   The former of these conquests is
disdained by their own writers, who were ignorant of the fame
of Jupiter and Minos, but it has not been overlooked by the
Byzantine historians, who now begin to cast a clearer light on
the affairs of their own times.[94]   A band of Andalusian volunteers, discontented with the climate or government of Spain,
explored the adventures of the sea; but, as they sailed in no
more than ten or twenty galleys, their warfare must be branded
with the name of piracy.   As the subjects and sectaries of the
white party, they might lawfully invade the dominions of the
black caliphs.   A rebellious faction introduced them into Alexandria;[95] they cut in pieces both friends and foes, pillaged the
churches and the mosques, sold above six thousand Christian
captives, and maintained their station in the capital of Egypt,
till they were oppressed by the forces and the presence of Almamon himself.   From the mouth of the Nile to the Hellespont,
the islands and sea-coasts, both of the Greeks and Moslems,
were exposed to their depredations; they saw, they envied, they
tasted the fertility of Crete, and soon returned with forty galleys
to a more serious attack.   The Andalusians wandered over the
land fearless and unmolested; but, when they descended with
their plunder to the sea-shore, their vessels were in flames, and
their chief, Abu Caab, confessed himself the author of the mis- [Abu Hafs]

(Voyage du Levant, tom. i. lettre ii. et iii.), and Meursius (CRETA, in his works,
tom. iii. p. 343-544).   Although Crete is styled by Homer πίειρα, by Dionysius
λιπαρή τε καὶ εὔβοτος, I cannot conceive that mountainous island to surpass, or even
to equal, in fertility the greater part of Spain.

[94] The most authentic and circumstantial intelligence is obtained from the four
books of the Continuation of Theophanes, compiled by the pen or the command
of Constantine Porphyrogenitus, with the Life of his father Basil the Macedonian
(Scriptores post Theophanem, p. 1-162, a Francis. Combefis., Paris, 1685).   The
loss of Crete and Sicily is related, l. ii. p. 46-52.   To these we may add the secondary
evidence of Joseph Genesius (l. ii. p. 21, Venet. 1733 [p. 46-49, ed. Bonn]), George
Cedrenus (Compend. p. 506-508 [ii. p. 92 *sqq.* ed. Bonn]), and John Scylitzes
Curopalata (apud Baron. Annal. Eccles. A.D. 827, No. 24, &c.).   But the modern
Greeks are such notorious plagiaries that I should only quote a plurality of names.
[These historiographical implications are not quite correct.   Genesius is not a
"secondary" authority in relation to the Scriptores post Theophanem; on the
contrary, he is a source of the Continuation of Theophanes.   See above, Appendix
1 to vol. 5, p. 535; for the sources of Genesius himself, *ib.* p. 534.   The order of
"plagiarism" is (1) Genesius, (2) Continuation of Theophanes, (3) Scylitzes, (4)
Cedrenus.]

[95] Renaudot (Hist. Patriarch. Alex. p. 251-256, 268-270) has described the rav-
ages of the Andalusian Arabs in Egypt, but has forgot to connect them with the
conquest of Crete.   [Tabari places the conquest of Crete in A.H. 210.   The first expeditions probably belong to A.D. 824-5.   Cp. A. Vasil'ev, Vizantiia i Araby, i. 46
sqq.]

chief. Their clamours accused his madness or treachery. "Of
what do you complain?" replied the crafty emir. "I have
brought you to a land flowing with milk and honey. Here is
your true country; repose from your toils, and forget the barren
place of your nativity." "And our wives and children?"
"Your beauteous captives will supply the place of your wives,
and in their embraces you will soon become the fathers of a
new progeny." The first habitation was their camp, with a
ditch and rampart, in the bay of Suda; but an apostate monk
led them to a more desirable position in the eastern parts; and
[Khandak] the name of Candax, their fortress and colony, had been extended to the whole island, under the corrupt and modern appellation of *Candia*. The hundred cities of the age of Minos
were diminished to thirty; and of these, only one, most probably
Cydonia, had courage to retain the substance of freedom and
the profession of Christianity. The Saracens of Crete soon repaired the loss of their navy; and the timbers of mount Ida
were launched into the main. During an hostile period, of one
hundred and thirty-eight years, the princes of Constantinople
attacked these licentious corsairs with fruitless curses and ineffectual arms.

and of
Sicily,
A.D. 827-878   The loss of Sicily [96] was occasioned by an act of superstitious
rigour. An amorous youth, who had stolen a nun from her
cloister, was sentenced by the emperor to the amputation of his
[A.D. 826] tongue. Euphemius [97] appealed to the reason and policy of the
Saracens of Africa; and soon returned with the Imperial purple,

[96] Δηλοῖ (says the continuator of Theophanes, l. ii. p. 51 [p. 32, ed. Bonn]) δὲ
ταῦτα σαφέστατα καὶ πλατικώτερον ἡ τότε γραφεῖσα Θεογνώστῳ καὶ εἰς χεῖρας ἐλθοῦσα
ἡμῶν. This [contemporary] history of the loss of Sicily is no longer extant. Muratori
(Annali d'Italia, tom. vii. p. 7, 19, 21, &c.) has added some circumstances from the
Italian chronicles. [For the Saracens in Sicily the chief modern work is M. Amari's
Storia dei Musulmani di Sicilia, in 3 vols. (1854-68). The same scholar published
a collection of Arabic texts relating to the history of Sicily (1857) and an Italian
translation thereof (Bibloteca arabo-sicula, versione italiana, 1880). There had been
several previous Saracen descents on Sicily: in A.D. 652 (the island was defended
by the Exarch Olympius); in A.D. 669 Syracuse was plundered. Both these invasions were from Syria. Then in A.D. 704 the descents from Africa began under
Mūsā with the destruction of an unnamed town on the west coast, which Amari
has identified with Lilybæum. The new town of Marsa-Ali (Marsala) took its
place. In 705 Syracuse was plundered again; and the island was repeatedly invaded in the eighth century. A. Holm has summarised these invasions in vol. 3
of his Geschichte Siciliens im Alterthum (1898), p. 316 *sqq.* See also Vasil'ev, *op.
cit.*, i. and ii.]

[97] [Euphemius revolted and declared himself Emperor in A.D. 826. See Amari
Storia d. Mus. i. 239 *sqq.* He was soon thrust aside by the Saracens. His name'
survives in the name of the town Calatafimi.]

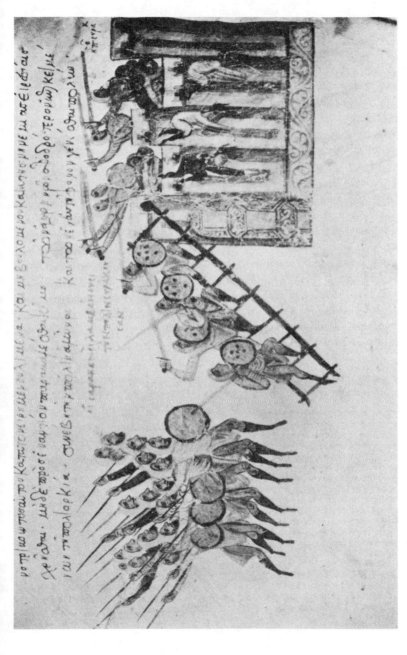

CAPTURE OF SYRACUSE BY THE SARACENS. FROM THE MS. OF SKYLITZES AT MADRID

a fleet of one hundred ships, and an army of seven hundred horse and ten thousand foot. They landed at Mazara near the [June 13, A.D. 827] ruins of the ancient Selinus; but, after some partial victories, Syracuse [98] was delivered by the Greeks, the apostate was slain before her walls, and his African friends were reduced to the necessity of feeding on the flesh of their own horses. In their turn they were relieved by a powerful [99] reinforcement of their brethren of Andalusia; the largest and western part of the island was gradually reduced, and the commodious harbour of Palermo was chosen for the seat of the naval and military power of the [A.D. 831] Saracens. Syracuse preserved about fifty years the faith which she had sworn to Christ and to Cæsar. In the last and fatal siege, her citizens displayed some remnant of the spirit which [Siege of Syracuse. A.D. 877-8] had formerly resisted the powers of Athens and Carthage. They stood about twenty days against the battering-rams and *catapultae*, the mines and tortoises of the besiegers; and the place might have been relieved, if the mariners of the Imperial fleet had not been detained at Constantinople in building a church to the Virgin Mary. The deacon Theodosius, with the bishop and clergy, was dragged in chains from the altar to Palermo, cast into a subterraneous dungeon, and exposed to the hourly peril of death or apostacy. His pathetic, and not inelegant, complaint may be read as the epitaph of his country.[100] From the Roman conquest to this final calamity, Syracuse, now [May 21, A.D. 878] dwindled to the primitive isle of Ortygia, had insensibly declined. Yet the relics were still precious; the plate of the cathedral weighed five thousand pounds of silver; the entire spoil was computed at one million of pieces of gold (about four hundred thousand pounds sterling); and the captives must out- [£600,000]

[98] The splendid and interesting tragedy of *Tancrede* would adapt itself much better to this epoch than to the date (A.D. 1005) which Voltaire himself has chosen. But I must gently reproach the poet for infusing into the Greek subjects the spirit of modern knights and ancient republicans.

[99] [Hardly powerful; the important help which led to the capture of Palermo came from Africa in A.D. 830. The invaders tried hard to take the fortress of Henna, but did not succeed till 859.]

[100] The narrative or lamentation of Theodosius is transcribed and illustrated by Pagi (Critica, tom. iii. p. 719, &c.). Constantine Porphyrogenitus (in Vit. Basil. c. 69, 70, p. 190-192) mentions the loss of Syracuse and the triumph of the demons. [The letter of Theodosius to his friend Leo on the capture of Syracuse is published in Hase's ed. of Leo Diaconus (Paris, 1819), p. 177 *sqq.*—It may be well to summarise the progress of the Saracen conquest of Sicily chronologically: Mazara captured 827; Mineo 828; Palermo 831; c. 840 Caltabellotta and other places; 847 Leontini; 848 Ragusa; 853 Camarina; 858 Cefalù; 859 Henna; 868-70 Malta; 878 Syracuse; 902 Taormina, Rametta, Catania.]

number the seventeen thousand Christians who were transported from the sack of Tauromenium into African servitude.   In Sicily the religion and language of the Greeks were eradicated; and such was the docility of the rising generation that fifteen thousand boys were circumcised and clothed on the same day with the son of the Fatimite caliph.   The Arabian squadrons issued from the harbours of Palermo, Biserta, and Tunis; an hundred and fifty towns of Calabria and Campania were attacked and pillaged; nor could the suburbs of Rome be defended by the name of the Cæsars and Apostles.   Had the Mahometans been united, Italy must have fallen an easy and glorious accession to the empire of the prophet.   But the caliphs of Bagdad had lost their authority in the West; the Aglabites and Fatimites usurped the provinces of Africa; their emirs of Sicily aspired to independence; and the design of conquest and dominion was degraded to a repetition of predatory inroads.[101]

In the sufferings of prostrate Italy, the name of Rome awakens a solemn and mournful recollection.   A fleet of Saracens from the African coast presumed to enter the mouth of the Tiber, and to approach a city which even yet, in her fallen state, was revered as the metropolis of the Christian world. The gates and ramparts were guarded by a trembling people; but the tombs and temples of St. Peter and St. Paul were left exposed in the suburbs of the Vatican and of the Ostian way. Their invisible sanctity had protected them against the Goths, the Vandals, and the Lombards; but the Arabs disdained both the gospel and the legend; and their rapacious spirit was approved and animated by the precepts of the Koran.   The Christian *idols* were stripped of their costly offerings; a silver altar was torn away from the shrine of St. Peter; and, if the bodies or the buildings were left entire, their deliverance must be imputed to the haste, rather than the scruples, of the Saracens.[102]   In their course along the Appian way, they pillaged Fundi and besieged Gayeta; but they had turned aside from the walls of Rome, and, by their divisions, the Capitol was

[101] The extracts from the Arabic histories of Sicily are given in Abulfeda (Annal. Moslem. p. 271-273) and in the first volume of Muratori's Scriptores Rerum Italicarum.   M. de Guignes (Hist. des Huns, tom. i. p. 363, 364) has added some important facts.

[102] [See the account in Gregorovius, Rome in the Middle Ages (E. T.), vol. 3, p. 87 *sqq*. Gregorovius describes the wealth of St. Peter's treasures at this time. Gibbon omits to mention that Guy of Spoleto relieved Rome.]

saved from the yoke of the prophet of Mecca. The same danger still impended on the heads of the Roman people; and their domestic force was unequal to the assault of an African emir. They claimed the protection of their Latin sovereign; but the Carlovingian standard was overthrown by a detachment of the barbarians; they meditated the restoration of the Greek emperors; but the attempt was treasonable, and the succour remote and precarious.[103] Their distress appeared to receive some aggravation from the death of their spiritual and temporal chiefs; but the pressing emergency superseded the forms and intrigues of an election; and the unanimous choice of pope [A.D. 847] Leo the Fourth[104] was the safety of the church and city. This pontiff was born a Roman; the courage of the first ages of the republic glowed in his breast; and, amidst the ruins of his country, he stood erect, like one of the firm and lofty columns that rear their heads above the fragments of the Roman forum. The first days of his reign were consecrated to the purification and removal of relics, to prayers and processions, and to all the solemn offices of religion, which served at least to heal the imagination, and restore the hopes, of the multitude. The public defence had been long neglected, not from the presumption of peace, but from the distress and poverty of the times. As far as the scantiness of his means and the shortness of his leisure would allow, the ancient walls were repaired by the command of Leo; fifteen towers, in the most accessible stations, were built or renewed; two of these commanded on either side the Tiber; and an iron chain was drawn across the stream, to impede the ascent of an hostile navy. The Romans were assured of a short respite by the welcome news that the siege of Gayeta had been raised and that a part of the enemy, with their sacrilegious plunder, had perished in the waves.

But the storm which had been delayed soon burst upon Victory and reign of Leo IV. A.D. 849

[103] One of the most eminent Romans (Gratianus, magister militum et Romani palatii superista) was accused of declaring, Quia Franci nihil nobis boni faciunt, neque adjutorium præbent, sed magis quæ nostra sunt violenter tollunt. Quare non advocamus Græcos, et cum eis fœdus pacis componentes, Francorum regem et gentem de nostro regno et dominatione expellimus? Anastasius in Leone IV. p. 199.

[104] Voltaire (Hist. Générale, tom. ii. c. 38, p. 124) appears to be remarkably struck with the character of pope Leo IV. I have borrowed his general expression; but the sight of the forum has furnished me with a more distinct and lively image.

them with redoubled violence. The Aglabite,[105] who reigned in Africa, and had inherited from his father a treasure and an army : a fleet of Arabs and Moors, after a short refreshment in the harbours of Sardinia, cast anchor before the mouth of the Tiber, sixteen miles from the city; and their discipline and numbers appeared to threaten, not a transient inroad, but a serious design of conquest and dominion. But the vigilance of Leo had formed an alliance with the vassals of the Greek empire, the free and maritime states of Gayeta, Naples, and Amalfi ; and in the hour of danger their galleys appeared in the port of Ostia, under the command of Cæsarius, the son of the Neapolitan duke, a noble and valiant youth, who had already vanquished the fleets of the Saracens. With his principal companions, Cæsarius was invited to the Lateran palace, and the dexterous pontiff affected to inquire their errand, and to accept, with joy and surprise, their providential succour. The city bands, in arms, attended their father at Ostia, where he reviewed and blessed his generous deliverers. They kissed his feet, received the communion with martial devotion, and listened to the prayer of Leo, that the same God who had supported St. Peter and St. Paul on the waves of the sea would strengthen the hands of his champions against the adversaries of his holy name. After a similar prayer, and with equal resolution, the Moslems advanced to the attack of the Christian galleys, which preserved their advantageous station along the coast. The victory inclined to the side of the allies, when it was less gloriously decided in their favour by a sudden tempest, which confounded the skill and courage of the stoutest mariners. The Christians were sheltered in a friendly harbour, while the Africans were scattered and dashed in pieces among the rocks and islands of an hostile shore. Those who escaped from shipwreck and hunger neither found nor deserved mercy at the hands of their implacable pursuers.[106] The sword and the gibbet reduced the dangerous multitude of captives; and the remainder was more usefully employed, to restore the

[League of the Southern cities]

---

[105] De Guignes, Hist. Générale des Huns, tom. i. p. 363, 364. Cardonne, Hist. de l'Afrique et de l'Espagne, sous la Domination des Arabes, tom. ii. p. 24, 25. I observe, and cannot reconcile, the difference of these writers in the succession of the Aglabites. [The Aghlabid who reigned at this time was Mohammad I. (840-856). For the succession see S. Lane-Poole, Mohammadan Dynasties, p. 37.]

[106] [The battle of Ostia is the subject of a fresco of Raffaelle in the Vatican.]

sacred edifices which they had attempted to subvert. The pontiff, at the head of the citizens and allies, paid his grateful devotion at the shrines of the apostles ; and, among the spoils of this naval victory, thirteen Arabian bows of pure and massy silver were suspended round the altar of the fishermen of Galilee. The reign of Leo the Fourth was employed in the defence and ornament of the Roman state: the churches were renewed and embellished; near four thousand pounds of silver were consecrated to repair the losses of St. Peter ; and his sanctuary was decorated with a plate of gold the weight of two hundred and sixteen pounds ; embossed with the portraits of the pope and emperor, and encircled with a string of pearls. Yet this vain magnificence reflects less glory on the character of Leo than the paternal care with which he rebuilt the walls of Horta and Ameria ; and transported the wandering inhabitants of Centumcellæ to his new foundation of Leopolis, twelve miles from the seashore.[107]   By his liberality a colony of Corsicans, with their wives and children, was planted in the station of Porto at the mouth of the Tiber ; the falling city was re- [Rebuilding of Portus] stored for their use, the fields and vineyards were divided among the new settlers; their first efforts were assisted by a gift of horses and cattle ; and the hardy exiles, who breathed revenge against the Saracens, swore to live and die under the standard of St. Peter. The nations of the West and North, who visited the threshold of the apostles, had gradually formed the large and populous suburb of the Vatican, and their various habitations were distinguished, in the language of the times, as the *schools* of the Greeks and Goths, of the Lombards and Saxons. But this venerable spot was still open to sacrilegious insult; the design of enclosing it with walls and towers exhausted all that authority could command or charity would supply; and the pious labour of four years was animated in every season, and

---

[107] Beretti (Chorographia Italiæ Medii Ævi, p. 106, 108) has illustrated Centumcellæ, Leopolis, Civitas Leonina, and the other places of the Roman duchy. [Leopolis never flourished. For the walls of the Leonine city see Gregorovius, *op. cit.*, p. 97 *sqq.* The fortification of the Vatican had been already designed and begun by Pope Leo III. " The line of Leo the Fourth's walls, built almost in the form of a horseshoe, is still in part preserved, and may be traced in the Borgo near the passage of Alexander the Sixth, near the Mint or the papal garden as far as the thick corner tower, also in the line of the Porta Pertusa, and.at the point where the walls form a bend between another corner tower and the Porta Fabrica." Gregorovius, *ib.*, p. 98.]

at every hour, by the presence of the indefatigable pontiff.   The
love of fame, a generous but worldly passion, may be detected
in the name of the *Leonine city*, which he bestowed on the
Vatican; yet the pride of the dedication was tempered with
Christian penance and humility.   The boundary was trod by
the bishop and his clergy, barefoot, in sackcloth and ashes; the
songs of triumph were modulated to psalms and litanies; the
walls were besprinkled with holy water; and the ceremony was
concluded with a prayer that, under the guardian care of the
apostles and the angelic host, both the old and the new Rome
might ever be preserved pure, prosperous, and impregnable.[108]

The emperor Theophilus, son of Michael the Stammerer,
was one of the most active and high-spirited princes who reigned
at Constantinople during the middle age.   In offensive or defensive war, he marched in person five times against the Saracens,
formidable in his attack, esteemed by the enemy in his losses
and defeats.   In the last of these expeditions he penetrated
into Syria, and besieged the obscure town of Sozopetra: the
casual birth-place of the caliph Motassem, whose father Harun
was attended in peace or war by the most favourite of his
wives and concubines.   The revolt of a Persian impostor employed at that moment the arms of the Saracen, and he could
only intercede in favour of a place for which he felt and acknowledged some degree of filial affection.   These solicitations
determined the emperor to wound his pride in so sensible a part.
Sozopetra was levelled with the ground, the Syrian prisoners
were marked or mutilated with ignominious cruelty, and a
thousand female captives were forced away from the adjacent
territory.   Among these a matron of the house of Abbas invoked, in an agony of despair, the name of Motassem; and the
insults of the Greeks engaged the honour of her kinsman to
avenge his indignity and to answer her appeal.   Under the
reign of the two elder brothers, the inheritance of the youngest
had been confined to Anatolia, Armenia, Georgia, and Circassia;

[108] The Arabs and the Greeks are alike silent concerning the invasion of Rome
by the Africans.   The Latin chronicles do not afford much instruction (see the
Annals of Baronius and Pagi).   Our authentic and contemporary guide for the
Popes of the ixth century is Anastasius, librarian of the Roman church.   His Life
of Leo IV. contains twenty-four pages (p. 175-199, edit. Paris); and, if a great
part consists of superstitious trifles, we must blame or commend his hero, who was
much oftener in a church than in a camp.   [Liber Pontificalis, ed. Duchesne, vol.
ii.   See above, vol. v. Appendix 1, p. 540.]

this frontier station had exercised his military talents ; and, among his accidental claims to the name of *Octonary*,[109] the most meritorious are the *eight* battles which he gained or fought against the enemies of the Koran. In this personal quarrel, the troops of Irak, Syria, and Egypt, were recruited from the tribes of Arabia and the Turkish hordes : his cavalry might be numerous, though we should deduct some myriads from the hundred and thirty thousand horses of the royal stables ; and the expense of the armament was computed at four millions sterling, or one hundred thousand pounds of gold. From Tarsus, the place of assembly, the Saracens advanced in three divisions along the high road of Constantinople : Motassem himself commanded the centre, and the vanguard was given to his son Abbas, who, in the trial of the first adventures, might succeed with the more glory, or fail with the least reproach. In the revenge of his injury, the caliph prepared to retaliate a similar affront. The father of Theophilus was a native of Amorium[110] in Phrygia ; the original seat of the imperial house had been adorned with privileges and monuments ; and, whatever might be the indifference of the people, Constantinople itself was scarcely of more value in the eyes of the sovereign and his court. The name of AMORIUM was inscribed on the shields of the Saracens ; and their three armies were again united under the walls of the devoted city. It had been proposed by the wisest counsellors to evacuate Amorium, to remove the inhabitants, and to abandon the empty structures to the vain resentment of the barbarians. The emperor embraced the more generous resolution of defending, in a siege and battle, the country of his ancestors. When the armies drew near, the front of the Mahometan line appeared to a Roman eye more closely planted with spears and javelins ; but the event of the

[109] The same number was applied to the following circumstance in the life of Motassem : he was the *eighth* of the Abbassides ; he reigned *eight* years, *eight* months, and *eight* days ; left *eight* sons, *eight* daughters, *eight* thousand slaves, *eight* millions of gold.

[110] Amorium is seldom mentioned by the old geographers, and totally forgotten in the Roman Itineraries. After the vith century it became an episcopal see, and at length the metropolis of the new Galatia [formed by Theodosius the Great] (Carol. Sancto Paulo, Geograph. Sacra, p. 234). The city rose again from its ruins, if we should read *Ammuria* not *Anguria*, in the text of the Nubian geographer, p. 236. [The site is near Hanza Hadji. See Hamilton, Researches in Asia Minor, i. p. 451 ; Ramsay, Asia Minor, p. 230-1. The battle described in the text was fought east of the Halys, near Dazimon (Tokat).]

action was not glorious on either side to the national troops. The Arabs were broken, but it was by the swords of thirty thousand Persians, who had obtained service and settlement in the Byzantine empire. The Greeks were repulsed and vanquished, but it was by the arrows of the Turkish cavalry; and, had not their bow-strings been damped and relaxed by the evening rain, very few of the Christians could have escaped with the emperor from the field of battle. They breathed at Dorylæum, at the distance of three days; and Theophilus, reviewing his trembling squadrons, forgave the common flight both of the prince and people. After this discovery of his weakness, he vainly hoped to deprecate the fate of Amorium : the inexorable caliph rejected with contempt his prayers and promises; and detained the Roman ambassadors to be the witnesses of his great revenge. They had nearly been the witnesses of his shame. The vigorous assaults of fifty-five days were encountered by a faithful governor, a veteran garrison, and a desperate people; and the Saracens must have raised the siege if a domestic traitor had not pointed to the weakest part of the wall, a place which was decorated with the statues of a lion and a bull. The vow of Motassem was accomplished with unrelenting rigour; tired, rather than satiated, with destruction, he returned to his new

[Samarra supersedes Bagdad for 55 years. A.D. 836-892] palace of Samara, in the neighbourhood of Bagdad, while the *unfortunate* [111] Theophilus implored the tardy and doubtful aid of his Western rival, the emperor of the Franks. Yet in the siege of Amorium above seventy thousand Moslems had perished; their loss had been revenged by the slaughter of thirty thousand Christians, and the sufferings of an equal number of captives, who were treated as the most atrocious criminals. Mutual necessity could sometimes extort the exchange or ransom of prisoners; [112] but in the national religious conflict of the two

---

[111] In the East he was styled Δυστυχής (Continuator Theophan. l. iii. p. 84 [p. 135, l. 10, ed. Bonn]) ; but such was the ignorance of the West that his ambassadors, in public discourse, might boldly narrate, de victoriis, quas adversus exteras bellando gentes cœlitus fuerat assecutus (Annalist. Bertinian. apud Pagi, tom. iii. p. 720 [Pertz, Mon. i. 434]). [For Samarrā op. Le Strange in Journal As. Soc. vol. 27, p. 36.—The siege of Amorion lasted only twelve days.]

[112] Abulpharagius (Dynast. p. 167, 168) relates one of these singular transactions on the bridge of the river Lamus [Lamas Su] in Cilicia, the limit of the two empires, and one day's journey westward of Tarsus (d'Anville, Géographie Ancienne, tom. ii. p. 91). Four thousand four hundred and sixty Moslems, eight hundred women and children, one hundred confederates, were exchanged for an equal number of Greeks. They passed each other in the middle of the bridge, and, when

empires peace was without confidence, and war without mercy. Quarter was seldom given in the field; those who escaped the edge of the sword were condemned to hopeless servitude or exquisite torture; and a Catholic emperor relates, with visible satisfaction, the execution of the Saracens of Crete, who were flayed alive, or plunged into caldrons of boiling oil.[113] To a point of honour Motassem had sacrificed a flourishing city, two hundred thousand lives, and the property of millions. The same caliph descended from his horse and dirtied his robe to relieve the distress of a decrepit old man, who with his laden ass had tumbled into a ditch. On which of these actions did he reflect with the most pleasure, when he was summoned by the angel of death?[114]

With Motassem, the eighth of the Abbassides, the glory of his family and nation expired. When the Arabian conquerors had spread themselves over the East, and were mingled with the servile crowds of Persia, Syria, and Egypt, they insensibly lost the freeborn and martial virtues of the desert. The courage of the South is the artificial fruit of discipline and prejudice; the active power of enthusiasm had decayed, and the mercenary forces of the caliphs were recruited in those climates of the North, of which valour is the hardy and spontaneous production. Of the Turks[115] who dwelt upon the Oxus and Jaxartes, the robust youths, either taken in war or purchased in trade, were educated in the exercises of the field and the profession of the Mahometan faith. The Turkish guards stood in arms round the

*Disorders of the Turkish guards.
A.D. 841-870, &c.*

they reached their respective friends, they shouted *Allah Acbar*, and *Kyrie Eleison.* Many of the prisoners of Amorium were probably among them, but in the same year (A.H. 231) the most illustrious of them, the forty-two martyrs, were beheaded by the caliph's order. [For exchanges of prisoners on the Lamos see also Theoph. Contin. p. 443, ed. Bonn. The hagiographical texts on the death of the distinguished captives taken at Amorium (A.D. 838) and martyred seven years later, have been edited by P. Nikitin : Skazaniia o 42 Amoriiskikh muchenikakh, in the Zapiski of Russian Imp. Academy, viii.ᵉ sér. vii. 2, 1905.]

[113] Constantin. Porphyrogenitus, in Vit. Basil. c. 61, p. 186. These Saracens were indeed treated with peculiar severity as pirates and renegadoes.

[114] For Theophilus, Motassem, and the Amorian war, see the Continuator of Theophanes (l. iii. p. 77-84 [p. 124 *sqq.* ed. Bonn]), Genesius (l. iii. p. 24-34 [p. 51 *sqq.*]), Cedrenus (528-532 [ii. 129 *sqq.* ed. Bonn]), Elmacin (Hist. Saracen. p. 180), Abulpharagius (Dynast. p. 165, 166), Abulfeda (Annal. Moslem. p. 191), d'Herbelot (Bibliot. Orientale, p. 639, 640).

[115] M. de Guignes, who sometimes leaps, and sometimes stumbles, in the gulf between Chinese and Mahometan story, thinks he can see that these Turks are the *Hoei-ke*, alias the *Kao-tche*, or *high-waggons;* that they were divided into fiftee hordes, from China and Siberia to the dominions of the caliphs and Samanides, &c. (Hist. des Huns, tom. iii. p. 1-33, 124-131).

throne of their benefactor, and their chiefs usurped the dominion of the palace and the provinces. Motassem, the first author of this dangerous example, introduced into the capital above fifty thousand Turks: their licentious conduct provoked the public indignation, and the quarrels of the soldiers and people induced the caliph to retire from Bagdad, and establish his own residence and the camp of his barbarian favourites at Samara on the Tigris, about twelve leagues above the city of Peace.[116] His son Motawakkel was a jealous and cruel tyrant; odious to his subjects, he cast himself on the fidelity of the strangers, and these strangers, ambitious and apprehensive, were tempted by the rich promise of a revolution. At the instigation, or at least in the cause, of his son, they burst into his apartment at the hour of supper, and the caliph was cut into seven pieces by the same swords which he had recently distributed among the guards of his life and throne. To this throne, yet streaming with a father's blood, Montasser was triumphantly led; but in a reign of six months he found only the pangs of a guilty conscience. If he wept at the sight of an old tapestry which represented the crime and punishment of the son of Chosroes; if his days were abridged by grief and remorse, we may allow some pity to a parricide, who exclaimed, in the bitterness of death, that he had lost both this world and the world to come. After this act of treason, the ensigns of royalty, the garment and walking staff of Mahomet, were given and torn away by the foreign mercenaries, who in four years created, deposed, and murdered three commanders of the faithful. As often as the Turks were inflamed by fear, or rage, or avarice, these caliphs were dragged by the feet, exposed naked to the scorching sun, beaten with iron clubs, and compelled to purchase, by the abdication of their dignity, a short reprieve of inevitable fate.[117] At length, however, the fury of the tempest was spent or

[Muta-wakkil. A.D. 847-861]

[Muntasir. A.D. 861-2]

[116] He changed the old name of Sumere, or Samara, into the fanciful title of *Ser-men-rai*, that which gives pleasure at first (d'Herbelot, Bibliothèque Orientale, p. 808; d'Anville, l'Euphrate et le Tigre, p. 97, 98). [*Surra men raā* = " who so saw, rejoiced ".]

[117] Take a specimen, the death of the caliph Motaz: Correptum pedibus retrahunt, et sudibus probe permulcant, et spoliatum laceris vestibus in sole collocant, præ cujus acerrimo æstu pedes alternis attollebat et demittebat. Adstantium aliquis misero colaphos continuo ingerebat, quos ille objectis manibus avertere studebat. . . . Quo facto traditus tortori fuit totoque triduo cibo potuque prohibitus. . . . Suffocatus, &c. (Abulfeda, p. 206). Of the caliph Mohtadi, he says, cervices ipsi perpetuis ictibus contundebant, testiculosque pedibus conculcabant (p. 208).

diverted; the Abbassides returned to the less turbulent residence of Bagdad ; the insolence of the Turks was curbed with a firmer and more skilful hand, and their numbers were divided and destroyed in foreign warfare. But the nations of the East had been taught to trample on the successors of the prophet; and the blessings of domestic peace were obtained by the relaxation of strength and discipline. So uniform are the mischiefs of military despotism that I seem to repeat the story of the prætorians of Rome.[118]

While the flame of enthusiasm was damped by the business, the pleasure, and the knowledge, of the age, it burned with concentrated heat in the breasts of the chosen few, the congenial spirits, who were ambitious of reigning either in this world or in the next. How carefully soever the book of prophecy had been sealed by the apostle of Mecca, the wishes, and (if we may profane the word) even the reason, of fanaticism might believe that, after the successive missions of Adam, Noah, Abraham, Moses, Jesus, and Mahomet, the same God, in the fulness of time, would reveal a still more perfect and permanent law. In the two hundred and seventy-seventh year of the Hegira, and in the neighbourhood of Cufa, an Arabian preacher, of the name of Carmath,[119] assumed the lofty and incomprehensible style of the Guide, the Director, the Demonstration, the Word, the Holy Ghost, the Camel, the Herald of the Messiah, who had conversed with him in a human shape, and the representative of Mohammed the son of Ali, of St.

Rise and progress of the Carmathians. A.D. 890-951

[Hamdān ibn Ashath]

---

[118] See under the reigns of Motassem, Motawakkel, Montasser, Mostain, Motaz, Mohtadi, and Motamed, in the Bibliothèque of d'Herbelot, and the now familiar annals of Elmacin, Abulpharagius, and Abulfeda. [Mustāin, A.D. 862-6 ; Matazz, A.D. 866-9 ; Muhtadi, A.D. 869-70 ; Mutamid, A.D. 870-92.]

[119] [The " Carmathian " movement has received its name, not from its originators, but from the man who placed himself at its head and organized it at Kūfa—Hamdān ibn Ashath, called Carmath. The true founder of the Carmathian movement was Abd Allāh ibn Maimun al-Kaddah, the active missionary of the Ismailite doctrine. This doctrine was that Ismail son of Jafar al-Sadik was the seventh imam from Ali ; and that Ismail's son Mohammad was the seventh prophet of the world (of the other six, Adam, &c., are mentioned above, in the text)—the Mahdi (or Messiah). Mohammad had lived in the second half of the eighth century, but he would come again. Abd Allāh and his missionaries propagated their doctrines far and wide ; they sought to convert Sunnites as well as Shiites, and even Jews and Christians. To the Jews they represented the Mahdi as Messias ; to the Christians as the Paraclete. Abd Allāh's son Ahmad continued his work, and it was one of his missionaries who converted Carmath. The new interpretations of the Koran mentioned in the text were due not to Carmath, but to Abd Allāh. See Weil's account, *op. cit.*, ii. p. 498 *sqq.*]

John the Baptist, and of the angel Gabriel. In his mystic volume, the precepts of the Koran were refined to a more spiritual sense; he relaxed the duties of ablution, fasting, and pilgrimage; allowed the indiscriminate use of wine and forbidden food; and nourished the fervour of his disciples by the daily repetition of fifty prayers. The idleness and ferment of the rustic crowd awakened the attention of the magistrates of Cufa; a timid persecution assisted the progress of the new sect; and the name of the prophet became more revered after his person had been withdrawn from the world. His twelve apostles dispersed themselves among the Bedoweens, "a race of men," says Abulfeda, "equally devoid of reason and of religion;" and the success of their preaching seemed to threaten Arabia with a new revolution. The Carmathians were ripe for rebellion, since they disclaimed the title of the house of Abbas and abhorred the worldly pomp of the caliphs of Bagdad. They were susceptible of discipline, since they vowed a blind and absolute submission to their imam, who was called to the prophetic office by the voice of God and the people. Instead of the legal tithes, he claimed the fifth of their substance and spoil; the most flagitious sins were no more than the type of disobedience; and the brethren were united and concealed by an oath of secrecy. After a bloody conflict, they prevailed in the province of Bahrein, along the Persian Gulf; far and wide, the tribes of the desert were subject to the sceptre, or rather to the sword, of Abu Said and his son Abu Taher; and these rebellious imams could muster in the field an hundred and seven thousand fanatics. The mercenaries of the caliph were dismayed at the approach of an enemy who neither asked nor accepted quarter; and the difference between them in fortitude and patience is expressive of the change which three centuries of prosperity had effected in the character of the Arabians. Such troops were discomfited in every action; the cities of Racca and Baalbec, of Cufa and Bassora, were taken and pillaged; Bagdad was filled with consternation; and the caliph trembled behind the veils of his palace. In a daring inroad beyond the Tigris, Abu Taher advanced to the gates of the capital with no more than five hundred horse. By the special order of Moctader, the bridges had been broken down, and the person or head of the rebel was expected every hour by the commander of the

Their military exploits. A.D. 900, &c.

[Abū Tahir Sulaiman]

[A.D. 923-924]

[A.D. 928]

faithful. His lieutenant, from a motive of fear or pity, apprised Abu Taher of his danger, and recommended a speedy escape. " Your master," said the intrepid Carmathian to the messenger, " is at the head of thirty thousand soldiers: three such men as these are wanting in his host: " at the same instant, turning to three of his companions, he commanded the first to plunge a dagger into his breast, the second to leap into the Tigris, and the third to cast himself headlong down a precipice. They obeyed without a murmur. " Relate," continued the imam, " what you have seen: before the evening your general shall be chained among my dogs." Before the evening, the camp was surprised and the menace was executed. The rapine of the Carmathians was sanctified by their aversion to the worship of Mecca: they robbed a caravan of pilgrims, and twenty thousand devout Moslems were abandoned on the [A.D. 906] burning sands to a death of hunger and thirst.[120] Another year they suffered the pilgrims to proceed without interruption ; but, in the festival of devotion, Abu Taher stormed the holy city and trampled on the most venerable relics of the Mahometan faith. Thirty thousand citizens and strangers were put to the sword; the sacred precincts were polluted by the burial of three thousand dead bodies; the well of Zemzem overflowed with blood; the golden spout was forced from its place; the veil of the Caaba was divided among these impious sectaries ; and the black stone, the first monument of the nation, was borne away in triumph to their capital. After this deed of sacrilege and cruelty, they continued to infest the confines of Irak, Syria, and Egypt; but the vital principle of enthusiasm had withered at the root. Their scruples or their avarice again opened the pilgrimage of Mecca and restored the black stone of the Caaba ; and it is needless to inquire into what factions they were broken, or by whose swords they were finally extirpated. The sect of the Carmathians may be considered as the second visible cause of the decline and fall of the empire of the caliphs.[121]

They pillage Mecca. A.D. 929

The third and most obvious cause was the weight and

Revolt of the provinces. A.D. 800-936

---

[120] [Abū Tahir also plundered pilgrim caravans in A.D. 924.]

[121] For the sect of the Carmathians, consult Elmacin (Hist. Saracen. p. 219, 224, 229, 231, 238, 241, 243), Abulpharagius (Dynast. p. 179-182), Abulfeda (Annal. Moslem. p. 218, 219, &c., 245, 265, 274), and d'Herbelot (Bibliothèque Orientale, p. 256-258, 635). I find some inconsistencies of theology and chronology, which it would not be easy nor of much importance to reconcile. [De Goeje, Mémoire sur les Carmathes du Bahraïn (1886).]

magnitude of the empire itself. The caliph Almamon might proudly assert that it was easier for him to rule the East and the West than to manage a chess-board of two feet square ; [122] yet I suspect that in both those games he was guilty of many fatal mistakes ; and I perceive that in the distant provinces the authority of the first and most powerful of the Abbassides was already impaired. The analogy of despotism invests the representative with the full majesty of the prince ; the division and balance of powers might relax the habits of obedience, might encourage the passive subject to inquire into the origin and administration of civil government. He who is born in the purple is seldom worthy to reign ; but the elevation of a private man, of a peasant perhaps, or a slave, affords a strong presumption of his courage and capacity. The viceroy of a remote kingdom aspires to secure the property and inheritance of his precarious trust ; the nations must rejoice in the presence of their sovereign ; and the command of armies and treasures are at once the object and the instrument of his ambition. A change was scarcely visible as long as the lieutenants of the caliph were content with their vicarious title ; while they solicited for themselves or their sons a renewal of the Imperial grant, and still maintained on the coin, and in the public prayers, the name and prerogative of the commander of the faithful. But in the long and hereditary exercise of power, they assumed the pride and attributes of royalty ; the alternative of peace or war, of reward or punishment, depended solely on their will ; and the revenues of their government were reserved for local services or private magnificence. Instead of a regular supply of men and money, the successors of the prophet were flattered with the ostentatious gift of an elephant, or a cast of hawks, a suit of silk hangings, or some pounds of musk and amber.[123]

The independent dynasties   After the revolt of Spain from the temporal and spiritual supremacy of the Abbassides, the first symptoms of disobedience

---

[122] Hyde, Syntagma Dissertat. tom. ii. p. 57, in Hist. Shahiludii. [Also : Al Nuwairi, in de Sacy, Exposé de la religion des Druzes, vol. i.]

[123] The dynasties of the Arabian empire may be studied in the Annals of Elmacin, Abulpharagius, and Abulfeda, under the *proper* years, in the dictionary of d'Herbelot, under the *proper* names. The tables of M. de Guignes (Hist. des Huns, tom. i.) exhibit a general chronology of the East, interspersed with some historical anecdotes ; but his attachment to national blood has sometimes confounded the order of time and place.

broke forth in the province of Africa. Ibrahim, the son of Aglab, the lieutenant of the vigilant and rigid Harun, bequeathed to the dynasty of the *Aglabites* the inheritance of his The Aglabites. A.D. 800-941 [909] name and power. The indolence or policy of the caliphs dissembled the injury and loss, and pursued only with poison the founder of the *Edrisites*,[124] who erected the kingdom and city The Edrisites. A.D. 829-907 of Fez on the shores of the western ocean.[125] In the East, the first dynasty was that of the *Taherites*,[126] the posterity of the The Taherites. A.D. 813-872 valiant Taher, who, in the civil wars of the sons of Harun, had served with too much zeal and success the cause of Almamon the younger brother. He was sent into honourable exile, to command on the banks of the Oxus; and the independence of his successors, who reigned in Chorasan till the fourth generation, was palliated by their modest and respectful demeanour, the happiness of their subjects, and the security of their frontier. They were supplanted by one of those adventurers so frequent in the annals of the East, who left his trade of a brazier (from The Soffarides. A.D. 872-902 whence the name of *Soffarides*) for the profession of a robber. In a nocturnal visit to the treasure of the prince of Sistan, Jacob, the son of Leith,[127] stumbled over a lump of salt, which he unwarily tasted with his tongue. Salt, among the Orientals,

[124] The Aglabites and Edrisites are the professed subject of M. de Cardonne (Hist. de l'Afrique et de l'Espagne sous la Domination des Arabes, tom. ii. p. 1-63). [The Aghlabid dynasty lasted from A.D. 800 to 909, when it gave way to the Fātimids. Its chief achievement was the conquest of Sicily. These princes also annexed Sardinia and Malta, and harried the Christian coasts of the Western Mediterranean.]

[125] To escape the reproach of error, I must criticize the inaccuracies of M. de Guignes (tom. i. p. 359) concerning the Edrisites. 1. The dynasty and city of Fez could not be founded in the year of the Hegira 173, since the founder was a *posthumous* child of a descendant of Ali, who fled from Mecca in the year 168. 2. This founder, Edris the son of Edris, instead of living to the improbable age of 120 years, A.H. 313, died A.H. 214, in the prime of manhood. 3. The dynasty ended A.H. 307, twenty-three years sooner than it is fixed by the historian of the Huns. See the accurate Annals of Abulfeda, p. 158, 159, 185, 238. [Idrīs, who founded the dynasty of the Idrīsids, was great-great-grandson of Alī. He revolted in Medīna against the caliph Mahdī in A.D. 785, and then he fled to Morocco, where he founded his dynasty (in A.D. 788), which expired in A.D. 985. For the succession cp. S. Lane-Poole, Mohammadan Dynasties, p. 35.]

[126] The dynasties of the Taherites and Soffarides, with the rise of that of the Samanides, are described in the original history and Latin version of Mirchond; yet the most interesting facts had already been drained by the diligence of M. d'Herbelot. [Tāhir was appointed governor of Khurāsān in A.D. 820; he and his successors professed to be vassals of the Caliphs.]

[127] [Yakūb, son of al-Layth, a coppersmith (saffār), conquered successively Fārs, Balkh, and Khurāsān. The Saffārid dynasty numbered only three princes: Yakūb, his brother Amr, and Amr's son Tāhir, whose power was confined to Sīstān, which he lost in A.D. 903. Cp. S. Lane-Poole, op. cit., p. 129, 130.]

is the symbol of hospitality, and the pious robber immediately retired without spoil or damage. The discovery of this honourable behaviour recommended Jacob to pardon and trust; he led an army at first for his benefactor, at last for himself, subdued Persia, and threatened the residence of the Abbassides. On his march towards Bagdad, the conqueror was arrested by a fever. He gave audience in bed to the ambassador of the caliph; and beside him on a table were exposed a naked scymetar, a crust of brown bread, and a bunch of onions. " If I die," said he, " your master is delivered from his fears. If I live, *this* must determine between us. If I am vanquished, I can return without reluctance to the homely fare of my youth."

From the height where he stood, the descent would not have
[A.D. 878] been so soft or harmless : a timely death secured his own repose and that of the caliph, who paid with the most lavish concessions the retreat of his brother Amrou to the palaces of Shiraz and Ispahan. The Abbassides were too feeble to contend, too proud to forgive : they invited the powerful dynasty
The Samanides. of the *Samanides*,[128] who passed the Oxus with ten thousand
A.D. 874-999 horse, so poor, that their stirrups were of wood ; so brave, that they vanquished the Soffarian army, eight times more numerous
[A.D. 900] than their own. The captive Amrou was sent in chains, a grateful offering to the court of Bagdad ; and, as the victor was content with the inheritance of Transoxiana and Chorasan, the realms of Persia returned for a while to the allegiance of the caliphs. The provinces of Syria and Egypt were twice dis-
The Toulonides. membered by their Turkish slaves, of the race of *Toulun* and
A.D. 868-905 *Ikshid*.[129] These barbarians, in religion and manners the country-

[128] [The Sāmānid dynasty, which held sway in Transoxiana and Persia, was founded by Nasr ben-Ahmad, great-grandson of Sāmān (a nobleman of Balkh). This dynasty lost Persia before the end of the 10th century and expired in A.D. 999. Cp. S. Lane-Poole, *op. cit.*, p. 131-3.]

[129] M. de Guignes (Hist. des Huns, tom. iii. p. 124-154) has exhausted the Toulonides and Ikshidites of Egypt, and thrown some light on the Carmathians and Hamadanites. [The Tūlūnid dynasty was founded by Ahmad, son of Tūlūn (a Turkish slave), who established his capital at the suburb of al-Katāi between Fustāt and the later Cairo. Syria was joined to Egypt under the government of Ahmad in A.D. 877.—Mohammad al-Ikhshīd, founder of the Ikhshīdid dynasty, was son of Tughj, a native of Farghānā. His government of Egypt began in A.D. 935 ; Syria was added in 941, and Mecca and Medīna in 942. Cp. S. Lane-Poole, *op. cit.*, p. 69. The Fātimids succeeded the Ikhshīdids in 969.—The influence of the Hamdānids in Mosul (Mōsil) may be dated from c. A.D. 873, but their independent rule there begins with Hasan (Nāsir ad-dawla) A.D. 929 and lasts till 991, when they gave way to the Buwayhids. In Aleppo, the Hamdānid dynasty lasted from A.D. 944 to 1003, and then gave way to the Fātimids. See S. Lane-Poole, *op. cit.*, p. 111-113.]

MOHAMMEDAN ART: THE MOSQUE OF TULUN AT CAIRO; 9TH CENTURY A.D.

men of Mahomet, emerged from the bloody factions of the palace to a provincial command and an independent throne : their names became famous and formidable in their time ; but the founders of these two potent dynasties confessed, either in words or actions, the vanity of ambition.   The first on his death-bed implored the mercy of God to a sinner, ignorant of the limits of his own power : the second, in the midst of four hundred thousand soldiers and eight thousand slaves, concealed from every human eye the chamber where he attempted to sleep.   Their sons were educated in the vices of kings ; and both Egypt and Syria were recovered and possessed by the Abbassides during an interval of thirty years.   In the decline of their empire, Mesopotamia, with the important cities of Mosul and Aleppo, was occupied by the Arabian princes of the tribe of *Hamadan*.   The poets of their court could repeat with-out a blush, that nature had formed their countenances for beauty, their tongues for eloquence, and their hands for liberality and valour ; but the genuine tale of the elevation and reign of the *Hamadanites* exhibits a scene of treachery, murder, and parricide.   At the same fatal period, the Persian kingdom was again usurped by the dynasty of the *Bowides*, by the sword of three brothers, who, under various names, were styled the support and columns of the state, and who, from the Caspian sea to the ocean, would suffer no tyrants but themselves. Under their reign, the language and genius of Persia revived, and the Arabs, three hundred and four years after the death of Mahomet, were deprived of the sceptre of the East.[130]

The Ikshid-ites. A.D. 934 [935]-968 [969]

The Hama-danites. A.D. 892-1001

The Bowides. A.D. 933 [932]-1055

Rahdi, the twentieth of the Abbassides, and the thirty-ninth of the successors of Mahomet, was the last who deserved the title of commander of the faithful :[131] the last (says Abulfeda)

Fallen state of the caliphs of Bagdad. A.D. 936, &c.

---

[130] [The three brothers, sons of Buwayh (a highland chief, who served the Zi-yārid lord of Jurjān), formed three principalities in the same year (932) : 1. Imād ad-dawla, in Fārs ; 2. Muizz ad-dawla in Irāk and Kirmān ; 3. Rukn ad-dawla in Rayy, Hamadhān, and Ispahān.   The third division of the Buwayhids lasted till 1023, when they were ousted by the Kākwayhids.   The dominions of the second passed under the lords of Fārs in 977 and again permanently in 1012 ; and the dynasty of Fārs survived until the conquest of the Seljūks.   See the table of the geographical distribution of the Buwayhids in S. Lane-Poole, *op. cit.*, p. 142.]

[131] Hic est ultimus chalifah qui multum atque sæpius pro concione perorarit. . . . Fuit etiam ultimus qui otium cum eruditis et facetis hominibus fallere hilari-terque agere soleret.   Ultimus tandem chalifarum cui sumtus, stipendia, reditus, et thesauri, culinæ, cæteraque omnis aulica pompa priorum chalifarum ad instar comparata fuerint.   Videbimus enim paullo post quam indignis et servilibus ludi-briis exagitati, quam ad humilem fortunam ultimumque contemptum abjecti fuerint

who spoke to the people, or conversed with the learned ; the last who, in the expense of his household, represented the wealth and magnificence of the ancient caliphs. After him, the lords of the eastern world were reduced to the most abject misery, and exposed to the blows and insults of a servile condition. The revolt of the provinces circumscribed their dominions within the walls of Bagdad ; but that capital still contained an innumerable multitude, vain of their past fortune, discontented with their present state, and oppressed by the demands of a treasury which had formerly been replenished by the spoil and tribute of nations. Their idleness was exercised by faction and controversy. Under the mask of piety, the rigid followers of Hanbal [132] invaded the pleasures of domestic life, burst into the houses of plebeians and princes, spilt the wine, broke the instruments, beat the musicians, and dishonoured, with infamous suspicions, the associates of every handsome youth. In each profession, which allowed room for two persons, the one was a votary, the other an antagonist, of Ali ; and the Abbassides were awakened by the clamorous grief of the sectaries, who denied their title and cursed their progenitors. A turbulent people could only be repressed by a military force ; but who could satisfy the avarice or assert the discipline of the mercenaries themselves? The African and the Turkish guards drew their swords against each other, and the chief commanders, the emirs al Omra,[133] imprisoned or deposed their sovereigns, and violated the sanctuary of the mosque and harem. If the caliphs escaped to the camp or court of any neighbouring prince, their deliverance was a change of servitude, till they were prompted by despair to invite the Bowides, the sultans of Persia, who silenced the factions of

hi quondam potentissimi totius terrarum Orientalium orbis domini. Abulfed. Annal. Moslem. p. 261. I have given this passage as the manner and tone of Abulfeda, but the cast of Latin eloquence belongs more properly to Reiske. The Arabian historian (p. 255, 257, 261-269, 283, &c.) has supplied me with the most interesting facts of this paragraph. [Rādī, A.D. 934-940.]

[132] Their master, on a similar occasion, shewed himself of a more indulgent and tolerating spirit. Ahmed Ebn Hanbal, the head of one of the four orthodox sects, was born at Bagdad A.H. 164, and died there A.H. 241. He fought and suffered in the dispute concerning the creation of the Koran.

[133] The office of vizir was superseded by the emir al Omra [amīr al-umarā] Imperator Imperatorum, a title first instituted by Rahdi [Weil quotes an instance of its use under al-Muktadir, Rādī's father, op. cit., ii. p. 559] and which merged at length in the Bowides and Seljukides ; vectigalibus et tributis et curiis per omnes regiones præfecit, jussitque in omnibus suggestis nominis ejus in concionibus mentionem fieri (Abulpharagius, Dynast. p. 199). It is likewise mentioned by Elmacin (p. 254, 255).

Bagdad by their irresistible arms.   The civil and military powers were assumed by Moezaldowlat, the second of the three [Muizz al-dawla] brothers, and a stipend of sixty thousand pounds sterling was assigned by his generosity for the private expense of the commander of the faithful.   But on the fortieth day, at the audience of the ambassadors of Chorasan, and in the presence of a trembling multitude, the caliph was dragged from his throne to a dungeon, by the command of the stranger, and the rude hands of his Dilemites.   His palace was pillaged, his eyes were put out, and the mean ambition of the Abbassides aspired to the vacant station of danger and disgrace.   In the school of adversity, the luxurious caliphs resumed the grave and abstemious virtues of the primitive times.   Despoiled of their armour and silken robes, they fasted, they prayed, they studied the Koran and the tradition of the Sonnites ; they performed with zeal and knowledge the functions of their ecclesiastical character. The respect of nations still waited on the successors of the apostle, the oracles of the law and conscience of the faithful ; and the weakness or division of their tyrants sometimes restored the Abbassides to the sovereignty of Bagdad.   But their misfortunes had been embittered by the triumph of the Fatimites, the real or spurious progeny of Ali.   Arising from the extremity of [Fatimids. A.D. 909-1171] Africa, these successful rivals extinguished in Egypt and Syria both the spiritual and temporal authority of the Abbassides ; and the monarch of the Nile insulted the humble pontiff on the banks of the Tigris.

In the declining age of the caliphs, in the century which [Enterprises of the Greeks. A.D. 960] elapsed after the war of Theophilus and Motassem, the hostile transactions of the two nations were confined to some inroads by sea and land, the fruits of their close vicinity and indelible hatred. But, when the Eastern world was convulsed and broken, the Greeks were roused from their lethargy by the hopes of conquest and revenge.   The Byzantine empire, since the accession of the Basilian race, had reposed in peace and dignity ; and they might encounter with their entire strength the front of some petty emir, whose rear was assaulted and threatened by his national foes of the Mahometan faith.   The lofty titles of the morning star, and the death of the Saracens,[134] were applied in the public

---

[134] Liutprand, whose choleric temper was embittered by his uneasy situation, suggests the names of reproach and contempt more applicable to Nicephorus than

acclamations to Nicephorus Phocas, a prince as renowned in the

Reduction
of Crete.
[A.D. 960] camp as he was unpopular in the city.   In the subordinate station
of great domestic, or general of the East, he reduced the island
of Crete, and extirpated the nest of pirates who had so long
defied, with impunity, the majesty of the empire.[135]   His military genius was displayed in the conduct and success of the
enterprise, which had so often failed with loss and dishonour.
The Saracens were confounded by the landing of his troops on
safe and level bridges, which he cast from the vessels to the
shore.   Seven months were consumed in the siege of Candia;
the despair of the native Cretans was stimulated by the frequent
aid of their brethren of Africa and Spain; and, after the massy
wall and double ditch had been stormed by the Greeks, an hopeless conflict was still maintained in the streets and houses of the
city.   The whole island was subdued in the capital, and a submissive people accepted, without resistance, the baptism of the
conqueror.[136]   Constantinople applauded the long-forgotten pomp
of a triumph; but the imperial diadem was the sole reward that
could repay the services, or satisfy the ambition, of Nicephorus.

The
Eastern
conquests
of Nice-
phorus
Phocas,
and John
Zimisces.
A.D. 963-975   After the death of the younger Romanus, the fourth in lineal
descent of the Basilian race, his widow Theophania [136a] successively married Phocas and his assassin John Zimisces, the two

the vain titles of the Greeks : Ecce venit stella matutina, surgit Eous, reverberat
obtutû solis radios, pallida Saracenorum mors, Nicephorus μέδων. • [Legatio, c. 10.]
    [135] Notwithstanding the insinuations of Zonaras, καὶ εἰ μή, &c. (tom. ii. l. xvi.
p. 197 [c. 23]) it is an undoubted fact that Crete was completely and finally subdued
by Nicephorus Phocas (Pagi, Critica, tom. iii. p. 873-875.   Meursius, Creta, l. iii. c.
7, tom. iii. p. 464, 465).   [The best account of the recovery of Crete will be found
in Schlumberger's Nicéphore Phocas, chap. 2.   There had been two ineffectual
expeditions against Crete in the same century ; in 902 (general Himerius), and in
949 (general Gongylus).   We are fortunate enough to possess many details of the
organisation of these expeditions in official accounts which are included in the so-
called Second Book of the de Caerimoniis (chap. 44 and 45 ; p. 651 sqq. ed. Bonn) ;
and these have been utilised by M. Schlumberger for his constructive description of
the expedition of 960.   The conquest of Crete was celebrated in an iambic poem
of 5 cantos by the Deacon Theodosius, a contemporary (publ. by F. Cornelius in
Creta Sacra (Venice, 1755) ; printed in the Bonn ed. of Leo Diaconus, p. 263 sqq.) ;
but it gives us little historical information.   Cp. Schlumberger, p. 84.]
    [136] A Greek life of St. Nicon [Metanoites], the Armenian, was found in the
Sforza library, and translated into Latin by the Jesuit Sirmond for the use of
cardinal Baronius.   This contemporary legend cast a ray of light on Crete and
Peloponnesus in the tenth century.   He found the newly recovered island, fœdis
detestandæ Agarenorum superstitionis vestigiis adhuc plenam ac refertam . . .
but the victorious missionary, perhaps with some carnal aid, ad baptismum omnes
veræque fidei disciplinam pepulit.   Ecclesiis per totam insulam ædificatis, &c.
(Annal. Eccles. A.D. 961).   [The Latin version in Migne, P. G. vol. 113, p. 975 sqq.
Also in the Vet. Scr. ampl. Coll. of Martène and Durand, 6, 837 sqq.]
    [136a] [Leg. Theophano.]

heroes of the age. They reigned as the guardians and colleagues
of her infant sons; and the twelve years of their military command form the most splendid period of the Byzantine annals.
The subjects and confederates, whom they led to war, appeared,
at least in the eyes of an enemy, two hundred thousand strong;
and of these about thirty thousand were armed with cuirasses.[137]
A train of four thousand mules attended their march; and their
evening camp was regularly fortified with an enclosure of iron
spikes. A series of bloody and undecisive combats is nothing
more than an anticipation of what would have been effected in
a few years by the course of nature; but I shall briefly prosecute
the conquests of the two emperors from the hills of Cappadocia
to the desert of Bagdad.[138] The sieges of Mopsuestia and Tarsus in Cilicia first expressed the skill and perseverance of their
troops, on whom, at this moment, I shall not hesitate to bestow
the name of Romans. In the double city of Mopsuestia, which
is divided by the river Sarus, two hundred thousand Moslems were
predestined to death or slavery,[139] a surprising degree of population, which must at least include the inhabitants of the dependent
districts. They were surrounded and taken by assault; but
Tarsus was reduced by the slow progress of famine; and no
sooner had the Saracens yielded on honourable terms than they
were mortified by the distant and unprofitable view of the naval
succours of Egypt. They were dismissed with a safe-conduct to
the confines of Syria; a part of the Christians had quietly lived
under their dominion; and the vacant habitations were replenished by a new colony. But the mosque was converted into
a stable; the pulpit was delivered to the flames; many rich
crosses of gold and gems, the spoils of Asiatic churches, were
made a grateful offering to the piety or avarice of the emperor; and he transported the gates of Mopsuestia and Tarsus,

Conquest of Cilicia

[Mopsuestia taken. A.D. 964]

[Tarsus. A.D. 965]

---

[137] [Elmacin, Hist. Saracen. p. 278, 279. Liutprand was disposed to depreciate
the Greek power, yet he owns that Nicephorus led against Assyria an army of
eighty thousand men.

[138] [For the Asiatic campaigns of Nicephorus and Tzimisces, see Schlumberger,
op. cit., and L'épopée byzantine; and K. Leonhardt, Kaiser Nicephorus II. Phokas
und die Hamdaniden, 960-969.]

[139] Ducenta fere millia hominum numerabat urbs (Abulfeda, Annal. Moslem.
p. 231) of Mopsuestia, or Masisa, Mampsysta, Mansista, Mamista, as it is corruptly,
or perhaps more correctly, styled in the middle ages (Wesseling, Itinerar. p. 580).
Yet I cannot credit this extreme populousness a few years after the testimony of the
emperor Leo, οὐ γὰρ πολυπληθία στρατοῦ τοῖς Κίλιξι βαρβάροις ἐστίν (Tactica, c. xviii.
in Meursii Oper. tom. vi. p. 817 [p. 980, ap. Migne, Patr. Gr. vol. 107)].

which were fixed in the wall of Constantinople, an eternal monument of his victory. After they had forced and secured the
narrow passes of mount Amanus, the two Roman princes repeatedly carried their arms into the heart of Syria. Yet, instead
of assaulting the walls of Antioch, the humanity or superstition
of Nicephorus appeared to respect the ancient metropolis of the
East : he contented himself with drawing round the city a line
of circumvallation ; left a stationary army ; and instructed his
lieutenant to expect, without impatience, the return of spring.
But in the depth of winter, in a dark and rainy night, an adventurous subaltern, with three hundred soldiers, approached the rampart, applied his scaling-ladders, occupied two adjacent towers,
stood firm against the pressure of multitudes, and bravely maintained his post till he was relieved by the tardy, though effectual,
support of his reluctant chief. The first tumult of slaughter and
rapine subsided ; the reign of Cæsar and of Christ was restored ;
and the efforts of an hundred thousand Saracens, of the armies
of Syria and the fleets of Afric, were consumed without effect
before the walls of Antioch.   The royal city of Aleppo was subject to Seifeddowlat, of the dynasty of Hamadan, who clouded
his past glory by the precipitate retreat which abandoned his
kingdom and capital to the Roman invaders.   In his stately
palace, that stood without the walls of Aleppo, they joyfully
seized a well-furnished magazine of arms, a stable of fourteen
hundred mules, and three hundred bags of silver and gold.   But
the walls of the city withstood the strokes of their battering-
rams ; and the besiegers pitched their tents on the neighbouring
mountain of Jaushan.   Their retreat exasperated the quarrel of
the townsmen and mercenaries ; the guard of the gates and ramparts was deserted ; and, while they furiously charged each other
in the market-place, they were surprised and destroyed by the
sword of a common enemy.   The male sex was exterminated by
the sword ; ten thousand youths were led into captivity ; the
weight of the precious spoil exceeded the strength and number
of the beasts of burthen ; the superfluous remainder was burnt ;
and, after a licentious possession of ten days, the Romans marched
away from the naked and bleeding city.   In their Syrian inroads
they commanded the husbandmen to cultivate their lands, that
they themselves, in the ensuing season, might reap the benefit :
more than an hundred cities were reduced to obedience ; and

eighteen pulpits of the principal mosques were committed to the flames, to expiate the sacrilege of the disciples of Mahomet. The classic names of Hierapolis, Apamea, and Emesa, revive for a moment in the list of conquest : the emperor Zimisces encamped in the Paradise of Damascus, and accepted the ransom of a submissive people ; and the torrent was only stopped by the impregnable fortress of Tripoli, on the sea-coast of Phœnicia. Since the days of Heraclius, the Euphrates, below the passage Passage of the Euphrates. [A.D. 974] of mount Taurus, had been impervious, and almost invisible, to the Greeks. The river yielded a free passage to the victorious Zimisces ; and the historian may imitate the speed with which he overran the once famous cities of Samosata, Edessa, Martyropolis, Amida,[140] and Nisibis, the ancient limit of the empire in the neighbourhood of the Tigris. His ardour was quickened by the desire of grasping the virgin treasures of Ecbatana,[141] a well-known name, under which the Byzantine writer has concealed the capital of the Abbassides. The consternation of the fugitives had already diffused the terror of his name; but the fancied riches of Bagdad had already been dissipated by the avarice and prodigality of domestic tyrants. The prayers of the Danger of Bagdad people, and the stern commands of the lieutenant of the Bowides, required the caliph to provide for the defence of the city. The helpless Mothi replied that his arms, his revenues, and his provinces had been torn from his hands, and that he was ready to abdicate a dignity which he was unable to support. The emir was inexorable ; the furniture of the palace was sold ; and the paltry price of forty thousand pieces of gold was instantly consumed in private luxury. But the apprehensions of Bagdad were relieved by the retreat of the Greeks ; thirst and hunger guarded the desert of Mesopotamia ; and the emperor, satiated

---

[140] The text of Leo the deacon, in the corrupt names of Emeta [Ἔμετ, p. 161, l. 19, ed. Bonn] and Myctarsim, reveals the cities of Amida and Martyropolis (Miafarekin [Μιεφαρκὶμ, ib. l. 21]. See Abulfeda, Geograph. p. 245, vers. Reiske). Of the former, Leo observes, urbs munita et illustris ; of the latter, clara atque conspicua opibusque et pecore, reliquis ejus provinciis [leg. provinciæ] urbibus atque oppidis longe præstans.

[141] Ut et Ecbatana pergeret Agarenorumque regiam everteret . . . aiunt enim urbium quæ usquam sunt ac toto orbe existunt felicissimam esse auroque ditissimam (Leo Diacon. apud Pagium, tom. iv. p. 34 [p. ,162, ed. Bonn]). This splendid description suits only with Bagdad, and cannot possibly apply either to Hamada, the true Ecbatana (d'Anville, Geog. Ancienne, tom. ii. p. 237), or Tauris, which has been commonly mistaken for that city. The name of Ecbatana, in the same indefinite sense, is transferred by a more classic authority (Cicero pro Lege Manilià, c. 4) to the royal seat of Mithridates, king of Pontus.

with glory, and laden with Oriental spoils, returned to Constantinople, and displayed, in his triumph, the silk, the aromatics, and
three hundred myriads of gold and silver.   Yet the powers of
the East had been bent, not broken, by this transient hurricane.
After the departure of the Greeks, the fugitive princes returned
to their capitals ; the subjects disclaimed their involuntary oaths
of allegiance ; the Moslems again purified their temples, and
overturned the idols of the saints and martyrs ; the Nestorians
and Jacobites preferred a Saracen to an orthodox master ; and
the numbers and spirit of the Melchites were inadequate to the
support of the church and state.   Of these extensive conquests,
[Cyprus Antioch, with the cities of Cilicia and the isle of Cyprus, was
recovered.
A.D. 965] alone restored, a permanent and useful accession to the Roman
empire.[142]

[142] See the annals of Elmacin, Abulpharagius, and Abulfeda, from A.H. 351 to
A.H. 361 ; and the reigns of Nicephorus Phocas and John Zimisces, in the Chronicles
of Zonaras (tom. ii. l. xvi. p. 199 [c. 24], l. xvii. 215 [c. 4]) and Cedrenus (Compend.
p. 649-684 [ii. p. 351 sqq. ed. Bonn]).   Their manifold defects are partly supplied
by the Ms. history of Leo the deacon, which Pagi obtained from the Benedictines,
and has inserted almost entire in a Latin version (Critica, tom. iii. p. 873, tom. iv.
p. 37).   [For Leo the deacon and the Greek text of his work, since published, see
above, vol. 5, Appendix 1, p. 535.]

CHAPTER LIII

State of the Eastern Empire in the Tenth Century—Extent and Division—Wealth and Revenue—Palace of Constantinople—Titles and Offices—Pride and Power of the Emperors—Tactics of the Greeks, Arabs, and Franks—Loss of the Latin Tongue—Studies and Solitude of the Greeks

A RAY of historic light seems to beam from the darkness of the tenth century. We open with curiosity and respect the royal volumes of Constantine Porphyrogenitus,[1] which he composed, at a mature age, for the instruction of his son, and which promise to unfold the state of the Eastern empire, both in peace and war, both at home and abroad. In the first of these works he minutely describes the pompous ceremonies of the church and palace of Constantinople, according to his own practice and that of his predecessors.[2] In the second he attempts an accurate survey of the provinces, the *themes*, as they were then denominated, both of Europe and Asia.[3] The system of Roman tactics, the discipline and order of

[Marginal notes:] Memorials of the Greek empire

Works of Constantine Porphyrogenitus. [The Ceremonies]

[The Themes]

---

[1] The epithet of Πορφυρογέννητος, Porphyrogenitus, born in the purple, is elegantly defined by Claudian :—

> Ardua privatos nescit fortuna Penates ;
> Et regnum cum luce dedit. Cognata potestas
> Excepit Tyrio venerabile pignus in ostro.

And Ducange, in his Greek and Latin Glossaries, produces many passages expressive of the same idea. [In connexion with the following account of the work of Constantine, the reader might have been reminded that the Continuation of Theophanes (and also the work of Genesius) were composed at the instigation of this Emperor, and that he himself wrote the Life of his grandfather Basil—a remarkable work whose tendency, credibility, and value have been fully discussed in A. Rambaud's L'empire grec au dixième siècle, p. 137-164.]

[2] A splendid Ms. of Constantine, de Ceremoniis Aulæ et Ecclesiæ Byzantinæ, wandered from Constantinople to Buda, Frankfort and Leipsic, where it was published in a splendid edition by Leich and Reiske (A.D. 1751[-1754] in folio), with such slavish praise as editors never fail to bestow on the worthy or worthless object of their toil. [See Appendix 1.]

[3] See, in the first volume of Banduri's Imperium Orientale, Constantinus de Thematibus, p. 1-24, de Administrando Imperio, p. 45-127, edit. Venet. The text

troops, and the military operations by land and sea, are explained in the third of these didactic collections, which may be ascribed to Constantine or his father Leo.[4]   In the fourth, of the administration of the empire, he reveals the secrets of the Byzantine policy, in friendly or hostile intercourse with the nations of the earth.   The literary labours of the age, the practical systems of law, agriculture, and history, might redound to the benefit of the subject and the honour of the Macedonian princes.   The sixty books of the *Basilics*,[5] the code and pandects of civil jurisprudence, were gradually framed in the three first reigns of that prosperous dynasty.   The art of agriculture had amused the leisure, and exercised the pens, of the best and wisest of the ancients; and their chosen precepts are comprised in the twenty books of the *Geoponics*,[6] of Constantine.   At his command, the historical examples of vice and virtue were methodized in fifty-three books,[7] and every citizen

[The Administration of the Empire]

[Augmentation of the Basilica]

[Edition of the Geoponics]

[Historical Encyclopædia]

of the old edition of Meursius is corrected from a Ms. of the royal library of Paris, which Isaac Causabon had formerly seen (Epist. ad Polybium, p. 10), and the sense is illustrated by two maps of William Deslisle, the prince of geographers till the appearance of the greater d'Anville. [On the Themes, see Appendix 3 ; on the treatise on the Administration, see Appendix 4.]

[4] The Tactics of Leo and Constantine are published with the aid of some new Mss. in the great edition of the works of Meursius, by the learned John Lami (tom. vi. p. 531-920, 1211-1417 ; Florent. 1745), yet the text is still corrupt and mutilated, the version is still obscure and faulty. [The Tactics of Constantine is little more than a copy of the Tactics of Leo, and was compiled by Constantine VIII., not by Constantine VII.] The Imperial library of Vienna would afford some valuable materials to a new editor (Fabric. Bibliot. Græc. tom. vi. p. 369, 370). [See Appendix 1.]

[5] On the subject of the *Basilics*, Fabricius (Bibliot. Græc. tom. xii. p. 425-514), and Heineccius (Hist. Juris Romani, p. 396-399), and Giannone (Istoria civile di Napoli, tom. i. p. 450-458), as historical civilians, may be usefully consulted. Forty-one books of this Greek code have been published, with a Latin version, by Charles Annibal Fabrottus (Paris, 1647) in seven volumes in folio ; four other books have since been discovered, and are inserted in Gerard Meerman's Novus Thesaurus Juris Civ. et Canon. tom. v. Of the whole work, the sixty books, John Leunclavius has printed (Basil, 1575) an *eclogue* or synopsis. The cxiii novels, or new laws, of Leo, may be found in the Corpus Juris Civilis. [See above, vol. 5, Appendix 11.]

[6] I have used the last and best edition of the Geoponics (by Nicolas Niclas, Leipsic, 1781, 2 vols. in octavo). [Recent edition by H. Beckh, 1895.] I read in the preface that the same emperor restored the long forgotten systems of rhetoric and philosophy ; and his two books of *Hippiatrica*, or Horse-physic, were published at Paris, 1530, in folio (Fabric. Bibliot. Græc. tom. vi. p. 493-500). [All that Constantine did for agriculture was to cause an unknown person to make a very bad copy of the *Geoponica* of Cassianus Bassus (a compilation of the 6th century). See Krumbacher (Gesch. der byz. Litt. p. 262), who observes that the edition produced at the instance of Constantine was so bad that the old copies must have risen in price.]

[7] Of these liii books, or titles, only two have been preserved and printed, de Legationibus (by Fulvius Ursinus, Antwerp, 1582, and Daniel Hœschelius, August.

might apply, to his contemporaries or himself, the lesson or the warning of past times. From the august character of a legislator, the sovereign of the East descends to the more humble office of a teacher and a scribe; and, if his successors and subjects were regardless of his paternal cares, *we* may inherit and enjoy the everlasting legacy.

A closer survey will indeed reduce the value of the gift, and the gratitude of posterity: in the possession of these Imperial treasures, we may still deplore our poverty and ignorance; and the fading glories of their authors will be obliterated by indifference or contempt. The Basilics will sink to a broken copy, a partial and mutilated version in the Greek language, of the laws of Justinian; but the sense of the old civilians is often superseded by the influence of bigotry; and the absolute prohibition of divorce, concubinage, and interest for money, enslaves the freedom of trade and the happiness of private life. In the historical book, a subject of Constantine might admire the inimitable virtues of Greece and Rome; he might learn to what a pitch of energy and elevation the human character had formerly aspired. But a contrary effect must have been produced by a new edition of the lives of the saints, which the great logothete, or chancellor of the empire, was directed to prepare; and the dark fund of superstition was enriched by the fabulous and florid legends of Simon the *Metaphrast*.[8]   The

Their imperfections

[Lives of the Saints and Acts of the Martyrs]

[Symeon]

Vindol. 1603) and de Virtutibus et Vitiis (by Henry Valesius, or de Valois, Paris, 1634). [We have also fragments of the titles περὶ γνωμῶν (De Sententiis), ed. by A. Mai, Scr. Vet. Nov. Collect. vol. 2; and περὶ ἐπιβουλῶν κατὰ βασιλέων γεγονυιῶν (De Insidiis), ed. C. A. Feder (1848-55). The collection was intended to be an Encyclopædia of historical literature. For the new edition of the Excerpta see above, vol. iv. p. 545.]

[8] The life and writings of Simon Metaphrastes are described by Hankius (de Scriptoribus Byzant. p. 410-460). This biographer of the saints indulged himself in a loose paraphrase of the sense or nonsense of more ancient acts. His Greek rhetoric is again paraphrased in the Latin version of Surius, and scarcely a thread can be now visible of the original texture. [The most recent investigations of Vasilievski and Ehrhard as to the date of Symeon Metaphrastes confirm the notice in the text. He flourished about the middle and second half of the 10th century; his hagiographical work was suggested by Constantine Porphyrogennetos and was probably composed during the reign of Nicephorus Phocas. Symeon is doubtless to be identified with Symeon Magister, the chronicler; see above, vol. 5, App. p. 533. (Cp. Krumbacher, Geschichte der byzantinischen Litteratur, p. 200.) Symeon's work was not an original composition; he collected and edited older works, lives of saints and acts of martyrs; he paraphrased them, improved their style, and adapted them to the taste of his contemporaries, but he did not invent new stories. His Life of Abercius has been strikingly confirmed by the discovery of the original inscription quoted in that life. The collection of Symeon was freely interpolated and augmented by new lives after his death, and the edition of Migne, P. G. 114, 115,

merits and miracles of the whole calendar are of less account in the eyes of a sage than the toil of a single husbandman, who multiplies the gifts of the Creator and supplies the food of his brethren.   Yet the royal authors of the *Geoponics* were more seriously employed in expounding the precepts of the destroying art, which has been taught since the days of Xenophon [9] as the

[Tactics of Leo and Constantine]

art of heroes and kings.   But the *Tactics* of Leo and Constantine are mingled with the baser alloy of the age in which they lived.   It was destitute of original genius ; they implicitly transcribe the rules and maxims which had been confirmed by victories.   It was unskilled in the propriety of style and method ; they blindly confound the most distant and discordant institutions, the phalanx of Sparta and that of Macedon, the legions of Cato and Trajan, of Augustus and Theodosius.   Even the use, or at least the importance, of these military rudiments, may be fairly questioned : their general theory is dictated by reason ; but the merit, as well as difficulty, consists in the application.   The discipline of a soldier is formed by exercise rather than by study ; the talents of a commander are appropriated to those calm though rapid minds, which nature produces to decide the fate of armies and nations : the former is the habit of a life, the latter the glance of a moment ; and the battles won by lessons of tactics may be numbered with the epic poems created from the rules of criticism.   The book of ceremonies is a recital, tedious yet imperfect, of the despicable pageantry which had infected the church and state since the gradual decay of the purity of the one and the power of the other.   A review of the themes or provinces might promise

116, does not represent the original work. To determine the compass of that original is of the highest importance, and this can only be done by a comparative study of numerous Mss. which contain portions of it. This problem has been solved in the main by A. Ehrhard, who found a clue in a Moscow Ms. of the 11th century.   He has published his results in a paper entitled Die Legendensammlung des Symeon Metaphrastes und ihr ursprünglicher Bestand, in the Festschrift zum elfhundertjährigen Jubiläum des deutschen Campo Santo in Rom, 1897.]

[9] According to the first book of the Cyropœdia, professors of tactics, a small part of the science of war, were already instituted in Persia, by which Greece must be understood.   A good edition of all the Scriptores Tactici would be a task not unworthy of a scholar.   His industry might discover some new Mss. and his learning might illustrate the military history of the ancients.   But this scholar should be likewise a soldier ; and, alas ! Quintus Icilius is no more. [Köchly and Rüstow have edited some of the Tactici in Greek and German (1853-5) ; but a complete *corpus* is a desideratum.]

such authentic and useful information as the curiosity of government only can obtain, instead of traditionary fables on the origin of the cities, and malicious epigrams on the vices of their inhabitants.[10] Such information the historian would have been pleased to record; nor should his silence be condemned if the most interesting objects, the population of the capital and provinces, the amount of the taxes and revenues, the numbers of subjects and strangers who served under the Imperial standard, have been unnoticed by Leo the Philosopher and his son Constantine. His treatise of the public administration is stained with the same blemishes; yet it is discriminated by peculiar merit; the antiquities of the nations may be doubtful or fabulous; but the geography and manners of the barbaric world are delineated with curious accuracy. Of these nations, Embassy the Franks alone were qualified to observe in their turn, and to prand. describe, the metropolis of the East. The ambassador of the [A.D. 968-9] great Otho, a bishop of Cremona, has painted the state of Constantinople about the middle of the tenth century; his style is glowing, his narrative lively, his observation keen ; and even the prejudices and passions of Liutprand are stamped with an original character of freedom and genius.[11] From this scanty fund of foreign and domestic materials I shall investigate the form and substance of the Byzantine empire : the provinces and wealth, the civil government and military force, the character and literature, of the Greeks, in a period of six hundred years, from the reign of Heraclius to the successful invasion of the Franks or Latins.

After the final division between the sons of Theodosius, the

[10] After observing that the demerit of the Cappadocians rose in proportion to their rank and riches, he inserts a more pointed epigram, which is ascribed to Demodocus :

$$\text{Καππαδόκην ποτ' ἔχιδνα κακὴ δάκεν, ἀλλὰ καὶ αὐτή}$$
$$\text{Κάτθανε, γευσαμένη αἵματος ἰοβόλου.}$$

The sting, is precisely the same with the French epigram against Fréron ; Un serpent mordit Jean Fréron—Eh bien ? Le serpent en mourut. But, as the Paris wits are seldom read in the Anthology, I should be curious to learn through what channel it was conveyed for their imitation (Constantin. Porphyrogen. de Themat. c. ii. Brunk, Analect. Græc. tom. ii. p. 56 [p. 21, ed. Bonn] ; Brodæi. Anthologia, l. ii. p. 244 [Anthol. Pal. xi. 237]). [Of Constantine's Book on the Themes, M. Rambaud observes : " C'est l'empire au viᵉ siècle, et non pas au xᵉ siècle, que nous trouvons dans son livre " (op. cit., p. 166).]

[11] The Legatio Liutprandi Episcopi Cremonensis ad Nicephorum Phocam is inserted in Muratori, Scriptores Rerum Italicarum, tom. ii. pars i. [In Pertz, Mon. Germ. Hist. (Scriptores), vol. 3. There is a convenient ed. of Liutprand's works by E. Dümmler in the Scriptores rerum Germanicarum, 1877.]

The
themes,
or pro-
vinces of
the empire,
and its
limits
in every
age swarms of barbarians from Scythia and Germany overspread the
provinces, and extinguished the empire, of ancient Rome.   The
weakness of Constantinople was concealed by extent of dominion;
her limits were inviolate, or at least entire; and the kingdom
of Justinian was enlarged by the splendid acquisition of Africa
and Italy.   But the possession of these new conquests was
transient and precarious; and almost a moiety of the Eastern
empire was torn away by the arms of the Saracens.   Syria and
Egypt were oppressed by the Arabian caliphs; and, after the
reduction of Africa, their lieutenants invaded and subdued the
Roman province which had been changed into the Gothic
monarchy of Spain.   The islands of the Mediterranean were not
inaccessible to their naval powers; and it was from their extreme
stations, the harbours of Crete and the fortresses of Cilicia, that
the faithful or rebel emirs insulted the majesty of the throne and
capital.   The remaining provinces, under the obedience of the
emperors, were cast into a new mould; and the jurisdiction of
the presidents, the consulars, and the counts was superseded by
the institution of the *themes*,[12] or military governments, which
prevailed under the successors of Heraclius, and are described
by the pen of the royal author.   Of the twenty-nine themes,
twelve in Europe and seventeen in Asia, the origin is obscure,
the etymology doubtful or capricious, the limits were arbitrary
and fluctuating; but some particular names that sound the most
strangely to our ear were derived from the character and attributes of the troops that were maintained at the expense, and for
the guard, of the respective divisions.   The vanity of the Greek
princes most eagerly grasped the shadow of conquest and the
memory of lost dominion.   A new Mesopotamia was created on
the Western side of the Euphrates; the appellation and prætor
of Sicily were transferred to a narrow slip of Calabria; and a
fragment of the duchy of Beneventum was promoted to the
style and title of the theme of Lombardy.   In the decline of
the Arabian empire, the successors of Constantine might indulge
their pride in more solid advantages.   The victories of Nice-

---

[12] See Constantine de Thematibus, in Banduri, tom. i. p. 1-30, who owns that the
word is οὐκ παλαιά.   Θέμα is used by Maurice (Stratagem. l. ii. c. 2) for a legion, from
whence the name was easily transferred to its post or province (Ducange, Gloss. Græc.
tom. i. p. 487, 488).   Some etymologies are attempted for the Opsician, Optimatian,
Thracesian, themes.   [For the history of the Themes, and Constantine's treatise, see
Appendix 3.]

phorus, John Zimisces, and Basil the Second, revived the fame
and enlarged the boundaries of the Roman name; the province
of Cilicia, the metropolis of Antioch, the islands of Crete and
Cyprus, were restored to the allegiance of Christ and Cæsar;
one third of Italy was annexed to the throne of Constantinople ;
the kingdom of Bulgaria was destroyed ; and the last sovereigns
of the Macedonian dynasty extended their sway from the sources
of the Tigris to the neighbourhood of Rome.   In the eleventh
century, the prospect was again clouded by new enemies and
new misfortunes; the relics of Italy were swept away by the
Norman adventurers; and almost all the Asiatic branches were
dissevered from the Roman trunk by the Turkish conquerors.
After these losses, the emperors of the Comnenian family continued to reign from the Danube to Peloponnesus, and from
Belgrade to Nice, Trebizond, and the winding stream of the
Meander.   The spacious provinces of Thrace, Macedonia, and
Greece, were obedient to their sceptre ; the possession of Cyprus,
Rhodes, and Crete was accompanied by the fifty islands of the
Ægean or Holy Sea ;[13] and the remnant of their empire trans-
cends the measure of the largest of the European kingdoms.

The same princes might assert with dignity and truth that of
all the monarchs of Christendom they possessed the greatest
city,[14] the most ample revenue, the most flourishing and populous General
state.   With the decline and fall of the empire, the cities of the populous-
West had decayed and fallen ; nor could the ruins of Rome, or ness
the mud walls, wooden hovels, and narrow precincts of Paris
and London, prepare the Latin stranger to contemplate the
situation and extent of Constantinople, her stately palaces and
churches, and the arts and luxury of an innumerable people.
Her treasures might attract, but her virgin strength had repelled,

---

[13] Ἅγιος [leg. ἅγιον] πέλαγος, as it is styled by the modern Greeks, from which the
corrupt names of Archipelago, l'Archipel, and the Arches, have been transformed by
geographers and seamen (d'Anville, Géographie Ancienne, tom. i. p. 281 ; Analyse de
la Carte de la Grece, p. 60).   The numbers of monks or caloyers in all the islands and
the adjacent mountain of Athos (Observations de Belon, fol. 32, verso), Monte Santo,
might justify the epithet of holy, ἅγιος, a slight alteration from the original αἰγαῖος, imposed by the Dorians, who, in their dialect, gave the figurative name of αἶγες, or
goats, to the bounding waves (Vossius, apud Cellarium, Geograph. Antiq. tom i. p. 829).
[αἶγες, waves, has, of course, nothing to do with αἴξ, a goat.   The derivations suggested
of Archipelago and ἅγιον πέλαγος are not acceptable.]
[14] According to the Jewish traveller who had visited Europe and Asia, Constantinople was equalled only by Bagdad, the great city of the Ismaelites (Voyage de Benjamin
de Tudèle, par Baratier, tom. i. c. 5, p. 36).

and still promised to repel, the audacious invasion of the Persian and Bulgarian, the Arab and the Russian. The provinces were less fortunate and impregnable; and few districts, few cities, could be discovered which had not been violated by some fierce barbarian, impatient to despoil, because he was hopeless to possess. From the age of Justinian the Eastern empire was sinking below its former level; the powers of destruction were more active than those of improvement; and the calamities of war were embittered by the more permanent evils of civil and ecclesiastical tyranny. The captive who had escaped from the barbarians was often stripped and imprisoned by the ministers of his sovereign: the Greek superstition relaxed the mind by prayer and emaciated the body by fasting; and the multitude of convents and festivals diverted many hands and many days from the temporal service of mankind. Yet the subjects of the Byzantine empire were still the more dexterous and diligent of nations; their country was blessed by nature with every advantage of soil, climate, and situation; and, in the support and restoration of the arts, their patient and peaceful temper was more useful than the warlike spirit and feudal anarchy of Europe. The provinces that still adhered to the empire were repeopled and enriched by the misfortunes of those which were irrecoverably lost. From the yoke of the caliphs, the Catholics of Syria, Egypt, and Africa, retired to the allegiance of their prince, to the society of their brethren: the moveable wealth, which eludes the search of oppression, accompanied and alleviated their exile; and Constantinople received into her bosom the fugitive trade of Alexandria and Tyre. The chiefs of Armenia and Scythia, who fled from hostile or religious persecution, were hospitably entertained; their followers were encouraged to build new cities and to cultivate waste lands; and many spots, both in Europe and Asia, preserved the name, the manners, or at least the memory, of these national colonies. Even the tribes of barbarians, who had seated themselves in arms on the territory of the empire, were gradually reclaimed to the laws of the church and state; and, as long as they were separated from the Greeks, their posterity supplied a race of faithful and obedient soldiers. Did we possess sufficient materials to survey the twenty-nine themes of the Byzantine monarchy, our curiosity might be satisfied with a chosen example: it is fortunate enough that the clearest light should be thrown on the most interesting province, and the name of PELOPONNESUS will awaken the attention of the classic reader.

As early as the eighth century, in the troubled reign of the Iconoclasts, Greece, and even Peloponnesus,[15] were overrun by some Sclavonian bands, who outstripped the royal standard of Bulgaria. The strangers of old, Cadmus, and Danaus, and Pelops, had planted in that fruitful soil the seeds of policy and learning; but the savages of the north eradicated what yet remained of their sickly and withered roots. In this irruption, the country and the inhabitants were transformed; the Grecian blood was contaminated; and the proudest nobles of Peloponnesus were branded with.the names of foreigners and *slaves*. By the diligence of succeeding princes, the land was in some measure purified from the barbarians; and the humble remnant was bound by an oath of obedience, tribute, and military service, which they often renewed and often violated. The siege of Patras was formed by a singular concurrence of the Sclavonians of Peloponnesus and the Saracens of Africa. In their last distress, a pious fiction of the approach of the prætor of Corinth revived the courage of the citizens. Their sally was bold and successful; the strangers embarked, the rebels submitted, and the glory of the day was ascribed to a phantom or a stranger, who fought in the foremost ranks under the character of St. Andrew the Apostle. The shrine which contained his relics was decorated with the trophies of victory, and the captive race was for ever devoted to the service and vassalage of the metropolitan church of Patras. By the revolt of two Sclavonian tribes in the neighbourhood of Helos and Lacedæmon, the peace of the peninsula was often disturbed. They sometimes insulted the weakness, and sometimes resisted the oppression, of the Byzantine government, till at length the approach of their hostile brethren extorted a golden bull to define the rights and obligations of the Ezzerites and Milengi, whose annual tribute was defined at twelve hundred pieces of gold. From

State of Peloponnesus Sclavonians

---

[15] Ἐσθλαβώθη δὲ πᾶσα ἡ χώρα καὶ γέγονε βάρβαρος, says Constantine (Thematibus, l. ii. c. 6, p. 25 [p. 53, ed. Bonn]) in a style as barbarous as the idea, which he confirms, as usual, by a foolish epigram. The epitomizer of Strabo likewise observes, καὶ νῦν δὲ πᾶσαν Ἤπειρον καὶ Ἑλλάδα σχεδὸν καὶ Μακεδονίαν, καὶ Πελοπόννησον Σκύθαι Σκλάβοι νέμονται (l. vii. p. 98, edit. Hudson): a passage which leads Dodwell a weary dance (Geograph. Minor. tom. ii. dissert. vi. p. 170-191) to enumerate the inroads of the Sclavi, and to fix the date (A.D. 980) of this petty geographer. [On the Slavonic element in Greece, see Appendix 7.]

these strangers the Imperial geographer has accurately distinguished a domestic and perhaps original race, who, in some degree, might derive their blood from the much-injured Helots.

Freemen of Laconia The liberality of the Romans, and especially of Augustus, had enfranchised the maritime cities from the dominion of Sparta ; and the continuance of the same benefit ennobled them with the title of *Eleuthero* or Free-Laconians.[16] In the time of Constantine Prophyrogenitus they had acquired the name of *Mainotes*, under which they dishonour the claim of liberty by the inhuman pillage of all that is shipwrecked on their rocky shores. Their territory, barren of corn, but fruitful of olives, extended to the Cape of Malea ; they accepted a chief or prince from the Byzantine prætor, and a light tribute of four hundred pieces of gold was the badge of their immunity rather than of their dependence. The freemen of Laconia assumed the character of Romans, and long adhered to the religion of the Greeks. By the zeal of the emperor Basil, they were baptized in the faith of Christ ; but the altars of Venus and Neptune had been crowned by these rustic votaries five hundred years after they were proscribed in the Roman world. In the theme of

Cities and revenue of Peloponnesus Peloponnesus[17] forty cities were still numbered, and the declining state of Sparta, Argos, and Corinth may be suspended in the tenth century, at an equal distance, perhaps, between their antique splendour and their present desolation. The duty of military service, either in person or by substitute, was imposed on the lands or benefices of the province ; a sum of five pieces of gold was assessed on each of the substantial tenants ; and the same capitation was shared among several heads of inferior value. On the proclamation of an Italian war, the Peloponnesians excused themselves by a voluntary oblation of one hundred pounds

[£4320] of gold (four thousand pounds sterling) and a thousand horses with their arms and trappings. The churches and monasteries furnished their contingent ; a sacrilegious profit was extorted from the sale of ecclesiastical honours ; and the indigent bishop of Leucadia[18] was made responsible for a pension of one hundred pieces of gold.[19]

---

[16] Strabon. Geograph. l. viii. p. 562 [5, § 5]. Pausanias, Græc. Descriptio, l. iii. c. 21, p. 264, 265. Plin. Hist. Natur. l. iv. c. 8.

[17] Constantin. de Administrando Imperio, l. ii. c. 50, 51, 52.

[18] The rock of Leucate was the southern promontory of his island and diocese. Had he been the exclusive guardian of the Lover's Leap, so well known to the

But the wealth of the province, and the trust of the revenue, were founded on the fair and plentiful produce of trade and manufactures; and some symptoms of liberal policy may be traced in a law which exempts from all personal taxes the mariners of Peloponnesus and the workmen in parchment and purple. This denomination may be fairly applied or extended to the manufactures of linen, woollen, and more especially of silk : the two former of which had flourished in Greece since the days of Homer; and the last was introduced perhaps as early as the reign of Justinian. These arts, which were exercised at Corinth, Thebes, and Argos, afforded food and occupation to a numerous people; the men, women and children were distributed according to their age and strength; and, if many of these were domestic slaves, their masters, who directed the work and enjoyed the profit, were of a free and honourable condition. The gifts which a rich and generous matron of Peloponnesus presented to the emperor Basil, her adopted son, were doubtless fabricated in the Grecian looms. Danielis bestowed a carpet of fine wool, of a pattern which imitated the spots of a peacock's tail, of a magnitude to overspread the floor of a new church, erected in the triple name of Christ, of Michael the archangel, and the prophet Elijah. She gave six hundred pieces of silk and linen, of various use and denomination; the silk was painted with the Tyrian die, and adorned by the labours of the needle; and the linen was so exquisitely fine that an entire piece might be rolled in the hollow of a cane.[20] In his description of the Greek manufactures, an historian of Sicily discriminates their price according to the weight and quality of the silk, the closeness of the texture, the beauty of the colours, and the taste and materials of the embroidery. A single, or even a double or treble, thread was thought sufficient for ordinary sale; but the union of six threads composed a piece of stronger and more costly workmanship. Among the

readers of Ovid (Epist. Sappho) and the Spectator, he might have been the richest prelate of the Greek church.

[19] Leucatensis mihi juravit episcopus, quotannis ecclesiam suam debere Nicephoro aureos centum persolvere, similiter et ceteras plus minusve secundum vires suas (Liutprand in Legat. p. 489 [c. 63]).

[20] See Constantine (in Vit. Basil. c. 74, 75, 76, p. 195, 197, in Script. post Theophanem), who allows himself to use many technical or barbarous words : barbarous, says he, τῇ τῶν πολλῶν ἀμαθίᾳ, καλὸν γὰρ ἐπὶ τούτοις κοινολεκτεῖν. Ducange labours on some ; but he was not a weaver.

colours, he celebrates, with affectation of eloquence, the fiery blaze of the scarlet, and the softer lustre of the green. The embroidery was raised either in silk or gold ; the more simple ornament of stripes or circles was surpassed by the nicer imitation of flowers ; the vestments that were fabricated for the palace or the altar often glittered with precious stones ; and the figures were delineated in strings of Oriental pearls.[21] Till the twelfth century, Greece alone, of all the countries of Christendom, was possessed of the insect who is taught by nature, and of the workmen who are instructed by art, to prepare this elegant luxury. But the secret had been stolen by the dexterity and diligence of the Arabs ; the caliphs of the East and West scorned to borrow from the unbelievers their furniture and apparel ; and two cities of Spain, Almeria and Lisbon, were famous for the manufacture, the use, and perhaps the exportation of silk. It was first introduced into Sicily by the Normans ; and this emigration of trade distinguishes the victory of Roger from the uniform and fruitless hostilities of every age. After the sack of Corinth, Athens, and Thebes, his lieutenant embarked with a captive train of weavers and artificers of both sexes, a trophy glorious to their masters and disgraceful to the Greek emperor.[22] The king of Italy was not insensible of the value of the present ; and, in the restitution of the prisoners, he exempted only the male and female manu-

transported from Greece to Italy

[21] The manufactures of Palermo, as they are described by Hugo Falcandus (Hist. Sicula in proem. in Muratori, Script. Rerum Italicarum, tom. v. p. 256), are a copy of those of Greece. Without transcribing his declamatory sentences, which I have softened in the text, I shall observe, that in this passage, the strange word *exarentasmata* is very properly changed for *exanthemata* by Carisius, the first editor. Falcandus lived about the year 1190.

[22] Inde ad interiora Græciæ progressi, Corinthum, Thebas, Athenas, antiquâ nobilitate celebres, expugnant ; et, maximâ ibidem prædâ direptâ, opifices etiam, qui sericos pannos texere solent, ob ignominiam Imperatoris illius suique principis gloriam captivos deducunt. Quos Rogerius, in Palermo Siciliæ metropoli collocans, artem texendi suos edocere præcepit ; et exhinc prædicta ars illa, prius a Græcis tantum inter Christianos habita, Romanis patere cœpit ingeniis (Otho Frisingen. de Gestis Frederici I. l. i. c. 33, in Muratori, Script. Ital. tom. vi. p. 668). This exception allows the bishop to celebrate Lisbon and Almeria in sericorum pannorum opificio prænobilissimæ (in Chron. apud Muratori, Annali d'Italia, tom. ix. p. 415). [On the manufacture of silk and the regulation of the silk trade and guilds of silk merchants at Constantinople, much light is thrown by the so-called Ἐπαρχικὸν βιβλίον, or Book of the Prefect of the City—an Imperial Edict published by M. Jules Nicole of Geneva in 1893, and attributed by him, without sufficient proof, to Leo VI. Cp. sects. iv.-viii. We find distinguished the *vestiopratai* who sold silk dresses ; the *prandiopratai* who· sold dresses imported from Syria or Cilicia ; the *metaxopratai*, silk merchants ; the *katartarioi*, silk manufacturers ; and *serikarioi*, silk weavers.]

facturers of Thebes and Corinth, who labour, says the Byzantine historian, under a barbarous lord, like the old Eretrians in the service of Darius.[23] A stately edifice, in the palace of Palermo, was erected for the use of this industrious colony; [24] and the art was propagated by their children and disciples to satisfy the increasing demand of the western world. The decay of the looms of Sicily may be ascribed to the troubles of the island and the competition of the Italian cities. In the year thirteen hundred and fourteen, Lucca alone, among her sister republics, enjoyed the lucrative monopoly.[25] A domestic revolution dispersed the manufactures of Florence, Bologna, Venice, Milan, and even the countries beyond the Alps; and, thirteen years after this event, the statutes of Modena enjoin the planting of mulberry trees and regulate the duties on raw silk.[26] The northern climates are less propitious to the education of the silk-worm; but the industry of France and England [27] is supplied and enriched by the productions of Italy and China.

I must repeat the complaint that the vague and scanty me- Revenue of morials of the times will not afford any just estimate of the the Greek empire taxes, the revenue, and the resources of the Greek empire. From every province of Europe and Asia the rivulets of gold and silver discharged into the Imperial reservoir a copious and perennial stream.[28] The separation of the branches from the trunk increased the relative magnitude of Constantinople; and the maxims of despotism contracted the state to the capital, the capital to the palace, and the palace to the royal person. A Jewish traveller, who visited the East in the twelfth century, is lost in his admiration of the Byzantine riches. " It is here," says Benjamin of Tudela, " in the queen of cities, that the

---

[23] Nicetas in Manuel. l. ii. c. 8, p. 65. He describes these Greeks as skilled εὐητρίους ὀθόνας ὑφαίνειν, as ἱστῷ προσανέχοντας τῶν ἐξαμίτων καὶ χρυσοπάστων στολῶν.

[24] Hugo Falcandus styles them nobiles officinas. The Arabs had not introduced silk, though they had planted canes and made sugar in the plain of Palermo.

[25] See the Life of Castruccio Casticani, not by Machiavel, but by his more authentic biographer Nicholas Tegrimi. Muratori, who has inserted it in the xith volume of his Scriptores, quotes this curious passage in his Italian Antiquities (tom. i. dissert. xxv. p. 378).

[26] From the Ms. statutes, as they are quoted by Muratori in his Italian Antiquities (tom. ii. dissert. xxx. p. 46-48).

[27] The broad silk manufacture was established in England in the year 1620 (Anderson's Chronological Deduction, vol. ii. p. 4) ; but it is to the revocation of the Edict of Nantes that we owe the Spitalfields colony.

[28] [And from the reign of Leo the Great in the 5th, to the capture of Constantinople at the beginning of the 13th, the gold coinage was never depreciated.]

tributes of the Greek empire are annually deposited, and the lofty towers are filled with precious magazines of silk, purple and gold. It is said that Constantinople pays each day to her sovereign twenty thousand pieces of gold; which are levied on the shops, taverns, and markets, on the merchants of Persia and Egypt, of Russia and Hungary, of Italy and Spain, who frequent the capital by sea and land." [29] In all pecuniary matters, the authority of a Jew is doubtless respectable; but as the three hundred and sixty-five days would produce a [£4,380,000] yearly income exceeding seven millions sterling, I am tempted to retrench at least the numerous festivals of the Greek calendar. The mass of treasure that was saved by Theodora and Basil the Second will suggest a splendid though indefinite idea of their supplies and resources. The mother of Michael, before she retired to a cloister, attempted to check or expose the prodigality of her ungrateful son by a free and faithful account of the wealth which he inherited: one hundred and nine thousand pounds of gold, and three hundred thousand of silver, the fruits of her own economy and that of her deceased husband.[30] The avarice of Basil is not less renowned than his valour and fortune: his victorious armies were paid and rewarded without breaking into the mass of two hundred thou- [£8,640,000] sand pounds of gold (about eight millions sterling) which he had buried in the subterraneous vaults of the palace.[31] Such accumulation of treasure is rejected by the theory and practice of modern policy; and we are more apt to compute the national riches by the use and abuse of the public credit. Yet the maxims of antiquity are still embraced by a monarch formidable to his enemies; by a republic respectable to her allies; and both have attained their respective ends, of military power and domestic tranquillity.

Whatever might be consumed for the present wants, or re-

---

[29] Voyage de Benjamin de Tudèle, tom. i. c. 5, p. 44-52. The Hebrew text has been translated into French by that marvellous child Baratier, who has added a volume of crude learning. The errors and fictions of the Jewish rabbi are not a sufficient ground to deny the reality of his travels. [Benjamin's Itinerary has been edited and translated by A. Asher, 2 vols., 1840. For his statements concerning Greece, cp. Gregorovius, Geschichte der Stadt Athen im Mittelalter, i. p. 200.]

[30] See the continuator of Theophanes (l. iv. p. 107 [p. 172, ed. Bonn]), Cedrenus (p. 544 [ii. p. 158, ed. Bonn]), and Zonaras (tom. ii. l. xvi. p. 157 [c. 2]).

[31] Zonaras (tom. ii. l. xvii. p. 225 [c. 8]), instead of pounds, uses the more classic appellation of talents, which, in a literal sense and strict computation, would multiply sixty-fold [sixfold] the treasure of Basil.

served for the future use, of the state, the first and most sacred Pomp and luxury of the emperors
demand was for the pomp and pleasure of the emperor; and
his discretion only could define the measure of his private expense.   The princes of Constantinople were far removed from
the simplicity of nature; yet, with the revolving seasons, they
were led by taste or fashion to withdraw to a purer air from the
smoke and tumult of the capital.   They enjoyed, or affected
to enjoy, the rustic festival of the vintage; their leisure was
amused by the exercise of the chase, and the calmer occupation
of fishing; and in the summer heats they were shaded from the
sun and refreshed by the cooling breezes from the sea.   The
coasts and islands of Asia and Europe were covered with their
magnificent villas; but, instead of the modest art which secretly
strives to hide itself and to decorate the scenery of nature, the
marble structure of their gardens served only to expose the
riches of the lord and the labours of the architect.   The successive casualties of inheritance and forfeiture had rendered the
sovereign proprietor of many stately houses in the city and
suburbs, of which twelve were appropriated to the ministers of
state; but the great palace,[32] the centre of the Imperial resi- The palace of Constan-
dence, was fixed during eleven centuries to the same position, tinople
between the hippodrome, the cathedral of St. Sophia, and the
gardens, which descended by many a terrace to the shores of
the Propontis.   The primitive edifice of the first Constantine

---

[32] For a copious and minute description of the Imperial palace, see the Con-
stantinop. Christiana (l. ii. c. 4, p. 113-123) of Ducange, the Tillemont of the middle
ages.   Never has laborious Germany produced two antiquarians more laborious
and accurate than these two natives of lively France.   [For recent works on the
reconstruction of the Imperial Palace, based on the Ceremonies of Constantine
Porphyrogennetos, see above, vol. 2, App. 8.   To these must now be added J.
Ebersolt, Le grand palais de Constantinople, 1910; and see also Bury, The Great
Palace, in Byzantinische Zeitschrift, vol. xx., 1911 (where Ebersolt's results are
criticized).   Though all attempts to reconstruct the plan must be highly problem-
atical till the site is excavated, the general distribution of the chief groups of
buildings may be conjectured with some probability.   The Daphne palace and the
other buildings of the original Constantinian palace lay in the north part of the
enclosure.   The Chrysotriklinos (see below, n. 36) lay considerably to the south-
east of these edifices, and was connected with the Hippodrome by two long halls
which ran from east to west, (a) the Lausiakos and (b) the triklinos of Justinian
(II.), commonly called "the Justinian".   The Justinian opened into the Skyla
(a vestibule) from which there was a door into the Hippodrome.   The new buildings of Theophilus (Trikonchos, Sigma, Phiale, &c., see below) were immediately
north and north-west of the Chrysotriklinos.   The palace of Magnaura lay on the
east side of the Augusteon, and outside the precincts of the Great Palace, though
immediately adjoining.]

was a copy or rival of ancient Rome ; the gradual improvements of his successors aspired to emulate the wonders of the old world,[33] and in the tenth century the Byzantine palace excited the admiration, at least of the Latins, by an unquestionable pre-eminence of strength, size, and magnificence.[34] But the toil and treasure of so many ages had produced a vast and irregular pile ; each separate building was marked with the character of the times and of the founder ; and the want of space might excuse the reigning monarch who demolished, perhaps with secret satisfaction, the works of his predecessors. The economy of the emperor Theophilus allowed a more free and ample scope for his domestic luxury and splendour. A favourite ambassador, who had astonished the Abbassides themselves by his pride and liberality, presented on his return the model of a palace, which the caliph of Bagdad had recently constructed on the banks of the Tigris. The model was instantly copied and surpassed ; the new buildings of Theophilus [35] were accompanied with gardens, and with five churches, one of which was conspicuous for size and beauty : it was crowned with three domes, the roof, of gilt brass, reposed on columns of Italian marble, and the walls were encrusted with marbles of various colours. In the face of the church, a semi-circular portico, of the figure and name of the Greek *sigma*, was supported by fifteen columns of Phrygian marble, and the subterraneous vaults were of a similar construction. The square before the sigma was decorated with a fountain, and the margin of the

[The Mystic Phiale]

---

[33] The Byzantine palace surpasses the Capitol, the palace of Pergamus, the Rufinian wood ($\phi\alpha\iota\delta\rho\grave{o}\nu$ $\check{\alpha}\gamma\alpha\lambda\mu\alpha$), the temple of Hadrian at Cyzicus, the Pyramids, the Pharus, &c., according to an epigram (Antholog. Græc. l. iv. p. 488, 489. Brodæi, apud Wechel) ascribed to Julian, ex-præfect of Egypt. Seventy-one of his epigrams, some lively, are collected in Brunck (Analect. Græc. tom. ii. p. 493-510) ; but this is wanting.

[34] Constantinopolitanum Palatium non pulchritudine solum, verum etiam fortitudine, omnibus quas unquam videram [*leg.* perspexerim] munitionibus præstat (Liutprand, Hist. l. v. c. 9 [= c. 21], p. 465).

[35] See the anonymous continuator of Theophanes (p. 59, 61, 86 [p. 94, 98, 139, ed. Bonn]), whom I have followed in the neat and concise abstract of Le Beau (Hist. du Bas. Empire, tom. xiv. p. 436, 438). [The chief building of Theophilus in the Great Palace was the Trikonchos (so called from its three apses) with its adjunct, the Sigma. It was not a church. It had an understorey, which from its acoustic property of rendering whispers audible was called $M\upsilon\sigma\tau\acute{\eta}\rho\iota o\nu$—"The Whispering Room". The palace, constructed on the model brought from Baghdad, was not part of the Great Palace ; it was built in the suburb of Bryas, on the Bithynian shore.]

bason was lined and encompassed with plates of silver. In the beginning of each season, the bason, instead of water, was replenished with the most exquisite fruits, which were abandoned to the populace for the entertainment of the prince. He enjoyed this tumultuous spectacle from a throne resplendent with gold and gems, which was raised by a marble staircase to the height of a lofty terrace. Below the throne were seated the officers of his guards, the magistrates, the chiefs of the factions of the circus; the inferior steps were occupied by the people, and the place below was covered with troops of dancers, singers, and pantomimes. The square was surrounded by the hall of justice, the arsenal, and the various offices of business and pleasure; and the *purple* chamber was named from the annual distribution of robes of scarlet and purple by the hand of the empress herself. The long series of the apartments was adapted to the seasons, and decorated with marble and porphyry, with painting, sculpture, and mosaics, with a profusion of gold, silver, and precious stones. His fanciful magnificence employed the skill and patience of such artists as the times could afford ; but the taste of Athens would have despised their frivolous and costly labours : a golden tree, with its leaves and branches, which sheltered a multitude of birds, warbling their artificial notes, and two lions of massy gold, and of the natural size, who looked and roared like their brethren of the forest. The successors of Theophilus, of the Basilian and Comnenian dynasties, were not less ambitious of leaving some memorial of their residence; and the portion of the palace most splendid and august was dignified with the title of the golden *triclinium*.[36] With becoming modesty, the rich and noble Greeks aspired to imitate their sovereign, and, when they passed through the

Furniture and attendance

[36] In aureo triclinio quæ præstantior est pars potentissime (*the usurper Romanus*) degens cæteras partes (*filiis*) distribuerat (Liutprand, Hist. l. v. c. 9 [= c. 21], p. 469). For this lax signification of Triclinium (ædificium tria vel plura κλίνη scilicet στέγη complectens) see Ducange (Gloss. Græc. et Observations sur Joinville, p. 240) and Reiske (ad Constantinum de Ceremoniis, p. 7). [The Gold Room (Χρυσοτρίκλινος), being near the imperial chambers, was more convenient for ordinary ceremonies than the more distant throne-rooms which were used only on specially solemn occasions. It was built by Justin II., and was probably modelled on the design of the Church of St. Sergius and Bacchus built by Justinian. (For the plan of this church see plate 5 in the atlas to Salzenberg's Altchristliche Baudenkmale von Constantinopel. Cp. Diehl, Manuel de l'art byzantin, 137. Ducange, Constant. Christ. II. p. 94-95, confounds the Chrysotriklinos with the Augusteus, another throne-room which was in the Daphne palace. The Chrysotriklinos was domed and had eight καμάραι or recesses off the central room.]

streets on horseback, in their robes of silk and embroidery, they were mistaken by the children for kings.[37]   A matron of Peloponnesus,[38] who had cherished the infant fortunes of Basil the Macedonian, was excited by tenderness or vanity to visit the greatness of her adopted son.   In a journey of five hundred miles from Patras to Constantinople, her age or indolence declined the fatigue of an horse or carriage; the soft litter or bed of Danielis was transported on the shoulders of ten robust slaves; and, as they were relieved at easy distances, a band of three hundred was selected for the performance of this service. She was entertained in the Byzantine palace with filial reverence and the honours of a queen; and, whatever might be the origin of her wealth, her gifts were not unworthy of the regal dignity. I have already described the fine and curious manufactures of Peloponnesus, of linen, silk, and woollen; but the most acceptable of her presents consisted in three hundred beautiful youths, of whom one hundred were eunuchs;[39] "for she was not ignorant," says the historian, "that the air of the palace is more congenial to such insects than a shepherd's dairy to the flies of the summer".   During her lifetime, she bestowed the greater part of her estates in Peloponnesus, and her testament instituted Leo, the son of Basil, her universal heir.   After the payment of the legacies, fourscore villas or farms were added to the Imperial domain; and three thousand slaves of Danielis were enfranchised by their new lord, and transplanted as a colony to the Italian coast.   From this example of a private matron, we may estimate the wealth and magnificence of the emperors.   Yet our enjoyments are confined by a narrow circle; and, whatsoever may be its value, the luxury of life is possessed with more innocence and safety by the master of his own, than by the steward of the public, fortune.

In an absolute government, which levels the distinctions of

[37] In equis vecti (says Benjamin of Tudela) regum filiis videntur persimiles. I prefer the Latin version of Constantine l'Empereur (p. 46) to the French of Baratier (tom. i. p. 49).

[38] See the account of her journey, munificence, and testament in the Life of Basil, by his grandson Constantine (c. 74, 75, 76, p. 195-197).

[39] *Carsamatium* [*leg.* carzimasium] (καρξιμάδες, Ducange, Gloss.) Græci vocant, amputatis virilibus et virgâ, puerum eunuchum quos [*leg.* quod] Verdunenses mercatores ob immensum lucrum facere solent et in Hispaniam ducere (Liutprand, l. vi. c. 3, p. 470).—The last abomination of the abominable slave-trade! Yet I am surprised to find in the xth century such active speculations of commerce in Lorraine.

noble and plebeian birth, the sovereign is the sole fountain of Honours and titles of the Imperial family honour; and the rank, both in the palace and the empire, depends on the titles and offices which are bestowed and resumed by his arbitrary will. Above a thousand years, from Vespasian to Alexius Comnenus,[40] the *Cæsar* was the second person, or at least the second degree, after the supreme title of *Augustus* was more freely communicated to the sons and brothers of the reigning monarch. To elude without violating his promise to a powerful associate, the husband of his sister, and, without giving himself an equal, to reward the piety of his brother Isaac, the crafty Alexius interposed a new and supereminent dignity. The happy flexibility of the Greek tongue allowed him to compound the names of Augustus and emperor (Sebastos and Autocrator), and the union produced the sonorous title of *Sebastocrator.* He was exalted above the Cæsar on the first step of the throne; the public acclamations repeated his name; and he was only distinguished from the sovereign by some peculiar ornaments of the head and feet. The emperor alone could assume the purple or red buskins, and the close diadem or tiara, which imitated the fashion of the Persian kings.[41] It

---

[40] See the Alexiad (l. iii. p. 78, 79 [c. 4]) of Anna Comnena, who, except in filial piety, may be compared to Mademoiselle de Montpensier. In her awful reverence for titles and forms, she styles her father 'Επιστημονάρχης, the inventor of this royal art, the τέχνη τεχνῶν, and ἐπιστήμη ἐπιστημῶν.

[41] Στέμμα, στέφανος, διάδημα; see Reiske, ad Ceremoniale, p. 14, 15. Ducange has given a learned dissertation on the crowns of Constantinople, Rome, France, &c. (sur Joinville, xxv. p. 289-303), but of his thirty-four models none exactly tally with Anna's description. [The Imperial costume may be best studied in Byzantine miniatures. It does not seem correct to describe the crown as a "high pyramidal cap"; the crowns represented in the paintings are not high or pyramidal. The diadems of the Empresses had not the cross or the pearl pendants. As Gibbon says, it was only the crown and the red boots which distinguished the Emperor; there were no distinctively Imperial robes. (1) On great state occasions the Emperor wore a long tunic (not necessarily purple) called a *divetesion* (διβητήσιον); and over it either a heavy mantle (χλαμύς) or a scarf (λῶρος) wound over the shoulders and round the arms. (2) As a sort of half-dress costume and always when he was riding the Emperor wore a different tunic, simpler and more convenient, called the *scaramangion* (σκαραμάγγιον) and over it a lighter cloak (σαγίον). (3) There was yet another lighter dress, the *colovion* (κολόβιον), a tunic with short sleeves to the elbow or no sleeves at all, which he wore on some occasions. All these official tunics were worn over the ordinary tunic (χιτών) of private life. The only satisfactory discussions of these Imperial costumes are to be found in Bieliaiev, Ezhednevnye i Voskresnye Priemy viz. Tsarei (=Byzantina, Bk. ii. 1893): for the σκαραμάγγιον, p. 8; κολόβιον, p. 26; διβητήσιον, p. 51-56; λῶρος (which corresponded to the Roman *trabea*), p. 213, 214, 301. For the θωράκιον which was worn on certain occasions instead of the διβητήσιον see *ib.* 197-8 (Basil ii. in the miniature mentioned below, note 54, seems to wear a gold θωράκιον). Bieliaiev explains the origin of διβητήσιον (διβιτήσιον) satisfactorily from Lat. *divitense* (p. 54).]

was an high pyramidal cap of cloth or silk, almost concealed by a profusion of pearls and jewels, the crown was formed by an horizontal circle and two arches of gold; at the summit, the point of their intersection, was placed a globe or cross, and two strings or lappets of pearl depended on either cheek. Instead of red, the buskins of the Sebastocrator and Cæsar were green; and on their *open* coronets or crowns the precious gems were more sparingly distributed. Beside and below the Cæsar, the fancy of Alexius created the *Panhypersebastos* and the *Protosebastos*, whose sound and signification will satisfy a Grecian ear. They imply a superiority and a priority above the simple name of Augustus; and this sacred and primitive title of the Roman prince was degraded to the kinsmen and servants of the Byzantine court. The daughter of Alexius applauds, with fond complacency, this artful gradation of hopes and honours; but the science of words is accessible to the meanest capacity; and this vain dictionary was easily enriched by the pride of his successors. To their favourite sons or brothers, they imparted the more lofty appellation of Lord or *Despot*, which was illustrated with new ornaments and prerogatives, and placed immediately after the person of the emperor himself. The five titles of 1. *Despot;* 2. *Sebastocrator;* 3. *Cæsar;* 4. *Panhypersebastos;* and, 5. *Protosebastos*, were usually confined to the princes of his blood; they were the emanations of his majesty; but, as they exercised no regular functions, their existence was useless, and their authority precarious.

Offices of the palace, the state, and the army   But in every monarchy the substantial powers of government must be divided and exercised by the ministers of the palace and treasury, the fleet and army. The titles alone can differ; and in the revolution of ages, the counts and præfects, the prætor and quæstor, insensibly descended, while their servants rose above their heads to the first honours of the state. 1. In a monarchy, which refers every object to the person of the prince, the care and ceremonies of the palace form the most respectable department. The *Curopalata*,[42] so illustrious

[42] Pars exstans curis, solo diademate dispar,
        Ordine pro rerum vocitatus *Cura-Palati;*
says the African Corippus (de Laudibus Justini, l. i. 136), and in the same century (the sixth) Cassiodorius represents him, who, virgâ aureâ decoratus, inter numerosa obsequia primus ante pedes regios incederet (Variar. vii. 5). But this great officer (unknown) ἀνεπίγνωστος, exercising no function, νῦν δὲ οὐδεμίαν, was cast down by

in the age of Justinian, was supplanted by the *Protovestiare*, whose primitive functions were limited to the custody of the wardrobe. From thence his jurisdiction was extended over the numerous menials of pomp and luxury; and he presided with his silver wand at the public and private audience. 2. In the ancient system of Constantine, the name of *Logothete*, or accountant, was applied to the receivers of the finances: the principal officers were distinguished as the Logothetes of the domain, of the posts, the army, the private and public treasure; and the *great Logothete*, the supreme guardian of the laws and revenues, is compared with the chancellor of the Latin monarchies.[43] His discerning eye pervaded the civil administration; and he was assisted, in due subordination, by the eparch or præfect of the city, the first secretary, and the keepers of the privy seal, the archives, and the red or purple ink which was reserved for the sacred signature of the emperor alone.[44] The introductor and interpreter of foreign ambassadors were the great *Chiauss*[45] and the *Dragoman*,[46] two names of Turkish

the modern Greeks to the xvth rank (Codin. c. 5, p. 65 [p. 35, ed. Bonn]). [It is not correct to say that the place of the Curopalates was taken by the protovestiarios. Curopalates was a title of rank, not of office. The care of the Palace devolved upon the Great Papias (ὁ μέγας παπίας), who was always a eunuch and held the rank of protospathar. He was a very important official, and had an assistant (also a eunuch) called "the Second" (ὁ δεύτερος). The protovestiarios was a eunuch who presided over the Imperial wardrobe (*sacra vestis*). As for the Curopalates he was in the 9th century the highest person at court next to the nobilissimus, who came immediately after the Cæsar. (Philotheus, ap. Const. Porph. de Cer. ii. 52, p. 711.) Only six persons were deemed worthy of sitting at the same table as the Emperor and Empress, namely, the Patriarch of Constantinople, the Cæsar, the Nobilissimus, the Curopalates, the Basileopator (cp. above, vol. v. p. 219), and the Zostê patricia or highest maid of honour. See Philotheus, *ib.* p. 726. On the ranks and offices in the 9th century see Bury, The Imperial Administrative System in the Ninth Century (Supp. Papers, I. of British Academy), 1911.]

[43] Nicetas (in Manuel. l. vii. c. i. [p. 262, ed. Bonn]) defines him ὡς ἡ Λατίνων [βούλεται] φωνὴ Καγκελλάριον, ὡς δ' Ἕλληνες εἴποιεν Λογοθέτην. Yet the epithet of μέγας was added by the elder Andronicus (Ducange, tom. i. p. 822, 823). [This is the Logothete τοῦ γενικοῦ who corresponded to the old Count of the Sacred Largesses (τὸ γενικόν = the Exchequer). For the history of the financial bureaux, compare Bury, *op. cit.*, 78 *sqq.* There were other Logothetes: the Logothete of the military chest (τοῦ στρατιωτικοῦ); the Logothete of the Dromos or Imperial post—a name which first occurs in the 8th century; the Logothete of the pastures (τῶν ἀγελῶν, "of the flocks").]

[44] From Leo I. (A.D. 470) the Imperial ink, which is still visible on some original acts, was a mixture of vermillion and cinnabar or purple. The Emperor's guardians, who shared in this prerogative, always marked in green ink the indiction and the month. See the Dictionnaire Diplomatique (tom. i. p. 511, 513), a valuable abridgment. [The keeper of the Imperial ink was entitled ὁ χαρτουλάριος τοῦ κανικλείου.]

[45] The Sultan sent a Σιαούς to Alexius (Anna Comnena, l. vi. p. 170; [c. 9] Ducange *ad loc.*), and Pachymer often speaks of the μέγας τζαούς (l. vii. c. 1, l. xii.

origin, and which are still familiar to the Sublime Porte.   3. From the humble style and service of guards, the *Domestics* insensibly rose to the station of generals; the military themes of the East and West, the legions of Europe and Asia, were often divided, till the *great Domestic* was finally invested with the universal and absolute command of the land forces.[47]   The *Protostrator*, in his original functions, was the assistant of the emperor when he mounted on horseback; he gradually became the lieutenant of the great Domestic in the field; and his jurisdiction extended over the stables, the cavalry, and the royal train of hunting and hawking.   The *Stratopedarch* was the great judge of the camp; the *Protospathaire*[48] commanded the guards; the *Constable*,[49] the great *Æteriarch*,[50] and the *Acolyth*[51] were the separate chiefs of the Franks, the barbarians, and the Varangi, or English, the mercenary strangers, who, in the decay of the national spirit, formed the nerve of the Byzantine armies.   4. The naval powers were under the command of the *great Duke*; in his absence they obeyed the *great Drungaire* of the fleet; and, in *his* place, the *Emir*, or *admiral*, a name of Saracen extraction,[52] but which has been naturalised in all the modern languages of Europe.   Of these officers, and of many more whom it would be useless to enumerate, the civil and military hierarchy was framed.   Their honours and emoluments, their dress and titles, their mutual salutations and respective pre-eminence, were balanced with more exquisite labour than would have fixed the constitution of a free people;

c. 30, l. xiii. c. 22).   The Chiaoush basha is now at the head of 700 officers (Rycaut's Ottoman Empire, p. 349, octavo edition).

[46] *Tagerman* is the Arabic name of an interpreter (d'Herbelot, p. 854, 855); πρῶτος τῶν ἑρμηνέων οὓς κοινῶς ὀνομάζουσι δραγομάνους, says Codinus (c. v. No. 70, p. 67).   See Villehardouin (No. 96), Busbequius (Epist. iv. p. 338), and Ducange (Observations sur Villehardouin and Gloss. Græc. et Latin).

[47] [There were various military commands (7 in the 9th century) with the title Domestic.   The three chief were the Domestic of the Schools, the Domestic of the Excubiti, and the Domestic of the Hikanatoi.   Cp. Bury, *op. cit.*, 47 *sqq.*]

[48] [The Πρωτοσπαθάριος τῶν βασιλικῶν.   But the term *protospatharios* by itself designated a rank, not an office; it was the rank below that of patrician and above that of *spatharocandidatus* (which in turn was superior to that of *spatharios*).]

[49] Κονόσταυλος, or κοντόσταυλος, a corruption from the Latin Comes stabuli, or the French Connétable.   In a military sense, it was used by the Greeks in the xith century, at least as early as in France.

[50] [ὁ ἑταιρειάρχης, cp. above, vol. v. p. 222, note 45.]

[51] [ἀκόλουθός, and if anglicized should be *acoluth*. ἀκολουθία meant a ceremony.]

[52] It was directly borrowed from the Normans.   In the xiith century, Giannone reckons the admiral of Sicily among the great officers.

and the code was almost perfect when this baseless fabric, the
monument of pride and servitude, was for ever buried in the
ruins of the empire.[53]

The most lofty titles and the most humble postures, which Adoration of the emperor
devotion has applied to the Supreme Being, have been prosti-
tuted by flattery and fear to creatures of the same nature with
ourselves. The mode of *adoration*,[54] of falling prostrate on the
ground and kissing the feet of the emperor, was borrowed by
Diocletian from Persian servitude; but it was continued and
aggravated till the last age of the Greek monarchy. Excepting
only on Sundays, when it was waived, from a motive of religious
pride, this humiliating reverence was exacted from all who
entered the royal presence, from the princes invested with the
diadem and purple, and from the ambassadors who represented
their independent sovereigns, the caliphs of Asia, Egypt, or Spain,
the kings of France and Italy, and the Latin emperors of ancient
Rome. In his transactions of business, Liutprand, bishop of Cremona,[55] asserted the free spirit of a Frank and the dignity of
his master Otho. Yet his sincerity cannot disguise the abase-
ment of his first audience. When he approached the throne, Reception of ambassadors
the birds of the golden tree began to warble their notes, which
were accompanied by the roarings of the two lions of gold.
With his two companions, Liutprand was compelled to bow and
to fall prostrate; and thrice he touched the ground with his
forehead. He arose; but, in the short interval, the throne had
been hoisted by an engine from the floor to the ceiling, the

[53] This sketch of honours and offices is drawn from George Codinus Curopalata,
who survived the taking of Constantinople by the Turks; his elaborate though
trifling work (de Officiis Ecclesiæ et Aulæ C. P.) has been illustrated by the notes
of Goar, and the three books of Gretser, a learned Jesuit. [For Codinus see Appendix
1.—Following "Codinus," Ducange and Gibbon, in the account in the text, have
given a description of the ministers and officials of the Byzantine court which confounds different periods in a single picture. The functions and the importance of
these dignitaries were constantly changing; but the history of each office throughout
the whole period has still to be written.]

[54] The respectful salutation of carrying the hand to the mouth, *ad os*, is the root
of the Latin word, *adoro adorare*. [This is to go too far back. *Adoro* comes
directly from *oro*.] See our learned Selden (vol. iii. p. 143-145, 942), in his Titles
of Honour. It seems, from the first books of Herodotus, to be of Persian origin.
[The adoration of the Basileus is vividly represented in a fine miniature in a Venetian
psalter, which shows the Emperor Basil II. in grand costume and men grovelling at
his feet. There is a coloured reproduction in Schlumberger's Nicéphore Phocas, p.
304.]

[55] The two embassies of Liutprand to Constantinople, all that he saw or suffered
in the Greek capital, are pleasantly described by himself (Hist. l. vi. c. 1-4, p. 469-
471. Legatio ad Nicephorum Phocam, p. 479-489).

Imperial figure appeared in new and more gorgeous apparel, and the interview was concluded in haughty and majestic silence. In this honest and curious narrative, the bishop of Cremona represents the ceremonies of the Byzantine court, which are still practised in the Sublime Porte, and which were preserved in the last age by the dukes of Moscovy or Russia. After a long journey by the sea and land, from Venice to Constantinople, the ambassador halted at the golden gate, till he was conducted by the formal officers to the hospitable palace prepared for his reception ; but this palace was a prison, and his jealous keepers prohibited all social intercourse, either with strangers or natives. At his first audience, he offered the gifts of his master, slaves, and golden vases, and costly armour. The ostentatious payment of the officers and troops displayed before his eyes the riches of the empire : he was entertained at a royal banquet,[56] in which the ambassadors of the nations were marshalled by the esteem or contempt of the Greeks : from his own table, the emperor, as the most signal favour, sent the plates which he had tasted ; and his favourites were dismissed with a robe of honour.[57] In the morning and evening of each day, his civil and military servants attended their duty in the palace ; their labour was repaid by the sight, perhaps by the smile, of their lord ; his commands were signified by a nod or a sign ; but all earthly greatness *stood* silent and submissive in his presence. In his regular or extraordinary processions through the capital, he unveiled his person to the public view ; the rites of policy were connected with those of religion, and his visits to the principal churches were regulated by the festivals of the Greek calendar. On the eve of these processions, the gracious or devout intention of the monarch was proclaimed by the heralds. The streets were cleared and purified ; the pavement was strewed with flowers ; the most precious furniture, the

Proces-
sions
and accla-
mations

[56] Among the amusements of the feast, a boy balanced, on his forehead, a pike, or pole, twenty-four feet long, with a cross bar of two cubits a little below the top. Two boys, naked, though cinctured (*campestrati*), together and singly, climbed, stood, played, descended, &c., ita me stupidum reddidit ; utrum mirabilius nescio (p. 470 [vi. c. 9]). At another repast, an homily of Chrysostom on the Acts of the Apostles was read elata voce non Latine (p. 483 [c. 29. The words *non Latine* do not occur in the text ; but there is a variant *Latina* for *elata*]).

[57] *Gala* is not improbably derived from Cala, or Caloat, in Arabic, a robe of honour (Reiske, Not. in Ceremon. p. 84). [*Gala* seems to be connected with *gallant*, O. Fr. *galant ;* and it is supposed that both words may be akin to N.H.G. *geil*, Gothic *gailjan* (to rejoice), χαίρω.]

gold and silver plate, and silken hangings were displayed from the windows and balconies, and a severe discipline restrained and silenced the tumult of the populace. The march was opened by the military officers at the head of their troops; they were followed in long order by the magistrates and ministers of the civil government: the person of the emperor was guarded by his eunuchs and domestics, and at the church door he was solemnly received by the patriarch and his clergy. The task of applause was not abandoned to the rude and spontaneous voices of the crowd. The most convenient stations were occupied by the bands of the blue and green factions of the circus;[58] and their furious conflicts, which had shaken the capital, were insensibly sunk to an emulation of servitude. From either side they echoed in responsive melody the praises of the emperor; their poets and musicians directed the choir, and *long life*[59] and victory were the burden of every song. The same acclamations were performed at the audience, the banquet, and the church; and, as an evidence of boundless sway, they were repeated in the Latin,[60] Gothic, Persian, French, and even English language,[61] by the mercenaries who sustained the real or fictitious character of those nations. By the pen of Constantine Porphyrogenitus this science of form and flattery has been reduced into a pompous and trifling volume,[62] which the vanity of succeeding times might enrich with an ample supplement. Yet the calmer reflection of a prince would surely suggest that the same acclamations were applied to every character and every reign; and, if

[58] [See above, vol. iv., Appendix 11, p. 567-8.]

[59] Πολυχρονίζειν is explained by εὐφημίζειν (Codin. c. 7, Ducange, Gloss. Græc. tom. i. p. 1199).

[60] Κωνσέρβετ Δέους ἡμπέριουμ βέστρουμ—βίκτωρ σῆς σέμπερ—βήβητε Δόμηνι Ἡμπεράτορες ἢν μούλτος ἄννος (Ceremon. [i.] c. 75, p. 215). The want of the Latin V obliged the Greeks to employ their β [it was not a shift; the pronunciation of β was then, as it is now, the same as that of v]; nor do they regard quantity. Till he recollected the true language, these strange sentences might puzzle a professor.

[61] Βάραγγοι κατὰ τὴν πατρίαν γλῶσσαν καὶ οὗτοι, ἤγουν Ἰγκλινιστὶ πολυχρονίζουσι (Codin. p. 90 [p. 57, ed. Bonn]). I wish he had preserved the words, however corrupt, of their English acclamation.

[62] For all these ceremonies, see the professed work of Constantine Porphyrogenitus, with the notes, or rather dissertations, of his German editors, Leich and Reiske. For the rank of the *standing* courtiers, p. 80 [c. 23 *ad fin.*], not. 23, 62, for the adoration, except on Sundays, p. 95, 240 [c. 39; c. 91 (p. 414, ed. Bonn)], not. 131, the processions, p. 2 [c. 1], &c., not. p. 3, &c., the acclamations, *passim*, not. 25, &c., the factions and Hippodrome, p. 177-214 [c. 68—c. 73], not. 9, 93, &c., the Gothic games, p. 221 [c. 83], not. 111, vintage, p. 217 [c. 78], not. 109. Much more information is scattered over the work.

he had risen from a private rank, he might remember that his own voice had been the loudest and most eager in applause, at the very moment when he envied the fortune, or conspired against the life, of his predecessor.[63]

Marriage of the Cæsars with foreign nations The princes of the North, of the nations, says Constantine, without faith or fame, were ambitious of mingling their blood with the blood of the Cæsars, by their marriage with a royal virgin, or by the nuptials of their daughters with a Roman prince.[64] The aged monarch, in his instructions to his son, reveals the secret maxims of policy and pride; and suggests the most decent reasons for refusing these insolent and unreasonable demands. Every animal, says the discreet emperor, is prompted by nature to seek a mate among the animals of his own species; and the human species is divided into various tribes, by the distinction of language, religion, and manners. A just regard to the purity of descent preserves the harmony of public and private life; but the mixture of foreign blood is the fruitful source of disorder and discord. Such has ever been the opinion and practice of the sage Romans; their jurisprudence proscribed the marriage of a citizen and a stranger; in the days of freedom and virtue, a senator would have scorned to match his daughter with a king; the glory of Mark Anthony was sullied by an Egyptian wife;[65] and the emperor Titus was compelled, by popular censure, to dismiss with reluctance the reluctant Bernice.[66] This perpetual interdict was ratified by the fabulous sanction of the great Constantine. The ambassadors of the nations, more especially of the unbelieving nations, were solemnly admonished that such strange alliances had been condemned by the founder *Imaginary law of Constantine* of the church and city. The irrevocable law was inscribed on the altar of St. Sophia; and the impious prince who should stain the majesty of the purple was excluded from the civil and ec-

[63] Et privato Othoni et nuper eadem dicenti nota adulatio (Tacit. Hist. i. 85).
[64] The xiiith chapter, de Administratione Imperii, may be explained and rectified by the Familiæ Byzantinæ of Ducange.
[65] Sequiterque nefas! Ægyptia conjunx (Virgil, Æneid. viii. 687 [*leg.* 686]). Yet this Egyptian wife was the daughter of a long line of kings. Quid te mutavit (says Antony in a private letter to Augustus)? an quod regimen ineo? Uxor mea est (Sueton. in August. c. 69). Yet I much question (for I cannot stay to inquire) whether the triumvir ever dared to celebrate his marriage either with Roman or Egyptian rites.
[66] Berenicem invitus invitam dimisit (Suetonius in Tito, c. 7). Have I observed elsewhere that this Jewish beauty was at this time above fifty years of age? The judicious Racine has most discreetly suppressed both her age and her country.

clesiastical communion of the Romans. If the ambassadors were
instructed by any false brethren in the Byzantine history, they
might produce three memorable examples of the violation of
this imaginary law : the marriage of Leo, or rather of his father,
Constantine the Fourth, with the daughter of the king of the
Chozars, the nuptials of the grand-daughter of Romanus with a
Bulgarian prince, and the union of Bertha of France or Italy
with young Romanus, the son of Constantine Porphyrogenitus
himself. To these objections three answers were prepared,
which solved the difficulty and established the law. I. The The first
deed and the guilt of Constantine Copronymus were acknow- A.D. 733
ledged. The Isaurian heretic, who sullied the baptismal font
and declared war against the holy images, had indeed embraced
a barbarian wife. By this impious alliance he accomplished the
measure of his crimes, and was devoted to the just censure of
the church and of posterity. II. Romanus could not be alleged The
as a legitimate emperor ; he was a plebeian usurper, ignorant of A.D. 941
the laws, and regardless of the honour, of the monarchy. His
son Christopher, the father of the bride, was the third in rank
in the college of princes, at once the subject and the accomplice of a rebellious parent. The Bulgarians were sincere and
devout Christians ; and the safety of the empire, with the redemption of many thousand captives, depended on this preposterous alliance. Yet no consideration could dispense from
the law of Constantine : the clergy, the senate, and the people
disapproved the conduct of Romanus ; and he was reproached,
both in his life and death, as the author of the public disgrace.
III. For the marriage of his own son with the daughter of The third.
Hugo, king of Italy, a more honourable defence is contrived by A.D. 943
the wise Porphyrogenitus. Constantine, the great and holy, esteemed the fidelity and valour of the Franks ;[67] and his prophetic spirit beheld the vision of their future greatness. They
alone were excepted from the general prohibition : Hugo king
of France was the lineal descendant of Charlemagne ;[68] and his

[67] Constantine was made to praise the εὐγένεια and περιφάνεια of the Franks,
with whom he claimed a private and public alliance. The French writers (Isaac
Casaubon in Dedicat. Polybii) are highly delighted with these compliments. [A
Monodia is extant which is composed by Imperial order for the young Romanus and
dedicated by him to Bertha. It had been published by S. Lambros in the Bulletin
de Correspondance hellénique, ii. 266 sqq. (1878).]

[68] Constantine Porphyrogenitus (de Admistrat. Imp. c. 26) exhibits a pedigree
and life of the illustrious king Hugo (περιβλέπτου ῥῆγος Οὕγωνος). A more correct

daughter Bertha inherited the prerogatives of her family and nation. The voice of truth and malice insensibly betrayed the fraud or error of the Imperial court. The patrimonial estate of Hugo was reduced from the monarchy of France to the simple county of Arles; though it was not denied that, in the confusion of the times, he had usurped the sovereignty of Provence and invaded the kingdom of Italy. His father was a private noble : and, if Bertha derived her female descent from the Carlovingian line, every step was polluted with illegitimacy or vice. The grandmother of Hugo was the famous Valdrada, the concubine, rather than the wife, of the second Lothair; whose adultery, divorce, and second nuptials had provoked against him the thunders of the Vatican. His mother, as she was styled, the great Bertha, was successively the wife of the count of Arles and the marquis of Tuscany : France and Italy were scandalized by her gallantries; and, till the age of threescore, her lovers, of every degree, were the zealous servants of her ambition. The example of maternal incontinence was copied by the king of Italy; and the three favourite concubines of Hugo were decorated with the classic names of Venus, Juno, and Semele.[69] The daughter of Venus was granted to the solicitations of the Byzantine court; her name of Bertha was changed to that of Eudoxia; and she was wedded, or rather betrothed, to young Romanus, the future heir of the empire of the East. The consummation of this foreign alliance was suspended by the tender age of the two parties; and, at the end of five years, the union was dissolved by the death of the virgin spouse. The second wife of the emperor Romanus was a maiden of plebeian, but of Roman birth; and their two daughters, Theophano and Anne, were given in marriage to the princes of the earth. The eldest was bestowed, as the pledge of peace, on the eldest son of the great Otho, who had solicited this alliance with arms and embassies. It might legally be questioned how far a Saxon was entitled to the privilege of the French nation; but every scruple was silenced

[Death of Bertha. A.D. 949]

Otho of Germany. A.D. 972

idea may be formed from the Criticism of Pagi, the Annals of Muratori, and the Abridgment of St. Marc, A.D. 925-946.

[69] After the mention of the three Goddesses, Liutprand very naturally adds, et quoniam non rex solus iis abutebatur, earum nati ex incertis patribus originem ducunt (Hist. l. iv. c. 6 [= c. 14]); for the marriage of the younger Bertha see Hist. l. v. c. 5 [= c. 14]; for the incontinence of the elder, dulcis exercitio Hymenæi, l. ii. c. 15 [= c. 55]; for the virtues and vices of Hugo, l. iii. c. 5 [=c. 19]. Yet it must not be forgot that the bishop of Cremona was a lover of scandal.

by the fame and piety of a hero who had restored the empire of the West. After the death of her father-in-law and husband, Theophano governed Rome, Italy, and Germany during the minority of her son, the third Otho; and the Latins have praised the virtues of an empress, who sacrificed to a superior duty the remembrance of her country.[70]   In the nuptials of her sister Anne, every prejudice was lost, and every consideration of dignity was superseded, by the stronger argument of necessity and fear.   A Pagan of the North, Wolodomir, great prince of Russia, aspired to a daughter of the Roman purple; and his claim was enforced by the threats of war, the promise of conversion, and the offer of a powerful succour against a domestic rebel.   A victim of her religion and country, the Grecian princess was torn from the palace of her fathers, and condemned to a savage reign and an hopeless exile on the banks of the Borysthenes, or in the neighbourhood of the Polar circle.[71]   Yet the marriage of Anne was fortunate and fruitful; the daughter of her grandson Jeroslaus was recommended by her Imperial descent; and the king of France, Henry I., sought a wife on the last borders of Europe and Christendom.[72]

Wolodomir of Russia [Vladimir of Kiev]. A.D. 988 [989]

[Yaroslav]

In the Byzantine palace, the emperor was the first slave of the ceremonies which he imposed, of the rigid forms which regulated each word and gesture, besieged him in the palace, and violated the leisure of his rural solitude.   But the lives and fortunes of millions hung on his arbitrary will; and the firmest minds, superior to the allurements of pomp and luxury, may be

Despotic power

---

[70] Licet illa Imperatrix Græca sibi et aliis fuisset satis utilis, et optima, &c., is the preamble of an inimical writer, apud Pagi, tom. iv. A.D. 989, No. 3.   Her marriage and principal actions may be found in Muratori, Pagi, and St. Marc, under the proper years.   [For the question as to the identity of Theophano, see above, vol. v. p. 225, note 49.   For her remarkably capable regency (a striking contrast to that of Agnes of Poictiers, mother of the Emperor Henry IV.) see Giesebrecht, Geschichte der deutschen Kaiserzeit, i. p. 611 *sqq.*]

[71] Cedrenus, tom. ii. p. 699 [ii. p. 444, ed. Bonn]; Zonaras, tom. ii. p. 221 [xvii. 7]; Elmacin, Hist. Saracenica, l. iii. c. 6; Nestor apud Levesque, tom. ii. p. 112 [Chron. Nestor, c. 42]; Pagi, Critica, A.D. 987, No. 6; a singular concourse! Wolodomir and Anne are ranked among the saints of the Russian church.   Yet we know his vices, and are ignorant of her virtues.   [For the date of Vladimir's marriage and conversion see below, chap. lv. p. 170, note 100.]

[72] Henricus primus duxit uxorem Scythicam [et] Russam, filiam regis Jeroslai. An embassy of bishops was sent into Russia, and the father gratanter filiam cum multis donis misit.   This event happened in the year 1051.   See the passages of the original chronicles in Bouquet's Historians of France (tom. xi. p. 29, 159, 161, 319, 384, 481).   Voltaire might wonder at this alliance; but he should not have owned his ignorance of the country, religion, &c., of Jeroslaus—a name so conspicuous in the Russian annals.

seduced by the more active pleasure of commanding their equals. The legislative and executive power were centered in the person of the monarch, and the last remains of the authority of the senate were finally eradicated by Leo the Philosopher.[73] A lethargy of servitude had benumbed the minds of the Greeks; in the wildest tumults of rebellion they never aspired to the idea of a free constitution; and the private character of the prince was the only source and measure of their public happiness. Superstition riveted their chains; in the church of St. Sophia, he was solemnly crowned by the patriarch; at the foot of the altar, they pledged their passive and unconditional

Coronation
oathobedience to his government and family. On his side he engaged to abstain as much as possible from the capital punishments of death and mutilation; his orthodox creed was subscribed with his own hand, and he promised to obey the decrees of the seven synods, and the canons of the holy church.[74] But the assurance of mercy was loose and indefinite: he swore, not to his people, but to an invisible judge, and, except in the inexpiable guilt of heresy, the ministers of heaven were always prepared to preach the indefeasible right, and to absolve the venial transgressions, of their sovereign. The Greek ecclesiastics were themselves the subjects of the civil magistrate; at the nod of a tyrant, the bishops were created, or transferred, or deposed, or punished with an ignominious death: whatever might be their wealth or influence, they could never succeed like the Latin clergy in the establishment of an independent republic; and the patriarch of Constantinople condemned, what he secretly envied, the temporal greatness of his Roman brother. Yet the exercise of boundless despotism is happily checked by the laws of nature and necessity. In proportion to his wisdom and virtue, the master of an empire is confined to the path of his sacred and laborious duty. In proportion to his vice and folly, he drops the sceptre too weighty for his hands; and the motions of the

---

[73] A constitution of Leo the philosopher (lxxviii. [Zachariä, Jus Græco-Rom. iii. p. 175]), ne senatus consulta amplius fiant, speaks the language of naked despotism, ἐξ οὗ τὸ μόναρχον κράτος τὴν τούτων ἀνῆπται διοικησιν, και ἄκαιρον καὶ μάταιον τὸ [leg. τὸν] ἄχρηστον μετὰ τῶν χρείαν παρεχομένων συνάπτεσθαι [leg. συντάττεσθαι].

[74] Codinus (de Officiis, c. xvii. p. 120, 121 [p. 87, ed. Bonn]) gives an idea of this oath so strong to the church πιστὸς και γνήσιος δοῦλος καὶ υἱὸς τῆς ἁγίας ἐκκλησίας, so weak to the people καὶ ἀπέχεσθαι φόνων καὶ ἀκρωτηριασμῶν καὶ [τῶν] ὁμοίων τούτοις κατὰ τὸ δυνατόν.

royal image are ruled by the imperceptible thread of some minister or favourite, who undertakes for his private interest to exercise the task of the public oppression. In some fatal moment, the most absolute monarch may dread the reason or the caprice of a nation of slaves; and experience has proved that whatever is gained in the extent, is lost in the safety and solidity, of regal power.

Whatever titles a despot may assume, whatever claims he may assert, it is on the sword that he must ultimately depend to guard him against his foreign and domestic enemies. From the age of Charlemagne to that of the Crusades, the world (for I overlook the remote monarchy of China) was occupied and disputed by the three great empires or nations of the Greeks, the Saracens, and the Franks. Their military strength may be ascertained by a comparison of their courage, their arts and riches, and their obedience to a supreme head, who might call into action all the energies of the state. The Greeks, far inferior to their rivals in the first, were superior to the Franks, and at least equal to the Saracens, in the second and third of these warlike qualifications. *Military force of the Greeks, the Saracens, and the Franks*

The wealth of the Greeks enabled them to purchase the service of the poorer nations, and to maintain a naval power for the protection of their coasts and the annoyance of their enemies.[75]   A commerce of mutual benefit exchanged the gold of Constantinople for the blood of the Sclavonians and Turks, the Bulgarians and Russians: their valour contributed to the victories of Nicephorus and Zimisces; and, if an hostile people pressed too closely on the frontier, they were recalled to the defence of their country and the desire of peace by the well-managed attack of a more distant tribe.[76]   The command of the Mediterranean, from the mouth of the Tanais to the *Navy of the Greeks*

---

[75] If we listen to the threats of Nicephorus to the ambassador of Otho : Nec est in mari domino tuo classium numerus.   Navigantium fortitudo mihi soli inest, qui eum classibus aggrediar, bello maritimas ejus civitates demoliar ; et quæ fluminibus sunt vicina redigam in favillam (Liutprand in Legat. ad Nicephorum Phocam, in Muratori, Scriptores Rerum Italicarum, tom. ii. pars i. p. 481 [c. 11]). He observes in another place [c. 45], qui cæteris præstant Venetici sunt et Amalphitani.

[76] Nec ipsa capiet eum (the emperor Otho) in quâ ortus est pauper et [gunnata, id est] pellicea Saxonia ; pecuniâ quâ pollemus omnes nationes super eum [ipsum] invitabimus ; et quasi Keramicum confringemus (Liutprand in Legat. p. 487 [c. 53]).   The two books, De administrando Imperio, perpetually inculcate the same policy.

columns of Hercules, was always claimed, and often possessed, by the successors of Constantine.   Their capital was filled with naval stores and dexterous artificers; the situation of Greece and Asia, the long coasts, deeps gulfs, and numerous islands accustomed their subjects to the exercise of navigation; and the trade of Venice and Amalfi supplied a nursery of seamen to the Imperial fleet.[77]   Since the time of the Peloponnesian and Punic wars, the sphere of action had not been enlarged ; and the science of naval architecture appears to have declined.   The art of constructing those stupendous machines which displayed three, or six, or ten, ranges of oars, rising above, or falling behind, each other, was unknown to the ship-builders of Constantinople, as well as to the mechanicians of modern days.[78] The *Dromones*[79] or light galleys of the Byzantine empire were content with two tier of oars; each tier was composed of five and twenty benches ; and two rowers were seated on each bench, who plied their oars on either side of the vessel.   To these we must add the captain or centurion, who, in time of action, stood erect with his armour-bearer on the poop, two steersmen at the helm, and two officers at the prow, the one to manage the anchor, the other to point and play against the enemy the tube of liquid fire.   The whole crew, as in the infancy of the art, performed the double service of mariners and soldiers; they were provided with defensive and offensive arms, with bows and arrows, which they used from the upper deck, with long pikes, which they pushed through the port-holes of the lower tier.   Sometimes, indeed, the ships of war were of a larger and more solid construction ; and the labours of combat and navigation were more regularly divided between seventy soldiers and two hundred and thirty mariners.   But for the most part they were of the light and manageable size;

[77] The xixth chapter of the Tactics of Leo (Meurs. Opera, tom. vi. p. 825-848), which is given more correct from a manuscript of Gudius, by the laborious Fabricius (Bibliot. Græc. tom. vi. p. 372-379), relates to the *Naumachia* or naval war. [On the Byzantine navy, compare Appendix 5.]

[78] Even of fifteen or sixteen rows of oars, in the navy of Demetrius Poliorcetes. These were for real use ; the forty rows of Ptolemy Philadelphus were applied to a floating palace, whose tonnage, according to Dr. Arbuthnot (Tables of Ancient Coins, &c., p. 231-236), is compared as $4\frac{1}{2}$ to one, with an English 100-gun ship.

[79] The Dromones of Leo, &c., are so clearly described with two tier of oars that I must censure the version of Meursius and Fabricius, who pervert the sense by a blind attachment to the classic appellation of *Triremes*.   The Byzantine historians are sometimes guilty of the same inaccuracy.

and, as the cape of Malea in Peloponnesus was still clothed with its ancient terrors, an Imperial fleet was transported five miles over land across the Isthmus of Corinth.[80]   The principles of maritime tactics had not undergone any change since the time of Thucydides : a squadron of galleys still advanced in a crescent, charged to the front, and strove to impel their sharp beaks against the feeble sides of their antagonists.   A machine for casting stones and darts was built of strong timbers in the midst of the deck; and the operation of boarding was effected by a crane that hoisted baskets of armed men.   The language of signals, so clear and copious in the naval grammar of the moderns, was imperfectly expressed by the various positions and colours of a commanding flag.   In the darkness of the night the same orders to chase, to attack, to halt, to retreat, to break, to form, were conveyed by the lights of the leading galley.   By land, the fire-signals were repeated from one mountain to another ; a chain of eight stations commanded a space of five hundred miles; and Constantinople in a few hours was apprised of the hostile motions of the Saracens of Tarsus.[81]   Some estimate may be formed of the power of the Greek emperors, by the curious and minute detail of the armament which was prepared for the reduction of Crete.   A fleet of one hundred and [A.D. 902] twelve galleys, and seventy-five vessels of the Pamphylian style, was equipped in the capital, the islands of the Ægean sea, and the sea-ports of Asia, Macedonia, and Greece.   It carried thirty-four thousand mariners, seven thousand three hundred and forty soldiers, seven hundred Russians, and five thousand and eighty-seven Mardaites, whose fathers had been transplanted from the mountains of Libanus.   Their pay, most probably of a month, was computed at thirty-four centenaries of gold, about one hundred and thirty-six thousand pounds sterling.   Our fancy is bewildered by the endless recapitulation of arms

---

[80] Constantin. Porphyrogen. in Vit. Basil. c. lxi. p. 185.   He calmly praises the stratagem as a βουλὴν συνετὴν καὶ σοφήν ; but the sailing round Peloponnesus is described by his terrified fancy as a circumnavigation of a thousand miles.

[81] The continuator of Theophanes (l. iv. p. 122, 123 [c. 35]) names the successive stations, the castle of Lulum near Tarsus, mount Argæus, Isamus, Ægilus, the hill of Mamas, Cyrisus [Cyrizus], Mocilus, the hill of Auxentius, the sun-dial of the Pharus of the great palace.   He affirms that the news were transmitted ἐν ἀκαρεῖ, in an indivisible moment of time.   Miserable amplification, which, by saying too much, says nothing.   How much more forcible and instructive would have been the definition of three or six or twelve hours !   [See above, vol. v. p. 213, note 34.]

and engines, of clothes and linen, of bread for the men and forage for the horses, and of stores and utensils of every description, inadequate to the conquest of a petty island, but amply sufficient for the establishment of a flourishing colony.[82]

Tactics and character of the Greeks

The invention of the Greek fire did not, like that of gunpowder, produce a total revolution in the art of war.   To these liquid combustibles the city and empire of Constantinople owed their deliverance; and they were employed in sieges and sea-fights with terrible effect.   But they were either less improved or less susceptible of improvement; the engines of antiquity, the catapultæ, balistæ, and battering-rams, were still of most frequent and powerful use in the attack and defence of fortifications; nor was the decision of battles reduced to the quick and heavy *fire* of a line of infantry, whom it were fruitless to protect with armour against a similar fire of their enemies.   Steel and iron were still the common instruments of destruction and safety; and the helmets, cuirasses, and shields of the tenth century did not, either in form or substance, essentially differ from those which had covered the companions of Alexander or Achilles.[83]   But, instead of accustoming the modern Greeks, like the legionaries of old, to the constant and easy use of this salutary weight, their armour was laid aside in light chariots, which followed the march, till, on the approach of an enemy, they resumed with haste and reluctance the unusual incumbrance.   Their offensive weapons consisted of swords, battle-axes, and spears; but the Macedonian pike was shortened a fourth of its length, and reduced to the more convenient measure of twelve cubits or feet.   The sharpness of the Scythian and Arabian arrows had been severely felt; and the emperors lament the decay of archery as a cause of the public misfortunes, and recommend, as an advice and a command, that the military youth, till the age of forty, should assiduously practise the

---

[82] See the Ceremoniale of Constantine Porphyrogenitus, l. ii. c. 44, p. 176-192 [*leg*. 376-392].   A critical reader will discern some inconsistencies in different parts of this account; but they are not more obscure or more stubborn than the establishment and effectives, the present and fit for duty, the rank and file and the private, of a modern return, which retain in proper hands the knowledge of these profitable mysteries.   [See above, p. 60, note 135.]

[83] See the fifth, sixth and seventh chapters, περὶ ὅπλων, περὶ ὁπλίσεως and περὶ γυμνασίας, in the Tactics of Leo, with the corresponding passages in those of Constantine.   [On the organization and tactics of the Byzantine army, see Oman's Art of War, ii. Bk. iv. chaps. ii. and iii.]

exercise of the bow.[84] The *bands*, or regiments, were usually
three hundred strong; and, as a medium between the extremes
of four and sixteen, the foot-soldiers of Leo and Constantine
were formed eight deep; but the cavalry charged in four ranks,
from the reasonable consideration that the weight of the front
could not be increased by any pressure of the hindermost horses.
If the ranks of the infantry or cavalry were sometimes doubled,
this cautious array betrayed a secret distrust of the courage of
the troops, whose numbers might swell the appearance of the
line, but of whom only a chosen band would dare to encounter
the spears and swords of the barbarians. The order of battle
must have varied according to the ground, the object and the
adversary; but their ordinary disposition, in two lines and a
reserve, presented a succession of hopes and resources most
agreeable to the temper as well as the judgment of the Greeks.[85]
In case of a repulse, the first line fell back into the intervals
of the second ; and the reserve, breaking into two divisions,
wheeled round the flanks to improve the victory or cover the
retreat. Whatever authority could enact was accomplished, at
least in theory, by the camps and marches, the exercises and
evolutions, the edicts and books, of the Byzantine monarch.[86]
Whatever art could produce from the forge, the loom, or the
laboratory, was abundantly supplied by the riches of the prince
and the industry of his numerous workmen. But neither
authority nor art could frame the most important machine, the
soldier himself; and, if the *ceremonies* of Constantine always
suppose the safe and triumphal return of the emperor,[87] his
tactics seldom soar above the means of escaping a defeat and
procrastinating the war.[88] Notwithstanding some transient

---

[84] They observe τῆς γὰρ τοξείας παντελῶς ἀμεληθείσης . . . ἐν τοῖς Ῥωμάνοις τὰ
πολλὰ νῦν εἴωθε σφάλματα γίνεσθαι (Leo, Tactic. p. 581 [6, § 5]; Constantin. p. 1216).
Yet such were not the maxims of the Greeks and Romans, who despised the loose
and distant practice of archery.

[85] Compare the passages of the Tactics, p. 669 and 721 and the xiith with the
xviiith chapter. [The strength of the army lay in the heavy cavalry.]

[86] In the preface to his Tactics, Leo very freely deplores the loss of discipline
and the calamities of the times, and repeats without scruple (Proem. p. 537) the reproaches of ἀμέλεια, ἀταξία, ἀγυμνασία, δειλία, &c., nor does it appear that the same
censures were less deserved in the next generation by the disciples of Constantine.

[87] See in the Ceremonial (l. ii. c. 19, p. 353) the form of the emperor's trump-
ling on the necks of the captive Saracens, while the singers chanted, "thou hast
made my enemies my footstool!" and the people shouted forty times the kyrie
eleison.

[88] Leo observes (Tactic. p. 668) that a fair open battle against any nation
whatsoever is ἐπισφαλές and ἐπικίνδυνον; the words are strong and the remark is

success, the Greeks were sunk in their own esteem and that of
their neighbours. A cold hand and a loquacious tongue was
the vulgar description of the nation; the author of the Tactics
was besieged in his capital ; and the last of the barbarians, who
trembled at the name of the Saracens or Franks, could proudly
exhibit the medals of gold and silver which they had extorted
from the feeble sovereign of Constantinople. What spirit their
government and character denied, might have been inspired in
some degree by the influence of religion; but the religion of
the Greeks could only teach them to suffer and to yield. The
emperor Nicephorus, who restored for a moment the discipline
and glory of the Roman name, was desirous of bestowing the
honours of martyrdom on the Christians, who lost their lives
in an holy war against the infidels. But this political law was
defeated by the opposition of the patriarch, the bishops, and
the principal senators ; and they strenuously urged the canons
of St. Basil, that all who were polluted by the bloody trade of
a soldier should be separated, during three years, from the
communion of the faithful.[89]

Character
and tactics
of the
Saracens These scruples of the Greeks have been compared with the
tears of the primitive Moslems when they were held back from
battle ; and this contrast of base superstition and high-spirited
enthusiasm unfolds to a philosophic eye the history of the rival
nations. The subjects of the last caliphs[90] had undoubtedly
degenerated from the zeal and faith of the companions of the
prophet. Yet their martial creed still represented the Deity as
the author of war;[91] the vital though latent spark of fanaticism still glowed in the heart of their religion, and among the
Saracens who dwelt on the Christian borders it was frequently
rekindled to a lively and active flame. Their regular force was

true ; yet, if such had been the opinion of the old Romans, Leo had never reigned
on the shores of the Thracian Bosphorus.

[89] Zonaras (tom. ii. 1. xvi. p. 202, 203 [c. 25]) and Cedrenus (Compend. p. 688
[ii. p. 369, ed. Bonn]), who relate the design of Nicephorus, most unfortunately apply
the epithet of γεννάιως to the opposition of the patriarch.

[90] The xviiith chapter of the tactics of the different nations is the most
historical and useful of the whole collection of Leo. The manners and arms of
the Saracens (Tactic. p. 809-817, and a fragment from the Medicean Ms. in the
preface of the vith volume of Meursius) the Roman emperor was too frequently called
upon to study.

[91] Παντὸς δὲ καὶ κακοῦ ἔργου τὸν Θεὸν αἴτιον ὑποτίθενται, καὶ πολέμοις χαίρειν λέγουσι
τὸν Θεὸν τὸν διασκόρπιζοντα ἔθνη τὰ τοὺς πολέμους θέλοντα. Leon. Tactic. p. 809 [c. 18,
§ 111].

formed of the valiant slaves who had been educated to guard
the person and accompany the standard of their lord; but the
Musulman people of Syria and Cilicia, of Africa and Spain, was
awakened by the trumpet which proclaimed an holy war
against the infidels. The rich were ambitious of death or
victory in the cause of God; the poor were allured by the
hopes of plunder; and the old, the infirm, and the women assumed their share of meritorious service by sending their
substitutes, with arms and horses, into the field. These
offensive and defensive arms were similar in strength and
temper to those of the Romans, whom they far excelled in the
management of the horse and the bow; the massy silver of
their belts, their bridles, and their swords, displayed the
magnificence of a prosperous nation, and, except some black
archers of the South, the Arabs disdained the naked bravery of
their ancestors. Instead of waggons, they were attended by a
long train of camels, mules, and asses; the multitude of these
animals, whom they bedecked with flags and streamers, appeared
to swell the pomp and magnitude of their host; and the
horses of the enemy were often disordered by the uncouth
figure and odious smell of the camels of the East. Invincible
by their patience of thirst and heat, their spirits were frozen by
a winter's cold, and the consciousness of their propensity to
sleep exacted the most rigorous precautions against the sur-
prises of the night. Their order of battle was a long square of
two deep and solid lines: the first of archers, the second of
cavalry. In their engagements by sea and land, they sustained with patient firmness the fury of the attack, and seldom
advanced to the charge till they could discern and oppress the
lassitude of their foes. But, if they were repulsed and broken,
they knew not how to rally or renew the combat; and their
dismay was heightened by the superstitious prejudice that God
had declared himself on the side of their enemies. The decline
and fall of the caliphs countenanced this fearful opinion; nor
were there wanting, among the Mahometans and Christians,
some obscure prophecies [92] which prognosticated their alternate

---

[92] Liutprand (p. 484, 485 [c. 39]) relates and interprets the oracles of the Greeks
and Saracens, in which, after the fashion of prophecy, the past is clear and historical, the future is dark, ænigmatical, and erroneous. From this boundary of light
and shade an impartial critic may commonly determine the date of the composition.

defeats.   The unity of the Arabian empire was dissolved, but
the independent fragments were equal to populous and powerful kingdoms; and in their naval and military armaments an
emir of Aleppo or Tunis might command no despicable fund of
skill and industry and treasure.   In their transactions of peace
and war with the Saracens, the princes of Constantinople too
often felt that these barbarians had nothing barbarous in their
discipline; and that, if they were destitute of original genius,
they had been endowed with a quick spirit of curiosity and
imitation.   The model was indeed more perfect than the copy;
their ships, and engines, and fortifications were of a less skilful
construction; and they confess, without shame, that the same
God, who has given a tongue to the Arabians, had more nicely
fashioned the hands of the Chinese and the heads of the
Greeks.[93]

The Franks
or Latins
A name of some German tribes between the Rhine and the
Weser had spread its victorious influence over the greatest part
of Gaul, Germany, and Italy; and the common appellation of
FRANKS[94] was applied by the Greeks and Arabians to the
Christians of the Latin church, the nations of the West, who
stretched beyond *their* knowledge to the shores of the Atlantic
Ocean.   The vast body had been inspired and united by the
soul of Charlemagne; but the division and degeneracy of his
race soon annihilated the Imperial power, which would have
rivalled the Cæsars of Byzantium and revenged the indignities
of the Christian name.   The enemies no longer feared, nor
could the subjects any longer trust, the application of a public
revenue, the labours of trade and manufactures in the military
service, the mutual aid of provinces and armies, and the naval
squadrons which were regularly stationed from the mouth of
the Elbe to that of the Tiber.   In the beginning of the tenth
century, the family of Charlemagne had almost disappeared;
his monarchy was broken into many hostile and independent

[93] The sense of this distinction is expressed by Abulpharagius (Dynast. p. 2,
62, 101); but I cannot recollect the passage in which it is conveyed by this lively
apophthegm.

[94] Ex Francis, quo nomine tam Latinos quam Teutones comprehendit, ludum
habuit (Liutprand in Legat. ad Imp. Nicephorum, p. 483, 484 [c. 33]).   This extension of the name may be confirmed from Constantine (de administrando Imperio,
l. ii. c. 27, 28) and Eutychius (Annal. tom. i. p. 55, 56), who both lived before the
crusades.   The testimonies of Abulpharagius (Dynast. p. 69) and Abulfeda
(Prefat. ad Geograph.) are more recent.

states; the regal title was assumed by the most ambitious chiefs; their revolt was imitated in a long subordination of anarchy and discord; and the nobles of every province disobeyed their sovereign, oppressed their vassals, and exercised perpetual hostilities against their equals and neighbours. Their private wars, which overturned the fabric of government, fomented the martial spirit of the nation. In the system of modern Europe, the power of the sword is possessed, at least in fact, by five or six mighty potentates; their operations are conducted on a distant frontier by an order of men who devote their lives to the study and practice of the military art; the rest of the country and community enjoys in the midst of war the tranquillity of peace, and is only made sensible of the change by the aggravation or decrease of the public taxes. In the disorders of the tenth and eleventh centuries, every peasant was a soldier, and every village a fortification; each wood or valley was a scene of murder and rapine; and the lords of each castle were compelled to assume the character of princes and warriors. To their own courage and policy they boldly trusted for the safety of their family, the protection of their lands, and the revenge of their injuries; and, like the conquerors of a larger size, they were too apt to transgress the privilege of defensive war. The powers of the mind and body were hardened by the presence of danger and the necessity of resolution; the same spirit refused to desert a friend and to forgive an enemy; and, instead of sleeping under the guardian care of the magistrate, they proudly disdained the authority of the laws. In the days of feudal anarchy, the instruments of agriculture and art were converted into the weapons of bloodshed : the peaceful occupations of civil and ecclesiastical society were abolished or corrupted; and the bishop who exchanged his mitre for an helmet was more forcibly urged by the manners of the times than by the obligation of his tenure.[95]

The love of freedom and of arms was felt, with conscious pride, by the Franks themselves, and is observed by the Greeks **Their character and tactics**

---

[95] On this subject of ecclesiastical and beneficiary discipline, Father Thomassin (tom. iii. l. i. c. 40, 45, 46, 47) may be usefully consulted. A general law of Charlemagne exempted the bishops from personal service ; but the opposite practice, which prevailed from the ixth to the xvth century, is countenanced by the example or silence of saints and doctors. . . . You justify your cowardice by the holy canons, says Rutherius of Verona ; the canons likewise forbid you to whore, and yet——

with some degree of amazement and terror. "The Franks," says the emperor Constantine, "are bold and valiant to the verge of temerity; and their dauntless spirit is supported by the contempt of danger and death. In the field and in close onset, they press to the front, and rush headlong against the enemy, without deigning to compute either his numbers or their own. Their ranks are formed by the firm connexions of consanguinity and friendship; and their martial deeds are prompted by the desire of saving or revenging their dearest companions. In their eyes a retreat is a shameful flight, and flight is indelible infamy." [96] A nation endowed with such high and intrepid spirit must have been secure of victory, if these advantages had not been counterbalanced by many weighty defects. The decay of their naval power left the Greeks and Saracens in possession of the sea, for every purpose of annoyance and supply. In the age which preceded the institution of knighthood, the Franks were rude and unskilful in the service of cavalry; [97] and in all perilous emergencies their warriors were so conscious of their ignorance that they chose to dismount from their horses and fight on foot. Unpractised in the use of pikes or of missile weapons, they were encumbered by the length of their swords, the weight of their armour, the magnitude of their shields, and, if I may repeat the satire of the meagre Greeks, by their unwieldy intemperance. Their independent spirit disdained the yoke of subordination, and abandoned the standard of their chief, if he attempted to keep the field beyond the term of their stipulation or service. On all sides they were open to the snares of an enemy, less brave, but more artful, than themselves. They might be bribed, for the barbarians were venal; or surprised in the night, for they neglected the precautions of a close encampment or vigilant sentinels. The fatigues of a summer's campaign exhausted their strength and patience, and they

---

[96] In the xviiith chapter of his Tactics, the emperor Leo has fairly stated the military vices and virtues of the Franks (whom Meursius ridiculously translates by *Galli*) and the Lombards, or Langobards. See likewise the xxvith Dissertation of Muratori de Antiquitatibus Italiæ medii Ævi.

[97] Domini tui milites (says the proud Nicephorus) equitandi ignari pedestris pugnæ sunt inscii; scutorum magnitudo, loricarum gravitudo, ensium longitudo, galearumque pondus neutrâ parte pugnare eos sinit; ac subridens, impedit, inquit, ac eos [*leg.* eos et] gastrimargia hoc est ventris ingluvies, &c. Liutprand in Legat. p. 480, 481 [c. 11].

sunk in despair if their voracious appetite was disappointed of a plentiful supply of wine and of food. This general character of the Franks was marked with some national and local shades, which I should ascribe to accident rather than to climate, but which were visible both to natives and to foreigners. An ambassador of the great Otho declared, in the palace of Constantinople, that the Saxons could dispute with swords better than with pens; and that they preferred inevitable death to the dishonour of turning their backs to an enemy.[98] It was the glory of the nobles of France that, in their humble dwellings, war and rapine were the only pleasure, the sole occupation, of their lives. They affected to deride the palaces, the banquets, the polished manners, of the Italians, who, in the estimate of the Greeks themselves, had degenerated from the liberty and valour of the ancient Lombards.[99]

By the well-known edict of Caracalla, his subjects, from Britain to Egypt, were entitled to the name and privilege of Romans, and their national sovereign might fix his occasional or permanent residence in any province of their common country. In the division of the East and West an ideal unity was scrupulously preserved, and in their titles, laws, and statutes the successors of Arcadius and Honorius announced themselves as the inseparable colleagues of the same office, as the joint sovereigns of the Roman world and city, which were bounded by the same limits. After the fall of the Western monarchy, the majesty of the purple resided solely in the princes of Constantinople; and

Oblivion of the Latin language

---

[98] In Saxoniâ certe scio . . . decentius ensibus pugnare quam calamis, et prius mortem obire quam hostibus terga dare (Liutprand, p. 482 [c. 22]).

[99] Φράγγοι τοίνυν καὶ Λογγίβαρδοι λόγον ἐλευθερίας περὶ πολλοῦ ποιοῦνται, ἀλλ᾽ οἱ μέν Λογγίβαρδοι τὸ πλέον τῆς τοιαύτης ἀρετῆς νῦν ἀπώλεσαν. Leonis Tactica, c. 18 [§ 80], p. 805. The emperor Leo died A.D. 911; an historical poem, which ends in 916 and appears to have been composed in 940 [between 915 and 922], by a native of Venetia, discriminates in these verses the manners of Italy and France :—

—— Quid inertia bello
Pectora (Ubertus ait) duris prætenditis armis,
O Itali ? Potius vobis sacra pocula cordi
Sæpius et stomachum nitidis laxare saginis
Elatasque domos rutilo fulcire metallo.
Non eadem Gallos similis vel cura remordet;
Vicinas quibus est studium devincere terras
Depressumque larem spoliis hinc inde coactis
Sustentare——

(Anonym. Carmen Panegyricum de Laudibus Berengarii Augusti, l. ii. in Muratori, Script. Rerum Italic. tom. ii. pars i. p. 393 [leg. 395] [in Pertz, Mon. Germ. Hist., iv. p. 189 sqq. New ed. by Dümmler, 1871]).

of these Justinian was the first, who, after a divorce of sixty
years, regained the dominion of ancient Rome and asserted, by
the right of conquest, the august title of Emperor of the Romans.[100]
A motive of vanity or discontent solicited one of his successors,
Constans the Second, to abandon the Thracian Bosphorus and to
restore the pristine honours of the Tiber: an extravagant project (exclaims the malicious Byzantine), as if he had despoiled
a beautiful and blooming virgin, to enrich, or rather to expose,
the deformity of a wrinkled and decrepit matron.[101]   But the
sword of the Lombards opposed his settlement in Italy; he
entered Rome, not as a conqueror, but as a fugitive, and, after a
visit of twelve days, he pillaged, and for ever deserted, the ancient
capital of the world.[102]   The final revolt and separation of Italy
was accomplished about two centuries after the conquests of
Justinian, and from his reign we may date the gradual oblivion
of the Latin tongue.   That legislator had composed his Institutes, his Code, and his Pandects, in a language which he
celebrates as the proper and public style of the Roman government, the consecrated idiom of the palace and senate of Constantinople, of the camps and tribunals of the East.[103]   But
this foreign dialect was unknown to the people and soldiers of
the Asiatic provinces, it was imperfectly understood by the
greater part of the interpreters of the laws and the ministers of
the state.   After a short conflict, nature and habit prevailed
over the obsolete institutions of human power : for the general
benefit of his subjects, Justinian promulgated his novels in the
two languages; the several parts of his voluminous jurisprudence

[100] Justinian, says the Historian Agathias (l. v. p. 157 [c. 14]), πρῶτος Ῥωμαίων
αὐτοκράτωρ ὀνόματι καὶ πράγματι.   Yet the specific title of Emperor of the Romans
was not used at Constantinople, till it had been claimed by the French and German
emperors of old Rome.
[101] Constantine Manasses reprobates this design in his barbarous verse [3836
sqq.] :

Τὴν πόλιν τὴν βασιλείαν ἀποκοσμῆσαι θέλων,
Καὶ τὴν ἀρχὴν χαρίσασθαι [τῇ] τριπεμπέλῳ Ῥώμῃ,
Ὡς εἴτις ἀβροστόλιστον ἀποκοσμήσει νύμφην,
Καὶ γραῦν τινα τρικόρωνον ὡς κόρην ὡραίσει.

and it is confirmed by Theophanes, Zonaras, Cedrenus, and the Historia Miscella :
Voluit in urbem Romam Imperium transferre (l. xix. p. 157, in tom. i. pars i. of the
Scriptores Rer. Ital. of Muratori).
[102] Paul. Diacon. l. v. c. 11, p. 480.   Anastasius in Vitis Pontificum, in Muratori's Collection, tom. iii. pars i. p. 141.
[103] Consult the preface of Ducange (ad Gloss. Græc. medii Ævi) and the Novels
of Justinian (vii. lxvi.).   The Greek language was κοινός, the Latin was πάτριος to
himself, κυριώτατος to the πολιτείας σχῆμα, the system of government.

were successively translated: [104] the original was forgotten, the version was studied, and the Greek, whose intrinsic merit deserved indeed the preference, obtained a legal as well as popular establishment in the Byzantine monarchy. The birth and residence of succeeding princes estranged them from the Roman idiom : Tiberius by the Arabs,[105] and Maurice by the Italians,[106] are distinguished as the first of the Greek Cæsars, as the founders of a new dynasty and empire ; the silent revolution was accomplished before the death of Heraclius ; and the ruins of the Latin speech were darkly preserved in the terms of jurisprudence and the acclamations of the palace. After the restoration of the Western empire by Charlemagne and the Othos, the names of Franks and Latins acquired an equal signification and extent ; and these haughty barbarians asserted, with some justice, their superior claim to the language and dominion of Rome. They insulted the aliens of the East who had renounced the dress and idiom of Romans ; and their reasonable practice will justify the frequent appellation of Greeks.[107] But this contemptuous appellation was indignantly rejected by the prince and people to whom it is applied. Whatsoever changes had been introduced by the lapse of ages, they alleged a lineal and unbroken succession from Augustus and Constantine ; and, in the lowest period of degeneracy and decay, the name of

The Greek emperors and their subjects retain and assert the name of Romans

---

[104] Οὐ μὴν ἀλλὰ καὶ Λατινικὴ λέξις καὶ φράσις εἰσέτι τοὺς νόμους [κρύπτουσα] τοὺς συνεῖναι ταύτην μὴ δυναμένους ἰσχυρῶς ἀπετείχιζε (Matth. Blastares, Hist. Juris. apud Fabric. Bibliot. Græc. tom. xii. p. 369). The Code and Pandects (the latter by Thalelæus) were translated in the time of Justinian (p. 258, 366). Theophilus, one of the original triumvirs, has left an elegant, though diffuse, paraphrase of the Institutes. [Edited by G. O. Reitz, 2 vols., 1752 ; G. A. Rhalles, 1836 ; E. C. Ferrini, 2 parts, 1884-88.] On the other hand, Julian, antecessor of Constantinople (A.D. 570), cxx. Novellas Græcas eleganti Latinitate donavit (Heineccius, Hist. J. R. p. 396), for the use of Italy and Africa.

[105] Abulpharagius assigns the viith Dynasty to the Franks or Romans, the viiith to the Greeks, the ixth to the Arabs. A tempore Augusti Cæsaris donec imperaret Tiberius Cæsar spatio circiter annorum 600 fuerunt Imperatores C. P. Patricii, et præcipua pars exercitus Romani ; extra quod, consiliarii, scribæ et populus, omnes Græci fuerunt ; deinde regnum etiam Græcanicum factum est (p. 96, vers. Pocock). The Christian and ecclesiastical studies of Abulpharagius gave him some advantage over the more ignorant *Moslems*.

[106] Primus ex Græcorum genere in Imperio confirmatus est [the right reading] ; or, according to another Ms. of Paulus Diaconus (l. iii. c. 15, p. 443), in Græcorum Imperio.

[107] Quia linguam, mores, vestesque mutastis, putavit Sanctissimus Papa (an audacious irony), ita vos [vobis] displicere Romanorum nomen [c. 51]. His nuncios [nuncii cum literis quibus], rogabant Nicephorum Imperatorem Græcorum, ut cum Othone Imperatore Romanorum amicitiam faceret (Liutprand in Legatione, p. 486 [c. 47]). [The citation is *verbally* inaccurate.]

Romans adhered to the last fragments of the empire of Constantinople.[108]

While the government of the East was transacted in Latin, the Greek was the language of literature and philosophy; nor could the masters of this rich and perfect idiom be tempted to envy the borrowed learning and imitative taste of their Roman disciples. After the fall of paganism, the loss of Syria and Egypt, and the extinction of the schools of Alexandria and Athens, the studies of the Greeks insensibly retired to some regular monasteries, and above all to the royal college of Constantinople, which was burnt in the reign of Leo the Isaurian.[109] In the pompous style of the age, the president of that foundation was named the Sun of Science: his twelve associates, the professors in the different arts and faculties, were the twelve signs of the zodiac; a library of thirty-six thousand five hundred volumes was open to their inquiries; and they could shew an ancient manuscript of Homer, on a roll of parchment one hundred and twenty feet in length, the intestines, as it was fabled, of a prodigious serpent.[110] But the seventh and eighth centuries were a period of discord and darkness; the library was burnt, the college was abolished, the Iconoclasts are represented as the foes of antiquity; and a savage ignorance and contempt of letters has disgraced the princes of the Heraclean and Isaurian dynasties.[111]

In the ninth century we trace the first dawnings of the restoration of science.[112] After the fanaticism of the Arabs had sub-

---

[108] By Laonicus Chalcocondyles, who survived the last siege of Constantinople, the account is thus stated (l. i. p. 3 [p. 6, ed. Bonn]) : Constantine transplanted his Latins of Italy to a Greek city of Thrace : they adopted the language and manners of the natives, who were confounded with them under the name of Romans. The kings of Constantinople, says the historian, ἐπὶ τῷ σφᾶς αὐτοὺς σεμνύνεσθαι Ῥωμαίων βασιλεῖς τε και αὐτοκράτορας ἀποκαλεῖν, Ἑλλήνων δὲ βασιλεῖς οὐκέτι οὐδαμῆ ἀξιοῦν.

[109] See Ducange (C. P. Christiana, l. ii. p. 150, 151), who collects the testimonies, not of Theophanes, but at least of Zonaras (tom. ii. l. xv. p. 104 [c. 3]), Cedrenus (p. 454 [i. 795, ed. Bonn]), Michael Glycas (p. 281 [p. 522, ed. Bonn]), Constantine Manasses (p. 87 [1. 4257]). After refuting the absurd charge against the emperor, Spanheim (Hist. Imaginum, p. 90-111), like a true advocate, proceeds to doubt or deny the reality of the fire, and almost of the library.

[110] According to Malchus (apud Zonar. l. xiv. p. 53 [leg. 52 ; c. 2]) this Homer was burnt in the time of Basiliscus. The Ms. might be renewed—but on a serpent's skin ? Most strange and incredible !

[111] The ἀλογία of Zonaras, the ἀργία καὶ ἀμαθία of Cedrenus, are strong words, perhaps not ill suited to these reigns.

[112] See Zonaras (l. xvi. p. 160, 161 [c. 4]) and Cedrenus (p. 549, 550 [ii. 168-9, ed. Bonn]). Like Friar Bacon, the philosopher Leo has been transformed by ignorance into a conjurer ; yet not so undeservedly, if he be the author of the oracles

sided, the caliphs aspired to conquer the arts, rather than the provinces, of the empire : their liberal curiosity rekindled the emulation of the Greeks, brushed away the dust from their ancient libraries, and taught them to know and reward the philosophers, whose labours had been hitherto repaid by the pleasure of study and the pursuit of truth. The Cæsar Bardas, the uncle of Michael the Third, was the generous protector of letters, a title which alone has preserved his memory and excused his ambition. A particle of the treasures of his nephew was sometimes diverted from the indulgence of vice and folly ; a school was opened in the palace of Magnaura ; and the presence of Bardas excited the emulation of the masters and students. At their head, was the philosopher Leo, archbishop of Thessalonica ; his profound skill in astronomy and the mathematics was admired by the strangers of the East ; and this occult science was magnified by vulgar credulity, which modestly supposes that all knowledge superior to its own must be the effect of inspiration or magic. At the pressing entreaty of the Cæsar, his friend, the celebrated Photius,[113] renounced the freedom of a secular and studious life, ascended the patriarchal throne, and was alter- [A.D. 858] nately excommunicated and absolved by the synods of the East and West. By the confession even of priestly hatred, no art or science, except poetry, was foreign to this universal scholar, who was deep in thought, indefatigable in reading, and eloquent in diction. Whilst he exercised the office of protospathaire, or captain of the guards, Photius was sent ambassador to the caliph of Bagdad.[114] The tedious hours of exile, perhaps of confine-

more commonly ascribed to the emperor of the same name. The physics of Leo in Ms. are in the library of Vienna (Fabricius, Bibliot. Græc. tom. vi. p. 366, tom. xii. p. 781). Quiescant ! [On the mathematical studies of Leo see Heiberg, der byzant. Mathematiker Leon, in Bibliot. Mathematica, N.F. i. 33 *sqq.*, 1887.]

[113] The ecclesiastical and literary character of Photius is copiously discussed by Hanckius (de Scriptoribus Byzant. p. 296-396) and Fabricius. [See Appendix 1.]

[114] Eἰς 'Ασσυρίους can only mean Bagdad, the seat of the caliph ; and the relation of his embassy might have been curious and instructive. But how did he procure his books ? A library so numerous could neither be found at Bagdad, nor transported with his baggage, nor preserved in his memory. Yet the last, however incredible, seems to be affirmed by Photius himself, ὅσας αὐτῶν ἡ μνημη διέσωζε. Camusat (Hist. Critique des Journaux, p. 87-94) gives a good account of the Myriobiblon. [Photius never held a military post. He was Protoasecretis—an office which corresponded in functions to that of the *primicerius notariorum* of earlier times (cp. Bury, *op. cit.*, 97 *sqq.*). He had the *rank* of protospatharios, but the insignia of this order were conferred on civil as well as military officials. Probably Photius began the *Bibliotheca* while he was in the East, and completed and revised it on his return to Constantinople].

ment, were beguiled by the hasty composition of his *Library*, a living monument of erudition and criticism. Two hundred and fourscore writers, historians, orators, philosophers, theologians, are reviewed without any regular method; he abridges their narrative or doctrine, appreciates their style and character, and judges even the fathers of the church with a discreet freedom, which often breaks through the superstition of the times. The emperor Basil, who lamented the defects of his own education, entrusted to the care of Photius his son and successor Leo the Philosopher ; and the reign of that prince and of his son Constantine Porphyrogenitus forms one of the most prosperous æras of the Byzantine literature. By their munificence the treasures of antiquity were deposited in the Imperial library ; by their pens, or those of their associates, they were imparted in such extracts and abridgments as might amuse the curiosity, without oppressing the indolence, of the public. Besides the *Basilics*, or code of laws, the arts of husbandry and war, of feeding or destroying the human species, were propagated with equal diligence; and the history of Greece and Rome was digested into fifty-three heads or titles, of which two only (of embassies, and of virtues and vices) have escaped the injuries of time. In every station, the reader might contemplate the image of the past world, apply the lesson or warning of each page, and learn to admire, perhaps to imitate, the examples of a brighter period. I shall not expatiate on the works of the Byzantine Greeks, who, by the assiduous study of the ancients, have deserved in some measure the remembrance and gratitude of the moderns. The scholars of the present age may still enjoy the benefit of the philosophical common-place book of Stobæus, the grammatical and historical lexicon of Suidas, the Chiliads of Tzetzes, which comprise six hundred narratives in twelve thousand verses, and the commentaries on Homer of Eustathius, archbishop of Thessalonica, who, from his horn of plenty, has poured the names and authorities of four hundred writers. From these originals, and from the numerous tribe of scholiasts and critics,[115]

---

[115] Of these modern Greeks, see the respective articles in the Bibliotheca Græca of Fabricius ; a laborious work, yet susceptible of a better method and many improvements : of Eustathius (tom. i. p. 289-292, 306-329 [for Eustathius see App. 1, and below, cap. lvi. p. 227]), of the Pselli (a diatribe of Leo Allatius, ad calcem tom. v. [reprinted in Migne, P. G. vol. 122]), of Constantine Porphyrogenitus (tom. vi. p. 486-509), of John Stobæus (tom. viii. 665-728), of Suidas (tom. ix. p. 620-827),

some estimate may be formed of the literary wealth of the
twelfth century; Constantinople was enlightened by the genius
of Homer and Demosthenes, of Aristotle and Plato; and in
the enjoyment or neglect of our present riches, we must envy
the generation that could still peruse the history of Theopompus,
the orations of Hyperides, the comedies of Menander,[116] and the
odes of Alcæus and Sappho. The frequent labour of illustration
attests not only the existence but the popularity of the Grecian
classics; the general knowledge of the age may be deduced from
the example of two learned females, the empress Eudocia, and
the princess Anna Comnena, who cultivated, in the purple, the
arts of rhetoric and philosophy.[117] The vulgar dialect of the

John Tzetzes (tom. xii. p. 245-273). Mr. Harris, in his Philological Arrangements,
opus senile, has given a sketch of this Byzantine learning (p. 287-300). [The elder
Psellus (flor. c. init. saec. ix.) is a mere name. For the life of the younger Psellus,
see above, vol. v. Appendix 1. John of Stoboi belongs to the 6th century. Of
Suidas (a Thessalian name) nothing is known, but his lexicographical work was
compiled in the 10th century. Its great importance is due to its biographical
notices and information on literary history. Much of the author's knowledge was
obtained at second hand through the collections of Constantine Porphyrogennetos.
Cp. Krumbacher, *op. cit.*, p. 567. Best ed. by G. Bernhardy (1834-53). The only
certain work of Isaac Tzetzes is a treatise on the metres of Pindar. He and his
younger brother John lived in the 12th century. John wrote, among other things,
an exegesis on Homer; scholia on Hesiod, Aristophanes, the Alexandra of Lyco-
phron, and the Halieutica of Oppian; a commentary on Porphyry's Eisagoge.
Most famous are his *Chiliads* (βίβλος Ιστορίας) in 12,674 political verses, containing
600 historical anecdotes, mythological stories, &c., and provided with marginal
scholia (ed. T. Kiessling, 1826). Extant letters of Tzetzes have been collected by
T. Pressel (1851).]
116 From obscure and hearsay evidence, Gerard Vossius (de Poetis Græcis, c. 6)
and Le Clerc (Bibliothèque Choisie, tom. xix. p. 285) mention a commentary of
Michael Psellus on twenty-four plays of Menander, still extant in Ms. at Constantinople. Yet such classic studies seem incompatible with the gravity or dulness of
a schoolman, who pored over the categories (de Psellis, p. 42), and Michael has
probably been confounded with Homerus *Sellius*, who wrote arguments to the
comedies of Menander. In the xth century, Suidas quotes fifty plays, but he often
transcribes the old scholiast of Aristophanes. [It is remarkable that of the five
authors, whose lost works Gibbon regrets, portions or fragments of three (some would
say, of four) have been recovered during the last century, in older texts than Eustathius or Photius can have possessed. Among the treasures preserved in Egyptian
Papyri are several speeches of Hyperides, considerable fragments of some of the
comedies of Menander, mutilated odes of Sappho; while a long text from the pen of
a fourth-century historian is supposed by some eminent critics to be a part of the
Hellenica of Theopompus.]
117 Anna Comnena may boast of her Greek style (τὸ Ἑλληνίζειν ἐς ἄκρον ἐσπουδα-
κυῖα), and Zonaras, her contemporary, but not her flatterer, may add with truth, γλῶτ-
ταν εἶχεν ἀκριβῶς Ἀττικίζουσαν. The princess was conversant with the artful dialogues
of Plato; and had studied the τετρακτύς, or *quadrivium* of astrology, geometry,
arithmetic, and music (see her preface to the Alexiad, with Ducange's notes). [Eudocia
Macrembolitissa, the wife of Constantine X., must be deposed from the place which
she has hitherto occupied in Byzantine literature, since it has been established that
the Ἰωνια (Violarium) was not compiled by her, but nearly five centuries later (c.
1543) by Constantine Palaeokappa. See P. Pulch, de Eudociae quod fertur Violario

city was gross and barbarous: a more correct and elaborate style distinguished the discourse, or at least the compositions, of the church and palace, which sometimes affected to copy the purity of the Attic models.

Decay of
taste and
genius

In our modern education, the painful though necessary attainment of two languages, which are no longer living, may consume the time and damp the ardour of the youthful student. The poets and orators were long imprisoned in the barbarous dialects of our Western ancestors, devoid of harmony or grace; and their genius, without precept or example, was abandoned to the rude and native powers of their judgment and fancy. But the Greeks of Constantinople, after purging away the impurities of their vulgar speech, acquired the free use of their ancient language, the most happy composition of human art, and a familiar knowledge of the sublime masters who had pleased or instructed the first of nations. But these advantages only tend to aggravate the reproach and shame of a degenerate people. They held in their lifeless hands the riches of their fathers, without inheriting the spirit which had created and improved that sacred patrimony: they read, they praised, they compiled, but their languid souls seemed alike incapable of thought and action. In the revolution of ten centuries, not a single discovery was made to exalt the dignity or promote the happiness of mankind. Not a single idea has been added to the speculative systems of antiquity, and a succession of patient disciples became in their turn the dogmatic teachers of the next servile generation. Not a single composition of history, philosophy, or literature, has been saved from oblivion by the intrinsic beauties of style or sentiment, of original fancy, or even of successful imitation. In prose, the least offensive of the Byzantine writers are absolved from censure by their naked and unpresuming simplicity; but the orators, most eloquent[118] in their own conceit, are the farthest removed from the models whom they affect to emulate. In every page our taste and reason are wounded by the choice of gigantic and obsolete words, a stiff and intricate phraseology, the discord of images, the childish play of false or unseasonable

(Strassburg, 1880) and Konstantin Palaeocappa, in Hermes 17, 177 *sqq.* (1882). Cp. Krumbacher, *op. cit.*, p. 579.]

[118] To censure the Byzantine taste, Ducange (Prefat. Gloss Græc. p. 17) strings the authorities of Aulus Gellius, Jerom, Petronius, George Hamartolus, Longinus; who give at once the precept and the example.

ornament, and the painful attempt to elevate themselves, to astonish the reader, and to involve a trivial meaning in the smoke of obscurity and exaggeration. Their prose is soaring to the vicious affectation of poetry: their poetry is sinking below the flatness and insipidity of prose. The tragic, epic, and lyric muses were silent and inglorious; the bards of Constantinople seldom rose above a riddle or epigram, a panegyric or tale; they forgot even the rules of prosody; and, with the melody of Homer yet sounding in their ears, they confound all measure of feet and syllables in the impotent strains which have received the name of *political* or city verses.[119] The minds of the Greeks were bound in the fetters of a base and imperious superstition, which extends her dominion round the circle of profane science. Their understandings were bewildered in metaphysical controversy; in the belief of visions and miracles, they had lost all principles of moral evidence; and their taste was vitiated by the homilies of the monks, an absurd medley of declamation and scripture. Even these contemptible studies were no longer dignified by the abuse of superior talents; the leaders of the Greek church were humbly content to admire and copy the oracles of antiquity, nor did the schools or pulpit produce any rivals of the fame of Athanasius and Chrysostom.[120]

In all the pursuits of active and speculative life, the emulation of states and individuals is the most powerful spring of the efforts and improvements of mankind. The cities of ancient Greece were cast in the happy mixture of union and independ-

Want of national emulation

---

[119] The *versus politici*, those common prostitutes, as, from their easiness, they are styled by Leo Allatius, usually consist of fifteen syllables. They are used by Constantine Manasses, John Tzetzes, &c. (Ducange, Gloss. Latin. tom. iii. p. i. p. 345, 346, edit. Basil, 1762). [All the verses which abandoned prosody and considered only accent may be called *political* ; but the most common form was the line of fifteen syllables with a diæresis after the eighth syllable ; the rhythm was :—

$$\cup \stackrel{\prime}{\_} \cup \stackrel{\prime}{\_} \cup \stackrel{\prime}{\_} \cup \stackrel{\prime}{\_} \mid \cup \stackrel{\prime}{\_} \cup \stackrel{\prime}{\_} \cup \stackrel{\prime}{\_} \cup$$

Proverbs in this form existed as early as the sixth century ; and in the Ceremonies of Constantine Porphyrogennetus we find a popular spring song in political verse, beginning (p. 367) :—

ἰδὲ τὸ ἔαρ τὸ γλυκὺ | πάλιν ἐπανατέλλει.

Cp. also above, vol. v. p. 212, note 32. The question has been much debated whether this kind of verse arose out of the ancient trochaic, or the ancient iambic, tetrameter. Cp. Krumbacher, *op. cit.* p. 650-1. The name political was probably applied because accentual verses were chanted by the citizens and the factions of the circus on public occasions to express pleasure or disapproval. We have examples from the sixth century.]

[120] As St. Bernard of the Latin, so St. John Damascenus in the viiith century is revered as the last father of the Greek, church.

ence, which is repeated on a larger scale, but in a looser form,
by the nations of modern Europe: the union of language, religion, and manners, which renders them the spectators and
judges of each other's merit;[121] the independence of government and interest, which asserts their separate freedom, and
excites them to strive for pre-eminence in the career of glory.
The situation of the Romans was less favourable; yet in the
early ages of the republic, which fixed the national character, a
similar emulation was kindled among the states of Latium and
Italy; and, in the arts and sciences, they aspired to equal or
surpass their Grecian masters.   The empire of the Cæsars
undoubtedly checked the activity and progress of the human
mind; its magnitude might, indeed, allow some scope for domestic competition; but, when it was gradually reduced, at first
to the East, and at last to Greece and Constantinople, the Byzantine subjects were degraded to an abject and languid temper,
the natural effect of their solitary and insulated state.   From
the North they were oppressed by nameless tribes of barbarians,
to whom they scarcely imparted the appellation of men.   The
language and religion of the more polished Arabs were an unsur-
mountable bar to all social intercourse.   The conquerors of
Europe were their brethren in the Christian faith; but the
speech of the Franks or Latins was unknown, their manners
were rude, and they were rarely connected, in peace or war,
with the successors of Heraclius.   Alone in the universe, the
self-satisfied pride of the Greeks was not disturbed by the comparison of foreign merit; and it is no wonder if they fainted in
the race, since they had neither competitors to urge their speed
nor judges to crown their victory.   The nations of Europe and
Asia were mingled by the expeditions to the Holy Land; and
it is under the Comnenian dynasty that a faint emulation of
knowledge and military virtue was rekindled in the Byzantine
empire.

[121] Hume's Essays, vol. i. p. 125.

CHAPTER LIV

Origin and Doctrine of the Paulicians—Their Persecution by the Greek Emperors—Revolt in Armenia, &c.—Transplantation into Thrace—Propagation in the West—The Seeds, Character, and Consequences, of the Reformation

I N the profession of Christianity, the variety of national characters may be clearly distinguished. The natives of Syria and Egypt abandoned their lives to lazy and contemplative devotion; Rome again aspired to the dominion of the world; and the wit of the lively and loquacious Greeks was consumed in the disputes of metaphysical theology. The incomprehensible mysteries of the Trinity and Incarnation, instead of commanding their silent submission, were agitated in vehement and subtle controversies, which enlarged their faith, at the expense, perhaps, of their charity and reason. From the council of Nice to the end of the seventh century, the peace and unity of the church was invaded by these spiritual wars; and so deeply did they effect the decline and fall of the empire that the historian has too often been compelled to attend the synods, to explore the creeds, and to enumerate the sects, of this busy period of ecclesiastical annals. From the beginning of the eighth century to the last ages of the Byzantine empire the sound of controversy was seldom heard; curiosity was exhausted, zeal was fatigued, and, in the decrees of six councils, the articles of the Catholic faith had been irrevocably defined. The spirit of dispute, however vain and pernicious, requires some energy and exercise of the mental faculties; and the prostrate Greeks were content to fast, to pray, and to believe, in blind obedience to the patriarch and his clergy. During a long dream of superstition, the Virgin and the Saints, their visions and miracles, their relics and images, were preached by the monks and worshipped by the people; and the appellation of people might be extended without in-

Supine superstition of the Greek church

justice to the first ranks of civil society. At an unseasonable moment the Isaurian emperors attempted somewhat rudely to awaken their subjects: under their influence, reason might obtain some proselytes, a far greater number was swayed by interest or fear; but the Eastern world embraced or deplored their visible [A.D. 843] deities, and the restoration of images was celebrated as the feast of orthodoxy. In this passive and unanimous state the ecclesiastical rulers were relieved from the toil, or deprived of the pleasure, of persecution. The Pagans had disappeared; the Jews were silent and obscure; the disputes with the Latins were rare and remote hostilities against a national enemy; and the sects of Egypt and Syria enjoyed a free toleration, under the shadow of the Arabian caliphs. About the middle of the seventh century, a branch of Manichæans was selected as the victims of spiritual tyranny: their patience was at length exasperated to despair and rebellion; and their exile has scattered over the West the seeds of reformation. These important events will justify some inquiry into the doctrine and story of the PAULICIANS: [1] and, as they cannot plead for themselves, our candid criticism will magnify the *good*, and abate or suspect the *evil*, that is reported by their adversaries.

Origin of the Paulicians or disciples of St. Paul. A.D. 660, &c.   The Gnostics, who had distracted the infancy, were oppressed by the greatness and authority, of the church. Instead of emulating or surpassing the wealth, learning, and numbers of the Catholics, their obscure remnant was driven from the capitals of the East and West, and confined to the villages and mountains along the borders of the Euphrates. Some vestige of the Marcionites may be detected in the fifth century; [2] but the numerous sects were finally lost in the odious name of the Manichæans; and these heretics, who presumed to reconcile the doctrines of Zoroaster and Christ, were pursued by the two religions with

[1] The errors and virtues of the Paulicians are weighed, with his usual judgment and candour, by the learned Mosheim (Hist. Ecclesiast. seculum ix. p. 311, &c.). He draws his original intelligence from Photius (contra Manichæos, l. i.) and Peter Siculus (Hist. Manichæorum). The first of these accounts has not fallen into my hands; the second, which Mosheim prefers, I have read in a Latin version inserted in the Maxima Bibliotheca Patrum (tom. xvi. p. 754-764) from the edition of the Jesuit Raderus (Ingolstadii, 1604, in 4to). [See Appendix 6.]

[2] In the time of Theodoret, the diocese of Cyrrhus, in Syria, contained eight hundred villages. Of these, two were inhabited by Arians and Eunomians, and eight by *Marcionites*, whom the laborious bishop reconciled to the Catholic church (Dupin, Bibliot. Ecclésiastique, tom. iv. p. 81, 82). [The existence of Marcionites at the end of the 6th century is attested by Theophylactus Simocatta.]

equal and unrelenting hatred. Under the grandson of Heraclius, in the neighbourhood of Samosata, more famous for the birth of Lucian than for the title of a Syrian kingdom, a reformer arose, esteemed by the *Paulicians* as the chosen messenger of truth. In his humble dwelling of Mananalis,[3] Constantine entertained a deacon, who returned from Syrian captivity, and received the inestimable gift of the New Testament, which was already concealed from the vulgar by the prudence of the Greek, and perhaps of the Gnostic, clergy.[4] These books became the measure of his studies and the rule of his faith; and the Catholics, who dispute his interpretation, acknowledge that his text was genuine and sincere. But he attached himself with peculiar devotion to the writings and character of St. Paul: the name of the Paulicians is derived by their enemies from some unknown and domestic teacher; but I am confident that they gloried in their affinity to the apostle of the Gentiles.[5] His disciples, Titus, Timothy, Sylvanus, Tychicus, were represented by Constantine and his fellow-labourers: the names of the apostolic churches were applied to the congregations which they assembled in Armenia and Cappadocia; and this innocent allegory revived the example and memory of the first ages.[6] In the gospel, and Their Bible

[3] [The text of Petros Hegumenos (see Appendix 6) gives Καμάναλις, a mere misprint (notwithstanding Karapet Ter-Mkrttschian, Die Paulikianer, p. 5). For the identification of Mananalis with Kerachoban, on the Kinis Chai, S.E. of Erzerum, see Conybeare, Key of Truth, Introd. p. lxix.]

[4] Nobis profanis ista (*sacra Evangelia*) legere non licet sed sacerdotibus duntaxat, was the first scruple of a Catholic when he was advised to read the Bible (Petr. Sicul. p. 761).

[5] [Three derivations of *Paulician* were alleged. (1) From Paul of Samosata, son of a Manichæan woman; he was said to be the founder of the heresy; but the Paulicians themselves did not admit this and said that Silvanus was their true founder. See all the sources (cp. Appendix 6). But cp. Conybeare, *op. cit.* p. cvi. (2) This Paul was said to have a brother John; and, perhaps from a consciousness of the difficulty of deriving Paulician from Paulos (cp. Friedrich, Bericht über die Paulikianer, p. 93), it was proposed (see Photius, ed. Migne, P. G. 102, p. 17) to regard the word as a corruption of Παυλοιωάννης, "Paul-John". (3) From St. Paul (see Pseudo-Phot., ap. Migne, *ib.* p. 109).—The word is curiously formed; "followers of Paul" ought to be *Paulianoi*. It seems highly probable that the name *Paulician* was not used by the heretics themselves. George Mon. says "they call themselves Christians, but us Romans". "Paulikianos" must be formed from "Paulikios," an Armenian diminutive somewhat contemptuous (compare Kourtikios, &c.). It might then be suggested that the hypothetical Paulikios from whom the sect derived their nickname, is to be identified with Paul the Armenian, father of Gegnaesius, the third head of the Paulician church (see Photius, c. Man. p. 53, ap. Migne, P. G. 102; Petrus Sic. p. 1284, *ib.* 104).]

[6] [The seven teachers of the Paulicians were: (1) Constantine = Silvanus; (2) Simeon = Titus; (3) Gegnaesius = Timotheus (an Armenian); (4) Joseph = Epaphroditus; (5) Zacharias, rejected by some, and named the hireling Shepherd; (6) Baanes (an Armenian name, Vahan), nicknamed the Dirty; (7) Sergius = Tychicus.]

the epistles of St. Paul, his faithful follower investigated the creed of a primitive Christianity ; and, whatever might be the success, a protestant reader will applaud the spirit of the inquiry. But, if the scriptures of the Paulicians were pure, they were not perfect. Their founders rejected the two epistles of St. Peter,[7] the apostle of the circumcision, whose dispute with their favourite for the observance of the law could not easily be forgiven.[8] They agreed with their Gnostic brethren in the universal contempt for the Old Testament, the books of Moses and the prophets, which have been consecrated by the decrees of the Catholic church. With equal boldness, and doubtless with more reason, Constantine, the new Sylvanus, disclaimed the visions which, in so many bulky and splendid volumes, had been published by the Oriental sect;[9] the fabulous productions of the Hebrew patriarchs and the sages of the East; the spurious gospels, epistles, and acts, which in the first age had overwhelmed the orthodox code; the theology of Manes and the authors of the kindred heresies; and the thirty generations, or æons, which had been created by the fruitful fancy of Valentine. The Paulicians sincerely condemned the memory and opinions of the Manichæan sect, and complained of the injustice which impressed that invidious name on the simple votaries of St. Paul and of Christ.[10]

Their six churches were : (1) " Macedonia " = Cibossa near Colonea (founded by Silvanus and Titus); (2) " Achaia " = Mananalis (founded by Timotheus); (3) " the Philippians " (where?) (founded by Epaphroditus and Zacharias) ; (4) " the Laodiceans " = Argaus ; (5) " the Ephesians " = Mopsuestia ; (6) " The Colossians " = Κυνοχωρῖται or Κοινοχωρῖται (apparently like the 'Αστατοι, a particular sect). The 4th and 6th churches are thus given by George Mon. p. 607 (ed. Muralt), but Peter Sic. connects the Colossians with Argaus and equates the Laodiceans with the Kunochorites (those who dwell in τὴν τοῦ κυνὸς χώραν).]

[7] In rejecting the *second* epistle of St. Peter, the Paulicians are justified by some of the most respectable of the ancients and moderns (see Wetstein ad loc. ; Simon, Hist. Critique du Nouveau Testament, c. 17). They likewise overlooked the Apocalypse (Petr. Sicul. p. 756 [p. 1256, ap. Migne, P. G. 104]) ; but, as such neglect is not imputed as a crime, the Greeks of the ixth century must have been careless of the credit and honour of the Revelations.

[8] This contention, which has not escaped the malice of Porphyry, supposes some error and passion in one or both of the apostles. By Chrysostom, Jerom, and Erasmus, it is represented as a sham quarrel, a pious fraud, for the benefit of the Gentiles and the correction of the Jews (Middleton's Works, vol. ii. p. 1-20).

[9] Those who are curious of this heterodox library may consult the researches of Beausobre (Hist. Critique du Manichéisme, tom. i. p. 385-437). Even in Africa, St. Austin could describe the Manichæan books, tam multi, tam grandes, tam pretiosi codices (contra Faust. xiii. 14); but he adds, without pity, Incendite omnes illas membranas : and his advice had been rigorously followed.

[10] [The Greeks included the Paulicians, like the Marcionites, under the general title of Manichæans, because they supposed them to be dualists, assuming two first principles.]

Of the ecclesiastical chain, many links had been broken by The simplicity of their belief and worship the Paulician reformers; and their liberty was enlarged, as they reduced the number of masters at whose voice profane reason must bow to mystery and miracle. The early separation of the Gnostics had preceded the establishment of the Catholic worship; and against the gradual innovations of discipline and doctrine they were as strongly guarded by habit and aversion as by the silence of St. Paul and the evangelists. The objects which had been transformed by the magic of superstition appeared to the eyes of the Paulicians in their genuine and naked colours. An image made without hands was the common workmanship of a mortal artist, to whose skill alone the wood and canvas must be indebted for their merit or value. The miraculous relics were an heap of bones and ashes, destitute of life or virtue, or of any relation, perhaps, with the person to whom they were ascribed. The true and vivifying cross was a piece of sound or rotten timber; the body and blood of Christ, a loaf of bread and a cup of wine, the gifts of nature and the symbols of grace. The mother of God was degraded from her celestial honours and immaculate virginity; and the saints and angels were no longer solicited to exercise the laborious office of mediation in heaven and ministry upon earth. In the practice, or at least in the theory, of the sacraments, the Paulicians were inclined to abolish all visible objects of worship, and the words of the gospel were, in their judgment, the baptism and communion of the faithful. They indulged a convenient latitude for the interpretation of scripture; and, as often as they were pressed by the literal sense, they could escape to the intricate mazes of figure and allegory. Their utmost diligence must have been employed to dissolve the connexion between the Old and the New Testament; since they adored the latter as the oracles of God, and abhorred the former as the fabulous and absurd invention of men or dæmons. We cannot be surprised that they should have found in the gospel the orthodox mystery of the Trinity; but, instead of confessing the human nature and substantial sufferings of Christ, they amused their fancy with a celestial body that passed through the virgin like water through a pipe; with a fantastic crucifixion that eluded the vain and impotent malice of the Jews. A creed thus simple and spiritual was not adapted to the genius of the

They hold the two principles of the Magians and Manichæans

times ;[11] and the rational Christian, who might have been contented with the light yoke and easy burthen of Jesus and his apostles, was justly offended that the Paulicians should dare to violate the unity of God, the first article of natural and revealed religion. Their belief and their trust was in the Father of Christ, of the human soul, and of the invisible world. But they likewise held the eternity of matter: a stubborn and rebellious substance, the origin of a second principle, of an active being, who has created this visible world and exercises his temporal reign till the final consummation of death and sin.[12] The appearances of moral and physical evil had established the two principles in the ancient philosophy and religion of the East; from whence this doctrine was transfused to the various swarms of the Gnostics. A thousand shades may be devised in the nature and character of *Ahriman*, from a rival God to a subordinate dæmon, from passion and frailty to pure and perfect malevolence: but, in spite of our efforts, the goodness and the power of Ormusd are placed at the opposite extremities of the line; and every step that approaches the one must recede in equal proportion from the other.[13]

The establishment of the Paulicians in Armenia, Pontus, &c.

The apostolic labours of Constantine-Sylvanus soon multiplied the number of his disciples, the secret recompense of spiritual ambition. The remnant of the Gnostic sects, and especially the Manichæans of Armenia, were united under his standard; many Catholics were converted or seduced by his arguments; and he preached with success in the regions of Pontus[14] and Cappadocia, which had long since imbibed the

[11] The six capital errors of the Paulicians are defined by Peter Siculus (p. 756 [c. 10, p. 1253, 1256-7, ed. Migne]) with much prejudice and passion. [In the following order : (1) The two principles ; (2) the exclusion of the Virgin Mary from the number of " Good Folk " (cp. the Perfect of the Bogomils; see Appendix 6) ; and the doctrine that Christ's body came down from Heaven ; (3) the rejection of the Sacrament and (4) the Cross, and (5) the Old Testament, &c. ; (6) the rejection of the elders of the Church.]

[12] Primum illorum axioma est, duo rerum esse principia ; Deum malum et Deum bonum aliumque hujus mundi conditorem et principem, et alium futuri ævi (Petr. Sicul. p. 756 [c. 10, p. 1253, ed. Migne]). [One God was the Heavenly Father, who has not authority in this world but in the world to come ; the other was the world-maker (cosmopoiêtês), who governs the present world. Cp. George Mon. p. 721 ed. De Boor = p. 607, ed. Muralt.]

[13] Two learned critics, Beausobre (Hist. Critique du Manichéisme, l. i. 4, 5, 6) and Mosheim (Institut. Hist. Eccles. and de Rebus Christianis ante Constantinum, sec. i. ii. iii.), have laboured to explore and discriminate the various systems of the Gnostics on the subject of the two principles.

[14] The countries between the Euphrates and the Halys were possessed above 350 years by the Medes (Herodot. l. i. c. 103) and Persians ; and the kings of Pontus

religion of Zoroaster. The Paulician teachers were distinguished only by their scriptural names, by the modest title of fellow-pilgrims, by the austerity of their lives, their zeal or knowledge, and the credit of some extraordinary gifts of the Holy Spirit. But they were incapable of desiring, or at least of obtaining, the wealth and honours of the Catholic prelacy: such anti-christian pride they bitterly censured; and even the rank of elders or presbyters was condemned as an institution of the Jewish synagogue. The new sect was loosely spread over the provinces of Asia Minor to the westward of the Euphrates; six of their principal congregations represented the churches to which St. Paul had addressed his epistles; and their founder chose his residence in the neighbourhood of Colonia,[15] in the same district of Pontus which had been celebrated by the altars of Bellona[16] and the miracles of Gregory.[17] After a mission of twenty-seven years, Sylvanus, who had retired from the tolerating government of the Arabs, fell a sacrifice to Roman persecution. The laws of the pious emperors, which seldom touched the lives of less odious heretics, proscribed without mercy or disguise the tenets, the books, and the persons of the Montanists and Manichæans : the books were delivered to the flames; and all who should presume to secrete such writings, or to profess such opinions, were devoted to an ignominious death.[18] A

Persecution of the Greek emperors

were of the royal race of the Achæmenides (Sallust. Fragment. l. iii. with the French supplement, and notes of the President de Brosses).

[15] Most probably founded by Pompey after the conquest of Pontus. This Colonia, on the Lycus above Neo-Cæsarea, is named by the Turks Couleihisar, or Chonac, a populous town in a strong country (d'Anville, Géographie Ancienne, tom. ii. p. 34; Tournefort, Voyage du Levant, tom. iii. lettre xxi. p. 293). [Ramsay is inclined to identify Colonea with Kara Hissar (= Black Castle,¹ Μαυρόκαστρον, Attaliates, p. 125); Historical Geography of Asia Minor, p. 267, and cp. p. 57.]

[16] The temple of Bellona at Comana, in Pontus, was a powerful and wealthy foundation, and the high priest was respected as the second person in the kingdom. As the sacerdotal office had been occupied by his mother's family, Strabo (l. xii. p. 809 [2, § 3], 835, 836, 837 [3, § 32 *sqq.*]) dwells with peculiar complacency on the temple, the worship, and festival, which was twice celebrated every year. But the Bellona of Pontus had the features and character of the goddess, not of war, but of love.

[17] Gregory, bishop of Neo-Cæsarea (A.D. 240-265), surnamed Thaumaturgus or the Wonder-worker. An hundred years afterwards, the history or romance of his life was composed by Gregory of Nyssa, his namesake and countryman, the brother of the great St. Basil.

[18] Hoc cæterum ad sua egregia facinora divini atque orthodoxi Imperatores addiderunt, ut Manichæos Montanosque capitali puniri sententiâ juberent, eorumque libros, quocunque in loco inventi essent, flammis tradi ; quod siquis uspiam eosdem occultasse deprehenderetur, hunc eundem mortis pœnæ addici, ejusque bona in fiscum interri (Petr. Sicul. p. 759). What more could bigotry and persecution desire ?

Greek minister, armed with legal and military powers, appeared
at Colonia to strike the shepherd, and to reclaim, if possible,
the lost sheep. By a refinement of cruelty, Simeon placed
the unfortunate Sylvanus before a line of his disciples, who
were commanded, as the price of their pardon and the proof
of their repentance, to massacre their spiritual father. They
turned aside from the impious office ; the stones dropped from
their filial hands; and of the whole number only one executioner could be found, a new David, as he is styled by the
Catholics, who boldly overthrew the giant of heresy. This
apostate, Justus was his name, again deceived and betrayed his
unsuspecting brethren, and a new conformity to the acts of St.
Paul may be found in the conversion of Simeon: like the
apostle, he embraced the doctrine which he had been sent to
persecute, renounced his honours and fortunes, and acquired
among the Paulicians the fame of a missionary and a martyr.
They were not ambitious of martyrdom,[19] but, in a calamitous
period of one hundred and fifty years, their patience sustained
whatever zeal could inflict; and power was insufficient to
eradicate the obstinate vegetation of fanaticism and reason.
From the blood and ashes of the first victims, a succession of
teachers and congregations repeatedly arose; amidst their
foreign hostilities, they found leisure for domestic quarrels; they
preached, they disputed, they suffered; and the virtues, the ap-
[Sergius of parent virtues, of Sergius, in a pilgrimage of thirty-three years,
Tavia] are reluctantly confessed by the orthodox historians.[20] The
native cruelty of Justinian the Second was stimulated by a
pious cause; and he vainly hoped to extinguish, in a single

[19] It should seem that the Paulicians allowed themselves some latitude of
equivocation and mental reservation; till the Catholics discovered the pressing
questions, which reduced them to the alternative of apostacy or martyrdom (Petr.
Sicul. p. 760).
[20] The persecution is told by Petrus Siculus (p. 579-763) with satisfaction and
pleasantry. Justus *justa* persolvit. Simeon was not τίτος but κῆτος [cp. Petrus, c.
27, p. 1281, ed. Migne] (the pronunciation of the two vowels must have been nearly
the same), a great whale that drowned the mariners who mistook him for an island.
See likewise Cedrenus (p. 432-435 [i. 766 *sqq.*, ed. B.]). [Sergius seems to have
lived about the end of the eighth and the beginning of the ninth century ; but there
are some difficulties and confusions in the chronology. Cp. Ter-Mkrttschian, Die
Paulikianer, p. 17 *sqq.* There seems no reason to question the date assigned to the
founder Sylvanus by George Monachus, *viz.* the reigns of Constans II. and Constantine IV. And in that case there is no reason why Gegnaesius, the third head of
the Paulician Church, should not have lived under Leo III. (see Photius, p. 53, ap.
Migne, P. G. 102 ; Petrus Sic. p. 1284, *ib.* 104). The chronology holds together.]

conflagration, the name and memory of the Paulicians. By
their primitive simplicity, their abhorrence of popular superstition, the Iconoclast princes might have been reconciled to
some erroneous doctrines ; but they themselves were exposed
to the calumnies of the monks, and they chose to be the tyrants, lest they should be accused as the accomplices, of the
Manichæans. Such a reproach has sullied the clemency of
Nicephorus, who relaxed in their favour the severity of the
penal statutes, nor will his character sustain the honour of a
more liberal motive. The feeble Michael the First, the rigid
Leo the Armenian, were foremost in the race of persecution ;
but the prize must doubtless be adjudged to the sanguinary
devotion of Theodora, who restored the images to the Oriental
church. Her inquisitors explored the cities and mountains of
the lesser Asia, and the flatterers of the empress have affirmed
that, in a short reign, one hundred thousand Paulicians were
extirpated by the sword, the gibbet, or the flames. Her guilt
or merit has perhaps been stretched beyond the measure of
truth ; but, if the account be allowed, it must be presumed that
many simple Iconoclasts were punished under a more odious
name ; and that some, who were driven from the church, unwillingly took refuge in the bosom of heresy.

The most furious and desperate of rebels are the sectaries Revolt
of a religion long persecuted, and at length provoked. In an Paulicians.
holy cause they are no longer susceptible of fear or remorse : A.D. 845-880
the justice of their arms hardens them against the feelings
of humanity ; and they revenge their fathers' wrongs on the
children of their tyrants. Such have been the Hussites of
Bohemia and the Calvinists of France, and such, in the ninth
century, were the Paulicians of Armenia and the adjacent provinces.[21] They were first awakened to the massacre of a
governor and bishop, who exercised the Imperial mandate of
converting or destroying the heretics ; and the deepest recesses
of mount Argæus protected their independence and revenge.
A more dangerous and consuming flame was kindled by the
persecution of Theodora, and the revolt of Carbeas, a valiant
Paulician, who commanded the guards of the general of the [General of
the Ana-
tolic
Theme]

---

[21] Petrus Siculus (p. 763, 764), the continuator of Theophanes (l. iv. c. 4, p. 103,
104), Cedrenus (p. 541, 542, 545 [ii. 153 sqq., ed. B.]), and Zonaras (tom. ii. l. xvi.
p. 156 [c. 2]) describe the revolt and exploits of Carbeas and his Paulicians.

East. His father had been impaled by the Catholic inquisitors;
and religion, or at least nature, might justify his desertion and
revenge. Five thousand of his brethren were united by the
same motives; they renounced the allegiance of anti-christian
Rome ; a Saracen emir introduced Carbeas to the caliph; and
the commander of the faithful extended his sceptre to the
implacable enemy of the Greeks. In the mountains between

They
fortify
Tephrice

Siwas [22] and Trebizond he founded or fortified the city of
Tephrice,[23] which is still occupied by a fierce and licentious
people, and the neighbouring hills were covered with the
Paulician fugitives, who now reconciled the use of the Bible
and the sword. During more than thirty years, Asia was afflicted by the calamities of foreign and domestic war; in their
hostile inroads the disciples of St. Paul were joined with those
of Mahomet; and the peaceful Christians, the aged parent and
tender virgin, who were delivered into barbarous servitude,
might justly accuse the intolerant spirit of their sovereign. So
urgent was the mischief, so intolerable the shame, that even
the dissolute Michael, the son of Theodora, was compelled to

[A.D. 859]

march in person against the Paulicians : he was defeated under
the walls of Samosata; and the Roman emperor fled before the
heretics whom his mother had condemned to the flames.[24] The
Saracens fought under the same banners, but the victory was
ascribed to Carbeas; and the captive generals, with more than
an hundred tribunes, were either released by his avarice or
tortured by his fanaticism. The valour and ambition of Chrysocheir,[25] his successor, embraced a wider circle of rapine and

---

[22] [Sebastea.]

[23] Otter (Voyage en Turquie et en Perse, tom. ii.) is probably the only Frank
who has visited the independent Barbarians of Tephrice, now Divrigni [Devrik],
from whom he fortunately escaped in the train of a Turkish officer. [The Paulicians
first occupied and fortified (with the help of the Emir of Melitene) Argaûs and
Amara (Theoph. Cont. iv. 16, p. 166, ed. Bonn). Argaûs has been identified with
Argovan, on a tributary of the Euphrates, due north of Melitene, by J. G. C.
Anderson (Journal of Hellenic Studies, xvii. p. 27, 1897) ; and he places Amara (or
Abara) on a high pass on the road from Sebastea to Lycandus, nearly due south of
Sebastea. Tephrice lay S.E. from Sebastea on the road from that city to Satala.
" The secluded position of Divreky made it the seat of an almost independent band
of Kurds, when it was visited by Otter in 1743. Voyage en Turquie et en Perse, ii.
306." Finlay, ii. p. 169, note. See further, for the site, Guy Le Strange in Journ.
R. Asiat. Soc. vol. 28 (1896). The Arabic name was Abrīk.]

[24] [For this expedition see Theoph. Contin. iv. c. 23.]

[25] In the history of Chrysocheir, Genesius (Chron. p. 67-70, edit. Venet. [leg. 57-
60 ; p. 121 sqq., ed. Bonn]) has exposed the nakedness of the empire. Constantine
Porphyrogenitus (in Vit. Basil. c. 37-43, p. 166-171) has displayed the glory of his

revenge. In alliance with his faithful Moslems, he boldly penetrated into the heart of Asia; the troops of the frontier and
the palace were repeatedly overthrown; the edicts of persecution were answered by the pillage of Nice and Nicomedia, of
Ancyra and Ephesus; nor could the apostle St. John protect and pillage
from violation his city and sepulchre. The cathedral of Ephesus Asia Minor
was turned into a stable for mules and horses; and the Paulicians vied with the Saracens in their contempt and abhorrence
of images and relics. It is not unpleasing to observe the
triumph of rebellion over the same despotism which has disdained the prayers of an injured people. The emperor Basil,
the Macedonian, was reduced to sue for peace, to offer a ransom
for the captives, and to request, in the language of moderation
and charity, that Chrysocheir would spare his fellow-Christians,
and content himself with a royal donative of gold and silver
and silk-garments. " If the emperor," replied the insolent
fanatic, " be desirous of peace, let him abdicate the East, and
reign without molestation in the West. If he refuse, the
servants of the Lord will precipitate him from the throne."
The reluctant Basil suspended the treaty, accepted the defiance,
and led his army into the land of heresy, which he wasted with
fire and sword. The open country of the Paulicians was ex- [c. A.D.
posed to the same calamities which they had inflicted; but, 871-2]
when he had explored the strength of Tephrice, the multitude
of the barbarians, and the ample magazines of arms and provisions, he desisted with a sigh from the hopeless siege.[26] On
his return to Constantinople he laboured, by the foundation of
convents and churches, to secure the aid of his celestial patrons,
of Michael the archangel and the prophet Elijah; and it was
his daily prayer that he might live to transpierce, with three
arrows, the head of his impious adversary. Beyond his expectations, the wish was accomplished: after a successful inroad,
Chrysocheir was surprised and slain in his retreat; and the

---

grandfather. Cedrenus (p. 570-573 [ii. p. 209 sqq., ed. B.]) is without their passions
or their knowledge.

[26] [In regard to this campaign of Basil (in 871 or 872) it was generally supposed
that he crossed the Euphrates, as the Continuator of Theophanes states (p. 269).
But J. G. C. Anderson has shown that this must be a mistake and that the scene of
the whole campaign was west of the Euphrates (Classical Review, April, 1896, p. 139).
Basil's object (after his failure at Tephrice) was to capture Melitene, the chief
Saracen stronghold of the Cis-Euphratesian territory in Asia Minor. Theoph.
Contin. ib.]

[A.D. 874-5] rebel's head was triumphantly presented at the foot of the throne. On the reception of this welcome trophy, Basil instantly called for his bow, discharged three arrows with unerring aim, and accepted the applause of the court, who hailed the victory of the royal archer. With Chrysocheir, the glory of the Paulicians faded and withered;[27] on the second expedition of the emperor, the impregnable Tephrice was deserted by the heretics, who sued for mercy or escaped to the borders. The city was ruined, but the spirit of independence survived in the mountains; the Paulicians defended, above a century, their religion and liberty, infested the Roman limits, and maintained their perpetual alliance with the enemies of the empire and the gospel.

Their decline

About the middle of the eighth century, Constantine, surnamed Copronymus by the worshippers of images, had made an expedition into Armenia, and found, in the cities of Melitene and Theodosiopolis, a great number of Paulicians, his kindred heretics. As a favour or punishment, he transplanted them from the banks of the Euphrates to Constantinople and Thrace; and by this emigration their doctrine was introduced and diffused in Europe.[28] If the sectaries of the metropolis were soon mingled with the promiscuous mass, those of the country struck a deep root in a foreign soil. The Paulicians of Thrace resisted the storms of persecution, maintained a secret correspondence with their Armenian brethren, and gave aid and comfort to their preachers, who solicited, not without success, the infant faith of the Bulgarians.[29] In the tenth century, they were restored and multiplied by a more powerful colony, which John Zimisces[30] transported from the Chalybian hills to the valleys

Their transplantation from Armenia to Thrace

---

[27] Συναπεμαράνθη πᾶσα ἡ ἀνθοῦσα τῆς Τεφρικῆς εὐανδρία [p. 212]. How elegant is the Greek tongue, even in the mouth of Cedrenus! [Cp. the continuation of George Mon. p. 841, ed. Bonn.]

[28] Copronymus transported his συγγενεῖς, heretics; and thus ἐπλατύνθη ἡ αἵρεσις Παυλικιανῶν, says Cedrenus (p. 463 [ii. p. 10]), who has copied the annals of Theophanes. [Sub A.M. 6247.]

[29] Petrus Siculus, who resided nine months at Tephrice (A.D. 870) for the ransom of captives (p. 764), was informed of their intended mission, and addressed his preservative, the Historia Manichæorum, to the new archbishop of the Bulgarians (p. 754 [p. 1241, ed. Migne]). [For Petrus Siculus, cp. Appendix 6.]

[30] The colony of Paulicians and Jacobites, transplanted by John Zimisces (A.D. 970) from Armenia to Thrace, is mentioned by Zonaras (tom. ii. l. xvii. p. 209 [c. 1]) and Anna Comnena (Alexiad, l. xiv. p. 450, &c. [c. 8]). [This colonisation must have taken place *after* the conquest of Eastern Bulgaria and the war with Sviatoslav; and therefore not before A.D. 973. Cp. Schlumberger, L'épopée byzantine,

of Mount Hæmus. The Oriental clergy, who would have preferred the destruction, impatiently sighed for the absence, of the Manichæans; the warlike emperor had felt and esteemed their valour; their attachment to the Saracens was pregnant with mischief; but, on the side of the Danube, against the barbarians of Scythia, their service might be useful and their loss would be desirable. Their exile in a distant land was softened by a free toleration; the Paulicians held the city of Philippopolis and the keys of Thrace; the Catholics were their subjects; the Jacobite emigrants their associates: they occupied a line of villages and castles in Macedonia and Epirus; and many native Bulgarians were associated to the communion of arms and heresy. As long as they were awed by power and treated with moderation, their voluntary bands were distinguished in the armies of the empire; and the courage of these *dogs*, ever greedy of war, ever thirsty of human blood, is noticed with astonishment, and almost with reproach, by the pusillanimous Greeks. The same spirit rendered them arrogant and contumacious: they were easily provoked by caprice or injury; and their privileges were often violated by the faithless bigotry of the government and clergy. In the midst of the Norman war, two thousand five hundred Manichæans deserted the standard of Alexius Comnenus,[31] and retired to their native homes. He dissembled till the moment of revenge; invited the chiefs to a friendly conference; and punished the innocent and guilty by imprisonment, confiscation, and baptism. In an interval of peace, the emperor undertook the pious office of reconciling them to the church and state: his winter quarters were fixed at Philippopolis; and the thirteenth apostle, as he is styled by his pious daughter, consumed whole days and nights in theological controversy. His arguments were fortified, their obstinacy was melted, by the honours and rewards which he bestowed on the most eminent proselytes; and a new city, surrounded with gardens, enriched with immunities, and

p. 181. Scylitzes (= Cedrenus, ii. p. 382) says that it was Thomas, Patriarch of Antioch, who suggested the transplantation. He realised that in the Eastern provinces the Paulicians were dangerous allies of the Saracens.]

[31] The Alexiad of Anna Comnena (l. v. p. 131 [c. 3], l. vi. p. 154, 155 [c. 2], l. xiv. p. 450-457 [c. 8, 9], with the annotations of Ducange) records the transactions of her apostolic father with the Manichæans, whose abominable heresy she was desirous of refuting.

dignified with his own name, was founded by Alexius, for the residence of his vulgar converts.   The important station of Philippopolis was wrested from their hands; the contumacious leaders were secured in a dungeon or banished from their country; and their lives were spared by the prudence, rather than the mercy, of an emperor at whose command a poor and [A.D. 1111] solitary heretic was burnt alive before the church of St. Sophia.[32] But the proud hope of eradicating the prejudices of a nation was speedily overturned by the invincible zeal of the Paulicians, who ceased to dissemble or refused to obey.   After the departure and death of Alexius, they soon resumed their civil and religious laws.   In the beginning of the thirteenth century, their pope or primate (a manifest corruption) resided on the confines of Bulgaria, Croatia, and Dalmatia, and governed by his vicars the filial congregations of Italy and France.[33]   From that æra, a minute scrutiny might prolong and perpetuate the chain of tradition.   At the end of the last age, the sect or colony still inhabited the valleys of mount Hæmus, where their ignorance and poverty were more frequently tormented by the Greek clergy than by the Turkish government.   The modern Paulicians have lost all memory of their origin; and their religion is disgraced by the worship of the cross, and the practice of bloody sacrifice, which some captives have imported from the wilds of Tartary.[34]

Their introduction into Italy and France   In the West, the first teachers of the Manichæan theology had been repulsed by the people, or suppressed by the prince. The favour and success of the Paulicians in the eleventh and twelfth centuries must be imputed to the strong, though secret, discontent which armed the most pious Christians against the

[32] Basil, a monk, and the author of the Bogomiles, a sect of Gnostics, who soon vanished (Anna Comnena, Alexiad, l. xv. p. 486-494 [c. 8, 9, 10]; Mosheim, Hist. Ecclesiastica, p. 420).   [This Basil was not "the author of the Bogomils". *Bogomil* is the Slavonic equivalent of the Greek name *Theophilos;* and Bogomil, who founded the sect, lived in the tenth century under the Bulgarian prince Peter (regn. 927-969).   There arose soon two Bogomil churches : the Bulgarian, and that of the Dragoviči; and from these two all the other later developments started.   Rački seeks the name of the second church among the Macedonian Dragoviči on the Vardar; while Golubinski identifies them with Dragoviči in the neighbourhood of Philippopolis.   See Jireček, Gesch. der Bulgaren, p. 176.   For the Bogomilian doctrines, see Appendix 6.]
[33] Matt. Paris, Hist. Major, p. 267.   This passage of our English historian is alleged by Ducange in an excellent note on Villehardouin (No. 208), who found the Paulicians at Philippopolis the friends of the Bulgarians.
[34] See Marsigli, Stato Militare dell' Impero Ottomano, p. 24.

church of Rome. Her avarice was oppressive, her despotism
odious; less degenerate perhaps than the Greeks in the worship
of saints and images, her innovations were more rapid and
scandalous; she had rigorously defined and imposed the doctrine
of transubstantiation: the lives of the Latin clergy were more
corrupt, and the Eastern bishops might pass for the successors
of the apostles, if they were compared with the lordly prelates
who wielded by turns the crosier, the sceptre, and the sword.
Three different roads might introduce the Paulicians into the
heart of Europe. After the conversion of Hungary, the pilgrims
who visited Jerusalem might safely follow the course of the
Danube; in their journey and return they passed through Philipp-
popolis; and the sectaries, disguising their name and heresy,
might accompany the French or German caravans to their respective countries. The trade and dominion of *Venice* pervaded
the coast of the Adriatic, and the hospitable republic opened
her bosom to foreigners of every climate and religion. Under
the Byzantine standard, the Paulicians were often transported to
the Greek provinces of Italy and Sicily; in peace and war they
freely conversed with strangers and natives, and their opinions
were silently propagated in Rome, Milan, and the kingdoms beyond the Alps.[35] It was soon discovered that many thousand
Catholics of every rank, and of either sex, had embraced the
Manichæan heresy; and the flames which consumed twelve
canons of Orleans was the first act and signal of persecution.
The Bulgarians,[36] a name so innocent in its origin, so odious in
its application, spread their branches over the face of Europe.
United in common hatred of idolatry and Rome, they were con-

---

[35] The introduction of the Paulicians into Italy and France is amply discussed
by Muratori (Antiquitat. Italiæ medii Ævi, tom. v. dissert. lx. p. 81-152) and
Mosheim (p. 379-382, 419-422). Yet both have overlooked a curious passage of
William the Apulian, who clearly describes them in a battle between the Greeks and
Normans, A.D. 1040 (in Muratori, Script. Rerum Ital. tom. v. p. 256).
    Cum Græcis aderant quidam quos pessimus error
      Fecerat amentes, et ab ipso nomen habebant.
But he is so ignorant of their doctrine as to make them a kind of Sabellians or
Patripassians. [It is thought that the Bogomilian doctrine travelled westward chiefly
by the provinces of southern Italy; Jireček, *op. cit.*, p. 212.]

[36] *Bulgari, Boulgres, Bougres*, a national appellation, has been applied by the
French as a term of reproach to usurers and unnatural sinners. The *Paterini*, or
Patelini, has been made to signify a smooth and flattering hypocrite, such as
l'Avocat Patelin of that original and pleasant farce (Ducange, Gloss. Latinitat.
medii et infimi Ævi). [The word is said to be derived from Pataria, a suburb of
Milan.] The Manichæans were likewise named *Cathari*, or the pure, by corruption,
Gazari, &c.

nected by a form of episcopal and presbyterian government; their various sects were discriminated by some fainter or darker shades of theology; but they generally agreed in the two principles: the contempt of the Old Testament, and the denial of the body of Christ, either on the cross or in the eucharist. A confession of simple worship and blameless manners is extorted from their enemies; and so high was their standard of perfection that the increasing congregations were divided into two classes of disciples, of those who practised and of those who aspired.

Persecu-
tion
of the Albi-
geois. A.D.
1200, &c.
It was in the country of the Albigeois,[37] in the southern provinces of France, that the Paulicians were most deeply implanted; and the same vicissitudes of martyrdom and revenge which had been displayed in the neighbourhood of the Euphrates were repeated in the thirteenth century on the banks of the Rhone. The laws of the Eastern emperors were revived by Frederic the Second. The insurgents of Tephrice were represented by the barons and cities of Languedoc: Pope Innocent III. surpassed the sanguinary fame of Theodora. It was in cruelty alone that her soldiers could equal the heroes of the crusades, and the cruelty of her priests was far excelled by the founders of the inquisition: [38] an office more adapted to confirm, than to refute, the belief of an evil principle. The visible assemblies of the Paulicians, or Albigeois, were extirpated by fire and sword; and the bleeding remnant escaped by flight, concealment, or catholic conformity. But the invincible spirit which they had kindled still

[37] Of the laws, crusade, and persecution against the Albigeois, a just, though general, idea is expressed by Mosheim (p. 477-481). The detail may be found in the ecclesiastical historians, ancient and modern, Catholics and Protestants; and among these Fleury is the most impartial and moderate. [C. Schmidt, Histoire et doctrine de la secte des Cathares, 2 vols., 1849. Rački, Bogomili i Catareni, Agram, 1869. These sectaries begin to appear in southern Gaul about A.D. 1017. Their chief seat was Toulouse; they were called *Albigeois* from the town of Albi, and *Tisserands* because many weavers embraced the doctrine. For the Ritual of the Albigeois, preserved in a Lyons Ms., see Conybeare, Key of Truth, App. vi. Cp. below, Appendix 6.]

[38] The Acts (Liber Sententiarum) of the Inquisition of Toulouse (A.D. 1307-1323) have been published by Limborch (Amstelodami, 1692), with a previous History of the Inquisition in general. They deserved a more learned and critical editor. As we must not calumniate even Satan, or the Holy Office, I will observe that, of a list of criminals which fills nineteen folio pages, only fifteen men and four women were delivered to the secular arm. [In an annotation on this note Dr. Smith says: "Dr. Maitland, in his Facts and Documents Relating to the Ancient Albigenses and Waldenses, remarks (p. 217, note) that Gibbon ought to have said *thirty-two* men and *eight* women". For the Albigeois and the persecution see A. Luchaire, Innocent III., Croisade, 1905; Devic and Vaissete, Histoire de Languedoc, vol. viii., 1876; Barrau and Darragon, Histoire des Croisades contre les Albigeois, 2 vols., 1840.]

lived and breathed in the Western world. In the state, in the church, and even in the cloister, a latent succession was preserved of the disciples of St. Paul ; who protested against the tyranny of Rome, embraced the Bible as the rule of faith, and purified their creed from all the visions of the Gnostic theology. The struggles of Wickliff in England, of Huss in Bohemia, were premature and ineffectual ; but the names of Zuinglius, Luther, and Calvin are pronounced with gratitude as the deliverers of nations.

A philosopher, who calculates the degree of their merit and the value of their reformation, will prudently ask from what articles of faith, *above* or *against* our reason, they have enfranchised the Christians ; for such enfranchisement is doubtless a benefit so far as it may be compatible with truth and piety. After a fair discussion we shall rather be surprised by the timidity, than scandalized by the freedom, of our first reformers.[39] With the Jew, they adopted the belief and defence of all the Hebrew scriptures, with all their prodigies, from the garden of Eden to the visions of the prophet Daniel ; and they were bound, like the Catholics, to justify against the Jews the abolition of a divine law. In the great mysteries of the Trinity and Incarnation the reformers were severely orthodox : they freely adopted the theology of the four or the six first councils ; and, with the Athanasian creed, they pronounced the eternal damnation of all who did not believe the Catholic faith. Transubstantiation, the invisible change of the bread and wine into the body and blood of Christ, is a tenet that may defy the power of argument and pleasantry ; but, instead of consulting the evidence of their senses, of their sight, their feeling, and their taste, the first Protestants were entangled in their own scruples, and awed by the words of Jesus in the institution of the sacrament. Luther maintained a *corporeal*, and Calvin a *real*, presence of Christ in the eucharist ; and the opinion of Zuinglius, that it is no more than a spiritual communion, a simple memorial, has slowly prevailed in the reformed churches.[40] But the loss of

Character and consequences of the reformation

[39] The opinions and proceedings of the reformers are exposed in the second part of the general history of Mosheim ; but the balance, which he has held with so clear an eye, and so steady an hand, begins to incline in favour of his Lutheran brethren.
[40] Under Edward VI. our reformation was more bold and perfect : but in the fundamental articles of the church of England a strong and explicit declaration

one mystery was amply compensated by the stupendous doctrines of original sin, redemption, faith, grace, and predestination, which have been strained from the epistles of St. Paul. These subtle questions had most assuredly been prepared by the fathers and schoolmen; but the final improvement and popular use may be attributed to the first reformers, who enforced them as the absolute and essential terms of salvation. Hitherto the weight of supernatural belief inclines against the Protestants; and many a sober Christian would rather admit that a wafer is God, than that God is a cruel and capricious tyrant.

Yet the services of Luther and his rival are solid and important; and the philosopher must own his obligations to these fearless enthusiasts.[41] I. By their hands the lofty fabric of superstition, from the abuse of indulgences to the intercession of the Virgin, has been levelled with the ground. Myriads of both sexes of the monastic profession were restored to the liberty and labours of social life. An hierarchy of saints and angels, of imperfect and subordinate deities, were stripped of their temporal power, and reduced to the enjoyment of celestial happiness; their images and relics were banished from the church; and the credulity of the people was no longer nourished with the daily repetition of miracles and visions. The imitation of Paganism was supplied by a pure and spiritual worship of prayer and thanksgiving, the most worthy of man, the least unworthy of the Deity. It only remains to observe whether such sublime simplicity be consistent with popular devotion; whether the vulgar, in the absence of all visible objects, will not be inflamed by enthusiasm, or insensibly subside in languor and indifference. II. The chain of authority was broken, which restrains the bigot from thinking as he pleases, and the slave from speaking as he thinks; the popes, fathers, and councils were no longer the supreme and infallible judges of the world; and each Christian was taught to acknowledge no law but the scriptures, no interpreter but his own conscience. This freedom, however, was the consequence, rather than the design, of the

against the real presence was obliterated in the original copy, to please the people, or the Lutherans, or Queen Elizabeth (Burnet's History of the Reformation, vol. ii. p. 82, 128, 302).

[41] "Had it not been for such men as Luther and myself," said the fanatic Whiston to Halley the philosopher, " you would now be kneeling before an image of St. Winifred."

Reformation. The patriot reformers were ambitious of succeeding the tyrants whom they had dethroned. They imposed with equal rigour their creeds and confessions; they asserted the right of the magistrate to punish heretics with death. The pious or personal animosity of Calvin proscribed in Servetus [42] the guilt of his own rebellion; [43] and the flames of Smithfield, in which he was afterwards consumed, had been kindled for the Anabaptists by the zeal of Cranmer. [44] The nature of the tiger was the same, but he was gradually deprived of his teeth and fangs. A spiritual and temporal kingdom was possessed by the Roman pontiff; the Protestant doctors were subjects of an humble rank, without revenue or jurisdiction. *His* decrees were consecrated by the antiquity of the Catholic church; *their* arguments and disputes were submitted to the people; and their appeal to private judgment was accepted, beyond their wishes, by curiosity and enthusiasm. Since the days of Luther and Calvin, a secret reformation has been silently working in the bosom of the reformed churches; many weeds of prejudice were eradicated; and the disciples of Erasmus [45] diffused a spirit of freedom and moderation. The liberty of conscience has been

[42] The article of *Servet* in the Dictionnaire Critique of Chauffepié is the best account which I have seen of this shameful transaction. See likewise the Abbé d'Artigny, Nouveaux Mémoires d'Histoire, &c., ii. p. 55-154. [The remarkable theological heresies of Servet were as obnoxious to the Protestants as to the Catholics. For an account of his system see H. Tollin's Das Lehrsystem Michael Servets, in 3 vols. (1876-8). The documents of the trial of Servet may be conveniently consulted in the edition of Calvin's works by Baum, Cunitz, and Reuss, vol. 8. There is a good account of the transaction in Roget's Histoire du peuple de Genève, vol. 4 (1877).]
[43] I am more deeply scandalized at the single execution of Servetus, than at the hecatombs which have blazed in the Auto da Fès of Spain and Portugal. 1. The zeal of Calvin seems to have been envenomed by personal malice, and perhaps envy. He accused his adversary before their common enemies, the judges of Vienna, and betrayed, for his destruction, the sacred trust of a private correspondence. 2. The deed of cruelty was not varnished by the pretence of danger to the church or state. In his passage through Geneva, Servetus was an harmless stranger, who neither preached, nor printed, nor made proselytes. 3. A Catholic inquisitor yields the same obedience which he requires, but Calvin violated the golden rule of doing as he would be done by : a rule which I read in a moral treatise of Isocrates (in Nicocle, tom. i. p. 93, edit. Battie), four hundred years before the publication of the gospel. ᾅ πάσχοντες ὑφ' ἑτέρων ὀργίζεσθε, ταῦτα τοῖς ἄλλοις μὴ ποιεῖτε. [The part taken by Calvin in the transaction seems to have been chiefly the furnishing of the documents on which Servetus was condemned.]
[44] See Burnet, vol. ii. p. 84-86. The sense and humanity of the young king were oppressed by the authority of the primate.
[45] Erasmus may be considered as the father of rational theology. After a slumber of an hundred years, it was revived by the Arminians of Holland, Grotius, Limborch, and Le Clerc; in England by Chillingworth, the latitudinarians of Cambridge (Burnet, Hist. of own Times, vol. i. p. 261-268, octavo edition), Tillotson, Clarke, Hoadley, &c.

claimed as a common benefit, an inalienable right;[46] the free governments of Holland[47] and England[48] introduced the practice of toleration; and the narrow allowance of the laws has been enlarged by the prudence and humanity of the times. In the exercise, the mind has understood the limits of its powers, and the words and shadows that might amuse the child can no longer satisfy his manly reason. The volumes of controversy are overspread with cobwebs; the doctrine of a Protestant church is far removed from the knowledge or belief of its private members; and the forms of orthodoxy, the articles of faith, are subscribed with a sigh or a smile by the modern clergy. Yet the friends of Christianity are alarmed at the boundless impulse of inquiry and scepticism. The predictions of the Catholics are accomplished; the web of mystery is unravelled by the Arminians, Arians, and Socinians, whose numbers must not be computed from their separate congregations; and the pillars of revelation are shaken by those men who preserve the name without the substance of religion, who indulge the licence without the temper of philosophy.[49]

[46] I am sorry to observe that the three writers of the last age, by whom the rights of toleration have been so nobly defended, Bayle, Leibnitz, and Locke, are all laymen, and philosophers.

[47] See the excellent chapter of Sir William Temple on the Religion of the United Provinces. I am not satisfied with Grotius (de Rebus Belgicis, Annal. l. i. p. 13, 14, edit. in 12mo), who improves the Imperial laws of persecution, and only condemns the bloody tribunal of the inquisition.

[48] Sir William Blackstone (Commentaries, vol. iv. p. 33, 54) explains the law of England as it was fixed at the Revolution. The exceptions of Papists, and of those who deny the Trinity, would still leave a tolerable scope for persecution, if the national spirit were not more effectual than an hundred statutes.

[49] I shall recommend to public animadversion two passages in Dr. Priestly, which betray the ultimate tendency of his opinions. At the first of these (Hist. of the Corruptions of Christianity, vol. i. p. 275, 276) the priest, at the second (vol. ii. p. 484) the magistrate, may tremble !

SILK TEXTILE OF THE 11TH CENTURY AT VICH, WITH IMPERIAL
TWO-HEADED EAGLE

FROM A WATER-COLOUR BY HERR PAUL SCHULZE, VICTORIA AND ALBERT MUSEUM

CHAPTER LV

The Bulgarians—Origin, Migrations, and Settlement of the Hungarians—Their inroads in the East and West—The monarchy of Russia—Geography and Trade—Wars of the Russians against the Greek Empire—Conversion of the Barbarians

UNDER the reign of Constantine the grandson of Heraclius, the ancient barrier of the Danube, so often violated and so often restored, was irretrievably swept away by a new deluge of barbarians. Their progress was favoured by the caliphs, their unknown and accidental auxiliaries: the Roman legions were occupied in Asia ; and, after the loss of Syria, Egypt, and Africa, the Cæsars were twice reduced to the danger and disgrace of defending their capital against the Saracens. If, in the account of this interesting people, I have deviated from the strict and original line of my undertaking, the merit of the subject will hide my transgression or solicit my excuse. In the East, in the West, in war, in religion, in science, in their prosperity, and in their decay, the Arabians press themselves on our curiosity : the first overthrow of the church and empire of the Greeks may be imputed to their arms ; and the disciples of Mahomet still hold the civil and religious sceptre of the Oriental world. But the same labour would be unworthily bestowed on the swarms of savages who, between the seventh and the twelfth century, descended from the plains of Scythia, in transient inroad or perpetual emigration.[1] Their names are uncouth, their origins doubtful, their actions obscure, their superstition was blind, their valour brutal, and the uniformity of their

---

[1] *All* the passages of the Byzantine history which relate to the barbarians are compiled, methodized, and transcribed, in a Latin version, by the laborious John Gotthelf Stritter, in his " Memoriæ Populorum ad Danubium, Pontum Euxinum, Paludem Mæotidem, Caucasum, Mare Caspium, et inde magis ad Septemtriones incolentium ". Petropoli, 1771-1779 ; in four tomes, or six volumes, in 4to. But the fashion has not enhanced the price of these raw materials.

public and private lives was neither softened by innocence nor refined by policy. The majesty of the Byzantine throne repelled and survived their disorderly attacks; the greater part of these barbarians has disappeared without leaving any memorial of their existence, and the despicable remnant continues, and may long continue, to groan under the dominion of a foreign tyrant. From the antiquities of, I. *Bulgarians*, II. *Hungarians*, and III. *Russians*, I shall content myself with selecting such facts as yet deserve to be remembered. The conquests of the, IV., Normans, and the monarchy of the, V., Turks, will naturally terminate in the memorable Crusades to the Holy Land, and the double fall of the city and empire of Constantine.

I. In his march to Italy, Theodoric [2] the Ostrogoth had trampled on the arms of the Bulgarians. After this defeat, the name and the nation are lost during a century and a half; [3] and it may be suspected that the same or a similar appellation was revived by strange colonies from the Borysthenes, the Tanais, or the Volga. A king of the ancient Bulgaria [4] bequeathed to his five sons a last lesson of moderation and concord. It was received as youth has ever received the counsels of age and experience: the five princes buried their father; divided his subjects and cattle; forgot his advice; separated from each other; and wandered in quest of fortune, till we find the most adventurous in the heart of Italy, under the protection of the exarch of Ravenna. [5] But the stream of emigration was directed or impelled towards the capital. The modern Bulgaria, along the southern banks of the Danube, was stamped with the name and image which it has

---

[2] [Above] Hist. vol. iv. p. 190.

[3] [For the Bulgarians see above, vol. iv. Appendix 16, p. 573. They continued to live north of the Danube and formed part of the Avar empire in the latter half of the sixth century. They appear as the subjects of the Chagan in Theophylactus Simocatta.]

[4] Theophanes, p. 296-299 [*sub* A.M. 6171]. Anastasius, p. 113 [p. 225 *sqq.* ed. de Boor]. Nicephorus, C. P. p. 22, 23 [p. 33, 34, ed. de Boor]. Theophanes places the old Bulgaria on the banks of the Atell or Volga [old Bulgaria lay between the rivers Volga and Kama. There is still a village called Bolgary in the province of Kazan]; but he deprives himself of all geographical credit by discharging that river into the Euxine Sea.

[5] Paul. Diacon. de Gestis Langobard. l. v. c. 29, p. 881, 882. The apparent difference between the Lombard historian and the above-mentioned Greeks is easily reconciled by Camillo Pellegrino (de Ducatu Beneventano, dissert. vii. in the Scriptores Rerum Ital. tom. v. p. 186, 187) and Beretti (Chorograph. Italiæ medii Ævi, p. 273, &c.). This Bulgarian colony was planted in a vacant district of Samnium [at Bovianum, Sergna, and Sipicciano], and learned the Latin, without forgetting their native, language.

retained to the present hour; the new conquerors successively acquired, by war or treaty, the Roman provinces of Dardania, Thessaly, and the two Epirus';[6] the ecclesiastical supremacy was translated from the native city of Justinian; and, in their prosperous age, the obscure town of Lychnidus, or Achrida, was honoured with the throne of a king and a patriarch.[7] The unquestionable evidence of language attests the descent of the Bulgarians from the original stock of the Sclavonian, or more properly Slavonian, race;[8] and the kindred bands of Servians, Bosnians, Rascians, Croatians, Walachians,[9] &c. followed either the standard or the example of the leading tribe. From the Euxine to the Adriatic, in the state of captives or subjects, or allies or enemies, of the Greek empire, they overspread the land; and the national appellation of the SLAVES [10] has been degraded

---

[6] These provinces of the Greek idiom and empire are assigned to the Bulgarian kingdom in the dispute of ecclesiastical jurisdiction between the patriarchs of Rome and Constantinople (Baronius, Annal. Eccles. A.D. 869, No. 75).

[7] The situation and royalty of Lychnidus, or Achrida, are clearly expressed in Cedrenus (p. 713 [ii. p. 468, ed. B.]). The removal of an archbishop or patriarch from Justinianea prima, to Lychnidus, and at length to Ternovo, has produced some perplexity in the ideas or language of the Greeks (Nicephorus Gregoras, l. ii. c. 2, p. 14, 15; Thomassin, Discipline de l'Eglise, tom. i. l. i. c. 19, 23); and a Frenchman (d'Anville) is more accurately skilled in the geography of their own country (Hist. de l'Académie des Inscriptions, tom. xxxi.).

[8] Chalcocondyles, a competent judge, affirms the identity of the language of the Dalmatians, Bosnians, Servians, *Bulgarians*, Poles (de Rebus Turcicis, l. x. p. 283 [p. 530, ed. Bonn]), and elsewhere of the Bohemians (l. ii. p. 38 [p. 73, *ib.*]). The same author has marked the separate idiom of the Hungarians. [The Bulgarian conquerors adopted the language of their Slavonic subjects, but they were not Slavs. See Appendix 8.]

[9] See the work of John Christopher de Jordan, de Originibus Sclavicis, Vindobonæ, 1745, in four parts, or two volumes in folio. His collections and researches are useful to elucidate the antiquities of Bohemia and the adjacent countries; but his plan is narrow, his style barbarous, his criticism shallow, and the Aulic counsellor is not free from the prejudices of a Bohemian. [The statement in the text can partly stand, if it is understood that " kindred bands " means kindred to the Slavs who formed the chief population of the Bulgarian Kingdom—not to the Bulgarian c nquerors. The Servians, Croatians, &c., were Slavs. But in no case does it apply to the Walachians, who ethnically were probably Illyrians—descended at least from those peoples who inhabited Dacia and Illyricum, before the coming of the Slavs. There was a strong Walachian population in the Bulgarian kingdom which extended north of the Danube (see Appendix 11); and it has been conjectured that the Walachians even gave the Bulgarians a king—*Sabinos*, a name of Latin sound. But this seems highly doubtful; and compare Appendix 9.]

[10] Jordan subscribes to the well-known and probable derivation from *Slava, laus, gloria*, a word of familiar use in the different dialects and parts of speech, and which forms the termination of the most illustrious names (de Originibus Sclavicis, pars i. p. 40, pars iv. p. 101, 102). [This derivation has been generally abandoned, and is obviously unlikely. Another, which received the approbation of many, explained the name Slovanie (sing. Slovanjn) from *slovo*, " a word," in the sense of ὁμόγλωττοι, people who speak one language—opposed to Niemi, " the dumb " (non-Slavs, Germans). But this too sounds improbable, and has been

by chance or malice from the signification of glory to that of
servitude.[11] Among these colonies, the Chrobatians,[12] or Croats,
who now attend the motions of an Austrian army, are the descendants of a mighty people, the conquerors and sovereigns of
Dalmatia. The maritime cities, and of these the infant republic
of Ragusa, implored the aid and instructions of the Byzantine
court : they were advised by the magnanimous Basil to reserve
a small acknowledgment of their fidelity to the Roman empire,
and to appease, by an annual tribute, the wrath of these irresistible barbarians. The kingdom of Croatia was shared by
eleven *Zoupans*, or feudatory lords; and their united forces
were numbered at sixty thousand horse and one hundred thousand foot. A long sea-coast, indented with capacious harbours,
covered with a string of islands, and almost in sight of the
Italian shores, disposed both the natives and strangers to the
practice of navigation. The boats or brigantines of the Croats
were constructed after the fashion of the old Liburnians; one
hundred and eighty vessels may excite the idea of a respectable
navy; but our seamen will smile at the allowance of ten, or
twenty, or forty, men for each of these ships of war. They
were gradually converted to the more honourable service of
commerce ; yet the Sclavonian pirates were still frequent and
dangerous; and it was not before the close of the tenth century

rightly rejected by Schafarik, who investigates the name at great length (Slawische
Alterthümer, ii. p. 25 *sqq.*). The original form of the name was Slované or Slovené.
The form "Sclavonian," which is still often used in English books, ought to be
discarded (as Gibbon suggests) ; the guttural does not belong to the word, but
was inserted by the Greeks, Latins, and Orientals (Σκλάβος, Sclavus, Saklab,
Sakalibé, &c.). By the analogy of other names similarly formed, Schafarik shows
convincingly that the name was originally local, meaning "the folk who dwelled
in Slovy," cp. p. 43-45. The discovery of this hypothetical Slovy is another question.
In the Chronicle of Nestor, Slovene is used in the special sense of a tribe about
Novgorod, as well as in the general sense of Slav.]

[11] This conversion of a national into an appellative name appears to have arisen
in the viiith century, in the Oriental France [*i.e.* East Francia, or Franconia : towards
the end of the eighth century, cp. Schafarik, *op. cit.*, ii. p. 325-6] ; where the princes
and bishops were rich in Sclavonian captives, not of the Bohemian (exclaims Jordan)
but of Sorabian race. From thence the word was extended to general use, to the
modern languages, and even to the style of the last Byzantines (see the Greek and
Latin Glossaries of Ducange). The confusion of the Σέρβλοι, or Servians, with the
Latin *Servi* was still more fortunate and familiar (Constant. Porphyr. de Administrando Imperio, c. 32, p. 99). [Serb is supposed to have been the oldest national
name of the Slavs, on the evidence of Procopius (B. G. iii. 14), who says that the
Slavs and Antæ had originally one name, Σπόροι, which is frequently explained as
= Srbs. Schafarik, *op. cit.*, i. p. 93-99.]

[12] The emperor Constantine Porphyrogenitus, most accurate for his own times,
most fabulous for preceding ages, describes the Sclavonians of Dalmatia (c. 29-86).

that the freedom and sovereignty of the Gulf were effectually vindicated by the Venetian republic.[13] The ancestors of these Dalmatian kings were equally removed from the use and abuse of navigation; they dwelt in the White Croatia, in the inland regions of Silesia and Little Poland, thirty days' journey, according to the Greek computation, from the sea of darkness.

The glory of the Bulgarians [14] was confined to a narrow scope both of time and place. In the ninth and tenth centuries they reigned to the south of the Danube; but the more powerful nations that had followed their emigration repelled all return to the north and all progress to the west. Yet, in the obscure catalogue of their exploits, they might boast an honour which had hitherto been appropriated to the Goths: that of slaying in battle one of the successors of Augustus and Constantine. The emperor Nicephorus had lost his fame in the Arabian, he lost his life in the Sclavonian, war. In his first operations he advanced with boldness and success into the centre of Bulgaria, and burnt the *royal court*, which was probably no more than an edifice and village of timber. But, while he searched the spoil and refused all offers of treaty, his enemies collected their spirits and their forces; the passes of retreat were insuperably barred; and the trembling Nicephorus was heard to exclaim: "Alas, alas! unless we could assume the wings of birds, we cannot hope to escape". Two days he waited his fate in the inactivity of despair; but, on the morning of the third, the Bulgarians surprised the camp; and the Roman prince, with the great officers of the empire, were slaughtered in their tents. A.D. 811 The body of Valens had been saved from insult; but the head of Nicephorus was exposed on a spear, and his skull, enchased with gold, was often replenished in the feasts of victory. The Greeks bewailed the dishonour of the throne; but they acknowledged the just punishment of avarice and cruelty. This savage

First kingdom of the Bulgarians. A.D. 640-1017

[The war of Nic phorus with Krum]

[Pliska]

---

[13] See the anonymous Chronicle of the xith century, ascribed to John Sagorninus (p. 94-102), and that composed in the xivth by the Doge Andrew Dandolo (Script. Rerum Ital. tom. xii. p. 227-230) : the two oldest monuments of the history of Venice.

[14] The first kingdom of the Bulgarians may be found, under the proper dates, in the Annals of Cedrenus and Zonaras. The Byzantine materials are collected by Stritter (Memoriæ Populorum, tom. ii. pars ii. p. 441-647), and the series of their kings is disposed and settled by Ducange (Fam. Byzant. p. 305-318). [For an ancient Bulgarian list of the early Bulgarian kings, see Appendix 9. For the migration and establishment south of the Danube, and extent of the kingdom, cp. Appendix 8.]

cup was deeply tinctured with the manners of the Scythian wilderness; but they were softened before the end of the same century by a peaceful intercourse with the Greeks, the possession of a cultivated region, and the introduction of the Christian worship.[15] The nobles of Bulgaria were educated in the schools and palace of Constantinople; and Simeon,[16] a youth of the royal line, was instructed in the rhetoric of Demosthenes and the logic of Aristotle. He relinquished the profession of a monk for that of a king and warrior; and in his reign, of more than forty years,[17] Bulgaria assumed a rank among the civilised powers of the earth. The Greeks, whom he repeatedly attacked, derived a faint consolation from indulging themselves in the reproaches of perfidy and sacrilege. They purchased the aid of the Pagan Turks; but Simeon, in a second battle, redeemed the loss of the first, at a time when it was esteemed a victory to elude the arms of that formidable nation. The Servians [18] were overthrown, made captive, and dispersed; and those who

A.D. 888-927, or 922

[A.D. 893]

[Turks = Hungarians]

[A.D. 924]

---

[15] [In the year after his victory over Nicephorus, the Bulgarian prince Krum captured the towns of Mesembria and Develtus, and in the following year inflicted a crushing defeat on Michael I. at Versinicia near Hadrianople (June, 813) and proceeded to besiege Constantinople. He retired, having devastated the country, but prepared to besiege the capital again in 814. His death was a relief to the Emperor Leo V. (see above, vol. 5, p. 206), who had taken the field and gained at Mesembria a bloody victory over the Bulgarians. The prince Giom Omurtag, who came to the throne in 814-5, made a treaty with Leo for 30 years; and peace was maintained with few interruptions for more than 75 years, till the accession of Simeon. Omurtag is called *Mortagon* by the Greek chroniclers, and Ombritag by Theophylactus of Ochrida; but the right form of the name is furnished by his own inscriptions (see Appendix 10). Omurtag's youngest son Malamir came to the throne. He was succeeded by his nephew Boris (circa A.D. 852-888), whose reign is memorable for the conversion of Bulgaria to Christianity (see Appendix 12).]

[16] Simeonem [emi-argon, id est] semi-Græcum esse aiebant, eo quod a pueritiâ Byzantii Demosthenis rhetoricam et Aristotelis syllogismos didicerat [*leg.* didicerit] (Liutprand, l. iii. c. 8 [= c. 29]). He says in another place, Simeon, fortis, bellator, Bulgariæ [*leg.* Bulgariis] præerat; Christianus sed vicinis Græcis valde inimicus (l. i. c. 2 [= c. 5]). [It is important to notice that native Slavonic literature flourished under Simeon—the result of the invention of Slavonic alphabets (see Appendix 12). Simeon himself—anticipating Constantine Porphyrogennetos—instituted the compilation of a Sbornik or encyclopædia (theological, philosophical, historical), extracted from 20 Greek writers. The Presbyter Grigori translated the chronicle of John Malalas into Slavonic. John the Exarch wrote a *Shestodnev* (Hexaemeron), an account of the Creation. The monk Chrabr wrote a little treatise on the invention of the Cyrillic alphabet (cp. Appendix 12): and other works (chiefly theological) of the same period are extant.]

[17] [Simeon came to the throne in 892-893, and died May 27, 927.]

[18] [That is, *Servia* in the strict sense, excluding the independent Servian principalities of Zachlumia, Trevunia, Diocletia, as well as the Narentans. See Const. Porph., De Adm. Imp., chaps. 32-36. The boundary of Bulgaria against Servia in Simeon's time seems to have followed the Drin; it left Belgrade, Prishtina, Nitzch and Lipljan in Bulgaria.]

visited the country before their restoration could discover no
more than fifty vagrants, without women or children, who extorted a precarious subsistence from the chase.   On classic
ground, on the banks of the Achelöus, the Greeks were defeated ; [A.D. 917,
their horn was broken by the strength of the barbaric Hercules.[19]   Aug. 20]
He formed the siege of Constantinople; and, in a personal
conference with the emperor, Simeon imposed the conditions of
peace.   They met with the most jealous precautions; the royal
galley was drawn close to an artificial and well-fortified platform ;
and the majesty of the purple was emulated by the pomp of the
Bulgarian.   " Are you a Christian? " said the humble Romanus.
" It is your duty to abstain from the blood of your fellow-Christians.   Has the thirst of riches seduced you from the blessings
of peace?   Sheathe your sword, open your hand, and I will
satiate the utmost measure of your desires."   The reconciliation
was sealed by a domestic alliance ;[20] the freedom of trade was
granted or restored ; the first honours of the court were secured
to the friends of Bulgaria, above the ambassadors of enemies or
strangers ;[21] and her princes were dignified with the high and

[19] ――Rigidum fera dextera cornu
            Dum tenet, infregit truncâque a fronte revellit.
Ovid (Metamorph. ix. 1-100) has boldly painted the combat of the river-god and the
hero ; the native and the stranger. [The battle was fought near Anchialos in
Bulgaria (Leo Diac. p. 124). There was a river named Achelous in the neighbourhood (Theoph. Contin. p. 389 ; cp. Pseudo-Sym. Mag. p. 724), and the name misled
Gibbon.   Cp. Finlay, ii. p. 288, note.]
[20] [The peace was concluded after Simeon's death in A.D. 927. Th. Uspenski
has published (in the Lietopis ist. phil. obschestva, of the Odessa University.   Viz.
Otd. ii., 1894, p. 48 sqq.) a curious jubilant sermon preached at Constantinople on
the occasion of the conclusion of the peace.   It presents great difficulties, owing to
the allusiveness of its style, which has been ingeniously discussed by Uspenski, who
is tempted to identify the anonymous author with Nicolaus Mysticus, the Patriarch,
a correspondent of the Tsar Simeon.   But chronology seems to exclude this supposition ; for Nicolaus died in 925 ; and, though the preliminaries to the peace may
have occupied a considerable time, the sermon must have been composed after the
death of Simeon in 927 (as Uspenski seems to forget in his concluding remarks, p.
123).]
[21] The ambassador of Otho was provoked by the Greek excesses, cum Christo-
phori filiam Petrus Bulgarorum Vasileus conjugem duceret, Symphona, id est
consonantia, scripto [al. consonantia scripta], juramento firmata sunt, ut omnium
gentium Apostolis, id est nunciis, penes nos Bulgarorum Apostoli præponantur,
honorentur, diligantur (Liutprand in Legatione, p. 482 [c. 19]).   See the Ceremoniale of Constantine of Porphyrogenitus, tom. i. p. 82 [c. 24, p. 139, ed. Bonn],
tom. ii. p. 429, 430, 434, 435, 443, 444, 446, 447 [c. 52, p. 740, 742, 743, 749, 751,
767, 771, 772, 773], with the annotations of Reiske.   [Bulgarian rulers before
Simeon were content with the title Knez.   Simeon first assumed the title tsar (from
tsesar, ts'sar ; = Cæsar).   It may have been remembered that Terbel had been made
a Cæsar by Justinian II. (Nicephorus, p. 42, ed. de Boor).   The Archbishopric of
Bulgaria was raised to the dignity of a Patriarchate.   Simeon's residence was Great
Peristhlava ; see below, p. 167, note 90.]

invidious title of *basileus*, or emperor. But this friendship was soon disturbed: after the death of Simeon, the nations were A.D. 950, &c. again in arms; his feeble successors were divided [22] and extinguished; and, in the beginning of the eleventh century, the second Basil, who was born in the purple, deserved the appellation of conqueror of the Bulgarians.[23] His avarice was in some measure gratified by a treasure of four hundred thousand pounds sterling (ten thousand pounds weight of gold) which he found in the palace of Lychnidus. His cruelty inflicted a cool and exquisite vengeance on fifteen thousand captives who had been guilty of the defence of their country: they were deprived of sight; but to one of each hundred a single eye was left, that

---

[22] [In A.D. 963 Shishman of Trnovo revolted, and founded an independent kingdom in Macedonia and Albania. Thus there were now two Bulgarian kingdoms and two tsars.]

[23] [The kingdom of Eastern Bulgaria had been conquered first by the Russians and then by the Emperor Tzimisces (see below, p. 167), but Western Bulgaria survived, and before 980, Samuel, son of Shishman, came to the throne. His capital was at first Prespa, but he afterwards moved to Ochrida. His aim was to recover Eastern Bulgaria and conquer Greece; and for thirty-five years he maintained a heroic struggle against the Empire. Both he and his great adversary Basil were men of iron, brave, cruel, and unscrupulous; and Basil was determined not merely to save Eastern, but to conquer Western, Bulgaria. In the first war (976-986) the Bulgarians were successful. Samuel pushed southward and, after repeated attempts which were repulsed, captured Larissa in Thessaly and pushed on to the Isthmus. This was in A.D. 986. To cause a diversion and relieve Greece, Basil marched on Sofia, but was caught in a trap and having endured immense losses escaped with difficulty. After this defeat Eastern Bulgaria was lost to the Empire. (The true date of the capture of Larissa and the defeat of Basil, A.D. 986, has been established, against the old date 981, by the evidence of the Strategikon of Kekaumenos,—for which see above, vol. 5, p. 536. Cp. Schlumberger, L'épopée Byzantine, p. 686. On this first Bulgarian war, see also the Vita Niconis, ap. Martène et Durand, ampl. Coll. 6, 837 *sqq.*; and a contemporary poem of John Geometres, Migne, P. G. vol. 106, p. 934, and cp. p. 920, a piece on the *Cometopulos*, *i.e.* Samuel, with a pun on κομήτης, "comet".) There was a cessation of hostilities for ten years. The second war broke out in A.D. 996. Samuel invaded Greece, but returning he was met by a Greek army in the plain of the Spercheios north of Thermopylæ, and his whole host was destroyed in a night surprise. In A.D. 1000 Basil recovered Eastern Bulgaria, and in the following year South-western Macedonia (Vodena, Berrœa). Again hostilities languished for over ten years; Basil was occupied in the east. In A.D. 1014, the third war began; on July 29 Nicephorus Xiphias gained a brilliant victory over the Bulgarian army at Bielasica (somewhere in the neighbourhood of the river Strumica); Samuel escaped to Prilêp, but died six weeks later. The struggle was sustained weakly under Gabriel Roman (Samuel's son) and John Vladislav, his murderer and successor, last Tsar of Ochrida, who fell, besieging Durazzo, in 1018. The Bulgarians submitted, and the whole Balkan peninsula was once more imperial. If Samuel had been matched with a less able antagonist than Basil, he would have succeeded in effecting what was doubtless his aim, the union of all the Slavs south of the Danube into a great empire. For a fuller account of these wars see Finlay, vol. ii.; and for the first war, Schlumberger, *op. cit.*, chap. x. Jireček, Gesch. der Bulgaren, p. 192-8, is remarkably brief. There is a fuller study of the struggle by Rački in the Croatian tongue (1875).]

he might conduct his blind century to the presence of their king. Their king is said to have expired of grief and horror; the nation was awed by this terrible example; the Bulgarians were swept away from their settlements, and circumscribed within a narrow province; the surviving chiefs bequeathed to their children the advice of patience and the duty of revenge. [Death of Tsar Samuel. A.D. 1014, Sept. 15]

II. When the black swarm of Hungarians first hung over Europe, about nine hundred years after the Christian æra, they were mistaken by fear and superstition for the Gog and Magog of the Scriptures, the signs and forerunners of the end of the world.[24] Since the introduction of letters, they have explored their own antiquities with a strong and laudable impulse of patriotic curiosity.[25] Their rational criticism can no longer be amused with a vain pedigree of Attila and the Huns; but they complain that their primitive records have perished in the Tartar war; that the truth or fiction of their rustic songs is long since forgotten; and that the fragments of a rude chronicle[26] must be painfully reconciled with the contemporary though foreign intelligence of the Imperial geographer.[27] Magiar is the national and Oriental denomination of the Hungarians; but, among the tribes of Scythia, they are distinguished by the Greeks under the proper and peculiar name of Turks, as the descendants of that mighty people who had conquered and reigned from [Emigration of the Hungarians. A.D. 884] [Magyar]

[24] A bishop of Wurtzburg [leg. Verdun] submitted this opinion to a reverend abbot; but he more gravely decided that Gog and Magog were the spiritual persecutors of the church; since Gog signifies the roof, the pride of the Heresiarchs, and Magog what comes from the roof, the propagation of their sects. Yet these men once commanded the respect of mankind (Fleury, Hist. Eccles. tom. xi. p. 594, &c.).

[25] The two national authors, from whom I have derived the most assistance, are George Pray (Dissertationes ad Annales veterum Hungarorum, &c., Vindobonæ, 1775, in folio) and Stephen Katona (Hist. Critica Ducum et Regum Hungariæ stirpis Arpadianæ, Pæstini, 1778-1781, 5 vols. in octavo). The first embraces a large and often conjectural space; the latter, by his learning, judgment, and perspicuity, deserves the name of a critical historian.

[26] The author of this Chronicle is styled the notary of king Béla. Katona has assigned him to the twelfth century, and defends his character against the hypercriticism of Pray. This rude annalist must have transcribed some historical records, since he could affirm with dignity, rejectis falsis fabulis rusticorum, et garrulo cantu joculatorum. In the xvth century, these fables were collected by Thurotzius, and embellished by the Italian Bonfinius. See the Preliminary Discourse in the Hist. Critica Ducum, p. 7-33. [Cp. Appendix 13.]

[27] See Constantine de Administrando Imperio, c. 3, 4, 13, 38-42. Katona has nicely fixed the composition of this work to the years 949, 950, 951 (p. 4-7). [Cp. App. 4.] The critical historian (p. 34-107) endeavours to prove the existence, and to relate the actions, of a first duke Almus, the father of Arpad, who is tacitly rejected by Constantine. [Constantine, c. 38, says that Arpad was elected chief, and not his father Salmutzes (Almos).]

China to the Volga. The Pannonian colony preserved a correspondence of trade and amity with the Eastern Turks on the
confines of Persia; and after a separation of three hundred
and fifty years, the missionaries of the king of Hungary discovered and visited their ancient country near the banks of the
Volga. They were hospitably entertained by a people of pagans
and savages, who still bore the name of Hungarians; conversed
in their native tongue, recollected a tradition of their long-lost
brethren, and listened with amazement to the marvellous tale
of their new kingdom and religion. The zeal of conversion was
animated by the interest of consanguinity; and one of the
greatest of their princes had formed the generous, though fruitless, design of replenishing the solitude of Pannonia by this
domestic colony from the heart of Tartary.[28] From this primitive country they were driven to the West by the tide of war
and emigration, by the weight of the more distant tribes, who
at the same time were fugitives and conquerors. Reason or
fortune directed their course towards the frontiers of the Roman
empire; they halted in the usual stations along the banks of the
great rivers; and in the territories of Moscow, Kiow, and Moldavia some vestiges have been discovered of their temporary
residence. In this long and various peregrination, they could
not always escape the dominion of the stronger; and the purity
of their blood was improved or sullied by the mixture of a foreign
race; from a motive of compulsion or choice, several tribes of
the Chazars were associated to the standard of their ancient
vassals; introduced the use of a second language;[29] and obtained
by their superior renown the most honourable place in the front
of battle. The military force of the Turks and their allies
marched in seven equal and artificial divisions; each division
was formed of thirty thousand eight hundred and fifty-seven
warriors, and the proportion of women, children, and servants
supposes and requires at least a million of emigrants. Their
public councils were directed by seven *vayvods*,[30] or hereditary
chiefs; but the experience of discord and weakness recommended
the more simple and vigorous administration of a single person.

---

[28] Pray (Dissert. p. 37-39, &c.) produces and illustrates the original passages of
the Hungarian missionaries, Bonfinius and Æneas Silvius.
[29] [Cp. Appendix 13.]
[30] [Voivods, " war-leaders," a Slavonic word. Cp. Appendix 13.]

The sceptre which had been declined by the modest Lebedias, was granted to the birth or merit of Almus and his son Arpad, and the authority of the supreme khan of the Chazars confirmed the engagement of the prince and people: of the people to obey his commands, of the prince to consult their happiness and glory.

With this narrative we might be reasonably content, if the penetration of modern learning had not opened a new and larger prospect of the antiquities of nations. The Hungarian language stands alone, and as it were insulated, among the Sclavonian dialects; but it bears a close and clear affinity to the idioms of the *Fennic* race,[31] of an obsolete and savage race, which formerly occupied the northern regions of Asia and Europe. The genuine appellation of *Ugri* or *Igours* is found on the Western confines of China,[32] their migration to the banks of the Irtish is attested by Tartar evidence,[33] a similar name and language are detected in the southern parts of Siberia,[34] and the remains of the Fennic tribes are widely, though thinly, scattered from the sources of the Oby to the shores of Lapland.[35] The consanguinity of the Hungarians and Laplanders would display the powerful energy of climate on the children of a common parent; the lively contrast between the bold adventurers who are intoxicated with the wines of the Danube, and the wretched fugitives who are immersed beneath the snows of the polar circle. Arms and freedom have ever been the ruling,

Their Fennic origin

---

[31] Fischer, in the Quæstiones Petropolitanæ de Origine Ungrorum, and Pray, Dissertat. i. ii. iii. &c., have drawn up several comparative tables of the Hungarian with the Fennic dialects. The affinity is indeed striking, but the lists are short; the words are purposely chosen; and I read in the learned Bayer (Comment. Academ. Betropol. tom. x. p. 374) that, although the Hungarian has adopted many Fennic words (innumeras voces), it essentially differs toto genio et naturâ. [Cp. Appendix 13.]

[32] In the region of Turfan, which is clearly and minutely described by the Chinese geographers (Gaubil, Hist. du Grand Gengiscan, p. 13 ; De Guignes, Hist. des Huns, tom. ii. p. 31, &c.).

[33] Hist. Généalogique des Tartars, par Abulghazi Bahadur Khan, partie ii. p. 90-98.

[34] In their journey to Pekin, both Isbrand Ives (Harris's Collection of Voyages and Travels, vol. ii. p. 920, 921) and Bell (Travels, vol. i. p. 174) found the Vogulitz in the neighbourhood of Tobolsky. By the tortures of the etymological art, *Ugur* and *Vogul* are reduced to the same name; the circumjacent mountains really bear the appellation of *Ugrian ;* and of all the Fennic dialects the Vogulian is the nearest to the Hungarian (Fischer, Dissert. i. p. 20-30. Pray, Dissert. ii. p. 31-34). [It is quite true that the Vogulian comes closest to the Hungarian.]

[35] The eight tribes of the Fennic race are described in the curious work of M. Levesque (Hist. des Peuples soumis à la Domination de la Russie, tom. i. p. 361-561).

though too often the unsuccessful, passion of the Hungarians, who are endowed by nature with a vigorous constitution of soul and body.[36] Extreme cold has diminished the stature and congealed the faculties of the Laplanders; and the Arctic tribes, alone among the sons of men, are ignorant of war and unconscious of human blood: an happy ignorance, if reason and virtue were the guardians of their peace![37]

Tactics and manners of the Hungarians and Bulgarians. A.D. 900, &c.
It is the observation of the Imperial author of the Tactics[38] that all the Scythian hordes resembled each other in their pastoral and military life, that they all practised the same means of subsistence, and employed the same instruments of destruction. But he adds that the two nations of Bulgarians and Hungarians were superior to their brethren, and similar to each other, in the improvements, however rude, of their discipline and government; their visible likeness determines Leo to confound his friends and enemies in one common description; and the picture may be heightened by some strokes from their contemporaries of the tenth century. Except the merit and fame of military prowess, all that is valued by mankind appeared vile and contemptible to these barbarians, whose native fierceness was stimulated by the consciousness of numbers and freedom. The tents of the Hungarians were of leather, their garments of fur; they shaved their hair and scarified their faces ; in speech they were slow, in action prompt, in treaty perfidious; and they shared the common reproach of barbarians, too ignorant to conceive the importance of truth, too proud to deny or palliate the breach of their most solemn engagements. Their simplicity has been praised; yet they abstained only from the luxury they had never known ; whatever they saw, they coveted; their

[36] This picture of the Hungarians and Bulgarians is chiefly drawn from the Tactics of Leo, p. 796-801 [c. 18], and the Latin Annals, which are alleged by Baronius, Pagi, and Muratori, A.D. 889, &c.

[37] Buffon, Hist. Naturelle, tom. v. p. 6, in 12mo. Gustavus Adolphus attempted, without success, to form a regiment of Laplanders. Grotius says of these Arctic tribes, arma arcus et pharetra, sed adversus feras (Annal. l. iv. p. 236) ; and attempts, after the manner of Tacitus, to varnish with philosophy their brutal ignorance.

[38] Leo has observed that the government of the Turks was monarchical, and that their punishments were rigorous (Tactics, p. 896 [18, § 46], ἀπηνεῖς καὶ βαρεῖας). Regino (in Chron. A.D. 889) mentions theft as a capital crime, and his jurisprudence is confirmed by the original code of St. Stephen (A.D. 1016). If a slave were guilty, he was chastised, for the first time, with the loss of his nose, or a fine of five heifers ; for the second, with the loss of his ears, or a similar fine ; for the third, with death ; which the freeman did not incur till the fourth offence, as his first penalty was the loss of liberty (Katona, Hist. Regum Hungar. tom. i. p. 231, 232).

desires were insatiate, and their sole industry was the hand of violence and rapine.   By the definition of a pastoral nation, I have recalled a long description of the economy, the warfare, and the government that prevail in that stage of society; I may add that to fishing as well as to the chase the Hungarians were indebted for a part of their subsistence; and, since they *seldom* cultivated the ground, they must, at least in their new settlements, have sometimes practised a slight and unskilful husbandry.   In their emigrations, perhaps in their expeditions, the host was accompanied by thousands of sheep and oxen, which increased the cloud of formidable dust, and afforded a constant and wholesome supply of milk and animal food.   A plentiful command of forage was the first care of the general, and, if the flocks and herds were secure of their pastures, the hardy warrior was alike insensible of danger and fatigue.   The confusion of men and cattle that overspread the country exposed their camp to a nocturnal surprise, had not a still wider circuit been occupied by their light cavalry, perpetually in motion to discover and delay the approach of the enemy.   After some experience of the Roman tactics, they adopted the use of the sword and spear, the helmet of the soldier, and the iron breast-plate of his steed; but their native and deadly weapon was the Tartar bow ; from the earliest infancy, their children and servants were exercised in the double science of archery and horsemanship; their arm was strong ; their aim was sure; and, in the most rapid career, they were taught to throw themselves backwards, and to shoot a volley of arrows into the air.   In open combat, in secret ambush, in flight or pursuit, they were equally formidable ; an appearance of order was maintained in the foremost ranks, but their charge was driven forwards by the impatient pressure of succeeding crowds.   They pursued, headlong and rash, with loosened reins and horrific outcries ; but, if they fled, with real or dissembled fear, the ardour of a pursuing foe was checked and chastised by the same habits of irregular speed and sudden evolution.   In the abuse of victory, they astonished Europe, yet smarting from the wounds of the Saracen and the Dane ; mercy they rarely asked, and more rarely bestowed ; both sexes were accused as equally inaccessible to pity, and their appetite for raw flesh might countenance the popular tale that they drank the blood and feasted on the hearts of the slain. Yet the Hungarians were not devoid of those principles of justice and humanity which nature has implanted in every bosom. The licence of public and private injuries was restrained by laws and punishments ; and in the security of an open camp theft is the most tempting and the most dangerous offence. Among the barbarians there were many whose spontaneous virtue supplied their laws and corrected their manners, who performed the duties, and sympathized with the affections, of social life.

Establishment and inroads of the Hungarians. A.D. 889

After a long pilgrimage of flight or victory, the Turkish hordes approached the common limits of the French and Byzantine empires. Their first conquests and final settlements extended on either side of the Danube above Vienna, below Belgrade, and beyond the measure of the Roman province of Pannonia, or the modern kingdom of Hungary.[39] That ample and fertile land was loosely occupied by the Moravians, a Sclavonian name and tribe, which were driven by the invaders into the compass of a narrow province. Charlemagne had stretched a vague and nominal empire as far as the edge of Transylvania ; but, after the failure of his legitimate line, the dukes of Moravia forgot their obedience and tribute to the monarchs of Oriental France.[40] The bastard Arnulph was provoked to invite the arms of the Turks ; they rushed through the real or figurative wall which his indiscretion had thrown open ; and the king of Germany has been justly reproached as a traitor to the civil and ecclesiastical society of the Christians. During the life of Arnulph, the Hun-

A.D. 900, &c. garians were checked by gratitude or fear ; but in the infancy of his son Lewis they discovered and invaded Bavaria ; and such was their Scythian speed that, in a single day, a circuit of fifty miles was stripped and consumed. In the battle of Augsburg,

[39] See Katona, Hist. Ducum Hungar. p. 321-352. [One of the most important consequences of the Hungarian invasion and final settlement in these regions was the permanent separation of the Northern from the Southern Slavs. In the eighth and ninth centuries the Slavs formed an unbroken line from the Baltic to the Cretan sea. This line was broken by the Magyar wedge.]

[40] [In the latter part of the ninth century, Moravia under Sviatopolk or Svatopluk was a great power, the most formidable neighbour of the Western Empire. It looked as if he were going to found a great Slavonic empire. For the adoption of the Christian faith see Appendix 12. He died in 894, and under his incompetent son the power of Great Moravia declined, and was blotted out from the number of independent states by the Hungarians about A.D. 906. The annihilation of Moravia might be a relief to the Franks who had originally (before Svatopluk's death) called in the Magyars against the Moravians, but they found—at least for some time to come—more terrible foes in the Magyars.]

the Christians maintained their advantage till the seventh hour
of the day; they were deceived and vanquished by the flying
stratagems of the Turkish cavalry.   The conflagration spread
over the provinces of Bavaria, Swabia, and Franconia; and the
Hungarians [41] promoted the reign of anarchy by forcing the
stoutest barons to discipline their vassals and fortify their castles.
The origin of walled towns is ascribed to this calamitous period;
nor could any distance be secure against an enemy who, almost
at the same instant, laid in ashes the Helvetian monastery of
St. Gall, and the city of Bremen on the shores of the northern
ocean.   Above thirty years the Germanic empire, or kingdom,
was subject to the ignominy of tribute; and resistance was disarmed by the menace, the serious and effectual menace, of dragging the women and children into captivity and of slaughtering
the males above the age of ten years.   I have neither power nor
inclination to follow the Hungarians beyond the Rhine; but I
must observe with surprise that the southern provinces of France
were blasted by the tempest, and that Spain, behind her Pyrenees,
was astonished at the approach of these formidable strangers.[42]
The vicinity of Italy had tempted their early inroads; but, from A.D. 900
their camp on the Brenta, they beheld with some terror the
apparent strength and populousness of the new-discovered
country.   They requested leave to retire; their request was
proudly rejected by the Italian king; and the lives of twenty
thousand Christians paid the forfeit of his obstinacy and rashness.
Among the cities of the West, the royal Pavia was conspicuous
in fame and splendour; and the pre-eminence of Rome itself
was only derived from the relics of the apostles.   The Hungarians appeared; Pavia was in flames; forty-three churches A.D. 924
were consumed; and, after the massacre of the people, they
spared about two hundred wretches who had gathered some

---

[41] Hungarorum gens, cujus omnes fere nationes expertæ [sunt] sævitiam, &c., is
the preface of Liutprand (l. i. c. 2 [= c. 5]), who frequently expatiates on the
calamities of his own times.   See l. i. c. 5 [= c. 13]; l. ii. c. 1, 2, 4, 5, 6, 7 [= c. 2-5,
3 sqq. 21]; l. iii. c. 1, &c.; l. v. c. 8 [= c. 19], 15 [= c. 33], in Legat. p. 485 [c. 45].
His colours are glaring, but his chronology must be rectified by Pagi and Muratori.
For these early invasions of the Western Empire by the Hungarians see E. Dümmler,
Geschichte des ostfränkischen Reichs, ii. 437 sqq., 543 sqq.   The terrible defeat of
the Bavarians under Margrave Liutpold took place on July 5, 907.]
[42] The three bloody reigns of Arpad, Zoltan, and Toxus are critically illustrated
by Katona (Hist. Ducum, &c. p. 107-499).   His diligence has searched both natives
and foreigners; yet to the deeds of mischief, or glory, I have been able to add the
destruction of Bremen (Adam Bremensis, i. 43 [leg. 54]).

bushels of gold and silver (a vague exaggeration) from the smoking ruins of their country.   In these annual excursions from the Alps to the neighbourhood of Rome and Capua, the churches, that yet escaped, resounded with a fearful litany: " Oh! save and deliver us from the arrows of the Hungarians!" But the saints were deaf or inexorable; and the torrent rolled forwards, till it was stopped by the extreme land of Calabria.[43] A composition was offered and accepted for the head of each Italian subject; and ten bushels of silver were poured forth in the Turkish camp.   But falsehood is the natural antagonist of violence; and the robbers were defrauded both in the numbers of the assessment and the standard of the metal.   On the side of the East the Hungarians were opposed in doubtful conflict by the equal arms of the Bulgarians, whose faith forbade an alliance with the Pagans, and whose situation formed the barrier of the

A.D. 925 Byzantine empire.   The barrier was overturned; the emperor of Constantinople beheld the waving banners of the Turks; and one of their boldest warriors presumed to strike a battle-axe into the golden gate.   The arts and treasures of the Greeks diverted the assault; but the Hungarians might boast, on their retreat, that they had imposed a tribute on the spirit of Bulgaria and the majesty of the Cæsars.[44]   The remote and rapid operations of the same campaign appear to magnify the powers and numbers of the Turks; but their courage is most deserving of praise since a light troop of three or four hundred horse would often attempt and execute the most daring inroads to the gates o:

[43] Muratori has considered with patriotic care the danger and resources o Modena. The citizens besought St. Geminianus, their patron, to avert, by hi intercession, the *rabies, flagellum*, &c.

Nunc te rogamus, licet servi pessimi,
Ab Ungerorum nos defendas jaculis.

The bishop erected walls for the public defence, not contra dominos serenc (Antiquitat. Ital. med. Ævi, tom. i. dissertat. i. p. 21, 22), and the song of th nightly watch is not without elegance or use (tom. iii. diss. xl. p. 709). The Italia annalist has accurately traced the series of their inroads (Annali d'Italia, tom. vii p. 365, 367, 393, 401, 437, 440 ; tom. viii. p. 19, 41, 52, &c.).

[44] Both the Hungarian and Russian annals suppose that they besieged, c attacked, or insulted Constantinople (Pray, dissertat. x. p. 239 ; Katona, His Ducum, p. 354-360), and the fact is *almost* confessed by the Byzantine historiar (Leo Grammaticus, p. 506 [p. 322, ed. Bonn] ; Cedrenus, tom. ii. p. 629 [ii. p. 31⟨ ed. Bonn]), yet, however glorious to the nation, it is denied or doubted by the crit cal historian, and even by the notary of Béla. Their scepticism is meritorious they could not safely transcribe or believe the rusticorum fabulas ; but Katon might have given due attention to the evidence of Liutprand ; Bulgarorum genter atque *Graecorum* tributariam fecerant (Hist. l. ii. c. 4, p. 435 [= c. 7]).

Thessalonica and Constantinople. At this disastrous æra of the ninth and tenth centuries, Europe was afflicted by a triple scourge from the North, the East, and the South; the Norman, the Hungarian, and the Saracen sometimes trod the same ground of desolation; and these savage foes might have been compared by Homer to the two lions growling over the carcase of a mangled stag.[45]

The deliverance of Germany and Christendom was achieved by the Saxon princes, Henry the Fowler and Otho the Great, who, in two memorable battles, for ever broke the power of the Hungarians.[46] The valiant Henry was roused from a bed of sickness by the invasion of his country; but his mind was vigorous and his prudence successful. "My companions," said he on the morning of the combat, "maintain your ranks, receive on your bucklers the first arrows of the Pagans, and prevent their second discharge by the equal and rapid career of your lances." They obeyed, and conquered; and the historical picture of the castle of Merseburg expressed the features, or at least the character, of Henry, who, in an age of ignorance, entrusted to the finer arts the perpetuity of his name.[47] At the end of twenty years, the children of the Turks who had fallen by his sword invaded the empire of his son; and their force is defined, in the lowest estimate, at one hundred thousand horse. They were invited by domestic faction; the gates of Germany were treacherously unlocked; and they spread, far beyond the

[marginal notes:] Victory of Henry the Fowler. A.D. 934 [933]

[Battle of Riada]

of Otho the Great. A.D. 955 [August 10]

---

[45] ————λέονθ᾽ ὥς δηρινθήτην,
"Ὧτ᾽ ὄρεος κορυφῇσι περὶ κταμένης ἐλάφοιο
᾽Αμφω πεινάοντε μέγα φρονέοντε μάχεσθον. [Il. 16, 756.]

[46] They are amply and critically discussed by Katona (Hist. Ducum, p. 360-368, 427-470). Liutprand (l. ii. c. 8, 9 [= c. 24-31]) is the best evidence for the former, and Witichind (Annal. Saxon. l. iii. [c. 34-49]) of the latter; but the critical historian will not even overlook the horn of a warrior, which is said to be preserved at Jazberin.

[47] Hunc vero triumphum, tam laude quam memoriâ dignum, ad Meresburgum rex in superiori cœnaculo domus per ζωγραφίαν, id est, picturam, notari [leg. notare] præcepit, adeo ut rem veram potius quam verisimilem videas : an high encomium (Liutprand, l. ii. c. 9 [= c. 31]). Another palace in Germany had been painted with holy subjects by the order of Charlemagne ; and Muratori may justly affirm, nulla sæcula fuere in quibus pictores desiderati fuerint (Antiquitat. Ital. medii Ævi, tom. ii. dissert. xxiv. p. 360, 361). Our domestic claims to antiquity of ignorance and original imperfection (Mr. Walpole's lively words) are of a much more recent date (Anecdotes of Painting, vol. i. p. 2, &c.). [This victory is commonly called the battle of Merseburg ; but it was fought at Riada (according to Widukind, i. 38, who in such a matter is the best authority), and Riada probably corresponds to Rietheburg, where the streams of the Unstrut and Helme meet. The event should be called the battle of Riada. The Italian Liutprand who names Merseburg is not such a good witness as the Saxon historian.]

Rhine and the Meuse, into the heart of Flanders. But the vigour and prudence of Otho dispelled the conspiracy; the princes were made sensible that, unless they were true to each other, their religion and country were irrecoverably lost; and the national powers were reviewed in the plains of Augsburg. They marched and fought in eight legions,[48] according to the division of provinces and tribes; the first, second, and third were composed of Bavarians; the fourth of Franconians; the fifth of Saxons, under the immediate command of the monarch;

[Battle of the Lech-feld] the sixth and seventh consisted of Swabians; and the eighth legion, of a thousand Bohemians, closed the rear of the host. The resources of discipline and valour were fortified by the arts of superstition, which, on this occasion, may deserve the epithets of generous and salutary. The soldiers were purified with a fast; the camp was blessed with the relics of saints and martyrs; and the Christian hero girded on his side the sword of Constantine, grasped the invincible spear of Charlemagne, and waved the banner of St. Maurice, the præfect of the Thebæan legion. But his firmest confidence was placed in the holy lance,[49] whose point was fashioned of the nails of the cross, and which his father had extorted from the king of Burgundy by the threats of war and the gift of a province. The Hungarians were expected in the front;[50] they secretly passed the Lech, a river of Bavaria that falls into the Danube; turned the rear of the Christian army; plundered the baggage and disordered the legions of Bohemia and Swabia. The battle was restored by the Franconians, whose duke, the valiant Conrad, was pierced with an arrow as he rested from his fatigues; the Saxons fought under the eyes of their king; and his victory surpassed, in merit and importance, the triumphs of the last two hundred years. The loss of the Hungarians was still greater in the flight than in the action; they were encompassed by the rivers

---

[48] [Giesebrecht has made it probable that by legion Widukind (iii. 44) meant a company of 1000 men. Geschichte der deutschen Kaiserzeit, i. p. 831.]

[49] See Baronius, Annal. Eccles. A.D. 929, No. 2-5. The lance of Christ is taken from the best evidence, Liutprand (l. iv. c. 12 [= c. 25]), Sigebert, and the acts of St. Gerard; but the other military relics depend on the faith of the Gesta Anglorum post Bedam, l. ii. c. 8.

[50] [The best account of the battle is in Widukind. The other sources are Annales Sangallenses majores; Flodoard; Continuator Reginonis; Ruotger; and a later but noteworthy account in the Vita Udalrici by Gerhard. See E. Dümmler, Kaiser Otto der Grosse (in the Jahrbb. der deutschen Geschichte), 1876 (p. 256 sqq.), and Giesebrecht, op. cit. (p. 418 sqq.), for details of the battle.]

of Bavaria; and their past cruelties excluded them from the hope of mercy. Three captive princes were hanged at Ratisbon, the multitude of prisoners was slain or mutilated, and the fugitives, who presumed to appear in the face of their country, were condemned to everlasting poverty and disgrace.[51] Yet the spirit of the nation was humbled, and the most accessible passes of Hungary were fortified with a ditch and rampart. Adversity suggested the counsels of moderation and peace; the robbers of the West acquiesced in a sedentary life; and the next generation was taught, by a discerning prince, that far more might be gained A.D. 972 by multiplying and exchanging the produce of a fruitful soil. The native race, the Turkish or Fennic blood, was mingled with new colonies of Scythian or Sclavonian origin; [52] many thousands of robust and industrious captives had been imported from all the countries of Europe; [53] and, after the marriage of Geisa with a Bavarian princess, he bestowed honours and estates on the nobles of Germany.[54] The son of Geisa was invested with the regal title, and the house of Arpad reigned three hundred years in the kingdom of Hungary. But the freeborn barbarians were not dazzled by the lustre of the diadem, and the people asserted

---

[51] Katona, Hist. Ducum Hungariæ, p. 500, &c.

[52] Among these colonies we may distinguish, 1. The Chazars, or Cabari, who joined the Hungarians on their march (Constant. de Admin. Imp. c. 39, 40, p. 108, 109). [The name of the Kabars, a Khazar people, survives in the name of the two Kabar-dahs (Kabar-hills).] 2. The Jazyges, Moravians, and Siculi, whom they found in the land; the last were [according to Simon de Kéza, c. 4] perhaps a remnant of the Huns of Attila, and were entrusted with the guard of the borders. Siculus (Zaculus in Simon de Kéza) is the equivalent, in chroniclers' Latin, of Székely (plural, Székelyek), which is generally derived from szék, seat, abode. Hunfalvy (Magyarország Ethnographiája, p. 302) explains the word as "beyond the habitations," a name which might be applied to people of a march district. The word would thus be formed like Erdély (= Erdö-ely, beyond the forest), the Hungarian name of Transylvania. Their German neighbours call the Székelyek Szeklers.] 3. The Russians, who, like the Swiss in France, imparted a general name to the royal porters. 4. The Bulgarians, whose chiefs (A.D. 956) were invited, cum magnâ multitudine Hismahelitarum. Had any of these Sclavonians embraced the Mahometan religion? 5. The Bisseni and Cumans, a mixed multitude of Patzinacites, Uzi, Chazars, &c. who had spread to the lower Danube. Bisseni = Patzinaks; Cumans = Uzi.] The last colony of 40,000 Cumans, A.D. 1239, was received and converted by the kings of Hungary, who derived from that tribe a new regal appellation (Pray, Dissert. vi. vii. p. 109-173; Katona, Hist. Ducum, p. 95-99, 252-264, 476, 479-483, &c.).

[53] Christiani autem, quorum pars major populi est, qui ex omni parte mundi illuc tracti sunt captivi, &c. Such was the language of Piligrinus, the first missionary who entered Hungary, A.D. 973. Pars major is strong. Hist. Ducum, p. 517.

[54] The fideles Teutonici of Geisa are authenticated in old charters; and Katona, with his usual industry, has made a fair estimate of these colonies, which had been so loosely magnified by the Italian Ranzanus (Hist. Critic. Ducum, p. 667-681).

their indefeasible right of choosing, deposing, and punishing the hereditary servant of the state.

Origin of
the Rus-
sian mon-
archy
III. The name of Russians [55] was first divulged, in the ninth century, by an embassy from Theophilus, emperor of the East, to the emperor of the West, Lewis, the son of Charlemagne. The Greeks were accompanied by the envoys of the great duke, or chagan, or *czar*, of the Russians. In their journey to Con-

A.D. 839
stantinople, they had traversed many hostile nations; and they hoped to escape the dangers of their return by requesting the French monarch to transport them by sea to their native country. A closer examination detected their origin : they were the brethren of the Swedes and Normans, whose name was already odious and formidable in France; and it might justly be appre- hended that these Russian strangers were not the messengers of peace but the emissaries of war. They were detained, while the Greeks were dismissed; and Lewis expected a more satis- factory account, that he might obey the laws of hospitality or prudence, according to the interest of both empires. [56]   The Scandinavian origin of the people, or at least the princes of Russia, may be confirmed and illustrated by the national annals [57] and the general history of the North. The Normans, who had so long been concealed by a veil of impenetrable darkness, suddenly burst forth in the spirit of naval and military enter- prise. The vast, and, as it is said, the populous, regions of Denmark, Sweden, and Norway were crowded with independent chieftains and desperate adventurers, who sighed in the laziness of peace, and smiled in the agonies of death. Piracy was the exercise, the trade, the glory and the virtue, of the Scandina-

[55] Among the Greeks, this national appellation has a singular form 'Ρῶs, as an undeclinable word, of which many fanciful etymologies have been suggested. [Cp Appendix 14.] I have perused, with pleasure and profit, a dissertation de Origin Russorum (Comment. Academ. Petropolitanæ, tom. viii. p. 388-436) by Theophilu Sigefrid Bayer, a learned German, who spent his life and labours in the service o Russia. A geographical tract of d'Anville, de l'Empire de Russie, son Origine, e ses Accroissemens (Paris, 1772, in 12mo), has likewise been of use.

[56] See the entire passage (dignum, says Bayer, ut aureis in tabulis figatur) in th Annales Bertiniani Francorum (in Script. Ital. Muratori, tom. ii. pars i. p. 52 [Pertz, Mon. Germ. Hist. i. 434]), A.D. 839, twenty-two years before the æra of Ruric In the tenth century, Liutprand (Hist. l. v. c. 6 [= c. 15]) speaks of the Russians an Normans as the same Aquilonares homines of a red complexion.

[57] My knowledge of these annals is drawn from M. Levesque, Histoire de Russie Nestor, the first and best of these ancient annalists, was a monk of Kiow, who die in the beginning of the twelfth century; but his chronicle was obscure, till it wa published at Petersburgh, 1767, in 4to. Levesque, Hist. de Russie, tom. i. p. 16 Coxe's Travels, vol. ii. p. 184. [See Appendix 1.]

vian youth. Impatient of a bleak climate and narrow limits, they started from the banquet, grasped their arms, sounded their horn, ascended their vessels, and explored every coast that promised either spoil or settlement. The Baltic was the first scene of their naval achievements; they visited the eastern shores, the silent residence of Fennic and Sclavonian tribes, and the primitive Russians of the lake Ladoga paid a tribute, the skins of white squirrels, to these strangers, whom they saluted with the title of *Varangians*,[58] or Corsairs. Their superiority in arms, discipline, and renown, commanded the fear and reverence of the natives. In their wars against the more inland savages, the Varangians condescended to serve as friends and auxiliaries, and gradually, by choice or conquest, obtained the dominion of a people whom they were qualified to protect. Their tyranny was expelled, their valour was again recalled, till at length, Ruric,[59] a Scandinavian chief, became the father of a dynasty A.D. 862 which reigned above seven hundred years. His brothers extended his influence; the example of service and usurpation was imitated by his companions[60] in the southern provinces of Russia; and their establishments, by the usual methods of war and assassination, were cemented into the fabric of a powerful monarchy.

As long as the descendants of Ruric were considered as aliens The Varangians of and conquerors, they ruled by the sword of the Varangians, Constantinople distributed estates and subjects to their faithful captains, and

[58] Theophil. Sig. Bayer de Varagis (for the name is differently spelt), in Comment. Academ. Petropolitanæ, tom. iv. p. 275-311. [The Varangians, in the proper and original sense of the word, meant the Scandinavians. In the chronicle of Nestor, the Baltic Sea is the sea of the Variazi (c. 4). Endless attempts have been made, chiefly by Russian scholars, to find other identifications (such as Slavs, Khazars, Finns); but all these attempts were eminently unsuccessful. The geographical meaning of Varangia has been brought out most clearly in a passage in the Book of Advice which is annexed to the Strategicon of Cecaumenos (see above, vol. 5, p. 536). In § 246 (p. 97, ed. Vasilievski and Jernstedt) Harold Hardrada is called the " son of the king of Varangia," *i.e.* Norway. The formation of the Varangian guard at Constantinople, and the inclusion in it of other Teutons (Danes, English, &c.), led to an extension of the meaning of Varangian from its original limitation to Norwegians or Scandinavians. Schafarik (ii. 72) derives the name from *vara*, *vaere*, a compact; the meaning would be *fœderati*.]

[59] [The name is Scandinavian (old Norse Hraerikr). Riuric founded Novgorod (Nestor, c. 15) ; died in 879.]

[60] [This refers to the story of Oskold and Dir, boyars of Riuric, and their establishment at Kiev ; see Nestor, c. 15, 16, 18. Oleg, who succeeded Riuric at Novgorod, is stated in this chronicle to have marched against Kiev and put Oskold and Dir to death (A.D. 881). It was doubtless Oleg who united Novgorod and Kiev, but it has been questioned whether Oskold and Dir were real personages. The Arabic writer Masūdī mentions " Dir " as a powerful Slav king.]

supplied their numbers with fresh streams of adventurers from the Baltic coast.[61] But, when the Scandinavian chiefs had struck a deep and permanent root into the soil, they mingled with the Russians in blood, religion, and language, and the first Waladimir had the merit of delivering his country from these foreign mercenaries. They had seated him on the throne; his riches were insufficient to satisfy their demands; but they listened to his pleasing advice that they should seek, not a more grateful, but a more wealthy master; that they should embark for Greece, where, instead of the skins of squirrels, silk and gold would be the recompense of their service. At the same time, the Russian prince admonished his Byzantine ally to disperse and employ, to recompense and restrain, these impetuous children of the North. Contemporary writers have recorded the introduction, name, and character of the *Varangians*: each day they rose in confidence and esteem; the whole body was assembled at Constantinople to perform the duty of guards; and their strength was recruited by a numerous band of their countrymen from the island of Thule. On this occasion the vague appellation of Thule is applied to England; and the new Varangians were a colony of English and Danes who fled from the yoke of the Norman conqueror. The habits of pilgrimage and piracy had approximated the countries of the earth; these exiles were entertained in the Byzantine court; and they preserved, till the last age of the empire, the inheritance of spotless loyalty and the use of the Danish or English tongue. With their broad and double-edged battle-axes on their shoulders, they attended the Greek emperor to the temple, the senate, and the hippodrome; he slept and feasted under their trusty guard; and the keys of the palace, the treasury, and the capital were held by the firm and faithful hands of the Varangians.[62]

---

[61] Yet, as late as the year 1018, Kiow and Russia were still guarded ex fugitivorum servorum robore confluentium, et maxime Danorum. Bayer, who quotes (p. 292) the Chronicle of Dithmar [Thietmar] of Merseburg, observes that it was unusual for the Germans to enlist in a foreign service.

[62] Ducange has collected from the original authors the state and history of the Varangi at Constantinople (Glossar. Med. et Infimæ Græcitatis, sub voce Βάραγγοι; Med. et Infimæ Latinitatis, sub voce *Vagri*; Not. ad. Alexiad. Annæ Comnenæ, p. 256, 257, 258; Notes sur Villehardouin, p. 296-299). See likewise the annotations of Reiske to the Ceremoniale Aulæ Byzant. of Constantine, tom. ii. p. 149, 150. Saxo Grammaticus affirms that they spoke Danish; but Codinus maintains them till the fifteenth century in the use of their native English: Πολυχρονίζουσι οἱ Βάραγγοι κατὰ τὴν πάτριον γλῶσσαν αὐτῶν ἤτοι Ἰγκλην ιστί.

In the tenth century, the geography of Scythia was extended
far beyond the limits of ancient knowledge; and the monarchy of the Russians obtains a vast and conspicuous place in the map of Constantine.[63] The sons of Ruric were masters of the spacious province of Wolodomir, or Moscow; and, if they were confined on that side by the hordes of the East, their western frontier in those early days was enlarged to the Baltic sea and the country of the Prussians. Their northern reign ascended above the sixtieth degree of latitude, over the Hyperborean regions, which fancy had peopled with monsters, or clouded with eternal darkness. To the south they followed the course of the Borysthenes, and approached with that river the neighbourhood of the Euxine Sea. The tribes that dwelt, or wandered, in this ample circuit were obedient to the same conqueror, and insensibly blended into the same nation. The language of Russia is a dialect of the Sclavonian; but, in the tenth century, these two modes of speech were different from each other; and, as the Sclavonian prevailed in the South, it may be presumed that the original Russians of the North, the primitive subjects of the Varangian chief, were a portion of the Fennic race.[64] With the emigration, union, or dissolution of the wandering tribes, the loose and indefinite picture of the Scythian desert has continually shifted. But the most ancient map of Russia affords some places which still retain their name and position; and the two capitals, Novogorod [65] and Kiow,[66] are coeval with the first age of the mon-

[63] The original record of the geography and trade of Russia is produced by the emperor Constantine Porphyrogenitus (de Administrat. Imperii, c. 2, p. 55, 56, c. 9, p. 59-61, c. 13, p. 63-67, c. 37, p. 106, c. 42, p. 112, 113), and illustrated by the diligence of Bayer (de Geographiâ Russiæ vicinarumque Regionum circiter A.C. 948, in Comment. Academ. Petropol. tom. ix. p. 367-422, tom. x. p. 371-421), with the aid of the chronicles and traditions of Russia, Scandinavia, &c.

[64] [There were peoples of Finnic race in Livonia and Ingria, between Novgorod and the Baltic; and east of Novgorod the Finnic circle reached down to the Oka, south of Moskowa. The most southerly of these peoples were the Muromians, whose town was Murom; north of these were the Merians, whose town was Rostov; and further north were the Ves, who lived about the White Lake (Bielo-ozero). The Muromians, the Merians, and Ves were in loose subjection to Riuric (Nestor, c. 15).]

[65] The haughty proverb : " Who can resist God and the great Novogorod ? " is applied by M. Levesque (Hist. de Russie, tom. i. p. 60) even to the times that preceded the reign of Ruric. In the course of his history he frequently celebrates this republic, which was suppressed A.D. 1475 (tom. ii. p. 252-266). That accurate traveller, Adam Olearius, describes (in 1635) the remains of Novogorod, and the route by sea and land of the Holstein ambassadors (tom. i. p. 123-129).

[66] In hâc magnâ civitate, quæ est caput regni, plus trecentæ ecclesiæ habentur et nundinæ octo, populi etiam ignota manus (Eggehardus ad A.D. 1018, apud

archy. Novogorod had not yet deserved the epithet of great, nor the alliance of the Hanseatic league, which diffused the streams of opulence and the principles of freedom. Kiow could not yet boast of three hundred churches, an innumerable people, and a degree of greatness and splendour, which was compared with Constantinople by those who had never seen the residence of the Cæsars. In their origin, the two cities were no more than camps or fairs, the most convenient stations in which the barbarians might assemble for the occasional business of war or trade. Yet even these assemblies announce some progress in the arts of society ; a new breed of cattle was imported from the southern provinces; and the spirit of commercial enterprise pervaded the sea and land from the Baltic to the Euxine, from the mouth of the Oder to the port of Constantinople. In the days of idolatry and barbarism, the Sclavonic city of Julin was frequented and enriched by the Normans, who had prudently secured a free mart of purchase and exchange.[67] From this harbour, at the entrance of the Oder, the corsair, or merchant, sailed in forty-three days to the eastern shores of the Baltic, the most distant nations were intermingled, and the holy groves of Curland *are said* to have been decorated with *Grecian* and Spanish gold.[68] Between the sea and Novogorod an easy intercourse was discovered: in the summer, through a gulf, a lake, and a navigable river; in the winter season, over the hard and

Bayer, tom. ix. p. 412 [Ekkehardus Uraugiensis, Chronicon, ap. Pertz, Mon. vi.]). He likewise quotes (tom. x. p. 397) the words of the Saxon annalist [Adam of Bremen, ii. c. 19], Cujus (*Russiae*) metropolis est Chive, æmula sceptri Constantinopolitani quæ est clarissimum decus Græciæ. The fame of Kiow, especially in the xith century, had reached the German and the Arabian geographers.

[67] In Odoræ ostio quâ Scythicas alluit paludes, nobilissima civitas ulinum [*leg.* Jumne], celeberrimam Barbaris et Græcis qui sunt in circuitu præstans stationem ; est sane maxima omnium quas Europa claudit civitatum (Adam Bremensis, Hist. Eccles. p. 19 [ii. 19]). A strange exaggeration even in the xith century. The trade of the Baltic, and the Hanseatic league, are carefully treated in Anderson's Historical Deduction of Commerce ; at least in *our* language, I am not acquainted with any book so satisfactory. [Jumne lies near Wollin.]

[68] According to Adam of Bremen (de Situ Daniæ, p. 58), the old Curland extended eight days' journey along the coast ; and by Peter Teutoburgicus (p. 68, A.D. 1326) Memel is defined as the common frontier of Russia, Curland, and Prussia. Aurum ibi plurimum (says Adam) [. . .] divinis auguribus atque necromanticis omnes domus sunt plenæ . . . a toto orbe ibi responsa petuntur maxime ab Hispanis (forsan *Zupanis*, id est regulis Lettoviæ [other conjectures are : *Cispanis* and *his paganis*]) et Græcis [c. 16]. The name of Greeks was applied to the Russians even before their conversion : an imperfect conversion, if they still consulted the wizards of Curland (Bayer, tom. x. p. 378, 402, &c. ; Grotius, Prolegomen. ad Hist. Goth. p. 99).

level surface of boundless snows. From the neighbourhood of
that city, the Russians descended the streams that fall into
the Borysthenes; their canoes, of a single tree, were laden with
slaves of every age, furs of every species, the spoil of their bee-
hives, and the hides of their cattle; and the whole produce of
the North was collected and discharged in the magazines of
Kiow. The month of June was the ordinary season of the departure of the fleet; the timber of the canoes was framed into
the oars and benches of more solid and capacious boats; and
they proceeded without obstacle down the Borysthenes, as far
as the seven or thirteen ridges of rocks, which traverse the bed,
and precipitate the waters, of the river. At the more shallow
falls it was sufficient to lighten the vessels; but the deeper
cataracts were impassable; and the mariners, who dragged their
vessels and their slaves six miles over land, were exposed in this
toilsome journey to the robbers of the desert.[69] At the first
island below the falls, the Russians celebrated the festival of
their escape; at a second, near the mouth of the river, they
repaired their shattered vessels for the longer and more perilous
voyage of the Black Sea. If they steered along the coast, the
Danube was accessible; with a fair wind they could reach in
thirty-six or forty hours the opposite shores of Anatolia; and
Constantinople admitted the annual visit of the strangers of the
North. They returned at the stated season with a rich cargo
of corn, wine, and oil, the manufactures of Greece, and the
spices of India. Some of their countrymen resided in the
capital and provinces; and the national treaties protected the
persons, effects, and privileges of the Russian merchant.[70]

[69] Constantine [de adm. Imp. c. 9] only reckons seven cataracts, of which he
gives the Russian and Sclavonic names; but thirteen are enumerated by the Sieur
de Beauplan, a French engineer, who had surveyed the course and navigation of
the Dnieper or Borysthenes (Description de Ukraine, Rouen, 1660, a thin quarto),
but the map is unluckily wanting in my copy. [See Appendix 15.]

[70] Nestor apud Levesque, Hist. de Russie, tom. i. p. 78-80 [caps. 21, 22, 27, 35].
From the Dnieper or Borysthenes, the Russians went to Black Bulgaria, Chazaria,
and *Syria*. To Syria, how? where? when? May we not, instead of Συρία, read
Συανία? (de Administrat. Imp. c. 42, p. 113). The alteration is slight; the position
of Suania, between Chazaria and Lazica, is perfectly suitable; and the name was
still used in the xith century (Cedren. tom. ii. p. 770). [Four treaties are cited
in the old Russian chronicle: (1) A.D. 907 (Nestor, c. 21) with Oleg; (2) A.D. 911
(*ib.* c. 22) with Oleg; (3) A.D. 945 (*ib.* c. 27) with Igor; (4) A.D. 970 (*ib.* c. 36)
with Sviatoslav. There is no doubt that the texts of the last three treaties inserted
by the chronicler are genuine. According to custom, duplicates of the documents
in Greek and in the language of the other contracting party were drawn up. These
treaties have attracted much attention from Russian scholars. Two investigations

Naval ex-
peditions
of the
Russians
against
Constanti-
nople

But the same communication which had been opened for the benefit, was soon abused for the injury, of mankind. In a period of one hundred and ninety years, the Russians made four attempts to plunder the treasures of Constantinople; the event was various, but the motive, the means, and the object were the same in these naval expeditions.[71] The Russian traders had seen the magnificence and tasted the luxury of the city of the Cæsars. A marvellous tale, and a scanty supply, excited the desires of their savage countrymen : they envied the gifts of nature which their climate denied; they coveted the works of art which they were too lazy to imitate and too indigent to purchase : the Varangian princes unfurled the banners of piratical adventure, and their bravest soldiers were drawn from the nations that dwelt in the northern isles of the ocean.[72] The image of their naval armaments was revived in the last century in the fleets of the Cossacks, which issued from the Borysthenes to navigate the same seas for a similar purpose.[73] The Greek appellation of monoxyla, or single canoes, might be justly applied to the bottom of their vessels. It was scooped out of the long stem of a beech or willow, but the slight and narrow foundation was raised and continued on either side with planks, till it attained the length of sixty, and the height of about twelve, feet. These boats were built without a deck, but with two rudders and a mast; to move with sails and oars; and to contain from forty to seventy men, with their arms, and provisions of fresh water and salt fish. The first trial of the Russians was made

deserve special mention : a paper of Sergieevich in the Zhurnal Minist. Nar. Prosv. January, 1882, and an article of Dimitriu in Vizantiiski Vremennik, ii. p. 531 sqq. (1893). The transaction of A.D. 907, before the walls of Constantinople, was merely a convention, not a formal treaty ; and Dimitriu shows that the negotiation of A.D. 911 was doubtless intended to convert the spirit of this convention into an international treaty, signed and sealed. But he also makes it probable that this treaty of A.D. 911 did not receive its final ratification from Oleg and his boyars, and consequently was not strictly binding. But it proved a basis for the treaty of 945, which was completed with the full diplomatic forms and which refers back to it.]
   [71] The wars of the Russians and Greeks in the ixth, xth, and xith centuries are related in the Byzantine Annals, especially those of Zonaras and Cedrenus ; and all their testimonies are collected in the Russica of Stritter, tom. ii. pars ii. p. 939-1044.
   [72] Προσεταιρισάμενος δὲ καὶ συμμαχικὸν οὐκ ὀλίγον ἀπὸ τῶν κατοικούντων ἐν τοῖς προσαρκτίοις τοῦ Ὠκεανοῦ νήσοις ἐθνῶν. Cedrenus, in Compend. p. 758 [ii. 551, ed B.].
   [73] See Beauplan (Description de l'Ukraine, p. 54-61). His descriptions are lively, his plans accurate, and, except the circumstance of fire-arms, we may read old Russians for modern Cossacks.

with two hundred boats; but, when the national force was exerted, they might arm against Constantinople a thousand or twelve hundred vessels. Their fleet was not much inferior to the royal navy of Agamemnon, but it was magnified in the eyes of fear to ten or fifteen times the real proportion of its strength and numbers. Had the Greek emperors been endowed with foresight to discern, and vigour to prevent, perhaps they might have sealed with a maritime force the mouth of the Borysthenes. Their indolence abandoned the coast of Anatolia to the calamities of a piratical war, which, after an interval of six hundred years, again infested the Euxine; but, as long as the capital was respected, the sufferings of a distant province escaped the notice both of the prince and the historian. The storm, which had swept along from the Phasis and Trebizond, at length burst on the Bosphorus of Thrace: a strait of fifteen miles, in which the rude vessels of the Russian might have been stopped and destroyed by a more skilful adversary. In their first enter- The first. prise [74] under the prince of Kiow, they passed without opposition, [860] and occupied the port of Constantinople in the absence of the emperor Michael, the son of Theophilus. Through a crowd of [Michael perils he landed at the palace stairs, and immediately repaired to III.] a church of the Virgin Mary.[75] By the advice of the patriarch,

[74] It is to be lamented that Bayer has only given a Dissertation de Russorum *primâ* Expeditione Constantinopolitanâ (Comment. Academ. Petropol. tom. vi. p. 365-391). After disentangling some chronological intricacies, he fixes it in the years 864 or 865, a date which might have smoothed some doubts and difficulties in the beginning of M. Levesque's history. [The true date of the Russian attack on Constantinople is given in a short Chronicle first printed by F. Cumont in "Anecdota Bruxellensia I. Chroniques quelques byzantines du Mscr. 11376 "; and has been established demonstratively by C. de Boor (Byz. Zeitsch. iv. p. 445 *sqq*.). It is June 18, 860; the old date 865 or 866 was derived from the Chronicle of Pseudo-Symeon (p. 674, ed. Bonn : cp. above, vol. 5, p. 534); but it has been proved by Hirsch that the dates of this chronicle had no authority. The same source which gives the right date asserts that the Russians were defeated and annihilated (ἠφανίσθησαν) by the Christians with the help of the Virgin. It seems certain that they experienced a severe defeat *after* their retreat from the walls. Two homilies delivered by Photius on the occasion of this attack were published by Nauck in 1867 and again by C. Müller in Frag. Hist. Graec. v. 2, p. 162 *sqq*. The first was spoken in the moment of terror before the Emperor's arrival ; the second after the rescue. But the second makes no mention of the destruction of the hostile armament ; hence de Boor shows that it must have been delivered immediately after the retreat of the barbarians from the walls, but before their destruction. Another contemporary notice of the event is found in the life of Ignatius by Nicetas (see above, vol. 5, p. 532), Migne, P. G. 105, p. 512. The chronicle of Nestor makes Oskold and Dir (see above, note 60) the leaders of the expedition.]

[75] When Photius wrote his encyclic epistle on the conversion of the Russians, the miracle was not yet sufficiently ripe ; he reproaches the nation as εἰs ὠμότητα καὶ μιαιφονίαν [πάντας] δευτέρους ταττόμενον. [See Photii Epistolæ, ed. Valettas, p. 178.]

her garment, a precious relic, was drawn from the sanctuary and dipped in the sea; and a seasonable tempest, which determined the retreat of the Russians, was devoutly ascribed to the The
second.
A.D. 904 [907] Mother of God.[76]   The silence of the Greeks may inspire some doubt of the truth, or at least of the importance, of the second attempt of Oleg, the guardian of the sons of Ruric.[77]   A strong barrier of arms and fortifications defended the Bosphorus : they were eluded by the usual expedient of drawing the boats over the isthmus; and this simple operation is described in the national chronicles as if the Russian fleet had sailed over dry The third.
A.D. 941 land with a brisk and favourable gale.   The leader of the third armament, Igor, the son of Ruric, had chosen a moment of weakness and decay, when the naval powers of the empire were employed against the Saracens.   But, if courage be not wanting, the instruments of defence are seldom deficient.   Fifteen broken and decayed galleys were boldly launched against the enemy; but, instead of the single tube of Greek fire usually planted on the prow, the sides and stern of each vessel were abundantly supplied with that liquid combustible.   The engineers were dexterous; the weather was propitious; many thousand Russians, who chose rather to be drowned than burnt, leaped into the sea; and those who escaped to the Thracian shore were inhumanly slaughtered by the peasants and soldiers.   Yet one third of the canoes escaped into shallow water; and the next spring Igor was again prepared to retrieve his disgrace and claim his revenge.[78]   After a long peace, Jaroslaus, the great-grandson The fourth.
A.D. 1043 of Igor, resumed the same project of a naval invasion.   A fleet, under the command of his son, was repulsed at the entrance of the Bosphorus by the same artificial flames.   But in the rashness of pursuit the vanguard of the Greeks was encompassed

---

[76] Leo Grammaticus, p. 463, 464 [p. 241, ed. B.].   Constantini Continuator, in Script. post Theophanem, p. 121, 122 [p. 196-7, ed. B.]   Simeon Logothet. p. 445, 446 [p. 674-5, ed. B.].   Georg. Monach. p. 535, 536 [826, ed. B.].   Cedrenus, tom. ii. p. 551 [ii. 173, ed. B.].   Zonaras, tom. ii. p. 162 [xvi. 5].
[77] See Nestor [c. 21] and Nicon, in Levesque's Hist. de Russie, tom. i. p. 74-80. Katona (Hist. Ducum, p. 75-79) uses his advantage to disprove this Russian victory, which would cloud the siege of Kiow by the Hungarians.
[78] Leo Grammaticus, p. 506, 507 [p. 323, ed. B.]; Incert. Contin. p. 263, 264 [p. 424]; Simeon Logothet. p. 490, 491 [p. 746-7, ed. B.]; Georg. Monach. p. 588, 589 [p. 914, ed. B.].; Cedren. tom. ii. p. 629 [ii. 316, ed. B.]; Zonaras, tom. ii. p. 190, 191 [xvi. 16]; and Luitprand, l. v. c. 6 [= c. 15], who writes from the narratives of his father-in-law, then ambassador at Constantinople, and corrects the vain exaggeration of the Greeks. [Nestor, c. 26.]

by an irresistible multitude of boats and men; their provision
of fire was probably exhausted; and twenty-four galleys were
either taken, sunk, or destroyed.[79]
Yet the threats or calamities of a Russian war were more
frequently diverted by treaty than by arms. In these naval hostilities every disadvantage was on the side of the Greeks; their
savage enemy afforded no mercy; his poverty promised no spoil;
his impenetrable retreat deprived the conqueror of the hopes of
revenge; and the pride or weakness of empire indulged an
opinion that no honour could be gained or lost in the intercourse
with barbarians. At first their demands were high and inadmis-
sible, throo pounds of gold for each soldier or mariner of the
fleet; the Russian youth adhered to the design of conquest and
glory; but the counsels of moderation were recommended by
the hoary sages. " Be content," they said, " with the liberal [A.D. 944]
offers of Cæsar; is it not far better to obtain without a combat
the possession of gold, silver, silks, and all the objects of our
desires? Are we sure of victory? Can we conclude a treaty
with the sea? We do not tread on the land; we float on the
abyss of water, and a common death hangs over our heads." [80]
The memory of these Arctic fleets that seemed to descend from
the Polar circle left a deep impression of terror on the Imperial
city. By the vulgar of every rank, it was asserted and believed
that an equestrian statue in the square of Taurus was secretly
inscribed with a prophecy, how the Russians, in the last days,
should become masters of Constantinople.[81] In our own time,
a Russian armament, instead of sailing from the Borysthenes,
has circumnavigated the continent of Europe; and the Turkish
capital has been threatened by a squadron of strong and lofty

Negotia-
tions and
prophecy

---

[79] I can only appeal to Cedrenus (tom. ii. p. 758, 759 [ii. 551, ed. B.]) and Zonaras
(tom. ii. p. 253, 254 [xvii. 24]), but they grow more weighty and credible as they
draw near to their own times. [Cp. Nestor, c. 56.]
[80] Nestor, apud Levesque, Hist. de Russie, tom. i. p. 87. [This advice was
given by his counsellors to Igor in A.D. 944. See Nestor, c. 27; p. 25, ed. Miklosich.]
[81] This brazen statue, which had been brought from Antioch, and was melted
down by the Latins, was supposed to represent either Joshua or Bellerophon, an
odd dilemma. See Nicetas Choniates (p. 413, 414 [p. 848, ed. Bonn]), Codinus (de
Originibus [leg. de Signis] C. P. p. 24 [p. 43, ed. B.]), and the anonymous writer de
Antiquitat. C. P. (Banduri, Imp. Orient. tom. i. p. 17, 18) who lived about the year
1100. They witness the belief of the prophecy; the rest is immaterial. [The prophecy is not mentioned in the passage of Nicetas; and " Codinus " is merely a
copyist of the anonymous Πάτρια τῆς Κωνσταντινοπόλεως edited by G. Banduri (see
above, vol. ii. Appendix 8). Therefore (as Smith rightly pointed out in his annotation
to this note) there is only one witness.]

ships of war, each of which, with its naval science and thundering artillery, could have sunk or scattered an hundred canoes, such as those of their ancestors. Perhaps the present generation may yet behold the accomplishment of the prediction, of a rare prediction, of which the style is unambiguous and the date unquestionable.

Reign of Swato-slaus. A.D. 955-973

By land the Russians were less formidable than by sea ; and, as they fought for the most part on foot, their irregular legions must often have been broken and overthrown by the cavalry of the Scythian hordes. Yet their growing towns, however slight and imperfect, presented a shelter to the subject and a barrier to the enemy: the monarchy of Kiow, till a fatal partition, assumed the dominion of the North ; and the nations from the Volga to the Danube were subdued or repelled by the

[Sviatoslav. A.D. 945-972]

arms of Swatoslaus,[82] the son of Igor, the son of Oleg, the son of Ruric. The vigour of his mind and body was fortified by the hardships of a military and savage life. Wrapt in a bear-skin Swatoslaus usually slept on the ground, his head reclining on a saddle ; his diet was coarse and frugal, and, like the heroes of Homer,[83] his meat (it was often horse-flesh) was broiled or roasted on the coals. The exercise of war gave stability and discipline to his army ; and it may be presumed that no soldier

[A.D. 967]

was permitted to transcend the luxury of his chief. By an embassy from Nicephorus, the Greek emperor, he was moved to

[Circa £64,800]

undertake the conquest of Bulgaria, and a gift of fifteen hundred pounds of gold was laid at his feet to defray the expense, or reward the toils, of the expedition.[84] An army of sixty thousand men

---

[82] The life of Swatoslaus, or Sviateslaf, or Sphendosthlabus [the form in Greek writers], is extracted from the Russian Chronicles by M. Levesque (Hist. de Russie, tom. i. pp. 94-107). [Nestor, c. 32-36. Sviatoslav was born in A.D. 942 (cp. Nestor, c. 27) ; his independent reign began about A.D. 965, in which year he made an expedition against the Khazars (ib. 32).]

[83] This resemblance may be clearly seen in the ninth book of the Iliad (205-221), in the minute detail of the cookery of Achilles. By such a picture a modern epic poet would disgrace his work and disgust his reader ; but the Greek verses are harmonious ; a dead language can seldom appear low or familiar ; and at the distance of two thousand seven hundred years we are amused with the primitive manners of antiquity.

[84] [The Bulgarian Tsar Peter, successor of Simeon, made a treaty with the Empire in A.D. 927. He stipulated to prevent the Hungarians from invading the Empire, and in return he was to receive an annual subsidy ; and the contract was sealed by his marriage with the granddaughter of Romanus. Peter, a feeble prince, wished to preserve the treaty, but he was not able to prevent some Magyar invasions (A.D. 959, 962, 967) ; and the strong and victorious Nicephorus refused to pay the subsidies any longer. He saw that the time had come to reassert the power of the

was assembled and embarked; they sailed from the Borysthenes to the Danube; their landing was effected on the Mæsian shore; and, after a sharp encounter, the swords of the Russians prevailed against the arrows of the Bulgarian horse. The vanquished king sunk into the grave; his children were made [Jan. 30, captive;[85] and his dominions as far as mount Hæmus, were subdued or ravaged by the northern invaders. But, instead of relinquishing his prey and performing his engagements, the Varangian prince was more disposed to advance than to retire; and, had his ambition been crowned with success, the seat of empire in that early period might have been transferred to a more temperate and fruitful climate. Swatoslaus enjoyed and acknowledged the advantages of his new position, in which he could unite, by exchange or rapine, the various productions of the earth. By an easy navigation he might draw from Russia the native commodities of furs, wax, and hydromel; Hungary supplied him with a breed of horses and the spoils of the West; and Greece abounded with gold, silver, and the foreign luxuries which his poverty had affected to disdain. The bands of Patzinacites, Chozars, and Turks repaired to the standard of

Empire against Bulgaria. He advanced against Peter in 967 (this is the right date; others place it in 966), but unaccountably retreated without accomplishing anything. He then sent Calocyres to Kiev to instigate Sviatoslav against Bulgaria. The envoy was a traitor, and conceived the idea of making Sviatoslav's conquest of Bulgaria a means of ascending himself the throne of Constantinople. Sviatoslav conquered the north of Bulgaria in the same year (Nestor, c. 32), and established his residence at Peristhlava (near Tulcea, on south arm of the Danube delta; to be distinguished from Great Peristhlava, see below, note 90). Drster (Silistria) alone held out against the Russians. Sviatoslav wintered at Peristhlava, but was obliged to return to Russia in the following year (968) to deliver Kiev, which was besieged by the Patzinaks (Nestor, c. 33). A few months later his mother Olga died (ib. c. 34), and then Sviatoslav returned to Bulgaria, which he purposed to make the centre of his dominions. Leo Diaconus (v. c. 2, 3; p. 77-79) and the Greek writers do not distinguish the first and second Russian invasions of Sviatoslav; hence the narrative of Gibbon is confused. For these events see Jireček, Geschichte der Bulgaren, p. 186-7; Hilferding, Geschichte der Serben und Bulgaren, i. 127 sqq.; and (very fully told in) Schlumberger, Nicéphore Phocas, c. xii. and c. xv.]

[85] [Before Peter's death, in Jan. A.D. 969, Nicephorus, aware of the treachery of his ambassador Calocyres who had remained with Sviatoslav, and afraid of the ambition of the Russian prince, changed his policy; and, though he had called Russia in to subdue Bulgaria, he now formed a treaty with Bulgaria to keep Russia out. The basis of this treaty (Leo Diac. p. 7-9) was a contract of marriage between the two young Emperors, Basil and Constantine, and two Bulgarian princesses. Then the death of Peter supervened. David the son of Shishman the Tsar of western Bulgaria (cp. above, p. 142, note 22) made an attempt to seize eastern Bulgaria, but was anticipated by Peter's young son, Boris. Then Sviatoslav returned to Bulgaria (see last note). During his absence Little Peristhlava seems to have been regained by the Bulgarians and he had to recapture it. Then he went south and took Great Peristhlava; and captured Boris and his brother Romanus, A.D. 969.]

[Calocyres] victory; and the ambassador of Nicephorus betrayed his trust, assumed the purple, and promised to share with his new allies the treasures of the Eastern world. From the banks of the Danube the Russian prince pursued his march as far as Hadrianople; a formal summons to evacuate the Roman province was dismissed with contempt; and Swatoslaus fiercely replied that Constantinople might soon expect the presence of an enemy and a master.

His defeat by John Zimisces. A.D. 970-973

Nicephorus could no longer expel the mischief which he had introduced;[86] but his throne and wife were inherited by John Zimisces,[87] who, in a diminutive body, possessed the spirit and abilities of an hero. The first victory of his lieutenants deprived the Russians of their foreign allies, twenty thousand of whom were either destroyed by the sword or provoked to revolt or tempted to desert.[88] Thrace was delivered, but seventy thousand barbarians were still in arms; and the legions that had been recalled from the new conquests of Syria prepared, with the return of the spring, to march under the banners of a warlike prince, who declared himself the friend and avenger of the injured Bulgaria. The passes of mount Hæmus had been left

[86] [Nicephorus was assassinated Dec. 10, A.D. 969. Lines of his admirer John Geometres, bishop of Melitene, written soon after his death, attest the apprehensions of the people of Constantinople at the threatening Russian invasions. " Rise up," he cries to the dead sovereign, " gather thine army; for the Russian host is speeding against us; the Scythians are throbbing for carnage," &c. The piece is quoted by Scylitzes (Cedrenus, ii. p. 378, ed. Bonn) and is printed in Hase's ed. of Leo Diac. (p. 453, ed. B.). Evidently these verses were written just after the capture of Philippopolis by the Russians, and the horrible massacre of the inhabitants, in early spring A.D. 970, when the Russian plunderers were already approaching the neighbourhood of the capital. John Tzimisces, before he took the field, sent two embassies to Sviatoslav, commanding him to leave not only the Imperial provinces but Bulgaria (cp. Lambin in the Mémoires de l'Acad. de St. Petersburg, 1876, p. 119 sqq.). In preparing for his campaign, Tzimisces formed a new regiment of chosen soldiers, which he called the Immortals (Leo Diac. p. 107). For the Russian wars of Tzimisces see Schlumberger, L'épopée Byzantine, chaps. i., ii., iii.; and Bielov's study (cited below, note 88).]

[87] This singular epithet is derived from the Armenian language, and Τζιμισκῆς is interpreted in Greek by μουζακίτζης, or μοιρακίτζης. As I profess myself equally ignorant of these words, I may be indulged in the question in the play, " Pray which of you is the interpreter? " From the context they seem to signify Adolescentulus (Leo Diacon. l. iv. Ms. apud Ducange, Glossar. Græc. p. 1570 [Bk. v. c. 9, p. 92, ed. Bonn]). [Tshemshkik would be the Armenian form. It is supposed to be derived from a phrase meaning a red boot.]

[88] [The first victory was gained by the general Bardas Sclerus in the plains near Arcadiopolis; it saved Constantinople. M. Bielov in a study of this war (Zhurnal Min. Nar. Prosv., vol. 170, 1876, p. 168 sqq.) tried to show that the Russians were victorious, but (as M. Schlumberger rightly thinks) he is unsuccessful in proving this thesis.]

DEFEAT OF THE RUSSIANS BEFORE DRISTRA IN THE REIGN OF JOHN ZIMISCES. FROM THE MS. OF SKYLITZES AT MADRID

unguarded; they were instantly occupied; the Roman vanguard
was formed of the *immortals* (a proud imitation of the Persian
style); the emperor led the main body of ten thousand five hun- [A.D. 972]
dred foot;[89] and the rest of his forces followed in slow and cautious
array with the baggage and military engines.   The first exploit
of Zimisces was the reduction of Marcianopolis, or Peristhlaba,[90]
in two days: the trumpet sounded; the walls were scaled; eight
thousand five hundred Russians were put to the sword;[91] and
the sons of the Bulgarian king were rescued from an ignominious
prison, and invested with a nominal diadem.   After these repeated losses, Swatoslaus retired to the strong post of Dristra,
on the banks of the Danube, and was pursued by an enemy who
alternately employed the arms of celerity and delay.   The By- [Siege of
zantine galleys ascended the river; the legions completed a line Drster be-
of circumvallation;[92] and the Russian prince was encompassed, gins. April
assaulted, and famished, in the fortifications of the camp and 25]
city.   Many deeds of valour were performed; several desperate
sallies were attempted; nor was it till after a siege of sixty-five
days that Swatoslaus yielded to his adverse fortune.   The liberal [July 25]
terms which he obtained announce the prudence of the victor,
who respected the valour, and apprehended the despair, of an
unconquered mind.   The great duke of Russia bound himself
by solemn imprecations to relinquish all hostile designs; a safe
passage was opened for his return; the liberty of trade and

[89] [For the date (A.D. 972) of this splendid expedition of Tzimisces, cp. Schlumberger, *op. cit.*, p. 82.   Nestor places it in A.D. 971 (c. 36).]
[90] In the Sclavonic tongue, the name of Peristhlaba implied the great or illustrious city, μεγάλη καὶ οὖσα καὶ λεγομένη, says Anna Comnena (Alexiad, l. vii. p. 194
[c. 3]).   From its position between mount Hæmus and the lower Danube, it
appears to fill the ground, or at least the station, of Marcianopolis.   The situation
of Durostolus, or Dristra, is well known and conspicuous (Comment. Academ.
Petropol. tom. ix. p. 415, 416; D'Anville, Geographie Ancienne, tom. i. p. 307,
311).   [Great Peristhlava was situated at Eski Stambul, 22 kilometers south of
Shumla.   Marcianopolis was much farther east; some of its ruins have been traced
near the modern village of Dievna (about 30 kils. west of Varna as the crow flies).
Tzimisces called Peristhlava after himself Joannopolis, but the city rapidly decayed
after this period.   He called Drster Theodoropolis, in honour of St. Theodore
the Megalomartyr, who was supposed to have fought in the Roman ranks in the
last great fight at Drster on July 23.   Thereby hangs a problem.   The Greek writers
say that the day of the battle was the feast of St. Theodore; but his feast falls on
June 8.   Cp. Muralt, Essai de Chronologie byzantine, ad ann.]
[91] [The Greek sources for the capture of Peristhlava (and for the whole campaign)
are Leo the Deacon and Scylitzes.   The numbers (given by Scylitzes) are very
doubtful.]
[92] [A battle was fought outside Silistria and the Russians discomfited, in April 23,
before the siege began.]

navigation was restored; a measure of corn was distributed to each of his soldiers; and the allowance of twenty-two thousand measures attests the loss and the remnant of the barbarians.[93] After a painful voyage, they again reached the mouth of the Borysthenes; but their provisions were exhausted; the season was unfavourable; they passed the winter on the ice; and, before they could prosecute their march, Swatoslaus was surprised and oppressed by the neighbouring tribes, with whom the Greeks entertained a perpetual and useful correspondence.[94] Far different was the return of Zimisces, who was received in his capital like Camillus or Marius, the saviours of ancient Rome. But the merit of the victory was attributed by the pious emperor to the Mother of God; and the image of the Virgin Mary, with the divine infant in her arms, was placed on a triumphal car, adorned with the spoils of war and the ensigns of Bulgarian royalty. Zimisces made his public entry on horseback; the diadem on his head, a crown of laurel in his hand; and Constantinople was astonished to applaud the martial virtues of her sovereign.[95]

Conversion of Russia. A.D. 864   Photius of Constantinople, a patriarch whose ambition was equal to his curiosity, congratulates himself and the Greek church on the conversion of the Russians.[96] Those fierce and bloody barbarians had been persuaded by the voice of reason and religion to acknowledge Jesus for their God, the Christian missionaries for their teachers, and the Romans for their friends and brethren. His triumph was transient and premature. In the various fortune of their piratical adventures, some Russian chiefs might allow themselves to be sprinkled with the waters of baptism; and a Greek bishop, with the name of metropolitan, might administer the sacraments in the church of Kiow to a congrega-

---

[93] [For the treaty see above, p. 159, note 70.]

[94] The political management of the Greeks, more especially with the Patzinacites, is explained in the seven first chapters de Administratione Imperii.

[95] In the narrative of this war, Leo the Deacon (apud Pagi, Critica, tom. iv. A.D. 968-973 [Bk. vi. c. 3-13]) is more authentic and circumstantial than Cedrenus (tom. ii. p. 660-683) and Zonaras (tom. ii. p. 205-214 [xvi. 27-xvii. 3]). These declaimers have multiplied to 308,000 and 330,000 men those Russian forces of which the contemporary had given a moderate and consistent account.

[96] Phot. Epistol. ii. No. 35, p. 58, edit. Montacut [Ep. 4, ed. Valettas, p. 178]. It was unworthy of the learning of the editor to mistake the Russian nation, τὸ Ρῶς, for a war-cry of the Bulgarians; nor did it become the enlightened patriarch to accuse the Sclavonian idolaters τῆς Ἑλληνικῆς καὶ ἀθέου δόξης. They were neither Greeks nor atheists. [Ἑλληνικός = pagan.]

tion of slaves and natives. But the seed of the Gospel was sown on a barren soil : many were the apostates, the converts were few ; and the baptism of Olga may be fixed as the æra of Russian Christianity.[97] A female, perhaps of the basest origin, who could revenge the death, and assume the sceptre, of her husband Igor, must have been endowed with those active virtues which command the fear and obedience of barbarians. In a moment of foreign and domestic peace, she sailed from Kiow to Constantinople; and the emperor Constantine Porphyrogenitus has described with minute diligence the ceremonial of her reception in his capital and palace. The steps, the titles, the salutations, the banquet, the presents, were exquisitely adjusted, to gratify the vanity of the stranger, with due reverence to the superior majesty of the purple.[98] In the sacrament of baptism, she received the venerable name of the empress Helena; and her conversion might be preceded or followed by her uncle, two interpreters, sixteen damsels, of an higher, and eighteen of a lower, rank, twenty-two domestics or ministers, and forty-four Russian merchants, who composed the retinue of the great princess Olga. After her return to Kiow and Novogorod, she firmly persisted in her new religion; but her labours in the propagation of the Gospel were not crowned with success; and both her family and nation adhered with obstinacy or indifference to the gods of their fathers. Her son Swatoslaus was apprehensive of the scorn and ridicule of his companions; and her grandson Wolodomir devoted his youthful zeal to multiply and decorate the monuments of ancient worship. The savage deities of the North were still propitiated with human sacrifices : in the choice of the victim, a citizen was preferred to a stranger, a Christian to an idolater; and the father who defended his son from the sacerdotal knife was involved in the same doom by the rage of a fanatic tumult. Yet the lessons and example of the

Baptism of Olga. A.D. 955 [957]

---

[97] M. Levesque has extracted, from old chronicles and modern researches, the most satisfactory account of the religion of the *Slavi*, and the conversion of Russia (Hist. de Russie, tom. i. p. 35-54, 59, 92, 93, 113-121, 124-129, 148, 149, &c.). [Nestor, c. 31.]

[98] See the Ceremoniale Aulæ Byzant. tom. ii. c. 15, p. 343-345 : the style of Olga, or Elga [Old Norse, *Helga*], is 'Αρχόντισσα Ρωσίας. For the chief of barbarians the Greeks whimsically borrowed the title of an Athenian magistrate, with a female termination which would have astonished the ear of Demosthenes. [In the account of the Ceremony of Olga's reception her baptism is not mentioned ; it was indeed irrelevant.]

pious Olga had made a deep though secret impression on the minds of the prince and people: the Greek missionaries continued to preach, to dispute, and to baptize; and the ambassadors or merchants of Russia compared the idolatry of the woods with the elegant superstition of Constantinople. They had gazed with admiration on the dome of St. Sophia: the lively pictures of saints and martyrs, the riches of the altar, the number and vestments of the priests, the pomp and order of the ceremonies; they were edified by the alternate succession of devout silence and harmonious song; nor was it difficult to persuade them that a choir of angels descended each day from heaven to join in the devotion of the Christians.[99] But the conversion of Wolodomir was determined, or hastened, by his desire of a Roman bride. At the same time, and in the city of Cherson, the rites of baptism and marriage were celebrated by the Christian pontiff; the city he restored to the emperor Basil, the brother of his spouse; but the brazen gates were transported, as it is said, to Novogorod, and erected before the first church as a trophy of his victory and faith.[100] At his despotic

Of Wolodo-
mir.   A.D.
988 [989]

[99] See an anonymous fragment published by Banduri (Imperium Orientale, tom. ii. p. 112, 113), de Conversione Russorum. [Reprinted in vol. iii. of Bonn ed. of Constantine Porph. p. 357 *sqq.*; but since published in a fuller form from a Patmos Ms. by W. Regel in Analecta Byzantino-Russica, p. 44 *sqq.* (1891). But the narrative is a later compilation and mixes up together (Regel, *op. cit.*, p. xxi.) the story of the earlier conversion by Photius, and the legend of the introduction of the Slavonic alphabet by Cyril and Methodius.]

[100] Cherson, or Corsun, is mentioned by Herberstein (apud Pagi, tom. iv. p. 56) as the place of Wolodomir's baptism and marriage; and both the tradition and the gates are still preserved at Novogorod. Yet an observing traveller transports the brazen gates from Magdeburg in Germany (Coxe's Travels into Russia, &c. vol. i. p. 452), and quotes an inscription, which seems to justify his opinion. The modern reader must not confound this old Cherson of the Tauric or Crimæan peninsula [situated on the southern shore of the bay of Sebastopol] with a new city of the same name, which had arisen near the mouth of the Borysthenes, and was lately honoured by the memorable interview of the empress of Russia with the emperor of the West. [Till recently, the date of the marriage and conversion of Vladimir was supposed to be A.D. 988. The authority is the Russian chronicle of "Nestor," which contains the fullest (partly legendary) account (c. 42). Vladimir captured Cherson, and sent an embassy, demanding the hand of the princess Anne, and threatening to attack Constantinople if it were refused. Vasilievski showed (in a paper in the Zhurnal Min. Nar. Prosv. 184 (1876), p. 156) from the notice in Leo Diaconus (p. 175, ed. Bonn), and Baron von Rosen (in his book of extracts from the annals of Yahia (1883), note 169), that Cherson was captured in A.D. 989 (c. June); and it follows that the marriage and conversion cannot have been celebrated before the autumn of 989. The fragment which is sometimes called "Notes of the Greek toparch of Gothia," which was published by Hase (notes to Leo Diaconus, p. 496 *sqq.*, ed. Bonn), belongs to a somewhat earlier period. The text has been republished by F. Westberg, with translation and commentary (die Fragmente des Toparcha Goticus, Zapiski of Imp. Acad. of Science, St. Petersburg, viiie sér., v. 2, 1901), and he fixes the date of the events described to A.D. 960-965.]

command, Peroun, the god of thunder, whom he had so long
adored, was dragged through the streets of Kiow; and twelve
sturdy barbarians battered with clubs the misshapen image,
which was indignantly cast into the waters of the Borysthenes.
The edict of Wolodomir had proclaimed that all who should refuse the rites of baptism would be treated as the enemies of
God and their prince; and the rivers were instantly filled with
many thousands of obedient Russians, who acquiesced in the
truth and excellence of a doctrine which had been embraced by
the great duke and his boyars.[101]　In the next generation the
relics of paganism were finally extirpated; but, as the two
brothers of Wolodomir had died without baptism, their bones
were taken from the grave and sanctified by an irregular and
posthumous sacrament.

In the ninth, tenth, and eleventh centuries of the Christian
æra, the reign of the gospel and of the church was extended
over Bulgaria, Hungary, Bohemia, Saxony, Denmark, Norway,
Sweden, Poland, and Russia.[102]　The triumphs of apostolic zeal
were repeated in the iron age of Christianity; and the northern
and eastern regions of Europe submitted to a religion more
different in theory than in practice from the worship of their
native idols. A laudable ambition excited the monks, both of
Germany and Greece, to visit the tents and huts of the barbarians; poverty, hardships, and dangers, were the lot of the
first missionaries; their courage was active and patient; their
motive pure and meritorious; their present reward consisted in
the testimony of their conscience and the respect of a grateful
people; but the fruitful harvest of their toils was inherited and
enjoyed by the proud and wealthy prelates of succeeding times.
The first conversions were free and spontaneous: an holy life
and an eloquent tongue were the only arms of the missionaries;
but the domestic fables of the pagans were silenced by the
miracles and visions of the strangers; and the favourable temper
of the chiefs was accelerated by the dictates of vanity and
interest.　The leaders of nations, who were saluted with the

Chris-
tianity of
the North.
A.D. 800-
1100

---

[101] [The adoption of Christianity in Russia was facilitated by the fact that there
was no sacerdotal caste to oppose it. This point is insisted on by Kostomarov,
Russische Geschichte in Biographien, i. 5.]
[102] Consult the Latin text, or English version, of Mosheim's excellent History
of the Church, under the first head or section of each of these centuries.

titles of kings and saints,[103] held it lawful and pious to impose the Catholic faith on their subjects and neighbours: the coast of the Baltic, from Holstein to the gulf of Finland, was invaded under the standard of the cross; and the reign of idolatry was closed by the conversion of Lithuania in the fourteenth century. Yet truth and candour must acknowledge that the conversion of the North imparted many temporal benefits both to the old and the new Christians. The rage of war, inherent to the human species, could not be healed by the evangelic precepts of charity and peace; and the ambition of Catholic princes has renewed in every age the calamities of hostile contention. But the admission of the barbarians into the pale of civil and ecclesiastical society delivered Europe from the depredations, by sea and land, of the Normans, the Hungarians, and the Russians, who learned to spare their brethren and cultivate their possessions.[104] The establishment of law and order was promoted by the influence of the clergy ; and the rudiments of art and science were introduced into the savage countries of the globe. The liberal piety of the Russian princes engaged in their service the most skilful of the Greeks, to decorate the cities and instruct the inhabitants ; the dome and the paintings of St. Sophia were rudely copied in the churches of Kiow [105] and Novogorod ; the writings of the fathers were translated into the Sclavonic idiom ; and three hundred noble youths were invited or compelled to attend the lessons of the college of Jaroslaus.[106] It should appear that Russia might have derived an early and rapid improvement from her peculiar connection with the church and state of

[Yaroslav. A.D. 1015-1054]

103 In the year 1000, the ambassadors of St. Stephen received from pope Sylvester the title of King of Hungary, with a diadem of Greek workmanship. It had been designed for the duke of Poland; but the Poles, by their own confession, were yet too barbarous to deserve an *angelical* and *apostolical* crown (Katona, Hist. Critic. Regum Stirpis Arpadianæ, tom. i. p. 1-20).

104 Listen to the exultations of Adam of Bremen (A.D. 1080), of which the substance is agreeable to truth : Ecce illa ferocissima Danorum, &c. natio . . . jamdudum novit in Dei laudibus Alleluia resonare . . . Ecce populus ille piraticus . . . suis nunc finibus contentus est. Ecce patria [illa] horribilis semper inaccessa propter cultum idolorum . . . prædicatores veritatis ubique certatim admittit, &c. &c. (de Situ Daniæ, &c. p. 40, 41, edit. Elzevir [c. 42] : a curious and original prospect of the north of Europe, and the introduction of Christianity).

105 [The great monument of Yaroslav's reign is the church of St. Sophia at Kiev, built by Greek masons. A smaller church, also dedicated to the Holy Wisdom, was built at Novgorod on the pattern of the Kiev church by his son Vladimir in 1045.]

106 [For Yaroslav's taste for books, see Nestor, c. 55.]

Constantinople [107] which in that age so justly despised the ignorance of the Latins.   But the Byzantine nation was servile, solitary, and verging to an hasty decline; after the fall of Kiow, the navigation of the Borysthenes was forgotten ; the great princes of Wolodomir and Moscow were separated from the sea and Christendom ; and the divided monarchy was oppressed by the ignominy and blindness of Tartar servitude.[108]   The Sclavonic and Scandinavian kingdoms, which had been converted by the Latin missionaries, were exposed, it is true, to the spiritual jurisdiction and temporal claims of the popes ; [109] but they were united, in language and religious worship, with each other, and with Rome; they imbibed the free and generous spirit of the European republic, and gradually shared the light of knowledge which arose on the western world.

[107] [It is important to notice the growth of monasticism in Russia in the 11th century.   The original hearth and centre of the movement was at Kiev in the Pestcherski or Crypt Monastery, famous for the Saint Theodosius [ob. 1074] whose biography was written by Nestor.   Kostomarov (op. cit., p. 18 sqq.) has a readable chapter on the subject.]

[108] The great princes removed in 1156 from Kiow, which was ruined by the Tartars in 1240.   Moscow became the seat of empire in the xivth century.   See the first and second volumes of Levesque's History, and Mr. Coxe's Travels into the North, tom. i. p. 241, &c.

[109] The ambassadors of St. Stephen had used the reverential expressions of *regnum oblatum, debitam obedientiam,* &c. which were most rigorously interpreted by Gregory VII. ; and the Hungarian Catholics are distressed between the sanctity of the pope and the independence of the crown (Katona, Hist. Critica, tom. i. p. 20-25, tom. ii. p. 304, 346, 360, &c.).

CHAPTER LVI

The Saracens, Franks, and Greeks, in Italy—First Adventures and Settlement of the Normans—Character and Conquests of Robert Guiscard, Duke of Apulia—Deliverance of Sicily by his brother Roger—Victories of Robert over the Emperors of the East and West—Roger, king of Sicily, invades Africa and Greece—The Emperor Manuel Comnenus—Wars of the Greeks and Normans— Extinction of the Normans

Conflict of the Saracens, Latins, and Greeks, in Italy. A.D. 840-1017

THE three great nations of the world, the Greeks, the Saracens, and the Franks, encountered each other on the theatre of Italy.[1] The southern provinces, which now compose the kingdom of Naples, were subject, for the most part, to the Lombard dukes and princes of Beneventum:[2] so powerful in war that they checked for a moment the genius of Charlemagne; so liberal in peace that they maintained in their capital an academy of thirty-two philosophers and grammarians. The division of this flourishing state produced the rival principalities of Benevento, Salerno, and Capua;[3] and the

---

[1] For the general history of Italy in the ixth and xth centuries, I may properly refer to the vth, vith, and viith books of Sigonius de Regno Italiæ (in the second volume of his works, Milan, 1732) ; the Annals of Baronius, with the Criticism of Pagi ; the viith and viiith books of the Istoria Civile del Regno di Napoli of Giannone ; the viith and viiith volumes (the octavo edition) of the Annali d'Italia of Muratori, and the iid volume of the Abrégé Chronologique of M. de St. Marc, a work which, under a superficial title, contains much genuine learning and industry. But my long accustomed reader will give me credit for saying that I myself have ascended to the fountain-head, as often as such ascent could be either profitable or possible ; and that I have diligently turned over the originals in the first volumes of Muratori's great collection of the *Scriptores Rerum Italicarum.*

[2] Camillo Pellegrino, a learned Capuan of the last century, has illustrated the history of the duchy of Beneventum, in his two books, Historia Principum Longobardorum, in the Scriptores of Muratori, tom. ii. pars i. p. 221-345, and tom. v. p. 159-245.

[3] [The duchy of Beneventum first split up into two parts, an eastern and a western—the western under the name of the Principality of Salerno. Soon after this the Count of Capua threw off his allegiance to the Prince of Salerno ; so that the old duchy of Beneventum was represented by three independent states. For the

thoughtless ambition or revenge of the competitors invited the Saracens to the ruin of their common inheritance. During a calamitous period of two hundred years Italy was exposed to a repetition of wounds, which the invaders were not capable of healing by the union and tranquillity of a perfect conquest. Their frequent and almost annual squadrons issued from the port of Palermo, and were entertained with too much indulgence by the Christians of Naples; the more formidable fleets were prepared on the African coast; and even the Arabs of Andalusia were sometimes tempted to assist or oppose the Moslems of an adverse sect. In the revolution of human events, a new ambuscade was concealed in the Caudine forks, the fields of Cannæ were bedewed a second time with the blood of the Africans, and the sovereign of Rome again attacked or defended the walls of Capua and Tarentum. A colony of Saracens had been planted at Bari, which commands the entrance of the Adriatic Gulf; and their impartial depredations provoked the resentment, and conciliated the union, of the two emperors. An offensive alliance was concluded between Basil the Macedonian, the first of his race, and Lewis, the great-grandson of Charlemagne;[4] and each party supplied the deficiencies of his associate. It would have been imprudent in the Byzantine monarch to transport his stationary troops of Asia to an Italian campaign, and the Latin arms would have been insufficient, if *his* superior navy had not occupied the mouth of the Gulf. The fortress of Conquest Bari was invested by the infantry of the Franks, and by the of Bari. A.D. 871 cavalry and galleys of the Greeks; and, after a defence of four years, the Arabian emir submitted to the clemency of Lewis, who commanded in person the operations of the siege. This important conquest had been achieved by the concord of the East and West; but their recent amity was soon embittered by the mutual complaints of jealousy and pride. The Greeks assumed as their own the merit of the conquest and the pomp of the triumph; extolled the greatness of their powers, and affected to deride the intemperance and sloth of the handful of barbarians who appeared under the banners of the Carlovingian

---

history of Salerno see Schipa, Storia del principato Longobardo in Salerno, in the Arch. storico per le cose prov. Nap., 12, 1887. J. Gay, L'Italie méridionale et l'empire byzantin (867-1061), 1904.]

[4] See Constantin. Porphyrogen. de Thematibus, l. ii. c. xi. in Vit. Basil. c. 55, p. 181.

prince. His reply is expressed with the eloquence of indignation and truth: "We confess the magnitude of your preparations," says the great-grandson of Charlemagne. "Your armies
were indeed as numerous as a cloud of summer locusts, who
darken the day, flap their wings, and, after a short flight, tumble
weary and breathless to the ground. Like them, ye sunk
after a feeble effort; ye were vanquished by your own cowardice; and withdrew from the scene of action to injure and
despoil our Christian subjects of the Sclavonian coast. We were
few in number, and why were we few? Because, after a tedious
expectation of your arrival, I had dismissed my host, and retained only a chosen band of warriors to continue the blockade
of the city. If they indulged their hospitable feasts in the face
of danger and death, did these feasts abate the vigour of their
enterprise? Is it by your fasting that the walls of Bari have
been overturned? Did not these valiant Franks, diminished as
they were by languor and fatigue, intercept and vanquish the
three most powerful emirs of the Saracens? and did not their
defeat precipitate the fall of the city? Bari is now fallen;
Tarentum trembles; Calabria will be delivered; and, if we
command the sea, the island of Sicily may be rescued from the
hands of the infidels. My brother (a name most offensive to
the vanity of the Greek), accelerate your naval succours, respect
your allies, and distrust your flatterers."[5]

New pro-
vince of
the Greeks
in Italy.
A.D. 890

[Bari won
by the
Greeks.
A.D. 876]

These lofty hopes were soon extinguished by the death of
Lewis, and the decay of the Carlovingian house; and, whoever
might deserve the honour, the Greek emperors, Basil and his
son Leo, secured the advantage, of the reduction of Bari. The
Italians of Apulia and Calabria were persuaded or compelled to
acknowledge their supremacy, and an ideal line from mount
Garganus to the bay of Salerno leaves the far greater part of the
kingdom of Naples under the dominion of the eastern empire.
Beyond that line, the dukes or republics of Amalphi[6] and Naples,
who had never forfeited their voluntary allegiance, rejoiced in

---

[5] The original epistle of the emperor Lewis II. to the emperor Basil, a curious
record of the age, was first published by Baronius (Annal. Eccles. A.D. 871, No.
51-71) from the Vatican Ms. of Erchempert, or rather of the anonymous historian
of Salerno. [Printed also in Duchesne, Hist. Fr. scr. iii. p. 555.]

[6] See an excellent dissertation de Republicâ Amalphitanâ in the Appendix (p. 1-
42) of Henry Brenckmann's Historia Pandectarum (Trajecti ad Rhenum, 1722, in
4to). [Materials for the history of Naples are collected in Capasso's Monumenta
ad Neap. duc. histor. pertinentia, vol. i., 1881; vol. ii. 1, 1885, 2, 1892.]

the neighbourhood of their lawful sovereign; and Amalphi was enriched by supplying Europe with the produce and manufactures of Asia. But the Lombard princes of Benevento, Salerno, and Capua[7] were reluctantly torn from the communion of the Latin world, and too often violated their oaths of servitude and tribute. The city of Bari rose to dignity and wealth, as the metropolis of the new theme or province of Lombardy; the title of patrician, and afterwards the singular name of *Catapan*,[8] was assigned to the supreme governor; and the policy both of the church and state was modelled in exact subordination to the throne of Constantinople. As long as the sceptre was disputed by the princes of Italy, their efforts were feeble and adverse; and the Greeks resisted or eluded the forces of Germany, which descended from the Alps under the Imperial standard of the Othos. The first and greatest of those Saxon princes was compelled to relinquish the siege of Bari: the second, after the loss of his stoutest bishops and barons, escaped with honour from the bloody field of Crotona. On that day the scale of war was turned against the Franks by the valour of the Saracens.[9] These corsairs had indeed been driven by the

[Theme of Lagubardia]

Defeat of Otho III. [II.]. A.D. 983 [982]

[7] Your master, says Nicephorus, has given aid and protection principibus Capuano et Beneventano, servis meis, quos oppugnare dispono . . . Nova (potius *nota*) res est quod eorum patres et avi nostro Imperio tributa dederunt (Liutprand, in Legat. p. 484). Salerno is not mentioned, yet the prince changed his party about the same time, and Camillo Pellegrino (Script. Rer. Ital. tom. ii. pars i. p. 285) has nicely discerned this change in the style of the anonymous chronicle. On the rational ground of history and language, Liutprand (p. 480) had asserted the Latin claim to Apulia and Calabria. [The revival of East-Roman influence in Southern Italy in the last years of the ninth century is illustrated by the fact that an Imperial officer (of the rank of protospathar) resided at the court of the Dukes of Beneventum from A.D. 891. The allegiance of Naples, Amalfi, and Gaeta was indeed little more than nominal. For the history of Gaeta the chief source is the Codex Caietanus, published in the Tabularium Casinense (1890, 1892).]

[8] See the Greek and Latin Glossaries of Ducange (Κατεπάνω, *catapanus*), and his notes on the Alexias (p. 275). Against the contemporary notion, which derives it from Κατὰ πᾶν, *juxta omne*, he treats it as a corruption of the Latin *capitaneus*. Yet M. de St. Marc has accurately observed (Abrégé Chronologique, tom. ii. p. 924) that in this age the capitanei were not *captains*, but only nobles of the first rank, the great valvassors of Italy. [The Theme of Italy extended from the Ofanto in the north and the Bradano in the west to the southern point of Apulia, and included the south of Calabria (the old Bruttii). It must not be confounded with the Capitanata. It was probably about the year 1000 that the governors of the Theme of Italy conquered the land on the north side of their province, between the Ofanto and Fortore (see Heinemann, Gesch. der Normannem in Unter-Italien und Sicilien, i. p. 20). From the title of the governors, Katepanô, this conquest was called the Catepanata, and this became (through the influence of popular etymology) Capitanata.]

[9] Οὐ μόνον δια πολέμων ἀκριβῶς ἐκτεταγμένων το τοιοῦτον ὑπήγαγε τὸ ἔθνος (the Lombards), ἀλλὰ καὶ ἀγχινοίᾳ χρησάμενος καὶ δικαιοσύνῃ καὶ χρηστότητι, ἐπιεικῶς τε τοῖς

Byzantine fleets from the fortresses and coasts of Italy; but a sense of interest was more prevalent than superstition or resentment, and the caliph of Egypt had transported forty thousand Moslems to the aid of his Christian ally. The successors of Basil amused themselves with the belief that the conquest of Lombardy had been achieved, and was still preserved, by the justice of their laws, the virtues of their ministers, and the gratitude of a people whom they had rescued from anarchy and oppression. A series of rebellions might dart a ray of truth into the palace of Constantinople; and the illusions of flattery were dispelled by the easy and rapid success of the Norman adventurers.

Anecdotes   The revolution of human affairs had produced in Apulia and Calabria a melancholy contrast between the age of Pythagoras and the tenth century of the Christian æra. At the former period, the coast of Great Greece (as it was then styled) was planted with free and opulent cities: these cities were peopled with soldiers, artists, and philosophers; and the military strength of Tarentum, Sybaris, or Crotona was not inferior to that of a powerful kingdom. At the second æra, these once-flourishing provinces were clouded with ignorance, impoverished by tyranny, and depopulated by barbarian war; nor can we severely accuse the exaggeration of a contemporary that a fair and ample district was reduced to the same desolation which had covered the earth after the general deluge.[10] Among the hostilities of the Arabs, the Franks and the Greeks, in the southern Italy, I shall select two or three anecdotes expressive of their national manners. 1. It was the amusement of the Saracens to profane, as well as to A.D. 872   pillage, the monasteries and churches. At the siege of Salerno, a Musulman chief spread his couch on the communion-table, and on that altar sacrificed each night the virginity of a Christian

---

προσερχομένοις προσφερόμενος, καὶ τὴν ἐλευθερίαν αὐτοῖς πάσης τε δουλείας καὶ τῶν ἄλλων φορολογιῶν χαριζόμενος (Leon. Tactic. c. xv. p. 741). The little Chronicle of Beneventum (tom. ii. pars i. p. 280) gives a far different character of the Greeks during the five years (A.D. 891-896) that Leo was master of the city. [For good accounts of the expedition and defeat of Otto II. see Giesebrecht, Geschichte der deutschen Kaiserzeit, i. p. 595 sqq., Schlumberger, L'épopée byzantine, p. 502 sqq. Gay, op. cit., p. 327 sqq. The battle was fought in July 982, near Stilo, south of Croton.]

[10] Calabriam adeunt, eamque inter se divisam reperientes funditus depopulati sunt (or depopularunt), ita ut deserta sit velut in diluvio. Such is the text of Herempert, or Erchempert, according to the two editions of Carraccioli (Rer. Italic. Script. tom. v. p. 23), and of Camillo Pellegrino (tom. ii. p. 246). Both were extremely scarce, when they were reprinted by Muratori.

THE EMPEROR OTTO AND THE EMPRESS THEOPHANO BLESSED BY OUR
LORD: IVORY CARVING OF THE LATE 10TH CENTURY

MUSÉE DE CLUNY, PARIS

1un. As he wrestled with a reluctant maid, a beam in the roof was accidentally or dexterously thrown down on his head; and the death of the lustful emir was imputed to the wrath of Christ, which was at length awakened to the defence of his faithful spouse.[11] 2. The Saracens besieged the cities of Beneventum A.D. 874 and Capua: after a vain appeal to the successors of Charlemagne, the Lombards implored the clemency and aid of the Greek emperor.[12] A fearless citizen dropped from the walls, passed the intrenchments, accomplished his commission, and fell into the hands of the barbarians, as he was returning with the welcome news. They commanded him to assist their enterprise, and deceive his countrymen, with the assurance that wealth and honours should be the reward of his falsehood, and that his sincerity would be punished with immediate death. He affected to yield, but, as soon as he was conducted within hearing of the Christians on the rampart, "Friends and brethren," he cried with a loud voice, "be bold and patient, maintain the city; your sovereign is informed of your distress, and your deliverers are at hand. I know my doom, and commit my wife and children to your gratitude." The rage of the Arabs confirmed his evidence; and the self-devoted patriot was transpierced with an hundred spears. He deserves to live in the memory of the virtuous, but the repetition of the same story in ancient and modern times may sprinkle some doubts on the reality of this generous deed.[13] 3. The recital of the third incident may provoke a smile amidst A.D. 930 the horrors of war. Theobald, marquis of Camerino and

[11] Baronius (Annal. Eccles. A.D. 874, No. 2) has drawn this story from a Ms. of Erchempert, who died at Capua only fifteen years after the event. But the cardinal was deceived by a false title, and we can only quote the anonymous Chronicle of Salerno (Paralipomena, c. 110), composed towards the end of the xth century, and published in the second volume of Muratori's Collection. See the Dissertations of Camillo Pellegrino (tom. ii. pars i. 231-281, &c.).

[12] Constantine Porphyrogenitus (in Vit. Basil. c. 58, p. 183) is the original author of this story. He places it under the reigns of Basil and Lewis II.; yet the reduction of Beneventum by the Greeks is dated A.D. 891, after the decease of both of those princes.

[13] In the year 663, the same tragedy is described by Paul the Deacon (de Gestis Langobard. l. v. c. 7, 8, p. 870, 871, edit. Grot), under the walls of the same city of Beneventum. But the actors are different, and the guilt is imputed to the Greeks themselves, which in the Byzantine edition is applied to the Saracens. In the late war in Germany, M. d'Assas, a French officer of the regiment of Auvergne *is said* to have devoted himself in a similar manner. His behaviour is the more heroic, as mere silence was required by the enemy who had made him prisoner (Voltaire, Siècle de Louis XV. c. 33, tom. ix. p. 172).

Spoleto,[14] supported the rebels of Beneventum; and his wanton cruelty was not incompatible in that age with the character of an hero. His captives of the Greek nation or party were castrated without mercy, and the outrage was aggravated by a cruel jest, that he wished to present the emperor with a supply of eunuchs, the most precious ornaments of the Byzantine court. The garrison of the castle had been defeated in a sally, and the prisoners were sentenced to the customary operation. But the sacrifice was disturbed by the intrusion of a frantic female, who, with bleeding cheeks, dishevelled hair, and importunate clamours, compelled the marquis to listen to her complaint. "It is thus," she cried, "ye magnanimous heroes, that ye wage war against women, against women who have never injured ye, and whose only arms are the distaff and the loom?" Theobald denied the charge, and protested that, since the Amazons, he had never heard of a female war. "And how," she furiously exclaimed, "can you attack us more directly, how can you wound us in a more vital part, than by robbing our husbands of what we most dearly cherish, the source of our joys, and the hope of our posterity? The plunder of our flocks and herds I have endured without a murmur, but this fatal injury, this irreparable loss, subdues my patience, and calls aloud on the justice of heaven and earth." A general laugh applauded her eloquence; the savage Franks, inaccessible to pity, were moved by her ridiculous, yet rational despair; and, with the deliverance of the captives, she obtained the restitution of her effects. As she returned in triumph to the castle, she was overtaken by a messenger, to inquire, in the name of Theobald, what punishment should be inflicted on her husband, were he again taken in arms? "Should such," she answered without hesitation, "be his guilt and misfortune, he has eyes, and a nose, and hands, and feet. These are his own, and these he may deserve to forfeit by his personal offences. But let my lord be pleased to spare what his little handmaid presumes to claim as her peculiar and lawful property." [15]

---

[14] Theobald, who is styled *Heros* by Liutprand, was properly duke of Spoleto and marquis of Camerino, from the year 926 to 935. The title and office of marquis (commander of the march or frontier) was introduced into Italy by the French emperors (Abrégé Chronologique, tom. ii. p. 645-732, &c.).

[15] Liutprand, Hist. l. iv. c. iv. in the Rerum Italic. Script. tom. i. pars i. p. 453, 454. Should the licentiousness of the tale be questioned, I may exclaim, with

The establishment of the Normans in the kingdoms of Origin of
Naples and Sicily [16] is an event most romantic in its origin, mans in
and in its consequences most important both to Italy and the 1016
Eastern empire. The broken provinces of the Greeks, Lombards,
and Saracens were exposed to every invader, and every sea and
land were invaded by the adventurous spirit of the Scandinavian
pirates. After a long indulgence of rapine and slaughter, a fair
and ample territory was accepted, occupied, and named, by the
Normans of France; they renounced their gods for the God of the
Christians; [17] and the dukes of Normandy acknowledged themselves the vassals of the successors of Charlemagne and Capet.
The savage fierceness which they had brought from the snowy
mountains of Norway was refined, without being corrupted, in
a warmer climate; the companions of Rollo insensibly mingled
with the natives; they imbibed the manners, language, [18] and
gallantry of the French nation; and, in a martial age, the
Normans might claim the palm of valour and glorious achievements. Of the fashionable superstitions, they embraced with
ardour the pilgrimages of Rome, Italy, and the Holy Land. In
this active devotion, their minds and bodies were invigorated by
exercise: danger was the incentive, novelty the recompense;
and the prospect of the world was decorated by wonder, credu-

poor Sterne, that it is hard if I may not transcribe with caution what a bishop could
write without scruple !   What if I had translated, ut viris certetis testiculos ampu-
tare, in quibus nostri corporis refocillatio, &c. ?
[16] The original monuments of the Normans in Italy are collected in the vth
volume of Muratori, and among these we may distinguish the poem of William
Apulus (p. 245-278), and the history of Galfridus (*Jeffery*) Malaterra (p. 537-607).
Both were natives of France, but they wrote on the spot, in the age of the first conquerors (before A.D. 1100), and with the spirit of freemen.   It is needless to recapitulate the compilers and critics of Italian history, Sigonius, Baronius, Pagi,
Giannone, Muratori, St. Marc, &c. whom I have always consulted and never copied.
[See Appendix 1.   The best history of the Normans in Italy and Sicily is F.
Chalandon's Histoire de la domination en Italie et en Sicile, 2 vols., 1907.]
[17] Some of the first converts were baptized ten or twelve times, for the sake of
the white garments usually given at this ceremony.   At the funeral of Rollo, the
gifts to monasteries, for the repose of his soul, were accompanied by a sacrifice of
one hundred captives.   But in a generation or two the national change was pure
and general.
[18] The Danish language was still spoken by the Normans of Bayeux on the sea-
coast, at a time (A.D. 940) when it was already forgotten at Rouen, in the court
and capital.   Quem (Richard I.) confestim pater Baiocas mittens Botoni militiæ
suæ principi nutriendum tradidit, ut, ubi *linguâ* eruditus *Danicâ*, suis exterisque
hominibus sciret aperte dare responsa (Wilhelm. Gemeticensis de Ducibus Nor-
mannis, l. iii. c. 8, p. 623, edit. Camden).   Of the vernacular and favourite idiom
of William the Conqueror (A.D. 1035) Selden (Opera, tom. ii. p. 1640-1656) has
given a specimen, obsolete and obscure even to antiquarians and lawyers.

lity, and ambitious hope. They confederated for their mutual defence; and the robbers of the Alps, who had been allured by the garb of a pilgrim, were often chastised by the arm of a warrior. In one of these pious visits [19] to the cavern of mount Garganus in Apulia, which had been sanctified by the apparition of the archangel Michael,[20] they were accosted by a stranger in the Greek habit, but who soon revealed himself as a rebel, a fugitive, and a mortal foe of the Greek empire. His [Melus] name was Melo: [21] a noble citizen of Bari, who, after an unsuccessful revolt, was compelled to seek new allies and avengers of his country. The bold appearance of the Normans revived his hopes and solicited his confidence : they listened to the complaints, and still more to the promises, of the patriot. The assurance of wealth demonstrated the justice of his cause; and they viewed, as the inheritance of the brave, the fruitful land which was oppressed by effeminate tyrants. On their return to Normandy, they kindled a spark of enterprise ; and a small but intrepid band was freely associated for the deliverance of Apulia. They passed the Alps by separate roads, and in the disguise of pilgrims ; but in the neighbourhood of Rome they were saluted by the chief of Bari, who supplied the more indigent with arms [a.d. 1017] and horses, and instantly led them to the field of action. In the first conflict, their valour prevailed ; [22] but, in the second engagement, they were overwhelmed by the numbers and military

[19] [In a.d. 1016, as a Saracen fleet besieged Salerno, 40 Norman knights returning from the Holy Land disembarked in the neighbourhood, and hearing that the place was hard pressed offered their services to Prince Waimar. Their bravery delivered the town, and laden with rich presents they returned to Normandy, promising to induce their countrymen to visit the south and help in the defence of the land against the unbelievers. See Aimé, Ystorie de li Normant, i. c. 17 (and cp. H. Bresslau, Jahrbücher des deutschen Reichs unter Heinrich II., B. iii. Excurs. 4). Before the year was over, a certain Rudolf with his four brothers started to seek their fortune in the south ; when they reached Italy, they came to terms with Melus, the rebel of Bari, through the mediation of the Pope.]
[20] See Leandro Alberti (Descrizione d'Italia, p. 250) and Baronius (a.d. 493, No. 43). If the archangel inherited the temple and oracle, perhaps the cavern, of old Calchas the soothsayer (Strab. Geograph. l. vi. p. 435, 436), the Catholics (on this occasion) have surpassed the Greeks in the elegance of their superstition.
[21] [Melus was the leader of the anti-Greek party in Bari. His first revolt was for a time successful, but was put down in 1010 by the Catepan Basil Mesardonites.]
[22] [There were three battles. Melus and the Normans invaded the Capitanate in 1017. They gained a victory at Arenula on the river Fortore, and a second, more decisive, at Vaccaricia (near Troja). See Heinemann, op. cit., p. 36 (and Appendix). In the following year they suffered the great defeat on the plain of Cannæ, at the hands of the Catepan Basil Bojannes.]

engines of the Greeks, and indignantly retreated with their faces [A.D. 1018]
to the enemy. The unfortunate Melo ended his life, a suppliant [Death of
at the court of Germany : his Norman followers, excluded from A.D. 1020]
their native and their promised land, wandered among the hills
and valleys of Italy, and earned their daily subsistence by the
sword. To that formidable sword the princes of Capua, Beneventum, Salerno, and Naples, alternately appealed in their
domestic quarrels ; the superior spirit and discipline of the
Normans gave victory to the side which they espoused ; and
their cautious policy observed the balance of power, lest the
preponderance of any rival state should render their aid less important and their service less profitable. Their first asylum was
a strong camp in the depth of the marshes of Campania ; but they
were soon endowed by the liberality of the duke of Naples with
a more plentiful and permanent seat. Eight miles from his Founda-
residence, as a bulwark against Capua, the town of Aversa was Aversa.
built and fortified for their use ; [23] and they enjoyed as their own [1030]
the corn and fruits, the meadows and groves, of that fertile district. The report of their success attracted every year new
swarms of pilgrims and soldiers ; the poor were urged by necessity ; the rich were excited by hope ; and the brave and active
spirits of Normandy were impatient of ease and ambitious of
renown. The independent standard of Aversa afforded shelter
and encouragement to the outlaws of the province, to every
fugitive who had escaped from the injustice or justice of his
superiors ; and these foreign associates were quickly assimilated
in manners and language to the Gallic colony. The first
leader of the Normans was count Rainulf ; and, in the origin of
society, pre-eminence of rank is the reward and the proof of
superior merit.[24]

[23] [The settlement was assigned to Rainulf—one of Rudolph's brothers—by Duke
Sergius IV. of Naples. Aversa was founded in 1030 (Heinemann, op. cit., p. 58, note
2). Rainulf married the sister of Sergius, but after her death he deserted the cause
of Naples and went over to the interests of the foe, Pandulf of Capua, married his
niece and became his vassal,—Aversa being disputed territory between Naples and
Capua. But, when the Emperor Conrad visited Southern Italy in 1038, Pandulf was
deposed, and the county of Aversa was united with the principality of Salerno.
This, as Heinemann observes (p. 69), was a political event of the first importance.
The Norman settlement was formally recognized by the Emperor,—taken as it were
under the protection of the Western Empire.]
[24] See the first book of William Appulus. His words are applicable to every
swarm of barbarians and freebooters :

The Normans serve
in Sicily.
A.D. 1038
Since the conquest of Sicily by the Arabs, the Grecian emperors had been anxious to regain that valuable possession; but their efforts, however strenuous, had been opposed by the distance and the sea. Their costly armaments, after a gleam of success, added new pages of calamity and disgrace to the Byzantine annals; twenty thousand of their best troops were lost in a single expedition; and the victorious Moslems derided the policy of a nation, which entrusted eunuchs not only with the custody of their women, but with the command of their men.[25] After a reign of two hundred years, the Saracens were ruined by their divisions.[26] The emir disclaimed the authority of the king of Tunis; the people rose against the emir; the cities were usurped by the chiefs; each meaner rebel was independent in his village or castle; and the weaker of two rival brothers implored the friendship of the Christians.[27] In every service of danger the Normans were prompt and useful: and five hundred *knights*, or warriors on horseback, were enrolled by Arduin, the agent and interpreter of the Greeks, under the standard of [A.D. 1038] Maniaces, governor of Lombardy.[28] Before their landing, the brothers were reconciled; the union of Sicily and Africa were

> Si vicinorum quis *pernitiosus* ad illos
> Confugiebat, eum gratanter suscipiebant;
> Moribus et linguâ quoscumque venire videbant
> Informant propriâ; gens efficiatur ut una.

And elsewhere, of the native adventurers of Normandy:

> Pars parat, exiguæ vel opes aderant quia nullæ;
> Pars, quia de magnis majora subire volebant.

[25] Liutprand in Legatione, p. 485. Pagi has illustrated this event from the Ms. history of the deacon Leo (tom. iv. A.D. 965, No. 17-19).

[26] See the Arabian Chronicle of Sicily, apud Muratori, Script. Rerum Ital. tom. i. p. 253.

[27] [It was the emir Akhal who appealed to the Greeks to help him against his brother, Abū Hafs, who headed the Sicilian rebels. The latter were supported by the Zayrid Sultan of Tunis (Muizz ben Bādīs), and Akhal though he was supported by the Catepan of Italy and a Greek army in 1037 was shut up in Palermo, where he was murdered by his own followers. The statement in the text that "the brothers were reconciled" is misleading; but a prospect of such a reconciliation seems to have induced the Catepan to return to Italy without accomplishing much. Cp. Cedrenus, ii. p. 516; and Heinemann, *op. cit.*, p. 74. Meanwhile preparations had been made in Constantinople for an expedition to recover Sicily; and Maniaces arrived in Apulia and crossed over to the island in 1038.]

[28] [For a personal description of George Maniaces, a Hercules of colossal height (εἰς δέκατον ἀνεστηκὼς πόδα), see Psellus, Hist. p. 137-8 (ed. Sathas). According to Vámbéry the name *Maniakes* is Turkish and means *noble*. His memory survives at Syracuse in the Castel Maniaci, at the south point of Ortygia commanding the entrance to the Great Harbour. Maniaces was accompanied by another famous warrior, Harald Hardrada (brother of King Olaf of Norway), who was slain a quarter of a century later on English soil. Maniaces was the general of the expedition: he was not governor of the Theme of Lombardy.]

restored; and the Island was guarded to the water's edge.
The Normans led the van, and the Arabs of Messina felt the [Capture of Messina]
valour of an untried foe. In a second action, the emir of
Syracuse was unhorsed and transpierced by the *iron arm* of [Battle of Rametta. A.D. 1038]
William of Hauteville. In a third engagement, his intrepid
companions discomfited the host of sixty thousand Saracens, and [Battle of Troina. A.D. 1039]
left the Greeks no more than the labour of the pursuit: a
splendid victory; but of which the pen of the historian may
divide the merit with the lance of the Normans. It is, however, true that they essentially promoted the success of Maniaces,
who reduced thirteen cities, and the greater part of Sicily, under
the obedience of the emperor. But his military fame was
sullied by ingratitude and tyranny. In the division of the spoil
the deserts of his brave auxiliaries were forgotten; and neither
their avarice nor their pride could brook this injurious treatment.
They complained by the mouth of their interpreter; their
complaint was disregarded; their interpreter was scourged; the
sufferings were *his*; the insult and resentment belonged to *those*
whose sentiments he had delivered. Yet they dissembled till
they had obtained, or stolen, a safe passage to the Italian continent; their brethren of Aversa sympathized in their indignation, and the province of Apulia was invaded as the forfeit of
the debt.[29] Above twenty years after the first emigration, the [Their conquest of Apulia. A.D. 1040-1043]
Normans took the field with no more than seven hundred horse
and five hundred foot; and, after the recall of the Byzantine
legions[30] from the Sicilian war, their numbers are magnified to
the amount of threescore thousand men. Their herald proposed
the option of battle or retreat; "Of battle," was the unanimous
cry of the Normans; and one of their stoutest warriors, with a
stroke of his fist, felled to the ground the horse of the Greek

---

[29] Jeffrey Malaterra, who relates the Sicilian war and the conquest of Apulia
(l. i. c. 7, 8, 9, 19). The same events are described by Cedrenus (tom. ii. p. 741-
743, 755, 756) and Zonaras (tom. ii. p. 237, 238); and the Greeks are so hardened
to disgrace that their narratives are impartial enough.

[30] Cedrenus specifies the τάγμα of the Obsequium (Phrygia) and the μέρος of the
Thracesians (Lydia; consult Constantine de Thematibus, i. 3, 4, with Delisle's
map), and afterwards names the Pisidians and Lycaonians with the foederati.
The Normans under Rainulf were acting in common with, and at the instigation
of, the Lombard Arduin. They seized Melfi while the Catepan Michael Doceanus
was in Sicily seeking to retrieve the losses which the Greek cause had suffered since
the recall of Maniaces. From Melfi they conquered Ascoli and other places, and
Michael was forced to return to Italy. All this happened in A.D. 1040. Heinemann, *op. cit.*, p. 84.]

messenger.   He was dismissed with a fresh horse; the insult was concealed from the Imperial troops; but in two successive [A.D. 1041] battles [31] they were more fatally instructed of the prowess of their adversaries. In the plains of Cannæ, the Asiatics fled [May 4] from the adventurers of France; the Duke of Lombardy was made prisoner; the Apulians acquiesced in a new dominion; and the four places of Bari, Otranto, Brundusium, and Tarentum were alone saved in the shipwreck of the Grecian fortunes. From this æra, we may date the establishment of the Norman power, which soon eclipsed the infant colony of Aversa. Twelve counts [32] were chosen by the popular suffrage ; and age, birth, and merit were the motives of their choice. The tributes of their peculiar districts were appropriated to their use; and each count erected a fortress in the midst of his lands, and at the head of his vassals.   In the centre of the province, the common habitation of Melphi was reserved as the metropolis and citadel of the republic; an house and separate quarter was allotted to each of the twelve counts; and the national concerns were regulated by this military senate.   The first of his peers, their president and general, was entitled count of Apulia; and this [A.D. 1042] dignity was conferred on William of the Iron Arm, who, in the language of the age, is styled a lion in battle, a lamb in society, and an angel in council.[33]   The manners of his countrymen are

[31] [(1) On the Olivento (a tributary of the Ofanto), March 17, (2) near Monte Maggiore, in the plain of Cannæ, May 4, and (3) at Montepeloso, Sept. 3, 1041. See Heinemann, *op. cit.*, p. 358-61.]

[32] Omnes conveniunt ; et bis sex nobiliores,
Quos genus et gravitas morum decorabat et ætas,
Elegere duces.   Provectis ad comitatum
His alii parent.   Comitatus nomen honoris
Quo donantur erat.   Hi totas undique terras
Divisere sibi, ni sors inimica repugnet ;
Singula proponunt loca quæ contingere sorte
Cuique duci debent, et quæque tributa locorum.
And, after speaking of Melphi, William Appulus adds,
Pro numero comitum bis sex statuere plateas,
Atque domus comitum totidem fabricantur in urbe.
Leo Ostiensis (l. ii. c. 67) enumerates the divisions of the Apulian cities, which it is needless to repeat.

[33] Gulielm. Appulus, l. ii. c. 12, according to the reference of Giannone (Istoria Civile di Napoli, tom. ii. p. 31), which I cannot verify in the original.   The Apulian praises indeed his *validas vires, probitas animi*, and *vivida virtus ;* and declares that, had he lived, no poet could have equalled his merits (l. i. p. 258, l. ii. p. 259). He was bewailed by the Normans, quippe qui tanti consilii virum (says Malaterra, l. i. c. 12, p. 552) tam armis strenuum, tam sibi munificum, affabilem, morigeratum, ulterius se habere diffidebant.   [Having elected William, the Normans placed themselves under the suzerainty of Waimar of Salerno, who assumed the title of

fairly delineated by a contemporary and national historian.[34]
"The Normans," says Malaterra, "are a cunning and revengeful Character of the Normans people; eloquence and dissimulation appear to be their heredi- tary qualities: they can stoop to flatter; but, unless they are curbed by the restraint of law, they indulge the licentiousness of nature and passion.　Their princes affect the praise of popular munificence; the people observe the medium, or rather blend the extremes, of avarice and prodigality; and, in their eager thirst of wealth and dominion, they despise whatever they possess, and hope whatever they desire.　Arms and horses, the luxury of dress, the exercises of hunting and hawking,[35] are the delight of the Normans; but on pressing occasions they can endure with incredible patience the inclemency of every climate and the toil and abstinence of a military life."[36]

The Normans of Apulia were seated on the verge of the two Oppression of Apulia. A.D. 1046, &c. empires; and, according to the policy of the hour, they accepted the investiture of their lands from the sovereigns of Germany or Constantinople.[37]　But the firmest title of these adventurers was the right of conquest: they neither loved nor trusted; they were neither trusted nor beloved; the contempt of the princes was mixed with fear, and the fear of the natives was mingled with hatred and resentment.　Every object of desire, an horse, a woman, a garden, tempted and gratified the rapaciousness of

Prince of Apulia and Calabria.　William, Rainulf, and Waimar then proceeded to Melfi and divided the conquests.　Rainulf received, as an honorary present, Siponto and Mount Garganus; William got Ascoli; his brother, Drogo, Venosa, &c. &c., Aimé, Ystorie de li Normant, ii. 29, 30.　The extent of the Norman conquest in this first stage corresponds (Heinemann observes, p. 94) to the towns in the regions of the rivers Ofanto and Bradano.　"The valleys of these rivers were the natural roads to penetrate from Melfi eastward and southward into Greek territory."]

[34] The gens astutissima, injuriarum ultrix . . . adulari sciens . . . eloquentiis inserviens, of Malaterra (l. i. c. 3, p. 550) are expressive of the popular and pro- verbial character of the Normans.

[35] The hunting and hawking more properly belong to the descendants of the Norwegian sailors; though they might import from Norway and Iceland the finest casts of falcons.

[36] We may compare this portrait with that of William of Malmsbury (de Gestis Anglorum, l. iii. p. 101, 102), who appreciates, like a philosophic historian, the vices and virtues of the Saxons and Normans.　England was assuredly a gainer by the conquest.

[37] [The visit of the Emperor Henry III. to southern Italy in A.D. 1047 was of special importance.　He restored to Pandulf the principality of Capua, which Conrad II. had transferred to Waimar of Salerno.　Waimar had to resign his title of Prince of Apulia and Calabria, and his suzerainty over the Normans; while the Norman princes, Rainulf of Aversa and Drogo (William's successor), Count of Apulia, were elevated to be immediate vassals of the Empire.]

the strangers ; [38] and the avarice of their chiefs was only coloured by the more specious names of ambition and glory.   The twelve counts were sometimes joined in a league of injustice : in their domestic quarrels, they disputed the spoils of the people; the virtues of William were buried in his grave; and Drogo, his brother and successor, was better qualified to lead the valour, than to restrain the violence, of his peers.   Under the reign of Constantine Monomachus, the policy, rather than benevolence, of the Byzantine court attempted to relieve Italy from this adherent mischief, more grievous than a flight of barbarians ; [39] and Argyrus, the son of Melo, was invested for this purpose with the most lofty titles [40] and the most ample commission.   The memory of his father might recommend him to the Normans ; and he had already engaged their voluntary service to quell the revolt of Maniaces, and to avenge their own and the public injury.   It was the design of Constantine to transplant this warlike colony from the Italian provinces to the Persian war ; and the son of Melo distributed among the chiefs the gold and manufactures of Greece, as the first fruits of the Imperial bounty.   But his arts were baffled by the sense and spirit of the conquerors of Apulia : his gifts, or at least his proposals, were rejected ; and they unanimously refused to relinquish their possessions and their hopes for the distant prospect of Asiatic fortune.   After the means of persuasion had failed, Argyrus resolved to compel or to destroy : the Latin powers were solicited against the common enemy ; and an offensive alliance was formed of the pope and the two emperors of the East and West.   The throne of St. Peter was occupied by Leo

League of the pope and the two empires. A.D. 1049-1054

---

[38] The biographer of St. Leo IX. pours his holy venom on the Normans.   Videns indisciplinatam et alienam gentem Normannorum, crudeli et inauditâ rabie, et plusquam Paganâ impietate, adversus ecclesias Dei insurgere, passim Christianos trucidare, &c. (Wibert, c. 6).   The honest Apulian (l. ii. p. 259) says calmly of their accuser, Veris commiscens fallacia.

[39] The policy of the Greeks, revolt of Maniaces, &c. must be collected from Cedrenus (tom. ii. p. 757, 758), William Appulus (l. i. p. 257, 258, l. ii. p. 259), and the two chronicles of Bari, by Lupus Protospata (Muratori, Script. Ital. tom. v. p. 42, 43, 44), and an anonymous writer (Antiquitat. Italiæ medii Ævi, tom. i. p. 31-35). [This anonymous chronicle, called the Annales Barenses, compiled before A.D. 1071, is printed in Pertz, Mon. Germ. Hist. v. p. 51-56, with the corresponding text of " Lupus " opposite.]   This last is a fragment of some value.

[40] Argyrus received, says the anonymous Chronicle of Bari, Imperial letters, Fœderatus et Patriciatus, et Catapani et Vestatus.   In his annals, Muratori (tom. viii. p. 426) very properly reads, or interprets, Sevestatus, the title of Sebastos or Augustus.   But in his Antiquities, he was taught by Ducange to make it a palatine office, master of the wardrobe.

the Ninth, a simple saint,[41] of a temper most apt to deceive himself and the world, and whose venerable character would consecrate with the name of piety the measures least compatible with the practice of religion. His humanity was affected by the complaints, perhaps the calumnies, of an injured people; the impious Normans had interrupted the payment of tithes; and the temporal sword might be lawfully unsheathed against the sacrilegious robbers, who were deaf to the censures of the church. As a German of noble birth and royal kindred, Leo had free access to the court and confidence of the emperor Henry the Third; and in search of arms and allies his ardent zeal transported him from Apulia to Saxony, from the Elbe to the Tiber. During these hostile preparations, Argyrus indulged himself in the use of secret and guilty weapons; a crowd of Normans became the victims of public or private revenge; and the valiant Drogo was murdered in a church. But his spirit A.D. 1051 survived in his brother Humphrey, the third count of Apulia. The assassins were chastised; and the son of Melo, overthrown and wounded, was driven from the field to hide his shame behind the walls of Bari, and to await the tardy succour of his allies.

But the power of Constantine was distracted by a Turkish Expedition war; the mind of Henry was feeble and irresolute; and the of pope Leo IX. pope, instead of passing the Alps with a German army, was ac- against the companied only by a guard of seven hundred Swabians and Normans. A.D. 1053 some volunteers of Lorraine. In his long progress from Mantua to Beneventum, a vile and promiscuous multitude of Italians was enlisted under the holy standard;[42] the priest and the robber slept in the same tent; the pikes and crosses were intermingled in the front; and the natural saint repeated the lessons of his youth in the order of march, of encampment, and of combat. The Normans of Apulia could muster in the field no more

---

[41] A life of St. Leo IX., deeply tinged with the passions and prejudices of the age, has been composed by Wibert, printed at Paris, 1615, in octavo, and since inserted in the Collections of the Bollandists, of Mabillon, and of Muratori. [J. May, Untersuchungen über die Abfassungszeit und Glaubwürdigkeit von Wiberts Vita Leonis IX. (Offenburg, 1889).] The public and private history of that pope is diligently treated by M. de St. Marc (Abrégé, tom. ii. p. 140-210, and p. 25-95, second column).

[42] See the expedition of Leo IX. against the Normans. See William Appulus (l. ii. p. 259-261) and Jeffrey Malaterra (l. i. c. 13, 14, 15, p. 253) [and Aimé, iii. c. 40]. They are impartial, as the national is counterbalanced by the clerical prejudice. [For details, cp. Heinemann, op. cit., Appendix, p. 366 sqq.].

than three thousand horse, with an handful of infantry; the defection of the natives intercepted their provisions and retreat; and their spirit, incapable of fear, was chilled for a moment by superstitious awe. On the hostile approach of Leo, they knelt without disgrace or reluctance before their spiritual father. But the pope was inexorable; his lofty Germans affected to deride the diminutive stature of their adversaries; and the Normans were informed that death or exile was their only alternative. Flight they disdained, and, as many of them had been three days without tasting food, they embraced the assurance of a more easy and honourable death. They climbed [Battle of Civitate] the hill of Civitella, descended into the plain, and charged in three divisions the army of the pope. On the left and in the His defeat and captivity. June 18 centre, Richard count of Aversa, and Robert the famous Guiscard, attacked, broke, routed, and pursued the Italian multitudes, who fought without discipline and fled without shame. A harder trial was reserved for the valour of count Humphrey, who led the cavalry of the right wing. The Germans [43] have been described as unskilful in the management of the horse and lance; but on foot they formed a strong and impenetrable phalanx; and neither man nor steed nor armour could resist the weight of their long and two-handed swords. After a severe conflict, they were encompassed by the squadrons returning from the pursuit; and died in their ranks with the esteem of their foes and the satisfaction of revenge. The gates of Civitella were shut against the flying pope, and he was overtaken by the pious conquerors, who kissed his feet, to implore his blessing and the absolution of their sinful victory. The soldiers beheld in their enemy and captive the vicar of Christ; and, though we may suppose the policy of the chiefs, it is probable that they were infected by the popular superstition. In the calm of retirement, the well-meaning pope deplored the effusion of Christian blood, which must be imputed to his account; he felt, that he had been the author of sin and

---

[43] Teutonici, quia cæsaries et forma decoros
Fecerat egregia proceri corporis illos,
Corpora derident Normannica, quæ breviora
Esse videbantur.
The verses of the Apulian are commonly in this strain, though he heats himself a little in the battle. Two of his similes from hawking and sorcery are descriptive of manners.

scandal; and, as his undertaking had failed, the indecency of his military character was universally condemned.[44] With these dispositions, he listened to the offers of a beneficial treaty;[45] deserted an alliance which he had preached as the cause of God; and ratified the past and future conquests of the Normans. By whatever hands they had been usurped, the provinces of Apulia and Calabria were a part of the donation of Constantine and the patrimony of St. Peter; the grant and the acceptance confirmed the mutual claims of the pontiff and the adventurers. They promised to support each other with spiritual and temporal arms; a tribute or quit-rent of twelvepence was afterwards stipulated for every plough-land; and since this memorable transaction the kingdom of Naples has remained above seven hundred years a fief of the Holy See.[46]

The pedigree of Robert Guiscard[47] is variously deduced from the peasants and the dukes of Normandy: from the peasants, by the pride and ignorance of a Grecian princess;[48] from the

Origin of the papal investiture to the Normans

Birth and character of Robert Guiscard. A.D. 1020-1085

---

[44] Several respectable censures or complaints produced by M. de St. Marc (tom. ii. p. 200-204). As Peter Damianus, the oracle of the times, had denied the popes the right of making war, the hermit (lugens eremi incola) is arraigned by the cardinal, and Baronius (Annal. Eccles. A.D. 1053, No. 10-17) most strenuously asserts the two swords of St. Peter.

[45] [We have no contemporary evidence for the conditions which the Normans imposed on Leo, whom they detained in Beneventum. Heinemann thinks it probable (p. 143) that they required him to renounce the papal pretentions to sovereignty over territory in Apulia and Calabria, and to abandon his alliance with the Eastern Emperor. Leo, unable to bring himself to consent, remained at Beneventum till March, 1054; a severe illness (which proved fatal) filled him with a desire to return to Rome and induced him to consent to some at least of the Norman demands. Cp. Chalandon, op. cit., i. 142. He died on April 19. During his sojourn at Beneventum, he was engaged on a correspondence in connexion with the ecclesiastical quarrel—the final breach—with the Greek Church (see below, cap. lx.).]

[46] The origin and nature of the papal investitures are ably discussed by Giannone (Istoria Civile di Napoli, tom. ii. p. 37-49, 57-66) as a lawyer and antiquarian. Yet he vainly strives to reconcile the duties of patriot and Catholic, adopts an empty distinction of "Ecclesia Romana non dedit sed accepit," and shrinks from an honest but dangerous confession of the truth.

[47] The birth, character, and first actions of Robert Guiscard may be found in Jeffrey Malaterra (l. i. c. 3, 4, 11, 16, 17, 18, 38, 39, 40), William Appulus (l. ii. p. 260-262), William Gemeticensis or of Jumiegès (l. xi. c. 30, p. 663, 664, edit. Camden), and Anna Comnena (Alexiad. l. i. p. 23-27 [c. 10, 11], l. vi. p. 165, 166), with the annotations of Ducange (Not. in Alexiad. p. 230-232, 320), who has swept all the French and Latin Chronicles for supplemental intelligence.

[48] Ὁ δὲ Ῥομπέρτος (a Greek corruption [μπ is the regular symbol for the b sound in mediæval and modern Greek; β would represent v]) οὗτος ἦν Νορμάννος τὸ γένος, τὴν τύχην ἄσημος [i. c. 10]. . . . Again, ἐξ ἀφανοῦς πάνυ τύχης περιφανές. And elsewhere (l. iv. p. 84 [c. 1]), ἀπὸ ἐσχάτης πενίας καὶ τύχης ἀφανοῦς. Anna Comnena was born in the purple; yet her father was no more than a private though illustrious subject, who raised himself to the empire.

dukes by the ignorance and flattery of the Italian subjects.[49] His genuine descent may be ascribed to the second or middle order of private nobility.[50] He sprang from a race of *valvassors* or *bannerets* of the diocese of the Coutances, in the lower Normandy; the castle of Hauteville was their honourable seat; his father Tancred was conspicuous in the court and army of the duke; and his military service was furnished by ten soldiers or knights. Two marriages, of a rank not unworthy of his own, made him the father of twelve sons, who were educated at home by the impartial tenderness of his second wife. But a narrow patrimony was insufficient for this numerous and daring progeny; they saw around the neighbourhood the mischiefs of poverty and discord, and resolved to seek in foreign wars a more glorious inheritance. Two only remained to perpetuate the race and cherish their father's age; their ten brothers, as they successively attained the vigour of manhood, departed from the castle, passed the Alps, and joined the Apulian camp of the Normans. The elder were prompted by native spirit; their success encouraged their younger brethren; and the three first in seniority, William, Drogo, and Humphrey, deserved to be the chiefs of their nation, and the founders of the new republic. Robert was the eldest of the seven sons of the second marriage; and even the reluctant praise of his foes has endowed him with the heroic qualities of a soldier and a statesman. His lofty stature surpassed the tallest of his army; his limbs were cast in the true proportion of strength and gracefulness; and to the decline of life he maintained the patient vigour of health and the commanding dignity of his form. His complexion was ruddy, his shoulders were broad, his hair and beard were long and of a flaxen colour, his eyes sparkled with fire, and his voice, like that of Achilles, could impress obedience and terror amidst the tumult of battle. In the ruder ages of chivalry, such qualifications are not below the

[49] Giannone (tom. ii. p. 2) forgets all his original authors, and rests this princely descent on the credit of Inveges, an Augustine monk of Palermo, in the last century. They continue the succession of dukes from Rollo to William II. the Bastard or Conqueror, whom they hold (communemente si tiene) to be the father of Tancred of Hauteville; a most strange and stupendous blunder! The sons of Tancred fought in Apulia, before William II. was three years old (A.D. 1037).

[50] The judgment of Ducange is just and moderate: Certe humilis fuit ac tenuis Roberti familia, si ducalem et regium spectemus apicem, ad quem postea pervenit; quæ honesta tamen et præter nobilium vulgarium statum et conditionem illustris habita est, "quæ nec humi reperet nec altum quid tumeret" (Wilhelm Malmsbur. de Gestis Anglorum, l. iii. p. 107; Not. ad Alexiad. p. 230).

notice of the poet or historian; they may observe that Robert,
at once, and with equal dexterity, could wield in the right hand
his sword, his lance in the left; that in the battle of Civitella,
he was thrice unhorsed; and that in the close of that memorable
day he was adjudged to have borne away the prize of valour
from the warriors of the two armies.[51] His boundless ambition
was founded on the consciousness of superior worth; in the pursuit of greatness, he was never arrested by the scruples of justice
and seldom moved by the feelings of humanity; though not
insensible of fame, the choice of open or clandestine means was
determined only by his present advantage. The surname of
Guiscard[52] was applied to this master of political wisdom, which
is too often confounded with the practice of dissimulation and
deceit; and Robert is praised by the Apulian poet for excelling
the cunning of Ulysses and the eloquence of Cicero. Yet these
arts were disguised by an appearance of military frankness :
in his highest fortune, he was accessible and courteous to his
fellow-soldiers; and, while he indulged the prejudices of his new
subjects, he affected in his dress and manners to maintain the
ancient fashion of his country. He grasped with a rapacious,
that he might distribute with a liberal, hand; his primitive in-
digence had taught the habits of frugality; the gain of a
merchant was not below his attention; and his prisoners were
tortured with slow and unfeeling cruelty to force a discovery of
their secret treasure. According to the Greeks, he departed [c. a.d. 1046]
from Normandy with only five followers on horseback and thirty
on foot; yet even this allowance appears too bountiful; the
sixth son of Tancred of Hauteville passed the Alps as a pilgrim ;
and his first military band was levied among the adventurers of

---

[51] I shall quote with pleasure some of the best lines of the Apulian (l. ii. p.
270).

Pugnat utrâque manû, nec lancea cassa nec ensis
Cassus erat, quocunque manu deducere vellet.
Ter dejectus equo, ter viribus ipse resumptis,
Major in arma redit ; stimulos furor ipse ministrat.
Ut Leo cum frendens, &c.

. . . .
Nullus in hoc bello sicuti post bella probatum est
Victor vel victus, tam magnos edidit ictus.

[52] The Norman writers and editors most conversant with their own idiom inter-
pret *Guiscard*, or *Wiscard*, by *Callidus*, a cunning man. The root (*wise*) is familiar
to our ear ; and in the old word *Wiseacre* I can discern something of a similar
sense and termination. Τὴν ψυχὴν πανουργότατος is no bad translation of the
surname and character of Robert.

Italy. His brothers and countrymen had divided the fertile lands of Apulia; but they guarded their shares with the jealousy of avarice; the aspiring youth was driven forwards to the mountains of Calabria, and in his first exploits against the Greeks and the natives it is not easy to discriminate the hero from the robber. To surprise a castle or a convent, to ensnare a wealthy citizen, to plunder the adjacent villages for necessary food, were the obscure labours which formed and exercised the powers of his mind and body. The volunteers of Normandy adhered to his standard ; and, under his command, the peasants of Calabria assumed the name and character of Normans.

His ambition and success. A.D. 1054-1080   As the genius of Robert expanded with his fortune, he awakened the jealousy of his elder brother, by whom, in a transient quarrel, his life was threatened and his liberty restrained. After the death of Humphrey, the tender age of his sons excluded them from the command ; they were reduced to a private estate by the ambition of their guardian and uncle; [A.D. 1057] and Guiscard was exalted on a buckler, and saluted count of Apulia and general of the republic. With an increase of authority and of force, he resumed the conquest of Calabria, and soon aspired to a rank that should raise him for ever above the heads of his equals. By some acts of rapine or sacrilege he had incurred a papal excommunication : but Nicholas the Second was easily persuaded that the divisions of friends could terminate only in their mutual prejudice; that the Normans were the faithful champions of the Holy See; and it was safer to trust [Synod of Melfi. A.D. 1059, August 23] the alliance of a prince than the caprice of an aristocracy. A synod of one hundred bishops was convened at Melphi; and the count interrupted an important enterprise to guard the person and execute the decrees of the Roman pontiff. His gratitude and policy conferred on Robert and his posterity the ducal title,[53] with the investiture of Apulia, Calabria, and all the lands, both in Italy and Sicily, which his sword could rescue from the schismatic Greeks and the unbelieving Saracens.[54] This apostolic

---

[53] The acquisition of the ducal title by Robert Guiscard is a nice and obscure business. With the good advice of Giannone, Muratori, and St. Marc, I have endeavoured to form a consistent and probable narrative.

[54] Baronius (Annal. Eccles. A.D. 1059, No. 69) has published the original act. He professes to have copied it from the *Liber Censuum*, a Vatican Ms. Yet a Liber Censuum of the twelfth century has been printed by Muratori (Antiquit. medii Ævi, tom. v. p. 851-908), and the names of Vatican and Cardinal awaken the sus-

sanction might justify his arms ; but the obedience of a free and victorious people could not be transferred without their consent ; and Guiscard dissembled his elevation till the ensuing campaign had been illustrated by the conquest of Consenza and Reggio. In the hour of triumph, he assembled his troops, and solicited the Normans to confirm by their suffrage the judgment of the vicar of Christ ; the soldiers hailed with joyful acclamations their valiant duke ; and the counts, his former equals, pronounced the oath of fidelity, with hollow smiles and secret indignation. After this inauguration, Robert styled himself, " By the grace of God and St. Peter, duke of Apulia, Calabria, and hereafter of Sicily " ; and it was the labour of twenty years to deserve and realise these lofty appellations. Such tardy progress, in a narrow space, may seem unworthy of the abilities of the chief and the spirit of the nation ; but the Normans were few in number ; their resources were scanty ; their service was voluntary and precarious. The bravest designs of the Duke were sometimes opposed by the free voice of his parliament of barons ; the twelve counts of popular election conspired against his authority ; and against their perfidious uncle the sons of Humphrey demanded justice and revenge. By his policy and vigour, Guiscard discovered their plots, suppressed their rebellions, and punished the guilty with death or exile ; but in these domestic feuds his years, and the national strength, were unprofitably consumed. After the defeat of his foreign enemies, the Greeks, Lombards, and Saracens, their broken forces retreated to the strong and populous cities of the sea coast. They excelled in the arts of fortification and defence ; the Normans were accustomed to serve on horseback in the field, and their rude attempts could only succeed by the efforts of persevering courage. The resistance of Salerno was maintained above eight months ; the siege or blockade of Bari lasted near four years.[55] In these actions the Norman duke was the foremost in every danger ; in every fatigue the last and most patient. As he pressed the

[Duke of Apulia. A.D. 1060]

[May-Dec. A.D. 1076]
[A.D. 1068-71]

picions of a Protestant, and even of a philosopher. [The Liber Censuum, composed at the end of the 12th century (1192), contains the rent-roll of the Roman Church and various original documents, and the Lives of Popes beginning with Leo IX. The oldest Ms. does not contain the Lives. Muratori printed the whole compilation in Scr. Rer. Ital., 3, 1, p. 277 *sqq.* ; the edition in the Ant. Med. Æv. does not include the Lives.]

[55] [Not so long : August, 1068—April, 1071. The best source for the siege is Aimé, v. 27. Immediately before he laid siege to Bari, Robert captured Otranto.]

citadel of Salerno, an huge stone from the rampart shattered one of his military engines; and by a splinter he was wounded in the breast.   Before the gates of Bari, he lodged in a miserable hut or barrack, composed of dry branches, and thatched with straw : a perilous station, on all sides open to the inclemency of the winter and the spears of the enemy.[56]

His Italian conquests   The Italian conquests of Robert correspond with the limits of the present kingdom of Naples ; and the countries united by his arms have not been dissevered by the revolutions of seven hundred years.[57]   The monarchy has been composed of the Greek provinces Calabria and Apulia, of the Lombard principality of Salerno, the Republic of Amalphi,[58] and the inland dependencies of the large and ancient duchy of Beneventum. Three districts only were exempted from the common law of subjection : the first for ever, and the two last till the middle of the succeeding century.   The city and immediate territory of Benevento had been transferred, by gift or exchange, from the German emperor to the Roman pontiff; and, although this holy land was sometimes invaded, the name of St. Peter was finally more potent than the sword of the Normans.   Their first colony of Aversa subdued and held the state of Capua ; and her princes were reduced to beg their bread before the palace of their fathers. The dukes of Naples, the present metropolis, maintained the popular freedom, under the shadow of the Byzantine empire. Among the new acquisitions of Guiscard, the science of Salerno,[59] and the trade of Amalphi,[60] may detain for a moment the curiosity of the reader.   I.   Of the learned faculties jurisprudence

School of Salerno

[56] Read the life of Guiscard in the second and third books of the Apulian, the first and second books of Malaterra.
[57] The conquests of Robert Guiscard and Roger I., the exemption of Benevento and the twelve provinces of the kingdom, are fairly exposed by Giannone in the second volume of his Istoria Civile, l. ix., x., xi. and l. xvii. p. 460-470.   This modern division was not established before the time of Frederic II.
[58] [Amalfi acknowledged the lordship of Robert (" Duke of Amalfi ") from A.D. 1073.   Cp. Heinemann, op. cit., p. 268.]
[59] Giannone (tom. ii. p. 119-127), Muratori (Antiquitat. medii Ævi, tom. iii. dissert. xliv. p. 935, 936), and Tiraboschi (Istoria della Letteratura Italiana) have given an historical account of these physicians ; their medical knowledge and practice must be left to our physicians.
[60] At the end of the Historia Pandectarum of Henry Brenckmann (Trajecti ad Rhenum, 1722, in 4to), the indefatigable author has inserted two dissertations, de Republicâ Amalphitanâ, and de Amalphi a Pisanis direptâ, which are built on the testimonies of one hundred and forty writers.   Yet he has forgotten two most important passages of the embassy of Liutprand (A.D. 969), which compare the trade and navigation of Amalphi with that of Venice.

implies the previous establishment of laws and property; and theology may perhaps be superseded by the full light of religion and reason. But the savage and the sage must alike implore the assistance of physic; and, if *our* diseases are inflamed by luxury, the mischiefs of blows and wounds would be more frequent in the ruder ages of society. The treasures of Grecian medicine had been communicated to the Arabian colonies of Africa, Spain, and Sicily; and in the intercourse of peace and war a spark of knowledge had been kindled and cherished at Salerno, an illustrious city, in which the men were honest and the women beautiful.[61] A school, the first that arose in the darkness of Europe, was consecrated to the healing art;[62] the conscience of monks and bishops were reconciled to that salutary and lucrative profession; and a crowd of patients, of the most eminent rank and most distant climates, invited or visited the physicians of Salerno. They were protected by the Norman conquerors; and Guiscard, though bred in arms, could discern the merit and value of a philosopher. After a pilgrimage of thirty-nine years, Constantine, an African Christian, returned from Bagdad, a master of the language and learning of the Arabians; and Salerno was enriched by the practice, the lessons and the writings, of the pupil of Avicenna. The school of medicine has long slept in the name of an university;[63] but her

[61] Urbs Latii non est hâc delitiosior urbe,
Frugibus arboribus vinoque redundat; et unde
Non tibi poma, nuces, non pulchra palatia desunt,
Non species muliebris abest probitasque virorum.
(Gulielmus Appulus, l. iii. p. 267.)
[It has been commonly maintained that the medical school of Salerno owed its rise and development to Arabic influence. This view seems to be mistaken; documents published in De Renzi's *Collectio Salernitana* (1852) seem decidedly against it. See Rashdall's Universities in the Middle Ages, vol. i. p. 78 (chap. 3, p. 75 *sqq.* is devoted to Salerno). Rashdall is inclined to connect the revival of medical science in the 11th century at Salerno with the survival of the Greek language in those regions. Salerno went back to Hippocrates independently of Arabia; and it was when the Arabic methods in medicine became popular in the 13th century that the Salerno school declined.]

[62] [At the beginning of the 12th cent. Ordericus Vitalis describes the medical school of Salerno as existing *ab antiquo tempore* (Hist. Ecc. ii. Bk. 3, 11 in Migne, Patr. Lat., vol. 188, p. 260); see Rashdall, p. 77. The place was famous for its physicians in the 10th cent., and we have works of medical writers of Salerno from the early part of the 11th (*e.g.*, Gariopontus). The fullest account of the school is De Renzi's Storia documentata della scuola medica di Salerno. The school was first recognized by Frederick II., whose edict in 1231 appointed it as the examining body for candidates who desired to obtain the royal licence which he made compulsory for the practice of medicine.]

[63] [It was a school of doctors, in no way resembling a university. As Rashdall observes (*loc. cit.*, p. 82): "Salerno remains a completely isolated factor in the

precepts are abridged in a string of aphorisms, bound together in the Leonine verses, or Latin rhymes, of the twelfth century.[64]

Trade of Amalphi

II. Seven miles to the west of Salerno, and thirty to the south of Naples, the obscure town of Amalphi displayed the power and rewards of industry. The land, however fertile, was of narrow extent; but the sea was accessible and open; the inhabitants first assumed the office of supplying the western world with the manufactures and productions of the East; and this useful traffic was the source of their opulence and freedom. The government was popular under the administration of a duke and the supremacy of the Greek emperor. Fifty thousand citizens were numbered in the walls of Amalphi; nor was any city more abundantly provided with gold, silver, and the objects of precious luxury. The mariners who swarmed in her port excelled in the theory and practice of navigation and astronomy; and the discovery of the compass, which has opened the globe, is due to their ingenuity or good fortune. Their trade was extended to the coasts, or at least to the commodities, of Africa, Arabia, and India; and their settlements in Constantinople, Antioch, Jerusalem, and Alexandria acquired the privileges of independent colonies.[65] After three hundred years of prosperity, Amalphi was oppressed by the arms of the Normans, and sacked by the jealousy of Pisa; but the poverty of one thousand fisher-

academic polity of the Middle Ages. While its position as a school of medicine was, for two centuries at least, as unique as that of Paris in Theology and that of Bologna in Law, while throughout the Middle Ages no school of medicine except Montpellier rivalled its fame, it remained without influence in the development of Academic institutions."]

[64] Muratori carries their antiquity above the year (1066) of the death of Edward the Confessor, the *rex Anglorum* to whom they are addressed. Nor is this date affected by the opinion, or rather mistake, of Pasquier (Recherches de la France, l. vii. c. 2) and Ducange (Glossar. Latin.). The practice of rhyming, as early as the seventh century, was borrowed from the languages of the North and East (Muratori, Antiquitat. tom. iii. dissert. xl. p. 686-708). [Constantine translated the Aphorisms of Hippocrates from the Arabic version, c. A.D. 1080.]

[65] The description of Amalphi, by William the Apulian (l. iii. p. 267), contains much truth and some poetry; and the third line may be applied to the sailor's compass:

Nulla magis locuples argento, vestibus, auro
Partibus innumeris; hâc plurimus urbe moratur
Nauta *maris cælique vias aperire peritus.*
Huc et Alexandri diversa feruntur ab urbe
Regis, et Antiochi. Gens hæc freta plurima transit.
His [hio] Arabes, Indi, Siculi nascuntur et Afri.
Hæc gens est totum prope nobilitata per orbem,
Et mercanda ferens, et amans mercata referre.

men is yet dignified by the remains of an arsenal, a cathedral, and the palaces of royal merchants.

Roger, the twelfth and last of the sons of Tancred, had been long detained in Normandy by his own and his father's age. He accepted the welcome summons; hastened to the Apulian camp; and deserved at first the esteem, and afterwards the envy, of his elder brother.   Their valour and ambition were equal; but the youth, the beauty, the elegant manners, of Roger engaged the disinterested love of his soldiers and people.   So scanty was his allowance, for himself and forty followers, that he descended from conquest to robbery, and from robbery to domestic theft; and so loose were the notions of property that, by his own historian, at his special command, he is accused of stealing horses from a stable at Melphi.[66]   His spirit emerged from poverty and disgrace; from these base practices he rose to the merit and glory of a holy war; and the invasion of Sicily was seconded by the zeal and policy of his brother Guiscard.   After the retreat of the Greeks, the *idolaters*, a most audacious reproach of the Catholics, had retrieved their losses and possessions; but the deliverance of the island, so vainly undertaken by the forces of the Eastern empire, was achieved by a small and private band of adventurers. [67]   In the first attempt Roger braved, in an open boat, the real and fabulous dangers of Scylla and Charybdis; landed with only sixty soldiers on a hostile shore; drove the Saracens to the gates of Messina; and safely returned with the spoils of the adjacent country.   In the fortress of Trani, his active and patient courage were equally conspicuous.   In his old age he related with pleasure, that, by the distress of the

Marginal notes: Conquest of Sicily by count Roger. A.D. 1060-1090 — [A.D. 1060] — [Troina] — [A.D. 1062]

---

[66] Latrocinio armigerorum suorum in multis sustentabatur, quod quidem ad ejus ignominiam non dicimus; sed ipso ita præcipiente adhuc viliora et reprehensibiliora dicturi [*leg.* de ipso scripturi] sumus ut pluribus patescat quam laboriose et cum quantâ augustiâ a profundâ paupertate ad summum culmen divitiarum vel honoris attigerit.   Such is the preface of Malaterra (l. i. c. 25) to the horse-stealing.   From the moment (l. i. c. 19) that he has mentioned his patron Roger, the elder brother sinks into the second character.   Something similar in Velleius Paterculus may be observed of Augustus and Tiberius.

[67] Duo sibi proficua deputans, animæ scilicet et corporis, si terram idolis deditam ad cultum divinum revocaret (Galfrid. Malaterra, l. ii. c. 1).   The conquest of Sicily is related in the three last books, and he himself has given an accurate summary of the chapters (p. 544-546). [The Brevis historia liberationis Messanae, printed in Muratori, Scr. rer. It., 6, p. 614 *sqq.*, which ascribes the capture of Messina to this first descent of Roger, has been shown by Amari to be a concoction of the 18th century (Stor. dei Musulmani di Sicilia, iii. 56).   Messina was taken in the following year—1061, May.]

siege, himself and the countess his wife had been reduced to a single cloak or mantle, which they wore alternately; that in a sally his horse had been slain, and he was dragged away by the Saracens; but that he owed his rescue to his good sword, and had retreated with his saddle on his back, lest the meanest trophy might be left in the hands of the miscreants. In the siege of Trani, three hundred Normans withstood and repulsed the forces of the island. In the field of Ceramio,[68] fifty thousand horse and foot were overthrown by one hundred and thirty-six Christian soldiers, without reckoning St. George, who fought on horseback in the foremost ranks. The captive banners, with four camels, were reserved for the successors of St. Peter; and had these barbaric spoils been exposed not in the Vatican, but in the Capitol, they might have revived the memory of the Punic triumphs. These insufficient numbers of the Normans most probably denote their knights, the soldiers of honourable and equestrian rank, each of whom was attended by five or six followers in the field;[69] yet, with the aid of this interpretation, and after every fair allowance on the side of valour, arms, and reputation, the discomfiture of so many myriads will reduce the prudent reader to the alternative of a miracle or a fable. The Arabs of Sicily derived a frequent and powerful succour from their countrymen of Africa: in the siege of Palermo, the Norman cavalry was assisted by the galleys of Pisa; and, in the hour of action, the envy of the two brothers was sublimed to a generous and invincible emulation. After a war of thirty years,[70] Roger, with the title of great count, obtained the sovereignty of the largest and most fruitful island of the Mediterranean; and his administration displays a liberal and enlightened mind above the limits of his age and education. The Moslems were maintained in the free enjoyment of their religion and property;[71] a philosopher and physician of Mazara, of the race of Mahomet,

[Troina]

[A.D. 1063]

[A.D. 1071-2]

---

[68] [The fortress of Cerami was not far from Troina.]

[69] See the word *milites* in the Latin Glossary of Ducange.

[70] Of odd particulars, I learn from Malaterra that the Arabs had introduced into Sicily the use of camels (l. i. c. 33) and of carrier pigeons (c. 42), and that the bite of the tarantula provokes a windy disposition, quæ per anum inhoneste crepitando emergit: a symptom most ridiculously felt by the whole Norman army in their camp near Palermo (c. 36). I shall add an etymology not unworthy of the eleventh century: *Messana* is derived from *Messis*, the place from whence the harvests of the isle were sent in tribute to Rome (l. ii. c. 1).

[71] See the capitulation of Palermo in Malaterra, l. ii. c. 45, and Giannone, who remarks the general toleration of the Saracens (tom. ii. p. 72).

harangued the conqueror, and was invited to court; his geography of the seven climates was translated into Latin; and Roger, after a diligent perusal, preferred the work of the Arabian to the writings of the Grecian Ptolemy.[72] A remnant of Christian natives had promoted the success of the Normans; they were rewarded by the triumph of the cross. The island was restored to the jurisdiction of the Roman pontiff; new bishops were planted in the principal cities; and the clergy was satisfied by a liberal endowment of churches and monasteries. Yet the Catholic hero asserted the rights of the civil magistrate. Instead of resigning the investiture of benefices, he dexterously applied to his own profit the papal claims: the supremacy of the crown was secured and enlarged by the singular bull which declares the princes of Sicily hereditary and perpetual legates of the Holy See.[73]

To Robert Guiscard, the conquest of Sicily was more glorious than beneficial; the possession of Apulia and Calabria was inadequate to his ambition; and he resolved to embrace or create the first occasion of invading, perhaps of subduing, the Roman empire of the East.[74] From his first wife, the partner of his humble fortunes, he had been divorced under the pretence of consanguinity; and her son Bohemond was destined to imitate, rather than to succeed, his illustrious father. The second wife of Guiscard was the daughter of the princes of Salerno; the Lombards acquiesced in the lineal succession of their son Roger; their five daughters were given in honourable nuptials,[75] and

Robert invades the Eastern empire. A.D. 1081

[Sigelgaita]

---

[72] John Leo Afer, de Medicis et Philosophis Arabibus, c. 14, apud Fabric. Bibliot. Græc. tom. xiii. p. 278, 279. This philosopher is named Esseriph Essachalli, and he died in Africa, A.H. 516—A.D. 1122. Yet this story bears a strange resemblance to the Sherif al Edrissi, who presented his book (Geographia Nubiensis, see preface, p. 88, 90, 170) to Roger king of Sicily, A.H. 548—A.D. 1153 (d'Herbelot, Bibliothèque Orientale, p. 786; Prideaux's Life of Mahomet, p. 188; Petit de la Croix, Hist. de Gengiscan, p. 535, 536; Casiri, Bibliot. Arab. Hispan. tom. ii. p. 9-13), and I am afraid of some mistake.

[73] Malaterra remarks the foundation of the bishoprics (l. iv. c. 7) and produces the original of the bull (l. iv. c. 29). Giannone gives a rational idea of this privilege, and the tribunal of the monarchy of Sicily (tom. ii. p. 95-102); and St. Marc (Abrégé, tom. iii. p. 217-301, 1st column) labours the case with the diligence of a Sicilian lawyer.

[74] In the first expedition of Robert against the Greeks, I follow Anna Comnena (the ist, iiird, ivth, and vth books of the Alexiad), William Appulus (l. ivth and vth, p. 270-275), and Jeffrey Malaterra (l. iii. c. 13, 14, 24-29, 39). Their information is contemporary and authentic, but none of them were eye-witnesses of the war. [Monograph: Schwarz, Die Feldzüge Robert Guiscards gegen das byzantinische Reich, 1854.]

[75] One of them was married to Hugh, the son of Azzo, or Axo, a marquis of Lombardy, rich, powerful, and *noble* (Gulielm. Appul. l. iii. p. 267), in the xith

[Helena] one of them was betrothed, in a tender age, to Constantine, a beautiful youth, the son and heir of the emperor Michael.[76] But the throne of Constantinople was shaken by a revolution; the imperial family of Ducas was confined to the palace or the cloister ; and Robert deplored, and resented, the disgrace of his daughter and the expulsion of his ally. A Greek, who styled himself the father of Constantine, soon appeared at Salerno, and related the adventures of his fall and flight. That unfortunate friend was acknowledged by the duke, and adorned with the pomp and titles of Imperial dignity : in his triumphal progress through Apulia and Calabria, Michael[77] was saluted with the tears and acclamations of the people; and pope Gregory the Seventh exhorted the bishops to preach, and the Catholics to fight, in the pious work of his restoration.[78] His conversations with Robert were frequent and familiar ; and their mutual promises were justified by the valour of the Normans and the treasures of the East. Yet this Michael, by the confession of the Greeks and Latins, was a pageant and an impostor : a monk who had fled from his convent, or a domestic who had served in the palace. The fraud had been contrived by the subtle Guiscard ;[79] and he trusted that, after this pretender had given a decent colour to his arms, he would sink, at the nod of the

century, and whose ancestors in the xth and ixth are explored by the critical industry of Leibnitz and Muratori. From the two elder sons of the marquis Azzo are derived the illustrious lines of Brunswick and Este. See Muratori, Antichità Estense.

[76] Anna Comnena, somewhat too wantonly, praises and bewails that handsome boy, who, after the rupture of his barbaric nuptials (l. i. p. 23 [c. 10]), was betrothed as her husband ; he was ἄγαλμα φύσεως . . . Θεοῦ χειρῶν φιλοτίμημα . . . χρυσοῦ γένους ἀπορροή, &c. (p. 27 [c. 12]). Elsewhere, she describes the red and white of his skin, his hawk's eyes, &c. l. iii. p. 71 [c. 1]. [It had been proposed originally that Helena should marry another Constantine, a brother of Michael ; and there are extant two letters of this Emperor to Robert Guiscard, concerning the projected alliance, dating from 1073 (in the correspondence of Psellus, published by Sathas, Bibl. Gr. Med. Æv., 5, p. 385 sqq.). For criticism see Seger, Nikephorus Bryennios, p. 123-4 : Heinemann, op. cit., p. 394-6.]

[77] Anna Comnena, l. i. p. 28, 29 ; Gulielm. Appul. l. iv. p. 271 ; Galfrid. Malaterra, l. iii. c. 13, p. 579, 580. Malaterra is most cautious in his style; but the Apulian is bold and positive.

——Mentitus se Michaelem
Venerat a Danais quidam seductor ad illum.

As Gregory VII. had believed, Baronius, almost alone, recognises the emperor Michael (A.D. 1080, No. 44).

[78] [Registrum Epistolarum, of Gregory VII. (ap. Jaffé, Bibl. rer. Germ. ii.), viii. 6, p. 435.]

[79] [So the Greeks said. But probably this was not so. Robert saw through the imposture and took advantage of it ; but probably did not invent it.]

conqueror, into his primitive obscurity. But victory was the
only argument that could determine the belief of the Greeks;
and the ardour of the Latins was much inferior to their credulity: the Norman veterans wished to enjoy the harvest of their
toils, and the unwarlike Italians trembled at the known and
unknown dangers of a transmarine expedition. In his new
levies, Robert exerted the influence of gifts and promises, the
terrors of civil and ecclesiastical authority; and some acts of
violence might justify the reproach that age and infancy were
pressed without distinction into the service of their unrelenting
prince. After two years' incessant preparations, the land and
naval forces were assembled at Otranto, at the heel or extreme
promontory of Italy; and Robert was accompanied by his wife,
who fought by his side, his son Bohemond, and the representative of the emperor Michael. Thirteen hundred knights [80] of
Norman race or discipline formed the sinews of the army,
which might be swelled to thirty thousand [81] followers of every
denomination. The men, the horses, the arms, the engines,
the wooden towers, covered with raw hides, were embarked on
board one hundred and fifty vessels; the transports had been
built in the ports of Italy, and the galleys were supplied by the
alliance of the republic of Ragusa.

At the mouth of the Adriatic gulf, the shores of Italy and
Epirus incline towards each other. The space between Brundusium and Durazzo, the Roman passage, is no more than one
hundred miles; [82] at the last station of Otranto, it is contracted
to fifty; [83] and this narrow distance had suggested to Pyrrhus and

Siege of Durazzo. A.D. 1081, June 17

---

[80] Ipse armatæ militiæ non plusquam MCCC milites secum habuisse, ab eis qui
eidem negotio interfuerunt attestatur (Malaterra, l. iii. c. 24, p. 583). These are
the same whom the Apulian (l. iv. p. 273) styles the equestris gens ducis, equites
de gente ducis.

[81] Εἰς τριάκοντα χιλιάδας, says Anna Comnena (Alexias, l. i. p. 37 [c. 16]), and
her account tallies with the number and lading of the ships. Ivit in [leg. contra]
Dyrrachium cum xv millibus hominum, says the Chronicon Breve Normannicum
(Muratori, Scriptores, tom. v. p. 278). I have endeavoured to reconcile these
reckonings.

[82] The Itinerary of Jerusalem (p. 609, edit. Wesseling) gives a true and reasonable space of a thousand stadia, or one hundred miles, which is strangely doubled
by Strabo (l. vi. p. 433 [3, § 8]) and Pliny (Hist. Natur. iii. 16).

[83] Pliny (Hist. Nat. iii. 6, 16) allows quinquaginta millia for this brevissimus
cursus, and agrees with the real distance from Otranto to La Vallona, or Aulon
(d'Anville, Analyse de la Carte des Côtes de la Grèce, &c., p. 3-6). Hermolaus
Barbarus, who substitutes centum (Harduin, Not. lxvi. in Plin. l. iii.), might have
been corrected by every Venetian pilot who had sailed out of the gulf.

Pompey the sublime or extravagant idea of a bridge.   Before the
general embarkation, the Norman duke dispatched Bohemond
with fifteen galleys to seize or threaten the isle of Corfu, to
survey the opposite coast, and to secure an harbour in the neighbourhood of Vallona for the landing of the troops.   They passed
and landed without perceiving an enemy ; and this successful experiment displayed the neglect and decay of the naval power of
the Greeks.   The islands of Epirus and the maritime towns
were subdued by the arms or the name of Robert, who led his
fleet and army from Corfu (I use the modern appellation) [84] to
the siege of Durazzo.   That city, the western key of the
empire, was guarded by ancient renown and recent fortifications,
by George Palæologus, a patrician, victorious in the Oriental
wars, and a numerous garrison of Albanians and Macedonians,
who, in every age, have maintained the character of soldiers.
In the prosecution of his enterprise, the courage of Guiscard
was assailed by every form of danger and mischance.   In the
most propitious season of the year, as his fleet passed along the
coast, a storm of wind and snow unexpectedly arose: the
Adriatic was swelled by the raging blast of the south, and a
new shipwreck confirmed the old infamy of the Acroceraunian
rocks.[85]   The sails, the masts, and the oars were shattered or
torn away ; the sea and shore were covered with the fragments
of vessels, with arms and dead bodies; and the greatest part of
the provisions were either drowned or damaged.   The ducal
galley was laboriously rescued from the waves, and Robert
halted seven days on the adjacent cape, to collect the relics of
his loss and revive the drooping spirits of his soldiers.   The
Normans were no longer the bold and experienced mariners
who had explored the ocean from Greenland to Mount Atlas,
and who smiled at the petty dangers of the Mediterranean.
They had wept during the tempest; they were alarmed by the
hostile approach of the Venetians, who had been solicited by the
prayers and promises of the Byzantine court.   The first day's

---

[84] [Corfu, of course, is not a corruption of Kerkyra, but is the mediæval Greek
name Κορυφώ, which, originally applied to the hill-town (κορυφή), was extended to
designate the island.]

[85] Infames scopulos Acroceraunia, Horat. carm. i. 3.   The præcipitem Africum
decertantem Aquilonibus et rabiem Noti, and the monstra natantia of the Adriatic,
are somewhat enlarged ; but Horace trembling for the life of Virgil is an interesting
moment in the history of poetry and friendship.

action was not disadvantageous to Bohemond, a beardless youth,[86] who led the naval powers of his father. All night the galleys of the republic lay on their anchors in the form of a crescent; and the victory of the second day was decided by the dexterity of their evolutions, the station of their archers, the weight of their javelins, and the borrowed aid of the Greek fire. The Apulian and Ragusian vessels fled to the shore, several were cut from their cables and dragged away by the conqueror; and a sally from the town carried slaughter and dismay to the tents of the Norman duke. A seasonable relief was poured into Durazzo, and, as soon as the besiegers had lost the command of the sea, the islands and maritime towns withdrew from the camp the supply of tribute and provision. That camp was soon afflicted with a pestilential disease; five hundred knights perished by an inglorious death; and the list of burials (if all could obtain a decent burial) amounted to ten thousand persons. Under these calamities, the mind of Guiscard alone was firm and invincible: and, while he collected new forces from Apulia and Sicily, he battered, or scaled, or sapped, the walls of Durazzo. But his industry and valour were encountered by equal valour and more perfect industry. A moveable turret, of a size and capacity to contain five hundred soldiers, had been rolled forwards to the foot of the rampart; but the descent of the door or draw-bridge was checked by an enormous beam, and the wooden structure was instantly consumed by artificial flames.

While the Roman empire was attacked by the Turks in the East and the Normans in the West, the aged successor of Michael surrendered the sceptre to the hands of Alexius, an illustrious captain, and the founder of the Comnenian dynasty. The princess Anne, his daughter and historian, observes, in her affected style, that even Hercules was unequal to a double combat; and, on this principle she approves an hasty peace with the Turks, which allowed her father to undertake in person the relief of Durazzo. On his accession, Alexius found the camp without soldiers, and the treasury without money; yet such were the vigour and activity of his measures that, in six months, he

The army and march of the emperor Alexius. April-September

---

[86] Τῶν δὲ εἰς τὸν πώγωνα αὐτοῦ ἐφυβρισάντων (Alexias, l. iv. p. 106 [c. 2]). Yet the Normans shaved, and Venetians wore their beards; they must have derided the no-beard of Bohemond: an harsh interpretation! (Ducange, Not. ad Alexiad. p. 283).

assembled an army of seventy thousand men,[87] and performed a march of five hundred miles.   His troops were levied in Europe and Asia, from Peloponnesus to the Black Sea; his majesty was displayed in the silver arms and rich trappings of the companies of horseguards; and the emperor was attended by a train of nobles and princes, some of whom, in rapid succession, had been clothed with the purple, and were indulged by the lenity of the times in a life of affluence and dignity.   Their youthful ardour might animate the multitude; but their love of pleasure and contempt of subordination were pregnant with disorder and mischief; and their importunate clamours for speedy and decisive action disconcerted the prudence of Alexius, who might have surrounded and starved the besieging army.   The enumeration of provinces recalls a sad comparison of the past and present limits of the Roman world: the raw levies were drawn together in haste and terror; and the garrisons of Anatolia, or Asia Minor, had been purchased by the evacuation of the cities which were immediately occupied by the Turks.   The strength of the Greek army consisted in the Varangians, the Scandinavian guards, whose numbers were recently augmented by a colony of exiles and volunteers from the British island of Thule.   Under the yoke of the Norman conqueror, the Danes and English were oppressed and united: a band of adventurous youths resolved to desert a land of slavery; the sea was open to their escape; and, in their long pilgrimage, they visited every coast that afforded any hope of liberty and revenge.   They were entertained in the service of the Greek emperor; and their first station was in a new city on the Asiatic shore: but Alexius soon recalled them to the defence of his person and palace; and bequeathed to his successors the inheritance of their faith and valour.[88]   The name of a Norman invader revived the memory

---

[87] Muratori (Annali d'Italia, tom. ix. p. 136, 137) observes that some authors (Petrus Diacon. Chron. Casinen. l. iii. c. 49) compose the Greek army of 170,000 men, but that the *hundred* may be struck off, and that Malaterra reckons only 70,000 : a slight inattention.   The passage to which he alludes is in the Chronicle of Lupus Protospata (Script. Ital. tom. v. p. 45).   Malaterra (l. iv. c. 27) speaks in high, but indefinite, terms of the emperor, cum copiis innumerabilibus ; like the Apulian poet (l. iv. p. 272).
           More locustarum montes et plana teguntur.
[88] See William of Malmsbury, de Gestis Anglorum, l. ii. p. 92.   Alexius fidem Anglorum suscipiens præcipuis familiaritatibus suis eos applicabat, amorem eorum filio transcribens.   Ordericus Vitalis (Hist. Eccles. l. iv. p. 508, l. vii. p. 641) relates their emigration from England, and their service in Greece.

of their wrongs: they marched with alacrity against the national foe, and panted to regain in Epirus the glory which they had lost in the battle of Hastings. The Varangians were supported by some companies of Franks or Latins; and the rebels, who had fled to Constantinople from the tyranny of Guiscard, were eager to signalise their zeal and gratify their revenge. In this emergency, the emperor had not disdained the impure aid of the Paulicians or Manichæans of Thrace and Bulgaria; and these heretics united with the patience of martyrdom the spirit and discipline of active valour.[89] The treaty with the sultan had procured a supply of some thousand Turks; and the arrows of the Scythian horse were opposed to the lances of the Norman cavalry. On the report and distant prospect of these formidable numbers, Robert assembled a council of his principal officers. "You behold," said he, "your danger; it is urgent and inevitable. The hills are covered with arms and standards; and the emperor of the Greeks is accustomed to wars and triumphs. Obedience and union are our only safety; and I am ready to yield the command to a more worthy leader." The vote and acclamation, even of his secret enemies, assured him, in that perilous moment, of their esteem and confidence; and the duke thus continued: "Let us trust in the rewards of victory, and deprive cowardice of the means of escape. Let us burn our vessels and our baggage, and give battle on this spot, as if it were the place of our nativity and our burial." The resolution was unanimously approved; and, without confining himself to his lines, Guiscard awaited in battle-array the nearer approach of the enemy. His rear was covered by a small river; his right wing extended to the sea; his left to the hills; nor was he conscious, perhaps, that on the same ground Cæsar and Pompey had formerly disputed the empire of the world.[90]

Against the advice of his wisest captains, Alexius resolved to risk the event of a general action, and exhorted the garrison of Durazzo to assist their own deliverance by a well-timed sally from the town. He marched in two columns to surprise the Normans before day-break on two different sides: his light

Battle of Durazzo. A.D. 1081, October 18

---

[89] See the Apulian, l. i. p. 256. The character and story of these Manichæans has been the subject of the livth chapter.

[90] See the simple and masterly narrative of Cæsar himself (Comment. de Bell. Civil. iii. 41-75). It is a pity that Quintus Icilius (M. Guischard) did not live to analyse these operations, as he has done the campaigns of Africa and Spain.

cavalry was scattered over the plain ; the archers formed the
second line; and the Varangians claimed the honours of the
vanguard. In the first onset, the battle-axes of the strangers
made a deep and bloody impression on the army of Guiscard,
which was now reduced to fifteen thousand men. The Lombards
and Calabrians ignominiously turned their backs ; they fled towards the river and the sea; but the bridge had been broken
down to check the sally of the garrison, and the coast was lined
with the Venetian galleys, who played their engines among the
disorderly throng. On the verge of ruin, they were saved by
[Sigelgaita] the spirit and conduct of their chiefs. Gaita, the wife of Robert, is
painted by the Greeks as a warlike Amazon, a second Pallas ; less
skilful in arts, but not less terrible in arms, than the Athenian
goddess : [91] though wounded by an arrow, she stood her ground,
and strove, by her exhortation and example, to rally the
flying troops.[92] Her female voice was seconded by the more
powerful voice and arm of the Norman duke, as calm in action
as he was magnanimous in council : " Whither," he cried aloud,
" whither do ye fly? your enemy is implacable ; and death is
less grievous than servitude." The moment was decisive : as
the Varangians advanced before the line, they discovered the
nakedness of their flanks ; the main battle of the duke, of
eight hundred knights, stood firm and entire; they couched
their lances, and the Greeks deplore the furious and irresistible
shock of the French cavalry.[93] Alexius was not deficient in the
duties of a soldier or a general ; but he no sooner beheld the

[91] Πάλλας ἄλλη κἂν μὴ ᾿Αθήνη [Anna Comn., iv. c. 6], which is very properly
translated by the president Cousin (Hist. de Constantinople, tom. iv. p. 131 in 12mo),
qui combattoit comme une Pallas, quoiqu' elle ne fût pas aussi savante que celle
d'Athènes. The Grecian goddess was composed of two discordant characters, of
Neith, the workwoman of Sais in Egypt, and of a virgin Amazon of the Tritonian
Lake in Libya (Banier, Mythologie, tom. iv. p. 1-31 in 12mo).
[92] Anna Comnena (l. iv. p. 116 [c. 6]) admires, with some degree of terror, her
masculine virtues. They were more familiar to the Latins; and, though the
Apulian (l. iv. p. 273) mentions her presence and her wound, he represents her as
far less intrepid.
Uxor in hoc bello Roberti forte sagittâ
Quâdam læsa fuit; quo vulnere *territa* nullam
Dum sperabat opem se pœne *subegerat* hosti.
The last is an unlucky word for a female prisoner.
[93] ᾿Απὸ τῆς [μετὰ] τοῦ ῾Ρομπέρτου προηγησαμένης μάχης, γινώσκων τὴν πρώτην κατὰ
τῶν ἐναντίων ἱππασίαν τῶν Κελτῶν ἀνύποιστον (Anna, l. v. p. 133 [c. 3]), and elsewhere
καὶ γὰρ Κέλτος ἀνὴρ πᾶς ἐποχούμενος μὲν ἀνύποιστος τὴν ὁρμὴν καὶ τὴν θέαν ἐστίν (p.
140 [c. 6]). The pedantry of the princess in the choice of classic appellations encouraged Ducange to apply to his countrymen the characters of the ancient Gauls.

slaughter of the Varangians and the flight of the Turks, than he despised his subjects and despaired of his fortune. The princess Anne, who drops a tear on this melancholy event, is reduced to praise the strength and swiftness of her father's horse, and his vigorous struggle, when he was almost overthrown by the stroke of a lance, which had shivered the Imperial helmet. His desperate valour broke through a squadron of Franks who opposed his flight; and, after wandering two days and as many nights in the mountains, he found some repose of body, though not of mind, in the walls of Lychnidus. The victorious Robert reproached the tardy and feeble pursuit which had suffered the escape of so illustrious a prize; but he consoled his disappointment by the trophies and standards of the field, the wealth and luxury of the Byzantine camp, and the glory of defeating an army five times more numerous than his own. A multitude of Italians had been the victims of their own fears; but only thirty of his knights were slain in this memorable day. In the Roman host, the loss of Greeks, Turks, and English amounted to five or six thousand:[94] the plain of Durazzo was stained with noble and royal blood; and the end of the impostor Michael was more honourable than his life.

It is more than probable that Guiscard was not afflicted by the loss of a costly pageant, which had merited only the contempt and derision of the Greeks. After their defeat, they still persevered in the defence of Durazzo; and a Venetian commander supplied the place of George Palæologus, who had been imprudently called away from his station. The tents of the besiegers were converted into barracks, to sustain the inclemency of the winter; and in answer to the defiance of the garrison Robert insinuated that his patience was at least equal to their obstinacy.[95] Perhaps he already trusted to his secret correspondence with a Venetian noble, who sold the city for a rich and honourable marriage. At the dead of night several rope-ladders were dropped from the walls; the light Calabrians ascended in

Durazzo taken. A.D. 1082, Feb. 8 [21]

---

[94] Lupus Protospata (tom. iii. p. 45) says 6000 ; William the Apulian more than 5000 (l. iv. p. 273). Their modesty is singular and laudable : they might with so little trouble have slain two or three myriads of schismatics and infidels !

[95] The Romans had changed the inauspicious name of *Epi-damnus* to Dyrrachium (Plin. iii. 26), and the vulgar corruption of Duracium (see Malaterra) bore some affinity to *hardness*. One of Robert's names was Durand, *a durando* : Poor wit ! (Alberic. Monach. in Chron. apud Muratori, Annali d'Italia, tom. ix. p. 137).

silence; and the Greeks were awakened by the name and trumpets of the conqueror. Yet they defended the street three days against an enemy already master of the rampart; and near seven months elapsed between the first investment and the final surrender of the place. From Durazzo the Norman duke advanced into the heart of Epirus or Albania; traversed the first mountains of Thessaly; surprised three hundred English in the city of Castoria; approached Thessalonica; and made Constantinople tremble. A more pressing duty suspended the prosecution of his ambitious designs. By shipwreck, pestilence, and the sword, his army was reduced to a third of the original numbers; and, instead of being recruited from Italy, he was informed, by plaintive epistles, of the mischiefs and dangers which had been produced by his absence: the revolt of the cities and barons of Apulia; the distress of the pope; and the approach

Return of Robert [A.D. 1082] and actions of Bohemond or invasion of Henry king of Germany. Highly presuming that his person was sufficient for the public safety, he repassed the sea in a single brigantine, and left the remains of the army under the command of his son and the Norman counts, exhorting Bohemond to respect the freedom of his peers, and the counts to obey the authority of their leader. The son of Guiscard trod in the footsteps of his father; and the two destroyers are compared, by the Greeks, to the caterpillar and the locust, the last of whom devours whatever has escaped the teeth of the former.[96] After winning two battles against the emperor, he descended into the plain of Thessaly, and besieged Larissa, the fabulous realm of Achilles,[97] which contained the treasure and magazines of the Byzantine camp. Yet a just praise must not be refused to the fortitude and prudence of Alexius, who bravely struggled with the calamities of the times. In the poverty of the state, he presumed to borrow the superfluous ornaments of the churches; the desertion of the Manichæans was supplied by some tribes of Moldavia; a reinforcement of seven thousand

---

[96] Βρούχους καὶ ἀκρίδας εἶπεν ἄν τις αὐτοὺς [τὸν] πατέρα καὶ [τὸν] υἱόν (Anna, l. i. p. 35 [c. 14]). By these similes, so different from those of Homer, she wishes to inspire contempt as well as horror for the little noxious animal, a conqueror. Most unfortunately, the common sense, or common nonsense, of mankind resists her laudable design.

[97] Prodiit hâc auctor Trojanæ cladis Achilles.
The supposition of the Apulian (l. v. p. 275) may be excused by the more classic poetry of Virgil (Æneid II. 197), Larissæus Achilles, but it is not justified by the geography of Homer.

Turks replaced and revenged the loss of their brethren; and the
Greek soldiers were exercised to ride, to draw the bow, and to
the daily practice of ambuscades and evolutions. Alexius had
been taught by experience that the formidable cavalry of the
Franks on foot was unfit for action, and almost incapable of
motion ; [98] his archers were directed to aim their arrows at the
horse rather than the man; and a variety of spikes and snares
was scattered over the ground on which he might expect an
attack. In the neighbourhood of Larissa the events of war
were protracted and balanced. The courage of Bohemond was
always conspicuous, and often successful; but his camp was
pillaged by a stratagem of the Greeks; the city was impregnable; and the venal or discontented counts deserted his standard,
betrayed their trusts, and enlisted in the service of the emperor. Alexius returned to Constantinople with the advantage,
rather than the honour, of victory. After evacuating the conquests which he could no longer defend, the son of Guiscard embarked for Italy, and was embraced by a father who esteemed
his merit and sympathized in his misfortune.

Of the Latin princes, the allies of Alexius and enemies of The em-
Robert, the most prompt and powerful was Henry, the Third or Henry
Fourth, king of Germany and Italy, and future emperor of the invited
West. The epistle of the Greek monarch [99] to his brother is Greeks.
filled with the warmest professions of friendship, and the most A.D. 1081
lively desire of strengthening their alliance by every public and
private tie. He congratulates Henry on his success in a just
and pious war, and complains that the prosperity of his own
empire is disturbed by the audacious enterprises of the Norman
Robert. The list of his presents expresses the manners of the
age, a radiated crown of gold, a cross set with pearls to hang on

---

[98] The τῶν πεδίλων πρόδλματα, which incumbered the knights on foot, have been
ignorantly translated spurs (Anna Comnena, Alexias, l. v. p. 140 [c. 6]). Ducange
has explained the true sense by a ridiculous and inconvenient fashion, which lasted
from the xith to the xvth century. These peaks, in the form of a scorpion, were
sometimes two feet, and fastened to the knee with a silver chain.
[99] The epistle itself (Alexias, l. iii. p. 93, 94, 95 [c. 10]) well deserves to be read.
There is one expression, ἀστροπέλεκυν δεδεμένον μετὰ χρυσαφίου, which Ducange does
not understand ; I have endeavoured to grope out a tolerable meaning ; χρυσάφιον,
is a golden crown ; ἀστροπέλεκυς, is explained by Simon Portius (in Lexico Græco-
Barbar.) by κεραυνός, πρηστήρ, a flash of lightning. [Heinemann has shown that this
letter reached Henry IV. at Rome in June, 1081 (op. cit., p. 396-8). The embassy
is mentioned in Benzo's Panegyricus rhythmicus, probably composed at end of 1081
(printed in Pertz, Mon. Germ. Hist. xi. p. 591 sqq.).]

the breast, a case of relics with the names and titles of the saints, a vase of crystal, a vase of sardonyx, some balm, most probably of Mecca, and one hundred pieces of purple. To these he added a more solid present, of one hundred and forty-four thousand Byzantines of gold, with a further assurance of two hundred and sixteen thousand, so soon as Henry should have entered in arms the Apulian territories, and confirmed by an oath the league against the common enemy. The German,[100] who was already in Lombardy at the head of an army and a faction, accepted these liberal offers and marched towards the south : his speed was checked by the sound of the battle of Durazzo; but the influence of his arms or name, in the hasty return of Robert, was a full equivalent for the Grecian bribe. Henry was the severe adversary of the Normans, the allies and vassals of Gregory the Seventh, his implacable foe. The long quarrel of the throne and mitre had been recently kindled by the zeal and ambition of that haughty priest :[101] the king and the pope had degraded each other ; and each had seated a rival on the temporal or spiritual throne of his antagonist. After the defeat and death of his Swabian rebel, Henry descended into Italy, to assume the Imperial crown, and to drive from the Vatican the tyrant of the church.[102] But the Roman people adhered to the cause of Gregory : their resolution was fortified by supplies of men and money from Apulia ; and the city was thrice ineffectually besieged by the king of Germany. In the fourth year he corrupted, as it is said,

Besieges
Rome. A.D.
1081-1084;

<hr>

[100] For these general events I must refer to the general historians Sigonius, Baronius, Muratori, Mosheim, St. Marc, &c.

[101] The lives of Gregory VII. are either legends or invectives (St. Marc, Abrégé, tom. iii. p. 235, &c.), and his miraculous or magical performances are alike incredible to a modern reader. He will, as usual, find some instruction in Le Clerc (Vie de Hildebrand, Bibliot. ancienne et moderne, tom. viii.) and much amusement in Bayle (Dictionnaire Critique, *Grégoire* VII.). That pope was undoubtedly a great man, a second Athanasius, in a more fortunate age of the church. May I presume to add that the portrait of Athanasius is one of the passages of my history (vol. ii. p. 383 *sqq.*), with which I am the least dissatisfied ? [The nineteenth century produced an enormous Hildebrandine literature. The pioneer work was that of Johannes Voigt in 1815 ; Hildebrand als Papst Gregor VII. und sein Zeitalter. The Protestant author represented Gregory in the light of a reformer. Voigt's work led to an English monograph by J. W. Bowden : The Life and Pontificate of Gregory VII. (1840). Gfrörer, Papst Gregorius VII. und sein Zeitalter, 7 vols. (1859-61) ; W. Martens, Gregor VII. sein Leben und Wirken, 2 vols. (1894). See further the article on Gregory in the latest edition of the Encyclopædia Britannica.]

[102] Anna, with the rancour of a Greek schismatic, calls him [ὁ] κατάπτυστος οὗτος Πάπας (l. i. p. 32 [c. 13]), a pope, or priest, worthy to be spit upon ; and accuses him of scourging, shaving, perhaps of castrating, the ambassadors of Henry (p. 31, 33). But this outrage is improbable and doubtful (see the sensible preface of Cousin).

with Byzantine gold the nobles of Rome whose estates and castles
had been ruined by the war.   The gates, the bridges, and fifty
hostages were delivered into his hands; the antipope, Clement
the Third, was consecrated in the Lateran; the grateful pontiff
crowned his protector in the Vatican; and the emperor Henry A.D. 1084,
March 21,
fixed his residence in the Capitol, as the lawful successor of 24, 31
Augustus and Charlemagne.   The ruins of the Septizonium were
still defended by the nephew of Gregory: the pope himself was
invested in the castle of St. Angelo; and his last hope was in
the courage and fidelity of his Norman vassal.   Their friendship
had been interrupted by some reciprocal injuries and complaints;
but, on this pressing occasion, Guiscard was urged by the obligation of his oath, by his interest, more potent than oaths, by the
love of fame, and his enmity to the two emperors.   Unfurling
the holy banner, he resolved to fly to the relief of the prince
of the apostles: the most numerous of his armies, six thousand
horse and thirty thousand foot, was instantly assembled; and
his march from Salerno to Rome was animated by the public
applause and the promise of the divine favour.   Henry, invincible
in sixty-six battles, trembled at his approach; recollected some Flies before
Robert;
indispensable affairs that required his presence in Lombardy; May
exhorted the Romans to persevere in their allegiance; and hastily
retreated three days before the entrance of the Normans.   In
less than three years, the son of Tancred of Hauteville enjoyed
the glory of delivering the pope, and of compelling the two emperors of the East and West to fly before his victorious arms.[103]
But the triumph of Robert was clouded by the calamities of
Rome.   By the aid of the friends of Gregory, the walls had been
perforated or scaled; but the Imperial faction was still powerful
and active; on the third day, the people rose in a furious tumult;
and an hasty word of the conqueror, in his defence or revenge,
was the signal of fire and pillage.[104]   The Saracens of Sicily, the

[103] Sic uno tempore victi
Sunt terræ Domini duo : rex Alemannicus iste,
Imperii rector Romani maximus ille.
Alter ad arma ruens armis superatur ; et alter
Nominis auditi solâ formidine cessit.
It is singular enough that the Apulian, a Latin, should distinguish the Greek as
the ruler of the Roman empire (l. iv. p. 274).
[104] The narrative of Malaterra (l. iii. c. 37, p. 587, 588) is authentic, circumstantial, and fair.   Dux ignem exclamans urbe incensâ, &c.   The Apulian softens the
mischief (inde quibusdam ædibus exustis), which is again exaggerated in some
partial Chronicles (Muratori, Annali, tom. ix. p. 147).

subjects of Roger, and auxiliaries of his brother, embraced this fair occasion of rifling and profaning the holy city of the Christians: many thousands of the citizens, in the sight, and by the allies, of their spiritual father, were exposed to violation, captivity, or death; and a spacious quarter of the city, from the Lateran to the Coliseum, was consumed by the flames and devoted to perpetual solitude.[105] From a city, where he was now hated and might be no longer feared, Gregory retired to end his days in the palace of Salerno. The artful pontiff might flatter the vanity of Guiscard with the hope of a Roman or Imperial crown; but this dangerous measure, which would have inflamed the ambition of the Norman, must for ever have alienated the most faithful princes of Germany.

Second expedition of Robert into Greece.
A.D. 1084, October
The deliverer and scourge of Rome might have indulged himself in a season of repose; but, in the same year of the flight of the German emperor, the indefatigable Robert resumed the design of his eastern conquests. The zeal or gratitude of Gregory had promised to his valour the kingdoms of Greece and Asia;[106] his troops were assembled in arms, flushed with success, and eager for action. Their numbers, in the language of Homer, are compared by Anna to a swarm of bees;[107] yet the utmost and moderate limits of the powers of Guiscard have been already defined; they were contained on this second occasion in one hundred and twenty vessels; and, as the season was far advanced, the harbour of Brundusium[108] was preferred

---

[105] After mentioning this devastation, the Jesuit Donatus (de Româ veteri et novâ, l. iv. c. 8, p. 489) prettily adds, Duraret hodieque in Cœlio monte interque ipsum et Capitolium miserabilis facies prostratæ urbis, nisi in hortorum vinetorumque amœnitatem Roma resurrexisset ut perpetuâ viriditate contegeret vulnera et ruinas suas.

[106] The royalty of Robert, either promised or bestowed by the pope (Anna, l. i. p. 32 [c. 13]), is sufficiently confirmed by the Apulian (l. iv. p. 270).

Romani regni sibi promisisse coronam
Papa ferebatur.

Nor can I understand why Gretser, and the other papal advocates, should be displeased with this new instance of apostolic jurisdiction.

[107] See Homer, Iliad B (I hate this pedantic mode of quotation by the letter of the Greek alphabet), 87, &c. His bees are the image of a disorderly crowd: their discipline and public works seem to be the ideas of a later age (Virgil, Æneid l. i.).

[108] Gulielm. Appulus, l. v. p. 276. The admirable port of Brundusium was double; the outward harbour was a gulf covered by an island, and narrowing by degrees, till it communicated by a small gullet with the inner harbour, which embraced the city on both sides. Cæsar and nature have laboured for its ruin; and against such agents, what are the feeble efforts of the Neapolitan government? (Swinburne's Travels in the two Sicilies, vol. i. p. 384-390).

to the open road of Otranto.   Alexius, apprehensive of a second attack, had assiduously laboured to restore the naval forces of the empire; and obtained from the republic of Venice an important succour of thirty-six transports, fourteen galleys, and nine galeots or ships of extraordinary strength and magnitude. Their services were liberally paid by the licence or monopoly of trade, a profitable gift of many shops and houses in the port of Constantinople, and a tribute to St. Mark, the more acceptable, as it was the produce of a tax on their rivals of Amalphi.[109] By the union of the Greeks and Venetians, the Adriatic was covered with an hostile fleet; but their own neglect, or the vigilance of Robert, the, change of a wind, or the shelter of a mist, opened a free passage; and the Norman troops were safely disembarked on the coast of Epirus.   With twenty strong and well-appointed galleys, their intrepid duke immediately fought the enemy, and, though more accustomed to fight on horseback, he trusted his own life, and the lives of his brother and two sons, to the event of a naval combat.   The dominion of the sea was disputed in three engagements, in sight of the island of Corfu; in the two former, the skill and numbers of the allies were superior; but in the third the Normans obtained a final and complete victory.[110]   The light brigantines of the Greeks were scattered in ignominious flight; the nine castles of the Venetians maintained a more obstinate conflict; seven were sunk, two were taken; two thousand five hundred captives implored in vain the mercy of the victor; and the daughter of Alexius deplores the loss of thirteen thousand of his subjects or allies.   The want of experience had been supplied by the genius of Guiscard; and each evening, when he had sounded a retreat, he calmly explored the causes of his repulse, and invented new methods how to remedy his own defects and to baffle the advantages of the enemy.   The winter season suspended his progress; with the return of spring he again aspired

---

[109] [The golden Bull is printed in Tafel and Thomas, Urkunden zur älteren Handels- und Staatsgeschichte der Republik Venedigs, in Fontes rer. Aust. ii. 12, No. 23.]

[110] William of Apulia (l. v. p. 276) describes the victory of the Normans, and forgets the two previous defeats, which are diligently recorded by Anna Comnena (l. vi. p. 159, 160, 161 [c. 5]). In her turn, she invents or magnifies a fourth action, to give the Venetians revenge and rewards. Their own feelings were far different, since they deposed their doge, propter excidium stoli (Dandulus in Chron. in Muratori, Script. Rerum Italicarum, tom. xii. p. 249).

to the conquest of Constantinople; but, instead of traversing the hills of Epirus, he turned his arms against Greece and the islands, where the spoils would repay the labour, and where the land and sea forces might pursue their joint operations with vigour and effect. But, in the isle of Cephalonia, his projects were fatally blasted by an epidemical disease; Robert himself, in the seventieth year of his age, expired in his tent; and a suspicion of poison was imputed, by public rumour, to his wife, or to the Greek emperor.[111] This premature death might allow a boundless scope for the imagination of his future exploits: and the event sufficiently declares that the Norman greatness was founded on his life.[112] Without the appearance of an enemy, a victorious army dispersed or retreated in disorder and consternation; and Alexius, who had trembled for his empire, rejoiced in his deliverance. The galley which transported the remains of Guiscard was shipwrecked on the Italian shore; but the duke's body was recovered from the sea, and deposited in the sepulchre of Venusia,[113] a place more illustrious for the birth of Horace[114] than for the burial of the Norman heroes. Roger,

His death.
A.D. 1085,
July 17

[111] The most authentic writers, William of Apulia (l. v. 277), Jeffrey Malaterra (l. iii. c. 41, p. 589), and Romuald of Salerno (Chron. in Muratori, Script. Rerum Ital. tom. vii.), are ignorant of this crime so apparent to our countrymen William of Malmesbury (l. iii. p. 107) and Roger de Hoveden (p. 710 in Script. post Bedam), and the latter can tell how the just Alexius married, crowned, and burnt alive, his female accomplice. The English historian is indeed so blind that he ranks Robert Guiscard, or Wiscard, among the knights of Henry I. who ascended the throne fifteen years after the duke of Apulia's death. [When he died, Robert was on the point of sailing to Cephalonia, but he did not die in the island. He died (where he had made his winter quarters) at Bundicia on the river Glykys, on the coast of Epirus. Heinemann (op. cit., p. 401-3) treats the question in an acute appendix, and makes it probable that this Glykys is to be connected with the Γλυκὺς λιμήν, the name given by Strabo to the bay into which the Acheron flows—now called the bay of Phanari. He conjectures that Bundicia is the ancient Pandosia. The Chronicon breve Nortmannicum, sub ann., states that Guiscard died in Cassiopi and Romuald of Salerno says apud insulam Cassiopam; hence it has been supposed that the place was Cassiope, on the north side of the island of Corfu. Heinemann would connect " Cassiopa " with Cassiopia in Epirus. The statement that he died in Cephalonia is due to Anna Comnena (vi. 6) and Anon. Bar. sub ann., but is irreconcilable with the rest of the story.]

[112] The joyful Anna Comnena scatters some flowers over the grave of an enemy (Alexiad. l. vi. p. 162-166 [c. 6, 7]), and his best praise is the esteem and envy of William the Conqueror, the sovereign of his family. Græcia (says Malaterra) hostibus recedentibus libera læta quievit : Apulia tota sive Calabria turbatur.

[113] Urbs Venusina nitet tantis decorata sepulchris, is one of the last lines of the Apulian's poem (l. v. p. 278). William of Malmesbury (l. iii. p. 107) inserts an epitaph on Guiscard, which is not worth transcribing.

[114] Yet Horace had few obligations to Venusia : he was carried to Rome in his childhood (Serm. i. 6), and his repeated allusions to the doubtful limit of Apulia and Lucania (Carm. iii. 4; Serm. ii. 1) are unworthy of his age and genius.

his second son and successor, immediately sunk to the humble
station of a duke of Apulia: the esteem or partiality of his
father left the valiant Bohemond to the inheritance of his
sword. The national tranquillity was disturbed by his claims,
till the first crusade against the infidels of the East opened a
more splendid field of glory and conquest.[115]

Of human life the most glorious or humble prospects are
alike and soon bounded by the sepulchre. The male line of
Robert Guiscard was extinguished, both in Apulia and at
Antioch, in the second generation; but his younger brother
became the father of a line of kings; and the son of the great
count was endowed with the name, the conquests, and the spirit
of the first Roger.[116] The heir of that Norman adventurer was
born in Sicily: and, at the age of only four years, he succeeded
to the sovereignty of the island, a lot which reason might
envy, could she indulge for a moment the visionary, though
virtuous, wish of dominion. Had Roger been content with his
fruitful patrimony, an happy and grateful people might have
blessed their benefactor; and, if a wise administration could
have restored the prosperous times of the Greek colonies,[117]
the opulence and power of Sicily alone might have equalled the
widest scope that could be acquired and desolated by the sword
of war. But the ambition of the great count was ignorant of
these noble pursuits; it was gratified by the vulgar means of
violence and artifice. He sought to obtain the undivided
possession of Palermo, of which one moiety had been ceded
to the elder branch; struggled to enlarge his Calabrian limits
beyond the measure of former treaties; and impatiently watched

Reign and ambition of Roger, great count of Sicily. A.D. 1101-1154, Feb. 2

---

[115] See Giannone (tom. ii. p. 88-93) and the historians of the first crusade.

[116] The reign of Roger, and the Norman kings of Sicily, fills four books of the storia Civile of Giannone (tom. ii. l. xi.-xiv. p. 136-340), and is spread over the ninth and tenth volumes of the Italian Annals of Muratori. In the Bibliothèque Italique (tom. i. p. 175-222) I find an useful abstract of Capecelatro, a modern Neapolitan, who has composed, in two volumes, the history of his country from Roger I. to Frederic II. inclusive. [The old collection of authorities for Sicilian history by Fazellus (1579) was reissued at Catania in 1749-52. The Neapolitan collection of G. Del Re in 2 vols. (see below, note 118) includes some Sicilians. Some chronicles written in the Sicilian tongue were collected by Vincenzo de' Giovanni and published in 1865 (Cronache Siciliane dei secoli xiii.-xiv. c. xv.).]

[117] According to the testimony of Philistus and Diodorus, the tyrant Dionysius of Syracuse could maintain a standing force of 10,000 horse, 100,000 foot, and 400 galleys. Compare Hume (Essays, vol. i. p. 268, 435) and his adversary Wallace (Numbers of Mankind, p. 306, 307). The ruins of Agrigentum are the theme of every traveller, d'Orville, Reidesel, Swinburne, &c.

the declining health of his cousin William of Apulia, the grandson of Robert. On the first intelligence of his premature death,
Roger sailed from Palermo with seven galleys, cast anchor in
the bay of Salerno, received, after ten days' negotiation, an oath
of fidelity from the Norman capital, commanded the submission
of the barons, and extorted a legal investiture from the reluctant
popes, who could not long endure either the friendship or enmity
of a powerful vassal. The sacred spot of Benevento was respectfully spared, as the patrimony of St. Peter; but the reduction
of Capua and Naples completed the design of his uncle Guiscard ;
and the sole inheritance of the Norman conquests was possessed
by the victorious Roger. A conscious superiority of power and
merit prompted him to disdain the titles of duke and of count ;
and the isle of Sicily, with a third perhaps of the continent of
Italy, might form the basis of a kingdom [118] which would only
yield to the monarchies of France and England. The chiefs of
the nation who attended his coronation at Palermo might doubtless pronounce under what name he should reign over them ;
but the example of a Greek tyrant or a Saracen emir were
insufficient to justify his regal character; and the nine kings
of the Latin world [119] might disclaim their new associate, unless
he were consecrated by the authority of the supreme pontiff.
The pride of Anacletus was pleased to confer a title which the
pride of the Norman had stooped to solicit; [120] but his own
legitimacy was attacked by the adverse election of Innocent
the Second ; and, while Anacletus sat in the Vatican, the successful fugitive was acknowledged by the nations of Europe
The infant monarchy of Roger was shaken, and almost overthrown, by the unlucky choice of an ecclesiastical patron ; and

Duke of Apulia.
A.D. 1127

First king of Sicily.
A.D. 1130 Dec. 25—
A.D. 1139, July 25

[118] A contemporary historian of the acts of Roger, from the year 1127 to 1135
founds his title on merit and power, the consent of the barons, and the ancien
royalty of Sicily and Palermo, without introducing pope Anacletus (Alexand. Cœ
nobii Telesini Abbatis de Rebus gestis Regis Rogerii, lib. iv. in Muratori, Script
Rerum Ital. tom. v. p. 607-645 [printed with Italian translation, Del Re's Cronist
e scrittori sincroni Napolitani, vol. i. p. 85 *sqq.* (1845)]).

[119] The kings of France, England, Scotland, Castile, Arragon, Navarre, Sweden
Denmark, and Hungary. The three first were more ancient than Charlemagne
the three next were created by their sword, the three last by their baptism ; an
of these the king of Hungary alone was honoured or debased by a papal crown.

[120] Fazellus, and a crowd of Sicilians, had imagined a more early and indepen
dent coronation (A.D. 1130, May 1), which Giannone unwillingly rejects (tom. ii
p. 137-144). This fiction is disproved by the silence of contemporaries ; nor ca
it be restored by a spurious charter of Messina (Muratori, Annali d'Italia, tom. ix
p. 340 ; Pagi, Critica, tom. iv. p. 467, 468),

the sword of Lothaire the Second of Germany, the excommunications of Innocent, the fleets of Pisa, and the zeal of St. Bernard, were united for the ruin of the Sicilian robber. After a gallant resistance, the Norman prince was driven from the continent of Italy; a new duke of Apulia was invested by the pope and the emperor, each of whom held one end of the *gonfanon*, or flag-staff, as a token that they asserted their right and suspended their quarrel. But such jealous friendship was of short and precarious duration; the German armies soon vanished in disease and desertion;[121] the Apulian duke, with all his adherents, was exterminated by a conqueror who seldom forgave either the dead or the living; like his predecessor Leo the Ninth, the feeble though haughty pontiff became the captive and friend of the Normans; and their reconciliation was celebrated by the eloquence of Bernard, who now revered the title and virtues of the king of Sicily.

As a penance for his impious war against the successor of St. Peter, that monarch might have promised to display the banner of the cross, and he accomplished with ardour a vow so propitious to his interest and revenge. The recent injuries of Sicily might provoke a just retaliation on the heads of the Saracens; the Normans, whose blood had been mingled with so many subject streams, were encouraged to remember and emulate the naval trophies of their fathers, and in the maturity of their strength they contended with the decline of an African power. When the Fatimite caliph departed for the conquest of Egypt, he rewarded the real merit and apparent fidelity of his servant Joseph with a gift of his royal mantle and forty Arabian horses, his palace, with its sumptuous furniture, and the government of the kingdoms of Tunis and Algiers. The Zeirides,[122] the descendants of Joseph, forgot their allegiance and gratitude to a distant benefactor, grasped and abused the fruits of prosperity; and, after running the little course of an Oriental dynasty, were now fainting in their own weakness. On the

His conquests in Africa. A.D. 1122-1152

---

[121] Roger corrupted the second person of Lothaire's army, who sounded, or rather cried, a retreat; for the Germans (says Cinnamus, l. iii. c. i. p. 51) are ignorant of the use of trumpets. Most ignorant himself! [Cinnamus says that they did not use a trumpet; not that they were ignorant of its use.]

[122] See de Guignes, Hist. Générale des Huns, tom. i. p. 369-373, and Cardonne Hist. de l'Afrique, &c. sous la Domination des Arabes, tom. ii. p. 70-144. Their common original appears to be Novairi.

side of the land, they were pressed by the Almohades, the fanatic princes of Morocco, while the sea-coast was open to the enterprises of the Greeks and Franks, who, before the close of the eleventh century, had extorted a ransom of two hundred thousand pieces of gold. By the first arms of Roger, the island or rock of Malta, which has been since ennobled by a military and religious colony, was inseparably annexed to the crown of Sicily. Tripoli,[123] a strong and maritime city, was the next object of his attack ; and the slaughter of the males, the captivity of the females, might be justified by the frequent practice of the Moslems themselves. The capital of the Zeirides was named Africa from the country, and Mahadia [124] from the Arabian founder ; it is strongly built on a neck of land, but the imperfection of the harbour is not compensated by the fertility of the adjacent plain. Mahadia was besieged by George the Sicilian admiral, with a fleet of one hundred and fifty galleys, amply provided with men and the instruments of mischief ; the sovereign had fled, the Moorish governor refused to capitulate, declined the last and irresistible assault, and, secretly escaping with the Moslem inhabitants, abandoned the place and its treasures to the rapacious Franks. In successive expeditions, the king of Sicily or his lieutenants reduced the cities of Tunis, Safax, Capsia, Bona, and a long tract of the sea-coast ; [125] the fortresses were garrisoned, the country was tributary, and a boast, that it held Africa in subjection, might be inscribed with some flattery on the sword of Roger.[126] After his death, that sword was broken ; and these transmarine possessions were neglected, evacuated, or lost, under the troubled reign of his successor.[127] The triumphs of Scipio and Belisarius have proved

---

[123] Tripoli (says the Nubian geographer, or more properly the Sherif al Edrisi) urbs fortis, saxeo muro vallata, sita prope littus maris. Hanc expugnavit Rogerius, qui mulieribus captivis ductis, viros peremit.

[124] See the geography of Leo Africanus (in Ramusio, tom. i. fol. 74, verso, fol. 75, recto) and Shaw's Travels (p. 110), the viith book of Thuanus, and the xith of the Abbé de Vertot. The possession and defence of the place was offered by Charles V. and wisely declined by the knights of Malta.

[125] Pagi has accurately marked the African conquests of Roger ; and his criticism was supplied by his friend the Abbé Longuerue with some Arabic memorials (A.D. 1147, No. 26, 27, A.D. 1148, No. 16, A.D. 1153, No. 16).

[126] Appulus et Calaber, Siculus mihi servit et Afer. A proud inscription, which denotes that the Norman conquerors were still discriminated from their Christian and Moslem subjects.

[127] Hugo Falcandus (Hist. Sicula, in Muratori, Script. tom. vii. p. 270, 271) ascribes these losses to the neglect or treachery of the admiral Majo.

that the African continent is neither inaccessible nor invincible ; yet the great princes and powers of Christendom have repeatedly failed in their armaments against the Moors, who may still glory in the easy conquest and long servitude of Spain.

Since the decease of Robert Guiscard, the Normans had relinquished, above sixty years, their hostile designs against the empire of the East. The policy of Roger solicited a public and private union with the Greek princes, whose alliance would dignify his regal character; he demanded in marriage a daughter of the Comnenian family, and the first steps of the treaty seemed to promise a favourable event. But the contemptuous treatment of his ambassadors exasperated the vanity of the new monarch; and the insolence of the Byzantine court was expiated, according to the laws of nations, by the sufferings of a guiltless people.[128] With a fleet of seventy galleys George the admiral of Sicily appeared before Corfu ; and both the island and city were delivered into his hands by the disaffected inhabitants, who had yet to learn that a siege is still more calamitous than a tribute. In this invasion, of some moment in the annals of commerce, the Normans spread themselves by sea, and over the provinces of Greece ; and the venerable age of Athens, Thebes, and Corinth was violated by rapine and cruelty. Of the wrongs of Athens, no memorial remains. The ancient walls, which encompassed, without guarding, the opulence of Thebes, were scaled by the Latin Christians; but their sole use of the gospel was to sanctify an oath that the lawful owners had not secreted any relic of their inheritance or industry. On the approach of the Normans the lower town of Corinth was evacuated : the Greeks retired to the citadel, which was seated on a lofty eminence abundantly watered by the classic fountain of Pirene: an impregnable fortress, if the want of courage could be balanced by any advantages of art or nature. As soon as the besiegers had surmounted the labour (their sole labour) of climbing the hill, their general, from the commanding eminence, admired his own victory, and testified his gratitude to heaven by tearing from the altar the precious image of

His invasion of Greece.
A.D. 1146

---

[128] The silence of the Sicilian historians, who end too soon or begin too late, must be supplied by Otho of Frisingen, a German (de Gestis Frederici I. l. i. c. 33), in Muratori, Script. tom. vi. p. 668), the Venetian Andrew Dandulus (id. tom. xii. p. 282, 283), and the Greek writers Cinnamus (l. iii. c. 2-5) and Nicetas (in Manuel. l. ii. c. 2-6).

Theodore the tutelary saint. The silk weavers of both sexes, whom George transported to Sicily, composed the most valuable part of the spoil, and, in comparing the skilful industry of the mechanic with the sloth and cowardice of the soldier, he was heard to exclaim that the distaff and loom were the only weapons which the Greeks were capable of using. The progress of this naval armament was marked by two conspicuous events, the rescue of the king of France and the insult of the Byzantine capital. In his return by sea from an unfortunate crusade, Louis the Seventh was intercepted by the Greeks, who basely violated the laws of honour and religion. The unfortunate encounter of the Norman fleet delivered the royal captive ; and, after a free and honourable entertainment in the court of Sicily, Louis continued his journey to Rome and Paris.[129] In the absence of the emperor, Constantinople and the Hellespont were left without defence and without the suspicion of danger. The clergy and people, for the soldiers had followed the standard of Manuel, were astonished and dismayed at the hostile appearance of a line of galleys, which boldly cast anchor in the front of the Imperial city. The forces of the Sicilian admiral were inadequate to the siege or assault of an immense and populous metropolis; but George enjoyed the glory of humbling the Greek arrogance, and of marking the path of conquest to the navies of the West. He landed some soldiers to rifle the fruits of the royal gardens, and pointed with silver, or more probably with fire, the arrows which he discharged against the palace of the Cæsars.[130] This playful outrage of the pirates of Sicily, who had surprised an unguarded moment, Manuel affected to despise, while his martial spirit and the forces of the empire were awakened to revenge. The Archipelago and Ionian sea were covered with his squadrons and those of Venice ; but I know not by what favourable allowance of transports,

His admiral delivers Louis VII. of France

Insults Constantinople

The emperor Manuel repulses the Normans. A.D. 1148, 1149

---

[129] To this imperfect capture and speedy rescue, I apply the παρ' ὀλίγον ἦλθε τοῦ ἁλῶναι of Cinnamus, l. ii. c. 19, p. 49. Muratori, on tolerable evidence (Annali d'Italia, tom. ix. p. 420, 421), laughs at the delicacy of the French, who maintain, marisque nullo impediente periculo ad regnum proprium reversum esse : yet I observe that their advocate, Ducange, is less positive as the commentator on Cinnamus than as the editor of Joinville.

[130] In palatium regium sagittas igneas injecit, says Dandulus ; but Nicetas, l. ii. c. 8, p. 66, transforms them into βέλη ἀργεντέους ἔχοντα ἀτρακτούς, and adds that Manuel styled this insult παίγνιον and γέλωτα . . . ληστεύοντα. These arrows, by the compiler, Vincent de Beauvais, are again transmuted into gold.

victuallers, and pinnaces, our reason, or even fancy, can be reconciled to the stupendous account of fifteen hundred vessels,
which is proposed by a Byzantine historian. These operations
were directed with prudence and energy; in his homeward
voyage George lost nineteen of his galleys, which were separated
and taken; after an obstinate defence, Corfu implored the
clemency of her lawful sovereign; nor could a ship, a soldier of
the Norman prince, be found, unless as a captive, within the
limits of the Eastern empire. The prosperity and the health of
Roger were already in a declining state; while he listened in
his palace of Palermo to the messengers of victory or defeat, the
invincible Manuel, the foremost in every assault, was celebrated
by the Greeks or Latins as the Alexander or Hercules of the age.

A prince of such a temper could not be satisfied with having
repelled the insolence of a barbarian. It was the right and
duty, it might be the interest and glory, of Manuel to restore
the ancient majesty of the empire, to recover the provinces
of Italy and Sicily, and to chastise this pretended king, the
grandson of a Norman vassal.[131] The natives of Calabria were
still attached to the Greek language and worship, which had
been inexorably proscribed by the Latin clergy: after the loss
of her dukes, Apulia was chained as a servile appendage to the
crown of Sicily; the founder of the monarchy had ruled by the
sword; and his death had abated the fear, without healing the
discontent, of his subjects; the feudal government was always
pregnant with the seeds of rebellion; and a nephew of Roger
himself invited the enemies of his family and nation. The
majesty of the purple, and a series of Hungarian and Turkish
wars, prevented Manuel from embarking his person in the
Italian expedition. To the brave and noble Palæologus, his
lieutenant, the Greek monarch entrusted a fleet and army; the
siege of Bari was his first exploit; and, in every operation, gold
as well as steel was the instrument of victory. Salerno, and
some places along the Western coast, maintained their fidelity
to the Norman king; but he lost in two campaigns the greater
part of his continental possessions; and the modest emperor,
disdaining all flattery and falsehood, was content with the re-

He reduces
Apulia and
Calabria.
A.D. 1155

---

[131] For the invasion of Italy, which is almost overlooked by Nicetas, see the
more polite history of Cinnamus (l. iv. c. 1-15, p. 78-101), who introduces a diffuse
narrative by a lofty profession, περὶ τῆς Σικελίας τε καὶ τῆς Ἰταλῶν ἐσκέπτετο γῆς, ὡς
καὶ ταύτας Ῥωμαίοις ἀνασώσαιτο [iii. 5].

duction of three hundred cities or villages of Apulia and Calabria, whose names and titles were inscribed on all the walls of the palace.

His design of acquiring Italy and the Western empire. A.D. 1155-1174, &c.

The prejudices of the Latins were gratified by a genuine or fictitious donation under the seal of the German Cæsars;[132] but the successor of Constantine soon renounced this ignominious pretence, claimed the indefeasible dominion of Italy, and professed his design of chasing the barbarians beyond the Alps. By the artful speeches, liberal gifts, and unbounded promises of their Eastern ally, the free cities were encouraged to persevere in their generous struggle against the despotism of Frederic Barbarossa; the walls of Milan were rebuilt by the contributions of Manuel; and he poured, says the historian, a river of gold into the bosom of Ancona, whose attachment to the Greeks was fortified by the jealous enmity of the Venetians.[133] The situation and trade of Ancona rendered it an important garrison in the heart of Italy; it was twice besieged by the arms of Frederic; the Imperial forces were twice repulsed by the spirit of freedom; that spirit was animated by the ambassador of Constantinople; and the most intrepid patriots, the most faithful servants, were rewarded by the wealth and honours of the Byzantine court.[134] The pride of Manuel disdained and rejected a barbarian colleague; his ambition was excited by the hope of stripping the purple from the German usurpers, and of establishing, in the West, as in the East, his lawful title of sole emperor of the Romans. With this view, he solicited the alliance of the people and the bishop of Rome. Several of the nobles embraced the cause of the Greek monarch; the splendid nuptials of his niece with Odo Frangipani secured the support of that powerful family,[135] and his royal standard or

<hr>

[132] The Latin, Otho (de Gestis Frederici I. l. ii. c. 30, p. 734), attests the forgery; the Greek, Cinnamus (l. i. c. 4, p. 78), claims a promise of restitution from Conrad and Frederic. An act of fraud is always credible when it is told of the Greeks.

[133] Quod Anconitani Græcum imperium nimis diligerent . . . Veneti speciali odio Anconam oderunt. The cause of love, perhaps of envy, were the beneficia, flumen aureum of the emperor; and the Latin narrative is confirmed by Cinnamus (l. iv. c. 14, p. 98).

[134] Muratori mentions the two sieges of Ancona: the first, in 1167, against Frederic I. in person (Annali, tom. x. p. 39, &c.), the second, in 1173, against his lieutenant Christian, archbishop of Mentz, a man unworthy of his name and office (p. 76, &c.). It is of the second siege that we possess an original narrative, which he has published in his great collection (tom. vi. p. 921-946).

[135] We derive this anecdote from an anonymous chronicle of Fossa Nova, published by Muratori (Script. Ital. tom. vii. p. 874). [=Annales Ceccanenses, in Pertz, Mon. Germ. Hist. xix. 276 sqq.]

image was entertained with due reverence in the ancient metropolis.[136] During the quarrel between Frederic and Alexander the Third, the pope twice received in the Vatican the ambassadors of Constantinople. They flattered his piety by the long-promised union of the two churches, tempted the avarice of his venal court, and exhorted the Roman pontiff to seize the just provocation, the favourable moment, to humble the savage insolence of the Alemanni, and to acknowledge the true representative of Constantine and Augustus.[137]

But these Italian conquests, this universal reign, soon escaped from the hand of the Greek emperor. His first demands were eluded by the prudence of Alexander the Third, who paused on this deep and momentous revolution,[138] nor could the pope be seduced by a personal dispute to renounce the perpetual inheritance of the Latin name. After his re-union with Frederic, he spoke a more peremptory language, confirmed the acts of his predecessors, excommunicated the adherents of Manuel, and pronounced the final separation of the churches, or at least the empires, of Constantinople and Rome.[139] The free cities of Lombardy no longer remembered their foreign benefactor, and, without preserving the friendship of Ancona, he soon incurred the enmity of Venice.[140] By his own avarice, or the complaints of his subjects, the Greek emperor was provoked to arrest the persons, and confiscate the effects, of the Venetian merchants. This violation of the public faith exasperated a free and commercial people: one hundred galleys were launched and armed in as many days; they swept the coasts of Dalmatia and Greece; but, after some mutual wounds, the war was terminated by an agreement, inglorious to the empire, insufficient for the republic; and a complete vengeance of these and of fresh injuries was

Failure of his designs

---

[136] The βασίλειον σημεῖον of Cinnamus (l. iv. c. 14, p. 99) is susceptible of this double sense. A standard is more Latin, an image more Greek.

[137] Nihilominus quoque petebat, ut quia occasio justa et tempus opportunum et acceptabile se obtulerant, Romani corona imperii a sancto apostolo sibi redderetur; quoniam non ad Frederici Alamanni, sed ad suum jus asseruit pertinere (Vit. Alexandri III. a Cardinal. Arragoniæ, in Script. Rerum Ital. tom. iii. par. i. p. 458). His second embassy was accompanied cum immensâ multitudine pecuniarum.

[138] Nimis alta et perplexa sunt (Vit. Alexandri III. p. 460, 461), says the cautious pope.

[139] Μηδὲν μέσον εἶναι λέγων Ῥώμῃ τῇ νεωτέρᾳ [νεοτέρᾳ in the quarto ed. vol. v. p. 636] πρὸς τὴν πρεσβυτέραν πάλαι ἀποῤῥαγεισῶν (Cinnamus, l. iv. c. 14, p. 99).

[140] In his vith book, Cinnamus describes the Venetian war, which Nicetas has not thought worthy of his attention. The Italian accounts, which do not satisfy our curiosity, are reported by the annalist Muratori, under the years 1171, &c.

reserved for the succeeding generation. The lieutenant of
Manuel had informed his sovereign that he was strong enough
to quell any domestic revolt of Apulia and Calabria ; but that
his forces were inadequate to resist the impending attack of the
king of Sicily. His prophecy was soon verified; the death of
Palæologus devolved the command on several chiefs, alike eminent in rank, alike defective in military talents; the Greeks
were oppressed by land and sea; and a captive remnant, that
escaped the swords of the Normans and Saracens, abjured all
future hostility against the person or dominions of their conqueror.[141] Yet the king of Sicily esteemed the courage and
constancy of Manuel, who had landed a second army on the
Italian shore; he respectfully addressed the new Justinian,
solicited a peace or truce of thirty years, accepted as a gift
the regal title, and acknowledged himself the military vassal of
the Roman empire.[142] The Byzantine Cæsars acquiesced in this
shadow of dominion, without expecting, perhaps without desiring, the service of a Norman army ; and the truce of thirty
years was not disturbed by any hostilities between Sicily and
Constantinople. About the end of that period, the throne of
Manuel was usurped by an inhuman tyrant, who had deserved
the abhorrence of his country and mankind : the sword of
William the Second, the grandson of Roger, was drawn by a
fugitive of the Comnenian race ; and the subjects of Andronicus
might salute the strangers as friends, since they detested their
sovereign as the worst of enemies. The Latin historians [143] expatiate on the rapid progress of the four counts who invaded
Romania with a fleet and army, and reduced many castles and
cities to the obedience of the king of Sicily. The Greeks [144]

Peace with the Normans. A.D. 1156

Last war of the Greeks and Normans. A.D. 1185

---

[141] This victory is mentioned by Romuald of Salerno (in Muratori, Script. Ital.
tom. vii. p. 198). It is whimsical enough that in the praise of the king of Sicily
Cinnamus (l. iv. c. 13, p. 97, 98) is much warmer and more copious than Falcandus
(p. 268, 270). But the Greek is fond of description, and the Latin historian is not
fond of William the Bad.

[142] For the epistle of William I. see Cinnamus (l. iv. c. 15, p. 101, 102) and
Nicetas (l. ii. c. 8). It is difficult to affirm whether these Greeks deceived themselves, or the public, in these flattering portraits of the grandeur of the empire.

[143] I can only quote of original evidence, the poor chronicles of Sicard of Cremona (p. 603), and of Fossa Nova (p. 875), as they are published in the viith tome
of Muratori's historians. The king of Sicily sent his troops contra nequitiam Andronici . . . ad acquirendum imperium C. P. They were capti aut confusi . . .
decepti captique, by Isaac.

[144] By the failure of Cinnamus, we are now reduced to Nicetas (in Andronico, l.
i. c. 7 8, 9, l. ii. c. i. in Isaac, Angelo, l. i. c. 1-4), who now becomes a respectable

accuse and magnify the wanton and sacrilegious cruelties that were perpetrated in the sack of Thessalonica, the second city of the empire. The former deplore the fate of those invincible but unsuspecting warriors, who were destroyed by the arts of a vanquished foe. The latter applaud, in songs of triumph, the repeated victories of their countrymen on the sea of Marmora or Propontis, on the banks of the Strymon, and under the walls of Durazzo. A revolution, which punished the crimes of Andronicus, had united against the Franks the zeal and courage of the successful insurgents: ten thousand were slain in battle, and Isaac Angelus, the new emperor, might indulge his vanity or vengeance in the treatment of four thousand captives. Such was the event of the last contest between the Greeks and Normans: before the expiration of twenty years, the rival nations were lost or degraded in foreign servitude; and the successors of Constantine did not long survive to insult the fall of the Sicilian monarchy.

The sceptre of Roger successively devolved to his son and grandson: they might be confounded under the name of William; they are strongly discriminated by the epithets of the *bad* and the *good;* but these epithets, which appear to describe the perfection of vice and virtue, cannot strictly be applied to either of the Norman princes. When he was roused to arms by danger and shame, the first William did not degenerate from the valour of his race; but his temper was slothful; his manners were dissolute; his passions headstrong and mischievous; and the monarch is responsible, not only for his personal vices, but for those of Majo, the great admiral, who abused the confidence, and conspired against the life, of his benefactor. From the Arabian conquest, Sicily had imbibed a deep tincture of Oriental manners; the despotism, the pomp, and even the harem, of a sultan; and a Christian people was oppressed and insulted by the ascendant of the eunuchs, who openly professed, or secretly cherished, the religion of Mahomet. An eloquent historian of the times [145] has delineated the misfortunes of

William I., the Bad, king of Sicily. Feb. 26— A.D. 1154, A.D. 1166, May 7

contemporary. As he survived the emperor and the empire, he is above flattery; but the fall of Constantinople exasperated his prejudices against the Latins. For the honour of learning I shall observe that Homer's great commentator, Eustathius, archbishop of Thessalonica, refused to desert his flock. [For Eustathius and his work on the siege of Thessalonica see Appendix 1.]

[145] The Historia Sicula of Hugo Falcandus, which properly extends from 1154 to 1169, is inserted in the viith volume of Muratori's Collection (tom. vii.

his country: [146] the ambition and fall of the ungrateful Majo; the revolt and punishment of his assassins; the imprisonment and deliverance of the king himself; the private feuds that arose from the public confusion; and the various forms of calamity and discord which afflicted Palermo, the island, and the continent, during the reign of William the First, and the minority of his son. The youth, innocence, and beauty of William the Second [147] endeared him to the nation: the factions were reconciled; the laws were revived; and, from the manhood to the premature death of that amiable prince, Sicily enjoyed a short season of peace, justice, and happiness, whose value was enhanced by the remembrance of the past and the dread of futurity. The legitimate male posterity of Tancred of Hauteville was extinct in the person of the second William; but his aunt, the daughter of Roger, had married the most powerful prince of the age; and Henry the Sixth, the son of Frederic Barbarossa, descended from the Alps, to claim the Imperial crown and the inheritance of his wife. Against the unanimous wish of a free people, this inheritance could only be acquired by arms; and I am pleased to transcribe the style and sense of the historian Falcandus, who writes at the moment and on the spot, with the feelings of a patriot, and the prophetic eye of a statesman. "Constantia, the daughter of Sicily, nursed from her cradle in the pleasures and plenty, and

William II., the Good. A.D. 1166, May 7 —A.D. 1189, Nov. 16

Lamentation of the historian Falcandus

p. 259-344), and preceded by an eloquent preface or epistle (p. 251-258) de Calamitatibus Siciliæ. [Re-edited by Del Re in Cronisti e scrittori sincroni napoletani, 1845.] Falcandus has been styled the Tacitus of Sicily; and, after a just but immense abatement, from the first to the twelfth century, from a senator to a monk, I would not strip him of his title: his narrative is rapid and perspicuous, his style bold and elegant, his observation keen; he had studied mankind, and feels like a man. I can only regret the narrow and barren field on which his labours have been cast. [Cp. Appendix 1. For the history of Sicily from the accession of William the Bad to 1177, see F. Holzach, Die auswärtige Politik des Königreichs Sicilien 1154-1177 (1892).]

[146] The laborious Benedictines (l'Art de verifier les Dates, p. 896) are of opinion that the true name of Falcandus is Fulcandus, or Foucault. According to them, Hugues Foucault, a Frenchman by birth, and at length abbot of St. Denys, had followed into Sicily his patron Stephen de la Perche, uncle to the mother of William II. archbishop of Palermo, and great chancellor of the kingdom. Yet Falcandus has all the feelings of a Sicilian; and the title of *Alumnus* (which he bestows on himself) appears to indicate that he was born, or at least educated, in the island. [See Appendix 1.]

[147] Falcand. p. 303. Richard de St. Germano begins his history from the death and praises of William II. After some unmeaning epithets, he thus continues: Legis et justitiæ cultus tempore suo vigebat in regno; suâ erat quilibet sorte contentus (were they mortals?); ubique pax, ubique securitas, nec latronum metuebat viator insidias, nec maris nauta offendicula piratarum (Script. Rerum Ital. tom. vii. p. 969).

educated in the arts and manners, of this fortunate isle, departed long since to enrich the barbarians with our treasures, and now returns with her savage allies, to contaminate the beauties of her venerable parent. Already I behold the swarms of angry barbarians; our opulent cities, the places flourishing in a long peace, are shaken with fear, desolated by slaughter, consumed by rapine, and polluted by intemperance and lust. I see the massacre or captivity of our citizens, the rapes of our virgins and matrons.[148] In this extremity (he interrogates a friend) how must the Sicilians act? By the unanimous election of a king of valour and experience, Sicily and Calabria might yet be preserved;[149] for in the levity of the Apulians, ever eager for new revolutions, I can repose neither confidence nor hope.[150] Should Calabria be lost, the lofty towers, the numerous youth, and the naval strength, of Messina[151] might guard the passage against a foreign invader. If the savage Germans coalesce with the pirates of Messina; if they destroy with fire the fruitful region, so often wasted by the fires of mount Ætna,[152] what resource will be left for the interior parts of the island, these noble cities which should never be violated by the hostile footsteps of a barbarian?[153] Catana has again been overwhelmed by an earthquake; the ancient virtue of Syracuse expires in poverty and solitude;[154] but Palermo is still crowned with a diadem,

---

[148] Constantia, primis a cunabulis in deliciarum tuarum affluentiâ diutius educata, tuisque institutis [instituta], doctrinis et moribus informata, tandem opibus tuis Barbaros delatura [ditatura] discessit; et nunc cum ingentibus copiis [. . .] revertitur, ut pulcherrima [pulcherrimæ] nutricis ornamenta [. . .] barbaricâ foeditate contaminet . . . Intueri mihi jam videor turbulentas barbarorum acies . . . civitates opulentas et loca diuturnâ pace florentia, metu concutere, cæde vastare, rapinis atterere, et foedare luxuriâ: [occurrunt] hinc cives aut [resistendo] gladiis intercepti, aut [. . .] servitute depressi [illinc], virgines [. . .] constupratæ, matronæ, &c. [p. 253-4].

[149] Certe si regem [sibi] non dubiæ virtutis elegerint, nec a Saracenis Christiani [leg. a Christianis Saraceni] dissentiant, poterit rex creatus rebus licet quasi desperatis et [fere] perditis subvenire, et incursus hostium, si prudenter egerit, propulsare.

[150] In Apulis, qui, semper novitate gaudentes, novarum rerum studiis aguntur, nihil arbitror spei aut fiduciæ reponendum.

[151] Si civium tuorum virtutem et audaciam attendas, . . . murorum etiam ambitum densis turribus circumseptum.

[152] Cum crudelitate piraticâ Theutonum confligat atrocitas, et inter ambustos lapides, et Æthnæ flagrantis incendia, &c.

[153] Eam partem, quam nobilissimarum civitatum fulgor illustrat, quæ et toti regno singulari meruit privilegio præeminere, nefarium esset . . . vel barbarorum ingressu pollui. I wish to transcribe his florid, but curious, description of the palace, city, and luxuriant plain of Palermo.

[154] Vires non suppetunt, et conatus tuos tam inopia civium, quam paucitas bellatorum elidunt.

and her triple walls inclose the active multitudes of Christians and Saracens. If the two nations, under one king, can unite for their common safety, they may rush on the barbarians with invincible arms. But, if the Saracens, fatigued by a repetition of injuries, should now retire and rebel; if they should occupy the castles of the mountains and sea-coast, the unfortunate Christians, exposed to a double attack, and placed as it were between the hammer and the anvil, must resign themselves to hopeless and inevitable servitude."[155] We must not forget that a priest here prefers his country to his religion; and that the Moslems, whose alliance he seeks, were still numerous and powerful in the state of Sicily.

Conquest of the kingdom of Sicily by the emperor Henry VI. A.D. 1194

The hopes, or at least the wishes, of Falcandus were at first gratified by the free and unanimous election of Tancred, the grandson of the first king, whose birth was illegitimate, but whose civil and military virtues shone without a blemish. During four years, the term of his life and reign, he stood in arms on the farthest verge of the Apulian frontier, against the powers of Germany; and the restitution of a royal captive, of Constantia herself, without injury or ransom, may appear to surpass the most liberal measure of reason. After his decease, the kingdom of his widow and infant son fell without a struggle; and Henry pursued his victorious march from Capua to Palermo. The political balance of Italy was destroyed by his success; and, if the pope and the free cities had consulted their obvious and real interest, they would have combined the powers of earth and heaven to prevent the dangerous union of the German empire with the kingdom of Sicily. But the subtle policy, for which the Vatican has so often been praised or arraigned, was on this occasion blind and inactive; and, if it were true that Celestine the Third had kicked away the Imperial crown from the head

---

[155] At vero, quia difficile est Christianos in tanto rerum turbine, sublato regis timore Saracenos non opprimere, si Saraceni [. . .] injuriis fatigati ab eis cœperint dissidere, et castella forte maritima vel montanas munitiones occupaverint; ut hinc cum Theutonicis summâ [sit] virtute pugnandum, illinc Saracenis crebris insultibus occurrendum, quid putas acturi sunt Siculi inter has depressi angustias, et velut inter malleum et incudem multo cum discrimine constituti? hoc utique agent quod poterunt, ut se Barbaris miserabili conditione dedentes, in eorum se conferant potestatem. O utinam plebis et [ac] procerum, Christianorum et Saracenorum vota conveniant; ut regem sibi concorditer eligentes, [irruentes] barbaros totis viribus, toto conamine, totisque desideriis proturbare contendant. The Normans and Sicilians appear to be confounded.

of the prostrate Henry,[156] such an act of impotent pride could serve only to cancel an obligation and provoke an enemy. The Genoese, who enjoyed a beneficial trade and establishment in Sicily, listened to the promise of his boundless gratitude and speedy departure;[157] their fleet commanded the straits of Messina, and opened the harbour of Palermo; and the first act of this government was to abolish the privileges, and to seize the property, of these imprudent allies. The last hope of Falcandus was defeated by the discord of the Christians and Mahometans: they fought in the capital; several thousands of the latter were slain; but their surviving brethren fortified the mountains, and disturbed above thirty years the peace of the island. By the policy of Frederic the Second, sixty thousand Saracens were transplanted to Nocera in Apulia. In their wars against the Roman church, the emperor and his son Mainfroy were strengthened and disgraced by the service of the enemies of Christ; and this national colony maintained their religion and manners in the heart of Italy, till they were extirpated, at the end of the thirteenth century, by the zeal and revenge of the house of Anjou.[158] All the calamities which the prophetic orator had deplored were surpassed by the cruelty and avarice of the German conqueror. He violated the royal sepulchres, and explored the secret treasures of the palace, Palermo, and the whole kingdom: the pearls and jewels, however precious, might be easily removed; but one hundred and sixty horses were laden with the gold and silver of Sicily.[159] The young

---

[156] The testimony of an Englishman, of Roger de Hoveden (p. 689), will lightly weigh against the silence of German and Italian history (Muratori, Annali d'Italia, tom. x. p. 156). The priests and pilgrims, who returned from Rome, exalted, by every tale, the omnipotence of the holy father.

[157] Ego enim in eo cum Teutonicis manere non debeo (Caffari, Annal. Genuenses, in Muratori, Script. Rerum Italicarum, tom. vi. p. 367, 368).

[158] For the Saracens of Sicily and Nocera, see the Annals of Muratori (tom. x. p. 149, and A.D. 1223, 1247), Giannone (tom. ii. p. 385), and of the originals, in Muratori's Collection, Richard de St. Germano (tom. vii. p. 996), Matteo Spinelli de Giovenazzo (tom. vii. p. 1064), Nicholas de Jamsilla (tom. x. p. 494), and Matteo Villani (tom. xiv. l. vii. p. 103). The last of these insinuates that, in reducing the Saracens of Nocera, Charles II. of Anjou employed rather artifice than violence.

[159] Muratori quotes a passage from Arnold of Lubec (l. iv. c. 20). Reperit thesauros absconditos, et omnem lapidum pretiosorum et gemmarum gloriam, ita ut oneratis 160 somariis gloriose ad terram suam redierit. Roger de Hoveden, who mentions the violation of the royal tomb and corpses, computes the spoil of Salerno at 200,000 ounces of gold (p. 746). On these occasions, I am almost tempted to exclaim with the listening maid in La Fontaine, "Je voudrois bien avoir ce qui manque".

king, his mother and sisters, and the nobles of both sexes, were separately confined in the fortresses of the Alps; and, on the slightest rumour of rebellion, the captives were deprived of life, of their eyes, or of the hope of posterity. Constantia herself was touched with sympathy for the miseries of her country; and the heiress of the Norman line might struggle to check her despotic husband, and to save the patrimony of her new-born son, of an emperor so famous in the next age under the name of Frederic the Second. Ten years after this revolution, the French monarchs annexed to their crown the duchy of Normandy; the sceptre of her ancient dukes had been transmitted, by a grand-daughter of William the Conqueror, to the house of Plantagenet; and the adventurous Normans, who had raised so many trophies in France, England, and Ireland, in Apulia, Sicily, and the East, were lost, either in victory or servitude, among the vanquished nations.

Final extinction of the Normans.
A.D. 1204

MOHAMMEDAN ORNAMENT. ABOVE, CARVED FRIEZE FROM THE MOSQUE
ESH SHABÎYEH ALEPPO (A.D. 1150); BELOW, INSCRIPTION AT MAYAFARKIN

CHAPTER LVII

The Turks of the House of Seljuk—Their Revolt against Mahmud, Conqueror of Hindostan—Togrul subdues Persia, and protects the Caliphs—Defeat and Captivity of the Emperor Romanus Diogenes by Alp Arslan—Power and Magnificence of Malek Shah—Conquest of Asia Minor and Syria—State and Oppression of Jerusalem—Pilgrimages to the Holy Sepulchre

FROM the isle of Sicily the reader must transport himself The Turks beyond the Caspian Sea, to the original seat of the Turks or Turkmans, against whom the first crusade was principally directed. Their Scythian empire of the sixth century was long since dissolved; but the name was still famous among the Greeks and Orientals; and the fragments of the nation, each a powerful and independent people, were scattered over the desert from China to the Oxus and the Danube: the colony of Hungarians was admitted into the republic of Europe, and the thrones of Asia were occupied by slaves and soldiers of Turkish extraction. While Apulia and Sicily were subdued by the Norman lance, a swarm of these northern shepherds overspread the kingdoms of Persia: their princes of the race of Seljuk erected a splendid and solid empire from Samarcand to the confines of Greece and Egypt; and the Turks have maintained their dominion in Asia Minor till the victorious crescent has been planted on the dome of St. Sophia.

One of the greatest of the Turkish princes was Mamood or Mahmud, the Gaznevide, A.D. 997-1028 the Gaznevide, who reigned in the eastern provinces Mahmud,[1] the Gaznevide, who reigned in the eastern provinces

[1] I am indebted for his character and history to d'Herbelot (Bibliothèque Orientale, *Mahmud*, p. 533-537), M. de Guignes (Histoire des Huns, tom. iii. p. 155-173), and our countryman, Colonel Alexander Dow (vol. i. p. 23-83). In the two first volumes of his History of Hindostan, he styles himself the translator of the Persian Ferishta; but in his florid text it is not easy to distinguish the version and the original. [This work of Dow has been superseded by the translation of Colonel

[Subukti-
gin]

of Persia one thousand years after the birth of Christ. His father Sebectagi was the slave of the slave of the slave of the commander of the faithful. But in this descent of servitude, the first degree was merely titular, since it was filled by the sovereign of Transoxiana and Chorasan, who still paid a nominal allegiance to the caliph of Bagdad. The second rank was that of a minister of state, a lieutenant of the Samanides,[2] who broke, by his revolt, the bonds of political slavery. But the third step was a state of real and domestic servitude in the family of that rebel; from which Sebectagi, by his courage and dexterity, ascended to the supreme command of the city and province of Gazna,[3] as the son-in-law and successor of his grateful master. The falling dynasty of the Samanides was at first protected, and at last overthrown, by their servants; and, in the public disorders, the fortune of Mahmud continually increased. For him, the title of *sultan*[4] was first invented; and his kingdom was enlarged from Transoxiana to the neighbourhood of Ispahan, from the shores of the Caspian to the mouth of the Indus. But the principal source of his fame and riches was the holy war which he waged against the Gentoos of Hindostan. In this

Briggs: "History of the Mahomedan Power in India till the year 1612, translated from the original Persian of Mohamed Kasim Ferishta," in 4 vols., 1829. Cp. his remarks on Dow's work in the Preface, vol. i. p. vi. vii.]

[2] The dynasty of the Samanides continued 125 years, A.D. 874-999, under ten princes. See their succession and ruin, in the Tables of M. de Guignes (Hist. des Huns, tom. i. p. 404-406). They were followed [south of the Oxus] by the Gaznevides, A.D. 999-1183. (See tom. i. p. 239, 240.) His division of nations often disturbs the series of time and place.

[3] Gaznah hortos non habet; est emporium et domicilium mercaturæ Indicæ. Abulfedæ Geograph. Reiske, tab. xxiii. p. 349; d'Herbelot, p. 364. It has not been visited by any modern traveller. [Subuktigīn conquered Būst and Kusdār in A.D. 978. For the story of his rise, cp. Nizām al-Mulk, Siasset Nameh, tr. Schefer, p. 140 sqq.]

[4] By the ambassador of the caliph of Bagdad, who employed an Arabian or Chaldaic word that signifies *lord* and *master* (d'Herbelot, p. 825). It is interpreted Αὐτοκράτωρ, Βασιλεὺς Βασιλέων, by the Byzantine writers of the eleventh century; and the name (Σουλτανός, Soldanus) is familiarly employed in the Greek and Latin languages, after it had passed from the Gaznevides to the Seljukides, and other emirs of Asia and Egypt. Ducange (Dissertation xvi. sur Joinville, p. 238-240, Gloss. Græc. et Latin.) labours to find the title of sultan in the ancient kingdom of Persia; but his proofs are mere shadows; a proper name in the Themes of Constantine (ii. 11), an anticipation of Zonaras, &c. and a medal of Kai Khosrou, not (as he believes) the Sassanide of the vith, but the Seljukide of Iconium of the xiiith, century (de Guignes, Hist. des Huns, tom. i. p. 246). [The title *sultan*, for the captain of the bodyguard, was introduced at least as early as the reign of Mutawakkil, in the middle of the 9th century. It has been conjectured (by Vámbéry) that the name of one of the sons of the Hungarian chief Arpad, Ζάλτας, is really *sultan*. The old Vienna chronicle gives his name as *Zoltan*, and the scribe of King Béla, as *Zulta*.]

foreign narrative I may not consume a page; and a volume would scarcely suffice to recapitulate the battles and sieges of his twelve expeditions. Never was the Musulman hero dismayed by the inclemency of the seasons, the height of the mountains, the breadth of the rivers, the barrenness of the desert, the multitudes of the enemy, or the formidable array of their elephants of war.[5] The sultan of Gazna surpassed the limits of the conquests of Alexander; after a march of three months, over the hills of Cashmir and Thibet, he reached the famous city of Kinnoge,[6] on the Upper Ganges; and, in a naval combat on one of the branches of the Indus, he fought and vanquished four thousand boats of the natives. Delhi, Lahor, and Multan were compelled to open their gates; the fertile kingdom of Guzarat attracted his ambition and tempted his stay; and his avarice indulged the fruitless project of discovering the golden and aromatic isles of the Southern Ocean. On the payment of a tribute, the *rajahs* preserved their dominions; the people, their lives and fortunes ; but to the religion of Hindostan the zealous Musulman was cruel and inexorable; many hundred temples, or pagodas, were levelled with the ground; many thousand idols were demolished; and the servants of the prophet were stimulated and rewarded by the precious materials of which they were composed. The pagoda of Sumnat was situated on the promontory of Guzarat, in the neighbourhood of Diu, one of the last remaining possessions of the Portuguese.[7] It was endowed with the revenue of two thousand villages; two thousand Brahmins were consecrated to the service of the Deity, whom they washed each morning and evening in water from

His twelve expeditions into Hindostan

[Kanauj]

[Somnath. A.D. 1024]

---

[5] Ferishta (apud Dow, Hist. of Hindostan, vol. i. p. 49) mentions the report of a *gun* in the Indian army. But, as I am slow in believing this premature (A.D. 1008) use of artillery, I must desire to scrutinise first the text and then the authority of Ferishta, who lived in the Mogul court in the last century. [Briggs (*op. cit.*, vol. i. p. 47) translates, in the passage to which Gibbon refers, " naphtha-balls " and " arrows " ; the original words being *nupth* and *khudung*. But in other Mss. the variants are formed : *tope* (a gun) and *toofung* (a musket). These readings must be due to interpolators. Probably Bābar first introduced guns into Upper India in 1526. Cp. the note of Briggs.]

[6] Kinnoge or Canouge (the old Palimbothra) is marked in latitude 27° 3′, longitude 80° 13′. See d'Anville (Antiquité de l'Inde, p. 60-62), corrected by the local knowledge of Major Rennell (in his excellent Memoir on his map of Hindostan, p. 37-43), 300 jewellers, 30,000 shops for the areca nut, 60,000 bands of musicians, &c. (Abulfed. Geograph. tab. xv. p. 274; Dow, vol. i. p. 16) will allow an ample deduction. [Palimbothra is supposed to be Patna.]

[7] The idolaters of Europe, says Ferishta (Dow, vol. i. p. 66). Consult Abulfeda (p. 272) and Rennell's map of Hindostan.

the distant Ganges : the subordinate ministers consisted of three hundred musicians, three hundred barbers, and five hundred dancing girls, conspicuous for their birth and beauty.. Three sides of the temple were protected by the ocean, the narrow isthmus was fortified by a natural or artificial precipice ; and the city and adjacent country were peopled by a nation of fanatics. They confessed the sins and the punishment of Kinnoge and Delhi ; but, if the impious stranger should presume to approach *their* holy precincts, he would surely be overwhelmed by a blast of the divine vengeance. By this challenge the faith of Mahmud was animated to a personal trial of the strength of this Indian deity. Fifty thousand of his worshippers were pierced by the spear of the Moslems: the walls were scaled; the sanctuary was profaned; and the conqueror aimed a blow of his iron mace at the head of the idol. The trembling Brahmins are said to have offered ten millions sterling [8] for his ransom; and it was urged by the wisest counsellors that the destruction of a stone image would not change the hearts of the Gentoos, and that such a sum might be dedicated to the relief of the true believers. "Your reasons," replied the Sultan, "are specious and strong; but never in the eyes of posterity shall Mahmud appear as a merchant of idols." He repeated his blows, and a treasure of pearls and rubies, concealed in the belly of the statue, explained in some degree the devout prodigality of the Brahmins. The fragments of the idol were distributed to Gazna, Mecca, and Medina. Bagdad listened to the edifying tale; and Mahmud was saluted by the caliph with the title of guardian of the fortune and faith of Mahomet.

His character

From the paths of blood, and such is the history of nations, I cannot refuse to turn aside to gather some flowers of science or virtue. The name of Mahmud the Gaznevide is still venerable in the East : his subjects enjoyed the blessings of prosperity and peace; his vices were concealed by the veil of religion; and two familiar examples will testify his justice and magnanimity. I. As he sat in the Divan, an unhappy subject bowed before the throne to accuse the insolence of a Turkish soldier who had driven him from his house and bed. "Suspend your clamours," said Mahmud, "inform me of his next visit and ourself in person

___

[8] [Not ten millions sterling, but " crores of gold ". Briggs, p. 72, translates " a quantity of gold ".]

will judge and punish the offender." The sultan followed his guide, invested the house with his guards, and, extinguishing the torches, pronounced the death of the criminal, who had been seized in the act of rapine and adultery. After the execution of his sentence, the lights were rekindled, Mahmud fell prostrate in prayer, and, rising from the ground, demanded some homely fare, which he devoured with the voraciousness of hunger. The poor man, whose injury he had avenged, was unable to suppress his astonishment and curiosity; and the courteous monarch condescended to explain the motives of this singular behaviour. "I had reason to suspect that none except one of my sons could dare to perpetrate such an outrage; and I extinguished the lights, that my justice might be blind and inexorable. My prayer was a thanksgiving on the discovery of the offender; and so painful was my anxiety that I had passed three days without food since the first moment of your complaint." II. The Sultan of Gazna had declared war against the dynasty of the Bowides, the sovereigns of the western Persia ; he was disarmed by an epistle of the sultana mother, and delayed his invasion till the manhood of her son.[9] "During the life of my husband," said the artful regent, "I was ever apprehensive of your ambition; he was a prince and a soldier worthy of your arms. He is now no more; his sceptre has passed to a woman and a child, and you *dare not* attack their infancy and weakness. How inglorious would be your conquest, how shameful your defeat! and yet the event of war is in the hand of the Almighty." Avarice was the only defect that tarnished the illustrious character of Mahmud; and never has that passion been more richly satisfied. The Orientals exceed the measure of credibility in the account of millions of gold and silver, such as the avidity of man has never accumulated ; in the magnitude of pearls, diamonds, and rubies, such as have never been produced by the workmanship of nature.[10] Yet the soil of Hindostan is impregnated with precious minerals; her trade, in every age, has attracted the gold and silver of the

---

[9] D'Herbelot, Bibliothèque Orientale, p. 527.   Yet these letters, apophthegms, &c., are rarely the language of the heart, or the motives of public action.

[10] For instance, a ruby of four hundred and fifty miskals (Dow, vol. i. p. 53) or six pounds three ounces : the largest in the treasury of Delhi weighed seventeen miskals (Voyages de Tavernier, partie ii. p. 280).   It is true that in the East all coloured stones are called rubies (p. 355), and that Tavernier saw three larger and more precious among the jewels de notre grand roi, le plus puissant et plus magnifique de tous les Rois de la terre (p. 376).

world; and her virgin spoils were rifled by the first of the Mahometan conquerors. His behaviour, in the last days of his life, evinces the vanity of these possessions, so laboriously won, so dangerously held, and so inevitably lost. He surveyed the vast and various chambers of the treasury of Gazna; burst into tears; and again closed the doors, without bestowing any portion of the wealth which he could no longer hope to preserve. The following day he reviewed the state of his military force : one hundred thousand foot, fifty-five thousand horse, and thirteen hundred elephants of battle.[11] He again wept the instability of human greatness; and his grief was embittered by the hostile progress of the Turkmans, whom he had introduced into the heart of his Persian kingdom.

Manners and emigration of the Turks or Turkmans.
A.D. 980-1028 In the modern depopulation of Asia, the regular operation of government and agriculture is confined to the neighbourhood of cities; and the distant country is abandoned to the pastoral tribes of Arabs, Curds, and *Turkmans*.[12] Of the last-mentioned people, two considerable branches extend on either side of the Caspian Sea : the western colony can muster forty thousand soldiers; the eastern, less obvious to the traveller, but more strong and populous, has increased to the number of one hundred thousand families. In the midst of civilised nations, they preserve the manners of the Scythian desert, remove their encampments with the change of seasons, and feed their cattle among the ruins of palaces and temples. Their flocks and herds are their only riches; their tents, either black or white, according to the colour of the banner, are covered with felt, and of a circular form; their winter apparel is a sheep-skin; a robe of cloth or cotton their summer garment : the features of the men are harsh and ferocious; the countenance of their women is soft and pleasing. Their wandering life maintains the spirit and exercise of arms; they fight on horseback; and their courage is displayed in frequent contests with each other and with their neighbours. For the licence of pasture they pay a slight tribute to the sove-

---

[11] Dow, vol. i. p. 65. The sovereign of Kinnoge is said to have possessed 2500 elephants (Abulfed. Geograph. tab. xv. p. 274). From these Indian stories the reader may correct a note in my first volume (p. 226) ; or from that note he may correct these stories.

[12] See a just and natural picture of these pastoral manners, in the history of William, archbishop of Tyre (l. i. c. vii. in the Gesta Dei per Francos, p. 633, 634), and a valuable note by the editor of the Histoire Généalogique des Tatars, p. 535-538.

reign of the land; but the domestic jurisdiction is in the hands of the chiefs and elders. The first emigration of the eastern Turkmans, the most ancient of their race, may be ascribed to the tenth century of the Christian æra.[13] In the decline of the caliphs, and the weakness of their lieutenants, the barrier of the Jaxartes was often violated: in each invasion, after the victory or retreat of their countrymen, some wandering tribe, embracing the Mahometan faith, obtained a free encampment in the spacious plains and pleasant climate of Transoxiana and Carizme. The Turkish slaves who aspired to the throne encouraged these emigrations, which recruited their armies, awed their subjects and rivals, and protected the frontier against the wilder natives of Turkestan; and this policy was abused by Mahmud the Gaznevide beyond the example of former times. He was admonished of his error by a chief of the race of Seljuk, who dwelt in the territory of Bochara. The sultan had enquired what supply of men he could furnish for military service. "If you send," replied Ismael, "one of these arrows into our camp, fifty thousand of your servants will mount on horseback." "And if that number," continued Mahmud, "should not be sufficient?" "Send this second arrow to the horde of Balik, and you will find fifty thousand more." "But," said the Gaznevide, dissembling his anxiety, "if I should stand in need of the whole force of your kindred tribes?" "Dispatch my bow," was the last reply of Ismael, "and, as it is circulated around, the summons will be obeyed by two hundred thousand horse." The apprehension of such formidable friendship induced Mahmud to transport the most obnoxious tribes into the heart of Chorasan, where they would be separated from their brethren by the river Oxus, and inclosed on all sides by the walls of obedient cities. But the face of the country was an object of temptation rather than terror; and the vigour of government was relaxed by the absence and death of the sultan of Gazna. The shepherds were converted into robbers; the bands of robbers were collected into an army of conquerors; as far as Ispahan and the Tigris, Persia was afflicted by their predatory

---

[13] The first emigrations of the Turkmans, and doubtful origin of the Seljukians, may be traced in the laborious history of the Huns, by M. de Guignes (tom. i. Tables Chronologiques, l. v. tom. iii. l. vii. ix. x.), and the Bibliothèque Orientale of d'Herbelot (p. 799-802, 897-901), Elmacin (Hist. Saracen. p. 331-333), and Abul-pharagius (Dynast. p. 221, 222).

inroads; and the Turkmans were not ashamed or afraid to measure their courage and numbers with the proudest sovereigns of Asia. Massoud, the son and successor of Mahmud, had too
[Emirs] long neglected the advice of his wisest Omrahs. "Your enemies," they repeatedly urged, "were in their origin a swarm of ants; they are now little snakes; and, unless they be instantly crushed, they will acquire the venom and magnitude of serpents." After some alternatives of truce and hostility, after the repulse or partial success of his lieutenants, the sultan marched in person against the Turkmans, who attacked him on all sides with barbarous shouts and irregular onset. "Massoud," says the Persian historian,[14] "plunged singly to oppose the torrent of gleaming arms, exhibiting such acts of gigantic force
They defeat the Gaznevides, and subdue Persia. A.D. 1038 [1039] [Battle of Damghan] and valour as never king had before displayed. A few of his friends, roused by his words and actions, and that innate honour which inspires the brave, seconded their lord so well that, wheresoever he turned his fatal sword, the enemies were mowed down or retreated before him. But now, when victory seemed to blow on his standard, misfortune was active behind it; for, when he looked round, he beheld almost his whole army, excepting that body he commanded in person, devouring the paths of flight." The Gaznevide was abandoned by the cowardice or treachery of some generals of Turkish race; and this memorable day of Zendecan[15] founded in Persia the dynasty of the shepherd kings.[16]

The victorious Turkmans immediately proceeded to the elec-

[14] Dow, Hist. of Hindostan, vol. i. p. 89, 95-98. I have copied this passage as a specimen of the Persian manner ; but I suspect that by some odd fatality the style of Ferishta has been improved by that of Ossian. [The translation of Briggs, i. 110, is as follows : " The king undismayed even by the defection of his officers gallantly rode his horse to the spot where he perceived the conflict most bloody, performing prodigies of valour, unequalled perhaps by any sovereign ; but his efforts were vain ; for, when he looked round, he beheld nearly the whole of his army, excepting the body which he commanded in person, in full flight ".]

[15] The Zendekan of d'Herbelot (p. 1028), the Dindaka of Dow (vol. i. p. 97), is probably the Dandanekan of Abulfeda (Geograph. p. 345, Reiske), a small town of Chorasan, two days' journey from Marû [Persian, Merv], and renowned through the East for the production and manufacture of cotton.

[16] The Byzantine historians (Cedrenus, tom. ii. p. 766, 767 [ii. p. 566, ed. Bonn] ; Zonaras, tom. ii. p. 255 [xvii. 25] ; Nicephorus Bryennius, p. 21 [p. 26, ed. B.]) have confounded, in this revolution, the truth of time and place, of names and persons, of causes and events. The ignorance and errors of these Greeks (which I shall not stop to unravel) may inspire some distrust of the story of Cyaxares and Cyrus, as it is told by their most eloquent predecessors.

tion of a king; and, if the probable tale of a Latin historian [17] Dynasty of the Seljukians. deserves any credit, they determined by lot the choice of their A.D. 1038- new master. A number of arrows were successively inscribed 1152 with the name of a tribe, a family, and a candidate; they were drawn from the bundle by the hand of a child; and the important prize was obtained by Togrul Beg, the son of Michael, the son of Seljuk, whose surname was immortalised in the greatness of his posterity. The sultan Mahmud, who valued himself on his skill in national genealogy, professed his ignorance of the family of Seljuk; yet the father of that race appears to have been a chief of power and renown.[18] For a daring intrusion into the harem of his prince, Seljuk was banished from Turkestan; with a numerous tribe of his friends [at Jend] and vassals, he passed the Jaxartes, encamped in the neighbourhood of Samarcand, embraced the religion of Mahomet,[19] and acquired the crown of martyrdom in a war against the infidels. His age, of an hundred and seven years, surpassed the life of his son, and Seljuk adopted the care of his two grandsons, Togrul and Jaafar; the eldest of whom, at the age of forty-five, was in- [Chaghar] vested with the title of sultan, in the royal city of Nishabur. Reign and character The blind determination of chance was justified by the virtues of Togrul of the successful candidate. It would be superfluous to praise 1038-1063 the valour of a Turk; and the ambition of Togrul [20] was equal to his valour. By his arms, the Gaznevides were expelled from the eastern kingdoms of Persia, and gradually driven to the banks of the Indus, in search of a softer and more wealthy conquest. In the West he annihilated the dynasty of the Bowides; and the sceptre of Irak passed from the Persian to the Turkish nation.

---

[17] Willerm. Tyr. l. i. c. 7, p. 633 [ed. Bongars.]. The divination by arrows is ancient and famous in the East.

[18] D'Herbelot, p. 801. Yet, after the fortune of his posterity, Seljuk became the thirty-fourth in lineal descent from the great Afrasiab, emperor of Touran (p. 800). The Tartar pedigree of the house of Zingis gave a different cast to flattery and fable; and the historian Mirkhond derives the Seljukides from Alankavah, the virgin mother (p. 801, col. 2). If they be the same as the *Zalzuts* of Abulghazi Bahader Khan (Hist. Généalogique, p. 148), we quote in their favour the most weighty evidence of a Tartar prince himself, the descendant of Zingis, Alankavah, or Alancu, and Oguz Khan.

[19] [The Seljúks were possibly Christians, before they were converted to Islamism; the names Michael, Jonas, Moses, which some of them bore, may point to this. Cp. Cahun, Intr. à l'histoire de l'Asie, p. 170.]

[20] By a slight corruption, Togrul Beg is the Tangroli-pix of the Greeks. His reign and character are faithfully exhibited by d'Herbelot (Bibliothèque Orientale, p. 1027, 1028) and de Guignes (Hist. des Huns, tom. iii. p. 189-201).

The princes who had felt, or who feared, the Seljukian arrows, bowed their heads in the dust; by the conquest of Aderbijan, [A.D. 1054] or Media, he approached the Roman confines; and the shepherd presumed to dispatch an ambassador, or herald, to demand the tribute and obedience of the emperor of Constantinople.[21]   In his own dominions, Togrul was the father of his soldiers and people; by a firm and equal administration Persia was relieved from the evils of anarchy; and the same hands which had been imbrued in blood became the guardians of justice and the public peace.   The more rustic, perhaps the wisest, portion of the Turkmans[22] continued to dwell in the tents of their ancestors; and, from the Oxus to the Euphrates, these military colonies were protected and propagated by their native princes.   But the Turks of the court and city were refined by business and softened by pleasure; they imitated the dress, language, and manners of Persia; and the royal palaces of Nishabur and Rei displayed the order and magnificence of a great monarchy.   The most deserving of the Arabians and Persians were promoted to the honours of the state; and the whole body of the Turkish nation embraced with fervour and sincerity the religion of Mahomet.   The northern swarms of barbarians, who overspread both Europe and Asia, have been irreconcilably separated by the consequences of a similar conduct.   Among the Moslems, as among the Christians, their vague and local traditions have yielded to the reason and authority of the prevailing system, to the fame of antiquity, and the consent of nations.   But the triumph of the Koran is more pure and meritorious, as it was not assisted by any visible splendour of worship which might allure the Pagans by some resemblance of idolatry.   The first of the Seljukian sultans was conspicuous by his zeal and faith : each day he repeated the five prayers which are enjoined to the true believers; of each week, the two first days were consecrated by an extraordinary fast;

---

[21] Cedrenus, tom. ii. p. 774, 775 [ii. p. 580, ed. B.].   Zonaras, tom. ii. p. 257 [xvii. 25].   With their usual knowledge of Oriental affairs, they describe the ambassador as a *sherif*, who, like the syncellus of the patriarch, was the vicar and successor of the caliph.

[22] From William of Tyre, I have borrowed this distinction of Turks and Turkmans, which at least is popular and convenient.   The names are the same, and the addition of *man* is of the same import in the Persic and Teutonic idioms. Few critics will adopt the etymology of James de Vitry (Hist. Hierosol. l. i. c. 11, p. 1061), of Turcomani, quasi *Turci* et *Comani*, a mixed people.

and in every city a mosch was completed, before Togrul presumed to lay the foundations of a palace.[23]
With the belief of the Koran, the son of Seljuk imbibed a lively reverence for the successor of the prophet. But that sublime character was still disputed by the caliphs of Bagdad and Egypt, and each of the rivals was solicitous to prove his title in the judgment of the strong, though illiterate, barbarians. Mahmud the Gaznevide had declared himself in favour of the line of Abbas ; and had treated with indignity the robe of honour which was presented to the Fatimite ambassador. Yet the ungrateful Hashemite had changed with the change of fortune ; he applauded the victory of Zendecan, and named the Seljukian sultan his temporal vicegerent over the Moslem world. As Togrul executed and enlarged this important trust, he was called to the deliverance of the caliph Cayem, and obeyed the holy summons, which gave a new kingdom to his arms.[24] In the palace of Bagdad, the commander of the faithful still slumbered, a venerable phantom. His servant or master, the prince of the Bowides, could no longer protect him from the insolence of meaner tyrants ; and the Euphrates and Tigris were oppressed by the revolt of the Turkish and Arabian emirs. The presence of a conqueror was implored as a blessing ; and the transient mischiefs of fire and sword were excused as the sharp but salutary remedies which alone could restore the health of the republic. At the head of an irresistible force, the sultan of Persia marched from Hamadan : the proud were crushed, the prostrate were spared ; the prince of the Bowides disappeared ; the heads of the most obstinate rebels were laid at the feet of Togrul ; and he inflicted a lesson of obedience on the people of Mosul and Bagdad. After the chastisement of the guilty and the restoration of peace, the royal shepherd accepted the reward of his labours ; and a solemn comedy represented the triumph of religious prejudice over barbarian power.[25] The Turkish sultan embarked on the Tigris, landed at the gate of Racca, and made his public

He delivers the caliph of Bagdad. A.D. 1055

[Al-Kaim]

His investiture

---

[23] Hist. Générale des Huns, tom. iii. p. 165, 166, 167. M. de Guignes quotes Abulmahasen, an historian of Egypt.
[24] Consult the Bibliothèque Orientale, in the articles of the *Abbassides, Caher,* and *Caiem,* and the Annals of Elmacin and Abulpharagius.
[25] For this curious ceremony, I am indebted to M. de Guignes (tom. iii. p. 197, 198), and that learned author is obliged to Bondari, who composed in Arabic the history of the Seljukides (tom. v. p. 365). I am ignorant of his age, country and character.

entry on horseback. At the palace-gate he respectfully dismounted, and walked on foot, preceded by his emirs without arms. The caliph was seated behind his black veil ; the black garment of the Abbassides was cast over his shoulders, and he held in his hand the staff of the apostle of God. The conqueror of the East kissed the ground, stood some time in a modest posture, and was led towards the throne by the vizir and an interpreter. After Togrul had seated himself on another throne, his commission was publicly read, which declared him the temporal lieutenant of the vicar of the prophet. He was successively invested with seven robes of honour, and presented with seven slaves, the natives of the seven climates of the Arabian empire. His mystic veil was perfumed with musk; two crowns were placed on his head; two scymetars were girded on his side, as the symbols of a double reign over the East and West. After this inauguration, the sultan was prevented from prostrating himself a second time; but he twice kissed the hand of the commander of the faithful, and his titles were proclaimed by the voice of heralds and the applause of the Moslems.[26] In a second visit to Bagdad, the Seljukian prince again rescued the caliph from his enemies; and devoutly, on foot, led the bridle of his mule from the prison to the palace. Their alliance was cemented by the marriage of Togrul's sister with the successor of the prophet. Without reluctance he had introduced a Turkish virgin into his harem; but Cayem proudly refused his daughter to the sultan, disdained to mingle the blood of the Hashemites with the blood of a Scythian shepherd; and protracted the negotiation many months, till the gradual diminution of his revenue admonished him that he was still in the hands of a master. The royal

and death. nuptials were followed by the death of Togrul himself;[27] as he
A.D. 1063 left no children, his nephew Alp Arslan succeeded to the title and prerogatives of sultan; and his name, after that of the caliph, was pronounced in the public prayers of the Moslems. Yet in this revolution the Abbassides acquired a larger measure of liberty and power. On the throne of Asia, the Turkish monarchs were less jealous of the domestic administration of Bagdad; and the

---

[26] [Weil, Geschichte der Chalifen, iii. p. 99.]
[27] Eodem anno (A.H. 455) obiit princeps Togrulbecus . . . rex fuit clemens, prudens, et peritus regnandi, cujus terror corda mortalium invaserat, ita ut obedirent ei reges atque ad ipsum scriberent. Elmacin, Hist. Saracen. p. 342, vers. Erpenii.

commanders of the faithful were relieved from the ignominious vexations to which they had been exposed by the presence and poverty of the Persian dynasty.

Since the fall of the caliphs, the discord and degeneracy of the Saracens respected the Asiatic provinces of Rome ; which, by the victories of Nicephorus, Zimisces, and Basil, had been extended as far as Antioch and the eastern boundaries of Armenia. Twenty-five years after the death of Basil, his successors were suddenly assaulted by an unknown race of barbarians, who united the Scythian valour with the fanaticism of new proselytes and the art and riches of a powerful monarchy.[28]   The myriads of Turkish horse overspread a frontier of six hundred miles from Taurus to Arzeroum, and the blood of one hundred and thirty thousand Christians was a grateful sacrifice to the Arabian prophet. Yet the arms of Togrul did not make any deep or lasting impression on the Greek empire. The torrent rolled away from the open country ; the sultan retired without glory or success from the siege of an Armenian city; the obscure hostilities were continued or suspended with a vicissitude of events; and the bravery of the Macedonian legions renewed the fame of the conqueror of Asia.[29]   The name of Alp Arslan, the valiant lion, is expressive of the popular idea of the perfection of man ; and the successor of Togrul displayed the fierceness and generosity of the royal animal. He passed the Euphrates at the head of the Turkish cavalry, and entered Cæsarea, the metropolis of Cappadocia, to which he had been attracted by the fame and wealth of the temple of St. Basil. The solid structure resisted the destroyer ; but he carried away the doors of the shrine incrusted with gold and pearls, and profaned the relics of the tutelar saint, whose mortal frailties were now covered by the venerable rust of antiquity. The final conquest

The Turks invade the Roman empire. A.D. 1050

Reign of Alp Arslan. A.D. 1063-1072

[28] For these wars of the Turks and Romans, see in general the Byzantine histories of Zonaras and Cedrenus, Scylitzes the continuator of Cedrenus, and Nicephorus Bryennius Cæsar. The two first of these were monks, the two latter statesmen ; yet such were the Greeks that the difference of style and character is scarcely discernible. For the Orientals, I draw as usual on the wealth of d'Herbelot (see titles of the first Seljukides) and the accuracy of de Guignes (Hist. des Huns, tom. iii. l. x.).

[29] Ἐφέρετο γὰρ ἐν Τούρκοις λόγος, ὡς εἴη πεπρωμένον καταστραφῆναι τὸ Τούρκων γένος ἀπὸ τῆς τοιαύτης δυνάμεως, ὁποίαν ὁ Μακεδὼν Ἀλέξανδρος ἔχων κατεστρέψατο Ἰέρσας. Cedrenus, tom. ii. p. 791 [ii. p. 611, ed. B.]. The credulity of the vulgar is always probable ; and the Turks had learned from the Arabs the history or legend of Escander Dulcarnein (d'Herbelot, p. 317, &c.).

Conquest of Armenia and Georgia. a.d. 1065-1068 of Armenia and Georgia was achieved by Alp Arslan. In Armenia, the title of a kingdom and the spirit of a nation [30] were annihilated; the artificial fortifications were yielded by the mercenaries of Constantinople; by strangers without faith, veterans without pay or arms, and recruits without experience or discipline. The loss of this important frontier was the news of a day; and the Catholics were neither surprised nor displeased that a people so deeply infected with the Nestorian and Eutychian errors had been delivered by Christ and his mother into the hands of the infidels.[31] The woods and valleys of mount Caucasus were more strenuously defended by the native Georgians [32] or Iberians: but the Turkish sultan and his son Malek were indefatigable in this holy war; their captives were compelled to promise a spiritual as well as temporal obedience; and, instead of their collars and bracelets, an iron horse-shoe, a badge of ignominy, was imposed on the infidels who still adhered to the worship of their fathers. The change, however, was not sincere or universal; and, through ages of servitude, the Georgians have maintained the succession of their princes and bishops. But a race of men, whom nature has cast in her most perfect mould, is degraded by poverty, ignorance, and vice; their profession, and still more their practice, of Christianity is an empty name; and, if they have emerged from heresy, it is only because they are too illiterate to remember a metaphysical creed.[33]

[30] [And the culture. Ani which had passed under the dominion of the Empire in 1046 was captured by Alp Arslan in 1064 (July 6). Kars was then ceded by its trembling prince to the Empire in exchange for Camendav in the mountains of Cilicia; but it had hardly been occupied by the Imperialists before it was taken by the Turks.]

[31] Οἱ καὶ [leg. τὴν] Ἰβηρίαν καὶ Μεσοποταμίαν καὶ Ἀρμενίαν οἰκοῦσιν [leg. καὶ Μεσοποταμίαν μέχρι Λυκανδοῦ καὶ Μελιτηνῆς καὶ τὴν παρακειμένην οἰκοῦσιν Ἀρμενίαν] καὶ οἱ τὴν Ἰουδαικην τοῦ Νεστορίου καὶ τῶν Ἀκεφάλων θρησκεύουσιν αἵρεσιν (Scylitzes, ad calcem Cedreni, tom. ii. p. 834 [ii. p. 687, ed. B.], whose ambiguous construction shall not tempt me to suspect that he confounded the Nestorian and Monophysite heresies). He familiarly talks of the μῆνις, χόλος, ὀργή, Θεοῦ, qualities, as I should apprehend, very foreign to the perfect Being; but his bigotry is forced to confess that they were soon afterwards discharged on the orthodox Romans.

[32] Had the name of Georgians been known to the Greeks (Stritter, Memoriæ Byzant. tom. iv. Iberica), I should derive it from their agriculture, as the Σκύθαι γεωργοί of Herodotus (l. iv. c. 18, p. 289, edit. Wesseling). But it appears only since the crusades, among the Latins (Jac. a Vitriaco, Hist. Hierosol. c. 79, p. 1095) and Orientals (d'Herbelot, p. 407), and was devoutly borrowed from St. George of Cappadocia.

[33] Mosheim, Institut. Hist. Eccles. p. 632. See in Chardin's Travels (tom. i. p. 171-175) the manners and religion of this handsome but worthless nation. See

The false or genuine magnanimity of Mahmud the Gaznevide The emperor Romanus Diogenes. A.D. 1068-1071 was not imitated by Alp Arslan ; and he attacked, without scruple, the Greek empress Eudocia and her children.   His alarming progress compelled her to give herself and her sceptre to the hand of a soldier; and Romanus Diogenes was invested with the Imperial purple.   His patriotism, and perhaps his pride, [1st campaign, A.D. 1068 ; 2nd campaign, A.D. 1069] urged him from Constantinople within two months after his accession ; and the next campaign he most scandalously took the field during the holy festival of Easter.   In the palace, Diogenes was no more than the husband of Eudocia; in the camp, he was the emperor of the Romans, and he sustained that character with feeble resources and invincible courage. By his spirit and success, the soldiers were taught to act, the subjects to hope, and the enemies to fear.   The Turks had penetrated into the heart of Phrygia; but the sultan himself had resigned to his emirs the prosecution of the war; and their numerous detachments were scattered over Asia in the security of conquest.   Laden with spoil and careless of discipline, they were separately surprised and defeated by the Greeks ; the activity of the emperor seemed to multiply his presence; and, while they heard of his expedition to Antioch, the enemy felt his sword on the hills of Trebizond.   In three laborious campaigns, the Turks were driven beyond the Euphrates; [34] in the fourth and last, Romanus undertook the deliverance of Armenia.   The desolation of the land obliged him to transport a supply of two months' provisions ; and he marched forwards to the siege of Malazkerd, [35] an important fortress in the midway between the modern cities of Arzeroum and Van.   His army amounted, at the least, to one hundred thousand men.   The troops of Constantinople were reinforced by the disorderly mul-

the pedigree of their princes from Adam to the present century, in the Tables of M. de Guignes (tom. i. p. 433-438).

   [34] [In the first two campaigns Romanus led the army himself.   For the geography of these military operations see J. G. C. Anderson's paper in the Journal of Hellenic Studies, xvii. p. 36-39 (1897).   In the third campaign (A.D. 1070) Manuel Comnenus was entrusted with the command.]

   [35] This city is mentioned by Constantine Porphyrogenitus (de Administrat. Imperii, l. ii. c. 44, p. 119) and the Byzantines of the xith century, under the name of Mantzikierte, and by some is confounded with Theodosiopolis; but Delisle, in his notes and maps, has very properly fixed the situation.   Abulfeda (Geograph. tab. xviii. p. 310) describes Malasgerd as a small town, built with black stone, supplied with water, without trees, &c.   [Manzikert is on the Murad Tchai, north of Lake Van.]

titudes of Phrygia and Cappadocia; but the real strength was composed of the subjects and allies of Europe, the legions of Macedonia, and the squadrons of Bulgaria; the Uzi, a Moldavian horde, who were themselves of the Turkish race;[36] and, above all, the mercenary and adventurous bands of French and Normans. Their lances were commanded by the valiant Ursel of Baliol, the kinsman or father of the Scottish kings,[37] and were allowed to excel in the exercise of arms, or, according to the Greek style, in the practice of the Pyrrhic dance.

Defeat of the Romans. A.D. 1071, August [Battle of Manzikert]

On the report of this bold invasion, which threatened his hereditary dominions, Alp Arslan flew to the scene of action at the head of forty thousand horse.[38] His rapid and skilful evolutions distressed and dismayed the superior numbers of the Greeks; and in the defeat of Basilacius, one of their principal

[36] The Uzi of the Greeks (Stritter, Memor. Byzant. tom. iii. p. 923-948) are the Gozz of the Orientals (Hist. des Huns, tom. ii. p. 522, tom. iii. p. 133, &c.). They appear on the Danube and the Volga, in Armenia, Syria and Chorasan, and the name seems to have been extended to the whole Turkman race. [The Uzi were a Turkish horde akin to the Patzinaks. They are mentioned by Constantine Porphyrogennetos (in the De Adm. Imp.) as living in his time beyond the Patzinaks and the Khazars. They are the same as the Cumani (Komanoi in Anna Comnena, &c.); and are called Polovtsi in the old Russian Chronicle. The Hungarians call them Kúnok. They first appeared in Russia in A.D. 1055 (Nestor, c. 59). Then they drove the Patzinaks out of Atelkuzu, the land of which *they* had formerly dispossessed the Hungarians, into Walachia. Sixty thousand of them crossed the Danube in 1065, but were for the most part cut to pieces, with the help of the Patzinaks; some of the remnant were settled in Macedonia. A glossary of the Cumanian language has been accidentally preserved in a Ms. which Petrarch presented to the Library of St. Mark. It was published by Klaproth in Mémoires relatifs à l'Asia, iii. (title: Alphabetum Persicum Comanicum et Latinum) and has been edited by Count Géza Kuun, Codex Cumanicus, 1880. It establishes the Turkish character of the Uzes.]

[37] Urselius (the Russelius of Zonaras) is distinguished by Jeffrey Malaterra (l. i. c. 33) among the Norman conquerors of Sicily, and with the surname of *Baliol;* and our own historians will tell how the Beliols came from Normandy to Durham, built Bernard's Castle on the Tees, married an heiress of Scotland, &c. Ducange (Not. ad Nicephor. Bryennium. l. ii. No. 4) has laboured the subject in honour of the president de Bailleul, whose father had exchanged the sword for the gown. [For the history of Ursel and his Norman realm in Asia Minor see Nicephorus Bryennius, p. 73 *sqq.*, and Attaleiates, p. 184 *sqq.* Cp. Hirsch, Forschungen zur deutschen Geschichte, 8, p. 232 *sqq.*]

[38] Elmacin (p. 343, 344) assigns this probable number, which is reduced by Abulpharagius to 15,000 (p. 227) and by d'Herbelot (p. 102) to 12,000 horse. But the same Elmacin gives 300,000 men to the emperor, of whom Abulpharagius says, cum centum hominum millibus, multisque equis et magnâ pompâ instructus. The Greeks abstain from any definition of numbers. [The Byzantine army was not prepared to cope with the extraordinarily rapid motions of the Turks; Gibbon brings this point out. But it should be added that the army in any case was inclined to be insubordinate, and Romanus had difficulty in handling it. Moreover there was treachery in his camp. There seems no doubt however that he fought the battle rashly. Cp. Finlay, iii. 33; and C. W. Oman, History of the Art of War, vol. 2, p. 217-19.]

generals, he displayed the first example of his valour and clemency. The imprudence of the emperor had separated his forces after the reduction of Malazkerd. It was in vain that he attempted to recal the mercenary Franks: they refused to obey his summons; he disdained to await their return; the desertion of the Uzi filled his mind with anxiety and suspicion; and against the most salutary advice he rushed forward to speedy and decisive action. Had he listened to the fair proposals of the sultan, Romanus might have secured a retreat, perhaps a peace; but in these overtures he supposed the fear or weakness of the enemy, and his answer was conceived in the tone of insult and defiance. "If the barbarian wishes for peace, let him evacuate the ground which he occupies for the encampment of the Romans, and surrender his city and palace of Rei as a pledge of his sincerity." Alp Arslan smiled at the vanity of the demand, but he wept the death of so many faithful Moslems; and, after a devout prayer, proclaimed a free permission to all who were desirous of retiring from the field. With his own hands he tied up his horse's tail, exchanged his bow and arrow for a mace and scymetar, clothed himself in a white garment, perfumed his body with musk, and declared that, if he were vanquished, that spot should be the place of his burial.[39] The sultan himself had affected to cast away his missile weapons; but his hopes of victory were placed in the arrows of the Turkish cavalry, whose squadrons were loosely distributed in the form of a crescent. Instead of the successive lines and reserves of the Grecian tactics, Romanus led his army in a single and solid phalanx, and pressed with vigour and impatience the artful and yielding resistance of the barbarians. In this desultory and fruitless combat, he wasted the greater part of a summer's day, till prudence and fatigue compelled him to return to his camp. But a retreat is always perilous in the face of an active foe; and no sooner had the standard been turned to the rear than the phalanx was broken by the base cowardice, or the baser jealousy, of Andronicus, a rival prince, who disgraced his birth and the purple of the Cæsars.[40] The Turkish

---

[39] The Byzantine writers do not speak so distinctly of the presence of the sultan; he committed his forces to an eunuch, had retired to a distance, &c. Is it ignorance, or jealousy, or truth?

[40] He was the son of the Cæsar John Ducas, brother of the emperor Constantine (Ducange, Fam. Byzant. p. 165). Nicephorus Bryennius applauds his virtues, and

squadrons poured a cloud of arrows on this moment of confusion and lassitude; and the horns of their formidable crescent were closed in the rear of the Greeks. In the destruction of the army and pillage of the camp, it would be needless to mention the number of the slain or captives. The Byzantine writers deplore the loss of an inestimable pearl: they forget to mention that, in this fatal day, the Asiatic provinces of Rome were irretrievably sacrificed.

Captivity and deliverance of the emperor

As long as a hope survived, Romanus attempted to rally and save the relics of his army. When the centre, the Imperial station, was left naked on all sides, and encompassed by the victorious Turks, he still, with desperate courage, maintained the fight till the close of day, at the head of the brave and faithful subjects who adhered to his standard. They fell around him; his horse was slain; the emperor was wounded; yet he stood alone and intrepid, till he was oppressed and bound by the strength of multitudes. The glory of this illustrious prize was disputed by a slave and a soldier: a slave who had seen him on the throne of Constantinople, and a soldier whose extreme deformity had been excused on the promise of some signal service. Despoiled of his arms, his jewels, and his purple, Romanus spent a dreary and perilous night on the field of battle, amidst a disorderly crowd of the meaner barbarians. In the morning the royal captive was presented to Alp Arslan, who doubted of his fortune, till the identity of the person was ascertained by the report of his ambassadors, and by the more pathetic evidence of Basilacius, who embraced with tears the feet of his unhappy sovereign. The successor of Constantine, in a plebeian habit, was led into the Turkish divan, and commanded to kiss the ground before the lord of Asia. He reluctantly obeyed; and Alp Arslan, starting from his throne, is said to have planted his foot on the neck of the Roman emperor.[41] But the fact is doubtful; and, if, in this moment of insolence, the sultan complied with a national custom, the

extenuates his faults (l. i. p. 30, 38, l. ii. p. 53 [p. 41, 54, 76, ed. Bonn]). Yet he owns his enmity to Romanus, οὐ πάνυ δὲ φιλίως ἔχων προς βασιλέα. Scylitzes speaks more explicitly of his treason.

[41] This circumstance, which we read and doubt in Scylitzes and Constantine Manasses, is more prudently omitted by Nicephorus and Zonaras. [The reader may remember how the Emperor Justinian II. placed his feet on the necks of his rivals Leontius and Apsimar. Finlay (iii. 34) rebukes Gibbon for his scepticism here.]

rest of his conduct has extorted the praise of his bigoted foes, and may afford a lesson to the most civilised ages. He instantly raised the royal captive from the ground ; and, thrice clasping his hand with tender sympathy, assured him that his life and dignity should be inviolate in the hands of a prince who had learned to respect the majesty of his equals and the vicissitudes of fortune. From the divan Romanus was conducted to an adjacent tent, where he was served with pomp and reverence by the officers of the sultan, who, twice each day, seated him in the place of honour at his own table. In a free and familiar conversation of eight days, not a word, not a look, of insult escaped from the conqueror ; but he severely censured the unworthy subjects who had deserted their valiant prince in the hour of danger, and gently admonished his antagonist of some errors which he had committed in the management of the war. In the preliminaries of negotiation, Alp Arslan asked him what treatment he expected to receive, and the calm indifference of the emperor displays the freedom of his mind. " If you are cruel," said he, "you will take my life; if you listen to pride, you will drag me at your chariot wheels; if you consult your interest, you will accept a ransom, and restore me to my country."—"And what," continued the sultan, "would have been your own behaviour, had fortune smiled on your arms ? " The reply of the Greek betrays a sentiment, which prudence, and even gratitude, should have taught him to suppress. " Had I vanquished," he fiercely said, "I would have inflicted on thy body many a stripe." The Turkish conqueror smiled at the insolence of his captive ; observed that the Christian law inculcated the love of enemies and forgiveness of injuries; and nobly declared that he would not imitate an example which he condemned. After mature deliberation, Alp Arslan dictated the terms of liberty and peace, a ransom of a million, an annual tribute of three hundred and sixty thousand pieces of gold,[42] the marriage of the royal children, and the deliverance of all the Moslems who were in the power of the Greeks. Romanus, with a sigh, subscribed this treaty, so disgraceful to the majesty

---

[42] The ransom and tribute are attested by reason and the Orientals. The other Greeks are modestly silent ; but Nicephorus Bryennius dares to affirm that the terms were οὐκ ἀναξίας 'Ρωμαίων ἀρχῆς, and that the emperor would have preferred death to a shameful treaty.

of the empire; he was immediately invested with a Turkish robe of honour; his nobles and patricians were restored to their sovereign; and the sultan, after a courteous embrace, dismissed him with rich presents and a military guard. No sooner did he reach the confines of the empire than he was informed that the palace and provinces had disclaimed their allegiance to a captive: a sum of two hundred thousand pieces was painfully collected; and the fallen monarch transmitted this part of his ransom, with a sad confession of his impotence and disgrace. The generosity, or perhaps the ambition, of the sultan prepared to espouse the cause of his ally; but his designs were prevented by the defeat, imprisonment, and death of Romanus Diogenes.[43]

Death of Alp Arslan. A.D. 1072   In the treaty of peace it does not appear that Alp Arslan extorted any province or city from the captive emperor; and his revenge was satisfied with the trophies of his victory, and the spoils of Anatolia from Antioch to the Black Sea. The fairest part of Asia was subject to his laws; twelve hundred princes, or the sons of princes, stood before his throne; and two hundred thousand soldiers marched under his banners. The sultan disdained to pursue the fugitive Greeks; but he meditated the more glorious conquest of Turkestan, the original seat of the house of Seljuk. He moved from Bagdad to the banks of the Oxus; a bridge was thrown over the river; and twenty days were consumed in the passage of his troops. But the progress of the great king was retarded by the governor of Berzem; and Joseph the Carizmian presumed to defend his fortress against the powers of the East. When he was produced a captive in the royal tent, the sultan, instead of praising his valour, severely reproached his obstinate folly; and the in-

---

[43] The defeat and captivity of Romanus Diogenes may be found in John Scylitzes ad calcem Cedreni, tom. ii. p. 835-843 [ii. p. 689 sqq. ed. B.]. Zonaras, tom. ii. p. 281-284 [xvii. 13, 14, 15]. Nicephorus Bryennius, l. i. p. 25-32 [p. 33 sqq. ed. B.]. Glycas, p. 325-327 [p. 607 sqq. ed. B.]. Constantine Manasses, p. 134 [p. 280, ed. B.]. Elmacin, Hist. Saracen. p. 343, 344. Abulpharag. Dynast. p. 227. D'Herbelot, p. 102, 103. De Guignes, tom. iii. p. 207-211. Besides my old acquaintance, Elmacin and Abulpharagius, the historian of the Huns has consulted Abulfeda, and his epitomizer, Benschounah, a Chronicle of the Caliphs, by Soyouthi, Abulmahasen of Egypt, and Novairi of Africa. [See also the Chronicle of Michael Attaleiates, p. 152 sqq. ed. Bonn. On the battle Finlay, vol. iii. p. 32-4, and Gfrörer, Byzantinische Geschichten, vol. iii. chap. 28; Oman, cited above, note 38; cp. too Seger, Nikephoros Bryennios, p. 41 sqq. Gfrörer insists (p. 785) on the statement of Elmacin that the battle was fought at Zahra (Zareshad? east of Manzikert).]

solent replies of the rebel provoked a sentence, that he should be fastened to four stakes and left to expire in that painful situation. At this command the desperate Carizmian, drawing a dagger, rushed headlong towards the throne: the guards raised their battle-axes; their zeal was checked by Alp Arslan, the most skilful archer of the age; he drew his bow, but his foot slipped, the arrow glanced aside, and he received in his breast the dagger of Joseph, who was instantly cut in pieces. The wound was mortal; and the Turkish prince bequeathed a dying admonition to the pride of kings. "In my youth," said Alp Arslan, "I was advised by a sage to humble myself before God; to distrust my own strength; and never to despise the most contemptible foe. I have neglected these lessons; and my neglect has been deservedly punished. Yesterday, as from an eminence I beheld the numbers, the discipline, and the spirit of my armies, the earth seemed to tremble under my feet; and I said in my heart, surely thou art the king of the world, the greatest and most invincible of warriors. These armies are no longer mine; and, in the confidence of my personal strength, I now fall by the hand of an assassin."[44] Alp Arslan possessed the virtues of a Turk and a Musulman; his voice and stature commanded the reverence of mankind; his face was shaded with long whiskers; and his ample turban was fashioned in the shape of a crown. The remains of the sultan were deposited in the tomb of the Seljukian dynasty; and the passenger might read and meditate this useful inscription:[45] "O YE WHO HAVE SEEN THE GLORY OF ALP ARSLAN EXALTED TO THE HEAVENS, REPAIR TO MARU, AND YOU WILL BEHOLD IT BURIED IN THE DUST!" The annihilation of the inscription, and the tomb itself, more forcibly proclaims the instability of human greatness.

During the life of Alp Arslan, his eldest son had been acknow- Reign and prosperity of Malek Shah. A.D 1072-1092
ledged as the future sultan of the Turks. On his father's death, the inheritance was disputed by an uncle, a cousin, and a brother:

[44] This interesting death is told by d'Herbelot (p. 103, 104) and M. de Guignes (tom. iii. p. 212, 213) from their Oriental writers; but neither of them have transfused the spirit of Elmacin (Hist. Saracen. p. 344, 345).

[45] A critique of high renown (the late Dr. Johnson), who has severely scrutinised the epitaphs of Pope, might cavil in this sublime inscription at the words, "repair to Maru," since the reader must already be at Maru before he could peruse the inscription.

they drew their scymetars, and assembled their followers; and the triple victory of Malek Shah [46] established his own reputation and the right of primogeniture. In every age, and more especially in Asia, the thirst of power has inspired the same passions and occasioned the same disorders; but, from the long series of civil war, it would not be easy to extract a sentiment more pure and magnanimous than is contained in a saying of the Turkish prince. On the eve of the battle, he performed

[Tus] his devotions at Thous, before the tomb of the Imam Riza. As the sultan rose from the ground, he asked his vizir Nizam, who had knelt beside him, what had been the object of his secret petition : "That your arms may be crowned with victory," was the prudent and most probably the sincere answer of the minister. "For my part," replied the generous Malek, "I implored the Lord of Hosts that he would take from me my life and crown, if my brother be more worthy than myself to reign over the Moslems." The favourable judgment of heaven was ratified by the caliph; and for the first time the sacred title of Commander of the Faithful was communicated to a barbarian.[46a] But this barbarian, by his personal merit and the extent of his empire, was the greatest prince of his age. After the settlement of Persia and Syria, he marched at the head of innumerable armies to achieve the conquest of Turkestan, which had been undertaken by his father. In his passage of the Oxus, the boatmen, who had been employed in transporting some troops, complained that their payment was assigned on the revenues of Antioch. The sultan frowned at this preposterous choice, but he smiled at the artful flattery of his vizir. "It was not to postpone their reward that I selected those remote places, but to leave a memorial to posterity that under your reign Antioch and the Oxus were subject to the same sovereign." But this description of his limits was unjust and parsimonious : beyond the Oxus, he reduced to his obedience the cities of Bochara, Carizme, and Samarcand, and crushed each rebellious slave, or independent savage, who dared to resist. Malek passed the Sihon or

---

[46] The Bibliothèque Orientale has given the text of the reign of Malek (p. 542, 543, 544, 654, 655), and the Histoire Générale des Huns (tom. iii. p. 214-224) has added the usual measure of repetition, emendation, and supplement. Without these two learned Frenchmen, I should be blind indeed in the Eastern world.

[46a] [Not Commander of the Faithful (title reserved for Caliphs), but "Partner of the Commander of the Faithful".]

Jaxartes, the last boundary of Persian civilisation: the lords of Turkestan yielded to his supremacy; his name was inserted on the coins, and in the prayers, of Cashgar, a Tartar kingdom on the extreme borders of China. From the Chinese frontier, he stretched his immediate jurisdiction or feudatory sway to the west and south, as far as the mountains of Georgia, the neighbourhood of Constantinople, the holy city of Jerusalem, and the spicy groves of Arabia Felix. Instead of resigning himself to the luxury of his harem, the shepherd king, both in peace and war, was in action and in the field. By the perpetual motion of the royal camp, each province was successively blessed with his presence; and he is said to have perambulated twelve times the wide extent of his dominions, which surpassed the *Asiatic* reign of Cyrus and the caliphs. Of these expeditions, the most pious and splendid was the pilgrimage of Mecca; the freedom and safety of the caravans were protected by his arms; the citizens and pilgrims were enriched by the profusion of his alms; and the desert was cheered by the places of relief and refreshment, which he instituted for the use of his brethren. Hunting was the pleasure, and even the passion, of the sultan, and his train consisted of forty-seven thousand horses; but, after the massacre of a Turkish chase, for each piece of game, he bestowed a piece of gold on the poor, a slight atonement, at the expense of the people, for the cost and mischief of the amusement of kings. In the peaceful prosperity of his reign, the cities of Asia were adorned with palaces and hospitals, with mosques and colleges; few departed from his divan without reward, and none without justice. The language and literature of Persia revived under the house of Seljuk; [47] and, if Malek emulated the liberality of a Turk less potent than himself,[48] his palace might resound with the songs of an hundred poets. The sultan bestowed a more serious and learned care on

[47] See an excellent discourse at the end of Sir William Jones's History of Nadir Shah, and the articles of the poets, Amak, Anvari, Raschadi, &c. in the Bibliothèque Orientale.

[48] His name was Kheder Khan. Four bags were placed round his sopha, and, as he listened to the song, he cast handfuls of gold and silver to the poets (d'Herbelot, p. 107). All this may be true; but I do not understand how he could reign in Transoxiana in the time of Malek Shah, and much less how Kheder could surpass him in power and pomp. I suspect that the beginning, not the end, of the xith century is the true æra of his reign. [Kadr Khān (one of the Turki Ilak Khāns) ruled at Kāshghar and Yarkand at beginning of xith cent.; his coins exist.]

the reformation of the calendar, which was effected by a general assembly of the astronomers of the East. By a law of the prophet, the Moslems are confined to the irregular course of the lunar months; in Persia, since the age of Zoroaster, the revolution of the sun has been known and celebrated as an annual festival;[49] but, after the fall of the Magian empire, the intercalation had been neglected; the fractions of minutes and hours were multiplied into days; and the date of the Spring was removed from the sign of Aries to that of Pisces. The reign of Malek was illustrated by the *Gelalœan* æra; and all errors, either past or future, were corrected by a computation of time, which surpasses the Julian, and approaches the accuracy of the Gregorian, style.[50]

His death.
A.D. 1092

[A.D. 1063-1092]

In a period when Europe was plunged in the deepest barbarism, the light and splendour of Asia may be ascribed to the docility rather than the knowledge of the Turkish conquerors. An ample share of their wisdom and virtue is due to a Persian vizir, who ruled the empire under the reign of Alp Arslan and his son. Nizam, one of the most illustrious ministers of the East, was honoured by the caliph as an oracle of religion and science;[51] he was trusted by the sultan as the faithful vicegerent of his power and justice. After an administration of thirty years, the fame of the vizir, his wealth, and even his services, were transformed into crimes. He was overthrown by the insidious arts of a woman and a rival; and his fall was hastened by a rash declaration that his cap and ink-horn, the badges of his office, were connected by the divine decree with the throne and diadem of the sultan. At the age of ninety-

---

[49] See Chardin, Voyages en Perse, tom. ii. p. 235.

[50] The Gelalæan æra (Gelaleddin, Glory of the Faith, was one of the names or titles of Malek Shah) is fixed to the 15th of March, A.H. 471, A.D. 1079. Dr. Hyde has produced the original testimonies of the Persians and Arabians (de Religione veterum Persarum, c. 16, p. 200-211). [The reform of the calendar was the work of Malik's minister, Nizām al-Mulk.]

[51] [Nizām has left a memorial of himself in the Siasset Nameh, or "book of government," which has been published with a translation by Schefer. It throws great light on the history of the time and shows us how the Seljūks were already changing under the influence of Iranian civilisation and Islamism. In this respect it is very interesting to compare it with the *Kudatker Bilik* or Art of Government, a contemporary work (written c. 1069 at Kashgar) which shows the pure Turk spirit of central Asia. The comparison is drawn by Cahun (*op. cit.*, p. 182 *sqq.*). Among the Turks, for instance, women had great influence; but in the Siasset Nameh "religion is much, woman is nothing". For a sketch of the vizierate of Nizām, see Stanley Lane-Poole's Saladin (1898), chap. i.]

three years, the venerable statesman was dismissed by his master, accused by his enemies, and murdered by a fanatic: the last words of Nizam attested his innocence, and the remainder of Malek's life was short and inglorious. From Ispahan, the scene of this disgraceful transaction, the sultan moved to Bagdad, with the design of transplanting the caliph, and of fixing his own residence in the capital of the Moslem world. The feeble successor of Mahomet obtained a respite of ten days; and, before the expiration of the term, the barbarian was summoned by the angel of death. His ambassadors at Constantinople had asked in marriage a Roman princess; but the proposal was decently eluded; and the daughter of Alexius, who might herself have been the victim, expresses her abhorrence of this unnatural conjunction.[52] The daughter of the sultan was bestowed on the caliph Moctadi, with the imperious condition that, renouncing the society of his wives and concubines, he should for ever confine himself to this honourable alliance.

The greatness and unity of the Turkish empire expired in the person of Malek Shah. His vacant throne was disputed by his brother and his four sons; and, after a series of civil wars, the treaty which reconciled the surviving candidates confirmed a lasting separation in the *Persian* dynasty, the eldest and principal branch of the house of Seljuk. The three younger dynasties were those of *Kerman*, of *Syria*, and of *Roum* : the first of these commanded an extensive, though obscure,[53] dominion on the shores of the Indian Ocean;[54] the second expelled the Arabian princes of Aleppo and Damascus; and the third, our peculiar care, invaded the Roman provinces of Asia Minor. The generous policy of Malek contributed to their elevation; he allowed the

Division of the Seljukian empire

---

[52] She speaks of this Persian royalty as ἁπάσης κακοδαιμονέστερον πενίας. Anna Comnena was only nine years old at the end of the reign of Malek Shah (A.D. 1092), and, when she speaks of his assassination, she confounds the sultan with the vizir (Alexias, l. vi. p. 177, 178 [c. 12]).

[53] So obscure that the industry of M. de Guignes could only copy (tom. i. p. 244, tom. iii. part i. p. 269, &c.) the history, or rather list, of the Seljukides of Kerman, in Bibliothèque Orientale. They were extinguished before the end of the xiith century. [For the succession of the Seljūks of Kirmān, A.D. 1041-1187, see S. Lane-Poole, Mohammadan Dynasties, p. 153. The main line of the Seljūks, with a nominal overlordship over the younger branches, continued to rule in Irāk Ajam and Khurāsān and expired with Sinjar in A.D. 1157.]

[54] Tavernier, perhaps the only traveller who has visited Kerman, describes the capital as a great ruinous village, twenty-five days' journey from Ispahan, and twenty-seven from Ormus, in the midst of a fertile country (Voyages en Turquie et en Perse, p. 107, 110).

princes of his blood, even those whom he had vanquished in the field, to seek new kingdoms worthy of their ambition; nor was he displeased that they should draw away the more ardent spirits who might have disturbed the tranquillity of his reign. As the supreme head of his family and nation, the great sultan of Persia commanded the obedience and tribute of his royal brethren; the throne of Kerman and Nice, of Aleppo and Damascus; the Atabeks, and emirs of Syria and Mesopotamia, erected their standards under the shadow of his sceptre;[55] and the hordes of Turkmans overspread the plains of the western Asia. After the death of Malek, the bands of union and subordination were relaxed and finally dissolved; the indulgence of the house of Seljuk invested their slaves with the inheritance of kingdoms; and, in the Oriental style, a crowd of princes arose from the dust of their feet.[56]

Conquest of Asia Minor by the Turks. A.D. 1074-1084

A prince of the royal line, Cutulmish, the son of Izrail, the son of Seljuk, had fallen in a battle against Alp Arslan; and the humane victor had dropped a tear over his grave. His five sons, strong in arms, ambitious of power, and eager for revenge, unsheathed their scymetars against the son of Alp Arslan. The two armies expected the signal, when the caliph, forgetful of the majesty which secluded him from vulgar eyes, interposed his venerable mediation. "Instead of shedding the blood of your brethren, your brethren both in descent and faith, unite your forces in an holy war against the Greeks, the enemies of God and his apostle." They listened to his voice; the sultan embraced his rebellious kinsmen; and the eldest, the valiant Soliman, accepted the royal standard, which gave him the free conquest and hereditary command of the provinces of the Roman empire, from Arzeroum to Constantinople and the unknown regions of the West.[57] Accompanied by his four brothers, he

[55] It appears from Anna Comnena that the Turks of Asia Minor obeyed the signet and chiauss of the great sultan (Alexias, l. vi. p. 170 [c. 9]) and that the two sons of Soliman were detained in his court (p. 180 [c. 12]).

[56] This expression is quoted by Petit de la Croix (Vie de Gengiscan, p. 161) from some poet, most probably a Persian. [The slaves who were to conduct the affairs of the Seljūk princes generally became the governors or regents, atābegs, for their sons or heirs, and thus got the supreme power into their hands.]

[57] On the conquest of Asia Minor, M. de Guignes has derived no assistance from the Turkish or Arabian writers, who produce a naked list of the Seljukides of Roum. The Greeks are unwilling to expose their shame, and we must extort some hints from Scylitzes (p. 860, 863 [p. 731, 736, ed. B.]), Nicephorus Bryennius (p. 88, 91, 92, &c. 103, 104 [p. 130, p. 136, 137, p. 158 sqq. ed. B.]), and Anna Comnena

passed the Euphrates : the Turkish camp was soon seated in the neighbourhood of Kutaieh, in Phrygia; and his flying cavalry [Cotyæum] laid waste the country as far as the Hellespont and the Black Sea. Since the decline of the empire, the peninsula of Asia Minor had been exposed to the transient though destructive inroads of the Persians and Saracens; but the fruits of a lasting conquest were reserved for the Turkish sultan; and his arms were introduced by the Greeks, who aspired to reign on the ruins of their country. Since the captivity of Romanus, six years the feeble son of Eudocia had trembled under the weight of the Imperial crown, till the provinces of the East and West were lost in the same month by a double rebellion : of either [A.D. 1078] chief Nicephorus was the common name; but the surnames of Bryennius and Botoniates distinguish the European and Asiatic candidates. Their reasons, or rather their promises, were weighed in the divan; and, after some hesitation, Soliman declared himself in favour of Botoniates, opened a free passage to his troops in their march from Antioch to Nice, and joined the banner of the crescent to that of the cross. After his ally had ascended the throne of Constantinople, the sultan was hospitably entertained in the suburb of Chrysopolis or Scutari ; and a body of two thousand Turks was transported into Europe, to whose dexterity and courage the new emperor was indebted for the defeat and captivity of his rival Bryennius. But the conquest of Europe was dearly purchased by the sacrifice of Asia : Constantinople was deprived of the obedience and revenue of the provinces beyond the Bosphorus and Hellespont; and the regular progress of the Turks, who fortified the passes of the rivers and mountains, left not a hope of their retreat or expulsion. Another candidate implored the aid of the sultan : [58] Melissenus, [A.D. 1079] in his purple robes and red buskins, attended the motions of the Turkish camp; and the desponding cities were tempted by the summons of a Roman prince, who immediately surrendered them into the hands of the barbarians. These acquisitions were [A.D. 1081] confirmed by a treaty of peace with the emperor Alexius; his fear of Robert compelled him to seek the friendship of Soliman ; and it was not till after the sultan's death that he extended as

(Alexias, p. 91, 92, &c. [iii. c. 9], 168, &c. [vi. c. 9]) [and the History of Michael Attaleiates].

[58] [It was Melissenus who yielded Nicaea to Sulaiman.]

far as Nicomedia, about sixty miles from Constantinople, the eastern boundary of the Roman world.   Trebizond alone, defended on either side by the sea and mountains, preserved at the extremity of the Euxine the ancient character of a Greek colony, and the future destiny of a Christian empire.

The Seljukian kingdom of Roum

Since the first conquests of the caliphs, the establishment of the Turks in Anatolia, or Asia Minor, was the most deplorable loss which the church and empire had sustained.   By the propagation of the Moslem faith, Soliman deserved the name of *Gazi*, a holy champion; and his new kingdom of the Romans, or of *Roum*, was added to the tables of Oriental geography.   It is described as extending from the Euphrates to Constantinople, from the Black Sea to the confines of Syria ; pregnant with mines of silver and iron, of alum and copper, fruitful in corn and wine, and productive of cattle and excellent horses.[59]   The wealth of Lydia, the arts of the Greeks, the splendour of the Augustan age, existed only in books and ruins, which were equally obscure in the eyes of the Scythian conquerors.   Yet, in the present decay, Anatolia still contains *some* wealthy and populous cities ; and, under the Byzantine empire, they were far more flourishing in numbers, size, and opulence.   By the choice of the sultan, Nice, the metropolis of Bithynia, was preferred for his palace and fortress : the seat of the Seljukian dynasty of Roum was planted one hundred miles from Constantinople ; and the divinity of Christ was denied and derided in the same temple in which it had been pronounced by the first general synod of the Catholics.   The unity of God and the mission of Mahomet were preached in the mosques ; the Arabian learning was taught in the schools ; the Cadhis judged according to the law of the Koran ; the Turkish manners and language prevailed in the cities ; and Turkman camps were scattered over the plains and mountains of Anatolia.   On the hard conditions of tribute and servitude, the Greek Christians might enjoy the exercise of their religion ; but their most holy churches were profaned ; their priests and bishops were insulted ;[60] they were compelled to suffer the triumph of the

[59] Such is the description of Roum by Haiton the Armenian, whose Tartar history may be found in the collections of Ramusio and Bergeron [and in L. de Backer's L'extrême orient au moyen âge, p. 125 *sqq.*, 1877] (see Abulfeda, Geograph. climat. xvii. p. 301-305 [and P. Paris, in Hist. littéraire de France, t. 25, p. 479 *sqq.*, 1869]).

[60] Dicit eos quendam abusione Sodomiticâ intervertisse episcopum (Guibert. Abbat. Hist. Hierosol. l. i. p. 468).   It is odd enough that we should find a parallel

pagans and the apostacy of their brethren; many thousand children were marked by the knife of circumcision; and many thousand captives were devoted to the service or the pleasures of their masters.[61] After the loss of Asia, Antioch still maintained her primitive allegiance to Christ and Cæsar; but the solitary province was separated from all Roman aid, and surrounded on all sides by the Mahometan powers. The despair of Philaretus the governor prepared the sacrifice of his religion and loyalty, had not his guilt been prevented by his son, who hastened to the Nicene palace, and offered to deliver this valuable prize into the hands of Soliman. The ambitious sultan mounted on horseback, and in twelve nights (for he reposed in the day) performed a march of six hundred miles. Antioch was oppressed by the speed and secrecy of his enterprise; and the dependent cities, as far as Laodicea and the confines of Aleppo,[62] obeyed the example of the metropolis. From Laodicea to the Thracian Bosphorus, or arm of St. George, the conquests and reign of Soliman extended thirty days' journey in length, and in breadth about ten or fifteen, between the rocks of Lycia and the Black Sea.[63] The Turkish ignorance of navigation protected, for a while, the inglorious safety of the emperor; but no sooner had a fleet of two hundred ships been constructed by the hands of the captive Greeks, than Alexius trembled behind the walls of his capital. His plaintive epistles were dispersed over Europe, to excite the compassion of the Latins, and to paint the danger, the weakness, and the riches, of the city of Constantine.[64]

passage of the same people in the present age. "Il n'est point d'horreur que ces Turcs n'ayent commis, et semblables aux soldats effrenés, qui dans la sac d'une ville non contens de disposer de tout à leur gré pretendent encore aux succès les moins désirables, quelques Sipahis ont porté leurs attentats sur la personne du vieux rabbi de la synagogue, et celle de l'Archévêque Grec" (Mémoires du Baron de Tott, tom. ii. p. 193).

[61] The emperor, or abbot, describe the scenes of a Turkish camp as if they had been present. Matres correptæ in conspectu filiarum multipliciter repetitis diversorum coitibus vexabantur (is that the true reading?), cum filiæ assistentes carmina præcinere saltando cogerentur. Mox eadem passio ad filias, &c.

[62] See Antioch, and the death of Soliman, in Anna Comnena (Alexias, l. vi. p. 168, 169 [c. 9]), with the notes of Ducange.

[63] William of Tyre (l. i. c. 9, 10, p. 635) gives the most authentic and deplorable account of these Turkish conquests.

[64] In his epistle to the count of Flanders, Alexius seems to fall too low beneath his character and dignity; yet it is approved by Ducange (Not. ad Alexiad. p. 335, &c.) and paraphrased by the abbot Guibert, a contemporary historian. The Greek text no longer exists; and each translator and scribe might say with Guibert (p. 475), verbis vestita meis, a privilege of most indefinite latitude. [Guibert incorporates the substance of this letter, Recueil, H. Occ. iv. p. 131 *sqq.* The best edition of

State and
pilgrimage
of Jeru-
salem.
A.D. 638-
1099

But the most interesting conquest of the Seljukian Turks was that of Jerusalem,[65] which soon became the theatre of nations. In their capitulation with Omar, the inhabitants had stipulated the assurance of their religion and property; but the articles were interpreted by a master against whom it was dangerous to dispute; and in the four hundred years of the reign of the caliphs, the political climate of Jerusalem was exposed to the vicissitudes of storms and sunshine.[66] By the increase of proselytes and population, the Mahometans might excuse their usurpation of three-fourths of the city; but a peculiar quarter was reserved for the patriarch with his clergy and people; a tribute of two pieces of gold was the price of protection; and the sepulchre of Christ, with the church of the Resurrection, was still left in the hands of his votaries. Of these votaries, the most numerous and respectable portion were strangers to Jerusalem: the pilgrimages to the Holy Land had been stimulated, rather than suppressed, by the conquest of the Arabs; and the enthusiasm which had always prompted these perilous journeys was nourished by the congenial passions of grief and indignation. A crowd of pilgrims from the East and West continued to visit the holy sepulchre and the adjacent sanctuaries, more especially at the festival at Easter; and the Greeks and Latins, the Nestorians

---

the text (preserved only in Latin) is that of the Count de Riant (1877 and again 1879). A controversy has raged over the genuineness of the document. Riant rejects it as spurious (like Wilken, Raumer, and others). But it was accepted as genuine by Sybel, and has been defended more recently by Vasilievski (Zhurn. Min. Nar. Prosv. 164, p. 325 *sqq.*, 1872) and Hagenmeyer (Byz. Ztsch. vi. 1 *sqq.*, 1897). It is doubtless genuine. The objections brought against it are not weighty; and the critics who condemn it have offered no theory of its origin that is in the least probable. It is perfectly incredible that it was composed as a deliberate forgery in the year 1098-9 in the camp of the Crusaders, as Riant tries to establish. Its contents are absolutely inconsistent with this theory. It was probably written long *before* the First Crusade; and Hagenmeyer is probably right in assigning it to 1088, when the Empire was in danger from the Patzinaks, and some months after the personal interview of Alexius with Robert of Flanders at Berrœa. The letter, of course, has suffered seriously in the process of its translation into Latin.]

[65] Our best fund for the history of Jerusalem from Heraclius to the crusades is contained in two large and original passages of William, archbishop of Tyre (l. i. c. 1-10, l. xviii. c. 5, 6), the principal author of the Gesta Dei per Francos. M. de Guignes has composed a very learned Mémoire sur le Commerce des François dans le Levant avant les Croisades, &c. (Mém. de l'Académie des Inscriptions, tom. xxxvii. p. 467-500).

[66] Secundum Dominorum dispositionem plerumque lucida plerumque nubila recepit intervalla, et ægrotantis more temporum praesentium gravabatur aut respirabat qualitate (l. i. c. 3, p. 630). The Latinity of William of Tyre is by no means contemptible; but in his account of 490 years, from the loss to the recovery of Jerusalem, he exceeds the true account by thirty years.

and Jacobites, the Copts and Abyssinians, the Armenians and Georgians, maintained the chapels, the clergy, and the poor of their respective communions. The harmony of prayer in so many various tongues, the worship of so many nations in the common temple of their religion, might have afforded a spectacle of edification and peace; but the zeal of the Christian sects was embittered by hatred and revenge; and in the kingdom of a suffering Messiah, who had pardoned his enemies, they aspired to command and persecute their spiritual brethren. The pre-eminence was asserted by the spirit and numbers of the Franks; and the greatness of Charlemagne [67] protected both the Latin pilgrims, and the Catholics of the East. The poverty of Carthage, Alexandria, and Jerusalem was relieved by the alms of that pious emperor; and many monasteries of Palestine were founded or restored by his liberal devotion. Harun Alrashid, the greatest of the Abbassides, esteemed in his Christian brother a similar supremacy of genius and power; their friendship was cemented by a frequent intercourse of gifts and embassies; and the caliph, without resigning the substantial dominion, presented the emperor with the keys of the holy sepulchre, and perhaps of the city of Jerusalem. In the decline of the Carlovingian monarchy, the republic of Amalphi promoted the interest of trade and religion in the East. Her vessels transported the Latin pilgrims to the coasts of Egypt and Palestine, and deserved, by their useful imports, the favour and alliance of the Fatimite caliphs: [68] an annual fair was instituted on mount Calvary; and the Italian merchants founded the convent and hospital of St. John of Jerusalem, the cradle of the monastic and military order, which has since reigned in the isles of Rhodes and of Malta. Had the Christian pilgrims been content to revere the tomb of a prophet, the disciples of Mahomet, instead of blaming, would have imitated, their piety; but these rigid *Unitarians* were scandalized by a worship which represents the birth, death, and resurrection, of a God; the Catholic images were branded

[67] For the transactions of Charlemagne with the Holy Land, see Eginhard (de Vitâ Caroli Magni, c. 16, p. 79-82), Constantine Porphyrogenitus (de Administratione Imperii, l. ii. c. 26, p. 80), and Pagi (Critica, tom. iii. A.D. 800, No. 13, 14, 15).

[68] The caliph granted his privileges, Amalphitanis viris amicis et utilium introductoribus (Gesta Dei, p. 934). The trade of Venice to Egypt and Palestine cannot produce so old a title, unless we adopt the laughable translation of a Frenchman who mistook the two factions of the circus (Veneti et Prasini) for the Venetians and Parisians.

with the name of idols ; and the Moslems smiled with indignation [69] at the miraculous flame, which was kindled on the eve of Easter in the holy sepulchre.[70] This pious fraud, first devised in the ninth century,[71] was devoutly cherished by the Latin crusaders, and is annually repeated by the clergy of the Greek, Armenian, and Coptic sects,[72] who impose on the credulous spectators [73] for their own benefit and that of their tyrants. In every age, a principle of toleration has been fortified by a sense of interest; and the revenue of the prince and his emir was increased each year by the expense and tribute of so many thousand strangers.

Under the Fatimite caliphs. A.D. 969-1076

The revolution which transferred the sceptre from the Abbassides to the Fatimites was a benefit, rather than an injury, to the Holy Land. A sovereign resident in Egypt was more sensible of the importance of Christian trade; and the emirs of Palestine were less remote from the justice and power of the throne. But the third of these Fatimite caliphs was the

[Succeeds in Egypt. A.D. 996]

famous Hakem,[74] a frantic youth, who was delivered by his impiety and despotism from the fear either of God or man; and whose reign was a wild mixture of vice and folly. Regardless of the most ancient customs of Egypt, he imposed on the women an absolute confinement: the restraint excited the clamours of both sexes; their clamours provoked his fury; a part of Old Cairo was delivered to the flames; and the guards and citizens

[69] An Arabic chronicle of Jerusalem (apud Asseman. Bibliot. Orient. tom. i. p. 628, tom. iv. p. 368) attests the unbelief of the caliph and the historian ; yet Cantacuzene presumes to appeal to the Mahometans themselves for the truth of this perpetual miracle.

[70] In his Dissertations on Ecclesiastical History, the learned Mosheim has separately discussed this pretended miracle (tom. ii. p. 214-306), de lumine sancti sepulchri.

[71] William of Malmsbury (l. iv. c. ii. p. 209) quotes the Itinerary of the monk Bernard, an eye-witness, who visited Jerusalem A.D. 870. The miracle is confirmed by another pilgrim some years older ; and Mosheim ascribes the invention to the Franks soon after the decease of Charlemagne.

[72] Our travellers, Sandys (p. 134), Thévenot (p. 621-627), Maundrell (p. 94, 95), &c., describe this extravagant farce. The Catholics are puzzled to decide *when* the miracle ended and the trick began.

[73] The Orientals themselves confess the fraud, and plead necessity and edification (Mémoires du Chevalier d'Arvieux, tom. i. p. 140 ; Joseph Abudacni, Hist. Copt. c. 20) ; but I will not attempt, with Mosheim, to explain the mode. Our travellers have failed with the blood of St. Januarius at Naples.

[74] See d'Herbelot (Bibliot. Orientale, p. 411), Renaudot (Hist. Patriarch. Alex. p. 390, 397, 400, 401), Elmacin (Hist. Saracen. p. 321-323), and Marei (p. 384-386), an historian of Egypt, translated by Reiske from Arabic into German, and verbally interpreted to me by a friend. [Al-Hākim Abū-Alī al-Mansūr reigned in Egypt from 996 to 1020.]

were engaged many days in a bloody conflict. At first the caliph declared himself a zealous Musulman, the founder or benefactor of mosques and colleges: twelve hundred and ninety copies of the Koran were transcribed at his expense in letters of gold; and his edict extirpated the vineyards of the Upper Egypt. But his vanity was soon flattered by the hope of introducing a [Assumes divinity. new religion; he aspired above the fame of a prophet, and styled A.D. 1017] himself the visible image of the Most High God, who, after nine apparitions on earth, was at length manifest in his royal person. At the name of Hakem, the lord of the living and the dead, every knee was bent in religious adoration: his mysteries were performed on a mountain near Cairo; sixteen thousand converts had signed his profession of faith; and at the present hour, a free and warlike people, the Druses of mount Libanus, are persuaded of the life and divinity of a madman and tyrant.[75] In his divine character, Hakem hated the Jews and Christians, as the servants of his rivals; while some remains of prejudice or prudence still pleaded in favour of the law of Mahomet.[76] Both in Egypt and Palestine, his cruel and wanton persecution made some martyrs and many apostates: the common rights and special privileges of the sectaries were equally disregarded; and a general interdict was laid on the devotion of strangers and natives. The temple of the Christian world, the church of the Sacrilege of Hakem. Resurrection, was demolished to its foundations; the luminous A.D. 1009 prodigy of Easter was interrupted, and much profane labour was exhausted to destroy the cave in the rock, which properly constitutes the holy sepulchre. At the report of this sacrilege, the nations of Europe were astonished and afflicted; but, instead of

---

[75] The religion of the Druses is concealed by their ignorance and hypocrisy. Their secret doctrines are confined to the elect who profess a contemplative life; and the vulgar Druses, the most indifferent of men, occasionally conform to the worship of the Mahometans and Christians of their neighbourhood. The little that is, or deserves to be, known may be seen in the industrious Niebuhr (Voyages, tom. ii. p. 354-357) and the second volume of the recent and instructive Travels of M. de Volney. [The religion of the Druses has been thoroughly investigated by Silvestre de Sacy in his Exposé de la religion des Druses, in two volumes, 1838.]

[76] ["It was not in his 'divine character' that Hakem 'hated the Jews and Christians,' but in that of a Mahometan bigot, which he displayed in the earlier years of his reign. His barbarous persecutions and the burning of the church of the Resurrection at Jerusalem belong entirely to that period; and his assumption of divinity was followed by an edict of toleration to Jews and Christians. The Mahometans, whose religion he then treated with hostility and contempt, being far the most numerous, were his most dangerous enemies, and therefore the objects of his most inveterate hatred " (Milman, note to this passage).]

arming in the defence of the Holy Land, they contented themselves with burning or banishing the Jews, as the secret ad-
visers of the impious barbarian.[77] Yet the calamities of Jerusalem
were in some measure alleviated by the inconstancy or repentance of Hakem himself; and the royal mandate was sealed for
the restitution of the churches, when the tyrant was assassinated
by the emissaries of his sister. The succeeding caliphs resumed
the maxims of religion and policy; a free toleration was again
granted; with the pious aid of the emperor of Constantinople
the holy sepulchre arose from its ruins; and, after a short abstinence, the pilgrims returned with an increase of appetite to
the spiritual feast.[78] In the sea-voyage of Palestine, the dangers
were frequent and the opportunities rare; but the conversion
of Hungary opened a safe communication between Germany
and Greece. The charity of St. Stephen, the apostle of his
kingdom, relieved and conducted his itinerant brethren;[79] and
from Belgrade to Antioch they traversed fifteen hundred miles

Increase of pilgrim-ages. A.D. 1024, &c. of a Christian empire. Among the Franks, the zeal of pilgrimage prevailed beyond the example of former times; and the
roads were covered with multitudes of either sex and of every
rank, who professed their contempt of life, so soon as they should
have kissed the tomb of their Redeemer. Princes and prelates
abandoned the care of their dominions; and the numbers of
these pious caravans were a prelude to the armies which marched
in the ensuing age under the banner of the cross. About thirty
years before the first crusade, the archbishop of Mentz, with
the bishops of Utrecht, Bamberg, and Ratisbon, undertook this
laborious journey from the Rhine to the Jordan; and the multitude of their followers amounted to seven thousand persons. At Constantinople, they were hospitably entertained by
the emperor; but the ostentation of their wealth provoked the assault of the wild Arabs; they drew their swords with scrupulous
reluctance, and sustained a siege in the village of Capernaum,

---

[77] See Glaber, l. iii. c. 7, and the Annals of Baronius and Pagi, A.D. 1009.
[78] Per idem tempus ex universo orbe tam innumerabilis multitudo cœpit con-
fluere ad sepulchrum Salvatoris Hierosolymis, quantum nullus hominum prius
sperare poterat. Ordo inferioris plebis . . . mediocres . . . reges et comites . . .
præsules . . . mulieres multæ nobiles cum pauperioribus . . . Pluribus enim erat
mentis desiderium mori priusquam ad propria reverterentur (Glaber, l. iv. c. 6;
Bouquet, Historians of France, tom. x. p. 50).
[79] Glaber, l. iii. c. 1. Katona (Hist. Critic. Regum Hungariæ, tom. i. p. 304-
311) examines whether St. Stephen founded a monastery at Jerusalem.

till they were rescued by the venal protection of the Fatimite emir. After visiting the holy places, they embarked for Italy, but only a remnant of two thousand arrived in safety in their native land. Ingulphus, a secretary of William the Conqueror, was a companion of this pilgrimage : he observes that they sallied from Normandy, thirty stout and well-appointed horsemen ; but that they repassed the Alps, twenty miserable palmers, with the staff in their hand, and the wallet at their back.[80]

After the defeat of the Romans, the tranquillity of the Fatimite caliphs was invaded by the Turks.[81] One of the lieutenants of Malek Shah, Atsiz the Carizmian, marched into Syria at the head of a powerful army, and reduced Damascus by famine and the sword. Hems, and the other cities of the province, acknowledged the caliph of Bagdad and the sultan of Persia; and the victorious emir advanced without resistance to the banks of the Nile ; the Fatimite was preparing to fly into the heart of Africa; but the negroes of his guard and the inhabitants of Cairo made a desperate sally, and repulsed the Turk from the confines of Egypt. In his retreat, he indulged the licence of slaughter and rapine; the judge and notaries of Jerusalem were invited to his camp; and their execution was followed by the massacre of three thousand citizens. The cruelty or the defeat of Atsiz was soon punished by the sultan Toucush, the brother of Malek Shah, who, with a higher title and more formidable powers, asserted the dominion of Syria and Palestine. The house of Seljuk reigned about twenty years in Jerusalem ;[82] but the hereditary command of the holy city and

[margin: Conquest of Jerusalem by the Turks. A.D. 1076-1096]

[margin: [Hims, Emesa]]

---

[80] Baronius (A.D. 1064, No. 43-56) has transcribed the greater part of the original narratives of Ingulphus, Marianus, and Lambertus. [Descriptions of the Holy Land by pilgrims of the 12th century, translated into English, will be found in vols. iv. and v. of the Library of the Palestine Pilgrims' Text Society.]

[81] See Elmacin (Hist. Saracen. p. 349, 350) and Abulpharagius (Dynast. p. 237, vers. Pocock). M. de Guignes (Hist. des Huns, tom. iii. part i. p. 215, 216) adds the testimonies, or rather the names, of Abulfeda and Novairi.

[82] From the expedition of Isar Atsiz (A.H. 469, A.D. 1076) to the expulsion of the Ortokides (A.D. 1096). Yet William of Tyre (l. i. c. 6, p. 633) asserts that Jerusalem was thirty-eight years in the hands of the Turks ; and an Arabic chronicle, quoted by Pagi (tom. iv. p. 202), supposes that the city was reduced by a Carizmian general to the obedience of the caliph of Bagdad, A.H. 463, A.D. 1070. These early dates are not very compatible with the general history of Asia; and I am sure that, as late as A.D. 1064, the regnum Babylonicum (of Cairo) still prevailed in Palestine) Baronius, A.D. 1064, No. 56). [See Mujīr ad-Dīn, Histoire de Jérusalem, transl. Sauvaire (1876), p. 69-70 ; who states that Atsīz ibn Auk (the Khwarizmian governor of Damascus) took Jerusalem in 1070-1 and the Abbāsid caliph was proclaimed there two years later, and the Ortokids expelled in 1096.]

territory was entrusted or abandoned to the emir Ortok, the chief of a tribe [82a] of Turkmans, whose children, after their ex pulsion from Palestine, formed two dynasties on the borders o Armenia and Assyria.[83] The Oriental Christians and the Latin pilgrims deplored a revolution, which, instead of the regular government and old alliance of the caliphs, imposed on their necks the iron yoke of the strangers of the north.[84] In his court and camp the great sultan had adopted in some degree the arts and manners of Persia; but the body of the Turkish nation, and more especially the pastoral tribes, still breathed the fierceness of the desert. From Nice to Jerusalem, the western countries of Asia were a scene of foreign and domestic hostility; and the shepherds of Palestine, who held a precarious sway on a doubtful frontier, had neither leisure nor capacity to await the slow profits of commercial and religious freedom. The pilgrims, who, through innumerable perils, had reached the gates of Jerusalem, were the victims of private rapine or public oppression, and often sunk under the pressure of famine and disease, before they were permitted to salute the holy sepulchre. A spirit of native barbarism, or recent zeal, prompted the Turkmans to insult the clergy of every sect; the patriarch was dragged by the hair along the pavement and cast into a dungeon, to extort a ransom from the sympathy of his flock; and the divine worship in the church of the Resurrection was often disturbed by the savage rudeness of its masters. The pathetic tale excited the millions of the West to march under the standard of the Cross to the relief of the Holy Land; and yet how trifling is the sum of these accumulated evils, if compared with the single act of the sacrilege of Hakem, which had been so patiently endured by the Latin Christians! A slighter provocation inflamed the more irascible temper of their descendants: a new spirit had arisen of religious chivalry and papal dominion; a nerve was touched of exquisite feeling; and the sensation vibrated to the heart of Europe.

[82a] [Family.]   [83] De Guignes, Hist. des Huns, tom. i. p. 249-252.
[84] Willerm. Tyr. l. i. c. 8, p. 634, who strives hard to magnify the Christian grievances. The Turks exacted an *aureus* from each pilgrim! The *caphar* of the Franks is now fourteen dollars; and Europe does not complain of this voluntary tax.

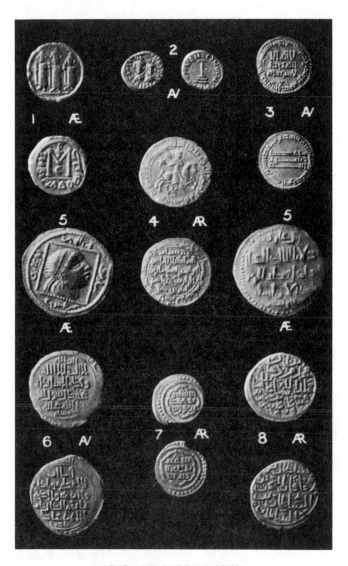

ARAB AND TURKISH COINS

CHAPTER LVIII

*Origin and Numbers of the First Crusade—Characters of the
Latin Princes—Their March to Constantinople—Policy
of the Greek Emperor Alexius—Conquest of Nice, Antioch,
and Jerusalem, by the Franks—Deliverance of the Holy
Sepulchre—Godfrey of Bouillon, first King of Jerusalem
—Institutions of the French or Latin Kingdom*

ABOUT twenty years after the conquest of Jerusalem by The first crusade. the Turks, the holy sepulchre was visited by an hermit A.D. 1095-1099. Peter of the name of Peter, a native of Amiens, in the pro- the Hermit vince of Picardy [1] in France. His resentment and sympathy were excited by his own injuries and the oppression of the Christian name ; he mingled his tears with those of the patriarch, and earnestly inquired if no hopes of relief could be entertained from the Greek emperors of the East. The patriarch exposed the vices and weakness of the successors of Constantine. "I will rouse," exclaimed the hermit, "the martial nations of Europe in your cause;" and Europe was obedient to the call of the hermit. The astonished patriarch dismissed him with epistles of credit and complaint ; and no sooner did he land at Bari than Peter hastened to kiss the feet of the Roman Pontiff. His stature was small, his appearance contemptible ; but his eye was keen and lively ; and he possessed that vehemence of speech which seldom fails to impart the persuasion of the soul.[2] He was born of a gentleman's

---

[1] Whimsical enough is the origin of the name of *Picards*, and from thence of *Picardie*, which does not date earlier than A.D. 1200. It was an academical joke, an epithet first applied to the quarrelsome humour of those students, in the university of Paris, who came from the frontier of France and Flanders (Valesii Notitia Galliarum, p. 447 ; Longuerue, Description de la France, p. 54).

[2] William of Tyre (l. i. c. 11, p. 637, 638) thus describes the hermit: Pusillus, persona contemptibilis, vivacis ingenii, et oculum habens perspicacem gratumque, et sponte fluens ei non deerat eloquium. See Albert Aquensis, p. 185. Guibert, p. 482. Anna Comnena in Alexiad. l. x. p. 284 [c. 5], &c. with Ducange's notes, p. 349. [In the writers who are contemporary with the First Crusade there is not a

family (for we must now adopt a modern idiom), and his
military service was under the neighbouring counts of Boulogne,
the heroes of the first crusade. But he soon relinquished the
sword and the world ; and, if it be true that his wife, however
noble, was aged and ugly, he might withdraw, with the less
reluctance, from her bed to a convent, and at length to an
hermitage. In this austere solitude, his body was emaciated,
his fancy was inflamed ; whatever he wished, he believed ;
whatever he believed, he *saw* in dreams and revelations.
From Jerusalem the pilgrim returned an accomplished fanatic ;
but, as he excelled in the popular madness of the times, Pope
Urban the Second received him as a prophet, applauded his
glorious design, promised to support it in a general council,
and encouraged him to proclaim the deliverance of the Holy
Land. Invigorated by the approbation of the Pontiff, his
zealous missionary traversed, with speed and success, the provinces of Italy and France. His diet was abstemious, his
prayers long and fervent, and the alms which he received with
one hand, he distributed with the other; his head was bare,
his feet naked, his meagre body was wrapt in a coarse garment ; he bore and displayed a weighty crucifix; and the ass
on which he rode was sanctified in the public eye by the
service of the man of God. He preached to innumerable
crowds in the churches, the streets, and the high-ways : the
hermit entered with equal confidence the palace and the
cottage ; and the people, for all was people, were impetuously
moved by his call to repentance and arms. When he painted
the sufferings of the natives and pilgrims of Palestine, every
heart was melted to compassion; every breast glowed with
indignation, when he challenged the warriors of the age to
defend their brethren and rescue their Saviour : his ignorance of
art and language was compensated by sighs, and tears, and
ejaculations ; and Peter supplied the deficiency of reason by
loud and frequent appeals to Christ and his mother, to the
saints and angels of paradise, with whom he had personally

word of Peter the Hermit instigating Pope Urban, nor is he mentioned as present
at the Council of Clermont. The story first appears in Albert of Aix and a little
later in the Chanson d'Antioche (of the Pilgrim Richard, c. 1145), which has been
edited by P. Paris, 1848. See Hagenmeyer, Peter der Eremite, 1879. After the
Council of Clermont Peter was active in preaching the Crusade in his own country
in the north-east of France, as we know from Guibertus.]

conversed.   The most perfect orator of Athens might have
envied the success of his eloquence: the rustic enthusiast inspired the passions which he felt, and Christendom expected
with impatience the counsels and decrees of the supreme
Pontiff.

The magnanimous spirit of Gregory the Seventh had already
embraced the design of arming Europe against Asia; the
ardour of his zeal and ambition still breathes in his epistles.
From either side of the Alps, fifty thousand Catholics had enlisted under the banner of St. Peter;[3] and his successor reveals
his intention of marching at their head against the impious
sectaries of Mahomet.   But the glory or reproach of executing,
though not in person, this holy enterprise was reserved for
Urban the Second,[4] the most faithful of his disciples.   He
undertook the conquest of the East, whilst the larger portion
of Rome was possessed and fortified by his rival, Guibert of
Ravenna, who contended with Urban for the name and honours of the pontificate.   He attempted to unite the powers of
the West, at a time when the princes were separated from
the church, and the people from their princes, by the excommunication which himself and his predecessors had thundered
against the emperor and the king of France.   Philip the First,
of France, supported with patience the censures which he had
provoked by his scandalous life and adulterous marriage.
Henry the Fourth, of Germany, asserted the right of investitures, the prerogative of confirming his bishops by the delivery
of the ring and crosier.   But the emperor's party was crushed
in Italy by the arms of the Normans and the Countess
Mathilda ; and the long quarrel had been recently envenomed

Urban II.
in the
council of
Placentia.
A.D. 1095,
March

---

[3] Ultra quinquaginta millia, si me possunt in expeditione pro duce et pontifice
habere, armatâ manu volunt in inimicos Dei insurgere, et ad sepulchrum Domini
ipso ducente pervenire (Gregor. vii. epist. ii. 31, in tom. xii. p. 322, Concil.).
[4] See the original lives of Urban II. by Pandulphus Pisanus and Bernardus
Guido [in his Vitae Pontificum Romanorum; Bernard flourished at the beginning
of the 14th century], in Muratori, Rer. Ital. Script. tom. iii. pars i. p. 352, 353.
The continuation of the Liber Pontificalis from Gregory VII. to Honorius II. was
ascribed by Baronius to Pandulfus of Pisa, and this view was adopted in Muratori's
edition.   But Giesebrecht has shown that the lives of Gregory VII., Victor III.,
and Urban II. are independent compositions and probably the work of the Cardinal
Petrus Pisanus.   The lives of Gelasius II., Calixtus II., and Honorius II. were
written by Pandulf, the nephew of Hugh of Alatri.   See Giesebrecht, Allgemeine
Monatschrift, 1852, p. 260 *sqq*., and Geschichte der deutschen Kaiserzeit, iii. p.
1067-8 (5th ed.).—On Urban II. cp. M. F. Stern, Biographie des Papstes Urban II.,
1883.]

by the revolt of his son Conrad, and the shame of his wife,[5] who, in the synods of Constance and Placentia, confessed the manifold prostitutions to which she had been exposed by an husband regardless of her honour and his own.[6] So popular was the cause of Urban, so weighty was his influence, that the council which he summoned at Placentia [7] was composed of two hundred bishops of Italy, France, Burgundy, Swabia, and Bavaria. Four thousand of the clergy, and thirty thousand of the laity, attended this important meeting; and, as the most spacious cathedral would have been inadequate to the multitude, the session of seven days was held in a plain adjacent to the city. The ambassadors of the Greek emperor, Alexius Comnenus, were introduced to plead the distress of their sovereign, and the danger of Constantinople, which was divided only by a narrow sea from the victorious Turks, the common enemy of the Christian name. In their suppliant address, they flattered the pride of the Latin princes; and, appealing at once to their policy and religion, exhorted them to repel the barbarians on the confines of Asia rather than to expect them in the heart of Europe. At the sad tale of the misery and perils of their Eastern brethren, the assembly burst into tears; the most eager champions declared their readiness to march; and the Greek ambassadors were dismissed with the assurance of a speedy and powerful succour. The relief of Constantinople was included in the larger and most distant project of the deliver-

---

[5] She is known by the different names of Praxes, Eupræcia, Eufrasia, and Adelais [generally called Praxedis in the sources]; and was the daughter of a Russian prince [Vsevlad of Kiev], and the widow of a Margrave of Brandenburg. Struv. Corpus Hist. Germanicæ, p. 340.

[6] Henricus odio eam cœpit habere : ideo incarceravit eam, et concessit ut plerique vim ei inferrent ; imo filium hortans ut eam subagitaret (Dodechin, Continuat. Marian. Scot. [i.e. the Annales S. Disibodi falsely ascribed to a certain Abbot Dodechin and erroneously supposed.to be a continuation of the Chronicle of Marianus Scotus] apud Baron. A.D. 1093, No. 4). In the synod of Constance, she is described by Bertholdus, rerum inspector : quæ se tantas et tam inauditas fornicationum spurcitias, et a tantis passam fuisse conquesta est, &c. And again at Placentia : satis misericorditer suscepit, eo quod ipsam tantas spurcitias non tam commississe quam invitam pertulisse pro certo cognoverit Papa cum sanctâ synodo. Apud Baron. A.D. 1093, No. 4, 1094, No. 3. A rare subject for the infallible decision of a Pope and council! These abominations are repugnant to every principle of human nature, which is not altered by a dispute about rings and crosiers. Yet it should seem that the wretched woman was tempted by the priests to relate or subscribe some infamous stories of herself and her husband.

[7] See the narrative and acts of the synod of Placentia, Concil. tom. xii. p. 821, &c. [Mansi, Concil. xx. p. 804, and cp. Pertz, Mon. Germ. Hist., 8, p. 474, for a notice appended to the Acts.]

ance of Jerusalem ; but the prudent Urban adjourned the final
decision to a second synod, which he proposed to celebrate in
some city of France in the autumn of the same year. The
short delay would propagate the flame of enthusiasm; and his
firmest hope was in a nation of soldiers,[8] still proud of the pre-
eminence of their name, and ambitious to emulate their hero
Charlemagne,[9] who, in the popular romance of Turpin,[10] had
achieved the conquest of the Holy Land. A latent motive of
affection or vanity might influence the choice of Urban. He
was himself a native of France, a monk of Clugny, and the
first of his countrymen who ascended the throne of St. Peter.
The Pope had illustrated his family and province. Nor is there
perhaps a more exquisite gratification than to revisit, in a conspicuous dignity, the humble and laborious scenes of our
youth.

It may occasion some surprise that the Roman pontiff Council of
should erect, in the heart of France, the tribunal from whence A.D. 1095,
he hurled his anathemas against the king; but our surprise will November
vanish, so soon as we form a just estimate of a king of France
of the eleventh century.[11] Philip the First was the great-grandson of Hugh Capet, the founder of the present race, who, in the

---

[8] Guibert, himself a Frenchman, praises the piety and valour of the French
nation, the author and example of the crusades : Gens nobilis, prudens, bellicosa,
dapsilis, et nitida.—Quos enim ·Britones, *Anglos*, Ligures, si bonis eos moribus
videamus, non illico *Francos homines* appellemus ? (p. 478). He owns, however,
that the vivacity of the French degenerates into petulance among foreigners (p.
483), and vain loquaciousness (p. 502).

[9] Per viam quam jamdudum Carolus Magnus, mirificus rex Francorum [*leg.*
Franciae], aptari fecit usque C. P. (Gesta Francorum, p. 1, Robert. Monach. Hist.
Hicros. l. i. p. 33, &c.).

[10] John Tilpinus, or Turpinus, was Archbishop of Rheims, A.D. 773. After the
year 1000, this romance was composed in his ·name by a monk of the borders of
France and Spain ; and such was the idea of ecclesiastical merit that he describes
himself as a fighting and drinking priest ! Yet the book of lies was pronounced
authentic by Pope Calixtus II. (A.D. 1122), and is respectfully quoted by the abbot
Suger, in the great Chronicles of St. Denys (Fabric. Bibliot. Latin. medii Ævi, edit.
Mansi, tom. iv. p. 161). [The most important critical work on Turpin's romance
(Historia de vita Caroli Magni et Rolandi eius nepotis, is the title) is that of Gaston
Paris, De Pseudo-Turpino (1865), who makes it probable that the first part (cc. 1-5)
was composed in the 11th century by a Spaniard, and the second part (c. 1110) by a
monk at Vienne. The most recent edition is that of F. Castets, 1880. There were
several old French translations. One, for instance, was edited by F. A. Wulff
(Chronique dite de Turpin, 1881), and two others by T. Auracher (1876, 1877).
There is an English translation by T. Rodd (History of Charles the Great and
Orlando ascribed to Turpin, 1812, 2 vols.).]

[11] See Etat de la France, by the Count de Boulainvilliers, tom. i. p. 180-182,
and the second volume of the Observations sur l'Histoire de France, by the Abbé
de Mably.

decline of Charlemagne's posterity, added the regal title to his patrimonial estates of Paris and Orleans.   In this narrow compass he was possessed of wealth and jurisdiction; but, in the rest of France, Hugh and his first descendants were no more than the feudal lords of about sixty dukes and counts, of independent and hereditary power,[12] who disdained the control of laws and legal assemblies, and whose disregard of their sovereign was revenged by the disobedience of their inferior vassals.   At Clermont, in the territories of the count of Auvergne,[13] the pope might brave with impunity the resentment of Philip; and the council which he convened in that city was not less numerous or respectable than the synod of Placentia.[14]   Besides his court and council of Roman cardinals, he was supported by thirteen archbishops and two hundred and twenty-five bishops;[15] the number of mitred prelates was computed at four hundred; and the fathers of the church were blessed by the saints, and enlightened by the doctors, of the age.   From the adjacent kingdoms a martial train of lords and knights of power and renown attended the council,[16] in high expectation of its resolves; and such was the ardour of zeal and curiosity that the city was filled, and many thousands, in the month of November, erected their tents or huts in the open field.   A session of eight days produced some useful or edifying canons for the reformation of manners; a severe censure was pronounced against the licence of private war; the Truce of God[17] was confirmed, a suspension of hostilities

---

[12] In the provinces to the south of the Loire, the first *Capetians* were scarcely allowed a feudal supremacy. On all sides, Normandy, Bretagne, Aquitain, Burgundy, Lorraine, and Flanders contracted the name and limits of the *proper* France. See Hadrian. Vales. Notitia Galliarum.

[13] These counts, a younger branch of the dukes of Aquitain, were at length despoiled of the greatest part of their country by Philip Augustus. The bishops of Clermont gradually became princes of the city. Mélanges tirés d'une grande Bibliothèque, tom. xxxvi. p. 288, &c.

[14] See the acts of the council of Clermont, Concil. tom. xii. p. 829, &c. [Mansi, Concilia, xx. p. 815 *sqq.*]

[15] [Thirteen archbishops, eighty bishops, and ninety abbots, Giesebrecht, *op. cit.*, iii. p. 667, following Cencius Camerarius (Mansi, xx. 908), and the Pope himself (*ib.*, 829).]

[16] Confluxerunt ad concilium e multis regionibus viri, potentes et honorati, innumeri quamvis cingulo laicalis militiæ superbi (Baldric, an eye-witness, p. 86-88. Robert. Mon. p. 31, 32. Will. Tyr. i. 14, 15, p. 639-641. Guibert, p. 478-480. Fulcher. Caront. p. 382).

[17] The Truce of God (Treva, or Treuga Dei) was first invented in Aquitain, A.D. 1032; blamed by some bishops as an occasion of perjury, and rejected by the Normans as contrary to their privileges (Ducange, Gloss. Latin. tom. vi. p. 682-685). [Kluckhohn, Geschichte des Gottesfriedens.]

uring four days of the week; women and priests were placed
under the safeguard of the church; and a protection of three
years was extended to husbandmen and merchants, the defence-
ess victims of military rapine. But a law, however venerable
be the sanction, cannot suddenly transform the temper of the
imes; and the benevolent efforts of Urban deserve the less
praise, since he laboured to appease some domestic quarrels
that he might spread the flames of war from the Atlantic to
the Euphrates. From the synod of Placentia the rumour of his
great design had gone forth among the nations; the clergy, on
their return, had preached in every diocese the merit and
glory of the deliverance of the Holy Land; and, when the pope
ascended a lofty scaffold in the market-place of Clermont, his
eloquence was addressed to a well-prepared and impatient
audience. His topics were obvious, his exhortation was vehement, his success inevitable. The orator was interrupted by
the shout of thousands, who with one voice, and in their rustic
idiom, exclaimed aloud, "God wills it, God wills it!"[18] "It
is indeed the will of God," replied the pope; "and let this
memorable word, the inspiration surely of the Holy Spirit, be
for ever adopted as your cry of battle, to animate the devotion
and courage of the champions of Christ. His cross is the symbol
of your salvation; wear it, a red, a bloody cross, as an external
mark on your breasts or shoulders, as a pledge of your sacred
and irrevocable engagement." The proposal was joyfully accepted; great numbers both of the clergy and laity impressed
on their garments the sign of the cross,[19] and solicited the pope
to march at their head. This dangerous honour was declined
by the more prudent successor of Gregory, who alleged the schism
of the church, and the duties of his pastoral office, recommend-

---

[18] *Deus vult, Deus vult !* was the pure acclamation of the clergy who understood
Latin (Robert. Mon. l. i. p. 32). By the illiterate laity, who spoke the *Provincial*
or *Limousin* idiom, it was corrupted to *Deus lo volt*, or *Diex el volt*. See Chron.
Casinense, l. iv. c. 11, p. 497, in Muratori, Script. Rerum Ital. tom. iv., and Ducange
(Dissertat. xi. p. 207 sur Joinville, and Gloss. Lat. tom. ii. p. 690), who, in his pre-
face, produces a very difficult specimen of the dialect of Rovergue, A.D. 1100, very
near, both in time and place, to the council of Clermont (p. 15, 16). [See Sybel,
Geschichte des ersten Kreuzzuges, p. 185 *sqq.*]

[19] Most commonly on their shoulders, in gold, or silk, or cloth, sewed on their
garments. In the first crusade, all were red; in the third, the French alone preserved that colour, while green crosses were adopted by the Flemings, and white
by the English (Ducange, tom. ii. p. 651). Yet in England the red ever appears
the favourite, and, as it were, the national, colour of our military ensigns and uni-
forms.

ing to the faithful, who were disqualified by sex or profession, by age or infirmity, to aid, with their prayers and alms, the personal service of their robust brethren. The name and powers of his legate he devolved on Adhemar, bishop of Puy, the first who had received the cross at his hands. The foremost of the temporal chiefs was Raymond, count of Toulouse, whose ambassadors in the council excused the absence, and pledged the honour, of their master. After the confession and absolution of their sins, the champions of the cross were dismissed with a superfluous admonition to invite their countrymen and friends; and their departure for the Holy Land was fixed to the festival of the Assumption, the fifteenth of August, of the ensuing year.[20]

Justice of the Crusades

So familiar, and as it were so natural, to man is the practice of violence that our indulgence allows the slightest provocation, the most disputable right, as a sufficient ground of national hostility. But the name and nature of an *holy war* demands a more rigorous scrutiny; nor can we hastily believe that the servants of the Prince of Peace would unsheath the sword of destruction, unless the motives were pure, the quarrel legitimate, and the necessity inevitable. The policy of an action may be determined from the tardy lessons of experience; but, before we act, our conscience should be satisfied of the justice and propriety of our enterprise. In the age of the crusades, the Christians, both of the East and West, were persuaded of their

[20] Bongarsius, who has published the original writers of the crusades, adopts, with much complacency, the fanatic title of Guibertus, Gesta Dei per Francos; though some critics propose to read Gesta *Diaboli* per Francos (Hanoviæ, 1611, two vols. in folio). I shall briefly enumerate, as they stand in this collection [superseded by the Recueil des historiens des Croisades; Historiens occidentaux, vols. 1-5, 1841-1895], the authors whom I have used for the first crusade. I. Gesta Francorum [Recueil, 3, p. 121 sqq.]. II. Robertus Monachus [ib. 3, p. 717 sqq.]. III. Baldricus [ib. 4, p. 1 sqq.]. IV. Raimundus de Agiles [ib. 3, p. 235 sqq.]. V. Albertus Aquensis [ib. 4, p. 265 sqq.]. VI. Fulcherius Carnotensis [ib. 3, p. 311 sqq.]. VII. Guibertus [ib. 4, p. 113 sqq.]. VIII. Willielmus Tyriensis [ib. 1, No. 3]. Muratori has given us, IX. Radulphus Cadomensis de Gestis Tancredi (Script. Rer. Ital. tom. v. p. 285-333 [Recueil, 3, p. 603 sqq.]), and X. Bernardus Thesaurarius de Acquisitione Terræ Sanctæ (tom. vii. p. 664-848 [ib. 2, p. 483 sqq.]). The last of these was unknown to a late French historian, who has given a large and critical list of the writers of the crusades (Esprit des Croisades, tom. i. p. 13-141), and most of whose judgments my own experience will allow me to ratify. It was late before I could obtain a sight of the French historians collected by Duchesne. I. Petri Tudebodi Sacerdotis Sivracensis [of Sivrai in Poitou; flor. c. A.D. 1100] Historia de Hierosolymitano Itinere (tom. iv. p. 773-815 [Recueil, 3, p. 1 sqq.; French translation by S. de Goy, 1878]) has been transfused into the first anonymous writer of Bongarsius [rather, the Gesta Francorum were incorporated and augmented by Peter. So Sybel; but otherwise Klein in his monograph Raimund von Aguilers, 1892]. II. The Metrical History of the First Crusade, in vii. books (p. 890-912), is of small value or account.

lawfulness and merit; their arguments are clouded by the perpetual abuse of scripture and rhetoric; but they seem to insist on the right of natural and religious defence, their peculiar title to the Holy Land, and the impiety of their Pagan and Mahometan foes.[21]   I. The right of a just defence may fairly include our civil and spiritual allies: it depends on the existence of danger; and that danger must be estimated by the twofold consideration of the malice and the power of our enemies.   A pernicious tenet has been imputed to the Mahometans, the duty of *extirpating* all other religions by the sword.   This charge of ignorance and bigotry is refuted by the Koran, by the history of the Musulman conquerors, and by their public and legal toleration of the Christian worship.   But it cannot be denied that the Oriental churches are depressed under their iron yoke; that, in peace and war, they assert a divine and indefeasible claim of universal empire; and that, in their orthodox creed, the unbelieving nations are continually threatened with the loss of religion or liberty.   In the eleventh century, the victorious arms of the Turks presented a real and urgent apprehension of these losses. They had subdued, in less than thirty years, the kingdoms of Asia, as far as Jerusalem and the Hellespont; and the Greek empire tottered on the verge of destruction.   Besides an honest sympathy for their brethren, the Latins had a right and interest in the support of Constantinople, the most important barrier of the West; and the privilege of defence must reach to prevent, as well as to repel, an impending assault.   But this salutary purpose might have been accomplished by a moderate succour; and our calmer reason must disclaim the innumerable hosts and remote operations which overwhelmed Asia and depopulated Europe.   II. Palestine could add nothing to the strength or safety of the Latins; and fanaticism alone could pretend to justify the conquest of that distant and narrow province.   The Christians affirmed that their inalienable title to the promised land had been sealed by the blood of their divine Saviour: it was their right and duty to rescue their inheritance from the unjust possessors, who profaned his sepulchre and oppressed the

---

[21] If the reader will turn to the first scene of the First Part of Henry IV., he will see in the text of Shakespeare the natural feelings of enthusiasm; and in the notes Dr. Johnson the workings of a bigoted though vigorous mind, greedy of every pretence to hate and persecute those who dissent from his creed.

pilgrimage of his disciples.   Vainly would it be alleged that the
pre-eminence of Jerusalem and the sanctity of Palestine have
been abolished with the Mosaic law; that the God of the Christians is not a local deity; and that the recovery of Bethlehem or
Calvary, his cradle or his tomb, will not atone for the violation
of the moral precepts of the gospel.   Such arguments glance
aside from the leaden shield of superstition; and the religious
mind will not easily relinquish its hold on the sacred ground of
mystery and miracle.   III.   But the holy wars which have been
waged in every climate of the globe, from Egypt to Livonia,
and from Peru to Hindostan, require the support of some more
general and flexible tenet.   It has been often supposed, and
sometimes affirmed, that a difference of religion is a worthy
cause of hostility; that obstinate unbelievers may be slain or subdued by the champions of the cross; and that grace is the sole
fountain of dominion as well as of mercy.   Above four hundred
years before the first crusade, the eastern and western provinces
of the Roman empire had been acquired about the same time,
and in the same manner, by the barbarians of Germany and
Arabia.   Time and treaties had legitimated the conquests of the
Christian Franks; but, in the eyes of their subjects and neighbours, the Mahometan princes were still tyrants and usurpers,
who, by the arms of war or rebellion, might be lawfully driven
from their unlawful possession.[22]

Spiritual
motives
and indul-
gences

As the manners of the Christians were relaxed, their discipline of penance[23] was enforced; and, with the multiplication of
sins, the remedies were multiplied.   In the primitive church, a
voluntary and open confession prepared the work of atonement.   In the middle ages, the bishops and priests interrogated
the criminal; compelled him to account for his thoughts, words
and actions; and prescribed the terms of his reconciliation with
God.   But, as this discretionary power might alternately be
abused by indulgence and tyranny, a rule of discipline was
framed, to inform and regulate the spiritual judges.   This mode

[22] The Sixth Discourse of Fleury on Ecclesiastical History (p. 223-261) contain
an accurate and rational view of the causes and effects of the crusades.

[23] The penance, indulgences, &c. of the middle ages are amply discussed by
Muratori (Antiquitat. Italiæ medii Ævi, tom. v. dissert. lxviii. p. 709-768) and by
M. Chais (Lettres sur les Jubilés et les Indulgences, tom. ii: lettres 21 and 22, p
478-556), with this difference, that the abuses of superstition are mildly, perhaps
faintly, exposed by the learned Italian, and peevishly magnified by the Dutch
minister.

of legislation was invented by the Greeks; their *penitentials* [24] were translated, or imitated, in the Latin church; and, in the time of Charlemagne, the clergy of every diocese were provided with a code, which they prudently concealed from the knowledge of the vulgar. In this dangerous estimate of crimes and punishments, each case was supposed, each difference was remarked, by the experience or penetration of the monks; some sins are enumerated which innocence could not have suspected, and others which reason cannot believe; and the more ordinary offences of fornication and adultery, of perjury and sacrilege, of rapine and murder, were expiated by a penance which, according to the various circumstances, was prolonged from forty days to seven years. During this term of mortification, the patient was healed, the criminal was absolved, by a salutary regimen of fasts and prayers; the disorder of his dress was expressive of grief and remorse; and he humbly abstained from all the business and pleasure of social life. But the rigid execution of these laws would have depopulated the palace, the camp, and the city; the barbarians of the West believed and trembled; but nature often rebelled against principle; and the magistrate laboured without effect to enforce the jurisdiction of the priest. A literal accomplishment of penance was indeed impracticable: the guilt of adultery was multipled by daily repetition; that of homicide might involve the massacre of a whole people; each act was separately numbered; and, in those times of anarchy and vice, a modest sinner might easily incur a debt of three hundred years. His insolvency was relieved by a commutation, or *indulgence*: a year of penance was appreciated at twenty-six *solidi* [25] of silver, about four pounds sterling, for the rich; at three solidi, or nine shillings, for the indigent: and these alms were soon appropriated to the use of the church, which derived, from the redemption of sins, an inexhaustible source of opulence and dominion. A debt of three hundred years, or twelve hundred pounds, was enough to impoverish a plentiful fortune;

[24] Schmidt (Histoire des Allemands, tom. ii. p. 211-220, 452-462) gives an abstract of the Penitential of Rhegino [ed. Wasserschleben, 1840] in the ixth [c. A.D. 906], and of Burchard [Migne, Patr. Lat. 140, p. 537 *sqq.*] in the xth, century. In one year, five and thirty murders were perpetrated at Worms.

[25] Till the xiith century, we may support the clear account of xii *denarii*, or pence, to the *solidus*, or shilling; and xx *solidi* to the pound weight of silver, about the pound sterling. Our money is diminished to a third, and the French to a fiftieth, of this primitive standard.

the scarcity of gold and silver was supplied by the alienation of land ; and the princely donations of Pepin and Charlemagne are expressly given for the *remedy* of their soul. It is a maxim of the civil law, That whosoever cannot pay with his purse must pay with his body; and the practice of flagellation was adopted by the monks, a cheap, though painful, equivalent. By a fantastic arithmetic, a year of penance was taxed at three thousand lashes ; [26] and such was the skill and patience of a famous hermit, St. Dominic of the Iron Cuirass,[27] that in six days he could discharge an entire century, by a whipping of three hundred thousand stripes. His example was followed by many penitents of both sexes ; and, as a vicarious sacrifice was accepted, a sturdy disciplinarian might expiate on his own back the sins of his benefactors.[28] These compensations of the purse and the person introduced, in the eleventh century, a more honourable mode of satisfaction. The merit of military service against the Saracens of Africa and Spain had been allowed by the predecessors of Urban the Second. In the council of Clermont, that Pope proclaimed a plenary indulgence to those who should enlist under the banner of the cross: the absolution of *all* their sins, and a full receipt for *all* that might be due of canonical penance.[29] The cold philosophy of modern times is incapable of feeling the impression that was made on a sinful and fanatic world. At the voice of their pastor, the robber, the incendiary, the homicide, arose by thousands to redeem their souls, by repeating on the infidels the same deeds which they had exercised against their Christian brethren ; and the terms of atonement were eagerly embraced by offenders of every rank and denomination. None

[26] Each century of lashes was sanctified with the recital of a psalm ; and the whole psalter, with the accompaniment of 15,000 stripes, was equivalent to five years.

[27] The Life and Achievements of St. Dominic Loricatus was composed by his friend and admirer, Peter Damianus [Acta Sanctorum, 14th October, 6 ; p. 621 sqq.]. See Fleury, Hist. Ecclés. tom. xiii. p. 96-104 ; Baronius, A.D. 1056, No. 7, who observes from Damianus, how fashionable, even among ladies of quality (sublimis generis), this expiation (purgatorii genus) was grown.

[28] At a quarter, or even half, a rial a lash, Sancho Panza was a cheaper and possibly not a more dishonest workman. I remember, in Père Labat (Voyages en Italie, tom. vii. p. 16-29), a very lively picture of the *dexterity* of one of these artists.

[29] Quicunque pro solâ devotione, non pro honoris vel pecuniæ adeptione, ad liberandam ecclesiam Dei Jerusalem profectus fuerit, iter illud pro omni pœnitentiâ reputetur. Canon. Concil. Claromont. ii. p. 829. Guibert styles it, novum salutis genus (p. 471), and is almost philosophical on the subject.

rere pure; none were exempt from the guilt and penalty of
in; and those who were the least amenable to the justice of
god and the church were the best entitled to the temporal
nd eternal recompense of their pious courage. If they fell, the
pirit of the Latin clergy did not hesitate to adorn their tomb
vith the crown of martyrdom; [30] and, should they survive, they
ould expect without impatience the delay and increase of their
leavenly reward. They offered their blood to the Son of God,
vho had laid down his life for their salvation: they took up the
ross, and entered with confidence into the way of the Lord.
Iis providence would watch over their safety; perhaps his
isible and miraculous power would smooth the difficulties of
heir holy enterprise. The cloud and pillar of Jehovah had
narched before the Israelites into the promised land. Might
iot the Christians more reasonably hope that the rivers would
pen for their passage; that the walls of the strongest cities
vould fall at the sound of their trumpets; and that the sun
vould be arrested in his mid-career, to allow them time for the
lestruction of the infidels?

Of the chiefs and soldiers who marched to the holy sepul- Temporal
                                                           and carnal
hre, I will dare to affirm that all were prompted by the spirit motives
if enthusiasm, the belief of merit, the hope of reward, and the
ssurance of divine aid. But I am equally persuaded that in
nany it was not the sole, that in some it was not the leading,
rrinciple of action. The use and abuse of religion are feeble to
item, they are strong and irresistible to impel, the stream of
iational manners. Against the private wars of the barbarians,
heir bloody tournaments, licentious loves, and judicial duels,
he popes and synods might ineffectually thunder. It is a more
asy task to provoke the metaphysical disputes of the Greeks,
o drive into the cloister the victims of anarchy or despotism, to
ianctify the patience of slaves and cowards, or to assume the
nerit of the humanity and benevolence of modern Christians.
War and exercise were the reigning passions of the Franks or
Latins; they were enjoined, as a penance, to gratify those pas-
ions, to visit distant lands, and to draw their swords against
he nations of the East. Their victory, or even their attempt,

[30] Such at least was the belief of the crusaders, and such is the uniform style
f the historians (Esprit des Croisades, tom. iii. p. 477); but the prayers for the
epose of their souls is inconsistent in orthodox theology with the merits of
nartyrdom.

would immortalise the names of the intrepid heroes of the cross ; and the purest piety could not be insensible to the most splendid prospect of military glory. In the petty quarrels of Europe, they shed the blood of their friends and countrymen, for the acquisition perhaps of a castle or a village. They could march with alacrity against the distant and hostile nations who were devoted to their arms : their fancy already grasped the golden sceptres of Asia; and the conquest of Apulia and Sicily by the Normans might exalt to royalty the hopes of the most private adventurer. Christendom, in her rudest state, must have yielded to the climate and cultivation of the Mahometan countries; and their natural and artificial wealth had been magnified by the tales of pilgrims and the gifts of an imperfect commerce. The vulgar, both the great and small, were taught to believe every wonder, of lands flowing with milk and honey, of mines and treasures, of gold and diamonds, of palaces of marble and jasper, and of odoriferous groves of cinnamon and frankincense. In this earthly paradise each warrior depended on his sword to carve a plenteous and honourable establishment, which he measured only by the extent of his wishes.[31] Their vassals and soldiers trusted their fortunes to God and their master : the spoils of a Turkish emir might enrich the meanest follower of the camp; and the flavour of the wines, the beauty of the Grecian women,[32] were temptations more adapted to the nature, than to the profession, of the champions of the cross. The love of freedom was a powerful incitement to the multitudes who were oppressed by feudal or ecclesiastical tyranny. Under this holy sign, the peasants and burghers, who were attached to the servitude of the glebe, might escape from an haughty lord, and transplant themselves and their families to a land of liberty. The monk might release himself from the discipline of his convent ; the debtor might suspend the accumulation of

---

[31] The same hopes were displayed in the letters of the adventurers, ad animandos qui in Franciâ resederant. Hugh de Reiteste could boast that his share amounted to one abbey and ten castles, of the yearly value of 1500 marks, and that he should acquire an hundred castles by the conquest of Aleppo (Guibert, p. 554, 555).

[32] In his genuine or fictitious letter to the Count of Flanders, Alexius mingles with the danger of the church, and the relics of saints, the auri et argenti amor and pulcherrimarum fœminarum voluptas (p. 476) ; as if, says the indignant Guibert, the Greek women were handsomer than those of France. [For the letter see above, p. 261, note 64.]

usury and the pursuit of his creditors ; and outlaws and male-
factors of every cast might continue to brave the laws and elude
the punishment of their crimes.[33]

These motives were potent and numerous : when we have Influence
singly computed their weight on the mind of each individual, of example
we must add the infinite series, the multiplying powers of example and fashion. The first proselytes became the warmest
and most effectual missionaries of the cross: among their friends
and countrymen they preached the duty, the merit, and the
recompense of their holy vow ; and the most reluctant hearers
were insensibly drawn within the whirlpool of persuasion and
authority. The martial youths were fired by the reproach or
suspicion of cowardice; the opportunity of visiting with an army
the sepulchre of Christ was embraced by the old and infirm, by
women and children, who consulted rather their zeal than their
strength ; and those who in the evening had derided the folly of
their companions were the most eager, the ensuing day, to tread
in their footsteps. The ignorance, which magnified the hopes,
diminished the perils, of the enterprise. Since the Turkish conquest, the paths of pilgrimage were obliterated ; the chiefs themselves had an imperfect notion of the length of the way and the
state of their enemies ; and such was the stupidity of the people
that, at the sight of the first city or castle beyond the limits of
their knowledge, they were ready to ask, whether that was not
the Jerusalem, the term and object of their labours. Yet the
more prudent of the crusaders, who were not sure that they
should be fed from heaven with a shower of quails or manna,
provided themselves with those precious metals which, in every
country, are the representatives of every commodity. To defray,
according to their rank, the expenses of the road, princes alienated their provinces, nobles their lands and castles, peasants their
cattle and the instruments of husbandry. The value of property
was depreciated by the eager competition of multitudes; while
the price of arms and horses was raised to an exorbitant height,
by the wants and impatience of the buyers.[34] Those who re-

[33] See the privileges of the *Crucesignati*, freedom from debt, usury, injury,
secular justice, &c. The pope was their perpetual guardian (Ducange, tom. ii. p. 651,
652).

[34] Guibert (p. 481) paints in lively colours this general emotion. He was one of
the few contemporaries who had genius enough to feel the astonishing scenes that
were passing before their eyes. Erat itaque videre miraculum caro omnes emere,
atque vili vendere, &c.

mained at home, with sense and money, were enriched by the epidemical disease : the sovereigns acquired at a cheap rate the domains of their vassals ; and the ecclesiastical purchasers completed the payment by the assurance of their prayers. The cross, which was commonly sewed on the garment, in cloth or silk, was inscribed by some zealots on their skin ; an hot iron, or indelible liquor, was applied to perpetuate the mark; and a crafty monk, who showed the miraculous impression on his breast, was repaid with the popular veneration and the richest benefices of Palestine.[35]

Departure of the first crusaders. A.D. 1096, March, May, &c. The fifteenth of August had been fixed in the council of Clermont for the departure of the pilgrims; but the day was anticipated by the thoughtless and needy crowd of plebeians ; and I shall briefly dispatch the calamities which they inflicted and suffered, before I enter on the more serious and successful enterprise of the chiefs. Early in the spring, from the confines of France and Lorraine, about sixty thousand of the populace of both sexes flocked round the first missionary of the crusade, and pressed him with clamorous importunity to lead them to the holy sepulchre. The hermit, assuming the character, without the talents or authority, of a general, impelled or obeyed the forward impulse of his votaries along the banks of the Rhine and Danube. Their wants and numbers soon compelled them to separate, and his lieutenant, Walter the Pennyless,[36] a valiant though needy soldier, conducted a vanguard of pilgrims, whose condition may be determined from the proportion of eight horsemen to fifteen thousand foot. The example and footsteps of Peter were closely pursued by another fanatic, the monk Godescal, whose sermons had swept away fifteen or twenty thousand peasants from the villages of Germany. Their rear was again pressed by an herd of two hundred thousand, the most stupid and savage refuse of the people, who mingled with their devotion a brutal licence of rapine, prostitution, and drunkenness. Some counts and gentlemen, at the head of three thousand horse, attended the motions of the multitude to partake in the spoil ; but their genuine leaders (may we credit such folly ?) were a goose and a goat, who were carried in the

---

[35] Some instances of these *stigmata* are given in the Esprit des Croisades (tom. iii. p. 169, &c.), from authors whom I have not seen.

[36] [Along with his uncle Walter de Poissy.]

front, and to whom these worthy Christians ascribed an infusion of the divine Spirit.[37] Of these and of other bands of enthusiasts, the first and most easy warfare was against the Jews, the murderers of the Son of God. In the trading cities of the Moselle and the Rhine, their colonies were numerous and rich ; and they enjoyed, under the protection of the emperor and the bishops, the free exercise of their religion.[38] At Verdun, Treves, Mentz, Spires, Worms, many thousands of that unhappy people were pillaged and massacred ;[39] nor had they felt a more bloody stroke since the persecution of Hadrian. A remnant was saved by the firmness of their bishops, who accepted a feigned and transient conversion; but the more obstinate Jews opposed their fanaticism to the fanaticism of the Christians, barricadoed their houses, and, precipitating themselves, their families, and their wealth, into the rivers or the flames, disappointed the malice, or at least the avarice, of their implacable foes.

Between the frontiers of Austria and the seat of the Byzantine monarchy, the crusaders were compelled to traverse an interval of six hundred miles ; the wild and desolate countries of Hungary [40] and Bulgaria. The soil is fruitful, and intersected with rivers ; but it was then covered with morasses and forests, which spread to a boundless extent, whenever man has ceased to exercise his dominion over the earth. Both nations had imbibed the rudiments of Christianity ; the Hungarians were ruled by their native princes ; the Bulgarians by a lieutenant of the

Their destruction in Hungary and Asia. A.D. 1096

---

[37] Fuit et aliud scelus detestabile in hâc congregatione pedestris populi stulti et vesanæ levitatis, . . . *anserem* quendam divino Spiritu asserebant afflatum, et *capellam* non minus eodem repletam, et has sibi duces [hujus] secundæ viæ fecerant, &c. (Albert. Aquensis, l. i. c. 31, p. 196). Had these peasants founded an empire, they might have introduced, as in Egypt, the worship of animals, which their philosophic descendants would have glossed over with some specious and subtle allegory.

[38] Benjamin of Tudela describes the state of his Jewish brethren from Cologne along the Rhine : they were rich, generous, learned, hospitable, and lived in the eager hope of the Messiah (Voyage, tom. i. p. 243-245, par Baratier). In seventy years (he wrote about A.D. 1170) they had recovered from these massacres.

[39] These massacres and depredations on the Jews, which were renewed at each crusade, are *coolly* related. It is true that St. Bernard (epist. 363, tom. i. p. 329) admonishes the Oriental Franks, non sunt persequendi Judæi, non sunt trucidandi. The contrary doctrine had been preached by a *rival* monk.

[40] See the contemporary description of Hungary in Otho of Frisingen [Gesta Friderici], l. ii. c. 31, in Muratori, Script. Rerum Italicarum, tom vi. p. 665, 666. [This work of Otto, along with the continuation by Rahewin, has been edited in Pertz, Mon. Germ. Hist. xx. p. 347 *sqq.* ; and (by G. Waitz) in Scr. rer. Germ., 1884.]

Greek emperor; but on the slightest provocation, their ferocious nature was rekindled, and ample provocation was afforded by the disorders of the first pilgrims. Agriculture must have been unskilful and languid among a people, whose cities were built of reeds and timber, which were deserted in the summer-season for the tents of hunters and shepherds. A scanty supply of provisions was rudely demanded, forcibly seized, and [In Servia] greedily consumed; and, on the first quarrel, the crusaders gave a loose to indignation and revenge. But their ignorance of the country, of war, and of discipline exposed them to every snare. The Greek præfect of Bulgaria commanded a regular force; at the trumpet of the Hungarian king, the eighth or the tenth of his martial subjects bent their bows and mounted on horseback; their policy was insidious, and their retaliation on these pious robbers was unrelenting and bloody.[41] About a third of the naked fugitives, and the hermit Peter was of the number, escaped to the Thracian mountains; and the emperor, who respected the pilgrimage and succour of the Latins, conducted [Arrival at Constantinople. Aug. 1, A.D. 1096] them by secure and easy journeys to Constantinople, and advised them to wait the arrival of their brethren. For a while they remembered their faults and losses; but no sooner were they revived by the hospitable entertainment than their venom was again inflamed; they stung their benefactor, and neither gardens nor palaces nor churches [41a] were safe from their depredations. For his own safety, Alexius allured them to pass over to the Asiatic side of the Bosphorus; but their blind impetuosity soon urged them to desert the station which he had assigned,[41b] and to rush headlong against the Turks, who occupied the road of Jerusalem. The hermit, conscious of his shame, had with-

---

[41] The old Hungarians, without excepting Turotzius, are ill informed of the first crusade, which they involve in a single passage. Katona, like ourselves, can only quote the writers of France; but he compares with local science the ancient and modern geography. *Ante portam Cyperon*, is Sopron, or Poson; *Mallevilla*, Zemlin; *Fluvius Maroe*, Savus; *Lintax*, Leith; *Mesebroch*, or *Marseburg*, Ouar, or Moson; *Tollenburg*, Pragg (De Regibus Hungariæ, tom. iii. p. 19-53). [The Hungarian king Caloman treated the pilgrims well. But a few stragglers belonging to the host of Walter were plundered at Semlin, and their arms were hung up on the wall. The army of Peter the Hermit, arriving later, saw the arms of their forerunners, and took vengeance by attacking and occupying the town. Both the host of Peter and that of Walter lost a great many men in conflicts in Bulgaria.]

[41a] [In the suburbs; they were not admitted into the city.]

[41b] [Their station was Nicomedia and its neighbourhood (Gesta Fr. ii. 4), including Civetot (Albert, i. 16; Gesta Fr. ii. 8) and Helenopolis (Anna, x. 6).]

45 To save time and space, I shall represent, in a short table, the particular references to the great events of the first crusade. [In cases where the author cites by the *pages* of Bongarsius, the chapters are added within square brackets, so that the reader may be able easily to refer to the Recueil des historiens de Croisades, or any other text. In the case of Baldric the pages of the edition in the Recueil (Hist. Occ. vol. iv.) are given.]

	The Crowd.	The Chiefs.	The Road to Constantinople.	Alexius.	Nice and Asia Minor.	Edessa.	Antioch.	The Battle.	The Holy Lance.	Conquest of Jerusalem.
I. Gesta Francorum	p. 1, 2 [l. i, 2]	p. 2 [i. 2, 3]	p. 2, 3 [i. 3, 4]	p. 4, 5 [ii. 1-4]	p. 5-7 [ii. 7-iv. 2]	—	p. 9-15 [iv. 5-27]	p. 15-22 [iv. 28-40]	p. 18-20 [iv. 35, 38]	p. 26-29 [iv. 49-55]
II. Robertus Monachus	p. 33, 34 [i. 4, 5]	p. 35, 36 [ii. 1-5]	p. 36, 37 [ii. 7-14]	p. 37, 38 [ii. 14-19]	p. 39-45 [iii. 1-26]	[cp. iii. 23]	p. 45-55 [iii. 29-v. 14]	p. 56-66 [vi. 4-vii. 19]	p. 61, 62 [vii. 1-3]	p. 74-81 [ix. 1-26]
III. Baldricus	89 [p. 17]	— [p. 17]	p. 91-93 [p. 20-23]	p. 91-94 [p. 20-25]	p. 94-101 [p. 26-39]	—	p. 101, 111 [p. 39-58]	p. 111-122 [p. 59-79]	p. 116-119 [p. 67-68, 78, 75]	p. 130-138 [p. 96-111]
IV. Raimundus des Agiles	—	—	p. 139, 140 [c. 1, 2]	p. 140, 141 [c. 2, 3]	p. 142 [c. 3, 4]	—	p. 142-149 [c. 5-9]	p. 149-155 [c. 10-17]	p. 150, 152, 156 [c. 10, 13, 18]	p. 173-183 [c. 20-21]
V. Albertus Aquensis	l. i, c. 7-31 [leg. 30]	[ii. 1]	l. ii. c. 1-8	{l. ii. c. 9-19}	{l. ii. c. 20-48, l. iii. c. 1-4}	{l. iii. c. 5-32, l. iv. 9-12, l. v. 15-22}	{l. iii. c. 33-66; iv. 1-26}	l. iv. c. 7-56	l. iv. c. 43	{l. v. c. 45, 46, l. vi. c. 1-50}
VI. Fulcherius Carnotensis	p. 384 [i. 2]	[i. 6]	p. 385, 386 [i. 6-8]	p. 386 [i. 9]	p. 387-389 [i. 9-18]	p. 389, 390 [i. 14]	p. 390-392 [i. 15-17]	p. 392-395 [i. 19-23]	392 [i. 18]	p. 396-400 [i. 25-28]
VII. Guibertus	p. 482, 485 [ii. 8-11]	[485-7] [ii. 12-19]	p. 485, 489 [ii. 12-iii. 3]	p. 485-490 [ii. 12-iii. 4]	p. 491-493, 498 [iii. 4-8; iv. 2]	p. 496, 497 [iii. 18]	p. 498, 506, 512 [iv. 3, 14; v. 8]	p. 512-523 [v. 9-vi. 10]	p. 520, 530, 538 [vi. 1, 22, 34]	p. 523-587 [vi. 11-vii. 11]
VIII. Willermus Tyrensis	l. i, c. 18-30	l. i, c. 17	{l. i. ii. c. 1-4, 18, 17, 22}	l. ii. c. 5-23	{l. iii. c. 1-12, l. iv. c. 13-25}	l. iv. c. 1-6	{l. iv. c. 9-24, l. v. 1-28}	l. vi. c. 1-28	l. vi. c. 14	{l. vii. c. 1-25, l. viii. c. 1-24}
IX. Radulphus Cadomensis	—	c. 1, 3, 15	c. 4-7, 17	{c. 8-13, 18, 19}	c. 14-16, 21-47	—	c. 48-71	c. 72-91	c. 100-109	c. 111-138
X. Bernardus Thesaurarius	c. 7-11	—	c. 11-20	c. 11-20	c. 21-25	c. 26	c. 27-38	c. 39-52	c. 45	c. 54-77

drawn from the camp to Constantinople; and his lieutenant, Walter the Pennyless, who was worthy of a better command, attempted, without success, to introduce some order and prudence among the herd of savages. They separated in quest of prey, and themselves fell an easy prey to the arts of the Sultan. By a rumour that their foremost companions were rioting in the spoils of his capital, Soliman tempted the main body to descend into the plain of Nice; they were overwhelmed by the Turkish arrows; and a pyramid of bones[42] informed their companions of the place of their defeat. Of the first crusaders, three hundred thousand had already perished, before a single city was rescued from the infidels, before their graver and more noble brethren had completed the preparations of their enterprise.[43]

[Gualterius Sinehabere]

[leg. Kilij Arslan]

The chiefs of the first crusade

I. Godfrey of Bouillon

None of the great sovereigns of Europe embarked their persons in the first crusade. The emperor Henry the Fourth was not disposed to obey the summons of the pope; Philip the First of France was occupied by his pleasures; William Rufus of England by a recent conquest; the kings of Spain were engaged in a domestic war against the Moors; and the northern monarchs of Scotland, Denmark,[44] Sweden, and Poland, were yet strangers to the passions and interests of the South. The religious ardour was more strongly felt by the princes of the second order, who held an important place in the feudal system. Their situation will naturally cast, under four distinct heads, the review of their names and characters; but I may escape some needless repetition by observing at once that courage and the exercise of arms are the common attribute of these Christian adventurers. I. The first rank both in war and council is justly due to Godfrey of Bouillon; and happy would it have been for the crusaders, if they had trusted themselves to the sole conduct of that accomplished hero, a worthy representative of Charle-

---

[42] Anna Comnena (Alexias, l. x. p. 287 [c. 6]) describes this ὀστῶν κολωνός as a mountain, ὑψηλὸν και βάθος καὶ πλάτος ἀξιολογώτατον [ἀπολαμβάνον]. In the siege of Nice, such were used by the Franks themselves as the materials of a wall. [It was near the river Dracon, which had been fixed as the boundary between the Empire and Rūm.]

[43] [See table on previous page.]

[44] The author of the Esprit des Croisades has doubted, and might have disbelieved, the crusade and tragic death of Prince Sueno, with 1500 or 15,000 Danes, who was cut off by Sultan Soliman in Cappadocia, but who still lives in the poem of Tasso (tom. iv. p. 111-115).

magne, from whom he was descended in the female line. His
father was of the noble race of the counts of Boulogne: Brabant,
the lower province of Lorraine,[45] was the inheritance of his
mother; and, by the emperor's bounty, he was himself invested
with that ducal title, which has been improperly transferred to
his lordship of Bouillon in the Ardennes.[46] In the service of
Henry the Fourth he bore the great standard of the empire,
and pierced with his lance the breast of Rodolph, the rebel
king: Godfrey was the first who ascended the walls of Rome;
and his sickness, his vow, perhaps his remorse for bearing arms
against the pope, confirmed an early resolution of visiting the
holy sepulchre, not as a pilgrim, but a deliverer. His valour was
matured by prudence and moderation; his piety, though blind,
was sincere; and, in the tumult of a camp, he practised the real
and fictitious virtues of a convent. Superior to the private factions of the chiefs, he reserved his enmity for the enemies of
Christ; and, though he gained a kingdom by the attempt, his
pure and disinterested zeal was acknowledged by his rivals.
Godfrey of Bouillon[47] was accompanied by his two brothers,
by Eustace the elder, who had succeeded to the county of
Boulogne, and by the younger, Baldwin, a character of more ambiguous virtue. The Duke of Lorraine was alike celebrated
on either side of the Rhine; from birth and education, he
was equally conversant with the French and Teutonic languages:
the barons of France, Germany, and Lorraine assembled their
vassals; and the confederate force that marched under his
banner was composed of fourscore thousand foot and about
ten thousand horse. II. In the parliament that was held
at Paris, in the king's presence, about two months after the
council of Clermont, Hugh, count of Vermandois, was the most

II. Hugh of
Verman-
dois,
Robert of
Normandy,
Robert of
Flanders,
Stephen of
Chartres,
&c.

[45] The fragments of the kingdoms of Lotharingia, or Lorraine, were broken into
the two duchies, of the Moselle, and of the Meuse; the first has preserved its name,
which in the latter has been changed into that of Brabant (Vales. Notit. Gall. p.
283-288). [Lothringen had been divided into Upper and Lower in the latter part
of the reign of Otto I. The two duchies were again united, under Conrad II., in
the hands of Duke Gozelo; but on his death in 1044 were separated, going to his
two sons, by permission of Henry III.]

[46] See, in the description of France, by the Abbé de Longuerue, the articles of
Boulogne, part i. p. 54; *Brabant*, part ii. p. 47, 48; *Bouillon*, p. 134. On his departure, Godfrey sold or pawned Bouillon to the church for 1300 marks.

[47] See the family character of Godfrey in William of Tyre, l. ix. c. 5-8; his
previous design in Guibert (p. 485); his sickness and vow in Bernard. Thesaur.
(c. 78).

conspicuous of the princes who assumed the cross.   But the
appellation of *the Great* was applied, not so much to his merit or
possessions (though neither were contemptible), as to the royal
birth of the brother of the king of France.[48]   Robert, duke
of Normandy, was the eldest son of William the Conqueror;
but on his father's death he was deprived of the kingdom of
England, by his own indolence and the activity of his brother
Rufus.   The worth of Robert was degraded by an excessive
levity and easiness of temper; his cheerfulness seduced him to
the indulgence of pleasure; his profuse liberality impoverished
the prince and people; his indiscriminate clemency multiplied
the number of offenders; and the amiable qualities of a
private man became the essential defects of a sovereign.   For
the trifling sum of ten thousand marks he mortgaged Normandy during his absence to the English usurper;[49] but his
engagement and behaviour in the holy war announced in Robert
a reformation of manners, and restored him in some degree to
the public esteem.   Another Robert was count of Flanders, a
royal province, which, in this century, gave three queens to the
thrones of France, England, and Denmark.   He was surnamed
the Sword and Lance of the Christians ; but in the exploits of a
soldier he sometimes forgot the duties of a general.   Stephen,
count of Chartres, of Blois, and of Troyes, was one of the richest
princes of the age; and the number of his castles has been compared to the three hundred and sixty-five days of the year.   His
mind was improved by literature; and, in the council of the
chiefs, the eloquent Stephen[50] was chosen to discharge the office
of their president.   These four were the principal leaders of the
French, the Normans, and the pilgrims of the British isles ; but
the list of the barons, who were possessed of three or four towns,

---

[48] Anna Comnena supposes that Hugh [Οὖβος] was proud of his nobility,
riches, and power (l. x. p. 288 [c. 7]); the two last articles appear more equivocal ;
but an εὐγένεια, which, seven hundred years ago, was famous in the palace
of Constantinople, attests the ancient dignity of the Capetian family of France.

[49] Will. Gemeticensis [of Jumièges ; c. A.D. 1027 ; the end of Bk. 7 and Bk. 8
are not by William], l. vii. c. 7, p. 672, 673, in Camden. Normanicis [in Migne, Pat.
Lat. 149, p. 779 *sqq.*].   He pawned the duchy for one hundredth part of the
present yearly revenue.   Ten thousand marks may be equal to five hundred
thousand livres, and Normandy annually yields fifty-seven millions to the king
(Necker, Administration des finances, tom. i. p. 287).

[50] His original letter to his wife [Adela] is inserted in the Spicilegium of Dom.
Luc. d'Acheri, tom. iv. and quoted in the Esprit des Croisades, tom. i. p. 63.
[This and another letter (entitled Ep. ex castris obsidionis Nicaenae anno 1098) are
printed in the Recueil, Hist. Occ. 3, p. 883 *sqq.*]

would exceed, says a contemporary, the catalogue of the Trojan war.[51] III. In the south of France, the command was assumed by Adhemar, bishop of Puy, the Pope's legate, and by Raymond, count of St. Giles and Toulouse, who added the prouder titles of duke of Narbonne and marquis of Provence. The former was a respectable prelate, alike qualified for this world and the next. The latter was a veteran warrior, who had fought against the Saracens of Spain, and who consecrated his declining age, not only to the deliverance, but to the perpetual service, of the holy sepulchre. His experience and riches gave him a strong ascendant in the Christian camp, whose distress he was often able, and sometimes willing, to relieve. But it was easier for him to extort the praise of the infidels than to preserve the love of his subjects and associates. His eminent qualities were clouded by a temper, haughty, envious, and obstinate; and, though he resigned an ample patrimony for the cause of God, his piety, in the public opinion, was not exempt from avarice and ambition.[52] A mercantile rather than a martial spirit prevailed among his *provincials*,[53] a common name, which included the natives of Auvergne and Languedoc,[54] the vassals of the kingdom of Burgundy or Arles. From the adjacent frontier of Spain he drew a band of hardy adventurers; as he marched through Lombardy, a crowd of Italians flocked to his standard; and his united force consisted of one hundred thousand horse and foot. If Raymond was the first to enlist, and the last to depart, the delay may be excused by the greatness of his preparation and the promise of an everlasting farewell. IV. The name of Bohemond, the son of Robert Guiscard, was already famous by his double victory over the Greek emperor;

---

[51] Unius enim, duum, trium, seu quatuor oppidorum dominos quis numeret? quorum tanta fuit copia, ut non vix totidem Trojana obsidio coegisse putetur. (Ever the lively and interesting Guibert, p. 486.)

[52] It is singular enough that Raymond of St. Giles, a second character in the genuine history of the crusades, should shine as the first of heroes in the writings of the Greeks (Anna Comnen. Alexiad. l. x. xi. [Anna calls him *Isangeles*]) and the Arabians (Longueruana, p. 129).

[53] Omnes de Burgundiâ, et Alverniâ, et Vasconiâ, et Gothi (of *Languedoc*), provinciales appellabantur cæteri vero Francigenæ, et hoc in exercitu; inter hostes autem Franci dicebantur. Raymond de Agiles, p. 144.

[54] The town of his birth, or first appanage, was consecrated to St. Ægidius, whose name, as early as the first crusade, was corrupted by the French into St. Gilles or St. Giles. It is situate in the Lower Languedoc, between Nismes and the Rhone, and still boasts a collegiate church of the foundation of Raymond (Mélanges tirés d'une grande Bibliothèque, tom. xxxvii. p. 51).

but his father's will had reduced him to the principality o
Tarentum and the remembrance of his Eastern trophies, till h
was awakened by the rumour and passage of the French pil
grims.   It is in the person of this Norman chief that we may
seek for the coolest policy and ambition, with a small allay
of religious fanaticism.   His conduct may justify a belief that
he had secretly directed the design of the pope, which he
affected to second with astonishment and zeal.   At the siege of
Amalphi, his example and discourse inflamed the passions of
a confederate army; he instantly tore his garment, to supply
crosses for the numerous candidates, and prepared to visit
Constantinople and Asia at the head of ten thousand horse
and twenty thousand foot.   Several princes of the Norman race
accompanied this veteran general; and his cousin Tancred [55]
was the partner, rather than the servant, of the war.   In the
accomplished character of Tancred we discover all the virtues
of a perfect knight,[56] the true spirit of chivalry, which inspired
the generous sentiments and social offices of man far better
than the base philosophy, or the baser religion, of the times.

Chivalry   Between the age of Charlemagne and that of the crusades, a
revolution had taken place among the Spaniards, the Normans,
and the French, which was gradually extended to the rest of
Europe.   The service of the infantry was degraded to the plebeians; the cavalry formed the strength of the armies, and the
honourable name of *miles*, or soldier, was confined to the gentlemen [57] who served on horseback and were invested with the

---

[55] The mother of Tancred was Emma, sister of the great Robert Guiscard; his
father, the marquis Odo the Good.   It is singular enough that the family and
country of so illustrious a person should be unknown; but Muratori reasonably
conjectures that he was an Italian, and perhaps of the race of the marquises of
Montferrat in Piedmont (Script. tom. v. p. 281, 282).   [But see below, p. 308, n.
86.]

[56] To gratify the childish vanity of the house of Este, Tasso has inserted in
his poem, and in the first crusade, a fabulous hero, the brave and amorous Rinaldo
(x. 75, xvii. 66-94).   He might borrow his name from a Rinaldo, with the Aquila
bianca Estense, who vanquished, as the standard-bearer of the Roman church,
the emperor Frederic I. (Storia Imperiale di Ricobaldo, in Muratori, Script. Ital.
tom. ix. p. 360; Ariosto, Orlando Furioso, iii. 30).   But, 1. The distance of sixty
years between the youth of the two Rinaldos destroys their identity.   2. The Storia
Imperiale is a forgery of the Conte Boyardo, at the end of the xvth century
(Muratori, p. 281-289).   3. This Rinaldo and his exploits are not less chimerical
than the hero of Tasso (Muratori, Antichità Estense, tom. i. p. 350).

[57] Of the words, *gentilis*, *gentilhomme*, *gentleman*, two etymologies are produced: 1. From the barbarians of the fifth century, the soldiers, and at length the
conquerors, of the Roman empire, who were vain of their foreign nobility; and,
2. From the sense of the civilians, who consider *gentilis* as synonymous with

character of knighthood. The dukes and counts, who had usurped the rights of sovereignty, divided the provinces among their faithful barons: the barons distributed among their vassals the fiefs or benefices of their jurisdiction; and these military tenants, the peers of each other and of their lord, composed the noble or equestrian order, which disdained to conceive the peasant or burgher as of the same species with themselves. The dignity of their birth was preserved by pure and equal alliances; their sons alone, who could produce four quarters or lines of ancestry, without spot or reproach, might legally pretend to the honour of knighthood; but a valiant plebeian was sometimes enriched and ennobled by the sword, and became the father of a new race. A single knight could impart, according to his judgment, the character which he received; and the warlike sovereigns of Europe derived more glory from this personal distinction than from the lustre of their diadem. This ceremony, of which some traces may be found in Tacitus and the woods of Germany,[58] was in its origin simple and profane; the candidate, after some previous trial, was invested with the sword and spurs; and his cheek or shoulder was touched with a slight blow, as an emblem of the last affront which it was lawful for him to endure. But superstition mingled in every public and private action of life; in the holy wars, it sanctified the profession of arms; and the order of chivalry was assimilated in its rights and privileges to the sacred orders of priesthood. The bath and white garment of the novice were an indecent copy of the regeneration of baptism; his sword, which he offered on the altar, was blessed by the ministers of religion; his solemn reception was preceded by fasts and vigils; and he was created a knight, in the name of God, of St. George, and of St. Michael the archangel. He swore to accomplish the duties of his profession; and education, example, and the public opinion were the inviolable guardians of his oath. As the champion of God and the ladies (I blush to unite such discordant names), he devoted himself to speak the truth; to maintain the right; to protect the distressed; to practise *courtesy*, a virtue less familiar to the ancients; to pursue the infidels; to despise the allurements of ease and

ingenuus. Selden inclines to the first, but the latter is more pure, as well as probable.
[58] Framea scutoque juvenem ornant. Tacitus, Germania, c. 13.

safety; and to vindicate in every perilous adventure the honour of his character.   The abuse of the same spirit provoked the illiterate knight to disdain the arts of industry and peace; to esteem himself the sole judge and avenger of his own injuries; and proudly to neglect the laws of civil society and military discipline.   Yet the benefits of this institution, to refine the temper of barbarians, and to infuse some principles of faith, justice, and humanity, were strongly felt, and have been often observed. The asperity of national prejudice was softened; and the community of religion and arms spread a similar colour and generous emulation over the face of Christendom.   Abroad in enterprise and pilgrimage, at home in martial exercise, the warriors of every country were perpetually associated; and impartial taste must prefer a Gothic tournament to the Olympic games of classic antiquity.[59]   Instead of the naked spectacles which corrupted the manners of the Greeks and banished from the stadium the virgins and the matrons, the pompous decoration of the lists was crowned with the presence of chaste and highborn beauty, from whose hands the conqueror received the prize of his dexterity and courage.   The skill and strength that were exerted in wrestling and boxing bear a distant and doubtful relation to the merit of a soldier; but the tournaments, as they were invented in France and eagerly adopted both in the East and West, presented a lively image of the business of the field. The single combats, the general skirmish, the defence of a pass or castle, were rehearsed as in actual service; and the contest, both in real and mimic war, was decided by the superior management of the horse and lance.   The lance was the proper and peculiar weapon of the knight; his horse was of a large and heavy breed; but this charger, till he was roused by the approaching danger, was usually led by an attendant, and he quietly rode a pad or palfrey of a more easy pace.   His helmet and sword, his greaves and buckler, it would be superfluous to describe; but I may remark that at the period of the crusades the armour was less ponderous than in later times; and that, instead of a massy cuirass, his breast was defended by an hauberk

---

[59] The athletic exercises, particularly the cœstus and pancratium, were condemned by Lycurgus, Philopœmen, and Galen, a lawgiver, a general, and a physician.   Against their authority and reasons, the reader may weigh the apology of Lucian, in the character of Solon.   See West on the Olympic Games, in his Pindar, vol. ii. p. 86-96, 245-248.

or coat of mail. When their long lances were fixed in the rest, the warriors furiously spurred their horses against the foe; and the light cavalry of the Turks and Arabs could seldom stand against the direct and impetuous weight of their charge. Each knight was attended to the field by his faithful squire, a youth of equal birth and similar hopes; he was followed by his archers and men at arms, and four, or five, or six soldiers were computed as the furniture of a complete *lance*. In the expeditions to the neighbouring kingdoms or the Holy Land, the duties of the feudal tenure no longer subsisted; the voluntary service of the knights and their followers was either prompted by zeal or attachment, or purchased with rewards and promises; and the numbers of each squadron were measured by the power, the wealth, and the fame of each independent chieftain. They were distinguished by his banner, his armorial coat, and his cry of war; and the most ancient families of Europe must seek in these achievements the origin and proof of their nobility. In this rapid portrait of chivalry, I have been urged to anticipate on the story of the crusades, at once an effect, and a cause, of this memorable institution.[60]

Such were the troops, and such the readers, who assumed the cross for the deliverance of the holy sepulchre. As soon as they were relieved by the absence of the plebeian multitude, they encouraged each other, by interviews and messages, to accomplish their vow and hasten their departure. Their wives and sisters were desirous of partaking the danger and merit of the pilgrimage; their portable treasures were conveyed in bars of silver and gold; and the princes and barons were attended by their equipage of hounds and hawks, to amuse their leisure and to supply their table. The difficulty of procuring subsistence for so many myriads of men and horses engaged them to separate their forces; their choice or situation determined the road; and it was agreed to meet in the neighbourhood of Constantinople, and from thence to begin their operations against the Turks. From the banks of the Meuse and the

March of the princes to Constantinople. A.D. 1096, August 15—A.D. 1097, May

---

[60] On the curious subject of knighthood, knights' service, nobility, arms, cry of war, banners, and tournaments, an ample fund of information may be sought in Selden (Opera, tom. iii. part 1: Titles of Honour, part ii. c. 1, 3, 5, 8), Ducange (Gloss. Latin. tom. iv. p. 398-412, &c.), Dissertations sur Joinville (i. vi.-xii. p. 127-142; p. 165-222), and M. de St. Palaye (Mémoires sur la Chevalerie). [Here the author anticipates a later age. At the time of the First Crusade, there was no chivalry, as here meant; knight signified a trooper.]

Moselle, Godfrey of Bouillon followed the direct way of Germany, Hungary, and Bulgaria; and, as long as he exercised the sole command, every step afforded some proof of his prudence and virtue. On the confines of Hungary he was stopped three weeks by a Christian people, to whom the name, or at least the abuse, of the cross was justly odious. The Hungarians still smarted with the wounds which they had received from the first pilgrims ; in their turn they had abused the right of defence and retaliation; and they had reason to apprehend a severe revenge from an hero of the same nation, and who was engaged in the same cause. But, after weighing the motives and the events, the virtuous duke was content to pity the crimes and misfortunes of his worthless brethren; and his twelve deputies, the messengers of peace, requested in his name a free passage and an equal market. To remove their suspicions, Godfrey trusted himself, and afterwards his brother, to the faith of [Coloman] Carloman, king of Hungary, who treated them with a simple but hospitable entertainment: the treaty was sanctified by their common gospel; and a proclamation, under pain of death, restrained the animosity and licence of the Latin soldiers. From Austria to Belgrade, they traversed the plains of Hungary, without enduring or offering an injury; and the proximity of Carloman, who hovered on their flanks with his numerous cavalry, was a precaution not less useful for their safety than for his own. They reached the banks of the Save; and no sooner had they passed the river than the king of Hungary restored the hostages and saluted their departure with the fairest wishes for the success of their enterprise. With the same conduct and discipline, Godfrey pervaded the woods of Bulgaria and the frontiers of Thrace; and might congratulate himself that he had almost reached the first term of his pilgrimage without drawing his sword against a Christian adversary. After an easy and pleasant journey through Lombardy, from Turin to Aquileia, Raymond and his provincials marched forty days through the savage country of Dalmatia [61] and Sclavonia.

---

[61] The Familiæ Dalmaticæ of Ducange are meagre and imperfect; the national historians are recent and fabulous, the Greeks remote and careless. In the year 1104, Coloman reduced the maritime country as far as Trau and Salona (Katona, Hist. Crit. tom. iii. p. 195-207). [For the journey see Knapp, Reisen durch die Balkanhalbinsel während des Mittelalters, in the Mittheilungen der k. k. geograph. Gesellschaft in Wien, xxiii., 1880.]

The weather was a perpetual fog; the land was mountainous and desolate; the natives were either fugitive or hostile; loose in their religion and government, they refused to furnish provisions or guides; murdered the stragglers; and exercised by night and day the vigilance of the count, who derived more security from the punishment of some captive robbers than from his interview and treaty with the prince of Scodra.[62] His march between Durazzo and Constantinople was harassed, without being stopped, by the peasants and soldiers of the Greek emperor; and the same faint and ambiguous hostility was prepared for the remaining chiefs, who passed the Adriatic from the coast of Italy. , Bohemond had arms and vessels, and foresight and discipline; and his name was not forgotten in the provinces of Epirus and Thessaly. Whatever obstacles he encountered were surmounted by his military conduct and the valour of Tancred; and, if the Norman prince affected to spare the Greeks, he gorged his soldiers with the full plunder of an heretical castle.[63] The nobles of France pressed forwards with the vain and thoughtless ardour of which their nation has been sometimes accused. From the Alps to Apulia, the march of Hugh the Great, of the two Roberts, and of Stephen of Chartres, through a wealthy country, and amidst the applauding Catholics, was a devout or triumphant progress: they kissed the feet of the Roman pontiff; and the golden standard of St. Peter was delivered to the brother of the French monarch.[64] But in this visit of piety and pleasure they neglected to secure the season and the means of their embarkation: the winter was insensibly lost; their troops were scattered and corrupted in the towns of Italy. They separately accomplished their passage, regardless of safety or dignity: and within nine months from the feast

---

[62] Scodras appears in Livy as the capital and fortress of Gentius, king of the Illyrians, arx munitissima, afterwards a Roman colony (Cellarius, tom. i. p. 393, 394). It is now called Iscodar, or Scutari (d'Anville, Géographie Ancienne, tom. i. p. 164). The sanjiak (now a ¡pasha) of Scutari, or¡ Schendeire, was the viiith under the Beglerbeg, of Romania, and furnished 600 soldiers on a revenue of 78,787 rix dollars (Marsigli, Stato Militare del Impero Ottomano, p. 128).

[63] In Pelagoniâ castrum hæreticum . . . spoliatum cum suis habitatoribus igne combussere. Nec id eis injuriâ contigit: quia illorum detestabilis sermo et cancer serpebat, jamque circumjacentes regiones suo pravo dogmate fœdaverat (Robert. Mon. p. 36, 37). After coolly relating the fact, the archbishop Baldric adds, as a phrase, Omnes siquidem illi viatores, Judaeos, hæreticos, Saracenos æqualiter habent exosos; quos omnes appellant inimicos Dei (p. 92).

[64] Ἀναλαβομενος ἀπὸ Ῥώμης τὴν χρυσῆν τοῦ Ἁγίου Πέτρου σημαίαν (Alexiad, l. x. p. 288 [c. 7]).

of the Assumption, the day appointed by Urban, all the Latin princes had reached Constantinople. But the Count of Vermandois was produced as a captive; his foremost vessels were scattered by a tempest; and his person, against the law of nations, was detained by the lieutenants of Alexius. Yet the arrival of Hugh had been announced by four-and-twenty knights in golden armour, who commanded the emperor to revere the general of the Latin Christians, the brother of the King of kings.[65]

Policy of the emperor Alexius Comnenus. A.D. 1096, December —A.D. 1097, May

In some Oriental tale I have read the fable of a shepherd, who was ruined by the accomplishment of his own wishes: he had prayed for water; the Ganges was turned into his grounds; and his flock and cottage were swept away by the inundation. Such was the fortune, or at least the apprehension, of the Greek emperor, Alexius Comnenus, whose name has already appeared in this history, and whose conduct is so differently represented by his daughter Anna[66] and by the Latin writers.[67] In the council of Placentia, his ambassadors had solicited a moderate succour, perhaps of ten thousand soldiers; but he was astonished by the approach of so many potent chiefs and fanatic nations. The emperor fluctuated between hope and fear, between timidity and courage; but in the crooked policy which he mistook for wisdom I cannot believe, I cannot discern, that he maliciously conspired against the life or honour of the French heroes. The promiscuous multitudes of Peter the Hermit were savage beasts, alike destitute of humanity and reason; nor was it possible for

---

[65] Ὁ Βασιλεὺς τῶν βασιλέων [Anna, x. c. 7, ad init. in Hugo's letter or message to Alexius], καὶ ἀρχηγὸς τοῦ Φραγγικοῦ στρατεύματος ἅπαντος [ib. c. 7, med., in the announcement of the four and twenty knights to the Duke of Dyrrachium]. This Oriental pomp is extravagant in a count of Vermandois; but the patriot Ducange repeats with much complacency (Not. ad Alexiad. p. 352, 353; Dissert. xxvii. sur Joinville, p. 315) the passages of Matthew Paris (A.D. 1254) and Froissard (vol. iv. p. 201), which style the King of France rex regum and chef de tous les rois Chrétiens.

[66] Anna Comnena was born on the 1st of December, A.D. 1083, indiction vii. (Alexiad, l. vi. p. 166, 167 [c. 8]). At thirteen, the time of the first crusade, she was nubile, and perhaps married to the younger Nicephorus Bryennius, whom she fondly styles τὸν ἐμὸν Καίσαρα (l. x. p. 295, 296 [c. 9]). Some moderns have *imagined* that her enmity to Bohemond [Βαϊμοῦντος] was the fruit of disappointed love. In the transactions of Constantinople and Nice, her partial accounts (Alex. l. x. xi. p. 283-317) may be opposed to the partiality of the Latins; but in their subsequent exploits she is brief and ignorant. [Cp. above, vol. 5, p. 537.]

[67] In their views of the character and conduct of Alexius, Maimbourg has favoured the *Catholic* Franks, and Voltaire has been partial to the *schismatic* Greeks. The prejudice of a philosopher is less excusable than that of a Jesuit.

Alexius to prevent or deplore their destruction. The troops of Godfrey and his peers were less contemptible, but not less suspicious, to the Greek emperor. Their motives *might* be pure and pious; but he was equally alarmed by his knowledge of the ambitious Bohemond and his ignorance of the Transalpine chiefs: the courage of the French was blind and headstrong; they might be tempted by the luxury and wealth of Greece, and elated by the view and opinion of their invincible strength; and Jerusalem might be forgotten in the prospect of Constantinople. After a long march and painful abstinence, the troops of Godfrey encamped in the plains of Thrace; they heard with indignation that their brother, the count of Vermandois, was imprisoned by the Greeks; and their reluctant Duke was compelled to indulge them in some freedom of retaliation and rapine. They were appeased by the submission of Alexius; he promised to supply their camp; and, as they refused, in the midst of winter, to pass the Bosphorus, their quarters were assigned among the gardens and palaces on the shores of that narrow sea. But an incurable jealousy still rankled in the minds of the two nations, who despised each other as slaves and barbarians. Ignorance is the ground of suspicion, and suspicion was inflamed into daily provocations; prejudice is blind, hunger is deaf; and Alexius is accused of a design to starve or assault the Latins on a dangerous post, on all sides encompassed with the waters.[68] Godfrey sounded his trumpets, burst the net, overspread the plain, and insulted the suburbs; but the gates of Constantinople were strongly fortified; the ramparts were lined with archers; and, after a doubtful conflict, both parties listened to the voice of peace and religion. The gifts and promises of the emperor insensibly soothed the fierce spirit of the western strangers; as a Christian warrior, he rekindled their zeal for the prosecution of their holy enterprise, which he engaged to second with his troops and treasures. On the return of spring, Godfrey was persuaded to occupy a pleasant and plentiful camp in Asia; and no sooner had he passed the Bosphorus, than the Greek vessels [Jan. 1097]

[68] Between the Black Sea, the Bosphorus, and the river Barbyses, which is deep in summer, and runs fifteen miles through a flat meadow. Its communication with Europe and Constantinople is by the stone-bridge of the *Blachernae* [close to St. Callinicus], which in successive ages was restored by Justinian and Basil (Gyllius de Bosphoro Thracio, l. ii. c. 3; Ducange, C. P. Christiana, l. iv. c. 2, p. 179).

were suddenly recalled to the opposite shore. The same polic
was repeated with the succeeding chiefs, who were swayed b
the example, and weakened by the departure, of their foremos
companions. By his skill and diligence, Alexius prevented th
union of any two of the confederate armies at the same momen
under the walls of Constantinople; and, before the feast of th
Pentecost, not a Latin pilgrim was left on the coast of Europe

He obtains the homage of the crusaders   The same arms which threatened Europe might deliver Asi
and repel the Turks from the neighbouring shores of th
Bosphorus and Hellespont. The fair provinces from Nice t
Antioch were the recent patrimony of the Roman emperor; an
his ancient and perpetual claim still embraced the kingdom
of Syria and Egypt. In his enthusiasm, Alexius indulged, o
affected, the ambitious hope of leading his new allies to subver
the thrones of the East; but the calmer dictates of reason an
temper dissuaded him from exposing his royal person to th
faith of unknown and lawless barbarians. His prudence, or hi
pride, was content with extorting from the French princes a
oath of homage and fidelity, and a solemn promise that the
would either restore, or hold, their Asiatic conquests as th
humble and loyal vassals of the Roman empire. Their inde
pendent spirit was fired at the mention of this foreign an
voluntary servitude; they successively yielded to the dextrou
application of gifts and flattery; and the first proselytes becam
the most eloquent and effectual missionaries to multiply th
companions of their shame. The pride of Hugh of Verman
dois was soothed by the honours of his captivity; and in th
brother of the French king the example of submission was pre
valent and weighty. In the mind of Godfrey of Bouillon, ever
human consideration was subordinate to the glory of God and
the success of the crusade. He had firmly resisted the tempta
tions of Bohemond and Raymond, who urged the attack and
conquest of Constantinople. Alexius esteemed his virtues, de
servedly named him the champion of the empire, and dignified
his homage with the filial name and the rights of adoption.[69]

[Arrival of Bohemond. April 26, 1097]   The hateful Bohemond was received as a true and ancient ally;
and, if the emperor reminded him of former hostilities, it was

[69] There were two sorts of adoption, the one by arms, the other by introducing
the son between the shirt and skin of his father. Ducange (sur Joinville, diss. xxii
p. 270) supposes Godfrey's adoption to have been of the latter sort. [The adoption
is mentioned by Albert, ii. 16.]

only to praise the valour that he had displayed, and the glory
that he had acquired, in the fields of Durazzo and Larissa.
The son of Guiscard was lodged and entertained, and served
with Imperial pomp: one day, as he passed through the gallery
of the palace, a door was carelessly left open to expose a pile of
gold and silver, of silk and gems, of curious and costly furniture,
that was heaped in seeming disorder from the floor to the roof
of the chamber. " What conquests," exclaimed the ambitious
miser, " might not be achieved by the possession of such a
treasure ! " "It is your own," replied a Greek attendant, who
watched the motions of his soul ; and Bohemond, after some
hesitation, condescended to accept this magnificent present.
The Norman was flattered by the assurance of an independent
principality ; and Alexius eluded, rather than denied, his daring
demand of the office of great domestic, or general, of the East.
The two Roberts, the son of the conqueror of England and
the kinsman of three queens,[70] bowed in their turn before the
Byzantine throne. A private letter of Stephen of Chartres
attests his admiration of the emperor, the most excellent and
liberal of men, who taught him to believe that he was a favourite, and promised to educate and establish his youngest son.
In his southern province, the count of St. Giles and Toulouse
faintly recognised the supremacy of the king of France, a prince
of a foreign nation and language. At the head of an hundred
thousand men, he declared that he was the soldier and servant
of Christ alone, and that the Greek might be satisfied with an
equal treaty of alliance and friendship. His obstinate resistance
enhanced the value and the price of his submission ; and he
shone, says the princess Anne, among the barbarians, as the
sun amidst the stars of heaven. His disgust of the noise and
insolence of the French, his suspicions of the designs of Bohemond, the emperor imparted to his faithful Raymond ; and that
aged statesman might clearly discern that, however false in
friendship, he was sincere in his enmity.[71] The spirit of
chivalry was last subdued in the person of Tancred ; and none
could deem themselves dishonoured by the imitation of that
gallant knight. He disdained the gold and flattery of the

[70] After his return, Robert of Flanders became the *man* of the King of England, for a pension of 400 marks. See the first act in Rymer's Fœdera.
[71] Sensit vetus regnandi, falsos in amore odia non fingere. Tacit. vi. 44.

Greek monarch; assaulted in his presence an insolent patrician
escaped to Asia in the habit of a private soldier; and yielded
with a sigh to the authority of Bohemond and the interest of
the Christian cause.   The best and most ostensible reason was
the impossibility of passing the sea and accomplishing their
vow, without the licence and the vessels of Alexius; but
they cherished a secret hope that, as soon as they trode the
continent of Asia, their swords would obliterate their shame
and dissolve the engagement, which on his side might not be
very faithfully performed.   The ceremony of their homage was
grateful to a people who had long since considered pride as the
substitute of power.   High on his throne, the emperor sat mute
and immoveable: his majesty was adored by the Latin princes
and they submitted to kiss either his feet or his knees, an
indignity which their own writers are ashamed to confess and
unable to deny.[72]

Insolence
of the
Franks Private or public interest suppressed the murmurs of the
dukes and counts; but a French baron (he is supposed to be
Robert of Paris [73]) presumed to ascend the throne, and to place
himself by the side of Alexius.   The sage reproof of Baldwin
provoked him to exclaim, in his barbarous idiom, "Who is this
rustic, that keeps his seat, while so many valiant captains are
standing round him?"   The emperor maintained his silence
dissembled his indignation, and questioned his interpreter con
cerning the meaning of the words, which he partly suspected
from the universal language of gesture and countenance.   Be
fore the departure of the pilgrims, he endeavoured to learn the
name and condition of the audacious baron.   "I am a French
man," replied Robert, "of the purest and most ancient nobility
of my country.   All that I know is, that there is a church in

[72] The proud historians of the crusades slide and stumble over this humiliating
step.   Yet, since the heroes knelt to salute the emperor as he sat motionless on
his throne, it is clear that they must have kissed either his feet or knees.   It is only
singular that Anna should not have amply supplied the silence or ambiguity of the
Latins.   The abasement of their princes would have added a fine chapter to the
Ceremoniale Aulæ Byzantinæ.

[73] He called himself Φράγγος καθαρὸς τῶν εὐγενῶν (Alexias, l. x. p. 301 [c. 11]).
What a title of noblesse of the xith century, if any one could now prove his inherit
ance!   Anna relates, with visible pleasure, that the swelling barbarian, Λατῖνο
τετυφωμένος, was killed, or wounded, after fighting in the front in the battle of
Dorylæum (l. xi. p. 317).   This circumstance may justify the suspicion of Ducange
(Not. p. 362) that he was no other than Robert of Paris, of the district most pecu
liarly styled the Duchy or Island of France (L'Isle de France).

THE EMPEROR NICEPHORUS BOTONIATES BETWEEN ST. JOHN
CHRYSOSTOM AND THE ARCHANGEL MICHAEL

MINIATURE OF THE 11TH CENTURY IN THE BIBLIOTHÈQUE NATIONALE, PARIS

ıy neighbourhood,[74] the resort of those who are desirous of ap-
roving their valour in single combat.   Till an enemy appears,
ıey address their prayers to God and his saints.   That church
have frequently visited, but never have I found an antagon-
·t who dared to accept my defiance." Alexius dismissed the
hallenger with some prudent advice for his conduct in the
'urkish warfare; and history repeats with pleasure this lively
xample of the manners of his age and country.

The conquest of Asia was undertaken and achieved by Alex- Their re-
ider, with thirty-five thousand Macedonians and Greeks; [75] and view and
numbers.
is best hope was in the strength and discipline of his phalanx A.D. 1097,
May
f infantry.   The principal force of the crusaders consisted in
ieir cavalry ; and, when that force was mustered in the plains
f Bithynia, the knights and their martial attendants on horse-
ack amounted to one hundred thousand fighting men com-
letely armed with the helmet and coat of mail.   The value of
iese soldiers deserved a strict and authentic account; and the
ower of European chivalry might furnish, in a first effort, this
ırmidable body of heavy horse.   A part of the infantry might
e enrolled for the service of scouts, pioneers, and archers; but
ıe promiscuous crowd were lost in their own disorder; and we
epend not on the eyes or knowledge, but on the belief and
ıncy, of a chaplain of count Baldwin,[76] in the estimate of six
undred thousand pilgrims able to bear arms, besides the priests
nd monks, the women and children, of the Latin camp.   The
:ader starts; and, before he is recovered from his surprise, I
ıall add, on the same testimony, that if all who took the cross
ad accomplished their vow, above SIX MILLIONS would have
ıigrated from Europe to Asia.   Under this oppression of faith,
derive some relief from a more sagacious and thinking writer,[77]

[74] With the same penetration, Ducange discovers his church to be that of St.
ausus, or Drosin, of Soissons, quem duello dimicaturi solent invocare : pugiles
ıi ad memoriam ejus (his tomb) pernoctant invictos reddit, ut et de Burgundiâ et
ıliâ tali necessitate confugiatur ed eum. Joan. Sariburiensis, epist. 139.

[75] There is some diversity on the numbers of his army ; but no authority can be
mpared with that of Ptolemy, who states it at five thousand horse and thirty
ousand foot (See Usher's Annales, p. 152).

[76] Fulcher. Carnotensis, p. 387.   He enumerates nineteen nations of different
ımes and languages (p. 389) ; but I do not clearly apprehend his difference
·tween the Franci and Galli, Itali and Apuli. Elsewhere (p. 385) he contemp-
ously brands the deserters.

[77] Guibert, p. 556.   Yet even his gentle opposition implies an immense multi-
.de.   By Urban II., in the fervour of his zeal, it is only rated at 300,000 pilgrims
.pist. xvi. Concil. tom. xii. p. 731).

who, after the same review of the cavalry, accuses the credulity
of the priest of Chartres, and even doubts whether the *Cisalpine*
regions (in the geography of a Frenchman) were sufficient to produce and pour forth such incredible multitudes. The coolest
scepticism will remember that of these religious volunteers great
numbers never beheld Constantinople and Nice. Of enthusiasm
the influence is irregular and transient; many were detained at
home by reason or cowardice, by poverty or weakness; and
many were repulsed by the obstacles of the way, the more insuperable as they were unforeseen to these ignorant fanatics.
The savage countries of Hungary and Bulgaria were whitened
with their bones; their vanguard was cut in pieces by the
Turkish sultan; and the loss of the first adventure, by the sword,
or climate, or fatigue, has already been stated at three hundred
thousand men. Yet the myriads that survived, that marched,
that pressed forwards on the holy pilgrimage were a subject of
astonishment to themselves and to the Greeks. The copious
energy of her language sinks under the efforts of the princess
Anne;[78] the images of locusts, of leaves and flowers, of the sands
of the sea, or the stars of heaven, imperfectly represent what she
had seen and heard; and the daughter of Alexius exclaims that
Europe was loosened from its foundations and hurled against
Asia. The ancient hosts of Darius and Xerxes labour under
the same doubt of a vague and indefinite magnitude; but I am
inclined to believe that a larger number has never been contained within the lines of a single camp than at the siege of
Nice, the first operation of the Latin princes. Their motives,
their characters, and their arms have been already displayed.
Of their troops, the most numerous portion were natives
of France; the Low Countries, the banks of the Rhine, and
Apulia, sent a powerful reinforcement; some bands of adven-

---

[78] Alexias, l. x. p. 283 [c. 5], 305 [c. 11]. Her fastidious delicacy complains of
their strange and inarticulate names; and indeed there is scarcely one that she has
not contrived to disfigure with the proud ignorance, so dear and familiar to a
polished people. I shall select only one example, *Sangeles*, for the count of St.
Giles. [Sangeles would be a near enough equivalent for St. Gilles, but it is
Isangeles; and the form of the corruption seems to have been determined by an
etymology complimentary to the count,—*ἰσάγγελος*, angelic. A reader, ignorant
of the pronunciation of modern Greek, might easily do injustice to Anna. The
modern Greek alphabet has no letters equivalent to *b* and *d* (β represents *v*, and δ
is aspirated, *dh*); and in order to reproduce these sounds they resort to the devices
of *μπ* and *ντ*. Thus *Robert* is quite correctly Ῥομπέρτος, and Γοντοφρέ is a near
transliteration of Godfrey (Godefroi).]

turers were drawn from Spain, Lombardy, and England;[79] and from the distant bogs and mountains of Ireland or Scotland[80] issued some naked and savage fanatics, ferocious at home, but unwarlike abroad. Had not superstition condemned the sacrilegious prudence of depriving the poorest or weakest Christian of the merit of the pilgrimage, the useless crowd, with mouths but without hands, might have been stationed in the Greek empire, till their companions had opened and secured the way of the Lord. A small remnant of the pilgrims, who passed the Bosphorus, was permitted to visit the holy sepulchre. Their northern constitution was scorched by the rays, and infected by the vapours, of a Syrian sun. They consumed, with heedless prodigality, their stores of water and provisions; their numbers exhausted the inland country; the sea was remote, the Greeks were unfriendly, and the Christians of every sect fled before the voracious and cruel rapine of their brethren. In the dire necessity of famine, they sometimes roasted and devoured the flesh of their infant or adult captives. Among the Turks and Saracens, the idolaters of Europe were rendered more odious by the name and reputation of cannibals; the spies who introduced themselves into the kitchen of Bohemond were shown several human bodies turning on the spit; and the artful Norman encouraged a report, which increased at the same time the abhorrence and the terror of the infidels.[81]

I have expatiated with pleasure on the first steps of the crusaders, as they paint the manners and character of Europe; but I shall abridge the tedious and uniform narrative of their

Siege of Nice. A.D. 1097, May 14—June 20 [19]

[79] William of Malmesbury (who wrote about the year 1130) has inserted in his history (l. iv. p. 130-154) a narrative of the first crusade ; but I wish that, instead of listening to the tenue murmur which had passed the British ocean (p. 143), he had confined himself to the numbers, families, and adventures of his countrymen. I find in Dugdale that an English Norman, Stephen, Earl of Albemarle and Holdernesse, led the rear-guard with Duke Robert, at the battle of Antioch (Baronage, part i. p. 61).

[80] Videres Scotorum apud se ferocium alias imbellium cuneos (Guibert, p. 471) ; the *crus intectum*, and *hispida chlamys*, may suit the Highlanders ; but the *finibus uliginosis* may rather apply to the Irish bogs. William of Malmesbury expressly mentions the Welsh and Scots, &c. (l. iv. p. 133), who quitted, the former venationem saltuum, the latter familiaritatem pulicum.

[81] This cannibal hunger, sometimes real, more frequently an artifice or a lie, may be found in Anna Comnena (Alexias, l. x. p. 288 [c. 7]), Guibert (p. 546), Radulph. Cadom. (c. 97). The stratagem is related by the author of the Gesta Francorum, the monk Robert, Baldric, and Raymond des Agiles, in the siege and famine of Antioch. [In the Romance of Richard Cœur de Lion (edited by Weber) Richard eats the heads of Saracens.]

blind achievements, which were performed by strength and are described by ignorance. From their first station in the neighbourhood of Nicomedia, they advanced in successive divisions, passed the contracted limit of the Greek empire, opened a road through the hills, and commenced, by the siege of his capital, their pious warfare against the Turkish sultan. His kingdom of Roum extended from the Hellespont to the confines of Syria and barred the pilgrimage of Jerusalem; his name was Kilidge-Arslan, or Soliman,[82] of the race of Seljuk, and son of the first conqueror; and, in the defence of a land which the Turks considered as their own, he deserved the praise of his enemies, by whom alone he is known to posterity. Yielding to the first impulse of the torrent, he deposited his family and treasure in Nice, retired to the mountains with fifty thousand horse, and twice descended to assault the camps or quarters of the Christian besiegers, which formed an imperfect circle of above six miles. The lofty and solid walls of Nice were covered by a deep ditch, and flanked by three hundred and seventy towers; and on the verge of Christendom the Moslems were trained in arms and inflamed by religion. Before this city, the French princes occupied their stations, and prosecuted their attacks without correspondence or subordination; emulation prompted their valour; but their valour was sullied by cruelty, and their emulation degenerated into envy and civil discord. In the siege of Nice the arts and engines of antiquity were employed by the Latins; the mine and the battering-ram, the tortoise, and the belfry or moveable turret, artificial fire, and the *catapult* and *balist*, the sling, and the cross-bow for the casting of stones and darts.[83] In the space of seven weeks much labour

[82] His Musulman appellation of Soliman is used by the Latins, and his character is highly embellished by Tasso. His Turkish name of Kilidge-Arslan (A.H. 485-500, A.D. 1192-1206; see de Guignes's Tables, tom. i. p. 245) is employed by the Orientals, and with some corruption by the Greeks; but little more than his name can be found in the Mahometan writers, who are dry and sulky on the subject of the first crusade (de Guignes, tom. iii. p. ii. p. 10-30). [This is not quite correct. Sulaimān died in 1086. After an interregnum of six years Kilij-Arslān, his son, succeeded in 1092, and reigned till 1106. The western historians confuse the two.]

[83] On the fortifications, engines, and sieges of the middle ages, see Muratori (Antiquitat. Italiæ, tom. ii. dissert. xxvi. p. 452-524). The *belfredus*, from whence our belfry, was the moveable tower of the ancients (Ducange, tom. i. p. 608). [See description of the *berefridus* in the Itinerarium regis Ricardi, iii. c. 6 (ed. Stubbs), and of the κριοφόρος χελώνη in Anna Comnena, xiii. c. 3; they are the same engine. Compare on the whole subject, Oman, Art of War, ii. p. 131 *sqq.*]

and blood were expended, and some progress, especially by
Count Raymond, was made on the side of the besiegers. But
the Turks could protract their resistance and secure their escape,
as long as they were masters of the lake Ascanius,[84] which
stretches several miles to the westward of the city. The means
of conquest were supplied by the prudence and industry of
Alexius; a great number of boats was transported on sledges
from the sea to the lake; they were filled with the most dex-
trous of his archers; the flight of the sultana was intercepted;
Nice was invested by land and water ; and a Greek emissary
persuaded the inhabitants to accept his master's protection, and
to save themselves, by a timely surrender, from the rage of the
savages of Europe. In the moment of victory, or at least of
hope, the crusaders, thirsting for blood and plunder, were awed
by the Imperial banner that streamed from the citadel, and
Alexius guarded with jealous vigilance this important conquest.
The murmurs of the chiefs were stifled by honour or interest;
and, after an halt of nine days, they directed their march towards
Phrygia, under the guidance of a Greek general, whom they [June 27]
suspected of secret connivance with the sultan. The consort
and the principal servants of Soliman had been honourably
restored without ransom, and the emperor's generosity to the
miscreants [85] was interpreted as treason to the Christian cause.

Soliman was rather provoked than dismayed by the loss of [Battle of
his capital; he admonished his subjects and allies of this strange Dorylæum. A.D. 1097,
invasion of the western barbarians; the Turkish emirs obeyed July 4 [1]]
the call of loyalty or religion; the Turkman hordes encamped
round his standard; and his whole force is loosely stated by the
Christians at two hundred, or even three hundred and sixty,
thousand horse. Yet he patiently waited till they had left behind them the sea and the Greek frontier, and, hovering on the
flanks, observed their careless and confident progress in two
columns, beyond the view of each other. Some miles before
they could reach Dorylæum in Phrygia, the left and least [Eski-
shehr]

---

[84] I cannot forbear remarking the resemblance between the siege and lake
of Nice with the operations of Hernan Cortez before Mexico. See Dr. Robertson,
Hist of America, l. v.

[85] *Mécréant*, a word invented by the French crusaders, and confined in that
language to its primitive sense. It should seem that the zeal of our ancestors
boiled higher, and that they branded every unbeliever as a rascal. A similar prejudice still lurks in the minds of many who think themselves Christians.

numerous division was surprised, and attacked, and almost oppressed, by the Turkish cavalry.[86] The heat of the weather, the clouds of arrows, and the barbarous onset overwhelmed the crusaders; they lost their order and confidence, and the fainting fight was sustained by the personal valour, rather than by the military conduct, of Bohemond, Tancred, and Robert of Normandy. They were revived by the welcome banners of duke Godfrey, who flew to their succour, with the count of Vermandois and sixty thousand horse, and was followed by Raymond of Toulouse, the bishop of Puy, and the remainder of the sacred army. Without a moment's pause they formed in new order, and advanced to a second battle. They were received with equal resolution; and, in their common disdain for the unwarlike people of Greece and Asia, it was confessed on both sides that the Turks and the Franks were the only nations entitled to the appellation of soldiers.[87] Their encounter was varied and balanced by the contrast of arms and discipline; of the direct charge, and wheeling evolutions; of the couched lance, and the brandished javelin; of a weighty broad-sword, and a crooked sabre; of cumbrous armour, and thin flowing robes;[87a] and of the long Tartar bow, and the *arbalist* or cross-bow, a deadly weapon, yet unknown to the Orientals.[88] As long as the horses were fresh and the quivers full, Soliman maintained the advantage of the day; and four thousand Christians were pierced by the Turkish arrows. In the evening, swiftness yielded to strength; on either side, the numbers were equal, or at least as great as

[86] Baronius has produced a very doubtful letter to his brother Roger (A.D. 1098, No. 15). The enemies consisted of Medes, Persians, Chaldeans; be it so. The first attack was, cum nostro incommodo; true and tender. But why Godfrey of Bouillon and Hugh *brothers*? Tancred is styled *filius*; of whom? certainly not of Roger, nor of Bohemond. [Tancred was a nephew of Bohemond, and a grand-nephew of Roger. His mother was Emma, Robert Guiscard's daughter; his father Marchisus (Gest. Fr. iv. 2 Marchisi filius), which conceivably does not mean a western Marquis but refers to the name of a Saracen emir, as P. Paris suggests, Chanson d'Antioch, ii. 372; but it is not easy to find a likely name.]

[87] Veruntamen dicunt se esse de Francorum generatione; et quia nullus homo naturaliter debet esse miles nisi Franci et Turci (Gesta Francorum, p. 7). The same community of blood and valour is attested by Archbishop Baldric (p. 99).

[87a] [The painted windows of the Church of St. Denys, made by order of the Abbot Suger in the 12th cent., reproduced in Montfaucon's Monuments, plate li. &c., illustrated the armour of the Saracens.]

[88] *Balista, Balestra, Arbalestre.* See Muratori, Antiq. tom. ii. p. 517-524. Ducange, Gloss. Latin. tom. i. p. 531, 532. In the time of Anna Comnena, this weapon, which she describes under the name of *tzangra*, was unknown in the East (l. x. p. 291 [c. 8]). By an humane inconsistency, the pope strove to prohibit it in Christian wars.

any ground could hold or any generals could manage; but in turning the hills the last division of Raymond and his *provincials* was led, perhaps without design, on the rear of an exhausted enemy; and the long contest was determined. Besides a nameless and unaccounted multitude, three thousand *pagan* knights were slain in the battle and pursuit; the camp of Soliman was pillaged; and in the variety of precious spoil the curiosity of the Latins was amused with foreign arms and apparel, and the new aspect of dromedaries and camels. The importance of the victory was proved by the hasty retreat of the sultan: reserving ten thousand guards of the relics of his army, Soliman evacuated the kingdom of Roum, and hastened to implore the aid, and kindle the resentment, of his Eastern brethren. In a march of five hundred miles, the crusaders traversed the Lesser Asia, through a wasted land and deserted towns, without either finding a friend or an enemy. The geographer [89] may trace the position of Dorylæum, Antioch of Pisidia, Iconium, Archelais, and Germanicia, and may compare those classic appellations with the modern names of Eskishehr the old city, Akshehr the white city, Cogni, Erekli,[89a] and Marash. As the pilgrims passed over a desert, where a draught of water is exchanged for silver, they were tormented by intolerable thirst; and on the banks of the first rivulet their haste and intemperance were still more pernicious to the disorderly throng. They climbed with toil and danger the steep and slippery sides of mount Taurus; many of the soldiers cast away their arms to secure their footsteps; and, had not terror preceded their van, the long and trembling file might have been driven down the precipice by an handful of resolute enemies. Two of their most respectable chiefs, the duke of Lorraine and the count of Toulouse, were carried in litters; Raymond was raised, as it is said, by miracle, from an hopeless malady; and Godfrey had been torn by a bear, as he pursued that rough and perilous chase in the mountains of Pisidia.

March through the Lesser Asia. July-September

[89] The curious reader may compare the classic learning of Cellarius and the geographical science of D'Anville. William of Tyre is the only historian of the crusades who has any knowledge of antiquity; and M. Otter trode almost in the footsteps of the Franks from Constantinople to Antioch (Voyage en Turquie et en Perse, tom. i. p. 35-88).

[89a] [Eregli is the ancient Heraclea, about 30 hours south-east of Iconium (Koniya). It was here that Tancred and Baldwin separated from the main army. Gesta Fr. x. 5.]

Baldwin
founds the
princi-
pality of
Edessa.
A.D. 1097-
1151

To improve the general consternation, the cousin of Bohemond and the brother of Godfrey were detached from the
main army, with their respective squadrons of five and of seven
hundred knights. They over-ran, in a rapid career, the hills
and sea-coast of Cilicia, from Cogni to the Syrian gates; the
Norman standard was first planted on the walls of Tarsus and
Malmistra; but the proud injustice of Baldwin at length provoked the patient and generous Italian, and they turned their
consecrated swords against each other in a private and profane
quarrel. Honour was the motive, and fame the reward, of
Tancred; but fortune smiled on the more selfish enterprise of
his rival.[90] He was called to the assistance of a Greek or

[Thoros]

Armenian tyrant, who had been suffered under the Turkish
yoke to reign over the Christians of Edessa. Baldwin accepted
the character of his son and champion; but no sooner was he
introduced into the city than he inflamed[91] the people to the
massacre of his father, occupied the throne and treasure, extended his conquests over the hills of Armenia and the plain
of Mesopotamia, and founded the first principality of the

[leg. forty-
six]

Franks or Latins, which subsisted fifty-four years beyond the
Euphrates.[92]

Siege of
Antioch.
A.D. 1097,
October 21
—A.D. 1098,
June 3

Before the Franks could enter Syria, the summer, and even
the autumn, were completely wasted: the siege of Antioch, or
the separation and repose of the army during the winter season,
was strongly debated in their council; the love of arms and the
holy sepulchre urged them to advance, and reason perhaps was
on the side of resolution, since every hour of delay abates the
fame and force of the invader and multiplies the resources of
defensive war. The capital of Syria was protected by the river
Orontes, and the *iron bridge* of nine arches derives its name
from the massy gates of the two towers which are constructed

---

[90] This detached conquest of Edessa is best represented by Fulcherius Carnotensis, or of Chartres (in the collections of Bongarsius, Duchesne, and Martenne),
the valiant chaplain of Count Baldwin (Esprit des Croisades, tom. i. p. 13-14). In
the disputes of that prince with Tancred, his partiality is encountered by the
partiality of Radulphus Cadomensis, the soldier and historian of the gallant marquis.
[See the Chronicle of Matthew of Edessa, tr. Dulaurier, p. 218-221.]

[91] [In the account of Matthew of Edessa, *ib.* p. 219-220, Baldwin did not
influence the people, but conspirators induced him to consent to their plan of
assassinating Thoros. The deed, however, was done, not by a band of conspirators,
but by " the inhabitants" in a mass; *ib.* p. 220.]

[92] See de Guignes, Hist. des Huns, tom. i. p. 456. [Edessa was taken in 1144
by Imād ad-dīn Zangī.]

at either end.[93] They were opened by the sword of the duke of
Normandy : his victory gave entrance to three hundred thousand crusaders, an account which may allow some scope for
losses and desertion, but which clearly detects much exaggeration in the review of Nice. In the description of Antioch [94] it is
not easy to define a middle term between her ancient magnificence, under the successors of Alexander and Augustus, and the
modern aspect of Turkish desolation. The Tetrapolis, or four
cities, if they retained their name and position, must have left
a large vacuity in a circumference of twelve miles; and that
measure, as well as the number of four hundred towers, are not
perfectly consistent with the five gates, so often mentioned in
the history of the siege. Yet Antioch must have still flourished
as a great and populous capital. At the head of the Turkish
emirs, Baghisian, a veteran chief, commanded in the place ; his [Yaghisi-
garrison was composed of six or seven thousand horse and fifteen   yan]
or twenty thousand foot : one hundred thousand Moslems are
said to have fallen by the sword, and their numbers were probably inferior to the Greeks, Armenians, and Syrians, who had
been no more than fourteen years the slaves of the house of
Seljuk. From the remains of a solid and stately wall it appears
to have arisen to the height of threescore feet in the valleys ;
and wherever less art and labour had been applied, the ground
was supposed to be defended by the river, the morass, and the
mountains. Notwithstanding these fortifications, the city had
been repeatedly taken by the Persians, the Arabs, the Greeks,
and the Turks ; [95] so large a circuit must have yielded many
pervious points of attack ; and, in a siege that was formed about
the middle of October, the vigour of the execution could alone
justify the boldness of the attempt. Whatever strength and
valour could perform in the field, was abundantly discharged by
the champions of the cross: in the frequent occasions of sallies,

---

[93] [About 3½ hrs. east of Antioch. See Hagenmeyer's note on Gesta Fr. xii. 1.
Compare Le Strange, Palestine under the Muslims, p. 60.]
[94] For Antioch, see Pococke (Description of the East, vol. ii. p. i. p. 188-193),
Otter (Voyage en Turquie, &c. tom. i. p. 81, &c.), the Turkish geographer (in Otter's
notes), the Index Geographicus of Schultens (ad calcem Bohadin. Vit. Saladin.),
and Abulfeda (Tabula Syriæ, p. 115-116, vers. Reiske). [Le Strange, Palestine
under the Muslims, p. 367-377.]
[95] [One of the most important fortifications for a besieger of Antioch to seize
was the tower of Bagrās, or St. Luke, which commanded the pass over Mount
Amanus to Alexandretta. It was fortified strongly by Nicephorus Phocas, when he
besieged the city in 968.]

of forage, of the attack and defence of convoys, they were often victorious; and we can only complain that their exploits are sometimes enlarged beyond the scale of probability and truth. The sword of Godfrey [96] divided a Turk from the shoulder to the haunch, and one half of the infidel fell to the ground, while the other was transported by his horse to the city gate. As Robert of Normandy rode against his antagonist, "I devote thy head," he piously exclaimed, " to the dæmons of hell," and that head was instantly cloven to the breast by the resistless stroke of his descending faulchion. But the reality or report of such gigantic prowess [97] must have taught the Moslems to keep within their walls, and against those walls of earth or stone the sword and the lance were unavailing weapons. In the slow and successive labours of a siege the crusaders were supine and ignorant, without skill to contrive, or money to purchase, or industry to use the artificial engines and implements of assault. In the conquest of Nice they had been powerfully assisted by the wealth and knowledge of the Greek emperor: his absence was poorly supplied by some Genoese and Pisan vessels that were attracted by religion or trade to the coast of Syria ; the stores were scanty, the return precarious, and the communication difficult and dangerous. Indolence or weakness had prevented the Franks from investing the entire circuit; and the perpetual freedom of two gates relieved the wants, and recruited the garrison, of the city. At the end of seven months, after the ruin of their cavalry, and an enormous loss by famine, desertion, and fatigue, the progress of the crusaders was imperceptible, and their success remote, if the Latin Ulysses, the artful and ambitious Bohemond, had not employed the arms of cunning and deceit. The Christians of Antioch were numerous and discontented: Phirouz, a Syrian renegado, had acquired the favour of the emir, and the command of three towers; and the

[Firur]

---

[96] Ensem elevat, eumque a sinistrâ parte scapularum tantâ virtute intorsit, ut quod pectus medium disjunxit spinam et vitalia interrupit ; et sic lubricus ensis super crus dextrum integer exivit ; sicque caput integrum cum dextrâ parte corporis immersit gurgite, partemque quæ equo præsidebat remisit civitati (Robert Mon. p. 50). Cujus ense trajectus, Turcus duo factus est Turci ; ut inferior alter in urbem equitaret, alter arcitenens in flumine nataret (Radulph. Cadom. c. 53, p. 304). Yet he justifies the deed by the *stupendis* viribus of Godfrey ; and William of Tyre covers it by obstupuit populus facti novitate . . . mirabilis (l. v. c. 6, p. 701). Yet it must not have appeared incredible to the knights of that age.

[97] See the exploits of Robert, Raymond, and the modest Tancred, who imposed silence on his squire (Radulph. Cadom. c. 53).

merit of his repentance disguised to the Latins, and perhaps
to himself, the foul design of perfidy and treason. A secret
correspondence, for their mutual interest, was soon established
between Phirouz and the prince of Tarento; and Bohemond
declared in the council of the chiefs that he could deliver the
city into their hands. But he claimed the sovereignty of
Antioch as the reward of his service; and the proposal which
had been rejected by the envy, was at length extorted from
the distress, of his equals. The nocturnal surprise was executed
by the French and Norman princes, who ascended in person
the scaling-ladders that were thrown from the walls; their
new proselyte, after the murder of his too scrupulous brother,
embraced and introduced the servants of Christ: the army
rushed through the gates; and the Moslems soon found that,
although mercy was hopeless, resistance was impotent. But
the citadel still refused to surrender; and the victors themselves were speedily encompassed and besieged by the innumerable forces of Kerboga, prince of Mosul, who, with twenty-eight
Turkish emirs, advanced to the deliverance of Antioch. Five
and twenty days the Christians spent on the verge of destruction ; and the proud lieutenant of the caliph and the sultan left
them only the choice of servitude or death.[98]   In this extremity Victory
they collected the relics of their strength, sallied from the town, crusaders.
and in a single memorable day annihilated or dispersed the host June 28
of Turks and Arabians, which they might safely report to have
consisted of six hundred thousand men.[99]   Their supernatural
allies I shall proceed to consider : the human causes of the
victory of Antioch were the fearless despair of the Franks; and
the surprise, the discord, perhaps the errors, of their unskilful
and presumptuous adversaries.   The battle is described with as

---

[98] After mentioning the distress and humble petition of the Franks, Abulpharagius adds the haughty reply of Codbuka, or Kerboga [Kawām ad-Dawla (pillar
of the realm) Kurbughā] ; "Non evasuri estis nisi per gladium" (Dynast. p. 242).
[In the Chanson d'Antioche, Kurbughā is mysteriously called Carbaran d'Oliferne.]
[99] In describing the host of Kerboga, most of the Latin historians, the author
of the Gesta (p. 17), Robert Monachus (p. 56), Baldric (p. 111), Fulcherius Carnotensis (p. 392), Guibert (p. 512), William of Tyre (l. vi. c. iii. p. 714), Bernard
Thesaurarius (c. 39, p. 695), are content with the vague expressions of infinita
multitudo, immensum agmen, innumerae copiae, or gentes, which correspond with
the μετὰ ἀναριθμήτων χιλιάδων of Anna Comnena (Alexias, l. xi. p. 318-320 [c. 4]).
The numbers of the Turks are fixed by Albert Aquensis at 200,000 (l. iv. c. x. p.
242), and by Radulphus Cadomensis at 400,000 horse (c. lxxii. p. 309). [Much
larger figures are given by Matthew of Edessa, c. clv. p. 221.]

much disorder as it was fought ; but we may observe the tent of Kerboga, a moveable and spacious palace, enriched with the luxury of Asia, and capable of holding above two thousand persons ; we may distinguish his three thousand guards, who were cased, the horses as well as men, in complete steel.

Their
famine and
distress at
Antioch In the eventful period of the siege and defence of Antioch, the crusaders were, alternately, exalted by victory or sunk in despair ; either swelled with plenty or emaciated with hunger. A speculative reasoner might suppose that their faith had a strong and serious influence on their practice; and that the soldiers of the cross, the deliverers of the holy sepulchre, prepared themselves by a sober and virtuous life for the daily contemplation of martyrdom.   Experience blows away this charitable illusion ; and seldom does the history of profane war display such scenes of intemperance and prostitution as were exhibited under the walls of Antioch.   The grove of Daphne no longer flourished ; but the Syrian air was still impregnated with the same vices; the Christians were seduced by every temptation [100] that nature either prompts or reprobates; the authority of the chiefs was despised ; and sermons and edicts were alike fruitless against those scandalous disorders, not less pernicious to military discipline than repugnant to evangelic purity.   In the first days of the siege and the possession of Antioch, the Franks consumed with wanton and thoughtless prodigality the frugal subsistence of weeks and months ; the desolate country no longer yielded a supply; and from that country they were at length excluded by the arms of the besieging Turks.   Disease, the faithful companion of want, was envenomed by the rains of the winter, the summer heats, unwholesome food, and the close imprisonment of multitudes.   The pictures of famine and pestilence are always the same, and always disgustful ; and our imagination may suggest the nature of their sufferings and their resources.   The remains of treasure or spoil were eagerly lavished in the purchase of the vilest nourishment ; and dreadful must have been the calamities of the poor, since, after paying three marks of silver for a goat, and fifteen for a lean camel,[101]

---

[100] See the tragic and scandalous fate of an archdeacon of royal birth, who was slain by the Turks as he reposed in an orchard, playing at dice with a Syrian concubine.

[101] The value of an ox rose from five solidi (fifteen shillings) at Christmas to two marks (four pounds), and afterwards much higher : a kid or lamb, from one

the count of Flanders was reduced to beg a dinner, and duke Godfrey to borrow an horse. Sixty thousand horses had been reviewed in the camp; before the end of the siege they were diminished to two thousand, and scarcely two hundred fit for service could be mustered on the day of battle. Weakness of body and terror of mind extinguished the ardent enthusiasm of the pilgrims; and every motive of honour and religion was subdued by the desire of life.[102] Among the chiefs three heroes may be found without fear or reproach : Godfrey of Bouillon was supported by his magnanimous piety; Bohemond by ambition and interest; and Tancred declared, in the true spirit of chivalry, that, as long as he was at the head of forty knights, he would never relinquish the enterprise of Palestine. But the count of Toulouse and Provence was suspected of a voluntary indisposition ; the duke of Normandy was recalled from the seashore by the censures of the church ; Hugh the Great, though he led the vanguard of the battle, embraced an ambiguous opportunity of returning to France; and Stephen, count of Chartres, basely deserted the standard which he bore, and the council in which he presided. The soldiers were discouraged by the flight of William, viscount of Melun, surnamed the *Carpenter*, from the weighty strokes of his axe ; and the saints were scandalized by the fall of Peter the Hermit, who, after arming Europe against Asia, attempted to escape from the penance of a necessary fast. Of the multitude of recreant warriors, the names (says an historian) are blotted from the book of life; and the opprobrious epithet of the rope-dancers was applied to the deserters who dropt in the night from the walls of Antioch. The emperor Alexius,[103] who seemed to advance to the succour of the Latins, was dismayed by the assurance of their hopeless condition. They expected their fate in silent despair; oaths and punishments were tried with-

---

shilling to eighteen of our present money : in the second famine, a loaf of bread, or the head of an animal, sold for a piece of gold. More examples might be produced ; but it is the ordinary, not the extraordinary, prices that deserve the notice of the philosopher.

[102] Alii multi quorum nomina non tenemus; quia, deleta de libro vitæ, præsenti operi non sunt inserenda (Will. Tyr. l. vi. c. v. p. 715). Guibert (p. 518-523) attempts to excuse Hugh the Great, and even Stephen of Chartres.

[103] See the progress of the crusade, the retreat of Alexius, the victory of Antioch, and the conquest of Jerusalem, in the Alexiad, l. xi. p. 317-327 [c. 3-6]. Anna was so prone to exaggeration that she magnifies the exploits of the Latins.

out effect; and, to rouse the soldiers to the defence of the walls, it was found necessary to set fire to their quarters.

Legend of the Holy Lance

For their salvation and victory, they were indebted to the same fanaticism which had led them to the brink of ruin. In such a cause, and in such an army, visions, prophecies, and miracles were frequent and familiar. In the distress of Antioch, they were repeated with unusual energy and success; St. Ambrose had assured a pious ecclesiastic that two years of trial must precede the season of deliverance and grace; the deserters were stopped by the presence and approaches of Christ himself; the dead had promised to arise and combat with their brethren; the Virgin had obtained the pardon of their sins; and their confidence was revived by a visible sign, the seasonable and splendid discovery of the HOLY LANCE. The policy of their chiefs has on this occasion been admired and might surely be excused; but a pious fraud is seldom produced by the cool conspiracy of many persons; and a voluntary impostor might depend on the support of the wise and the credulity of the people. Of the diocese of Marseilles, there was a priest of low cunning and loose manners, and his name was Peter Bartholemy. He presented himself at the door of the council-chamber, to disclose an apparition of St. Andrew, which had been thrice reiterated in his sleep, with a dreadful menace if he presumed to suppress the commands of Heaven. "At Antioch," said the apostle, "in the church of my brother St. Peter, near the high altar, is concealed the steel head of the lance that pierced the side of our Redeemer. In three days, that instrument of eternal, and now of temporal, salvation will be manifested to his disciples. Search, and ye shall find; bear it aloft in battle; and that mystic weapon shall penetrate the souls of the miscreants." The pope's legate, the bishop of Puy, affected to listen with coldness and distrust; but the revelation was eagerly accepted by count Raymond, whom his faithful subject, in the name of the apostle, had chosen for the guardian of the holy lance. The experiment was resolved; and on the third day, after a due preparation of prayer and fasting, the priest of Marseilles introduced twelve trusty spectators, among whom were the count and his chaplain; and the church doors were barred against the impetuous multitude. The ground was opened in the appointed place; but the workmen, who relieved each other, dug to the depth of twelve feet without discovering the object of their search. In the evening, when count Raymond had withdrawn to his post, and the weary assistants began to murmur, Bartholemy, in his shirt and without his shoes, boldly descended into the pit; the darkness of the hour and of the place enabled him to secrete and deposit the head of a Saracen lance, and the first sound, the first gleam, of the steel was saluted with a devout rapture. The holy lance was drawn from its recess, wrapt in a veil of silk and gold, and exposed to the veneration of the crusaders; their anxious suspense burst forth in a general shout of joy and hope, and the desponding troops were again inflamed with the enthusiasm of valour. Whatever had been the arts, and whatever might be the sentiments of the chiefs, they skilfully improved this fortunate revolution by every aid that discipline and devotion could afford. The soldiers were dismissed to their quarters, with an injunction to fortify their minds and bodies for the approaching conflict, freely to bestow their last pittance on themselves and their horses, and to expect with the dawn of day the signal of victory. On the festival of St. Peter and St. Paul, the gates of Antioch were thrown open; a martial psalm, " Let the Lord arise, and let his enemies be scattered! " was chaunted by a procession of priests and monks; the battle array was marshalled in twelve divisions, in honour of the twelve apostles; and the holy lance, in the absence of Raymond, was entrusted to the hands of his chaplain. The influence of this relic or trophy was felt by the servants, and perhaps by the enemies, of Christ;[104] and its potent energy was heightened by an accident, a stratagem, or a rumour, of a miraculous complexion. Three knights, in white garments and resplendent arms, either issued, or seemed to issue, from the hills: the voice of Adhemar, the pope's legate, proclaimed them as the martyrs St. George, St. Theodore, and St. Maurice; the tumult of battle allowed no time for doubt or scrutiny; and the welcome apparition dazzled the eyes or the imagination of a fanatic army. In the season of danger and triumph, the revelation, of Bartholemy of Marseilles was unanimously asserted; but, as soon as the temporary service was

Celestial warriors

---

[104] The Mahometan Aboulmahasen (apud de Guignes, tom. ii. p. 95) is more correct in his account of the holy lance than the Christians, Anna Comnena and Abulpharagius: the Greek princess confounds it with a nail of the cross (l. xi. p. 326 [c. 6]); the Jacobite primate, with St. Peter's staff (p. 242).

accomplished, the personal dignity and liberal alms which the count of Toulouse derived from the custody of the holy lance provoked the envy, and awakened the reason, of his rivals. A Norman clerk presumed to sift, with a philosophic spirit, the truth of the legend, the circumstances of the discovery, and the character of the prophet; and the pious Bohemond ascribed their deliverance to the merits and intercession of Christ alone. For a while the Provincials defended their national palladium with clamours and arms; and new visions condemned to death and hell the profane sceptics who presumed to scrutinise the truth and merit of the discovery. The prevalence of incredulity compelled the author to submit his life and veracity to the judgment of God. A pile of faggots, four feet high and fourteen feet long, was erected in the midst of the camp; the flames burnt fiercely to the elevation of thirty cubits; and a narrow path of twelve inches was left for the perilous trial. The unfortunate priest of Marseilles traversed the fire with dexterity and speed : but his thighs and belly were scorched by the intense heat; he expired the next day, and the logic of believing minds will pay some regard to his dying protestations of innocence and truth. Some efforts were made by the Provincials to substitute a cross, a ring, or a tabernacle, in the place of the holy lance, which soon vanished in contempt and oblivion.[105] Yet the revelation of Antioch is gravely asserted by succeeding historians; and such is the progress of credulity that miracles, most doubtful on the spot and at the moment, will be received with implicit faith at a convenient distance of time and space.

The state of the Turks or caliphs of Egypt

The prudence or fortune of the Franks had delayed their invasion till the decline of the Turkish empire.[106] Under the manly government of the three first sultans, the kingdoms of Asia were united in peace and justice; and the innumerable armies which they led in person were equal in courage, and superior in discipline, to the barbarians of the West. But at the time of the crusade, the inheritance of Malek Shah was dis-

---

[105] The two antagonists who express the most intimate knowledge and the strongest conviction of the *miracle*, and of the *fraud*, are Raymond des Agiles and Radulphus Cadomensis, the one attached to the Count of Toulouse, the other to the Norman prince. Fulcherius Carnotensis presumes to say, Audite fraudem et non fraudem ! and afterwards, Invenit lanceam, fallaciter occultatam forsitan. The rest of the herd are loud and strenuous.

[106] See M. de Guignes (tom. ii. p. ii. p. 223, &c.) ; and the articles of *Barkiarok, Mohammed, Sangiar*, in d'Herbelot.

puted by his four sons; their private ambition was insensible of the public danger; and, in the vicissitudes of their fortune, the royal vassals were ignorant, or regardless, of the true object of their allegiance. The twenty-eight emirs who marched with the standard of Kerboga were his rivals or enemies; their hasty levies were drawn from the towns and tents of Mesopotamia and Syria; and the Turkish veterans were employed or consumed in the civil wars beyond the Tigris. The caliph of Egypt embraced this opportunity of weakness and discord to recover his ancient possessions; and his sultan Aphdal besieged Jerusalem and Tyre, expelled the children of Ortok, and restored in Palestine the civil and ecclesiastical authority of the Fatimites.[107] They heard with astonishment of the vast armies of Christians that had passed from Europe to Asia, and rejoiced in the sieges and battles which broke the power of the Turks, the adversaries of their sect and monarchy. But the same Christians were the enemies of the prophet; and from the overthrow of Nice and Antioch, the motive of their enterprise, which was gradually understood, would urge them forward to the banks of the Jordan, or perhaps of the Nile. An intercourse of epistles and embassies, which rose and fell with the events of war, was maintained between the throne of Cairo and the camp of the Latins; and their adverse pride was the result of ignorance and enthusiasm. The ministers of Egypt declared in an haughty, or insinuated in a milder, tone that their sovereign, the true and lawful commander of the faithful, had rescued Jerusalem from the Turkish yoke; and that the pilgrims, if they would divide their numbers and lay aside their arms, should find a safe and hospitable reception at the sepulchre of Jesus. In the belief of their lost condition, the caliph Mostali despised their arms and imprisoned their deputies: the conquest and victory of Antioch prompted him to solicit those formidable champions with gifts of horses and silk robes, of vases, and purses of gold and silver; and, in his estimate of their merit or power, the first place was assigned to Bohemond, and the second to Godfrey. In either fortune the answer of the crusaders was firm and uniform: they disdained

---

[107] The emir, or sultan [really vezîr; called sultân in Egypt under the Fâtimids], Aphdal recovered Jerusalem and Tyre, A.H. 489 [1096] (Renaudot, Hist. Patriarch. Alexandrin. p. 478; De Guignes, tom. i. p. 249, from Abulfeda and Ben Schounah). Jerusalem ante adventum vestrum recuperavimus, Turcos ejecimus, say the Fatimite ambassadors.

to inquire into the private claims or possessions of the followers of Mahomet: whatsoever was his name or nation, the usurper of Jerusalem was their enemy; and, instead of prescribing the mode and terms of their pilgrimage, it was only by a timely surrender of the city and province, their sacred right, that he could deserve their alliance or deprecate their impending and irresistible attack.[108]

Delay of the Franks, A.D. 1098, July—A.D. 1099, May Yet this attack, when they were within the view and reach of their glorious prize, was suspended above ten months after the defeat of Kerboga. The zeal and courage of the crusaders were chilled in the moment of victory: and, instead of marching to improve the consternation, they hastily dispersed to enjoy the luxury, of Syria. The causes of this strange delay may be found in the want of strength and subordination. In the painful and various service of Antioch the cavalry was annihilated; many thousands of every rank had been lost by famine, sickness, and desertion; the same abuse of plenty had been productive of a third famine; and the alternative of intemperance and distress had generated a pestilence, which swept away above fifty thousand of the pilgrims. Few were able to command and none were willing to obey: the domestic feuds, which had been stifled by common fear, were again renewed in acts, or at least in sentiments, of hostility; the future of Baldwin and Bohemond excited the envy of their companions; the bravest knights were enlisted for the defence of their new principalities; and count Raymond exhausted his troops and treasures in an idle expedition into the heart of Syria.[109] The winter was consumed in discord and disorder; a sense of honour and religion was rekindled in the spring; and the private soldiers, less susceptible of ambition and jealousy, awakened with angry clamours

Their march to Jerusalem. A.D. 1099, May 13—June 6 the indolence of their chiefs. In the month of May, the relics of this mighty host proceeded from Antioch to Laodicea: about forty thousand Latins, of whom no more than fifteen hundred horse and twenty thousand foot were capable of immediate service. Their easy march was continued between Mount

---

[108] See the transactions between the caliphs of Egypt and the crusaders, in William of Tyre (l. iv. c. 24, l. vi. c. 19) and Albert Aquensis (l. iii. c. 59), who are more sensible of their importance than the contemporary writers.

[109] [Raymond captured Albara, and one of his men captured [the village of] Tell Mannas. They also attacked Maarra, but did not take it at the first attempt. Raymond and Bohemond captured it in December.]

Libanus and the sea-shore; their wants were liberally supplied by the coasting traders of Genoa and Pisa; and they drew large contributions from the emirs of Tripoli, Tyre, Sidon, Acre, and Cæsarea, who granted a free passage and promised to follow the example of Jerusalem. From Cæsarea [110] they advanced into the midland country; their clerks recognised the sacred geography of Lydda, Ramla, Emaus, and Bethlem; and, as soon as they descried the holy city, the crusaders forgot their toils, and claimed their reward.[111]

Jerusalem has derived some reputation from the number and importance of her memorable sieges. It was not till after a long and obstinate contest that Babylon and Rome could prevail against the obstinacy of the people, the craggy ground that might supersede the necessity of fortifications, and the walls and towers that would have fortified the most accessible plain.[112] These obstacles were diminished in the age of the crusades. The bulwarks had been completely destroyed, and imperfectly restored; the Jews, their nation and worship, were for ever banished; but nature is less changeable than man, and the site of Jerusalem, though somewhat softened and somewhat removed, was still strong against the assaults of an enemy. By the experience of a recent siege, and a three years' possession, the Saracens of Egypt had been taught to discern, and in some degree to remedy, the defects of a place which religion, as well as honour, forbade them to resign. Aladin or Iftikhar, the caliph's lieutenant, was entrusted with the defence; his policy strove to restrain the native Christians by the dread of their own ruin and that of the holy sepulchre; to animate the Moslems by the assurance of temporal and eternal rewards. His garrison is said to have consisted of forty thousand Turks and Arabians; and, if he could muster twenty thousand of the inhabitants, it must be confessed that the besieged were more

Siege and conquest of Jerusalem. A.D. 1099, June 7—July 15

[Iftikhar ad-dawla]

---

[110] [Before they reached Caesarea they were delayed by a three months' siege of Arka (a strong citadel under Mt. Lebanon, not far from Tripolis), which they left untaken.]

[111] The greatest part of the march of the Franks is traced, and most accurately traced, in Maundrell's Journey from Aleppo to Jerusalem (p. 11-67): un des meilleurs morceaux, sans contredit, qu'on ait dans ce genre (d'Anville, Mémoire sur Jérusalem, p. 27).

[112] See the masterly description of Tacitus (Hist. v. 11, 12, 13), who supposes that the Jewish lawgivers had provided for a perpetual state of hostility against the rest of mankind.

numerous than the besieging army.[113]   Had the diminished strength and numbers of the Latins allowed them to grasp the whole circumference of four thousand yards (about two English miles and a half),[114] to what useful purpose should they have descended into the valley of Ben Hinnom and torrent of Kedron,[115] or approached the precipices of the south and east, from whence they had nothing either to hope or fear?   Their siege was more reasonably directed against the northern and western sides of the city.   Godfrey of Bouillon erected his standard on the first swell of Mount Calvary; to the left, as far as St. Stephen's gate, the line of attack was continued by Tancred and the two Roberts; and count Raymond established his quarters from the citadel to the foot of Mount Sion, which was no longer included within the precincts of the city.   On the fifth day, the crusaders made a general assault, in the fanatic hope of battering down the walls without engines, and of scaling them without ladders.   By the dint of brutal force they burst the first barrier, but they were driven back with shame and slaughter to the camp; the influence of vision and prophecy was deadened by the too frequent abuse of those pious stratagems; and time and labour were found to be the only means of victory.   The time of the siege was indeed fulfilled in forty days, but they were forty days of calamity and anguish.   A repetition of the old complaint of famine may be imputed in some degree to the voracious or disorderly appetite of the Franks; but the stony soil of Jerusalem is almost destitute of

[113] The lively scepticism of Voltaire is balanced with sense and erudition by the French author of the Esprit des Croisades (tom. iv. p. 386-388), who observes that, according to the Arabians, the inhabitants of Jerusalem must have exceeded 200,000; that in the siege of Titus, Josephus collects 1,300,000 Jews; that they are stated by Tacitus himself at 600,000; and that the largest defalcation that his *accepimus* can justify will still leave them more numerous than the Roman army.

[114] Maundrell, who diligently perambulated the walls, found a circuit of 4630 paces, or 4167 English yards (p. 109, 110); from an authentic plan, d'Anville concludes a measure nearly similar, of 1960 French *toises* (p. 23-29), in his scarce and valuable tract.   For the topography of Jerusalem, see Reland (Palestina, tom. ii. p. 832-860).   [Cp. above, vol. 2, p. 479.   Guy Le Strange, Palestine under the Muslims, p. 83-223.]

[115] Jerusalem was possessed only of the torrent of Kedron, dry in summer, and of the little spring or brook of Siloe (Reland, tom. i. p. 294, 300).   Both strangers and natives complained of the want of water, which, in time of war, was studiously aggravated.   Within the city, Tacitus mentions a perennial fountain, an aqueduct, and cisterns for rain-water.   The aqueduct was conveyed from the rivulet Tekoe [Tekûa, 10 miles south of Jerusalem], or Etham, which is likewise mentioned by Bohadin (in Vit. Saladin. p. 238 [c. 157]).

water; the scanty springs and hasty torrents were dry in the summer season; nor was the thirst of the besiegers relieved, as in the city, by the artificial supply of cisterns and aqueducts. The circumjacent country is equally destitute of trees for the uses of shade or building; but some large beams were discovered in a cave by the crusaders: a wood near Sichem, the enchanted grove of Tasso,[116] was cut down; the necessary timber was transported to the camp, by the vigour and dexterity of Tancred; and the engines were framed by some Genoese artists, who had fortunately landed in the harbour of Jaffa. Two moveable turrets were constructed at the expense, and in the stations, of the duke of Lorraine and the count of Toulouse, and rolled forwards with devout labour, not to the most accessible, but to the most neglected, parts of the fortification. Raymond's tower was reduced to ashes by the fire of the besieged; but his colleague was more vigilant and successful; the enemies were driven by his archers from the rampart; the draw-bridge was let down; and on a Friday, at three in the [July 15] afternoon, the day and hour of the Passion, Godfrey of Bouillon stood victorious on the walls of Jerusalem. His example was followed on every side by the emulation of valour; and, about four hundred and sixty years after the conquest of Omar, the holy city was rescued from the Mahometan yoke. In the pillage of public and private wealth, the adventurers had agreed to respect the exclusive property of the first occupant; and the spoils of the great mosque, seventy lamps and massy vases of gold and silver, rewarded the diligence, and displayed the generosity, of Tancred. A bloody sacrifice was offered by his mistaken votaries to the God of the Christians; resistance might provoke, but neither age nor sex could mollify, their implacable rage; they indulged themselves three days in a promiscuous massacre;[117] and the infection of the dead bodies produced an epidemic disease. After seventy thousand Moslems had been put to the sword, and the harmless Jews had been burnt in their synagogue, they could still reserve a multitude of captives whom interest or lassitude persuaded them to

[116] Gierusalemme Liberata, canto xiii. It is pleasant enough to observe how Tasso has copied and embellished the minutest details of the siege.
[117] Besides the Latins, who are not ashamed of the massacre, see Elmacin (Hist. Saracen. p. 363), Abulpharagius (Dynast. p. 243), and M. de Guignes (tom. ii. p. ii. p. 99), from Aboulmahasen.

spare.   Of these savage heroes of the cross, Tancred alone betrayed some sentiments of compassion; yet we may praise the
more selfish lenity of Raymond, who granted a capitulation and
safe-conduct to the garrison of the citadel.[118]   The holy sepulchre was now free; and the bloody victors prepared to accomplish their vow.   Bareheaded and barefoot, with contrite hearts,
and in an humble posture, they ascended the hill of Calvary,
amidst the loud anthems of the clergy; kissed the stone which
had covered the Saviour of the world; and bedewed with tears
of joy and penitence the monument of their redemption.   This
union of the fiercest and most tender passions has been variously
considered by two philosophers: by the one,[119] as easy and
natural; by the other,[120] as absurd and incredible.   Perhaps it
is too rigorously applied to the same persons and the same hour:
the example of the virtuous Godfrey awakened the piety of his
companions; while they cleansed their bodies, they purified
their minds; nor shall I believe that the most ardent in
slaughter and rapine were the foremost in the procession to
the holy sepulchre.

Election
and reign
of Godfrey
of Bouil-
lon. A.D.
1099, July
23—A.D.
1100, July
18
Eight days after this memorable event, which Pope Urban
did not live to hear, the Latin chiefs proceeded to the election
of a king, to guard and govern their conquests in Palestine.
Hugh the Great and Stephen of Chartres had retired with some
loss of reputation, which they strove to regain by a second
crusade and an honourable death.   Baldwin was established at
Edessa, and Bohemond at Antioch; and the two Roberts, the
duke of Normandy[121] and the count of Flanders, preferred
their fair inheritance in the West to a doubtful competition or
a barren sceptre.   The jealousy and ambition of Raymond
were condemned by his own followers, and the free, the just,
the unanimous voice of the army proclaimed Godfrey of Bouillon

---

[118] The old tower Psephina, in the middle ages Neblosa, was named Castellum
Pisanum, from the patriarch Daimbert.   It is still the citadel, the residence of the
Turkish aga, and commands a prospect of the Dead Sea, Judea, and Arabia
(D'Anville, p. 19-23).   It was likewise called the Tower of David, πύργος παμμε-
γεθέστατος. [The Phasael of Josephus, B. J. 5, 4, 3.]

[119] Hume, in his History of England, vol. i. p. 311, 312, octavo edition.

[120] Voltaire, in his Essai sur l'Histoire Générale, tom. ii. c. 54, p. 345, 346.

[121] The English ascribe to Robert of Normandy, and the Provincials to Raymond of Toulouse, the glory of refusing the crown; but the honest voice of tradition has preserved the memory of the ambition and revenge (Villehardouin, No.
136) of the count of St. Giles.   He died at the siege of Tripoli, which was possessed
by his descendants.

the first and most worthy of the champions of Christendom. His magnanimity accepted a trust as full of danger as of glory; but in a city where his Saviour had been crowned with thorns the devout pilgrim rejected the name and ensigns of royalty; and the founder of the kingdom of Jerusalem contented himself with the modest title of Defender and Baron of the Holy Sepulchre. His government of a single year,[122] too short for the public happiness, was interrupted in the first fortnight by a summons to the field, by the approach of the vizir or sultan of Egypt, who had been too slow to prevent, but who was impatient to avenge, the loss of Jerusalem. His total overthrow in the battle of Ascalon sealed the establishment of the Latins in Syria, and signalised the valour of the French princes, who, in this action, bade a long farewell to the holy wars. Some glory might be derived from the prodigious inequality of numbers, though I shall not count the myriads of horse and foot on the side of the Fatimites; but, except three thousand Ethiopians or Blacks, who were armed with flails or scourges of iron, the barbarians of the South fled on the first onset, and afforded a pleasing comparison between the active valour of the Turks and the sloth and effeminacy of the natives of Egypt. After suspending before the holy sepulchre the sword and standard of the sultan, the new king (he deserves the title) embraced his departing companions, and could retain only with the gallant Tancred three hundred knights and two thousand foot-soldiers for the defence of Palestine. His sovereignty was soon attacked by a new enemy, the only one against whom Godfrey was a coward. Adhemar, Bishop of Puy, who excelled both in council and action, had been swept away in the last plague of Antioch; the remaining ecclesiastics preserved only the pride and avarice of their character; and their seditious clamours had required that the choice of a bishop should precede that of a king. The revenue and jurisdiction of the lawful patriarch were usurped by the Latin clergy; the exclusion of the Greeks and Syrians was justified by the reproach of heresy or schism;[123] and, under the iron yoke of their deliverers, the Oriental Christians regretted the tolerating government of the Arabian caliphs.

Battle of Ascalon. A.D. 1099, August 12

---

[122] See the election, the battle of Ascalon, &c. in William of Tyre, l. ix. c. 1-12, and the conclusion of the Latin historians of the first crusade.

[123] Renaudot, Hist. Patriarch. Alex. p. 479.

Daimbert, Archbishop of Pisa, had long been trained in the secret policy of Rome : he brought a fleet of his countrymen to the succour of the Holy Land, and was installed, without a competitor, the spiritual and temporal head of the church. The new patriarch [124] immediately grasped the sceptre which had been acquired by the toil and blood of the victorious pilgrims; and both Godfrey and Bohemond submitted to receive at his hands the investiture of their feudal possessions. Nor was this sufficient; Daimbert claimed the immediate property of Jerusalem and Jaffa : instead of a firm and generous refusal, the hero negotiated with the priest; a quarter of either city was ceded to the church ; and the modest bishop was satisfied with an eventual reversion of the rest, on the death of Godfrey without children, or on the future acquisition of a new seat at Cairo or Damascus.

The king-
dom of
Jerusalem.
A.D. 1099-
1187 [6] Without this indulgence, the conqueror would have almost been stripped of his infant kingdom, which consisted only of Jerusalem and Jaffa, with about twenty villages and towns of the adjacent country.[125] Within this narrow verge, the Mahometans were still lodged in some impregnable castles; and the husbandman, the trader, and the pilgrims were exposed to daily and domestic hostility. By the arms of Godfrey himself, and of the two Baldwins, his brother and cousin, who succeeded to the throne, the Latins breathed with more ease and safety ; and at length they equalled, in the extent of their dominions, though not in the millions of their subjects, the ancient princes of Judah and Israel.[126] After the reduction of the maritime

---

[124] See the claims of the patriarch Daimbert, in William of Tyre (l. ix. c. 15-18, x. 4, 7, 9), who asserts with marvellous candour the independence of the conquerors and kings of Jerusalem. [Arnulf was first elected Patriarch, but was deposed and replaced by Daimbert. Cp. Guibertus, vii. c. 15. Albert of Aix says that Daimbert owed his election chiefly to money, collectione potens pecuniae quam electione novae ecclesiae (vii. c. 7).]

[125] Willerm. Tyr. l. x. 19. The Historia Hierosolymitana of Jacobus a Vitriaco (l. i. c. 21-50) and the Secreta Fidelium Crucis of Marinus Sanutus (l. iii. p. 1) describe the state and conquests of the Latin kingdom of Jerusalem. [The work of Marinus (edited in Bongarsius, ii. p. 1 sqq.) was written A.D. 1306-1321. This Marinus Sanutus is distinguished as senior from his later namesake, author of the Chronicon Venetum. The first Book of the work of James de Vitry is printed in Bongarsius, i. p. 1047 sqq., along with Bk. iii., which is by a different author. Bk. ii. seems never to have been printed since the old edition of Moschus, 1597. For the history of the kingdom of Jerusalem, cp. below, p. 335, note 1.]

[126] An actual muster, not including the tribes of Levi and Benjamin, gave David an army of 1,300,000 or 1,574,000 fighting men ; which, with the addition of women, children, and slaves, may imply a population of thirteen millions, in a

cities of Laodicea, Tripoli, Tyre, and Ascalon,[127] which were powerfully assisted by the fleets of Venice, Genoa, and Pisa, and even of Flanders and Norway,[128] the range of sea-coast from Scanderoon to the borders of Egypt was possessed by the Christian pilgrims. If the prince of Antioch [129] disclaimed his supremacy, the counts of Edessa and Tripoli owned themselves the vassals of the king of Jerusalem : the Latins reigned beyond the Euphrates ; and the four cities of Hems, Hamah, Damascus, and Aleppo were the only relics of the Mahometan conquests in Syria.[130] The laws and language, the manners and titles, of the French nation and Latin church, were introduced into these transmarine colonies. According to the feudal jurisprudence, the principal states and subordinate baronies descended in the line of male and female succession ; [131] but the children of the first conquerors,[132] a motley and degenerate race,

country sixty leagues in length and thirty broad. The honest and rational Le Clerc (Comment. on 2 Samuel xxiv. and 1 Chronicles xxi.) æstuat angusto in limite, and mutters his suspicion of a false transcript,—a dangerous suspicion !

[127] These sieges are related, each in its proper place, in the great history of William of Tyre, from the ixth to the xviiith book, and more briefly told by Bernardus Thesaurarius (de Acquisitione Terræ Sanctæ, c. 89-98, p. 732-740). Some domestic facts are celebrated in the Chronicles of Pisa, Genoa, and Venice, in the vith, ixth, and xiith tomes of Muratori. [Baldwin I. took Tripoli in 1109 and gave it to Bertram, son of Raymond of Toulouse. Tyre surrendered in 1124. The year 1143 may be taken as the central year after which the kingdom begins to decline and the Christians have to fight not for conquest but for defence. Ascalon, however, was won ten years later (1153). In 1152 the County of Edessa was surrendered to Manuel Comnenus.]

[128] Quidam populus de insulis occidentis egressus, et maxime de eâ parte quæ Norvegia dicitur. William of Tyre (l. xi. c. 14, p. 804) marks their course per Britannicum mare et Calpen to the siege of Sidon.

[129] [For the history of the principality of Antioch, which deserves more attention than it has received, see E. Rey's Résumé chronologique de la histoire des princes d'Antioche, in the Revue de l'Orient Latin, iv. 321 sqq. (1896). The Bella Antiochena of Gualterius Cancellarius was printed in Bongarsius (vol. i.), but an improved text is published in the Recueil, vol. v. p. 81 sqq., and there is a new ed. by Hagenmeyer (1896).]

[130] Benelathir, apud de Guignes, Hist. des Huns, tom. ii. part ii. p. 150, 151, A.D. 1127. He must speak of the inland country.

[131] Sanut very sensibly descants on the mischiefs of female succession in a land, hostibus circumdata, ubi cuncta virilia et virtuosa esse deberent. Yet, at the summons, and with the approbation, of her feudal lord, a noble damsel was obliged to choose a husband and champion (Assises de Jérusalem, c. 242, &c.). See in M. de Guignes (tom. i. p. 441-471) the accurate and useful tables of these dynasties, which are chiefly drawn from the Lignages d'Outremer.

[132] They were called by derision Poullains, Pullani, and their name is never pronounced without contempt (Ducange, Gloss. Latin. tom. v. p. 535 ; and Observations sur Joinville, p. 84, 85 ; Jacob. à Vitriaco, Hist. Hierosol. l. i. c. 67, 72 ; and Sanut, l. iii. c. viii. c. 2, p. 182). Illustrium virorum qui ad Terræ Sanctæ . . . liberationem in ipsâ manserunt degeneres filii . . . in deliciis enutriti, molles et effœminati, &c. [The word does not necessarily imply mixture of blood ; it is

were dissolved by luxury of the climate; the arrival of new crusaders from Europe was a doubtful hope and a casual event. The service of the feudal tenures [133] was performed by six hundred and sixty-six knights, who might expect the aid of two hundred more under the banner of the count of Tripoli; and each knight was attended to the field by four squires or archers on horseback.[134] Five thousand and seventy-five *serjeants*, most probably foot-soldiers, were supplied by the churches and the cities; and the whole legal militia of the kingdom could not exceed eleven thousand men, a slender defence against the surrounding myriads of Saracens and Turks.[135] But the firmest bulwark of Jerusalem was founded on the knights of the Hospital of St. John,[136] and of the temple of Solomon; [137] on the strange association of a monastic and military life, which fanaticism might suggest, but which policy must approve. The

"used loosely as we use the word Creole" (Stubbs in Glossary to Itin. Regis Ricardi, p. 455).]

[133] This authentic detail is extracted from the Assises de Jérusalem (c. 324, 326-331). Sanut (l. iii. p. viii. c. i. p. 174) reckons only 518 knights and 5775 followers.

[134] The sum-total, and the division, ascertain the service of the three great baronies at 100 knights each; and the text of the Assises, which extends the number to 500, can only be justified by this supposition.

[135] Yet on great emergencies (says Sanut) the barons brought a voluntary aid; decentem comitivam militum juxta statum suum.

[136] William of Tyre (l. xviii. c. 3, 4, 5) relates the ignoble origin and early insolence of the Hospitalers, who soon deserted their humble patron, St. John the Eleemosynary, for the more august character of St. John the Baptist. (See the ineffectual struggles of Pagi, Critica, A.D. 1099, No. 14-18.) They assumed the profession of arms about the year 1120; the Hospital was *mater*, the Temple *filia;* the Teutonic order was founded A.D. 1190, at the siege of Acre (Mosheim, Institut. p. 389, 390). [The order of the Temple was founded about 1118. The Hospital was an older foundation, instituted by merchants of Amalfi for the relief of sick pilgrims; but as a military order it was younger than the Temple; in fact it was the foundation of the Templars which suggested the transformation of the Hospital into a military order. The Templars were distinguished by a white cloak and red cross, the Hospitallers by a white cross. Stubbs, dwelling on the degeneration of the Franks in Palestine at the time of the Second or Third Crusade, observes: "The only sound element in the country was the organization of the military orders. These procured a constant succession of fresh and healthy blood from Europe, they were not liable to the evils of minorities, their selfish interests were bound up with the strength of the kingdom. If one grand master fell another took his place. . . . It may be safely said that if Palestine could have been recovered and maintained by the Western powers it would have been by the knights of the Temple and the Hospital. If their system had been adopted, Palestine might have been still in Christian hands; or at least have continued so as long as Cyprus" (Introduction to Itin. Regis Ricardi, p. cvi. cvii.).]

[137] See St. Bernard de Laude Novæ Militiæ Templi, composed A.D. 1132-1136, in Opp. tom. i. p. ii. p. 547-563, edit. Mabillon. Venet. 1750. Such an encomium, which is thrown away on the dead Templars, would be highly valued by the historians of Malta.

flower of the nobility of Europe aspired to wear the cross, and to profess the vows, of these respectable orders; their spirit and discipline were immortal; and the speedy donation of twenty-eight thousand farms, or manors,[138] enabled them to support a regular force of cavalry and infantry for the defence of Palestine. The austerity of the convent soon evaporated in the exercise of arms; the world was scandalized by the pride, avarice, and corruption of these Christian soldiers; their claims of immunity and jurisdiction disturbed the harmony of the church and state; and the public peace was endangered by their jealous emulation. But in their most dissolute period, the knights of the Hospital and Temple maintained their fearless and fanatic character; they neglected to live, but they were prepared to die, in the service of Christ; and the spirit of chivalry, the parent and offspring of the crusades, has been transplanted by this institution from the holy sepulchre to the isle of Malta.[139]

The spirit of freedom, which pervades the feudal institutions, was felt in its strongest energy by the volunteers of the cross, who elected for their chief the most deserving of his peers. Amidst the slaves of Asia, unconscious of the lesson or example, a model of political liberty was introduced; and the laws of the French kingdom are derived from the purest source of equality and justice. Of such laws, the first and indispensable condition is the assent of those whose obedience they require, and for whose benefit they are designed. No sooner had Godfrey of Bouillon accepted the office of supreme magistrate than he solicited the public and private advice of the Latin pilgrims who were the best skilled in the statutes and customs of Europe. From these materials, with the counsel and approbation of the patriarch and barons, of the clergy and laity, Godfrey, composed the ASSISE OF JERUSALEM,[140] a precious monument of

Assise of Jerusalem. A.D. 1099-1369

---

[138] Matthew Paris, Hist. Major, p. 544. He assigns to the Hospitalers 19,000, to the Templars 9000 *maneria*, a word of much higher import (as Ducange has rightly observed) in the English than in the French idiom. *Manor* is a lordship *manoir* a dwelling.

[139] In the three first books of the Histoire des Chevaliers de Malthe, par l'Abbé de Vertot, the reader may amuse himself with a fair, and sometimes flattering, picture of the order, while it was employed for the defence of Palestine. The subsequent books pursue their emigrations to Rhodes and Malta.

[140] The Assises de Jérusalem, in old Law-French, were printed with Beaumanoir's Coutumes de Beauvoisis (Bourges and Paris, 1690, in folio), and illustrated by Gaspard Thaumas de la Thaumassière, with a comment and glossary. An

feudal jurisprudence. The new code, attested by the seals of
the king, the patriarch, and the viscount of Jerusalem, was
deposited in the holy sepulchre, enriched with the improvements of succeeding times, and respectfully consulted as often
as any doubtful question arose in the tribunals of Palestine.
With the kingdom and city all was lost; [141] the fragments of the
written law were preserved by jealous tradition,[142] and variable
practice, till the middle of the thirteenth century; the code
was restored by the pen of John d'Ibelin, count of Jaffa, one of
the principal feudatories; [143] and the final revision was accomplished in the year thirteen hundred and sixty-nine, for the use
of the Latin kingdom of Cyprus.[144]

Court of
peers

The justice and freedom of the constitution were maintained
by two tribunals of unequal dignity, which were instituted by
Godfrey of Bouillon after the conquest of Jerusalem. The
king, in person, presided in the upper court, the court of the
barons. Of these the four most conspicuous were the prince of
Galilee, the lord of Sidon and Cæsarea, and the counts of Jaffa
and Tripoli, who, perhaps with the constable and marshal,[145]

Italian version had been published in 1535, at Venice, for the use of the kingdom
of Cyprus. [The authoritative edition is that of the Comte de Beugnot : vol. i.
Assises de la Haute Cour, 1841; vol. ii. Assises de la Cour des bourgeois, 1843.]

[141] A la terre perdue, tout fut perdu, is the vigorous expression of the Assise (c.
281 [see Beugnot, vol. i. c. 47 in the Livre de Philippe de Navarre, p. 522 ; la
lettre fust perdue—et tout ce fust perdu quant Saladin prist Jerusalem]). Yet
Jerusalem capitulated with Saladin : the queen and the principal Christians departed in peace; and a code so precious and so portable could not provoke the
avarice of the conquerors. I have sometimes suspected the existence of this
original copy of the Holy Sepulchre, which might be invented to sanctify and
authenticate the traditionary customs of the French in Palestine. [See Appendix
16.]

[142] A noble lawyer, Raoul de Tabarie, denied the prayer of King Amauri (A.D.
1195-1205), that he would commit his knowledge to writing ; and frankly declared,
que de ce qu'il savoit ne feroit-il ja nul borjois son pareill, ne nul sage homme
lettré (c. 281).

[143] The compiler of this work, Jean d'Ibelin, was Count of Jaffa and Ascalon,
Lord of Baruth (Berytus) and Rames, and died A.D. 1266 (Sanut, l. iii. p. xii. c. 5,
8). The family of Ibelin, which descended from a younger brother of a count of
Chartres in France, long flourished in Palestine and Cyprus (see the Lignages de
de-ça Mer, or d'Outremer, c. 6, at the end of the Assises de Jérusalem, an original
book, which records the pedigrees of the French adventurers).

[144] By sixteen commissioners chosen in the states of the island, the work was
finished the 3d of November, 1369, sealed with four seals, and deposited in the
cathedral of Nicosia (see the preface to the Assises).

[145] The cautious John d'Ibelin argues, rather than affirms, that Tripoli is the
fourth barony, and expresses some doubt concerning the right or pretension of the
constable and marshal (c. 323 [c. 269, cp. c. 271]). [Tripoli was the fourth fief of
the *kingdom* of Jerusalem, but it was not a barony of the *principality* of Jerusalem.
The four fiefs of the kingdom were : (1) the principality of Jerusalem ; (2) the

were in a special manner the compeers and judges of each other. But all the nobles, who held their lands immediately of the crown, were entitled and bound to attend the king's court; and each baron exercised a similar jurisdiction in the subordinate assemblies of his own feudatories. The connection of lord and vassal was honourable and voluntary : reverence was due to the benefactor, protection to the dependent; but they mutually pledged their faith to each other, and the obligation on either side might be suspended by neglect or dissolved by injury. The cognisance of marriages and testaments was blended with religion and usurped by the clergy; but the civil and criminal causes of the nobles, the inheritance and tenure of their fiefs, formed the proper occupation of the supreme court. Each member was the judge and guardian both of public and private rights. It was his duty to assert with his tongue and sword the lawful claims of the lord ; but, if an unjust superior presumed to violate the freedom or property of a vassal, the confederate peers stood forth to maintain his quarrel by sword and deed. They boldly affirmed his innocence and his wrongs ; demanded the restitution of his liberty or his lands ; suspended, after a fruitless demand, their own service ; rescued their brother from prison ; and employed every weapon in his defence, without offering direct violence to the person of their lord, which was ever sacred in their eyes.[146] In their pleadings, replies, and rejoinders, the advocates of the court were subtile and copious ; but the use of argument and evidence was often superseded by judicial combat ; and the Assise of Jerusalem admits in many cases this barbarous institution, which has been slowly abolished by the laws and manners of Europe.

principality of Antioch ; (3) the county of Edessa ; (4) the county of Tripoli. The four baronies of the principality were : (1) the principality of Galilee ; (2) the lordship of Sidon and Cæsarea (Cæsarea being held as a fief of Sidon) ; (3) the county of Jaffa and Ascalon ; (4) the principality of Hebron or St. Abraham, to which was afterwards joined the lordship of Kerak and Montreal beyond the Jordan (including all the south of Palestine except Ascalon). There is a good map of the Principality of Jerusalem in the Eng. tr. of Behā ad-din in the Palestine Pilgrims Text Society.]
[146] Entre seignor et homme ne n'a que la foi ; . . . mais tant que l'homme doit à son seignor reverence en toutes choses (c. 206). Tous les hommes dudit royaume sont par la dite Assise tenus les uns as autres . . . et en celle manière que le seignor mette main ou face mettre au cors ou au fié d'aucun d'yaus sans esgard et sans connoissance de court, que tous les autres doivent venir devant le seignor, &c. (212). The form of their remonstrances is conceived with the noble simplicity of freedom.

Law of
judicial
combats
The trial by battle was established in all criminal cases which affected the life or limb or honour of any person; and in all civil transactions of or above the value of one mark of silver. It appears that in criminal cases the combat was the privilege of the accuser, who, except in a charge of treason, avenged his personal injury or the death of those persons whom he had a right to represent; but, wherever, from the nature of the charge, testimony could be obtained, it was necessary for him to produce witnesses of the fact. In civil cases, the combat was not allowed as the means of establishing the claim of the demandant; but he was obliged to produce witnesses who had, or assumed to have, knowledge of the fact. The combat was then the privilege of the defendant; because he charged the witness with an attempt by perjury to take away his right. He came, therefore, to be in the same situation as the appellant in criminal cases. It was not, then, as a mode of proof that the combat was received, nor as making negative evidence (according to the supposition of Montesquieu); [147] but in every case the right to offer battle was founded on the right to pursue by arms the redress of an injury; and the judicial combat was fought on the same principle, and with the same spirit, as a private duel. Champions were only allowed to women, and to men maimed or past the age of sixty. The consequence of a defeat was death to the person accused, or to the champion or witness, as well as to the accuser himself; but in civil cases the demandant was punished with infamy and the loss of his suit, while his witness and champion suffered an ignominious death. In many cases, it was in the option of the judge to award or to refuse the combat; but two are specified in which it was the inevitable result of the challenge: if a faithful vassal gave the lie to his compeer, who unjustly claimed any portion of their lord's demesnes; or if an unsuccessful suitor presumed to impeach the judgment and veracity of the court. He might impeach them, but the terms were severe and perilous: in the same day he successively fought *all* the members of the tribunal, even those who had been absent; a single defeat was followed by death and infamy; and, where none could hope for victory, it is highly probable that none would adventure the

---

[147] See l'Esprit des Loix, l. xxviii. In the forty years since its publication, no work has been more read and criticized; and the spirit of inquiry which it has excited is not the least of our obligations to the author.

trial. In the Assise of Jerusalem, the legal subtlety of the count of Jaffa is more laudably employed to elude, than to facilitate, the judicial combat, which he derives from a principle of honour rather than of superstition.[148]

Among the causes which enfranchised the plebeians from the yoke of feudal tyranny, the institution of cities and corporations is one of the most powerful; and, if those of Palestine are co-eval with the first crusade, they may be ranked with the most ancient of the Latin world. Many of the pilgrims had escaped from their lords under the banner of the cross; and it was the policy of the French princes to tempt their stay by the assurance of the rights and privileges of freemen. It is expressly declared in the Assise of Jerusalem that, after instituting, for his knights and barons, the court of Peers, in which he presided himself, Godfrey of Bouillon established a second tribunal, in which his person was represented by his viscount. The jurisdiction of this inferior court extended over the burgesses of the kingdom; and it was composed of a select number of the most discreet and worthy citizens, who were sworn to judge, according to the laws, of the actions and fortunes of their equals.[149] In the conquest and settlement of new cities, the example of Jerusalem was imitated by the kings and their great vassals; and above thirty similar corporations were founded before the loss of the Holy Land. Another class of subjects, the Syrians,[150] or Oriental Christians, were oppressed by the zeal of the clergy, and pro-tected by the toleration of the state. Godfrey listened to their reasonable prayer that they might be judged by their own national laws. A third court was instituted for their use, of limited and domestic jurisdiction; the sworn members were Syrians, in blood, language, and religion; but the office of the president (in Arabic, of the *rais*) was sometimes exercised by

Court of burgesses

Syrians

[148] For the intelligence of this obscure and obsolete jurisprudence (c. 80-111), I am deeply indebted to the friendship of a learned lord, who, with an accurate and discerning eye, has surveyed the philosophic history of law. By his studies, posterity might be enriched; the merit of the orator and the judge can be *felt* only by his contemporaries. [The reference is to Lord Loughborough.]

[149] Louis le Gros, who is considered as the father of this institution in France, did not begin his reign till nine years (A.D. 1108) after Godfrey of Bouillon (Assises, p. 2, 324). For its origin and effects, see the judicious remarks of Dr. Robertson (History of Charles V. vol. i. p. 30-36, 251-265, quarto edition).

[150] Every reader conversant with the historians of the crusades, will understand, by the peuple des Suriens, the Oriental Christians, Melchites, Jacobites, or Nesto-rians, who had all adopted the use of the Arabic language (vol. v. p. 151).

the viscount of the city. At an immeasurable distance below
the *nobles*, the *burgesses*, and the *strangers*, the Assise of Jerusalem condescends to mention the *villains* and *slaves*, the
peasants of the land and the captives of war, who were almost
equally considered as the objects of property. The relief or
protection of these unhappy men was not esteemed worthy of
the care of the legislator; but he diligently provides for the
recovery, though not indeed for the punishment, of the fugitives.
Like hounds, or hawks, who had strayed from the lawful owner,
they might be lost and claimed; the slave and falcon were of the
same value; but three slaves, or twelve oxen, were accumulated
to equal the price of the war-horse; and a sum of three hundred
pieces of gold was fixed, in the age of chivalry, as the equivalent
of the more noble animal.[151]

[151] See the Assises de Jérusalem (310-312). These laws were enacted as late as
the year 1358, in the kingdom of Cyprus. In the same century, in the reign of
Edward I., I understand, from a late publication (of his Book of Account), that the
price of a war-horse was not less exorbitant in England.

CHAPTER LIX

Preservation of the Greek Empire—Numbers, Passage, and Event of the Second and Third Crusades—St. Bernard —Reign of Saladin in Egypt and Syria—His Conquest of Jerusalem—Naval Crusades—Richard the First of England—Pope Innocent the Third; and the Fourth and Fifth Crusades—The Emperor Frederic the Second— Louis the Ninth of France; and the two last Crusades— Expulsion of the Latins or Franks by the Mamelukes

IN a style less grave than that of history, I should perhaps compare the Emperor Alexius [1] to the jackal, who is said to follow the steps, and to devour the leavings, of the lion. Whatever had been his fears and toils in the passage of the first crusade, they were amply recompensed by the subsequent benefits which he derived from the exploits of the Franks. His dexterity and vigilance secured their first conquest of Nice ; and from this threatening station the Turks were compelled to evacuate the neighbourhood of Constantinople. While the crusaders, with blind valour, advanced into the midland countries of Asia, the crafty Greek improved the favourable occasion when the emirs of the sea-coast were recalled to the standard of the Sultan. The Turks were driven from the isles of Rhodes and Chios : the cities of Ephesus and Smyrna, of Sardes, Philadelphia, and Laodicea, were restored to the empire, which Alexius enlarged from the Hellespont to the banks of the Mæander and the rocky shores of Pamphylia. The churches resumed their splendour ; the towns were rebuilt and fortified ;

Success of Alexius.
A.D. 1097-1118

---

[1] Anna Comnena relates her father's conquests in Asia Minor, Alexiad, l. xi. p. 321-325 [c. 5, 6], l. xiv. p. 419 [c. 1]; his Cilician war against Tancred and Bohemond, p. 328-342 [c. 7-12]; the war of Epirus, with tedious prolixity, l. xii. xiii. [c. 1-12], p. 345-406 ; the death of Bohemond, l. xiv. p. 419 [c. 1]. [The best complete history of the events described in this Chapter, from A.D. 1100 to 1291, is the work of Röhricht, Die Geschichte des Königreichs Jerusalem, 1898. See also W. B. Stevenson, the Crusaders in the East, 1907.]

and the desert country was peopled with colonies of Christians, who were gently removed from the more distant and dangerous frontier. In these paternal cares, we may forgive Alexius, if he forgot the deliverance of the holy sepulchre ; but, by the Latins, he was stigmatized with the foul reproach of treason and desertion. They had sworn fidelity and obedience to his throne ; but *he* had promised to assist their enterprise in person, or, at least, with his troops and treasures; his base retreat dissolved their obligations ; and the sword, which had been the instrument of their victory, was the pledge and title of their just independence. It does not appear that the emperor attempted to revive his obsolete claims over the kingdom of Jerusalem ;[2] but the borders of Cilicia and Syria were more recent in his possession, and more accessible to his arms. The great army of the crusaders was annihilated or dispersed ; the principality of Antioch was left without a head, by the surprise and captivity of Bohemond : his ransom had oppressed him with a heavy debt ; and his Norman followers were insufficient to repel the hostilities of the Greeks and Turks. In this distress, Bohemond embraced a magnanimous resolution, of leaving the defence of Antioch to his kinsman, the faithful Tancred, of arming the West against the Byzantine empire, and of executing the design which he inherited from the lessons and example of his father Guiscard. His embarkation was clandestine ; and, if we may credit a tale of the Princess Anne, he passed the hostile sea closely secreted in a coffin.[3] But his reception in France was dignified by the public applause and his marriage with the king's daughter ; his return was glorious, since the bravest spirits of the age enlisted under his veteran command ; and he repassed the Adriatic at the head of five thousand horse and forty thousand foot, assembled from the most remote climates of Europe.[4] The strength of Durazzo and prudence of Alexius,

---

[2] The kings of Jerusalem submitted, however, to a nominal dependence ; and in the dates of their inscriptions (one is still legible in the church of Bethlem) they respectfully placed before their own the name of the reigning emperor (Ducange, Dissertations sur Joinville, xxvii. p. 319).

[3] Anna Comnena adds that, to complete the imitation, he was shut up with a dead cock ; and condescends to wonder how the barbarian could endure the confinement and putrefaction. This absurd tale is unknown to the Latins.

[4] 'Απὸ Θούλης [Anna, xii. c. 9, cp. ii. c. 9], in the Byzantine Geography, must mean England ; yet we are more credibly informed that our Henry I. would not suffer him to levy any troops in his kingdom (Ducange, Not. ad Alexiad. p. 41).

the progress of famine and approach of winter, eluded his ambitious hopes ; and the venal confederates were seduced from his standard. A treaty of peace[5] suspended the fears of the Greeks ; and they were finally delivered by the death of an adversary whom neither oaths could bind nor dangers could appal nor prosperity could satiate. His children succeeded to the principality of Antioch ; but the boundaries were strictly defined, the homage was clearly stipulated, and the cities of Tarsus and Malmistra[6] were restored to the Byzantine emperors. Of the coast of Anatolia, they possessed the entire circuit from Trebizond to the Syrian gates. The Seljukian dynasty of Roum[7] was separated on all sides from the sea and their Musulman brethren ; the power of the sultans was shaken by the victories, and even the defeats, of the Franks; and after the loss of Nice they removed their throne to Cogni or Iconium, an obscure and inland town above three hundred miles from Constantinople.[8] Instead of trembling for their capital, the Comnenian princes waged an offensive war against the Turks, and the first crusade prevented the fall of the declining empire.

In the twelfth century, three great emigrations marched by land from the West to the relief of Palestine. The soldiers and pilgrims of Lombardy, France, and Germany were excited by the example and success of the first crusade.[9] Forty-eight years after the deliverance of the holy sepulchre, the emperor

Expeditions by land : the first crusade, A.D. 1101 ; the second of Conrad III. and Louis VII. A.D. 1147 ; the third of Frederic I. A.D. 1189

[5] The copy of the treaty (Alexiad, l. xiii. p. 406-416 [c. 12]) is an original and curious piece, which would require, and might afford, a good map of the principality of Antioch.

[6] [Mopsuestia, corrupted to Mampsista, Mansista, Mamista (Anna Comnena), whence Mamistra, Malmistra. In Turkish the form has become ultimately Missis ; in Arabic it is al-Missīsa.]

[7] See in the learned work of M. de Guignes (tom. ii. part ii.) the history of the Seljukians of Iconium, Aleppo, and Damascus, as far as it may be collected from the Greeks, Latins, and Arabians. The last are ignorant or regardless of the affairs of Roum.

[8] Iconium is mentioned as a station by Xenophon, and by Strabo [xii. 6, section 1] with the ambiguous title of Κωμόπολις (Cellarius, tom. ii. p. 121). Yet St. Paul found in that place a multitude (πλῆθος) of Jews and Gentiles. Under the corrupt name of Kunijah, it is described as a great city, with a river and gardens, three leagues from the mountains, and decorated (I know not why) with Plato's tomb (Abulfeda, tabul. xvii. p. 303, vers. Reiske ; and the Index Geographicus of Schultens from Ibn Said). [It is Soatra, not Iconium, that Strabo describes as Κωμόπολις in the passage to which Cellarius refers.]

[9] For this supplement to the first crusade, see Anna Comnena (Alexias, l. xi. p. 331 [c. 8], &c.) and the viiith book of Albert Aquensis [and Ekkehard of Aura, Hierosolymita, in Recueil, Hist. Occ. vol. v.].

and the French king, Conrad the Third and Louis the Seventh, undertook the second crusade to support the falling fortunes of the Latins.[10] A grand division of the third crusade was led by the emperor Frederic Barbarossa,[11] who sympathized with his brothers of France and England in the common loss of Jerusalem. These three expeditions may be compared in their resemblance of the greatness of numbers, their passage through the Greek empire, and the nature and event of their Turkish warfare ; and a brief parallel may save the repetition of a tedious narrative. However splendid it may seem, a regular story of the crusades would exhibit a perpetual return of the same causes and effects; and the frequent attempts for the defence and recovery of the Holy Land would appear so many faint and unsuccessful copies of the original.

Their
number

I. Of the swarms that so closely trod in the footsteps of the first pilgrims, the chiefs were equal in rank, though unequal in fame and merit, to Godfrey of Bouillon and his fellow-adventurers. At their head were displayed the banners of the dukes of Burgundy, Bavaria, and Aquitain : the first a descendant of Hugh Capet, the second a father of the Brunswick line; the archbishop of Milan, a temporal prince, transported, for the benefit of the Turks, the treasures and ornaments of his church and palace; and the veteran crusaders, Hugh the Great and Stephen of Chartres, returned to consummate their unfinished vow. The huge and disorderly bodies of their followers moved forwards in two columns; and, if the first consisted of two hundred and sixty thousand persons, the second might possibly amount to sixty thousand horse and one hundred thousand

---

[10] For the second crusade of Conrad III. and Louis VII. see William of Tyre (l. xvi. c. 18-29), Otho of Frisingen (l. i. c. 34-45, 59, 60), Matthew Paris (Hist. Major, p. 68), Struvius (Corpus Hist. Germanicæ, p. 372, 373), Scriptores Rerum Francicarum a Duchesne, tom. iv. ; Nicetas, in Vit. Manuel. l. i. c. 4, 5, 6, p. 41-48 ; Cinnamus, l. ii. p. 41-49 [p. 73 sqq., ed. Bonn]. [Among the western sources, Odo de Deogilo (Deuil), De Profectione Ludovici VII. regis Francorum in orientem, is important : Migne, Patrol. Lat. vol. 185, p. 1205 sqq. For a full enumeration of the sources, see Kugler, Studien zur Geschichte des zweiten Kreuzzuges 1866.]

[11] For the third crusade, of Frederic Barbarossa, see Nicetas in Isaac. Angel l. ii. c. 3-8, p. 257-266 ; Struv. (Corpus Hist. Germ. p. 414), and two historians, who probably were spectators, Tagino (in Scriptor. Freher. tom. i. p. 406-416, edit. Struv.) and the Anonymus de Expeditione Asiaticâ Fred. I. (in Canisii Antiq Lection. tom. iii. p. ii. p. 498-526, edit. Basnage). [A. Chroust, Tageno, Ansbert und die Historia Peregrinorum, 1892. Fischer, Geschichte des Kreuzzuges Kaiser Friedrichs I., 1870.]

foot.[12]   The armies of the second crusade might have claimed
the conquest of Asia: the nobles of France and Germany were
animated by the presence of their sovereigns; and both the
rank and personal characters of Conrad and Louis gave a dignity to their cause and a discipline to their force, which might
be vainly expected from the feudatory chiefs.   The cavalry of
the emperor, and that of the king, was each composed of
seventy thousand knights and their immediate attendants in
the field,[13] and, if the light-armed troops, the peasant infantry,
the women and children, the priests and monks, be rigorously
excluded, the full account will scarcely be satisfied with four
hundred thousand souls.   The West, from Rome to Britain, was
called into action; the kings of Poland and Bohemia obeyed
the summons of Conrad; and it is affirmed by the Greeks and
Latins that, in the passage of a strait or river, the Byzantine
agents, after a tale of nine hundred thousand, desisted from the
endless and formidable computation.[14]   In the third crusade, as
the French and English preferred the navigation of the Mediterranean, the host of Frederic Barbarossa was less numerous.
Fifteen thousand knights, and as many squires, were the flower
of the German chivalry; sixty thousand horse and one hundred
thousand foot were mustered by the emperor in the plains of
Hungary; and after such repetitions we shall no longer be
startled at the six hundred thousand pilgrims which credulity
has ascribed to this last emigration.[15]   Such extravagant reckon-

---

[12] Anne, who states these later swarms at 40,000 horse, and 100,000 foot, calls
them Normans, and places at their head two brothers of Flanders. The Greeks
were strangely ignorant of the names, families, and possessions of the Latin
princes.
[13] William of Tyre, and Matthew Paris, reckon 70,000 loricati in each of the
armies. [The same number is given by the Annals of Pöhlde (ad ann. 1147),
which were first published in Pertz, Mon. Germ. Hist., xvi. p. 48 sqq., in 1859.]
[14] The imperfect enumeration is mentioned by Cinnamus (ἐννενήκοντα μυριάδες)
[in connexion with the crossing of the Danube; Nicetas (p. 87, ed. Bonn) speaks
of a numbering at the crossing of the Hellespont], and confirmed by Odo de Diogilo
apud Ducange ad Cinnamum, with the more precise sum of 900,556. [The
Annals of Magdeburg give 650,000, and the Annals of Egmond 1,600,000.] Why
must therefore the version and comment suppose the modest and insufficient
reckoning of 90,000? Does not Godfrey of Viterbo (Pantheon, p. xix. in Muratori, tom. vii. p. 462) exclaim
——Numerum si poscere quæras—
Millia millena milites agmen erat?
[15] This extravagant account is given by Albert of Stade (apud Struvium, p. 414
[Chronicon; Pertz, Mon. xvi. p. 283 sqq.]); my calculation is borrowed from
Godfrey of Viterbo, Arnold of Lubeck [Chronica Slavorum, Pertz, Mon. Germ. Hist.,
xxi. p. 115 sqq.], apud eundem, and Bernard Thesaur. (c. 169, p. 804).   The original

ings prove only the astonishment of contemporaries; but their astonishment most strongly bears testimony to the existence of an enormous though indefinite multitude. The Greeks might applaud their superior knowledge of the arts and stratagems of war, but they confessed the strength and courage of the French cavalry and the infantry of the Germans;[16] and the strangers are described as an iron race, of gigantic stature, who darted fire from their eyes, and spilt blood like water on the ground. Under the banners of Conrad, a troop of females rode in the attitude and armour of men; and the chief of these Amazons, from their gilt spurs and buskins, obtained the epithet of the Golden-footed Dame.

Passage through the Greek empire

II. The numbers and character of the strangers was an object of terror to the effeminate Greeks, and the sentiment of fear is nearly allied to that of hatred. This aversion was suspended or softened by the apprehension of the Turkish power; and the invectives of the Latins will not bias our more candid belief that the Emperor Alexius dissembled their insolence, eluded their hostilities, counselled their rashness, and opened to their ardour the road of pilgrimage and conquest. But, when the Turks had been driven from Nice and the sea-coast, when the Byzantine princes no longer dreaded the distant sultans of Cogni, they felt with purer indignation the free and frequent passage of the western barbarians, who violated the majesty, and endangered the safety, of the empire. The second and third crusades were undertaken under the reign of Manuel Comnenus and Isaac Angelus. Of the former, the passions were always impetuous and often malevolent; and the natural union of a cowardly and a mischievous temper was exemplified in the latter, who, without merit or mercy, could punish a tyrant and occupy his throne. It was secretly, and perhaps tacitly, resolved by the prince and people to destroy, or at least to discourage, the pilgrims by every species of injury and oppression; and their want of prudence and discipline continually afforded the pretence or the

writers are silent. The Mahometans gave him 200,000 or 260,000 men (Bohadin, in Vit. Saladin. p. 110).

[16] I must observe that, in the second and third crusades, the subjects of Conrad and Frederic are styled by the Greeks and Orientals *Alamanni*. The Lechi and Tzechi of Cinnamus are the Poles and Bohemians; and it is for the French that he reserves the ancient appellation of Germans. He likewise names the Βρίττιοι, or Βριταννοί [Βρίττιοί τε καὶ Βρεταινοί, ii. 12].

opportunity. The Western monarchs had stipulated a safe passage and fair market in the country of their Christian brethren ; the treaty had been ratified by oaths and hostages ; and the poorest soldier of Frederic's army was furnished with three marks of silver to defray his expenses on the road. But every engagement was violated by treachery and injustice ; and the complaints of the Latins are attested by the honest confession of a Greek historian, who has dared to prefer truth to his country.[17] Instead of an hospitable reception, the gates of the cities, both in Europe and Asia, were closely barred against the crusaders ; and the scanty pittance of food was let down in baskets from the walls. Experience or foresight might excuse this timid jealousy ; but the common duties of humanity prohibited the mixture of chalk, or other poisonous ingredients, in the bread ; and, should Manuel be acquitted of any foul connivance, he is guilty of coining base money for the purpose of trading with the pilgrims. In every step of their march they were stopped or misled : the governors had private orders to fortify the passes, and break down the bridges against them ; the stragglers were pillaged and murdered ; the soldiers and horses were pierced in the woods by arrows from an invisible hand ; the sick were burnt in their beds ; and the dead bodies were hung on gibbets along the highways. These injuries exasperated the champions of the cross, who were not endowed with evangelical patience ; and the Byzantine princes, who had provoked the unequal conflict, promoted the embarkation and march of these formidable guests. On the verge of the Turkish frontiers, Barbarossa spared the guilty Philadelphia,[18] rewarded the hospitable Laodicea, and deplored the hard necessity that had stained his sword with any drops of Christian blood. In their intercourse with the monarchs of Germany and France, the pride of the Greeks was exposed to an anxious trial. They might boast that on the first interview the seat of Louis was a low stool beside the throne of Manuel ;[19] but no sooner had the French king transported his

---

[17] Nicetas was a child at the second crusade, but in the third he commanded against the Franks the important post of Philippopolis. Cinnamus is infected with national prejudice and pride.

[18] The conduct of the Philadelphians is blamed by Nicetas, while the anonymous German accuses the rudeness of his countrymen (culpâ nostrâ). History would be pleasant, if we were embarrassed only by such contradictions. It is likewise from Nicetas that we learn the pious and humane sorrow of Frederic.

[19] Χθαμαλὴ ἕδρα, which Cinnamus translates into Latin by the word Σελλίον. Ducange works very hard to save his king and country from such ignominy (sur

army beyond the Bosphorus than he refused the offer of a second conference, unless his brother would meet him on equal terms, either on the sea or land.   With Conrad and Frederic the ceremonial was still nicer and more difficult : like the successors of Constantine, they styled themselves Emperors of the Romans,[20] and firmly maintained the purity of their title and dignity.   The first of these representatives of Charlemagne would only converse with Manuel on horseback in the open field ; the second, by passing the Hellespont rather than the Bosphorus, declined the view of Constantinople and its sovereign.   An emperor who had been crowned at Rome was reduced in the Greek epistles to the humple appellation of *Rex*, or prince of the Alemanni ; and the vain and feeble Angelus affected to be ignorant of the name of one of the greatest men and monarchs of the age. While they viewed with hatred and suspicion the Latin pilgrims, the Greek emperors maintained a strict, though secret, alliance with the Turks and Saracens.   Isaac Angelus complained that by his friendship for the great Saladin he had incurred the enmity of the Franks ; and a mosque was founded at Constantinople for the public exercise of the religion of Mahomet.[21]

Turkish warfare

III. The swarms that followed the first crusade were destroyed in Anatolia by famine, pestilence, and the Turkish arrows : and the princes only escaped with some squadrons of horse to accomplish their lamentable pilgrimage.   A just opinion may be formed of their knowledge and humanity: of their knowledge, from the design of subduing Persia and Chorasan in their way to Jerusalem ; of their humanity, from the massacre of the Christian people, a friendly city, who came out to meet them with palms and crosses in their hands.   The arms of Conrad and Louis were less cruel and imprudent ; but the event of the second crusade was still more ruinous to Christendom ; and the Greek Manuel is accused by his own subjects of giving seasonable intelligence to the sultan, and treacherous guides to the Latin princes.   Instead of crushing the common foe, by a double

Joinville, dissertat. xxvii. p. 317-220).   Louis afterwards insisted on a meeting in mari ex æquo, not ex equo, according to the laughable readings of some Mss.

[20] Ego Romanorum imperator sum, ille Romaniorum (Anonym. Canis. p. 512). The public and historical style of the Greeks was 'Ρήξ . . . *princeps*. Yet Cinnamus owns, that 'Ιμπεράτωρ is synonymous to Βασιλεύς.

[21] In the epistles of Innocent III. (xiii. p. 184), and the History of Bohadin (p. 129, 130), see the views of a pope and a cadhi on this *singular* toleration.

attack at the same time but on different sides, the Germans were
urged by emulation, and the French were retarded by jealousy.
Louis had scarcely passed the Bosphorus when he was met by [October,
the returning emperor, who had lost the greatest part of his A.D. 1147]
army in glorious, but unsuccessful, actions on the banks of the
Mæander.[22]   The contrast of the pomp of his rival hastened the
retreat of Conrad : the desertion of his independent vassals reduced him to his hereditary troops ; and he borrowed some Greek
vessels to execute by sea the pilgrimage of Palestine.[23]   Without
studying the lessons of experience or the nature of war, the king
of France advanced through the same country to a similar fate.
The vanguard, which bore the royal banner and the oriflamme of
St. Denys,[24] had doubled their march with rash and inconsiderate
speed ; and the rear, which the king commanded in person, no
longer found their companions in the evening camp.   In darkness and disorder, they were encompassed, assaulted, and overwhelmed by the innumerable host of Turks, who, in the art [Near
of war, were superior to the Christians of the twelfth century. Laodicea]
Louis, who climbed a tree in the general discomfiture, was saved
by his own valour and the ignorance of his adversaries; and
with the dawn of day he escaped alive, but almost alone, to the
camp of the vanguard.   But, instead of pursuing his expedition
by land, he was rejoiced to shelter the relics of his army in the

---

[22] [This is quite inaccurate.   At Nicæa, Conrad divided his army.   About
15,000 took the coast route under Bishop Otto of Freising, the king's brother.
Conrad himself proceeded to Dorylæum with the main army ; but after a march
of eleven days want of supplies forced him to turn back.   The enemy harassed the
retreat, and 30,000 Germans are said to have perished.   Conrad met the French
army at Nicæa.]

[23] [This, too, is an inaccurate account.   Louis proceeded westward to Lopadium,
where he waited for Conrad, and the two kings advanced together (by Adramyttium,
Pergamum, and Smyrna) to Ephesus, where they spent Christmas, 1147, as
we learn from Conrad's letter to the abbot Wibald of Corvei (an important
source ; published in the collection of Wibald's letters, in Jaffé, Bib. rer. Germ.
i. no. 78).   Here Conrad fell ill, and returned to Constantinople on the Emperor's
invitation.   He set sail from Constantinople on March 10, 1148, and reached
Acre in April.   During their joint march Louis VII. appears to have shown
every consideration to his fellow-sovereign.   The other part of Conrad's army,
led by Otto of Freising, was cut to pieces near Mount Cadmus, south of Laodicea.
It is to this misfortune that Gibbon's "action on the banks of the Mæander " refers.
The same region was also disastrous to the army of Louis VII.]

[24] As counts of Vexin, the kings of France were the vassals and advocates of
the monastery of St. Denys.   The saint's peculiar banner, which they received
from the abbot, was of a square form and a red or *flaming* colour.   The *oriflamme*
appeared at the head of the French armies from the xiith to the xvth century
(Ducange sur Joinville, dissert. xviii. p. 244-253).

friendly seaport of Satalia.[25] From thence he embarked for Antioch; but so penurious was the supply of Greek vessels that they could only afford room for his knights and nobles; and the plebeian crowd of infantry was left to perish at the foot of the Pamphylian hills. The emperor and the king embraced and wept at Jerusalem; their martial trains, the remnant of mighty armies, were joined to the Christian powers of Syria, and a fruitless siege of Damascus was the final effort of the second crusade. Conrad and Louis embarked for Europe with the personal fame of piety and courage; but the Orientals had braved these potent monarchs of the Franks, with whose names and military forces they had been so often threatened.[26] Perhaps they had still more to fear from the veteran genius of Frederic the First, who in his youth had served in Asia under his uncle Conrad. Forty campaigns in Germany and Italy had taught Barbarossa to command; and his soldiers, even the princes of the empire, were accustomed under his reign to obey. As soon as he lost sight of Philadelphia and Laodicea, the last cities of the Greek frontier, he plunged into the salt and barren desert, a land (says the historian) of horror and tribulation.[27] During twenty days, every step of his fainting and sickly march was besieged by the innumerable hordes of Turkmans,[28] whose numbers and fury seemed after each defeat to multiply and inflame. The emperor continued to struggle and to suffer; and such was the measure of his calamities that, when he reached the gates of Iconium, no more than one thousand knights were able to serve on horseback. By a sudden and resolute assault, he defeated the guards, and stormed the capital, of the sultan,[29] who humbly sued for

---

[25] [The ancient Attalia. 's 'Αττάλειαν.]

[26] The original French histories of the second crusade are the Gesta Ludovici VII. published in the ivth volume of Duchesne's Collection. The same volume contains many original letters of the king, of Suger his minister, &c., the best documents of authentic history. [This work, the Gesta Ludovici VII., is a Latin translation from the Grandes Chroniques de France; in which the history of the reign of Louis VII. is based on the Historia Ludovici, an extract from the Continuatio Sangermanensis of Aimoin (written c. 1170-80). This original has been edited recently by A. Molinier, Vie de Louis le Gros par Suger (caps. 1-7 are the work of the Abbot Suger), 1887.]

[27] Terram horroris et salsuginis, terram siccam, sterilem, inamænam. Anonym. Canis. p. 517. The emphatic language of a sufferer.

[28] Gens innumera, sylvestris, indomita, prædones sine ductore. The sultan of Cogni might sincerely rejoice in their defeat. Anonym. Canis. p. 517-518.

[29] See in the anonymous writer in the collection of Canisius, Tagino, and Bohadin (Vit. Saladin. p. 119, 120, c. 70 [leg. 69]), the ambiguous conduct of Kilidge Arslan, sultan of Cogni, who hated and feared both Saladin and Frederic.

pardon and peace. The road was now open, and Frederic advanced in a career of triumph, till he was unfortunately drowned in a petty torrent of Cilicia.[30] The remainder of his Germans was consumed by sickness and desertion, and the emperor's son expired with the greatest part of his Swabian vassals at the siege of Acre. Among the Latin heroes, Godfrey of Bouillon and Frederic Barbarossa alone could achieve the passage of the Lesser Asia; yet even their success was a warning, and in the last and most experienced ages of the crusades every nation preferred the sea to the toils and perils of an inland expedition.[31]

The enthusiasm of the first crusade is a natural and simple event, while hope was fresh, danger untried, and enterprise congenial to the spirit of the times. But the obstinate perseverance of Europe may indeed excite our pity and admiration; that no instruction should have been drawn from constant and adverse experience; that the same confidence should have repeatedly grown from the same failures; that six succeeding generations should have rushed headlong down the precipice that was open before them; and that men of every condition should have staked their public and private fortunes on the desperate adventure of possessing or recovering a tomb-stone two thousand miles from their country. In a period of two centuries after the council of Clermont, each spring and summer produced a new emigration of pilgrim warriors for the defence of the Holy Land; but the seven great armaments or crusades were excited by some impending or recent calamity: the nations were moved by the authority of their pontiffs, and the example of their kings: their zeal was kindled, and their reason was silenced, by the voice of their holy orators; and among these Bernard,[32] the monk or the saint, may claim the most honourable

Obstinacy of the enthusiasm of the crusades

---

[30] The desire of comparing two great men has tempted many writers to drown Frederic in the river Cydnus, in which Alexander so imprudently bathed (Q. Curt. l. iii. c. 4, 5). But, from the march of the emperor, I rather judge that his Saleph is the Calycadnus, a stream of less fame, but of a longer course. [This judgment is right. Frederick was drowned in the Geuk Su or Calycadnus on his march from Laranda to Seleucia.]

[31] Marinus Sanutus, A.D. 1321, lays it down as a precept, Quod stolus ecclesiæ per terram nullâtenus est ducenda. He resolves, by the divine aid, the objection, or rather exception, of the first crusade (Secreta Fidelium Crucis, l. ii. pars ii. c. i. p. 37).

[32] The most authentic information of St. Bernard must be drawn from his own writings, published in a correct edition by Père Mabillon [2 vols., 1667], and reprinted at Venice, 1750, in six volumes in folio. Whatever friendship could recollect, or superstition could add, is contained in the two lives, by his disciples, in the vith

Character
and mis-
sion of St.
Bernard.
A.D. 1091-
1153
place.   About eight years before the first conquest of Jerusalem, he was born of a noble family in Burgundy; at the age of three and twenty, he buried himself in the monastery of Citeaux, then in the primitive fervour of the institution ; at the end of two years he led forth her third colony, or daughter, to the valley of Clairvaux [33] in Champagne ; and was content, till the hour of his death, with the humble station of abbot of his own community.   A philosophic age has abolished, with too liberal and indiscriminate disdain, the honours of these spiritual heroes. The meanest amongst them are distinguished by some energies of the mind ; they were at least superior to their votaries and disciples ; and in the race of superstition they attained the prize for which such numbers contended.   In speech, in writing, in action, Bernard stood high above his rivals and contemporaries; his compositions are not devoid of wit and eloquence; and he seems to have preserved as much reason and humanity as may be reconciled with the character of a saint.   In a secular life he would have shared the seventh part of a private inheritance; by a vow of poverty and penance, by closing his eyes against the visible world,[34] by the refusal of all ecclesiastical dignities, the abbot of Clairvaux became the oracle of Europe and the founder of one hundred and sixty convents.   Princes and pontiffs trembled at the freedom of his apostolical censure; France, England, and Milan consulted and obeyed his judgment in a schism of the church; the debt was repaid by the gratitude of Innocent the Second ; and his successor Eugenius the

volume : whatever learning and criticism could ascertain, may be found in the prefaces of the Benedictine editor. [Mabillon's collection contains 444 letters ; in Migne's Patr. Lat. vol. 182 there are 495.   The life and works have been translated into English by S. J. Eales, 1889.—Neander, Der heilige Bernhard und sein Zeitalter (new ed. 1890) ; J. Cotter Morrison, The Life and Times of St. Bernard of Clairvaux (new ed. 1884).   There are endless other monographs.]

[33] Clairvaux, surnamed the Valley of Absynth, is situate among the woods near Bar-sur-Aube in Champagne.   St. Bernard would blush at the pomp of the church and monastery ; he would ask for the library, and I know not whether he would be much edified by a tun of 800 muids (914 1-7th hogsheads), which almost rivals that of Heidelberg (Mélanges Tirés d'une Grande Bibliothèque, tom. xlvi. p. 15-20).

[34] The disciples of the saint (Vit. 1ma, l. iii. c. 2, p. 1232 ; Vit. 2da, c. 16, No. 45, p. 1383) record a marvellous example of his pious apathy.   Juxta lacum etiam Lausannensem totius diei itinere pergens, penitus non attendit, aut se videre non vidit.   Cum enim vespere facto de eodem lacu socii colloquerentur, interrogabat eos ubi lacus ille esset ; et mirati sunt universi.   To admire or despise St. Bernard as he ought, the reader, like myself, should have before the windows of his library the beauties of that incomparable landscape.

Third was the friend and disciple of the holy Bernard. It
was in the proclamation of the second crusade that he shone
as the missionary and prophet of God, who called the nations
to the defence of his holy sepulchre.[35] At the parliament of
Vézelay he spoke before the king; and Louis the Seventh, [A.D. 1146]
with his nobles, received their crosses from his hand. The
abbot of Clairvaux then marched to the less easy conquest
of the emperor Conrad: a phlegmatic people, ignorant of his [at Speyer]
language, was transported by the pathetic vehemence of his
tone and gestures; and his progress from Constance to Cologne
was the triumph of eloquence and zeal. Bernard applauds his
own success in the depopulation of Europe; affirms that cities
and castles were emptied of their inhabitants ; and computes
that only one man was left behind for the consolation of seven
widows.[36] The blind fanatics were desirous of electing him for
their general; but the example of the hermit Peter was before
his eyes; and, while he assured the crusaders of the divine
favour, he prudently declined a military command, in which
failure and victory would have been almost equally disgraceful
to his character.[37] Yet, after the calamitous event, the abbot
of Clairvaux was loudly accused as a false prophet, the author
of the public and private mourning; his enemies exulted, his
friends blushed, and his apology was slow and unsatisfactory.
He justifies his obedience to the commands of the pope; expatiates on the mysterious ways of Providence; imputes the
misfortunes of the pilgrims to their own sins; and modestly
insinuates that his mission had been approved by signs and
wonders.[38] Had the fact been certain, the argument would be

[35] Otho Frising. l. i. c. 4. Bernard, Epist. 363, ad Francos Orientales, Opp.
tom. i. p. 328. Vit. 1ma, l. iii. c. 4, tom. vi. p. 1235.

[36] Mandastis et obedivi . . . multiplicati sunt super numerum ; vacuantur urbes
et castella ; et *pene* jam non inveniunt quem apprehendant septem mulieres unum
virum ; adeo ubique viduæ vivis remanent viris. Bernard. Epist. p. 247 [*leg*. p.
246 ; *ep*. 247 ; p. 447 ap. Migne]. We must be careful not to construe *pene* as a
substantive.

[37] Quis ego sum ut disponam [castrorum] acies, ut egrediar ante facies arma-
torum, aut quid tam remotum a professione meâ, [etiam] si vires [suppeterent
etiam], si peritia [non deesset], &c. epist. 256, tom. i. p. 259 [*leg*. 258]. He speaks
with contempt of the hermit Peter, vir quidam, epist. 363 [p. 586 ap. Migne].

[38] Sic [*leg*. sed] dicunt forsitan iste, unde scimus quod a Domino sermo egressus
sit ? Quæ signa tu facis, ut credamus tibi ? Non est quod ad ista ipse respon-
deam ; parcendum verecundiæ meæ ; responde tu pro me, et pro te ipso, secundum
quæ vidisti et audisti [*leg*. audisti et vidisti], et [*leg*. aut certe] secundum quod te
[*leg*. tibi] inspiraverit Deus. Consolat. [De Consideratione ad Eugenium, iii.
Papam] l. ii. c. 1 [p. 744 ap. Migne] : Opp. tom. ii. p. 421-423.

decisive; and his faithful disciples, who enumerate twenty or thirty miracles in a day, appeal to the public assemblies of France and Germany, in which they were performed.[39]   At the present hour such prodigies will not obtain credit beyond the precincts of Clairvaux; but in the preternatural cures of the blind, the lame, or the sick, who were presented to the man of God, it is impossible for us to ascertain the separate shares of accident, of fancy, of imposture, and of fiction.

Progress of the Mahometans   Omnipotence itself cannot escape the murmurs of its discordant votaries; since the same dispensation which was applauded as a deliverance in Europe was deplored, and perhaps arraigned, as a calamity in Asia.   After the loss in Jerusalem the Syrian fugitives diffused their consternation and sorrow : Bagdad mourned in the dust; the Cadhi Zeineddin of Damascus tore his beard in the caliph's presence; and the whole divan shed tears at his melancholy tale.[40]   But the commanders of the faithful could only weep; they were themselves captives in the hands of the Turks; some temporal power was restored to the last age of the Abbassides ; but their humble ambition was confined to Bagdad and the adjacent province.   Their tyrants, the Seljukian sultans, had followed the common law of the Asiatic dynasties, the unceasing round of valour, greatness, discord, degeneracy, and decay : their spirit and power were unequal to the defence of religion ; and, in his distant realm of Persia, the Christians were strangers to the name and the arms of Sangiar, **The Atabeks of Syria [Guardians]** the last hero of his race.[41]   While the sultans were involved in the silken web of the harem, the pious task was undertaken by their slaves, the Atabeks,[42] a Turkish name, which, like the

---

[39] See the testimonies in Vita 1ma, l. iv. c. 5, 6.   Opp. tom. vi. p. 1258-1261, l. vi. c. 1-17, p. 1287-1314.

[40] Abulmahasen apud de Guignes, Hist. des Huns, tom. ii. p. ii. p. 99.

[41] See his *article* in the Bibliothèque Orientale of d'Herbelot, and de Guignes, tom. ii. p. i. p. 230-261.   Such was his valour that he was styled the second Alexander ; and such the extravagant love of his subjects that they prayed for the sultan a year after his decease.   Yet Sangiar might have been made prisoner by the Franks, as well as by the Uzes [Ghuzz].   He reigned near fifty years (A.D. 1103-1152), and was a munificent patron of Persian poetry.   [Muizz ad-din Abū-l-Hārith Sinjar, A.D. 1117-1157 ; his power was practically confined to Khurāsān.]

[42] See the Chronology of the Atabeks of Irak and Syria, in de Guignes, tom. i. p. 254; and the reigns of Zenghi and Noureddin in the same writer (tom. ii. p. ii. p. 147-221), who uses the Arabic text of Benelathir, Ben Schouna, and Abulfeda; the Bibliothèque Orientale, under the articles *Atabeks* and *Noureddin;* and the Dynasties of Abulpharagius, p. 250-267, vers. Pocock.   [For life of Zengī see Stanley Lane-Poole, Saladin, chaps. 3 and 4; for the genealogy of the Atabeks, the same writer's Mohammadan Dynasties.]

WEST END OF THE COURT OF THE GREAT MOSQUE AT DIARBEKR (AMIDA),
RECONSTRUCTED BY THE SELJUKS IN THE 12TH CENTURY FROM THE
REMAINS OF AN EARLIER CHRISTIAN BUILDING

Byzantine patricians, may be translated by Father of the Prince. Ascansar, a valiant Turk, had been the favourite of Malek Shah, [Aksunkur] from whom he received the privilege of standing on the right hand of the throne; but, in the civil wars that ensued on the monarch's death, he lost his head and the government of Aleppo. His domestic emirs persevered in their attachment to his son Zenghi, who proved his first arms against the Franks in the defeat of Antioch; thirty campaigns in the service of the caliph and sultan established his military fame; and he was invested with the command of Mosul, as the only champion that could avenge the cause of the prophet. The public hope was not disappointed: after a siege of twenty-five days, he stormed the city of Edessa, and recovered from the Franks their conquests beyond the Euphrates: [43] the martial tribes of Curdistan were subdued by the independent sovereign of Mosul and Aleppo: his soldiers were taught to behold the camp as their only country; they trusted to his liberality for their rewards; and their absent families were protected by the vigilance of Zenghi. At the head of these veterans, his son Noureddin gradually united the Mahometan powers; added the kingdom of Damascus to that of Aleppo, and waged a long and successful war against the Christians of Syria: he spread his ample reign from the Tigris to the Nile, and the Abbassides rewarded their faithful servant with all the titles and prerogatives of royalty. The Latins themselves were compelled to own the wisdom and courage, and even the justice and piety, of this implacable adversary. [44] In his life and government, the holy warrior revived the zeal and simplicity of the first caliphs. Gold and silk were banished from his palace; the use of wine from his dominions; the public revenue was scrupulously applied to the public service; and the frugal household of Noureddin was maintained from the legitimate share of the spoil, which he

Marginal notes: Zenghi. A.D. 1127-1145 [1146]

Noureddin. A.D. 1145 [1146]-1174

---

[43] William of Tyre (l. xvi. c. 4, 5, 7) describes the loss of Edessa, and the death of Zenghi. The corruption of his name into *Sanguin*, afforded the Latins a comfortable allusion to his *sanguinary* character and end, fit sanguine sanguinolentus.

[44] Noradinus [Nūr ad-dīn Mahmūd ibn Zangī] (says William of Tyre, l. xx. 33) maximus nominis et fidei Christianæ persecutor; princeps tamen justus, vafer, providus, et secundum gentis suæ traditiones religiosus. To this Catholic witness, we may add the primate of the Jacobites (Abulpharag. p. 267), quo non alter erat inter reges vitæ ratione magis laudabili, aut quæ pluribus justitiæ experimentis abundaret. The true praise of kings is after their death, and from the mouth of their enemies. [He won Damascus in 1154.]

vested in the purchase of a private estate. His favourite Sultana sighed for some female object of expense: "Alas," replied the king, "I fear God, and am no more than the treasurer of the Moslems. Their property I cannot alienate; but I still possess three shops in the city of Hems: these you may take, and these alone can I bestow." His chamber of justice was the terror of the great and the refuge of the poor. Some years after the sultan's death, an oppressed subject called aloud in the streets of Damascus, " O Noureddin, Noureddin, where art thou now? Arise, arise, to pity and protect us!" A tumult was apprehended, and a living tyrant blushed and trembled at the name of a departed monarch.

Conquest of Egypt by the Turks. A.D. 1163-1169   By the arms of the Turks and Franks, the Fatimites had been deprived of Syria. In Egypt the decay of their character and influence was still more essential. Yet they were still revered as the descendants and successors of the prophet; they maintained their visible state in the palace of Cairo; and their person was seldom violated by the profane eyes of subjects or strangers. The Latin ambassadors [45] have described their own introduction through a series of gloomy passages, and glittering porticoes; the scene was enlivened by the warbling of birds and the murmur of fountains; it was enriched by a display of rich furniture and rare animals; of the Imperial treasures, something was shown, and much was supposed; and the long order of unfolding doors was guarded by black soldiers and domestic eunuchs. The sanctuary of the presence-chamber was veiled with a curtain; and the vizir, who conducted the ambassadors, laid aside his scymetar, and prostrated himself three times on the ground; the veil was then removed; and they beheld the commander of the faithful, who signified his pleasure to the first slave of the throne. But this slave was his master; the vizirs or sultans had usurped the supreme administration of Egypt; the claims of the rival candidates were decided by arms; and the name of the most worthy, of the strongest, was inserted in the royal patent of command. The factions of Dargham and Shawer [46] alternately expelled each other from

[45] From the ambassador, William of Tyre (l. xix. c. 17, 18) describes the palace of Cairo. In the caliph's treasure were found, a pearl as large as a pigeon's egg, a ruby weighing seventeen Egyptian drams, an emerald a palm and a half in length, and many vases of crystal and porcelain of China (Renaudot, p. 536).

[46] [Shawar had been governor of Upper Egypt, Dirghām the chief of the guard; both became vezīrs.]

the capital and country; and the weaker side implored the dangerous protection of the Sultan of Damascus, or the king of Jerusalem, the perpetual enemies of the sect and monarchy of the Fatimites. By his arms and religion the Turk was most formidable; but the Frank, in an easy direct march, could advance from Gaza to the Nile; while the intermediate situation of his realm compelled the troops of Noureddin to wheel round the skirts of Arabia, a long and painful circuit, which exposed them to thirst, fatigue, and the burning winds of the desert. The secret zeal and ambition of the Turkish prince [First expedition to Egypt] aspired to reign in Egypt under the name of the Abbassides; but the restoration of the suppliant Shawer was the ostensible motive of the first expedition; and the success was entrusted to the emir Shiracouh,[47] a valiant and veteran commander. Dargham was oppressed and slain; but the ingratitude, the [A.D. 1164] jealousy, the just apprehensions, of his more fortunate rival, soon provoked him to invite the king of Jerusalem to deliver Egypt from his insolent benefactors. To this union, the forces [Bilbeys besieged for three months] of Shiracouh were unequal; he relinquished the premature conquest; and the evacuation of Belbeis, or Pelusium, was the condition of his safe retreat. As the Turks defiled before the enemy, and their general closed the rear, with a vigilant eye, and a battle-axe in his hand, a Frank presumed to ask him if he were not afraid of an attack? "It is doubtless in your power to begin the attack," replied the intrepid emir, "but rest assured that not one of my soldiers will go to paradise till he has sent an infidel to hell." His report of the riches of the land, the effeminacy of the natives, and the disorders of the government, revived the hopes of Noureddin; the caliph of Bagdad applauded the pious design; and Shiracouh descended [Second expedition to Egypt. A.D. 1167] into Egypt a second time with twelve thousand Turks and eleven thousand Arabs.[47a] Yet his forces were still inferior to the confederate armies of the Franks and Saracens; and I can discern an unusual degree of military art in his passage of the Nile, his retreat into Thebais, his masterly evolutions in the battle of Babain, the surprise of Alexandria, and his marches [Battle of al Babain] and counter-marches in the flats and valley of Egypt, from the

---

[47] [Asad ad-Dīn Abū l-Hārith Shīrkūh (= Lion of the Faith, Father of the Lion, Mountain Lion).]

[47a] [So William of Tyre; but Ibn al Athīr gives the total number as 2000.]

tropic to the sea. His conduct was seconded by the courage
of his troops, and on the eve of action a Mamaluke [48] exclaimed,
" If we cannot wrest Egypt from the Christian dogs, why do we
not renounce the honours and rewards of the sultan, and retire
to labour with the peasants, or to spin with the females of the
harem ? " Yet after all his efforts in the field,[49] after the
obstinate defence of Alexandria [50] by his nephew Saladin, an
honourable capitulation and retreat concluded the second enterprise of Shiracouh ; and Noureddin reserved his abilities for a
third and more propitious occasion. It was soon offered by the
[Amalric reigned, A.D. 1162-73] ambition and avarice of Amalric, or Amaury, king of Jerusalem,
who had imbibed the pernicious maxim that no faith should be
kept with the enemies of God.[50a] A religious warrior, the great
master of the hospital, encouraged him to proceed ; the emperor
of Constantinople either gave, or promised, a fleet to act with
the armies of Syria ; and the perfidious Christian, unsatisfied
with spoil and subsidy, aspired to the conquest of Egypt. In
this emergency the Moslems turned their eyes towards the
[Third expedition to Egypt. A.D. 1168-9] sultan of Damascus ; the vizir, whom danger encompassed on
all sides, yielded to their unanimous wishes, and Noureddin
seemed to be tempted by the fair offer of one third of the
[Fustat burned, Nov. 1168] revenue of the kingdom.[50b] The Franks were already at the gates
of Cairo ; but the suburbs, the old city, were burnt on their
approach ; they were deceived by an insidious negotiation ; and
their vessels were unable to surmount the barriers of the Nile.
They prudently declined a contest with the Turks in the midst
of an hostile country ; [50c] and Amaury retired into Palestine, with

[48] *Mamluc* [mamlūk], plur. *Mamalic* [mamālīk], is defined by Pocock (Prolegom. ad Abulpharag. p. 7), and d'Herbelot (p. 545), servum emptitium, seu qui
pretio numerato in domini possessionem cedit. They frequently occur in the wars
of Saladin (Bohadin, p. 236, &c.) ; and it was only the *Bahartie* [Bahrī ; that is,
of the river ; they are opposed to the Burjī (*of the fort*) Mamlūks who succeeded
them] Mamalukes that were first introduced into Egypt by his descendants
[namely by the Sultān Al-Sālih (1240-1249), who organized Turkish slaves as a
bodyguard].
[49] Jacobus a Vitriaco (p. 1116) gives the king of Jerusalem no more than 374
[*leg.* 370] knights. Both the Franks and the Moslems report the superior numbers
of the enemy ; a difference which may be solved by counting or omitting the
unwarlike Egyptians.
[50] It was the Alexandria of the Arabs, a middle term in extent and riches between the period of the Greeks and Romans, and that of the Turks (Savary, Lettres
sur l'Egypte, tom. i. p. 25, 26).
[50a] [Acc. to William of Tyre, Amalric was personally unwilling to undertake the
invasion.]
[50b] [This offer was made on the occasion of the *first* expedition.]
[50c] [They did not decline the contest, but the Turks evaded them.]

the shame and reproach that always adhere to unsuccessful injustice. After this deliverance, Shiracouh was invested with a robe of honour, which he soon stained with the blood of the unfortunate Shawer. For a while, the Turkish emirs condescended to hold the office of vizir; but this foreign conquest precipitated the fall of the Fatimites themselves; and the bloodless change was accomplished by a message and a word. The caliphs had been degraded by their own weakness and the tyranny of the vizirs: their subjects blushed, when the descendant and successor of the prophet presented his naked hand to the rude grip of a Latin ambassador; they wept when he sent the hair of his women, a sad emblem of their grief and terror, to excite the pity of the sultan of Damascus. By the command of Nou- End of the Fatimite reddin, and the sentence of the doctors, the holy names of caliphs. Abubeker, Omar, and Othman were solemnly restored; the A.D. 1171 caliph Mosthadi, of Bagdad, was acknowledged in the public prayers as the true commander of the faithful; and the green livery of the sons of Ali was exchanged for the black colour of the Abbassides. The last of his race, the caliph Adhed,[51] who survived only ten days, expired in happy ignorance of his fate; his [Sept. 13] treasures secured the loyalty of the soldiers, and silenced the murmurs of the sectaries; and in all subsequent revolutions Egypt has never departed from the orthodox tradition of the Moslems.[52]

The hilly country beyond the Tigris is occupied by the pas- Reign and character toral tribes of the Curds;[53] a people hardy, strong, savage, im- of Saladin. patient of the yoke, addicted to rapine, and tenacious of the A.D. 1171-1193 government of their national chiefs. The resemblance of name, situation, and manners seem to identify them with the Carduchians of the Greeks;[54] and they still defend against the

[51 [Al-Ādid Abū-Mohammad Abd-Allāh, A.D. 1160-71.]
[52 For this great revolution of Egypt, see William of Tyre (l. xix. 5-7, 12-31, xx. 5-12), Bohadin (in Vit. Saladin. p. 30-39), Abulfeda (in Excerpt. Schultens, p. 1-12), d'Herbelot (Bibliot. Orient. *Abhed, Fathemah,* but very incorrect), Renaudot (Hist. Patriarch. Alex. p. 522-525, 532-537), Vertot (Hist. des Chevaliers de Malthe, tom. i. p. 141-163, in 4to), and M. de Guignes (tom. ii. p. ii. p. 185-215).
[53 For the Curds, see de Guignes, tom. i. p. 416, 417, the Index Geographicus of Schultens, and Tavernier, Voyages, p. i. p. 308, 309. The Ayoubites [the name Ayyūb corresponds to Job] descended from the tribe of the Rawadiæi [Rawadīya], one of the noblest; but, as *they* were infected with the heresy of the Metempsychosis, the orthodox sultans insinuated that their descent was only on the mother's side, and that their ancestor was a stranger who settled among the Curds.
[54 See the ivth book of the Anabasis of Xenophon. The ten thousand suffered more from the arrows of the free Carduchians than from the splendid weakness of the Great King.

Ottoman Porte the antique freedom which they asserted against the successors of Cyrus. Poverty and ambition prompted them to embrace the profession of mercenary soldiers: the service of his father and uncle prepared the reign of the great Saladin;[55] and the son of Job or Ayub, a simple Curd, magnanimously smiled at his pedigree, which flattery deduced from the Arabian caliphs.[56] So unconscious was Noureddin of the impending ruin of his house that he constrained the reluctant youth to follow his uncle Shiracouh into Egypt; his military character was established by the defence of Alexandria ; and, if we may believe the Latins, he solicited and obtained from the Christian general the *profane* honours of knighthood.[57] On the death of Shiracouh, the office of grand vizir was bestowed on Saladin, as the youngest and least powerful of the emirs; but with the advice of his father, whom he invited to Cairo, his genius obtained the ascendant over his equals, and attached the army to his person and interest. While Noureddin lived, these ambitious Curds were the most humble of his slaves; and the indiscreet murmurs of the divan were silenced by the prudent Ayub, who loudly protested that at the command of the sultan he himself would lead his son in chains to the foot of the throne. " Such language," he added in private, " was prudent and proper in an assembly of your rivals; but we are now above fear and obedience; and the threats of Noureddin shall not extort the tribute of a sugar-cane." His seasonable death relieved them from the odious and doubtful conflict: his son, a minor of eleven years of age, was left for a while to the emirs of Damascus ; and the new lord of Egypt was decorated by the

[before 3rd expedition]

[2nd exped.]

[A.D. 1174]

---

[55] We are indebted to the Professor Schultens (Lugd. Bat. 1755, 1732, in folio) for the richest and most authentic materials, a life of Saladin (Salāh ad-Dīn], by his friend and minister the cadhi Bohadin [Bahā ad-Dīn], and copious extracts from the history of his kinsman, the Prince Abulfeda of Hamah. To these we may add, the article of *Salaheddin* in the Bibliothèque Orientale, and all that may be gleaned from the dynasties of Abulpharagius. [Also the articles in the Biographical dictionary of Ibn Khallikān, transl. by the Baron de Slane. Marin's Histoire de Saladin, publ. in 1758, is scholarly and well written. Stanley Lane-Poole, Saladin and the Fall of the Kingdom of Jerusalem, 1898, written from the original sources.]

[56] Since Abulfeda was himself an Ayoubite, he may share the praise, for imitating, at least tacitly, the modesty of the founder.

[57] Hist. Hierosol. in the Gesta Dei per Francos, p. 1152. [Itin. Reg. Ricard., i. c. 3 ; and cp. the romance L'ordene de chevalerie, in App. to Marin's Hist. de Saladin.] A similar example may be found in Joinville (p. 42, edition du Louvre) ; but the pious St. Louis refused to dignify infidels with the order of Christian knighthood (Ducange, Observations, p. 70).

caliph with every title [58] that could sanctify his usurpation in [A.D. 1175] the eyes of the people. Nor was Saladin long content with the possession of Egypt; he despoiled the Christians of Jerusalem, and the Atabeks of Damascus, Aleppo, and Diarbekir; Mecca [A.D. 1174-83] and Medina acknowledged him for their temporal protector; his brother subdued the distant regions of Yemen, or the Happy Arabia; and at the hour of his death his empire was spread from the African Tripoli to the Tigris, and from the Indian ocean to the mountains of Armenia. In the judgment of his character, the reproaches of treason and ingratitude strike forcibly on *our* minds, impressed as they are with the principle and experience of law and loyalty. But his ambition may in some measure be excused by the revolutions of Asia,[59] which had erased every notion of legitimate succession; by the recent example of the Atabeks themselves; by his reverence to the son of his benefactor; his humane and generous behaviour to the collateral branches; by *their* incapacity and *his* merits; by the approbation of the caliph, the sole source of all legitimate power; and, above all, by the wishes and interest of the people, whose happiness is the first object of government. In *his* virtues, and in those of his patron, they admired the singular union of the hero and the saint; for both Noureddin and Saladin are ranked among the Mahometan saints; and the constant meditation of the holy wars appears to have shed a serious and sober colour over their lives and actions. The youth of the latter [60] was addicted to wine and women; but his aspiring spirit soon renounced the temptations of pleasure for the graver follies of fame and dominion. The garment of Saladin was of coarse woollen; water was his only drink; and, while he emulated the temperance, he surpassed the chastity, of his Arabian

---

[58] In these Arabic titles, *religionis* [dīn] must always be understood; *Noureddin*, lumen r.; *Ezzodin*, decus; *Amadoddin*, columen; [*Bahā*,—lustre]: our hero's proper name was Joseph, and he was styled *Salahoddin*, salus; *Al Malichus Al Nasirus*, rex defensor; *Abu Medaffir* [Abū-l-Muzaffar], pater victoriæ. Schultens, Præfat. [Saladin was not acknowledged by the Caliph till A.D. 1175. He did not despoil Jerusalem nor the Atabegs of Damascus, who did not exist apart from Aleppo.]

[59] Abulfeda, who descended from a brother of Saladin, observes, from many examples, that the founders of dynasties took the guilt for themselves, and left the reward to their innocent collaterals (Excerpt. p. 10).

[60] See his life and character in Renaudot, p. 537-548. [There is no evidence for youthful dissipation on the part of Saladin, beyond his recorded resolve to renounce pleasure when he became vezīr of Egypt.]

prophet. Both in faith and practice he was a rigid Musulman he ever deplored that the defence of religion had not allowed him to accomplish the pilgrimage of Mecca; but at the stated hours, five times each day, the sultan devoutly prayed with his brethren; the involuntary omission of fasting was scrupulously repaid; and his perusal of the Koran on horseback, between the approaching armies, may be quoted as a proof, however ostentatious, of piety and courage.[61]   The superstitious doctrine of the sect of Shafei was the only study that he deigned to encourage; the poets were safe in his contempt; but all profane science was the object of his aversion; and a philosopher, who had vented some speculative novelties, was seized and strangled by the command of the royal saint. The justice of his divan was accessible to the meanest suppliant against himself and his ministers; and it was only for a kingdom that Saladin would deviate from the rule of equity. While the descendants of Seljuk and Zenghi held his stirrup, and smoothed his garments, he was affable and patient with the meanest of his servants. So boundless was his liberality, that he distributed twelve thousand horses at the siege of Acre; and, at the time of his death, no more than forty-seven drams of silver, and one piece of gold coin, were found in the treasury; yet in a martial reign, the tributes were diminished, and the wealthy citizens enjoyed, without fear or danger, the fruits of their industry. Egypt, Syria, and Arabia, were adorned by the royal foundations of hospitals, colleges, and mosques; and Cairo was fortified with a wall and citadel; but his works were consecrated to public use;[62] nor did the sultan indulge himself in a garden or palace of private luxury. In a fanatic age, himself a fanatic, the genuine virtues of Saladin commanded the esteem of the Christians; the emperor of Germany gloried in his friendship;[63] the Greek emperor solicited his alliance;[64] and the conquest of Jerusalem diffused, and perhaps magnified, his fame both in the East and West.

[61] His civil and religious virtues are celebrated in the first chapter of Bohadin (p. 4-30), himself an eye-witness and an honest bigot.

[62] In many works, particularly Joseph's well in the castle of Cairo, the sultan and the patriarch have been confounded by the ignorance of natives and travellers.

[63] Anonym. Canisii, tom. iii. p. ii. p. 504.

[64] Bohadin, p. 129, 130.

During its short existence, the kingdom of Jerusalem [65] was supported by the discord of the Turks and Saracens; and both the Fatimite caliphs and the sultans of Damascus were tempted to sacrifice the cause of their religion to the meaner considerations of private and present advantage. But the powers of Egypt, Syria, and Arabia were now united by an hero, whom nature and fortune had armed against the Christians. All without now bore the most threatening aspect; and all was feeble and hollow in the internal state of Jerusalem.[66] After the two first Baldwins, the brother and cousin of Godfrey of Bouillon, the sceptre devolved by female succession to Melisenda, daughter of the second Baldwin, and her husband Fulk, Count of Anjou, the father, by a former marriage, of our English Plantagenets. Their two sons, Baldwin the Third, and Amaury, waged a strenuous and not unsuccessful war against the infidels; but the son of Amaury, Baldwin the Fourth, was deprived by the leprosy, a gift of the crusades, of the faculties both of mind and body. His sister, Sybilla, the mother of Baldwin the Fifth, was his natural heiress. After the suspicious death of her child, she crowned her second husband, Guy of Lusignan, a prince of a handsome person, but of such base renown that his brother Jeffrey was heard to exclaim, "Since they have made *him* a king, surely

His conquest of the kingdom. A.D. 1187, July 3

[Baldwin I. A.D. 1100-18; Baldwin II. A.D. 1118-31]

[Fulk, 1131-43]

[Baldwin III. 1143-62; Amalric, 1163-73]

[Baldwin IV. 1174-85; Baldwin V. 1185-6]

[Guy, 1186-92]

---

[65] For the Latin kingdom of Jerusalem, see William of Tyre, from the ixth to the xxiid book. Jacob. a Vitriaco, Hist. Hierosolym. l. i. and Sanutus, Secreta Fidelium Crucis, l. iii. p. vi.-ix.

[66] [Some instructive observations have been made on the degeneracy of the race of the western settlers in Palestine, as a cause of the decline of the kingdom, by Stubbs (Itin. Regis. Ricardi, Introd. p. xcv. *sqq.*). "There were eleven kings of Jerusalem in the twelfth century; under the first four, who were all of European birth, the state was acquired and strengthened; under the second four, who were born in Palestine, the effects of the climate and the infection of Oriental habits were sadly apparent; of these four three were minors at the time of their accession, and one was a leper. The noble families which were not recruited, as the royal family was, with fresh members from Europe, fell more early into weakness and corruption. . . . The moral degradation of the Franks need not have entailed destruction from enemies not less degraded; and their inferiority in numbers would have been more than compensated by the successions of pilgrims. . . . But the shortness and precariousness of life was an evil without remedy and in its effects irreparable. Of these the most noticeable was perhaps one which would have arisen under any system, the difficulty of carrying on a fixed policy whilst the administrators were perpetually changing; but scarcely second to this was the influence in successions which was thrown into the hands of women. The European women were less exposed than the men to the injurious climate or to the fatigues of military service; and many of them having been born in Palestine were in a measure acclimatized. The feudal rights and burdens of heiress-ship, marriage, and dower, were strictly observed; consequently most of the heiresses lived to have two or three husbands and two or three families."]

they would have made *me* a god!" The choice was generally blamed; and the most powerful vassal, Raymond, count of Tripoli, who had been excluded from the succession and regency, entertained an implacable hatred against the king, and exposed his honour and conscience to the temptations of the sultan. Such were the guardians of the holy city: a leper, a child, a woman, a coward, and a traitor; yet its fate was delayed twelve years by some supplies from Europe, by the valour of the military orders, and by the distant or domestic avocations of their great enemy. · At length, on every side the sinking state was encircled and pressed by an hostile line; and the truce was violated by the Franks, whose existence it protected. A soldier of fortune, Reginald of Chatillon, had seized a fortress on the edge of the desert, from whence he pillaged the caravans, insulted Mahomet, and threatened the cities of Mecca and Medina. Saladin condescended to complain; rejoiced in the denial of justice; and, at the head of fourscore thousand horse and foot, invaded the Holy Land. The choice of Tiberias for his first siege was suggested by the count of Tripoli, to whom it belonged; and the king of Jerusalem was persuaded to drain his garrisons, and to arm his people, for the relief of that important place.[67] By the advice of the perfidious Raymond, the Christians were betrayed into a camp destitute of water; he fled on the first onset, with the curses of both nations;[68] Lusignan was overthrown, with the loss of thirty thousand men; and the wood of the true cross, a dire misfortune! was left in the power of the infidels. The royal captive was conducted to the tent of Saladin; and, as he fainted with thirst and terror, the generous victor presented him with a cup of sherbet cooled in snow, without suffering his companion, Reginald of Chatillon, to partake of this pledge of hospitality and pardon. "The

[67] Templarii ut apes bombabant et Hospitalarii ut venti stridebant, et barones se exitio offerebant, et Turcopuli (the Christian light troops) semet ipsi in ignem injiciebant (Ispahani de Expugnatione Kudsiticâ, p. 18, apud Schultens) : a specimen of Arabian eloquence, somewhat different from the style of Xenophon ! [80,000 as the number of Saladin's army must be an exaggeration. He had 12,000 regular levies. Perhaps his force amounted to 25 or 30 thousand. Oman (Art of War, ii. p. 322) puts it at 60 or 70 thousand. For a plan of the locality see *ib.* p. 326.]

[68] The Latins affirm, the Arabians insinuate, the treason of Raymond; but, had he really embraced their religion, he would have been a saint and a hero in the eyes of the latter. [The treachery of Raymond is not proved and is probably untrue. Cp. Ernoul, ed. Mas-Latrie, p. 169.]

person and dignity of a king," said the sultan, "are sacred; but this impious robber must instantly acknowledge the prophet, whom he has blasphemed, or meet the death which he has so often deserved." On the proud or conscientious refusal of the Christian warrior, Saladin struck him on the head with his scymetar, and Reginald was dispatched by the guards.[69] The trembling Lusignan was sent to Damascus to an honourable prison, and speedy ransom; but the victory was stained by the execution of two hundred and thirty knights of the hospital, the intrepid champions and martyrs of their faith. The kingdom was left without a head; and of the two grand masters of the military orders, the one was slain, and the other was made a prisoner. From all the cities, both of the sea-coast and the inland country, the garrisons had been drawn away for this fatal field. Tyre and Tripoli alone could escape the rapid inroad of Saladin; and three months after the battle of Tiberias he appeared in arms before the gates of Jerusalem.[70] [and the Temple]

He might expect that the siege of a city so venerable on earth and in heaven, so interesting to Europe and Asia, would rekindle the last sparks of enthusiasm; and that, of sixty thousand Christians, every man would be a soldier, and every soldier a candidate for martyrdom. But queen Sybilla trembled for herself and her captive husband; and the barons and knights, who had escaped from the sword and the chains of the Turks, displayed the same factious and selfish spirit in the public ruin. The most numerous portion of the inhabitants were composed of the Greek and Oriental Christians, whom experience had taught to prefer the Mahometan before the Latin yoke;[71] and the holy sepulchre attracted a base and needy crowd, without arms or courage, who subsisted only on the [and city of Jerusalem. A.D. 1187, October 2 [3]]

[69] Reaud, Reginald, or Arnold de Châtillon, is celebrated by the Latins in his life and death; but the circumstances of the latter are more distinctly related by Bohadin and Abulfeda; and Joinville (Hist. de St. Louis, p. 70) alludes to the practice of Saladin, of never putting to death a prisoner who had tasted his bread and salt. Some of the companions of Arnold had been slaughtered, and almost sacrificed, in a valley of Mecca, ubi sacrificia mactantur (Abulfeda, p. 32). [Reginald had been prince of Antioch in 1154 (by marriage with Constance, the heiress). He had been a prisoner at Aleppo for sixteen years, and, after his release, married another heiress, Stephanie of Hebron. He took part in the battle of Ramlah in which Saladin was vanquished in 1177.]
[70] Vertot, who well describes the loss of the kingdom and city (Hist. des Chevaliers de Malthe, tom. i. l. ii. p. 226-278), inserts two original epistles of a knight-templar.
[71] Renaudot, Hist. Patriarch. Alex. p. 545.

charity of the pilgrims. Some feeble and hasty efforts were
made for the defence of Jerusalem; but in the space of fourteen
days a victorious army drove back the sallies of the besieged
planted their engines, opened the wall to the breadth of fifteen
cubits, applied their scaling ladders, and erected on the breach
twelve banners of the prophet and the sultan. It was in vain
that a bare-foot procession of the queen, the women, and the
monks implored the Son of God to save his tomb and his in
heritance from impious violation. Their sole hope was in the
mercy of the conqueror, and to their first suppliant deputation
that mercy was sternly denied. " He had sworn to avenge the
patience and long-suffering of the Moslems; the hour of forgive
ness was elapsed, and the moment was now arrived to expiate
in blood, the innocent blood which had been spilt by Godfrey
and the first crusaders." But a desperate and successful
struggle of the Franks admonished the sultan that his triumph
was not yet secure; he listened with reverence to a solemn ad
juration in the name of the common Father of mankind; and
a sentiment of human sympathy mollified the rigour of fanati
cism and conquest. He consented to accept the city, and to
spare the inhabitants. The Greek and Oriental Christians were
permitted to live under his dominion; but it was stipulated, that
in forty days all the Franks and Latins should evacuate Jeru
salem, and be safely conducted to the sea-ports of Syria and
Egypt; that ten pieces of gold should be paid for each man
five for each woman, and one for every child; and that those
who were unable to purchase their freedom should be detained
in perpetual slavery. Of some writers it is a favourite and in
vidious theme to compare the humanity of Saladin with the
massacre of the first crusade. The difference would be merely
personal; but we should not forget that the Christians had
offered to capitulate, and that the Mahometans of Jerusalem
sustained the last extremities of an assault and storm. Justice
is indeed due to the fidelity with which the Turkish conqueror
fulfilled the conditions of the treaty; and he may be deservedly
praised for the glance of pity which he cast on the misery of
the vanquished. Instead of a rigorous exaction of his debt, he
accepted a sum of thirty thousand byzants, for the ransom
of seven thousand poor; two or three thousand more were dis
missed by his gratuitous clemency; and the number of slaves

was reduced to eleven or fourteen thousand persons. In his interview with the queen, his words, and even his tears, suggested the kindest consolations ; his liberal alms were distributed among those who had been made orphans or widows by the fortune of war; and, while the knights of the hospital were in arms against him, he allowed their more pious brethren to continue, during the term of a year, the care and service of the sick. In these acts of mercy, the virtue of Saladin deserves our admiration and love : he was above the necessity of dissimulation ; and his stern fanaticism would have prompted him to dissemble, rather than to affect, this profane compassion for the enemies of the Koran., After Jerusalem had been delivered from the presence of the strangers, the sultan made his triumphant entry, his banners waving in the wind, and to the harmony of martial music. The great mosque of Omar, which had been converted into a church, was again consecrated to one God and his prophet Mahomet; the walls and pavement were purified with rose-water ; and a pulpit, the labour of Noureddin, was erected in the sanctuary. But, when the golden cross that glittered on the dome was cast down, and dragged through the streets, the Christians of every sect uttered a lamentable groan, which was answered by the joyful shouts of the Moslems. In four ivory chests the patriarch had collected the crosses, the images, the vases, and the relics of the holy place : they were seized by the conqueror, who was desirous of presenting the caliph with the trophies of Christian idolatry. He was persuaded, however, to entrust them to the patriarch and prince of Antioch; and the pious pledge was redeemed by Richard of England, at the expense of fifty-two thousand byzants of gold.[72]

The nations might fear and hope the immediate and final expulsion of the Latins from Syria; which was yet delayed above a century after the death of Saladin.[73] In the career of

The third crusade, by sea. A.D. 1188

---

[72] For the conquest of Jerusalem, Bohadin (p. 67-75) and Abulfeda (p. 40-43) are our Moslem witnesses. Of the Christian, Bernard Thesaurarius (c. 151-167) is the most copious and authentic; see likewise Matthew Paris (p. 120-124). [See also Ibn al-Athīr; Imād ad-Dīn; Abū Shāma (in Goergens, Quellenbeiträge zur Geschichte der Kreuzzüge) ; De expugn. Terræ Sanctæ (cp. Appendix 1).]

[73] The sieges of Tyre and Acre are most copiously described by Bernard Thesaurarius (de Acquisitione Terræ Sanctæ, c. 167-179), the author of the Historia Hierosolymitana (p. 1150-1172, in Bongarsius), Abulfeda (p. 43-50), and Bohadin (p. 75-179).

[Tyre be-
sieged.
Nov. 9, a.d.
1187] victory, he was first checked by the resistance of Tyre; the troops and garrisons, which had capitulated, were imprudently conducted to the same port: their numbers were adequate to the defence of the place; and the arrival of Conrad of Montferrat inspired the disorderly crowd with confidence and union. His father, a venerable pilgrim, had been made prisoner in the battle of Tiberias; but that disaster was unknown in Italy and Greece, when the son was urged by ambition and piety to visit the inheritance of his royal nephew, the infant Baldwin. The view of the Turkish banners warned him from the hostile coast of Jaffa;[73a] and Conrad was unanimously hailed as the prince and champion of Tyre, which was already besieged by the conqueror of Jerusalem. The firmness of his zeal, and perhaps his knowledge of a generous foe, enabled him to brave the threats of the sultan, and to declare that, should his aged parent be exposed before the walls, he himself would discharge the first arrow, and glory in his descent from a Christian martyr.[74] The Egyptian fleet was allowed to enter the harbour of Tyre; but the chain was suddenly drawn, and five galleys were either sunk or taken;

[Siege
raised, Jan.
1, a.d. 1188] a thousand Turks were slain in a sally; and Saladin, after burning his engines, concluded a glorious campaign by a disgraceful retreat to Damascus. He was soon assailed by a more formidable tempest. The pathetic narratives, and even the pictures, that represented in lively colours the servitude and profanation of Jerusalem, awakened the torpid sensibility of Europe; the emperor, Frederic Barbarossa, and the kings of France and England assumed the cross; and the tardy magnitude of their armaments was anticipated by the maritime states of the Mediterranean and the Ocean. The skilful and provident Italians first embarked in the ships of Genoa, Pisa, and Venice. They were speedily followed by the most eager pilgrims of France, Normandy, and the Western Isles. The powerful succour of Flanders, Frise, and Denmark filled near an hundred vessels; and the northern warriors were distinguished in the field by a lofty stature and a ponderous battle-axe.[75] Their increasing

[73a] [It was at Acre that Conrad called.]
[74] I have followed a moderate and probable representation of the fact; by Vertot, who adopts without reluctance a romantic tale, the old marquis is actually exposed to the darts of the besieged.
[75] Northmanni et Gothi, et cæteri populi insularum quæ inter occidentem et septemtrionem sitæ sunt, gentes bellicosæ, corporis proceri, mortis intrepidæ,

multitudes could no longer be confined within the walls of Tyre, or remain obedient to the voice of Conrad. They pitied the misfortunes, and revered the dignity, of Lusignan, who was released from prison, perhaps to divide the army of the Franks. He proposed the recovery of Ptolemais, or Acre, thirty miles to the south of Tyre; and the place was first invested by two thousand horse and thirty thousand foot under his nominal command. I shall not expatiate on the story of this memorable siege, which lasted near two years, and consumed, in a narrow space, the forces of Europe and Asia. Never did the flame of enthusiasm burn with fiercer and more destructive rage; nor could the true believers, a common appellation, who consecrated their own martyrs, refuse some applause to the mistaken zeal and courage of their adversaries. At the sound of the holy trumpet, the Moslems of Egypt, Syria, Arabia, and the Oriental provinces assembled under the servant of the prophet:[76] his camp was pitched and removed within a few miles of Acre; and he laboured, night and day, for the relief of his brethren and the annoyance of the Franks. Nine battles, not unworthy of the name, were fought in the neighbourhood of Mount Carmel, with such vicissitude of fortune that in one attack the sultan forced his way into the city; [76a] that in one sally the Christians penetrated to the royal tent. By the means of divers and pigeons a regular correspondence was maintained with the besieged; and, as often as the sea was left open, the exhausted garrison was withdrawn, and a fresh supply was poured into the place. The Latin camp was thinned by famine, the sword, and the climate; but the tents of the dead were replenished with new pilgrims, who exaggerated the strength and speed of their approaching countrymen. The vulgar was astonished by the report that the pope himself, with an innumerable crusade, was advanced as far as Constantinople. The march of the emperor filled the East with more serious alarms; the obstacles which he encountered in Asia, and perhaps in Greece, were raised by the policy of Saladin; his joy on the death of Barbarossa was

Siege of Acre. A.D. 1189, July— A.D. 1191, July

bipennibus armatæ, navibus rotundis quæ Ysnachiæ [=esnecca, νάκκα] dicuntur advectæ.

[76] The historian of Jerusalem (p. 1108) adds the nations of the East from the Tigris to India, and the swarthy tribes of Moors and Getulians, so that Asia and Africa fought against Europe.

[76a] [More than once.]

measured by his esteem; and the Christians were rather dismayed than encouraged at the sight of the duke of Swabia and his wayworn remnant of five thousand Germans. At length, in the spring of the second year, the royal fleets of France and England cast anchor in the bay of Acre, and the siege was more vigorously prosecuted by the youthful emulation of the two kings, Philip Augustus and Richard Plantagenet. After every resource had been tried, and every hope was exhausted, the defenders of Acre submitted to their fate; a capitulation was granted, but their lives and liberties were taxed at the hard conditions of a ransom of two hundred thousand pieces of gold, the deliverance of one hundred nobles and fifteen hundred inferior captives, and the restoration of the wood of the holy cross. Some doubts in the agreement, and some delay in the execution, rekindled the fury of the Franks, and three thousand Moslems, almost in the sultan's view, were beheaded by the command of the sanguinary Richard.[77] By the conquest of Acre the Latin powers acquired a strong town and a convenient harbour; but the advantage was most dearly purchased. The minister and historian of Saladin computes, from the report of the enemy, that their numbers, at different periods, amounted to five or six hundred thousand; that more than one hundred thousand Christians were slain; that a far greater number was lost by disease or shipwreck; and that a small portion of this mighty host could return in safety to their native countries.[78]

Richard of England, in Palestine. A.D. 1191, 1192   Philip Augustus and Richard the First are the only kings of France and England who have fought under the same banners; but the holy service in which they were enlisted was incessantly disturbed by their national jealousy; and the two factions which they protected in Palestine were more averse to each other than to the common enemy. In the eyes of the Orientals the French monarch was superior in dignity and power; and, in the

---

[77] Bohadin, p. 180; and this massacre is neither denied nor blamed by the Christian historians. Alacriter jussa complentes (the English soldiers), says Galfridus a Vinesauf (l. iv. c. iv. p. 346), who fixes at 2700 the number of victims; who are multiplied to 5000 by Roger Hoveden (p. 697, 698). The humanity or avarice of Philip Augustus was persuaded to ransom his prisoners (Jacob. a Vitriaco, l. i. c. 98 [*leg.* 99], p. 1122).

[78] Bohadin, p. 14. He quotes the judgment of Balianus and the prince of Sidon, and adds, Ex illo mundo quasi hominum paucissimi redierunt. Among the Christians who died before St. John d'Acre, I find the English names of De Ferrers, Earl of Derby (Dugdale, Baronage, p. i. p. 260), Mowbray (idem, p. 124), de Mandevil, de Fiennes, St. John, Scrope, Pigot, Talbot, &c.

mperor's absence, the Latins revered him as their temporal
hief.[79] His exploits were not adequate to his fame. Philip
vas brave, but the statesman predominated in his character ;
he was soon weary of sacrificing his health and interest on a
barren coast ; the surrender of Acre became the signal of his [July, 1191]
leparture : nor could he justify this unpopular desertion by
eaving the duke of Burgundy, with five hundred knights and
en thousand foot, for the service of the Holy Land. The
King of England, though inferior in dignity, surpassed his rival
n wealth and military renown ;[80] and, if heroism be confined
o brutal and ferocious valour, Richard Plantagenet will stand
iigh among the heroes of the age. The memory of *Cœur de
Lion*, of the lion-hearted prince, was long dear and glorious to
his English subjects ; and, at the distance of sixty years, it was
celebrated in proverbial sayings by the grandsons of the Turks
and Saracens against whom he had fought : his tremendous
iame was employed by the Syrian mothers to silence their
nfants ; and, if an horse suddenly started from the way, his
ider was wont to exclaim, "Dost thou think King Richard is
n that bush ? "[81] His cruelty to the Mahometans was the
effect of temper and zeal ; but I cannot believe that a soldier, so
ree and fearless in the use of his lance, would have descended
o whet a dagger against his valiant brother, Conrad of Mont-
errat, who was slain at Tyre by some secret assassins.[82] After [A.D. 1192]
he surrender of Acre and the departure of Philip, the king of
England led the crusaders to the recovery of the sea-coast ;
and the cities of Cæsarea and Jaffa were added to the fragments

[79] Magnus hic apud eos, interque reges eorum tum virtute, tum majestate
minens . . . summus rerum arbiter (Bohadin, p. 159). He does not seem to have
nown the names either of Philip or Richard.
[80] Rex Angliæ præstrenuus . . . rege Gallorum minor apud eos censebatur
atione regni atque dignitatis ; sed tum divitiis florentior, tum bellicâ virtute multo
rat celebrior (Bohadin, p. 161). A stranger might admire those riches ; the
ational historians will tell with what lawless and wasteful oppression they were
ollected.
[81] Joinville, p. 17. Cuides-tu que ce soit le roi Richart ?
[82] Yet he was guilty in the opinion of the Moslems, who attest the confession
f the assassins that they were sent by the king of England (Bohadin, p. 225) ; and
is only defence is an absurd and palpable forgery (Hist. de l'Académie des
nscriptions, tom. xvi. p. 155-163), a pretended letter from the prince of the
assassins, the Sheich, or old man of the mountain, who justified Richard, by
assuming to himself the guilt or merit of the murder. [For the forged letter see
Röhricht, Regesta Regni Hierosol. 715. Cp. Itin. regis Ric. V. c. 26, where the old
nan of the mountain is called *Senior de Musse*, i.e., of Masyâf, a fort of the
assassins in the Ansarîya Mts. See S. Guyard, Un grand-maître des Assassins.]

of the kingdom of Lusignan. A march of one hundred miles

[At Asca-
lon. Jan.,
A.D. 1192]

[Battle of
Arsuf.
Sept. 7, A.D.
1191]

from Acre to Ascalon was a great and perpetual battle of eleven days.[83] In the disorder of his troops, Saladin remained on the field with seventeen guards, without lowering his standard or suspending the sound of his brazen kettle-drum : he again rallied and renewed the charge ; and his preachers or heralds called aloud on the *Unitarians* manfully to stand up against the Christian idolaters. But the progress of these idolaters was irresistible ; and it was only by demolishing the walls and buildings of Ascalon that the sultan could prevent them from occupying an important fortress on the confines of Egypt. During a severe winter the armies slept ; but in the spring the Franks advanced within a day's march of Jerusalem, under the leading standard of the English king ; and his active spirit intercepted a convoy, or caravan, of seven thousand camels. Saladin [84] had fixed his station in the holy city ; but the city was struck with consternation and discord : he fasted ; he prayed ;

[June, A.D.
1192]

he preached ; he offered to share the dangers of the siege ; but his Mamalukes, who remembered the fate of their companions at Acre, pressed the sultan with loyal or seditious clamours to preserve *his* person and *their* courage for the future defence of the religion and empire.[85] The Moslems were delivered by the sudden or, as they deemed, the miraculous retreat of the Christians ; [86] and the laurels of Richard were blasted by the prudence or envy of his companions. The hero, ascending an hill, and veiling his face, exclaimed with an indignant voice, " Those who are unwilling to rescue, are unworthy to view, the sepulchre of Christ ! " After his return to Acre, on the news that Jaffa was surprised by the sultan, he sailed with some merchant vessels, and leaped foremost on the beach ; the castle

---

[83] [The march was 60 miles from Acre to Jaffa, where there was a long halt. Richard approached twice within sight of Jerusalem, Jan. and June, 1192.]

[84] See the distress and pious firmness of Saladin, as they are described by Bohadin (p. 7-9 ; 235-237), who himself harangued the defenders of Jerusalem. Their fears were not unknown to the enemy (Jacob. a Vitriaco, l. i. c. 100, p. 1123 ; Vinisauf, l. v. c. 50, p. 399).

[85] Yet, unless the sultan, or an Ayoubite prince, remained in Jerusalem, nec Curdi Turcis, nec Turci essent obtemperaturi Curdis (Bohadin, p. 236). He draws aside a corner of the political curtain.

[86] Bohadin (p. 237), and even Jeffrey de Vinisauf (l. vi. c. 1-8, p. 403-409), ascribe the retreat to Richard himself ; and Jacobus a Vitriaco observes that, in his impatience to depart, in alterum virum mutatus est (p. 1123). Yet Joinville, a French knight, accuses the envy of Hugh, duke of Burgundy (p. 116), without supposing, like Matthew Paris, that he was bribed by Saladin.

was relieved by his presence; and sixty thousand Turks and Saracens fled before his arms. The discovery of his weakness provoked them to return in the morning; [86a] and they found him carelessly encamped before the gates with only seventeen knights and three hundred archers. Without counting their numbers, he sustained their charge; and we learn from the evidence of his enemies, that the king of England, grasping his lance, rode furiously along their front, from the right to the left wing, without meeting an adversary who dared to encounter his career.[87] Am I writing the history of Orlando or Amadis?

During these hostilities a languid and tedious negotiation [88] between the Franks and the Moslems was started, and continued, and broken, and again resumed, and again broken. Some acts of royal courtesy, the gift of snow and fruit, the exchange of Norway hawks and Arabian horses, softened the asperity of religious war: from the vicissitude of success the monarchs might learn to suspect that Heaven was neutral in the quarrel; nor, after the trial of each other, could either hope for a decisive victory.[89] The health both of Richard and Saladin appeared to be in a declining state; and they respectively suffered the evils of distant and domestic warfare: Plantagenet was impatient to punish a perfidious rival who had invaded Normandy in his

His treaty and departure. A.D. 1192, September

[86a] [Not exactly: four days later.]

[87] The expeditions to Ascalon, Jerusalem, and Jaffa are related by Bohadin (p. 184-249) and Abulfeda (p. 51, 52). The author of the Itinerary, or the monk of St. Albans, cannot exaggerate the Cadhi's account of the prowess of Richard (Vinisauf, l. vi. c. 14-24, p. 412-421; [Matthew Paris], Hist. Major, p. 137-143); and on the whole of this war there is a marvellous agreement between the Christian and Mahometan writers, who mutually praise the virtues of their enemies. [For Jaffa cp. the Chron. Anglicanum of Ralph of Coggeshall (Rolls Series), who was informed by Hugh Neville, an eye-witness.]

[88] See the progress of negotiation and hostility, in Bohadin (p. 207-260), who was himself an actor in the treaty. Richard declared his intention of returning with new armies to the conquest of the Holy Land; and Saladin answered the menace with a civil compliment (Vinisauf, l. vi. c. 28, p. 423).

[89] The most copious and original account of this holy war is Galfridi a Vinisauf Itinerarium Regis Anglorum Richardi et aliorum in Terram Hierosolymorum, in six books, published in the iid volume of Gale's Scriptores Hist. Anglicanæ (p. 247-429). [This work is still sometimes referred to under the name of Geoffrey Vinsauf, though Stubbs (who has edited it for the Rolls Series under the title Itinerarium Regis Ricardi, 1864) has demonstrated that it is not his work. It was written by an eye-witness of the capture of Jerusalem, and published between 1200 and 1220 (Stubbs, op. cit., Introduction, p. lxx.); and Stubbs advocates the authorship of a certain Richard, canon of the Holy Trinity in Aldgate (cp. App. 1).] Roger Hoveden [ed. Stubbs, 4 vols., 1868-71] and Matthew Paris [ed. Luard, 7 vols., 1872-83] afford likewise many valuable materials; and the former describes with accuracy the discipline and navigation of the English fleet. [Add Ralph of Coggeshall, Rolls Series; cp. Appendix 1.]

absence; and the indefatigable sultan was subdued by the cries of the people, who was the victim, and of the soldiers, who were the instruments, of his martial zeal. The first demands of the king of England were the restitution of Jerusalem, Palestine, and the true cross ; and he firmly declared that himself and his brother-pilgrims would end their lives in the pious labour, rather than return to Europe with ignominy and remorse. But the conscience of Saladin refused, without some weighty compensation, to restore the idols, or promote the idolatry, of the Christians: he asserted, with equal firmness, his religious and civil claim to the sovereignty of Palestine; descanted on the importance and sanctity of Jerusalem; and rejected all terms of the establishment, or partition, of the Latins. The marriage which Richard proposed, of his sister with the sultan's brother, was defeated by the difference of faith ; the princess abhorred the embraces of a Turk; and Adel, or Saphadin, would not easily renounce a plurality of wives. A personal interview was declined by Saladin, who alleged their mutual ignorance of each other's language; [89a] and the negotiation was managed with much art and delay by their interpreters and envoys. The final agreement was equally disapproved by the zealots of both parties, by the Roman pontiff, and the caliph of Bagdad. It was stipulated that Jerusalem and the holy sepulchre should be open, without tribute or vexation, to the pilgrimage of the Latin Christians; that, after the demolition of Ascalon, they should inclusively possess the sea coast from Jaffa to Tyre; that the count of Tripoli and the prince of Antioch should be comprised in the truce; and that, during three years and three months, all hostilities should cease. The principal chiefs of the two armies swore to the observance of the treaty; but the monarchs were satisfied with giving their word and their right hand ; and the royal Majesty was excused from an oath, which always implies some suspicion of falsehood and dishonour. Richard embarked for Europe, to seek a long captivity and a premature grave; and the space of a few months concluded the life and glories of Saladin. The Orientals describe his edifying death, which happened at Damascus; but they seem ignorant of the equal

[Joan]

Death of
Saladin.
A.D. 1193,
March 4

[89a] [Not the reason assigned. Saladin alleged unwillingness to fight with a king after a friendly interview.]

MOHAMMEDAN ART; THE MOSQUE AT MAYAFARKIN, ATTRIBUTED TO SALADIN

distribution of his alms among the three religions,[90] or of the display of a shroud, instead of a standard, to admonish the East of the instability of human greatness. The unity of empire was dissolved by his death; his sons were oppressed by the stronger arm of their uncle Saphadin; the hostile interests of the Sultans of Egypt, Damascus, and Aleppo[91] were again revived; and the Franks or Latins stood, and breathed, and hoped, in their fortresses along the Syrian coast.

The noblest monument of a conqueror's fame, and of the terror which he inspired, is the Saladine tenth, a general tax, which was imposed on the laity, and even the clergy, of the Latin church, for the service of the holy war. The practice was too lucrative to expire with the occasion; and this tribute became the foundation of all the tithes and tenths on ecclesiastical benefices which have been granted by the Roman pontiffs to Catholic sovereigns, or reserved for the immediate use of the apostolic see.[92] This pecuniary emolument must have tended to increase the interest of the Popes in the recovery of Palestine; after the death of Saladin they preached the crusade by their epistles, their legates, and their missionaries; and the accomplishment of the pious work might have been expected from the zeal and talents of Innocent the Third.[93] Under that young and ambitious priest the successors of St. Peter attained the full meridian of their greatness; and in a reign of eighteen years he exercised a despotic command over the emperors and kings, whom he raised and deposed; over the nations, whom an interdict of months or years deprived, for the offence of their rulers, of the exercise of Christian worship. In the council of the Lateran he acted as the ecclesiastical, almost as the temporal, sovereign of the East and West. It was at the feet of his legate that John of England surrendered his crown; and Innocent may boast of the two most signal triumphs over sense and

[margin note: Innocent III. A.D. 1198-1216]

---

[90] Even Vertot (tom. i. p. 251) adopts the foolish notion of the indifference of Saladin, who professed the Koran with his last breath.

[91] See the succession of the Ayoubites, in Abulpharagius (Dynast. p. 227, &c.), and the tables of M. de Guignes, l'Art de Vérifier les Dates, and the Bibliothèque Orientale.

[92] Thomassin (Discipline de l'Eglise, tom. iii. p. 311-374) has copiously treated of the origin, abuses, and restrictions of these *tenths*. A theory was started, but not pursued, that they were rightfully due to the pope, a tenth of the Levites' tenth to the high-priest (Selden on Tithes. See his Works, vol. iii. p. ii. p. 1083).

[93] See the Gesta Innocentii III. [by a contemporary] in Muratori, Script. Rer. Ital. (tom. iii. p. 486-568) [Migne, P. L. 214, p. xvii. *sqq.*].

humanity, the establishment of transubstantiation and the origin of the inquisition. At his voice, two crusades, the fourth and the fifth, were undertaken; but, except a king of Hungary, the princes of the second order were at the head of the pilgrims; the forces were inadequate to the design; nor did the effects correspond with the hopes and wishes of the pope and the people. The fourth crusade was diverted from Syria to Constantinople; and the conquest of the Greek or Roman empire by the Latins will form the proper and important subject of the next chapter. In the fifth,[94] two hundred thousand Franks were landed at the eastern mouth of the Nile. They reasonably hoped that Palestine must be subdued in Egypt, the seat and storehouse of the sultan; and, after a siege of sixteen months, the Moslems deplored the loss of Damietta. But the Christian army was ruined by the pride and insolence of the legate Pelagius, who, in the Pope's name, assumed the character of general; the sickly Franks were encompassed by the waters of the Nile and the Oriental forces; and it was by the evacuation of Damietta that they obtained a safe retreat, some concessions for the pilgrims, and the tardy restitution of the doubtful relic of the true cross. The failure may in some measure be ascribed to the abuse and multiplication of the crusades, which were preached at the same time against the pagans of Livonia, the Moors of Spain, the Albigeois of France, and the kings of Sicily of the Imperial family.[95] In these meritorious services the volunteers might acquire at home the same spiritual indulgence and a larger measure of temporal rewards; and even the popes, in their zeal against a domestic enemy, were sometimes tempted to forget the distress of their Syrian brethren. From the last age of the crusades they derived the occasional command of an

The fourth
crusade.
A.D. 1203

The fifth.
A.D. 1218

---

[94] See the vth crusade, and the siege of Damietta, in Jacobus a Vitriaco (l. iii. p. 1125-1149, in the Gesta Dei of Bongarsius),,an eye-witness, Bernard Thesaurarius (in Script. Muratori, tom. vii. p. 825-846, c. 190-207), a contemporary, and Sanutus (Secreta Fidel. Crucis, l. iii. p. xi. c. 4-9), a diligent compiler ; and of the Arabians, Abulpharagius (Dynast. p. 294), and the Extracts at the end of Joinville (p. 533, 537, 540, 547, &c.). [Also the Gesta obsidionis Damiatae in Muratori, S. R. I. 8, p. 1084 *sqq.* ; and Röhricht, Quinti belli sacri Script. min. p. 73 *sqq.*, 1879. Holder-Egger has vindicated the authorship for John Cadagnellus (Neues Archiv, 16, 287 *sqq.*, 1891).]

[95] To those who took the cross against Mainfroy, the pope (A.D. 1255) granted plenissimam peccatorum remissionem. Fideles mirabantur quod tantum eis promitteret pro sanguine Christianorum effundendo quantum pro cruore infidelium aliquando (Matthew Paris, p. 785). A high flight for the reason of the xiiith century !

army and revenue ; and some deep reasoners have suspected
that the whole enterprise, from the first synod of Placentia, was
contrived and executed by the policy of Rome. The suspicion
is not founded either in nature or in fact. The successors of
St. Peter appear to have followed, rather than guided, the impulse of manners and prejudice; without much foresight of the
seasons or cultivation of the soil, they gathered the ripe and
spontaneous fruits of the superstition of the times. They
gathered these fruits without toil or personal danger : in the
council of the Lateran, Innocent the Third declared an ambiguous resolution of animating the crusaders by his example ; but
the pilot of the sacred vessel could not abandon the helm ; nor
was Palestine ever blessed with the presence of a Roman
pontiff.[96]

The persons, the families, and estates of the pilgrims were The emper-
under the immediate protection of the popes ; and these spiritual II. in Pales-
patrons soon claimed the prerogative of directing their opera- tine. A.D.
tions and enforcing, by commands and censures, the accomplish- 1228
ment of their vow. Frederic the Second,[97] the grandson of
Barbarossa, was successively the pupil, the enemy, and the victim
of the church. At the age of twenty-one years, and in obedience
to his guardian Innocent the Third, he assumed the cross ; the
same promise was repeated at his royal and imperial coronations ;
and his marriage with the heiress of Jerusalem [98] for ever bound [Nov., A.D.
him to defend the kingdom of his son Conrad. But, as Frederic 1225]
advanced in age and authority, he repented of the rash engagements of his youth ; his liberal sense and knowledge taught him
to despise the phantoms of superstition and the crowns of Asia ;
he no longer entertained the same reverence for the successors
of Innocent ; and his ambition was occupied by the restoration
of the Italian monarchy from Sicily to the Alps. But the success

[96] This simple idea is agreeable to the good sense of Mosheim (Institut.
Hist. Eccles. p. 332) and the fine philosophy of Hume (Hist. of England, vol. i. p.
330).
[97] The original materials for the crusade of Frederic II. may be drawn from
Richard de St. Germano (in Muratori, Script. Rerum Ital. tom. vii. p. 1002-1013
[Chronica regni Siciliæ, a contemporary work preserved in two redactions : ed.
Pertz, Mon. Germ. Hist. xix. p. 323 sqq.; and Gaudenzi (in the Monumenti
Storici, published by the Società Napolitana di storia patria), 1888]), and
Matthew Paris (p. 286, 291, 300, 302, 304). The most rational moderns are
Fleury (Hist. Ecclés. tom. xvi.), Vertot (Chevaliers de Malthe, tom. i. l. iii.),
Giannone (Istoria Civile di Napoli, tom. ii. l. xvi.), and Muratori (Annali d'Italia,
tom. x.).
[98] [Yolande, daughter of John of Brienne.]

of this project would have reduced the popes to their primitive simplicity; and, after the delays and excuses of twelve years, they urged the emperor, with entreaties and threats, to fix the time and place of his departure for Palestine.   In the harbours of Sicily and Apulia, he prepared a fleet of one hundred galleys, and of one hundred vessels, that were framed to transport and land two thousand five hundred knights, with their horses and attendants; his vassals of Naples and Germany formed a powerful army; and the number of English crusaders was magnified to sixty thousand by the report of fame.   But the inevitable or affected slowness of these mighty preparations consumed the strength and provisions of the more indigent pilgrims; the multitude was thinned by sickness and desertion, and the sultry summer of Calabria anticipated the mischiefs of a Syrian campaign.   At length the emperor hoisted sail at [A.D. 1227] Brundusium, with a fleet and army of forty thousand men; but he kept the sea no more than three days; and his hasty retreat, which was ascribed by his friends to a grievous indisposition, was accused by his enemies as a voluntary and obstinate obedience. For suspending his vow was Frederic excommunicated by Gregory the Ninth; for presuming, the next year, to accomplish his vow, he was again excommunicated by the same pope.[99] While he served under the banner of the cross, a crusade was preached against him in Italy; and after his return he was compelled to ask pardon for the injuries which he had suffered. The clergy and military orders of Palestine were previously instructed to renounce his communion and dispute his commands; and in his own kingdom the emperor was forced to consent that the orders of the camp should be issued in the name of [March 18, A.D. 1229] God and of the Christian republic.   Frederic entered Jerusalem in triumph; and with his own hands (for no priest would perform the office) he took the crown from the altar of the holy sepulchre.   But the patriarch cast an interdict on the church which his presence had profaned; and the knights of the hospital and temple informed the sultan[100] how easily he might be surprised and slain in his unguarded visit to the river Jordan.   In such a state of fanaticism and faction, victory was hopeless and

---

[99] Poor Muratori knows what to think, but knows not what to say, " Chinò qui il capo," &c. p. 322.
[100] [Al-Kāmil Mohammad, 1218-1238.]

THE EMPEROR FREDERICK II, ENLARGED
FROM AN *AUGUSTALE*
BRITISH MUSEUM

defence was difficult; but the conclusion of an advantageous peace may be imputed to the discord of the Mahometans, and their personal esteem for the character of Frederic. The enemy of the church is accused of maintaining with the miscreants an intercourse of hospitality and friendship, unworthy of a Christian; of despising the barrenness of the land; and of indulging a profane thought that, if Jehovah had seen the kingdom of Naples, he never would have selected Palestine for the inheritance of his chosen people. Yet Frederic obtained from the sultan the restitution of Jerusalem, of Bethlem and Nazareth, of Tyre and Sidon; the Latins were allowed to inhabit and fortify the city; an equal code of civil and religious freedom was ratified for the sectaries of Jesus, and those of Mahomet; and, while the former worshipped at the holy sepulchre, the latter might pray and preach in the mosque of the temple,[101] from whence the prophet undertook his nocturnal journey to heaven. The clergy deplored this scandalous toleration; and the weaker Moslems were gradually expelled; but every rational object of the crusades was accomplished without bloodshed; the churches were restored, the monasteries were replenished; and, in the space of fifteen years, the Latins of Jerusalem exceeded the number of six thousand. This peace and prosperity, for which they were ungrateful to their benefactor, was terminated by the irruption of the strange and savage hordes of Carizmians.[102] Flying from the arms of the Moguls, those shepherds of the Caspian rolled headlong on Syria;[103] and the union of the Franks with the sultans of Aleppo, Hems, and Damascus was insufficient to stem the violence of the torrent. Whatever stood against them was cut off by the sword or dragged into captivity; the military orders were almost exterminated in a single battle; and in the pillage of the city, in the profanation of the holy sepulchre, the Latins confess and regret the modesty and discipline of the Turks and Saracens.

Of the seven crusades, the two last were undertaken by

Invasion of the Carizmians. A.D. 1243

[Battle of Gaza. A.D. 1244, Oct. 14]

---

[101] The clergy artfully confounded the mosque, or church of the temple, with the holy sepulchre; and their wilful error has deceived both Vertot and Muratori.

[102] The irruption of the Carizmians, or Corasmins, is related by Matthew Paris p. 546, 547), and by Joinville, Nangis, and the Arabians (p. 111, 112, 191, 192, 528, 530).

[103] [They were called in as allies by the Sultan of Egypt, As-Sālih Ayyūb.]

St. Louis, and the sixth cru- sade. A.D. 1248-1254

Louis the Ninth, king of France, who lost his liberty in Egypt, and his life on the coast of Africa. Twenty-eight years after his death, he was canonized at Rome; and sixty-five miracles were readily found, and solemnly attested, to justify the claim of the royal saint.[104] The voice of history renders a more honourable testimony, that he united the virtues of a king, an hero, and a man; that his martial spirit was tempered by the love of private and public justice; and that Louis was the father of his people, the friend of his neighbours, and the terror of the infidels. Superstition alone, in all the extent of her baleful influence,[105] corrupted his understanding and his heart; his devotion stooped to admire and imitate the begging friars of Francis and Dominic; he pursued with blind and cruel zeal the enemies of the faith; and the best of kings twice descended from his throne to seek the adventures of a spiritual knight-errant. A monkish historian would have been content to applaud the most despicable part of his character; but the noble and gallant Joinville,[106] who shared the friendship and captivity of Louis, has traced with the pencil of nature the free portrait of his virtues, as well as of his failings. From this intimate knowledge we may learn to suspect the political views of depressing their great vassals, which are so often imputed to the royal authors of the crusades. Above all the princes of the middle age, Louis the Ninth successfully laboured to restore the prerogatives of the crown; but it was at home, and not in the East, that he acquired for himself and his posterity; his vow was the result of enthusiasm and sickness; and, if he were the promoter, he was likewise the victim, of this holy madness.

[104] Read, if you can, the life and miracles of St. Louis, by the confessor of Queen Margaret (p. 291-523. Joinville, du Louvre).

[105] He believed all that Mother-church taught (Joinville, p. 10), but he cautioned Joinville against disputing with infidels. "L'omme lay," said he in his old language, "quand il ot medire de la loy Chrestienne, ne doit pas deffendre la loy Chrestienne ne mais que de l'espée, de quoi il doit donner parmi le ventre dedens, tant comme elle y peut entrer" (p. 12 [c. 10]).

[106] I have two editions of Joinville: the one (Paris, 1688) most valuable for the Observations of Ducange; the other (Paris, au Louvre, 1761) most precious for the pure and authentic text, a Ms. of which has been recently discovered. The last editor proves that the history of St. Louis was finished A.D. 1309, without explaining, or even admiring, the age of the author, which must have exceeded ninety years (Preface, p. xi., Observations de Ducange, p. 17). [Joinville's Histoire de Saint Louys IX. may be now most conveniently consulted in one of the editions of Natalis de Wailly (1867, 1874, &c.). The fine Paris edition of 1761 was edited by Mellot, Sallier, and Capperonnier, and included the Annals of William des Nangis.]

For the invasion of Egypt, France was exhausted of her troops and treasures; he covered the sea of Cyprus with eighteen hundred sails; the most modest enumeration amounts to fifty thousand men; and, if we might trust his own confession, as it is reported by Oriental vanity, he disembarked nine thousand five hundred horse, and one hundred and thirty thousand foot, who performed their pilgrimage under the shadow of his power.[107]

In complete armour, the oriflamme waving before him, Louis leaped foremost on the beach; and the strong city of Damietta, which had cost his predecessors a siege of sixteen months, was abandoned on the first assault by the trembling Moslems. But Damietta was the first and last of his conquests; and in the fifth and sixth crusades the same causes, almost on the same ground, were productive of similar calamities.[108] After a ruinous delay, which introduced into the camp the seeds of an epidemical disease, the Franks advanced from the sea-coast towards the capital of Egypt, and strove to surmount the unseasonable inundation of the Nile, which opposed their progress. Under the eye of their intrepid monarch, the barons and knights of France displayed their invincible contempt of danger and discipline: his brother, the count of Artois, stormed with inconsiderate valour the town of Massoura; and the carrier-pigeons announced to the inhabitants of Cairo, that all was lost. But a soldier, who afterwards usurped the sceptre, rallied the flying troops; the main body of Christians was far behind their vanguard; and Artois was overpowered and slain. A shower of Greek fire was incessantly poured on the invaders; the Nile was commanded by the Egyptian galleys, the open country by the Arabs; all provisions were intercepted; each day aggravated the sickness and famine; and about the same time a retreat was found to be necessary and impracticable. The Oriental writers confess that Louis might have escaped, if he would have deserted his subjects: he was made prisioner, with the

He takes
Damietta.
A.D. 1249
[May]

[A.D. 1250,
March]

---

107 Joinville, p. 32; Arabic Extracts, p. 549.

108 The last editors have enriched their Joinville with large and curious extracts from the Arabic historians, Macrizi, Abulfeda, &c. See likewise Abulpharagius (Dynast. p. 322-325), who calls him by the corrupt name of *Redefrans*. Matthew Paris (p. 683, 684) has described the rival folly of the French and English who fought and fell at Massoura. [Makrizi's important work is now accessible in Quatremère's French translation. See Appendix 1. The crusade has been recently narrated by E. J. Davis in a work entitled Invasion of Egypt in A.D. 1249 by Louis IX. of France and a History of the Contemporary Sultans of Egypt (1897).]

greatest part of his nobles; all who could not redeem their lives by service or ransom were inhumanly massacred; and the walls of Cairo were decorated with a circle of Christian heads.[109]

The king of France was loaded with chains; but the generous victor, a great-grandson of the brother of Saladin, sent a robe of honour to his royal captive; and his deliverance, with that of his soldiers, was obtained by the restitution of Damietta [110] and the payment of four hundred thousand pieces of gold. In a soft and luxurious climate, the degenerate children of the companions of Noureddin and Saladin were incapable of resisting the flower of European chivalry; they triumphed by the arms of their slaves or Mamalukes, the hardy natives of Tartary, who at a tender age had been purchased of the Syrian merchants, and were educated in the camp and palace of the sultan. But Egypt soon afforded a new example of the danger of prætorian bands; and the rage of these ferocious animals, who had been let loose on the strangers, was provoked to devour their benefactor. In the pride of conquest, Touran

Shah,[111] the last of his race, was murdered by his Mamalukes; and the most daring of the assassins entered the chamber of the captive king, with drawn scymetars, and their hands imbrued in the blood of their sultan. The firmness of Louis commanded their respect; [112] their avarice prevailed over cruelty

[109] Savary, in his agreeable Lettres sur l'Egypt, has given a description of Damietta (tom. i. lettre xxiii. p. 274-290) and a narrative of the expedition of St. Louis (xxv. p. 306). [In his Art of War, ii. p. 338-50, Oman gives a full áccount of the battle of Mansurah. He shows that the battle was lost because the reckless charge of Robert of Artois led to the separation of the cavalry and infantry; and it was only by a combination of cavalry and infantry that it was possible to deal with the horse-archers of the East.]

[110] For the ransom of St. Louis, a million of byzants was asked and granted; but the sultan's generosity reduced that sum to 800,000 byzants, which are valued by Joinville at 400,000 French livres of his own time, and expressed by Matthew Paris by 100,000 marks of silver (Ducange, Dissertation xx. sur Joinville).

[111] [Al-Muazzam Tūrān Shāh, A.D. 1249-50.]

[112] The idea of the emirs to choose Louis for their sultan is seriously attested by Joinville (p. 77, 78), and does not appear to me so absurd as to M. de Voltaire (Hist. Générale, tom. ii. p. 386, 387). The Mamalukes themselves were strangers, rebels, and equals; they had felt his valour, they hoped his conversion: and such a motion, which was not seconded, might be made perhaps by a secret Christian in their tumultuous assembly. [An interesting monument of Mamlūk history at this time is a coin of the Mamlūk queen, Shajar ad-Durr, the Tree of Pearls, who had risen from the condition of a slave. When the French landed in 1249, she concealed the death of her husband Sālih. After the battle of Mansurah, the heir died, and she was proclaimed queen, and reigned alone 2½ months. Then she married one Aibak; slew him; and was herself beaten to death by the slaves of a divorced wife of Aibak. The coin was struck at the moment of the discomfiture of St. Louis. See Stanley Lane-Poole, Coins and Medals, p. 158-161.]

and zeal; the treaty was accomplished; and the king of France, with the relics of his army, was permitted to embark for Palestine. He wasted four years within the walls of Acre, unable to visit Jerusalem, and unwilling to return without glory to his native country. [Return to France. A.D. 1254]

The memory of his defeat excited Louis, after sixteen years of wisdom and repose, to undertake the seventh and last of the crusades. His finances were restored, his kingdom was enlarged; a new generation of warriors had arisen, and he embarked with fresh confidence at the head of six thousand horse and thirty thousand foot. The loss of Antioch had provoked the enterprise; a wild hope of baptizing the King of Tunis tempted him to steer for the African coast; and the report of an immense treasure reconciled his troops to the delay of their voyage to the Holy Land. Instead of a proselyte he found a siege; the French panted and died on the burning sands; St. Louis expired in his tent; and no sooner had he closed his eyes than his son and successor gave the signal of the retreat.[113] "It is thus," says a lively writer, "that a Christian king died near the ruins of Carthage, waging war against the sectaries of Mahomet, in a land to which Dido had introduced the deities of Syria."[114] [His death before Tunis, in the seventh crusade. A.D. 1270, Aug. 25]

A more unjust and absurd constitution cannot be devised than that which condemns the natives of a country to perpetual servitude, under the arbitrary dominion of strangers and slaves. Yet such has been the state of Egypt above five hundred years. The most illustrious sultans of the Baharite and Borgite dynasties[115] were themselves promoted from the Tartar and Circassian bands; and the four-and-twenty beys or military chiefs, have ever been succeeded not by their sons but by their servants. They produce the great charter of their liberties, the [The Mamalukes of Egypt. A.D. 1250-1517]

---

[113] See the expedition in the Annals of St. Louis, by William de Nangis, p. 270-287, and the Arabic Extracts, p. 545, 555 of the Louvre edition of Joinville. [R. Steinfeld, Ludwigs des Heiligen Kreuzzug nach Tunis, 1270, und die Politik Karls I. von Sizilien (1896).]

[114] Voltaire, Hist. Générale, tom. ii. p. 391.

[115] The chronology of the two dynasties of Mamalukes, the Baharites, Turks or Tartars of Kipzak, and the Borgites, Circassians, is given by Pocock (Prolegom. ad Abulpharag. p. 6-31), and de Guignes (tom. i. p. 264-270) [see S. Lane-Poole, Mohammadan Dynasties, p. 80-83]; their history from Abulfeda, Macrizi, &c., to the beginning of the 15th century, by the same M. de Guignes (tom. iv. p. 110-328). [Weil's Gesch. der Chalifen, vols. 4 and 5.]

treaty of Selim the First with the republic ; [116] and the Othman emperor still accepts from Egypt a slight acknowledgment of tribute and subjection.[117] With some breathing intervals of peace and order, the two dynasties are marked as a period of rapine and bloodshed ; [118] but their throne, however shaken, reposed on the two pillars of discipline and valour ; their sway extended over Egypt, Nubia, Arabia, and Syria; their Mamalukes were multiplied from eight hundred to twenty-five thousand horse; and their numbers were increased by a provincial militia of one hundred and seven thousand foot, and the occasional aid of sixty-six thousand Arabs.[119] Princes of such power and spirit could not long endure on their coast an hostile and independent nation ; and, if the ruin of the Franks was postponed about forty years, they were indebted to the cares of an unsettled reign, to the invasion of the Mogols, and to the occasional aid of some warlike pilgrims. Among these, the English reader will observe the name of our first Edward, who assumed the cross in the lifetime of his father Henry. At the head of a thousand soldiers, the future conqueror of Wales and Scotland delivered Acre from a siege ; marched as far as Nazareth with an army of nine thousand men ; emulated the fame of his uncle Richard ; extorted, by his valour, a ten years' truce ; and escaped, with a dangerous wound, from the dagger of a fanatic *assassin*.[120] Antioch,[121] whose situation had been

---

[116] Savary, Lettres sur l'Egypt, tom. ii. lettre xv. p. 189-208. I much question the authenticity of this copy ; yet it is true that Sultan Selim concluded a treaty with the Circassians or Mamalukes of Egypt, and left them in possession of arms, riches, and power. See a new Abrégé de l'Histoire Ottomane, composed in Egypt, and translated by M. Digeon (tom. i. p. 55-58, Paris, 1781), a curious, authentic, and national history.

[117] [And Egypt was governed by a Turkish Pasha, whose power was limited by the council of beys.]

[118] Si totum quo regnum occupârunt tempus respicias, presertim quod fini propius, reperies illud bellis, pugnis, injuriis, ac rapinis refertum (Al Jannabi, apud Pocock, p. 31). The reign of Mohammed (A.D. 1311-1341) affords an happy exception (de Guignes, tom. iv. p. 208-210).

[119] They are now reduced to 8500 ; but the expense of each Mamaluke may be rated at 100 louis, and Egypt groans under the avarice and insolence of these strangers (Voyages de Volney, tom. i. p. 89-187).

[120] See Carte's History of England, vol. ii. p. 165-175, and his original authors, Thomas Wikes [Wykes; ed. by Luard, Annales Monastici, iv. 1869] and Walter Hemingford [Walterus Gisburniensis; ed. by H. C. Hamilton for the English Historical Society, 1848] (l. iii. c. 34, 35) in Gale's Collections (tom. ii. p. 97, 589-592). They are both ignorant of the Princess Eleanor's piety in sucking the poisoned wound, and saving her husband at the risk of her own life.

[121] Sanutus, Secret. Fidelium Crucis, l. iii. p. xii. c. 9, and de Guignes, Hist. des Huns, tom. iv. p. 143, from the Arabic historians.

less exposed to the calamities of the holy war, was finally Loss of Antioch. occupied and ruined by Bondocdar, or Bibars,[122] sultan of Egypt A.D. 1268, June 12 and Syria; the Latin principality was extinguished; and the first seat of the Christian name was dispeopled by the slaughter of seventeen, and the captivity of one hundred thousand, of her inhabitants. The maritime towns of Laodicea, Gabala, Tripoli, Berytus, Sidon, Tyre, and Jaffa, and the stronger castles of the Hospitalers and Templars, successively fell; and the whole existence of the Franks was confined to the city and colony of St. John of Acre, which is sometimes described by the more classic title of Ptolemais.

After the loss of Jerusalem, Acre,[123] which is distant about seventy miles, became the metropolis of the Latin Christians, and was adorned with strong and stately buildings, with aqueducts, an artificial port, and a double wall. The population was increased by the incessant streams of pilgrims and fugitives; in the pauses of hostility the trade of the East and West was attracted to this convenient station; and the market could offer the produce of every clime and the interpreters of every tongue. But in this conflux of nations every vice was propagated and practised; of all the disciples of Jesus and Mahomet, the male and female inhabitants of Acre were esteemed the most corrupt; nor could the abuse of religion be corrected by the discipline of law. The city had many sovereigns, and no government. The kings of Jerusalem and Cyprus, of the house of Lusignan, the princes of Antioch, the counts of Tripoli and Sidon, the great masters of the Hospital, the Temple, and the Teutonic order, the republics of Venice, Genoa, and Pisa, the pope's legate, the kings of France and England, assumed an independent command; seventeen tribunals exercised the power of life and death; every criminal was protected in the adjacent quarter; and the perpetual jealousy of the nations often burst forth in acts of violence and blood. Some adventurers, who disgraced the ensign of the cross, compensated their want of pay by the plunder of the Mahometan villages; nineteen Syrian merchants, who traded under the public faith, were despoiled and hanged by

---

[122] [Baybars al-Bundukdārī = the arbalestier.]
[123] The state of Acre is represented in all the chronicles of the times, and most accurately in John Villani, l. vii. c. 144, in Muratori, Scriptores Rerum Italicarum, tom. xiii. p. 337, 338.

the Christians; and the denial of satisfaction justified the arms of the sultan Khalil.   He marched against Acre, at the head of sixty thousand horse and one hundred and forty thousand foot; his train of artillery (if I may use the word) was numerous and weighty; the separate timbers of a single engine were transported in one hundred waggons; and the royal historian, Abulfeda, who served with the troops of Hamah, was himself a spectator of the holy war.   Whatever might be the vices of the Franks, their courage was rekindled by enthusiasm and despair; but they were torn by the discord of seventeen chiefs, and overwhelmed on all sides by the power of the sultan.   After a siege

The loss of
Acre and
the Holy
Land.   A.D.
1291, May
18 of thirty-three days, the double wall was forced by the Moslems; the principal tower yielded to their engines; the Mamalukes made a general assault; the city was stormed; and death or slavery was the lot of sixty thousand Christians.   The convent, or rather fortress, of the Templars resisted three days longer; but the great master was pierced with an arrow; and, of five hundred knights, only ten were left alive, less happy than the victims of the sword, if they lived to suffer on a scaffold in the unjust and cruel proscription of the whole order.   The king of Jerusalem, the patriarch and the great master of the Hospital effected their retreat to the shore; but the sea was rough, the vessels were insufficient; and great numbers of the fugitives were drowned before they could reach the isle of Cyprus, which might comfort Lusignan for the loss of Palestine.   By the command of the sultan, the churches and fortifications of the Latin cities were demolished; a motive of avarice or fear still opened the holy sepulchre to some devout and defenceless pilgrims; and a mournful and solitary silence prevailed along the coast which had so long resounded with the WORLD'S DEBATE.[124]

[124] See the final expulsion of the Franks, in Sanutus, l. ii. p. xii. c. 11-22. Abulfeda, Macrizi, &c., in de Guignes, tom. iv. p. 162, 164, and Vertot, tom. i. l. iii. p. 407-428.   [An important source for the siege of Acre is the anonymous *De Excidio urbis Acconis* (falsely ascribed to Adenulf of Anagnia) published in Martene and Durand, Ampliss. Collectio, vol. 5, p. 757 *sqq.*]

CHAPTER LX

*Schism of the Greeks and Latins—State of Constantinople—
Revolt of the Bulgarians—Isaac Angelus dethroned by
his brother Alexius — Origin of the Fourth Crusade —
Alliance of the French and Venetians with the son of
Isaac—Their naval expedition to Constantinople—The
two Sieges, and final Conquest of the City by the Latins*

THE restoration of the Western empire by Charlemagne Schism of
was speedily followed by the separation of the Greek the Greeks
and Latin churches.[1] A religious and national animosity still divides the two largest communions of the Christian
world; and the schism of Constantinople, by alienating her
most useful allies and provoking her most dangerous enemies,
has precipitated the decline and fall of the Roman empire in
the East.

In the course of the present history the aversion of the Their aver-
Greeks for the Latins has been often visible and conspicuous. sion to the
Latins
It was originally derived from the disdain of servitude, inflamed,
after the time of Constantine, by the pride of equality or dominion, and finally exasperated by the preference which their
rebellious subjects had given to the alliance of the Franks. In
every age the Greeks were proud of their superiority in profane
and religious knowledge; they had first received the light of
Christianity; they had pronounced the decrees of the seven
general councils; they alone possessed the language of Scripture
and philosophy; nor should the barbarians, immersed in the

[1] In the successive centuries, from the ixth to the xviiith, Mosheim traces the
schism of the Greeks, with learning, clearness, and impartiality : the *filioque*
(Institut. Hist. Eccles. p. 277); Leo III. p. 303; Photius, p. 307, 308; Michael
Cerularius, p. 370, 371, &c. [The relation between the eastern and western
churches is traced by Duchesne in his essay L'église grecque et le schisme grec,
in Eglises séparées, p. 163 *sqq.* L. Bréhier, Le Schisme oriental du XIe Siècle,
1899.]

darkness of the West,[2] presume to argue on the high and mysterious questions of theological science.   These barbarians despised, in their turn, the restless and subtle levity of the Orientals, the authors of every heresy; and blessed their own simplicity, which was content to hold the tradition of the apostolic church.   Yet, in the seventh century, the synods of Spain, and afterwards of France, improved or corrupted the Nicene creed, on the mysterious subject of the third person of the

Procession of the Holy Ghost Trinity.[3]   In the long controversies of the East, the nature and generation of the Christ had been scrupulously defined ; and the well-known relation of Father and Son seemed to convey a faint image to the human mind.   The idea of birth was less analogous to the Holy Spirit, who, instead of a divine gift or attribute, was considered by the Catholics as a substance, a person, a God ; he was not begotten, but, in the orthodox style, he *proceeded*. Did he proceed from the Father alone, perhaps *by* the Son? or from the Father *and* the Son?   The first of these opinions was asserted by the Greeks, the second by the Latins ; and the addition to the Nicene creed of the word *filioque* kindled the flame of discord between the Oriental and the Gallic churches. In the origin of the dispute the Roman pontiffs affected a character of neutrality and moderation ;[4] they condemned the innovation, but they acquiesced in the sentiment of their transalpine brethren; they seemed desirous of casting a veil of silence and charity over the superfluous research; and, in the correspondence of Charlemagne and Leo the Third, the Pope assumes the liberality of a statesman, and the prince descends to the passions and prejudices of a priest.[5]   But the orthodoxy

---

[2] Ἄνδρες δυσσεβεῖς καὶ ἀποτροπαῖοι, ἄνδρες ἐκ σκότους ἀναδύντες, τῆς γὰρ Ἑσπερίου μοίρας ὑπῆρχον γεννήματα (Phot. Epist. p. 47, edit. Montacut). The Oriental patriarch continues to apply the images of thunder, earthquake, hail, wild-boar, præcursors of Antichrist, &c. &c.

[3] The mysterious subject of the procession of the Holy Ghost is discussed in the historical, theological, and controversial sense, or nonsense, by the Jesuit Petavius (Dogmata Theologica, tom. ii. l. vii. p. 362-440). [The Greeks were right in saying that the *filioque* was an innovation on the symbolum recognized by the first four Councils.]

[4] Before the shrine of St. Peter he placed two shields of the weight of 94½ pounds of pure silver, on which he inscribed the text of both creeds (utroque symbolo), pro amore et *cauteld* orthodoxæ fidei (Anastas. in Leon. III. in Muratori, tom. iii. pars i. p. 208). His language most clearly proves that neither the filioque nor the Athanasian creed were received at Rome about the year 830.

[5] The Missi of Charlemagne pressed him to declare that all who rejected the *filioque*, at least the doctrine, must be damned. All, replies the Pope, are not capable of reaching the altiora mysteria ; qui potuerit, et non voluerit, salvus esse

of Rome spontaneously obeyed the impulse of her temporal policy; and the *filioque*, which Leo wished to erase, was transcribed in the symbol, and chaunted in the liturgy, of the Vatican. The Nicene and Athanasian creeds are held as the Catholic faith, without which none can be saved; and both Papists and Protestants must now sustain and return the anathemas of the Greeks, who deny the procession of the Holy Ghost from the Son, as well as from the Father. Such articles of faith are not susceptible of treaty; but the rules of discipline will vary in remote and independent churches; and the reason, even of divines, might allow that the difference is inevitable and harmless. The craft or superstition of Rome has imposed on her priests and deacons the rigid obligation of celibacy; among the Greeks, it is confined to the bishops; the loss is compensated by dignity or annihilated by age; and the parochial clergy, the papas, enjoy the conjugal society of the wives whom they have married before their entrance into holy orders. A question concerning the *Azyms* was fiercely debated in the eleventh century, and the essence of the Eucharist was supposed, in the East and West, to depend on the use of leavened or unleavened bread. Shall I mention in a serious history the furious reproaches that were urged against the Latins, who, for a long while, remained on the defensive? They neglected to abstain, according to the apostolical decree, from things strangled and from blood; they fasted, a Jewish observance! on the Saturday of each week; during the first week of Lent they permitted the use of milk and cheese;[6] their infirm monks were indulged in the taste of flesh; and animal grease was substituted for the want of vegetable oil; the holy chrism or unction in baptism was reserved to the episcopal order; the bishops, as the bridegrooms of their churches, were decorated with rings; their priests shaved their faces, and baptized by a single immersion. Such were the crimes which provoked the zeal of the patriarchs of Constantinople; and which were justified with equal zeal by the doctors of the Latin church.[7]

Variety of ecclesiastical discipline

non potest (Collect. Concil. tom. ix. p. 277-286). The *potuerit* would leave a large loop-hole of salvation !

[6] In France, after some harsher laws, the ecclesiastical discipline is now relaxed; milk, cheese and butter are become a perpetual, and eggs an annual, indulgence in Lent (Vie privée des François, tom. ii. p. 27-38).

[7] The original monuments of the schism, of the charges of the Greeks against the Latins, are deposited in the Epistles of Photius (Epist. Encyclica, ii. p. 47-61

Ambitious
quarrels of
Photius,
patriarch
of Con-
stanti-
nople, with
the Popes.
A.D. 857-886
Bigotry and national aversion are powerful magnifiers of every object of dispute ; but the immediate cause of the schism of the Greeks may be traced in the emulation of the leading prelates, who maintained the supremacy of the old metropolis superior to all, and of the reigning capital inferior to none, in the Christian world.   About the middle of the ninth century, Photius,[8] an ambitious layman, the captain of the guards and principal secretary, was promoted by merit and favour to the
more desirable office of patriarch of Constantinople.[9]   In science, even ecclesiastical science, he surpassed the clergy of the age ; and the purity of his morals has never been impeached ; but his ordination was hasty, his rise was irregular ; and Ignatius, his abdicated predecessor, was yet supported by the public compassion and the obstinacy of his adherents.   They appealed to the tribunal of Nicholas the First, one of the proudest and most aspiring of the Roman pontiffs, who embraced the welcome opportunity of judging and condemning his rival of the East.   Their quarrel was embittered by a conflict of jurisdiction over the king and nation of the Bulgarians ; nor was their recent conversion to Christianity of much avail to either prelate, unless he could number the proselytes among the subjects of his power.   With the aid of his court, the Greek patriarch was victorious; but in the furious contest he deposed, in his turn, the successor of St. Peter, and involved the Latin Church in the reproach of heresy and schism.   Photius sacrificed the peace of the world to a short and precarious reign; he fell with his patron, the Cæsar Bardas ;[10] and Basil the Macedonian performed an act of justice in the restoration of Ignatius, whose age and dignity had not been sufficiently respected.   From his monastery, or prison, Photius solicited the favour of the emperor by pathetic complaints and artful flattery ; and the eyes of his

---

[Ep. 4 in the ed. of Valettas, p. 165 *sqq.*] and of Michael Cerularius (Canisii Antiq. Lectiones, tom. iii. p. i. p. 281-324, edit. Basnage, with the prolix answer of Cardinal Humbert [in C. Will, Acta et scripta quae de controversiis ecclesiae graecae et latinae seculo xi. composita extant, p. 172 *sqq.* ; and in Migne, P. G. vol. 120, 752 *sqq.*]).

[8] The xth volume of the Venice edition of the Councils contains all the acts of the synods, and history of Photius ; they are abridged with a faint tinge of prejudice or prudence, by Dupin and Fleury. [The fullest modern history of Photius is Hergenröther's biography, cp. Appendix 1.]

[9] [As successor of Ignatius, who was deposed because he had offended the Emperor Michael III. and his uncle, Cæsar Bardas.]

[10] [Photius did not fall with Bardas ; he was deposed after the death of Michael III.]

rival were scarcely closed when he was again restored to the [A.D. 877] throne of Constantinople. After the death of Basil, he experienced the vicissitudes of courts and the ingratitude of a royal [A.D. 886] pupil; the patriarch was again deposed, and in his last solitary hours he might regret the freedom of a secular and studious [Photius died c. 891] life. In each revolution, the breath, the nod, of the sovereign had been accepted by a submissive clergy; and a synod of three hundred bishops was always prepared to hail the triumph, or to stigmatize the fall, of the holy or the execrable Photius.[11] By a delusive promise of succour or reward, the popes were tempted to countenance these various proceedings, and the synods of Constantinople were ratified by their epistles or legates. But the court and the people, Ignatius and Photius, were equally adverse to their claims; their ministers were insulted or imprisoned; the procession of the Holy Ghost was forgotten; Bulgaria was for ever annexed to the Byzantine throne; and the schism was prolonged by the rigid censure of all the multiplied ordinations of an irregular patriarch. The darkness and corruption of the tenth century suspended the intercourse, without reconciling the minds, of the two nations. But, when the Norman sword restored the churches of Apulia to the jurisdiction of Rome, the departing flock was warned, by a petulant epistle of the Grecian patriarch, to avoid and abhor the errors of the Latins. The rising majesty of Rome could no longer The popes excombrook the insolence of a rebel; and Michael Cerularius was municate excommunicated in the heart of Constantinople by the pope's the patriarch of legates. Shaking the dust from their feet, they deposited on Constantinople and the altar of St. Sophia a direful anathema,[12] which enumerates the Greeks. A.D. 1054, the seven mortal heresies of the Greeks, and devotes the guilty July 16 teachers, and their unhappy sectaries, to the eternal society of the devil and his angels. According to the emergencies of the church and state a friendly correspondence was sometimes resumed; the language of charity and concord was sometimes

---

[11] The synod of Constantinople, held in the year 869, is the viiith of the general councils, the last assembly of the East which is recognised by the Roman church. She rejects the synods of Constantinople of the years 867 and 879, which were, however, equally numerous and noisy; but they were favourable to Photius.

[12] See this anathema in the Councils, tom. xi. p. 1457-1460. [See Hergenröther, Photius, vol. iii. p. 730 *sqq.* for the conflict under Cerularius, and the work of Bréhier cited above, p. 381, n. 1. Cp. Gfrörer, Byzantinische Geschichten, vol. iii. cap. 23, p. 514 *sqq.*]

affected ; but the Greeks have never recanted their errors ; the popes have never repealed their sentence ; and from this thunderbolt we may date the consummation of the schism. It was enlarged by each ambitious step of the Roman pontiffs ; the emperors blushed and trembled at the ignominious fate of their royal brethren of Germany ; and the people was scandalized by the temporal power and military life of the Latin clergy.[13]

Enmity of the Greeks and Latins. A.D. 1100-1200

The aversion of the Greeks and Latins [14] was nourished and manifested in the three first expeditions to the Holy Land. Alexius Comnenus contrived the absence at least of the formidable pilgrims ; his successors, Manuel and Isaac Angelus, conspired with the Moslems for the ruin of the greatest princes of the Franks ; and their crooked and malignant policy was seconded by the active and voluntary obedience of every order of their subjects. Of this hostile temper a large portion may doubtless be ascribed to the difference of language, dress, and manners, which severs and alienates the nations of the globe. The pride, as well as the prudence, of the sovereign was deeply wounded by the intrusion of foreign armies, that claimed a right of traversing his dominions and passing under the walls of his capital ; his subjects were insulted and plundered by the rude strangers of the West ; and the hatred of the pusillanimous Greeks was sharpened by secret envy of the bold and pious enterprises of the Franks. But these profane causes of national enmity were fortified and inflamed by the venom of religious zeal. Instead of a kind embrace, an hospitable reception from their Christian brethren of the East, every tongue was taught to repeat the names of schismatic and heretic, more odious to an orthodox ear than those of pagan and infidel ; instead of being loved for the general conformity of faith and worship, they were abhorred for some rules of discipline, some questions of theology, in which themselves or their teachers might differ from the Oriental church. In the crusade of Louis the Seventh, the

---

[13] Anna Comnena (Alexiad, l. i. p. 31-33 [c. 13]) represents the abhorrence, not only of the church, but of the palace, for Gregory VII., the popes, and the Latin communion. The style of Cinnamus and Nicetas is still more vehement. Yet how calm is the voice of history compared with that of polemics !

[14] [The disputes over trivial points of theology and ceremony were the expression of the national enmity of the Greeks and Latins ; and this aversion was the deeper cause of the schism.]

Greek clergy washed and purified the altars which had been
defiled by the sacrifice of a French priest. The companions of
Frederic Barbarossa deplore the injuries which they endured,
both in word and deed, from the peculiar rancour of the bishops
and monks. Their prayers and sermons excited the people
against the impious barbarians ; and the patriarch is accused of
declaring that the faithful might obtain the redemption of all
their sins by the extirpation of the schismatics.[15] An enthusiast,
named Dorotheus, alarmed the fears, and restored the confidence, of the emperor, by a prophetic assurance that the
German heretic, after assaulting the gate of Blachernes, would
be made a signal example of the divine vengeance. The passage of these mighty armies were rare and perilous events ; but
the crusades introduced a frequent and familiar intercourse between the two nations, which enlarged their knowledge without
abating their prejudices. The wealth and luxury of Constan- The Latins
tinople demanded the productions of every climate ; these im- stantinople
ports were balanced by the art and labour of her numerous
inhabitants ; her situation invites the commerce of the world ;
and, in every period of her existence, that commerce has been
in the hands of foreigners. After the decline of Amalphi, the
Venetians, Pisans, and Genoese introduced their factories and
settlements into the capital of the empire ; their services were
rewarded with honours and immunities ; they acquired the possession of lands and houses ; their families were multiplied by
marriages with the natives ; and, after the toleration of a Mahometan mosque, it was impossible to interdict the churches of
the Roman rite.[16] The two wives of Manuel Comnenus [17] were
of the race of the Franks : the first, a sister-in-law of the Em-

[15] His anonymous historian (de Expedit. Asiat. Fred. I. in Canisii Lection. Antiq. tom. iii. pars ii. p. 511, edit. Basnage) mentions the sermons of the Greek
patriarch, quomodo Græcis injunxerat in remissionem peccatorum peregrinos oc-
cidere et delere de terrâ. Tagino observes (in Scriptores Freher. tom. i. p. 409,
edit. Struv.), Græci hæreticos nos appellant ; clerici et monachi dictis et factis per-
sequuntur. We may add the declaration of the emperor Baldwin fifteen years
afterwards : Hæc est (gens) quæ Latinos omnes non hominum nomine, sed canum
dignabatur ; quorum sanguinem effundere pene inter merita reputabant (Gesta
Innocent. III. c. 92, in Muratori, Script. Rerum Italicarum, tom. iii. pars i. p. 536).
There may be some exaggeration, but it was as effectual for the action and re-action
of hatred.
[16] See Anna Comnena (Alexiad, l. vi. p. 161, 162 [c. 5]), and a remarkable
passage of Nicetas (in Manuel. l. v. c. 9), who observes of the Venetians, κατὰ σμήνη
καὶ φρατρίας τὴν Κωνσταντινούπολιν τῆς οἰκείας ἠλλάξαντο, &c.
[17] Ducange, Fam. Byzant. p. 186, 187.

peror Conrad ; the second, a daughter of the prince of Antioch ; he obtained for his son Alexius, a daughter of Philip Augustus, king of France ; and he bestowed his own daughter on a Marquis of Montferrat, who was educated and dignified in the palace of Constantinople. The Greek encountered the arms, and aspired to the empire, of the West ; he esteemed the valour, and trusted the fidelity, of the Franks ;[18] their military talents were unfitly recompensed by the lucrative offices of judges and treasurers ; the policy of Manuel had solicited the alliance of the pope ; and the popular voice accused him of a partial bias to the nation and religion of the Latins.[19] During his reign, and that of his successor Alexius, they were exposed at Constantinople to the reproach of foreigners, heretics, and favourites ; and this triple guilt was severely expiated in the tumult which announced the return and elevation of Andronicus.[20]

their massacre. A.D. 1183 The people rose in arms ; from the Asiatic shore the tyrant dispatched his troops and galleys to assist the national revenge ; and the hopeless resistance of the strangers served only to justify the rage, and sharpen the daggers, of the assassins. Neither age nor sex nor the ties of friendship or kindred could save the victims of national hatred and avarice and religious zeal ; the Latins were slaughtered in their houses and in the streets ; their quarter was reduced to ashes ; the clergy were burnt in their churches, and the sick in their hospitals ; and some estimate may be formed of the slain from the clemency which sold above four thousand Christians in perpetual slavery to the Turks. The priests and monks were the loudest and most active in the destruction of the schismatics ; and they chaunted a thanksgiving to the Lord, when the head of a Roman cardinal, the pope's legate, was severed from his body, fastened to the tail

[18] Nicetas in Manuel. l. vii. c. 2. Regnante enim (Manuele) . . . apud eum tantam Latinus populus repererat gratiam ut neglectis Græculis suis tanquam viris mollibus et effœminatis, . . . solis Latinis grandia committeret negotia . . . erga eos profusâ liberalitate abundabat . . . ex omni orbe ad eum tanquam ad benefactorem nobiles et ignobiles concurrebant. Willerm. Tyr. xxii. c. 10.

[19] The suspicions of the Greeks would have been confirmed, if they had seen the political epistles of Manuel to pope Alexander III., the enemy of his enemy Frederic I., in which the emperor declares his wish of uniting the Greeks and Latins as one flock under one shepherd, &c. (see Fleury, Hist. Ecclés. tom. xv. p. 187, 213, 243).

[20] See the Greek and Latin Narratives in Nicetas (in Alexio Comneno, c. 10), and William of Tyre (l. xxii. c. 10-13) : the first, soft and concise ; the second, loud, copious, and tragical.

of a dog, and dragged with savage mockery through the city. The more diligent of the strangers had retreated, on the first alarm, to their vessels, and escaped through the Hellespont from the scene of blood. In their flight they burned and ravaged two hundred miles of the sea-coast; inflicted a severe revenge on the guiltless subjects of the empire; marked the priests and monks as their peculiar enemies; and compensated, by the accumulation of plunder, the loss of their property and friends. On their return, they exposed to Italy and Europe the wealth and weakness, the perfidy and malice of the Greeks, whose vices were painted as the genuine characters of heresy and schism. The scruples of the first crusaders had neglected the fairest opportunities of securing, by the possession of Constantinople, the way to the Holy Land; a domestic revolution invited and almost compelled the French and Venetians to achieve the conquest of the Roman empire of the East.

In the series of the Byzantine princes, I have exhibited the hypocrisy and ambition, the tyranny and fall of Andronicus, the last male of the Comnenian family who reigned at Constantinople. The revolution, which cast him headlong from the throne, saved and exalted Isaac Angelus,[21] who descended by the females from the same Imperial dynasty. The successor of a second Nero might have found it an easy task to deserve the esteem and affection of his subjects; they sometimes had reason to regret the administration of Andronicus. The sound and vigorous mind of the tyrant was capable of discerning the connection between his own and the public interest; and, while he was feared by all who could inspire him with fear, the unsuspected people and the remote provinces might bless the inexorable justice of their master. But his successor was vain and jealous of the supreme power, which he wanted courage and abilities to exercise; his vices were pernicious, his virtues (if he possessed any virtues) were useless, to mankind; and the Greeks, who imputed their calamities to his negligence, denied him the merit of any transient or accidental benefits of the times. Isaac slept on the throne, and was awakened only by the sound of pleasure; his vacant

Reign and character of Isaac Angelus. A.D. 1185-1195, Sept. 12

---

[21] The history of the reign of Isaac Angelus is composed, in three books, by the senator Nicetas (p. 288-290); and his offices of logothete, or principal secretary, and judge of the veil, or palace, could not bribe the impartiality of the historian. He wrote, it is true, after the fall and death of his benefactor. [Cp. above, vol. 5, p. 538.]

hours were amused by comedians and buffoons, and even to these buffoons the emperor was an object of contempt; his feasts and buildings exceeded the examples of royal luxury; the number of his eunuchs and domestics amounted to twenty thousand; and a daily sum of four thousand pounds of silver would swell to four millions sterling the annual expense of his household and table. His poverty was relieved by oppression; and the public discontent was inflamed by equal abuses in the collection and the application of the revenue. While the Greeks numbered the days of their servitude, a flattering prophet, whom he rewarded with the dignity of patriarch, assured him of a long and victorious reign of thirty-two years; during which he should extend his sway to mount Libanus, and his conquests beyond the Euphrates. But his only step towards the accomplishment of the prediction was a splendid and scandalous embassy to Saladin,[22] to demand the restitution of the holy sepulchre, and to propose an offensive and defensive league with the enemy of the Christian name. In these unworthy hands, of Isaac and his brother, the remains of the Greek empire crumbled into dust. The island of Cyprus, whose name excites the ideas of elegance and pleasure,

[Cyprus conquered by Richard. A.D. 1191]

was usurped by his namesake, a Comnenian prince; and, by a strange concatenation of events, the sword of our English Richard bestowed that kingdom on the house of Lusignan, a rich compensation for the loss of Jerusalem.[23]

[Revolt of the Bulgarians. A.D. 1186]

The honour of the monarchy and the safety of the capital were deeply wounded by the revolt of the Bulgarians and Wallachians. Since the victory of the second Basil, they had supported, above an hundred and seventy years, the loose dominion of the Byzantine princes; but no effectual measures had been adopted to impose the yoke of laws and manners on these savage tribes.[24] By the command of Isaac, their sole means of subsistence, their flocks and herds, were driven away,

[22] See Bohadin, Vit. Saladin. p. 129-131, 226, vers. Schultens. The ambassador of Isaac was equally versed in the Greek, French, and Arabic languages: a rare instance in those times. His embassies were received with honour, dismissed without effect, and reported with scandal in the West.

[23] [For Cyprus under the Lusignans, the chief work is L. de Mas-Latrie's Histoire de l'île de Chypre dans le règne des princes de la maison de Lusignan, 3 vols., 1855-61.]

[24] [For the Bulgarians and Wallachians in the 11th century, we have some interesting notices in the Strategicon of Cecaumenos (see vol. 5, Appendix, p. 536); especially the account of the revolt of the Wallachians of Thessaly (Great Vlachia) in A.D. 1066, c. 171 sqq.]

to contribute towards the pomp of the royal nuptials; and their fierce warriors were exasperated by the denial of equal rank and pay in the military service. Peter and Asan, two powerful chiefs, of the race of the ancient kings,[25] asserted their own rights and the national freedom ; their demoniac impostors proclaimed to the crowd that their glorious patron, St. Demetrius, had for ever deserted the cause of the Greeks ; and the conflagration spread from the banks of the Danube, to the hills of Macedonia and Thrace. After some faint efforts, Isaac Angelus and his brother acquiesced in their independence; and the imperial troops were soon discouraged by the bones of their fellow-soldiers, that were scattered along. the passes of mount Hæmus. By the arms and policy of John or Joannices, the second kingdom [John II. of Bulgaria was firmly established. The subtle barbarian sent A.D. 1197-1207] an embassy to Innocent the Third, to acknowledge himself a genuine son of Rome in descent and religion,[26] and humbly received from the pope the licence of coining money, the royal title, and a Latin archbishop or patriarch. The Vatican exulted in the spiritual conquest of Bulgaria, the first object of the schism ; and, if the Greeks could have preserved the prerogatives of the church, they would gladly have resigned the rights of the monarchy.

The Bulgarians were malicious enough to pray for the long life of Isaac Angelus, the surest pledge of their freedom and

[25] Ducange, Familiæ Dalmaticæ, p. 318-320. The original correspondence of the Bulgarian king and the Roman pontiff is inscribed in the Gesta Innocent. III. c. 66-82, p. 513-525. [For the foundation of the second Bulgarian (or Vlacho-Bulgarian) kingdom, see Jireček, Geschichte der Bulgaren, c. 14 ; Xénopol, Histoire des Roumains, p. 172 sqq., and L'empire valacho-bulgare in the Revue Historique, 47 (1897), p. 278 sqq. The two Asēns claimed to be descended from the old tsars ; but we cannot pay much regard to such a claim. The question is whether they were Bulgarians or Vlachs. The Roumanians would gladly believe that they were Vlachs ; and they appeal to an incident recorded by Nicetas (in Alex. Is. fil. i. c. 5, p. 617, ed. Bonn). A priest was taken prisoner, and he besought Asēn in Vlach, "which was also his language " (δεῖται τοῦ Ἀσᾶν ἀφεθῆναι, δι' ὁμοφωνίας ὡς ἴδρις τῆς τῶν Βλάχων φωνῆς). The natural inference from this piece of evidence is confirmed by the fact that (1) Pope Innocent III. in his correspondence with John Asēn II. (Calo-John) speaks to him as a Vlach or Roman (see next note) ; and (2) western historians assert that he was a Vlach (e.g. Villehardouin, Conquête de Constantinople, xliii. sect. 202, ce Johannis était un Blaque).]

[26] The pope acknowledges his pedigree, a nobili urbis Romæ prosapiâ genitores tui originem traxerunt. This tradition, and the strong resemblance of the Latin and Wallachian idioms, is explained by M. d'Anville (Etats de l'Europe, p. 258-262). The Italian colonies of the Dacia of Trajan were swept away by the tide of emigration from the Danube to the Volga, and brought back by another wave from the Volga to the Danube. Possible, but strange ! [Compare Appendix 11.]

Usurpa-
tion and
character
of Alexius
Angelus.
A.D. 1195—
1203, April
8
prosperity.   Yet their chiefs could involve in the same indiscriminate contempt the family and nation of the emperor.   " In all the Greeks," said Asan to his troops, " the same climate and character and education will be productive of the same fruits.   Behold my lance," continued the warrior, " and the long steamers that float in the wind.   They differ only in colour ; they are formed of the same silk, and fashioned by the same workman ; nor has the stripe that is stained in purple any superior price or value above its fellows." [27]   Several of these candidates for the purple successively rose and fell under the empire of Isaac : a general who had repelled the fleets of Sicily was driven to revolt and ruin by the ingratitude of the prince ; and his luxurious repose was disturbed by secret conspiracies and popular insurrections.   The emperor was saved by accident, or the merit of his servants : he was at length oppressed by an ambitious brother, who, for the hope of a precarious diadem, forgot the obligations of nature, of loyalty, and of friendship.[28] While Isaac in the Thracian valleys pursued the idle and solitary pleasures of the chase, his brother, Alexius Angelus, was invested with the purple by the unanimous suffrage of the camp ; the capital and the clergy subscribed to their choice ; and the vanity of the new sovereign rejected the name of his fathers for the lofty and royal appellation of the Comnenian race.   On the despicable character of Isaac I have exhausted the language of contempt; and can only add that in a reign of eight years the baser Alexius [29] was supported by the masculine vices of his wife Euphrosyne.   The first intelligence of his fall was conveyed to the late emperor by the hostile aspect and pursuit of the guards, no longer his own ; he fled before them above fifty [Stagira]   miles, as far as Stagyra in Macedonia; but the fugitive, without an object or a follower, was arrested, brought back to Constantinople, deprived of his eyes, and confined in a lonesome tower,

[27] This parable is in the best savage style; but I wish the Wallach had not introduced the classic name of Mysians, the experiment of the magnet or load-stone, and the passage of an old comic poet (Nicetas, in Alex. Comneno, l. i. p. 299, 300).

[28] The Latins aggravate the ingratitude of Alexius, by supposing that he had been released by his brother Isaac from Turkish captivity.   This pathetic tale had doubtless been repeated at Venice and Zara ; but I do not readily discover its grounds in the Greek historians.

[29] See the reign of Alexius Angelus, or Comnenus, in the three books of Nicetas, p. 291-352.

on a scanty allowance of bread and water. At the moment of the revolution, his son Alexius, whom he educated in the hope of empire, was twelve years of age.[30] He was spared by the usurper, and reduced to attend his triumph both in peace and war; but, as the army was encamped on the sea-shore, an Italian vessel facilitated the escape of the royal youth ; and, in the disguise of a common sailor, he eluded the search of his enemies, passed the Hellespont, and found a secure refuge in the isle of Sicily. After saluting the threshold of the apostles, and imploring the protection of Pope Innocent the Third, Alexius accepted the kind invitation of his sister Irene, the wife of Philip of Swabia, king of the Romans. But in his passage through Italy he heard that the flower of Western chivalry was assembled at Venice for the deliverance of the Holy Land; and a ray of hope was kindled in his bosom, that their invincible swords might be employed in his father's restoration.

About ten or twelve years after the loss of Jerusalem, the nobles of France were again summoned to the holy war by the voice of a third prophet, less extravagant, perhaps, than Peter the hermit, but far below St. Bernard in the merit of an orator and a statesman. An illiterate priest of the neighbourhood of Paris, Fulk of Neuilly,[31] forsook his parochial duty, to assume the more flattering character of a popular and itinerant missionary. The fame of his sanctity and miracles was spread over the land; he declaimed with severity and vehemence against the vices of the age; and his sermons, which he preached in the streets of Paris, converted the robbers, the usurpers, the prostitutes, and even the doctors and scholars of the university. No sooner did Innocent the Third ascend the chair of St. Peter than he proclaimed, in Italy, Germany, and France, the obligation of a new crusade.[32] The eloquent pontiff described the

The fourth crusade. A.D. 1198

---

[30] [Alexius is generally said to be the son of Margaret of Hungary, Isaac's second wife. But this is doubtful. Cp. Pears, Fall of Constantinople, p. 268, note 2.]

[31] See Fleury, Hist. Ecclés. tom. xvi. p. 26, &c., and Villehardouin, No. 1, with the observations of Ducange, which I always mean to quote with the original text.

[32] The contemporary life of Pope Innocent III., published by Baluze and Muratori (Scriptores Rerum Italicarum, tom. iii. pars i. p. 486-568), is most valuable for the important and original documents which are inserted in the text. The bull of the crusade may be read, c. 84, 85.

ruin of Jerusalem, the triumph of the Pagans, and the shame
of Christendom ; his liberality proposed the redemption of sins,
a plenary indulgence to all who should serve in Palestine,
either a year in person or two years by a substitute;[33] and,
among his legates and orators who blew the sacred trumpet,
Fulk of Neuilly was the loudest and most successful. The situation of the principal monarchs was averse to the pious summons.
The emperor Frederic the second was a child ; and his kingdom of Germany was disputed by the rival houses of Brunswick
and Swabia, the memorable factions of the Guelphs and Ghibe-
lines. Philip Augustus of France had performed, and could not
be persuaded to renew, the perilous vow ; but, as he was not
less ambitious of praise than of power, he cheerfully instituted
a perpetual fund for the defence of the Holy Land. Richard
of England was satiated with the glory and misfortunes of his
first adventure, and he presumed to deride the exhortations of
Fulk of Neuilly, who was not abashed in the presence of kings.
"You advise me," said Plantagenet, "to dismiss my three
daughters, pride, avarice, and incontinence: I bequeath them
to the most deserving; my pride to the knights-templars, my
avarice to the monks of Cisteaux, and my incontinence to the
prelates." But the preacher was heard and obeyed by the
great vassals, the princes of the second order ; and Theobald,
or Thibaut, count of Champagne, was the foremost in the holy
race. The valiant youth, at the age of twenty-two years,
was encouraged by the domestic examples of his father, who
marched in the second crusade, and of his elder brother, who
had ended his days in Palestine with the title of King of Jerusalem: two thousand two hundred knights owed service and
homage to his peerage;[34] the nobles of Champagne excelled in
all the exercises of war;[35] and, by his marriage with the heiress
of Navarre, Thibaut could draw a band of hardy Gascons from

embraced
by the
Barons of
France

[33] Por ce que cil pardon fut issi gran, si s'en esmeurent mult li cuers des genz
et mult s'en croisierent, porce que li pardons ere si gran. Villehardouin, No. 1
Our philosophers may refine on the cause of the crusades, but such were the genuine
feelings of a French knight.
[34] This number of fiefs (of which 1800 owed liege homage) was enrolled in the
church of St. Stephen at Troyes, and attested, A.D. 1213, by the marshal and butler
of Champagne (Ducange, Observ. p. 254).
[35] Campania . . . militiæ privilegio singularius excellit . . . in tyrociniis . .
prolusione armorum, &c. Ducange, p. 249, from the old Chronicle of Jerusalem
A.D. 1177-1199.

either side of the Pyrenæan mountains. His companion in
arms was Louis, count of Blois and Chartres; like himself of
regal lineage, for both the princes were nephews, at the same
time, of the kings of France and England. In a crowd of prelates and barons, who imitated their zeal, I distinguish the birth
and merit of Matthew of Montmorency ; the famous Simon of
Montfort, the scourge of the Albigeois; and a valiant noble,
Jeffrey of Villehardouin,[36] marshal of Champagne,[37] who has
condescended, in the rude idiom of his age and country,[38] to
write or dictate [39] an original narrative of the councils and
actions in which he bore a memorable part. At the same time,
Baldwin, count of Flanders, who had married the sister of
Thibaut, assumed the cross at Bruges, with his brother Henry
and the principal knights and citizens of that rich and industrious province.[40] The vow which the chiefs had pronounced in
churches, they ratified in tournaments ; the operations of war
were debated in full and frequent assemblies; and it was resolved to seek the deliverance of Palestine in Egypt, a country,
since Saladin's death, which was almost ruined by famine and
civil war. But the fate of so many royal armies displayed the
toils and perils of a land expedition; and, if the Flemings
dwelt along the ocean, the French barons were destitute of ships
and ignorant of navigation. They embraced the wise resolution
of choosing six deputies or representatives, of whom Villehardouin was one, with a discretionary trust to direct the motions,

[36] The name of Villehardouin was taken from a village and castle in the diocese
of Troyes, near the river Aube, between Bar and Arcis. The family was ancient
and noble ; the elder branch of our historian existed after the year 1400; the
younger, which acquired the principality of Achaia, merged in the house of Savoy
(Ducange, p. 235-245).
[37] This office was held by his father and his descendants, but Ducange has
not hunted it with his usual sagacity. I find that, in the year 1356, it was in the
family of Conflans; but these provincials have been long since eclipsed by the
national marshals of France.
[38] This language, of which I shall produce some specimens, is explained by
Vigenere and Ducange, in a version and glossary. The President des Brosses
(Méchanisme des Langues, tom. ii. p. 83) gives it as the example of a language
which has ceased to be French, and is understood only by grammarians.
[39] His age, and his own expression, moi que ceste oeuvre *dicta* (No. 62, &c.),
may justify the suspicion (more probable than Mr. Wood's on Homer) that he could
neither read nor write. Yet Champagne may boast of the two first historians, the
noble authors of French prose, Villehardouin and Joinville.
[40] The crusade and reigns of the counts of Flanders, Baldwin and his brother
Henry, are the subject of a particular history by the Jesuit Doutremens (Constanti-
nopolis Belgica, Turnaci, 1638, in 4to), which I have only seen with the eyes of
Ducange.

and to pledge the faith, of the whole confederacy. The maritime states of Italy were alone possessed of the means of transporting the holy warriors with their arms and horses; and the
six deputies proceeded to Venice, to solicit, on motives of piety
or interest, the aid of that powerful republic.

State of the Venetians. A.D. 697-1200   In the invasion of Italy by Attila, I have mentioned [41] the
flight of the Venetians from the fallen cities of the continent,
and their obscure shelter in the chain of islands that line the
extremity of the Adriatic gulf. In the midst of the waters,
free, indigent, laborious, and inaccessible, they gradually coal-
esced into a republic; the first foundations of Venice were laid
in the island of Rialto; and the annual election of the twelve
tribunes was superseded by the permanent office of a duke or
doge. On the verge of the two empires, the Venetians exult
in the belief of primitive and perpetual independence.[42] Against
the Latins, their antique freedom has been asserted by the sword,
and may be justified by the pen. Charlemagne himself resigned
all claim of sovereignty to the islands of the Adriatic gulf; his
son Pepin was repulsed in the attacks of the *lagunas*, or canals,
too deep for the cavalry, and too shallow for the vessels; and
in every age, under the German Cæsars, the lands of the republic
have been clearly distinguished from the kingdom of Italy.
But the inhabitants of Venice were considered by themselves,
by strangers, and by their sovereigns, as an inalienable portion
of the Greek empire;[43] in the ninth and tenth centuries, the

---

[41] History, &c. vol. iii. p. 488-490.

[42] The foundation and independence of Venice, and Pepin's invasion, are discussed by Pagi (Critica, tom. iii. A.D. 810, No. 4, &c.) and Beretti (Dissert.
Chorograph. Italiæ medii Ævi, in Muratori, Script. tom. x. p. 153). The two
critics have a slight bias, the Frenchman adverse, the Italian favourable, to the
republic.

[43] When the son of Charlemagne asserted his right of sovereignty, he was
answered by the loyal Venetians, ὅτι ἡμεῖς δοῦλοι θέλομεν εἶναι τοῦ Ῥωμαίων βασιλέως
(Constantin. Porphyrogenit. de Administrat. Imperii, pars ii. c. 28, p. 85); and the
report of the ixth establishes the fact of the xth century, which is confirmed by the
embassy of Liutprand of Cremona. The annual tribute, which the emperor allows
them to pay to the king of Italy, alleviates, by doubling, their servitude; but the
hateful word δοῦλοι must be translated, as in the charter of 827 (Laugier, Hist. de
Venise, tom. i. p. 67, &c.), by the softer appellation of *subditi*, or *fideles*. [The
relation of Venice to the Empire has been most recently investigated by E. Lentz.
He establishes the actual, not merely formal, dependence of Venice on Constantinople
up to about the years 836-40 (Das Verhältniss Venedigs zu Byzanz; Th. i., Venedig
als byzantinische Provinz, 1891). About that time the weakness of the Eastern
Empire enabled Venice gradually to work her way to a position of independence.
By military expeditions, undertaken on her own account, against the Slavonic pirates
of the Adriatic and the Saracens who carried their depredations to Dalmatia and

proofs of their subjection are numerous and unquestionable; and the vain titles, the servile honours, of the Byzantine court, so ambitiously solicited by their dukes, would have degraded the magistrates of a free people. But the bands of this dependence, which was never absolute or rigid, were imperceptibly relaxed by the ambition of Venice and the weakness of Constantinople. Obedience was softened into respect, privilege ripened into prerogative, and the freedom of domestic government was fortified by the independence of foreign dominion. The maritime cities of Istria and Dalmatia bowed to the sovereigns of the Adriatic; and, when they armed against the Normans in the cause of Alexius, the emperor applied, not to the duty of his subjects, but to the gratitude and generosity of his faithful allies. The sea was their patrimony;[44] the western parts of the Mediterranean, from Tuscany to Gibraltar, were indeed abandoned to their rivals of Pisa and Genoa; but the Venetians acquired an early and lucrative share of the commerce of Greece and Egypt. Their riches increased with the increasing demand of Europe; their manufactures of silk and glass, perhaps the institution of their bank, are of high antiquity; and they enjoyed the fruits of their industry in the magnificence of public and private life. To assert her flag, to avenge her injuries, to protect the freedom of navigation, the republic could launch and man a fleet of an hundred galleys; and the Greeks, the Saracens, and the Normans

the northern part of the Eastern Riviera, and by entering into independent compacts with the neighbouring cities of Italy, Venice changed her condition from that of a province to that of a responsible power, and, when the Eastern empire was stronger in the tenth century, it was impracticable to recall her to her former subordinate position, and the Emperors were perforce content with a nominal subjection. The man whose policy achieved this result was the Doge Peter Tradonicus. (Lentz, Der allmahliche Uebergang Venedigs von faktischer zu nomineller Abhängigkeit von Byzanz, in Byzantinische Zeitschrift, iii. p. 64 sqq., 1894.) The earliest independent treaty made by Venice was the Pactum Lotharii of 840: a treaty not with the Emperor Lothar, but with a number of Italian cities under the auspices of Lothar (see A. Fanta, Die Verträge der Kaiser mit Venedig bis zum Jahre 983: in Suppl. I. to the Mittheilungen des Inst. für österr. Geschichtsforschung, 1881; Kretschmayr, Geschichte von Venedig, i. 95 sq., and for the text Romanin, Storia documentata di Venezia, i. 356). For the latter relations of Venice with the Eastern Empire, especially in the 12th century, see C. Neumann in Byzantinische Zeitschrift, i. p. 366 sqq.; and for the development of Venetian commerce, and the bearings thereon of the Golden Bulls granted by the Emperors, Heyd, Histoire du commerce du Levant au moyen âge, 1885.]

[44] See the xxvth and xxxth dissertations of the Antiquitates Medii Ævi of Muratori. From Anderson's History of Commerce, I understand that the Venetians did not trade to England before the year 1323. The most flourishing state of their wealth and commerce in the beginning of the xvth century is agreeably described by the Abbé Dubos (Hist. de la Ligue de Cambray, tom. ii. p. 443-480).

were encountered by her naval arms.   The Franks of Syria
were assisted by the Venetians in the reduction of the sea-coast;
but their zeal was neither blind nor disinterested; and, in the
conquest of Tyre, they shared the sovereignty of a city, the
first seat of the commerce of the world.   The policy of Venice
was marked by the avarice of a trading, and the insolence of a
maritime power; yet her ambition was prudent; nor did she
often forget that, if armed galleys were the effect and safeguard,
merchant-vessels were the cause and supply, of her greatness.
In her religion she avoided the schism of the Greeks, without
yielding a servile obedience to the Roman pontiff; and a free
intercourse with the infidels of every clime appears to have
allayed betimes the fever of superstition.   Her primitive government was a loose mixture of democracy and monarchy; the
doge was elected by the votes of the general assembly: as long
as he was popular and successful, he reigned with the pomp and
authority of a prince ; but in the frequent revolutions of the
state he was deposed, or banished, or slain, by the justice or injustice of the multitude.   The twelfth century produced the
first rudiments of the wise and jealous aristocracy, which has
reduced the doge to a pageant, and the people to a cypher.[45]

Alliance of
the French
and Vene-
tians

When the six ambassadors of the French pilgrims arrived at
Venice, they were hospitably entertained in the palace of St.
Mark by the reigning duke: his name was Henry Dandolo ; [46]

[45] The Venetians have been slow in writing and publishing their history.   Their
most ancient monuments are, 1. The rude Chronicle (perhaps) of John Sagorninus
(Venezia, 1765, in 8vo), which represents the state and manners of Venice in the
year 1008.   [Johannes was chaplain of the Doge Peter II., at the beginning of the
11th century.   The name Sagorninus is due to an error as to the authorship.   The
chronicle has been edited by Monticolo in the Fonti per la storia d'Italia.   Cronache
Veneziane antich. i. p. 59 sqq., 1890.]   2. The larger history of the doge (1342-1354),
Andrew Dandolo, published for the first time in the xiith tom. of Muratori, A.D.
1738.   [H. Simonsfeld, Andreas Dandolo und seine Geschichtswerke, 1876.]   The
History of Venice, by the Abbé Laugier (Paris, 1728), is a work of some merit,
which I have chiefly used for the constitutional part.   [Romanin, Storia documentata
di Venezia, 10 vols., 1853-1861; H. Kretschmayr, Geschichte von Venedig, vol. i.
(comes down to death of Henry Dandolo), 1905.]

[46] Henry Dandolo was eighty-four at his election (A.D. 1192), and ninety-seven
at his death (A.D. 1205) [probably not quite so old].   See the Observations of Ducange sur Villehardouin, No. 204.   But this *extraordinary* longevity is not observed
by the original writers ; nor does there exist another example of an hero near an
hundred years of age.   Theophrastus might afford an instance of a writer of ninety-
nine ; but instead of ἐννενήκοντα (Procœm. ad Character.), I am much inclined to read
ἑβδομήκοντα, with his last editor Fischer, and the first thoughts of Casaubon.   It is
scarcely possible that the powers of the mind and body should support themselves
till such a period of life.

and he shone in the last period of human life as one of the most
illustrious characters of the time. Under the weight of years,
and after the loss of his eyes,[47] Dandolo retained a sound understanding and a manly courage ; the spirit of an hero, ambitious
to signalise his reign by some memorable exploits ; and the wisdom of a patriot, anxious to build his fame on the glory and
advantage of his country. He praised the bold enthusiasm and
liberal confidence of the barons and their deputies : in such a
cause, and with such associates, he should aspire, were he a private man, to terminate his life ; but he was the servant of the
republic, and some delay was requisite to consult, on this arduous
business, the judgment of his colleagues. The proposal of the
French was first debated by the six *sages* who had been recently
appointed to control the administration of the doge ; it was next
disclosed to the forty members of the council of state ; and finally
communicated to the legislative assembly of four hundred and
fifty representatives, who were annually chosen in the six
quarters of the city. In peace and war, the doge was still
the chief of the republic ; his legal authority was supported by
the personal reputation of Dandolo ; his arguments of public
interest were balanced and approved ; and he was authorised
to inform the ambassadors of the following conditions of the
treaty.[48] It was proposed that the crusaders should assemble
at Venice, on the feast of St. John of the ensuing year ; that
flat-bottomed vessels should be prepared for four thousand five
hundred horses, and nine thousand squires, with a number of
ships sufficient for the embarkation of four thousand five
hundred knights and twenty thousand foot ; that during a term
of nine months they should be supplied with provisions, and
transported to whatsoever coast the service of God and Christendom should require ; and that the republic should join the
armament with a squadron of fifty galleys. It was required
that the pilgrims should pay, before their departure, a sum of
eighty-five thousand marks of silver ; and that all conquests,

---

[47] The modern Venetians (Laugier, tom. ii. p. 119) accuse the emperor Manuel ;
but the calumny is refuted by Villehardouin and the old writers, who suppose that
Dandolo lost his eyes by a wound (No. 34, and Ducange).

[48] See the original treaty in the Chronicle of Andrew Dandolo, p. 323-326. [It
was agreed that Egypt should be the object of attack (see above, p. 395). A special
reason for this decision is said by Gunther (in Riant's Exuviae Sacrae, i. 71) to have
been the distress then prevailing in Egypt owing to the fact that the Nile had not
risen for five years.]

by sea and land, should be equally divided among the confederates. The terms were hard; but the emergency was pressing,
and the French barons were not less profuse of money than of
blood. A general assembly was convened to ratify the treaty;
the stately chapel and palace of St. Mark were filled with ten
thousand citizens; and the noble deputies were taught a new
lesson of humbling themselves before the majesty of the people.
"Illustrious Venetians," said the marshal of Champagne, "we
are sent by the greatest and most powerful barons of France,
to implore the aid of the masters of the sea for the deliverance
of Jerusalem. They have enjoined us to fall prostrate at your
feet; nor will we rise from the ground till you have promised
to avenge with us the injuries of Christ." The eloquence of
their words and tears,[49] their martial aspect and suppliant
attitude, were applauded by an universal shout; as it were,
says Jeffrey, by the sound of an earthquake. The venerable
doge ascended the pulpit, to urge their request by those motives
of honour and virtue which alone can be offered to a popular
assembly; the treaty was transcribed on parchment, attested
with oaths and seals, mutually accepted by the weeping and
joyful representatives of France and Venice, and dispatched to
Rome for the approbation of Pope Innocent the Third.[50] Two
thousand marks were borrowed of the merchants for the first
expenses of the armament. Of the six deputies, two repassed
the Alps to announce their success, while their four companions
made a fruitless trial of the zeal and emulation of the republics
of Genoa and Pisa.

[March,
A.D. 1201]

The execution of the treaty was still opposed by unforeseen
difficulties and delays.[51] The marshal, on his return to Troyes,

---

[49] A reader of Villehardouin must observe the frequent tears of the marshal
and his brother knights. Sachiez que la ot mainte lerme plorée de pitié (No. 17);
mult plorant (ibid.) ; mainte lerme plorée (No. 34) ; si orent mult pitié et plore-
rent mult durement (No. 60) ; i ot mainte lerme plorée de pitié (No. 202). They
weep on every occasion of grief, joy, or devotion.

[50] [Innocent approved with reserve (for he distrusted Venice, with good reason),
making a special condition that no Christian town should be attacked. Cp. Gesta
Innocentii, 84.]

[51] [In the meantime Venice had played the Crusaders false. It had been agreed
that the object of the expedition was to be Egypt. During the months which elapsed
between the treaty with the Crusaders (March, 1201) and the date they were to
assemble at Venice (June 24, 1202), the Republic negotiated with the sultan of Egypt;
her envoys concluded a treaty with him on May 13, 1202, and it was ratified at Venice
in July. By this treaty, Venice undertook that the Crusade should not attack
Egypt, and received in return important concessions : a quarter in Alexandria, and

was embraced and approved by Thibaut, count of Champagne, Assembly and departure of the crusade from Venice. A.D. 1202, Oct. 8 who had been unanimously chosen general of the confederates. But the health of that valiant youth already declined, and soon became hopeless; and he deplored the untimely fate which condemned him to expire, not in a field of battle, but on a bed of sickness. To his brave and numerous vassals the dying prince distributed his treasures; they swore in his presence to accomplish his vow and their own; but some there were, says the marshal, who accepted his gifts and forfeited their word. The more resolute champions of the cross held a parliament at Soissons for the election of a new general; but such was the incapacity, or jealousy, or reluctance, of the princes of France that none could be found both able and willing to assume the conduct of the enterprise. They acquiesced in the choice of a [August, A.D. 1201] stranger, of Boniface, marquis of Montferrat, descended of a race of heroes, and himself of conspicuous fame in the wars and negotiations of the times;[52] nor could the piety or ambition of the Italian chief decline this honourable invitation. After visiting the French court, where he was received as a friend and kinsman, the marquis, in the church of Soissons, was invested with the cross of a pilgrim and the staff of a general; and immediately repassed the Alps, to prepare for the distant expedition of the East.[53] About the festival of the Pentecost, he displayed his banner, and marched towards Venice at the head of the Italians: he was preceded or followed by the counts of Flanders and Blois, and the most respectable barons of France; and their numbers were swelled by the pilgrims of Germany,[54] whose object and motives were similar to their

the privilege that all pilgrims who visited the Holy Sepulchre under her protection should be safe (a privilege of great pecuniary value). It is clear that this treaty, carefully concealed, proves that the diversion of the Fourth Crusade was a deliberate plan and not an accident. The treaty was first exposed by Hopf (Ersch und Gruber, Enzyklopädie, vol. 85, p. 188). It is mentioned by Ernoul (William of Tyre's Continuator), Recueil, vol. 2, p. 250.]

[52] By a victory (A.D. 1191) over the citizens of Asti, by a crusade to Palestine, and by an embassy from the pope to the German princes (Muratori, Annali d'Italia, tom. x. p. 163, 202).

[53] [Boniface of Montferrat went in October, 1201, to the court of Philip of Swabia, who was son-in-law of Isaac Angelus; and he remained there till the first months of 1202, when he departed with an embassy to Pope Innocent to plead at Rome the cause of young Alexius. (See Gesta Innocentii, 84.) At Philip's court a plot was hatched. See below, note 63.]

[54] See the crusade of the Germans in the Historia C. P. of Gunther (Canisii Antiq. Lect. tom. iv. p. v. viii.), who celebrates the pilgrimage of his abbot Martin,

own.   The Venetians had fulfilled, and even surpassed, their engagements; stables were constructed for the horses, and barracks for the troops; the magazines were abundantly replenished with forage and provisions; and the fleet of transports, ships, and galleys was ready to hoist sail, as soon as the republic had received the price of the freight and armament.[55] But that price far exceeded the wealth of the crusaders who were assembled at Venice.   The Flemings, whose obedience to their court was voluntary and precarious, had embarked in their vessels for the long navigation of the ocean and Mediterranean; and many of the French and Italians had preferred a cheaper and more convenient passage from Marseilles and Apulia to the Holy Land.   Each pilgrim might complain that, after he had furnished his own contribution, he was made responsible for the deficiency of his absent brethren: the gold and silver plate of the chiefs, which they freely delivered to the treasury of St. Mark, was a generous but inadequate sacrifice; and, after all their efforts, thirty-four thousand marks were still wanting to complete the stipulated sum.   The obstacle was removed by the policy and patriotism of the doge,[56] who proposed to the barons that, if they would join their arms in reducing some revolted cities of Dalmatia, he would expose his person in the holy war, and obtain from the republic a long indulgence, till some wealthy conquest should afford the means of satisfying the debt.   After much scruple and hesitation, they chose rather to accept the offer than to relinquish the enterprise; and the first hostilities of the fleet and army were directed against Zara,[57] a strong city of the Sclavonian coast, which

one of the preaching rivals of Fulk of Neuilly.   His monastery, of the Cistercian order, was situate in the diocese of Basil.   [Gunther was prior of Päris in Elsass. The work has been separately edited by the Count de Riant, 1875.]

[55] [The price was 4 marks a horse and 2 a man; which, reckoning the mark at 52 francs, amounts to £180,000.   Pears, Fall of Constantinople, p. 234.]

[56] [According to Robert de Clari, the Venetians kept the Crusaders imprisoned in the island of S. Niccolò di Lido, and applied the screw of starvation.   *Two* proposals were then made; the first was, that the expedition should start for the East, and that the spoil of the first city d'outremer which they attacked should be appropriated to pay the debt to Venice; the second was that Zara should be attacked, but this was confided only to the chiefs and concealed from the mass of the host, until they reached the doomed city.   The account in the text, which represents the enterprise against Zara as started for the purpose of accommodating the difficulty, and the Venetians as honestly prepared at this stage to transport the Crusaders to the East, provided they were paid, is the account which Villehardouin successfully imposed upon the world.]

[57] Jadera, now Zara, was a Roman colony, which acknowledged Augustus for its parent.   It is now only two miles round, and contains five or six thousand in-

had renounced its allegiance to Venice and implored the protection of the king of Hungary.[58] The crusaders burst the chain or boom of the harbour; landed their horses, troops, and military engines; and compelled the inhabitants, after a defence of five days, to surrender at discretion; their lives were spared, but the revolt was punished by the pillage of their [Nov. 24] houses and the demolition of their walls. The season was far advanced; the French and Venetians resolved to pass the winter in a secure harbour and plentiful country; but their repose was disturbed by national and tumultuous quarrels of the soldiers and mariners. The conquest of Zara had scattered the seeds of discord and scandal; the arms of the allies had been stained in their outset with the blood, not of infidels, but of Christians; the king of Hungary and his new subjects were themselves enlisted under the banner of the cross, and the scruples of the devout were magnified by the fear or lassitude of the reluctant pilgrims. The pope had excommunicated the false crusaders, who had pillaged and massacred their brethren;[59] and only the marquis Boniface and Simon of Montfort escaped these spiritual thunders: the one by his absence from the siege, the other by his final departure from the camp. Innocent might absolve the simple and submissive penitents of France; but he was 'provoked by the stubborn reason of the Venetians, who refused to confess their guilt, to accept their pardon, or to allow, in their temporal concerns, the interposition of a priest.

The assembly of such formidable powers by sea and land had revived the hopes of young[60] Alexius; and, both at Venice and Zara, he solicited the arms of the crusaders for his own restoration and his father's[61] deliverance. The royal youth

Alliance of the crusaders with the Greek prince, the young Alexius

---

habitants; but the fortifications are strong, and it is joined to the mainland by a bridge. See the travels of the two companions, Spon and Wheler (Voyage de Dalmatie, de Grèce, &c. tom. i. p. 64-70; Journey into Greece, p. 8-14); the last of whom, by mistaking *Sestertia* for *Sestertii*, values an arch with statues and columns at twelve pounds. If in his time there were no trees near Zara, the cherry-trees were not yet planted which produce our incomparable *marasquin*.

[58] Katona (Hist. Critica Reg. Hungariæ, Stirpis Arpad. tom. iv. p. 536-558) collects all the facts and testimonies most adverse to the conquerors of Zara.

[59] See the whole transaction, and the sentiments of the pope, in the Epistles of Innocent III. Gesta, c. 86-88.

[60] A modern reader is surprised to hear of the valet de Constantinople, as applied to young Alexius on account of his youth, like the *infants* of Spain, and the *nobilissimus puer* of the Romans. The pages and *valets* of the knights were as noble as themselves (Villehardouin and Ducange, No. 36).

[61] The Emperor Isaac is styled by Villehardouin, *Sursac* (No. 35, &c.), which

was recommended by Philip, king of Germany; [62] his prayers and presence excited the compassion of the camp; and his cause was embraced and pleaded by the marquis of Montferrat [63] and the doge of Venice. A double alliance and the dignity of Cæsar had connected with the Imperial family the two elder brothers of Boniface; [64] he expected to derive a kingdom from the important service; and the more generous ambition of Dandolo was eager to secure the inestimable benefits of trade and dominion that might accrue to his country. [65] Their influence procured a favourable audience for the ambassadors of Alexius; and, if the magnitude of his offers excited some suspicion, the motives and rewards which he displayed might justify the delay and diversion of those forces which had been consecrated to the deliverance of Jerusalem. He promised, in his own and his father's name, that, as soon as they should be seated on the throne of Constantinople, they would terminate the long schism of the Greeks, and submit themselves and their people to the lawful supremacy of the Roman church. He engaged to recompense the labours and merits of the crusaders by the immediate payment of two hundred thousand marks of silver; to accompany them in person to Egypt; or, if it should be judged more advantageous, to maintain, during a year, ten

may be derived from the French *Sire*, or the Greek Κύρ (κύριος) melted into his proper name [from *Sire*; for Κύρ could not become *Sur*]; the farther corruptions of Tursac and Conserac will instruct us what licence may have been used in the old dynasties of Assyria and Egypt.

[62] [Whose court he visited A.D. 1201.]

[63] [The conduct of the Marquis of Montferrat was not more ingenuous than that of Dandolo. He was, no more than Dandolo, a genuine crusader; he used the crusaders for his own purpose, and that purpose was, from the beginning, to restore Alexius. The plan was arranged during the winter at the court of Philip of Swabia, to which Alexius had betaken himself after his escape from Constantinople; Boniface, as we have seen, was there too (above, p. 401, note 53); and there can be no doubt that there was a complete understanding between them. Cp. Gesta Innocentii, 83. Philip nursed the dream of a union of the eastern and the western empires. Thus Boniface and Dandolo (for different reasons) agreed on the policy of diverting their expedition to Constantinople long before it started; they hoodwinked the mass of the crusaders; and the difficulties about payment were pressed only for the purpose of accomplishing the ultimate object.]

[64] Reinier and Conrad: the former married Maria, daughter of the Emperor Manuel Comnenus; the latter was the husband of Theodora Angela, sister of the Emperors Isaac and Alexius. Conrad abandoned the Greek court and princess for the glory of defending Tyre against Saladin (Ducange, Fam. Byzant. p. 187, 203).

[65] Nicetas (in Alexio Comneno, l. iii. c. 9 [p. 715, ed. Bonn]) accuses the doge and Venetians as the first authors of the war against Constantinople, and considers only as a κῦμα ὑπὲρ [*leg.* ἐπὶ] κύματι the arrival and shameful offers of the royal exile.

thousand men, and, during his life, five hundred knights, for the service of the Holy Land. These tempting conditions were accepted by the republic of Venice; and the eloquence of the doge and marquis persuaded the counts of Flanders, Blois, and St. Pol, with eight barons of France, to join in the glorious enterprise. A treaty of offensive and defensive alliance was confirmed by their oaths and seals; and each individual, according to his situation and character, was swayed by the hope of public or private advantage ; by the honour of restoring an exiled monarch ; or by the sincere and probable opinion that their efforts in Palestine would be fruitless and unavailing, and that the acquisition of Constantinople must precede and prepare the recovery of Jerusalem. But they were the chiefs or equals of a valiant band of freemen and volunteers, who thought and acted for themselves ; the soldiers and clergy were divided ; and, if a large majority subscribed to the alliance, the numbers and arguments of the dissidents were strong and respectable.[66] The boldest hearts were appalled by the report of the naval power and impregnable strength of Constantinople ; and their apprehensions were disguised to the world, and perhaps to themselves, by the more decent objections of religion and duty. They alleged the sanctity of a vow, which had drawn them from their families and homes to rescue the holy sepulchre ; nor should the dark and crooked counsels of human policy divert them from a pursuit, the event of which was in the hands of the Almighty. Their first offence, the attack of Zara, had been severely punished by the reproach of their conscience and the censures of the pope ; nor would they again imbrue their hands in the blood of their fellow-Christians. The apostle of Rome had pronounced ; nor would they usurp the right of avenging with the sword the schism of the Greeks and the doubtful usurpation of the Byzantine monarch. On these principles or pretences, many pilgrims, the most distinguished for their valour and piety, withdrew from the camp ; and their retreat was less pernicious than the open or secret opposition of a discontented party, that laboured, on every occasion, to separate the army and disappoint the enterprise.

[66] Villehardouin and Gunther represent the sentiments of the two parties. The abbot Martin left the army at Zara, proceeded to Palestine, was sent ambassador to Constantinople, and became a reluctant witness of the second siege.

Voyage
from Zara
to Con-
stanti-
nople. A.D.
1203, April
7—June 24
Notwithstanding this defection, the departure of the fleet
and army was vigorously pressed by the Venetians, whose zeal
for the service of the royal youth concealed a just resentment to
his nation and family. They were mortified by the recent preference which had been given to Pisa, the rival of their trade;
they had a long arrear of debt and injury to liquïdate with the
Byzantine court ; and Dandolo might not discourage the popular
tale that he had been deprived of his eyes by the emperor
Manuel, who perfidiously violated the sanctity of an ambassador.
A similar armament, for ages, had not rode the Adriatic ; it was
composed of one hundred and twenty flat-bottomed vessels or
palanders for the horses; two hundred and forty transports
filled with men and arms; seventy store-ships laden with provisions ; and fifty stout galleys, well prepared for the encounter
of an enemy.[67] While the wind was favourable, the sky serene,
and the water smooth, every eye was fixed with wonder and
delight on the scene of military and naval pomp which cver-
spread the sea. The shields of the knights and squires, at
once an ornament and a defence, were arranged on either side
of the ships; the banners of the nations and families were displayed from the stern; our modern artillery was supplied by
three hundred engines for casting stones and darts; the fatigues
of the way were cheered with the sound of music; and the
spirits of the adventurers were raised by the mutual assurance that forty thousand Christian heroes were equal to the
conquest of the world.[68] In the navigation[69] from Venice and
Zara, the fleet was successfully steered by the skill and experi-

[67] The birth and dignity of Andrew Dandolo gave him the motive and the
means of searching in the archives of Venice the memorable story of his ancestor.
His brevity seems to accuse the copious and more recent narratives of Sanudo
(in Muratori, Script. Rerum Italicarum, tom. xx.), Blondus, Sabellicus, and
Rhamnusius.

[68] Villehardouin, No. 62. His feelings and expressions are original ; he often
weeps, but he rejoices in the glories and perils of war with a spirit unknown to a
sedentary writer.

[69] In this voyage, almost all the geographical names are corrupted by the Latins.
The modern appellation of Chalcis, and all Eubœa, is derived from its *Euripus*,
Evripo, Negri-po, Negropont, which dishonours our maps (d'Anville, Géographie
Ancienne, tom. i. p. 263). [Negroponte is a corruption of 'στὸν Εὔριπον (divided
στὸ Νεύριπον) with an attempt to make sense in the spirit of popular etymology ;
negroponte, "black bridge," being suggested to Italians by the bridge of Chalcis
connecting the island with the mainland. But we also find the intermediate form
Egripons (*e.g.*, in the letters of Pope Innocent). It is remarkable that in the 10th
century the town of Chalcis (or the whole island?) is called Χρῆπος (see Const.
Porphyr. de Cer. ii., c. 44, p. 657, ὁ ἄρχων Χρήπου), apparently from Εὔριπος.]

ence of the Venetian pilots ; at Durazzo the confederates first
landed on the territory of the Greek empire; the isle of Corfu
afforded a station and repose ;[70] they doubled, without accident,
the perilous cape of Malea, the southern point of Peloponnesus,
or the Morea ; made a descent in the islands of Negropont and
Andros ; and cast anchor at Abydus, on the Asiatic side of the
Hellespont. These preludes of conquest were easy and bloodless ; the Greeks of the provinces, without patriotism or courage,
were crushed by an irresistible force; the presence of the lawful heir might justify their obedience; and it was rewarded by
the modesty and discipline of the Latins. As they penetrated
through the Hellespont, the magnitude of their navy was com-
pressed in a narrow channel ; and the face of the waters was
darkened with innumerable sails. They again expanded in the
bason of the Propontis, and traversed that placid sea, till they
approached the European shore, at the abbey of St. Stephen,
three leagues to the west of Constantinople. The prudent
doge dissuaded them from dispersing themselves in a populous
and hostile land ; and, as their stock of provisions was reduced,
it was resolved, in the season of harvest, to replenish their
store-ships in the fertile islands of the Propontis. With this
resolution they directed their course ; but a strong gale and
their own impatience drove them to the eastward ; and so near
did they run to the shore and city that some volleys of stones
and darts were exchanged between the ships and the rampart.
As they passed along, they gazed with admiration on the capital
of the East, or, as it should seem, of the earth, rising from her
seven hills, and towering over the continents of Europe and Asia.
The swelling domes and lofty spires of five hundred palaces
and churches were gilded by the sun and reflected in the waters ;
the walls were crowded with soldiers and spectators, whose
numbers they beheld, of whose temper they were ignorant; and
each heart was chilled by the reflection that, since the beginning
of the world, such an enterprise had never been undertaken by
such an handful of warriors. But the momentary apprehension was dispelled by hope and valour; and every man, says the
marshal of Champagne, glanced his eye on the sword or lance

[70] [At Corfù, Alexius joined the army as a *protégé* of Boniface ; and here the
matter was first clearly brought before the Crusaders and hotly debated in an
assembly. See Robert de Clari, § 32, 33.]

which he must speedily use in the glorious conflict.[71] The Latins cast anchor before Chalcedon ; the mariners only were left in the vessels ; the soldiers, horses, and arms were safely landed ; and, in the luxury of an Imperial palace, the barons tasted the first-fruits of their success. On the third day, the fleet and army moved towards Scutari, the Asiatic suburb of Constantinople; a detachment of Greek horse was surprised and defeated by fourscore French knights; and, in a halt of nine days, the camp was plentifully supplied with forage and provisions.

Fruitless negotia- tion of the emperor In relating the invasion of a great empire, it may seem strange that I have not described the obstacles which should have checked the progress of the strangers. The Greeks, in truth, were an unwarlike people; but they were rich, industrious, and subject to the will of a single man, had that man been capable of fear when his enemies were at a distance, or of courage when they approached his person. The first rumour of his nephew's alliance with the French and Venetians was despised by the usurper Alexius; his flatterers persuaded him that in his contempt he was bold and sincere; and each evening, in the close of the banquet, he thrice discomfited the barbarians of the West. These barbarians had been justly terrified by the report of his naval power ; and the sixteen hundred fishing-boats of Constantinople[72] could have manned a fleet to sink them in the Adriatic, or stop their entrance in the mouth of the Hellespont. But all force may be annihilated by the negligence of the prince and the venality of his ministers. The great duke, or admiral, made a scandalous, almost a public, auction of the sails, the masts, and the rigging ; the royal forests were reserved for the more important purpose of the chase; and the trees, says Nicetas, were guarded by the eunuchs like the groves of religious worship.[73] From this dream of pride Alexius was awakened by the siege of Zara and the rapid advances of the

---

[71] Et sachiez que il ne ot si hardi cui le cuer ne fremist (c. 67). . . . . Chascuns regardoit ses armes . . . que par tems en aront mestier (c. 68). Such is the honesty of courage !

[72] Eandem urbem plus in solis navibus piscatorem abundare, quam illos in toto navigio. Habebat enim mille et sexcentas piscatorias naves . . . Bellicas autem sive mercatorias habebant infinitæ multitudinis et portum tutissimum. Gunther, Hist. C. P. c. 8, p. 10.

[73] Καθάπερ ἱερῶν ἀλσέων, εἰπεῖν δὲ καὶ θεοφυτεύτων παραδείσων ἐφείδοντο τουτωνί. Nicetas in Alex. Comneno, l. iii. c. 9, p. 348.

Latins: as soon as he saw the danger was real, he thought it inevitable, and his vain presumption was lost in abject despondency and despair. He suffered these contemptible barbarians to pitch their camp in the sight of the palace; and his apprehensions were thinly disguised by the pomp and menace of a suppliant embassy. The sovereign of the Romans was astonished (his ambassadors were instructed to say) at the hostile appearance of the strangers. If these pilgrims were sincere in their vow for the deliverance of Jerusalem, his voice must applaud, and his treasures should assist, their pious design; but, should they dare to invade the sanctuary of empire, their numbers, were they ten times more considerable, should not protect them from his just resentment. The answer of the doge and barons was simple and magnanimous: "In the cause of honour and justice," they said, "we despise the usurper of Greece, his threats, and his offers. *Our* friendship and *his* allegiance are due to the lawful heir, to the young prince who is seated among us, and to his father, the emperor Isaac, who has been deprived of his sceptre, his freedom, and his eyes, by the crime of an ungrateful brother. Let that brother confess his guilt and implore forgiveness, and we ourselves will intercede that he may be permitted to live in affluence and security. But let him not insult us by a second message; our reply will be made in arms, in the palace of Constantinople."

On the tenth day of their encampment at Scutari, the crusaders prepared themselves, as soldiers and as Catholics, for the passage of the Bosphorus. Perilous indeed was the adventure; the stream was broad and rapid; in a calm the current of the Euxine might drive down the liquid and unextinguishable fires of the Greeks; and the opposite shores of Europe were defended by seventy thousand horse and foot in formidable array. On this memorable day, which happened to be bright and pleasant, the Latins were distributed in six battles, or divisions; the first, or vanguard, was led by the count of Flanders, one of the most powerful of the Christian princes in the skill and number of his cross-bows. The four successive battles of the French were commanded by his brother Henry, the counts of St. Pol and Blois, and Matthew of Montmorency, the last of whom was honoured by the voluntary service of the marshal and nobles of Champagne. The sixth division, the rear-guard and reserve of

Passage of the Bosphorus. July 6

the army, was conducted by the marquis of Montferrat, at the head of the Germans and Lombards. The chargers, saddled, with their long caparisons dragging on the ground, were embarked in the flat *palanders;* [74] and the knights stood by the sides of their horses, in complete armour, their helmets laced, and their lances in their hands. Their numerous train of *serjeants* [75] and archers occupied the transports ; and each transport was towed by the strength and swiftness of a galley. The six divisions traversed the Bosphorus, without encountering an enemy or an obstacle; to land the foremost was the wish, to conquer or die was the resolution, of every division and of every soldier. Jealous of the pre-eminence of danger, the knights in their heavy armour leaped into the sea, when it rose as high as their girdle ; the serjeants and archers were animated by their valour ; and the squires, letting down the drawbridges of the palanders, led the horses to the shore. Before the squadrons could mount, and form, and couch their lances, the seventy thousand Greeks had vanished from their sight; the timid Alexius gave the example to his troops ; and it was only by the plunder of his rich pavilions that the Latins were informed that they had fought against an emperor. In the first consternation of the flying enemy, they resolved, by a double attack, to open the entrance of the harbour. The tower of Galata,[76] in the suburb of Pera, was attacked and stormed by the French, while the Venetians assumed the more difficult task of forcing the boom or chain that was stretched from that tower to the Byzan-

---

[74] From the version of Vigenère I adopt the well-sounding word *palander*, which is still used, I believe, in the Mediterranean. But had I written in French, I should have preferred the original and expressive denomination of *vessiers*, or *huissiers*, from the *huis*, or door, which was let down as a drawbridge ; but which, at sea, was closed into the side of the ship (see Ducange au Villehardouin, No. 14, and Joinville, p. 27, 28, édit. du Louvre).

[75] To avoid the vague expressions of followers, &c., I use, after Villehardouin, the word *serjeants* for all horsemen who were not knights. There were serjeants at arms, and serjeants at law ; and, if we visit the parade and Westminster-hall, we may observe the strange result of the distinction (Ducange, Glossar. Latin. *Servientes*, &c. tom. vi. p. 226-231).

[76] It is needless to observe that on the subject of Galata, the chain, &c., Ducange is accurate and full. Consult likewise the proper chapters of the C. P. Christiana of the same author. The inhabitants of Galata were so vain and ignorant that they applied to themselves St. Paul's Epistle to the Galatians. [The chain was fixed, on the city side, close to the gate of St. Eugenius. Part of the chain is still preserved in the court of the church of St. Irene. Cp. Mordtmann, Esquisse topographique de Constantinople, p. 49. A. van Millingen, Byzantine Constantinople, 222, 228 *sq.*]

tine shore.   After some fruitless attempts, their intrepid perseverance prevailed ; twenty ships of war, the relics of the
Grecian navy, were either sunk or taken ; the enormous and
massy links of iron were cut asunder by the shears, or broken
by the weight of the galleys ; [77] and the Venetian fleet, safe and
triumphant, rode at anchor in the port of Constantinople.   By
these daring achievements, a remnant of twenty thousand Latins
solicited the licence of besieging a capital which contained above
four hundred thousand inhabitants,[78] able, though not willing,
to bear arms in the defence of their country.   Such an account
would indeed suppose a population of near two millions ; but,
whatever abatement may be required in the numbers of the
Greeks, the *belief* of those numbers will equally exalt the fearless spirit of their assailants.

In the choice of the attack, the French and Venetians were First siege
divided by their habits of life and warfare.   The former affirmed and con-
with truth that Constantinople was most accessible on the side quest of Constanti-
of the sea and the harbour.   The latter might assert with honour nople by
that they had long enough trusted their lives and fortunes to a the Latins.
frail bark and a precarious element, and loudly demanded a trial July 7-18
of knighthood, a firm ground, and a close onset, either on foot
or horseback.   After a prudent compromise, of employing the
two nations by sea and land in the service best suited to their
character, the fleet covering the army, they both proceeded from
the entrance to the extremity of the harbour ; the stone-bridge
of the river was hastily repaired ; and the six battles of the
French formed their encampment against the front of the capital,
the basis of the triangle which runs about four miles from the
port to the Propontis.[79]   On the edge of a broad ditch, at the

---

[77] The vessel that broke the chain was named the Eagle, *Aquila* (Dandol.
Chronicon, p. 322), which Blondus (de Gestis Venet.) has changed into *Aquilo*,
the north wind.   Ducange, Observations, No. 83, maintains the latter reading ;
but he had not seen the respectable text of Dandolo ; nor did he enough consider
the topography of the harbour.   The south-east would have been a more effectual
wind.

[78] Quatre cens mil homes ou plus (Villehardouin, No. 134) must be understood
of *men* of a military age.   Le Beau (Hist. du Bas Empire, tom. xx. p. 417) allows
Constantinople a million of inhabitants, of whom 60,000 horse, and an infinite
number of foot-soldiers.   In its present decay the capital of the Ottoman empire
may contain 400,000 souls (Bell's Travels, vol. ii. p. 401, 402) ; but, as the Turks
keep no registers, and as circumstances are fallacious, it is impossible to ascertain
(Niebuhr, Voyage en Arabie, tom. i. p. 18, 19) the real populousness of their cities.

[79] On the most correct plans of Constantinople, I know not how to measure
more than 4000 paces.   Yet Villehardouin computes the space at three leagues (No.

foot of a lofty rampart, they had leisure to contemplate the difficulties of their enterprise. The gates to the right and left of their narrow camp poured forth frequent sallies of cavalry and light infantry, which cut off their stragglers, swept the country of provisions, sounded the alarm five or six times in the course of each day, and compelled them to plant a palisade, and sink an entrenchment, for their immediate safety. In the supplies and convoys the Venetians had been too sparing, or the Franks too voracious; the usual complaints of hunger and scarcity were heard, and perhaps felt; their stock of flour would be exhausted in three weeks; and their disgust of salt meat tempted them to taste the flesh of their horses. The trembling usurper was supported by Theodore Lascaris, his son-in-law, a valiant youth, who aspired to save and to rule his country; the Greeks, regardless of that country, were awakened to the defence of their religion; but their firmest hope was in the strength and spirit of the Varangian guards, of the Danes and English, as they are named in the writers of the times.[80] After ten days' incessant labour the ground was levelled, the ditch filled, the approaches of the besiegers were regularly made, and two hundred and fifty engines of assault exercised their various powers to clear the rampart, to batter the walls, and to sap the foundations. On the first appearance of a breach the scaling-ladders were applied; the numbers that defended the vantage-ground repulsed and oppressed the adventurous Latins; but they admired the resolution of fifteen knights and serjeants, who had gained the ascent, and maintained their perilous station till they were precipitated [July 17] or made prisoners by the Imperial guards. On the side of the harbour, the naval attack was more successfully conducted by the Venetians; and that industrious people employed every resource that was known and practised before the invention of gun-powder. A double line, three bow-shots in front, was formed by the galleys and ships; and the swift motion of the former was supported by the weight and loftiness of the latter, whose

---

86). If his eye were not deceived, he must reckon by the old Gallic league of 1500 paces, which might still be used in Champagne. [The length of the line of the land walls is over 7200 yards.]

[80] The guards, the Varangi, are styled by Villehardouin (No. 89, 95, &c.) Englois et Danois avec leurs haches. Whatever had been their origin, a French pilgrim could not be mistaken in the nations of which they were at that time composed. [Cp. below, Appendix 14.]

decks and poops and turret were the platforms of military engines, that discharged their shot over the heads of the first line. The soldiers, who leapt from the galleys on shore, immediately planted and ascended their scaling-ladders, while the large ships, advancing more slowly into the intervals, and lowering a drawbridge, opened a way through the air from their masts to the rampart. In the midst of the conflict, the doge, a venerable and conspicuous form, stood aloft, in complete armour, on the prow of his galley. The great standard of St. Mark was displayed before him; his threats, promises, and exhortations urged the diligence of the rowers; his vessel was the first that struck; and Dandolo was the first warrior on the shore. The nations admired the magnanimity of the blind old man, without reflecting that his age and infirmities diminished the price of life and enhanced the value of immortal glory. On a sudden, by an invisible hand (for the standard-bearer was probably slain), the banner of the republic was fixed on the rampart; twenty-five towers were rapidly occupied; and, by the cruel expedient of fire, the Greeks were driven from the adjacent quarter. The doge had dispatched the intelligence of his success, when he was checked by the danger of his confederates. Nobly declaring that he would rather die with the pilgrims than gain a victory by their destruction, Dandolo relinquished his advantage, recalled his troops, and hastened to the scene of action. He found the six weary diminutive *battles* of the French encompassed by sixty squadrons of the Greek cavalry, the least of which was more numerous than the largest of their divisions. Shame and despair had provoked Alexius to the last effort of a general sally; but he was awed by the firm order and manly aspect of the Latins; and, after skirmishing at a distance, withdrew his troops in the close of the evening. The silence or tumult of the night exasperated his fears; and the timid usurper, collecting a treasure of ten thousand pounds of gold, basely deserted his wife, his people, and his fortune; threw himself into a bark, stole through the Bosphorus, and landed in shameful safety in an obscure harbour of Thrace. As soon as they were apprised of his flight, the Greek nobles sought pardon and peace in the dungeon where the blind Isaac expected each hour the visit of the executioner. Again saved and exalted by the vicissitudes of fortune, the captive in his Imperial robes was replaced on the throne, and surrounded with prostrate slaves, whose real terror and affected joy he was incapable of discerning. At the dawn of day hostilities were suspended; and the Latin chiefs were surprised by a message from the lawful and reigning emperor, who was impatient to embrace his son and to reward his generous deliverers.[81]

Restoration of the Emperor Isaac Angelus, and his son Alexius. July 19
But these generous deliverers were unwilling to release their hostage, till they had obtained from his father the payment, or at least the promise, of their recompense. They chose four ambassadors, Matthew of Montmorency, our historian the marshal of Champagne, and two Venetians, to congratulate the emperor. The gates were thrown open on their approach, the streets on both sides were lined with the battle-axes of the Danish and English guard: the presence chamber glittered with gold and jewels, the false substitutes of virtue and power; by the side of the blind Isaac his wife was seated, the sister of the king of Hungary; and by her appearance the noble matrons of Greece were drawn from their domestic retirement and mingled with the circle of senators and soldiers. The Latins, by the mouth of the marshal, spoke like men conscious of their merits, but who respected the work of their own hands; and the emperor clearly understood that his son's engagement with Venice and the pilgrims must be ratified without hesitation or delay. Withdrawing into a private chamber with the empress, a chamberlain, an interpreter, and the four ambassadors, the father of young Alexius inquired with some anxiety into the nature of his stipulations: the submission of the Eastern empire to the pope, the succour of the Holy Land, and a present contribution of two hundred thousand marks of silver.—"These conditions are weighty," was his prudent reply; "they are hard to accept and difficult to perform. But no conditions can exceed the measure of your services and deserts." After this satisfactory assurance, the barons mounted on horseback, and introduced the heir of Constantinople to the city and palace: his youth and marvellous

[Aug. 1]
adventures engaged every heart in his favour, and Alexius was

---

[81] For the first siege and conquest of Constantinople, we may read the original letter of the crusaders to Innocent III. Gesta, c. 91, p. 533, 534; Villehardouin, No. 75-99; Nicetas in Alexio Comneno, l. iii. c. 10, p. 349-352; Dandolo, in Chron. p. 322. Gunther and his abbot Martin were not yet returned from their obstinate pilgrimage to Jerusalem, or St. John d'Acre, where the greatest part of the company had died of the plague.

solemnly crowned with his father in the dome of St. Sophia. In the first days of his reign, the people, already blessed with the restoration of plenty and peace, was delighted by the joyful catastrophe of the tragedy; and the discontent of the nobles, their regret, and their fears, were covered by the polished surface of pleasure and loyalty. The mixture of two discordant nations in the same capital might have been pregnant with mischief and danger; and the suburb of Galata, or Pera, was assigned for the quarters of the French and Venetians. But the liberty of trade and familiar intercourse was allowed between the friendly nations; and each day the pilgrims were tempted by devotion or curiosity to visit the churches and palaces of Constantinople. Their rude minds, insensible perhaps of the finer arts, were astonished by the magnificent scenery; and the poverty of their native towns enhanced the populousness and riches of the first metropolis of Christendom.[82] Descending from his state, young Alexius was prompted by interest and gratitude to repeat his frequent and familiar visits to his Latin allies; and in the freedom of the table, the gay petulance of the French sometimes forgot the emperor of the East.[83] In their more serious conferences, it was agreed that the re-union of the two churches must be the result of patience and time; but avarice was less tractable than zeal; and a large sum was instantly disbursed to appease the wants, and silence the importunity, of the crusaders.[84] Alexius was alarmed by the approaching hour of their departure; their absence might have relieved him from the engagement which he was yet incapable of performing; but his friends would have left him, naked and alone, to the caprice and prejudice of a perfidious nation. He wished to bribe their stay, the delay of a year,

[82] Compare, in the rude energy of Villehardouin (No. 66, 100), the inside and outside views of Constantinople, and their impression on the minds of the pilgrims : Cette ville (says he) que de totes les autres ére souveraine. See the parallel passages of Fulcherius Carnotensis, Hist. Hierosol. l. i. c. 4, and Will. Tyr. ii. 3, xx. 26.

[83] As they played at dice, the Latins took off his diadem, and clapped on his head a woollen or hairy cap, τὸ μεγαλοπρεπὲς καὶ παγκλέϊστον κατερρύπαινεν ὄνομα (Nicetas, p. 358). If these merry companions were Venetians, it was the insolence of trade and a commonwealth.

[84] Villehardouin, No. 101. Dandolo, p. 322. The Doge affirms that the Venetians were paid more slowly than the French; but he owns that the histories of the two nations differed on that subject. Had he read Villehardouin? The Greeks complained, however, quod totius Graeciæ opes transtulisset (Gunther, Hist. C. P. c. 13). See the lamentations and invectives of Nicetas (p. 355 [in Isaac. et Alex. c. 1]).

by undertaking to defray their expense and to satisfy, in their name, the freight of the Venetian vessels. The offer was agitated in the council of the barons; and, after a repetition of their debates and scruples, a majority of votes again acquiesced in the advice of the doge and the prayer of the young emperor. At the price of sixteen hundred pounds of gold, he prevailed on the marquis of Montferrat to lead him with an army round the provinces of Europe; to establish his authority, and pursue his uncle, while Constantinople was awed by the presence of Baldwin and his confederates of France and Flanders. The expedition was successful: the blind emperor exulted in the success of his arms, and listened to the predictions of his flatterers, that the same Providence which had raised him from the dungeon to the throne would heal his gout, restore his sight, and watch over the long prosperity of his reign. Yet the mind of the suspicious old man was tormented by the rising glories of his son; nor could his pride conceal from his envy that, while his own name was pronounced in faint and reluctant acclamations, the royal youth was the theme of spontaneous and universal praise.[85]

Quarrels of the Greeks and Latins　　By the recent invasion the Greeks were awakened from a dream of nine centuries; from the vain presumption that the capital of the Roman empire was impregnable to foreign arms. The strangers of the West had violated the city, and bestowed the sceptre, of Constantine: their Imperial clients soon became as unpopular as themselves: the well-known vices of Isaac were rendered still more contemptible by his infirmities; and the young Alexius was hated as an apostate, who had renounced the manners and religion of his country. His secret covenant with the Latins was divulged or suspected; the people, and especially the clergy, were devoutly attached to their faith and superstition; and every convent and every shop resounded with the danger of the church and the tyranny of the pope.[86] An empty treasury could ill supply the demands

---

[85] The reign of Alexius Comnenus occupies three books in Nicetas, p. 291-352. The short restoration of Isaac and his son is dispatched in five [four] chapters, p. 352-362.

[86] When Nicetas reproaches Alexius for his impious league, he bestows the harshest names on the pope's new religion, μεῖζον καὶ ἀτοπώτατον . . . παρεκτροπὴν πίστεως . . . τῶν τοῦ Πάπα προνομίων καινισμόν . . . μετάθεσίν τε καὶ μεταποίησιν τῶν παλαιῶν Ῥωμαίοις ἐθῶν (p. 348 [in Alex. iii. c. 9]). Such was the sincere language of every Greek to the last gasp of the empire.

of regal luxury and foreign extortion; the Greeks refused to
avert, by a general tax, the impending evils of servitude and
pillage; the oppression of the rich excited a more dangerous
and personal resentment; and, if the emperor melted the
plate, and despoiled the images, of the sanctuary, he seemed to
justify the complaints of heresy and sacrilege.   During the
absence of marquis Boniface and his Imperial pupil, Constantinople was visited with a calamity which might be justly imputed to the zeal and indiscretion of the Flemish pilgrims.[87]
In one of their visits to the city they were scandalized by the
aspect of a mosque or synagogue, in which one God was worshipped, without a partner or a son.[88]   Their effectual mode
of controversy was to attack the infidels with the sword, and
their habitation with fire; but the infidels and some Christian
neighbours presumed to defend their lives and properties;
and the flames which bigotry had kindled consumed the most
orthodox and innocent structures.   During eight days and
nights the conflagration spread above a league in front, from
the harbour to the Propontis, over the thickest and most
populous regions of the city.   It is not easy to count the
stately churches and palaces that were reduced to a smoking
ruin, to value the merchandise that perished in the trading
streets, or to number the families that were involved in the
common destruction.   By this outrage, which the doge and
the barons in vain affected to disclaim, the name of the Latins
became still more unpopular; and the colony of that nation,
above fifteen thousand persons, consulted their safety in a hasty
retreat from the city to the protection of their standard in the
suburb of Pera.   The emperor returned in triumph; but the
firmest and most dexterous policy would have been insufficient
to steer him through the tempest which overwhelmed the
person and government of that unhappy youth.   His own inclination and his father's advice attached him to his benefactors;
but Alexius hesitated between gratitude and patriotism, between
the fear of his subjects and of his allies.[89]   By his feeble and

---

[87] Nicetas (p. 355 [c. 2]) is positive in the charge, and specifies the Flemings
(Φλαμίονες), though he is wrong in supposing it an ancient name. Villehardouin
(No. 107) exculpates the barons, and is ignorant (perhaps affectedly ignorant) of
the names of the guilty.

[88] [The mosque of the Musulman merchants.]

[89] Compare the suspicions and complaints of Nicetas (p. 359-362 [c. 3, 4]) with

fluctuating conduct he lost the esteem and confidence of both ; and, while he invited the marquis of Montferrat to occupy the palace, he suffered the nobles to conspire, and the people to arm, for the deliverance of their country. Regardless of his painful situation, the Latin chiefs repeated their demands, resented his delays, suspected his intentions, and exacted a decisive answer of peace or war. The haughty summons was delivered by three French knights and three Venetian deputies, who girded their swords, mounted their horses, pierced through the angry multitude, and entered with a fearless countenance the palace and presence of the Greek emperor. In a peremptory tone they recapitulated their services and his engagements ; and boldly declared that, unless their just claims were fully and immediately satisfied, they should no longer hold him either as a sovereign or a friend. After this defiance, the first that had ever wounded an Imperial ear, they departed without betraying any symptoms of fear ; but their escape from a servile palace and a furious city astonished the ambassadors themselves ; and their return to the camp was the signal of mutual hostility.

The war
renewed.
A.D. 1204
Among the Greeks, all authority and wisdom were overborne by the impetuous multitude, who mistook their rage for valour, their numbers for strength, and their fanaticism for the support and inspiration of Heaven. In the eyes of both nations, Alexius was false and contemptible ; the base and spurious race of the Angeli was rejected with clamorous disdain ; and the people of Constantinople encompassed the senate, to demand at their hands a more worthy emperor. To every senator, conspicuous by his birth or dignity, they successively presented the purple ; by each senator the deadly garment was repulsed ; the contest lasted three days ; and we may learn from the historian Nicetas, one of the members of the assembly, that fear and weakness were the guardians of their loyalty. A phantom, who vanished in oblivion, was forcibly proclaimed by the crowd ; [90] but the author of the tumult, and the leader of the war, was a prince of the house of Ducas ; and his common ap-

the blunt charges of Baldwin of Flanders (Gesta Innocent. III. c. 92, p. 534), cum patriarchâ et mole nobilium, nobis promissis perjurus et mendax.

[90] His name was Nicholas Canabus : he deserved the praise of Nicetas, and the vengeance of Mourzoufle (p. 362 [c. 4]).

pellation of Alexius must be discriminated by the epithet of Mourzoufle,[91] which in the vulgar idiom expressed the close junction of his black and shaggy eye-brows. At once a patriot and a courtier, the perfidious Mourzoufle, who was not destitute of cunning and courage, opposed the Latins both in speech and action, inflamed the passions and prejudices of the Greeks, and insinuated himself into the favour and confidence of Alexius, who trusted him with the office of Great Chamberlain and tinged his buskins with the colours of royalty. At the dead of night he rushed into the bed-chamber with an affrighted aspect, exclaiming that the palace was attacked by the people and betrayed by the guards. Starting from his couch, the unsuspecting prince threw himself into the arms of his enemy, who had contrived his escape by a private staircase. But that staircase terminated in a prison; Alexius was seized, stripped, and loaded with chains; and, after tasting some days the bitterness of death, he was poisoned, or strangled, or beaten with clubs, at the command, and in the presence, of the tyrant. The emperor Isaac Angelus soon followed his son to the grave, and Mourzoufle, perhaps, might spare the superfluous crime of hastening the extinction of impotence and blindness. *Alexius and his father deposed by Mourzoufle. Feb. 8*

The death of the emperors, and the usurpation of Mourzoufle, had changed the nature of the quarrel. It was no longer the disagreement of allies who over-valued their services or neglected their obligations : the French and Venetians forgot their complaints against Alexius, dropt a tear on the untimely fate of their companion, and swore revenge against the perfidious nation who had crowned his assassin. Yet the prudent doge was still inclined to negotiate;[92] he asked as a debt, a subsidy, or a fine, fifty thousand pounds of gold, about two millions sterling ; nor would the conference have been abruptly broken, if the zeal or policy of Mourzoufle had not refused to sacrifice the Greek church to the safety of the state.[93] Amidst the in- *Second siege. January-April*

---

[91] Villehardouin (No. 116) speaks of him as a favourite, without knowing that he was a prince of the blood, *Angelus* and *Ducas*. Ducange, who pries into every corner, believes him to be the son of Isaac Ducas Sebastocrator, and second cousin of young Alexius.

[92] [From this time, Boniface, having lost his *protégé* Alexius, was no longer in cordial co-operation with the Doge. Dandolo carried out the rest of his plan himself. Cp. Pears, Fall of Constantinople, p. 334.]

[93] This negotiation, probable in itself, and attested by Nicetas (p. 365 [in Murz. c. 2]), is omitted as scandalous by the delicacy of Dandolo and Villehardouin.

vectives of his foreign and domestic enemies, we may discern that he was not unworthy of the character which he had assumed, of the public champion: the second siege of Constantinople was far more laborious than the first; the treasury was replenished, the discipline was restored, by a severe inquisition into the abuses of the former reign; and Mourzoufle, an iron mace in his hand, visiting the posts and affecting the port and aspect of a warrior, was an object of terror to his soldiers, at least, and to his kinsmen. Before and after the death of Alexius, the Greeks made two vigorous and well-conducted attempts to burn the navy in the harbour; but the skill and courage of the Venetians repulsed the fire-ships; and the vagrant flames wasted themselves without injury in the sea.[94] In a nocturnal sally the Greek emperor was vanquished by Henry, brother of the count of Flanders; the advantages of number and surprise aggravated the shame of his defeat; his buckler was found on the field of battle; and the Imperial standard,[95] a divine image of the Virgin, was presented, as a trophy and a relic, to the Cistercian monks, the disciples of St. Bernard. Near three months, without excepting the holy season of Lent, were consumed in skirmishes and preparations, before the Latins were ready or resolved for a general assault. The land-fortifications had been found impregnable; and the Venetian pilots represented that, on the shore of the Propontis, the anchorage was unsafe, and the ships must be driven by the current far away to the straits of the Hellespont: a prospect not unpleasing to the reluctant pilgrims, who sought every opportunity of breaking the army. From the harbour, therefore, the assault was determined by the assailants and expected by the besieged; and the emperor had placed his scarlet pavilions on a neighbouring height, to direct and animate the efforts of his troops. A fearless spectator, whose mind could entertain the ideas of pomp and pleasure, might have admired the long array of two embattled armies, which extended above half a league, the one on the ships

---

[94] Baldwin mentions both attempts to fire the fleet (Gest. c. 92, p. 534, 535); Villehardouin (No. 113-115) only describes the first. It is remarkable that neither of these warriors observe any peculiar properties in the Greek fire.

[95] Ducange (No. 119) pours forth a torrent of learning on the *Gonfanon Impérial*. This banner of the Virgin is shown at Venice as a trophy and relic; if it be genuine, the pious doge must have cheated the monks of Citeaux.

and galleys, the other on the walls and towers, raised above
the ordinary level by several stages of wooden turrets.   Their [April 9]
first fury was spent in the discharge of darts, stones, and fire,
from the engines ; but the water was deep; the French were
bold; the Venetians were skilful: they approached the walls ;
and a desperate conflict of swords, spears, and battle-axes was
fought on the trembling bridges that grappled the floating to
the stable batteries.   In more than an hundred places the
assault was urged and the defence was sustained; till the
superiority of ground and numbers finally prevailed, and the
Latin trumpets sounded a retreat.   On the ensuing days the [April 12]
attack was renewed with equal vigour and a similar event;
and in the night the doge and the barons held a council, apprehensive only for the public danger; not a voice pronounced
the words of escape or treaty ; and each warrior, according to
his temper, embraced the hope of victory or the assurance of
a glorious death.[96]   By the experience of the former siege, the
Greeks were instructed, but the Latins were animated; and
the knowledge that Constantinople *might* be taken was of
more avail than the local precautions which that knowledge
had inspired for its defence.   In the third assault two ships
were linked together to double their strength; a strong north
wind drove them on the shore; the bishops of Troyes and
Soissons led the van; and the auspicious names of the *Pilgrim*
and the *Paradise* resounded along the line.[97]   The episcopal
banners were displayed on the walls; an hundred marks of
silver had been promised to the first adventurers ; and, if their
reward was intercepted by death, their names have been immortalised by fame.   Four towers were scaled; three gates
were burst open; and the French knights, who might tremble
on the waves, felt themselves invincible on horseback on the
solid ground.   Shall I relate that the thousands who guarded
the emperor's person fled on the approach, and before the lance,
of a single warrior?   Their ignominious flight is attested by
their countryman Nicetas; an army of phantoms marched

---

[96] Villehardouin (No. 126) confesses that mult ere grant peril : and Guntherus
(Hist. C. P. c. 13) affirms that nulla spes victoriæ arridere poterat.   Yet the knight
despises those who thought of flight, and the monk praises his countrymen who
were resolved on death.

[97] Baldwin and all the writers honour the names of these two galleys, felici
auspicio.

with the French hero, and he was magnified to a giant in the eyes of the Greeks.[98]   While the fugitives deserted their posts and cast away their arms, the Latins entered the city under the banners of their leaders; the streets and gates opened for their passage; and either design or accident kindled a third conflagration, which consumed in a few hours the measure of three of the largest cities of France.[99]   In the close of the evening, the barons checked their troops and fortified their stations; they were awed by the extent and populousness of the capital, which might yet require the labour of a month, if the churches and palaces were conscious of their internal strength.   But in the morning a suppliant procession, with crosses and images, announced the submission of the Greeks and deprecated the wrath of the conquerors: the usurper escaped through the golden gate; the palaces of Blachernæ and Boucoleon were occupied by the count of Flanders and the marquis of Montferrat; and the empire, which still bore the name of Constantine and the title of Roman, was subverted by the arms of the Latin pilgrims.[100]

Pillage of Constantinople. [April 12, 13]

Constantinople had been taken by storm; and no restraints, except those of religion and humanity, were imposed on the conquerors by the laws of war.   Boniface, marquis of Montferrat, still acted as their general; and the Greeks, who revered his name as their future sovereign, were heard to exclaim in a lamentable tone, " Holy marquis-king, have mercy upon us ! " His prudence or compassion opened the gates of the city to the fugitives; and he exhorted the soldiers of the cross to spare the lives of their fellow-Christians.   The streams of blood that flow down the pages of Nicetas may be reduced to the slaughter

---

[98] With an allusion to Homer, Nicetas calls him ἐννέα ὀργυίας [ἐννεόργυιος], nine orgyæ, or eighteen yards high, a stature which would indeed have excused the terror of the Greek.   [In Murz. c. 2, p. 754, ed. B.]   On this occasion, the historian seems fonder of the marvellous than of his country, or perhaps of truth.   Baldwin exclaims in the words of the psalmist, Persequitur unus ex nobis centum alienos.

[99] Villehardouin (No. 130) is again ignorant of the authors of *this* more legitimate fire, which is ascribed by Gunther to a quidam comes Teutonicus (c. 14).   They seem ashamed, the incendiaries !

[100] For the second siege and conquest of Constantinople, see Villehardouin (No. 113-132), Baldwin's iid Epistle to Innocent III. (Gesta, c. 92, p. 534-537), with the whole reign of Mourzoufle in Nicetas (p. 363-375); and borrow some hints from Dandolo (Chron. Venet. p. 323-330) and Gunther (Hist. C. P. c. 14-18), who add the decorations of prophecy and vision.   The former produces an oracle of the Erythræan sybil, of a great armament on the Adriatic, under a blind chief, against Byzantium, &c.   Curious enough, were the prediction anterior to the fact.

of two thousand of his unresisting countrymen;[101] and the greater part was massacred, not by the strangers, but by the Latins who had been driven from the city, and who exercised the revenge of a triumphant faction. Yet of these exiles, some were less mindful of injuries than of benefits; and Nicetas himself was indebted for his safety to the generosity of a Venetian merchant. Pope Innocent the Third accuses the pilgrims of respecting, in their lust, neither age nor sex nor religious profession; and bitterly laments that the deeds of darkness, fornication, adultery, and incest were perpetrated in open day; and that noble matrons and holy nuns were polluted by the grooms and peasants of the Catholic camp.[102] It is indeed probable that the licence of victory prompted and covered a multitude of sins; but it is certain that the capital of the East contained a stock of venal or willing beauty, sufficient to satiate the desires of twenty thousand pilgrims; and female prisoners were no longer subject to the right or abuse of domestic slavery. The marquis of Montferrat was the patron of discipline and decency; the count of Flanders was the mirror of chastity : they had forbidden, under pain of death, the rape of married women, or virgins, or nuns; and the proclamation was sometimes invoked by the vanquished [103] and respected by the victors. Their cruelty and lust were moderated by the authority of the chiefs and feelings of the soldiers; for we are no longer describing an irruption of the northern savages; and, however ferocious they might still appear, time, policy, and religion had civilised the manners of the French, and still more of the Italians. But a free scope was allowed to their avarice, which was glutted, even in the holy week, by the pillage of Constantinople. The right of victory, unshackled by any promise or treaty, had confiscated the public and private wealth of the Greeks; and every hand, according to its size and strength,

---

[101] Ceciderunt tamen eâ die civium quasi duo millia, &c. (Gunther, c. 18). Arithmetic is an excellent touchstone to try the amplifications of passion and rhetoric.

[102] Quidam (says Innocent III. Gesta, c. 94, p. 538) nec religioni, nec ætati, nec sexui pepercerunt ; sed fornicationes, adulteria, et incestus in oculis omnium exercentes, non solum maritatas et viduas, sed et matronas et virgines Deoque dicatas, exposuerunt spurcitiis garcionum. Villehardouin takes no notice of these common incidents.

[103] Nicetas saved, and afterwards married, a noble virgin (p. 380 [in Urb. Capt., c. 3]), whom a soldier, ἐπὶ μάρτυσι πολλοῖς ὀνηδὸν ἐπιβρωμώμενος, had almost violated in spite of the ἐντολαί, ἐντάλματα εὖ γεγονότων.

might lawfully execute the sentence, and seize the forfeiture. A portable and universal standard of exchange was found in the coined and uncoined metals of gold and silver, which each captor at home or abroad might convert into the possessions most suitable to his temper and situation. Of the treasures which trade and luxury had accumulated, the silks, velvets, furs, the gems, spices and rich moveables, were the most precious, as they could not be procured for money in the ruder

Division of
the spoil countries of Europe. An order of rapine was instituted; nor was the share of each individual abandoned to industry or chance. Under the tremendous penalties of perjury, excommunication and death, the Latins were bound to deliver their plunder into the common stock: three churches were selected for the deposit and distribution of the spoil; a single share was allowed to a foot soldier; two for a serjeant on horseback; four to a knight; and larger proportions according to the rank and merit of the barons and princes. For violating this sacred engagement, a knight, belonging to the count of St. Paul, was hanged, with his shield and coat of arms round his neck: his example might render similar offenders more artful and discreet; but avarice was more powerful than fear; and it is generally believed that the secret far exceeded the acknowledged plunder. Yet the magnitude of the prize surpassed the largest scale of experience or expectation.[104] After the whole had been equally divided between the French and Venetians, fifty thousand marks were deducted to satisfy the debts of the former, and the demands of the latter. The residue of the French amounted to four hundred thousand marks of silver,[105] about eight hundred thousand pounds sterling; nor can I better appreciate the value of that sum in the public and private transactions of the age than by defining it at seven times the annual revenue of the kingdom of England.[106]

[104] Of the general mass of wealth, Gunther observes, ut de pauperibus et advenis cives ditissimi redderentur (Hist. C. P. c. 18); Villehardouin (No. 132 [250]), that since the creation, ne fu tant gaaignié dans [leg. en] une ville; Baldwin (Gesta, c. 92), ut tantum tota non videatur possidere Latinitas.

[105] Villehardouin, No. 133-135. Instead of 400,000, there is a various reading of 500,000. The Venetians had offered to take the whole booty, and to give 400 marks to each knight, 200 to each priest and horseman, and 100 to each foot-soldier: they would have been great losers (Le Beau, Hist. du Bas-Empire, tom. xx. p. 506 :—I know not from whence).

[106] At the council of Lyons (A.D. 1245) the English ambassadors stated the revenue of the crown as below that of the foreign clergy, which amounted to

In this great revolution, we enjoy the singular felicity of comparing the narratives of Villehardouin and Nicetas, the opposite feelings of the marshal of Champagne and the Byzantine senator.[107] At the first view, it should seem that the wealth of Constantinople was only transferred from one nation to another, and that the loss and sorrow of the Greeks is exactly balanced by the joy and advantage of the Latins. But in the miserable account of war the gain is never equivalent to the loss, the pleasure to the pain: the smiles of the Latins were transient and fallacious ; the Greeks for ever wept over the ruins of their country; and their real calamities were aggravated by sacrilege and mockery. , What benefits accrued to the conquerors from the three fires which annihilated so vast a portion of the buildings and riches of the city? What a stock of such things as could neither be used or transported was maliciously or wantonly destroyed! How much treasure was idly wasted in gaming, debauchery, and riot! And what precious objects were bartered for a vile price by the impatience or ignorance of the soldiers, whose reward was stolen by the base industry of the last of the Greeks! These alone who had nothing to lose might derive some profit from the revolution ; but the misery of the upper ranks of society is strongly painted in the personal adventures of Nicetas himself. His stately palace had been reduced to ashes in the second conflagration; and the senator, with his family and friends, found an obscure shelter in another house which he possessed near the church of St. Sophia. It was the door of this mean habitation that his friend, the Venetian merchant, guarded, in the disguise of a soldier, till Nicetas could save, by a precipitate flight, the relics of his fortune and the chastity of his daughter. In a cold wintry season these fugitives, nursed in the lap of prosperity, departed on foot; his wife was with child; the desertion of their slaves compelled them to carry their baggage on their own shoulders ; and their women, whom they placed in the centre, were exhorted to conceal their beauty with dirt, instead of adorning

60,000 marks a year (Matthew Paris, p. 451 ; Hume's History of England, vol. ii. p. 170).
[107] The disorders of the sack of Constantinople, and his own adventures, are feelingly described by Nicetas, p. 367-369, and in the Status Urb. C. P. p. 375-384. His complaints even of sacrilege are justified by Innocent III. (Gesta, c. 92) ; but Villehardouin does not betray a symptom of pity or remorse.

it with paint and jewels. Every step was exposed to insult
and danger ; the threats of the strangers were less painful than
the taunts of the plebeians, with whom they were now levelled ;
nor did the exiles breathe in safety till their mournful pilgrimage was concluded at Selymbria, above forty miles from the
capital. On the way they overtook the patriarch, without attendance, and almost without apparel, riding on an ass, and
reduced to a state of apostolical poverty, which, had it been
voluntary, might perhaps have been meritorious. In the
meanwhile his desolate churches were profaned by the licentiousness and party-zeal of the Latins. After stripping the
gems and pearls, they converted the chalices into drinking-
cups; their tables, on which they gamed and feasted, were
covered with the pictures of Christ and the saints; and they
trampled under foot the most venerable objects of the Christian worship. In the cathedral of St. Sophia the ample veil
of the sanctuary was rent asunder for the sake of the golden
fringe ; and the altar, a monument of art and riches, was broken
in pieces and shared among the captors.[108] Their mules and
horses were laden with the wrought silver and gilt carvings,
which they tore down from the doors and pulpit ; and, if the
beasts stumbled under the burden, they were stabbed by their
impatient drivers, and the holy pavement streamed with their
impure blood. A prostitute was seated on the throne of the
patriarch; and that daughter of Belial, as she is styled, sung
and danced in the church, to ridicule the hymns and processions
of the Orientals. Nor were the repositories of the royal dead
secure from violation; in the church of the Apostles the tombs
of the emperors were rifled ; and it is said that after six centuries the corpse of Justinian was found without any signs of
decay or putrefaction. In the streets the French and Flemings
clothed themselves and their horses in painted robes and flowing
head-dresses of linen; and the coarse intemperance of their
feasts[109] insulted the splendid sobriety of the East. To expose
the arms of a people of scribes and scholars, they affected to
display a pen, an ink-horn, and a sheet of paper, without dis-

Sacrilege and mock-ery

[108] [For the plunder of the church, see the Chronicle of Novgorod, in Hopf's
Chroniques Gréco-Romanes.]
[109] If I rightly apprehend the Greek of Nicetas's receipts, their favourite dishes
were boiled buttocks of beef, salt pork and pease, and soup made of garlic and sharp
or sour herbs (p. 382).

cerning that the instruments of science and valour were *alike* feeble and useless in the hands of the modern Greeks. Their reputation and their language encouraged them, how- Destruc-ever, to despise the ignorance, and to overlook the progress, statues of the Latins.[110] In the love of the arts the national difference was still more obvious and real; the Greeks preserved with reverence the works of their ancestors, which they could not imitate; and, in the destruction of the statues of Constantinople, we are provoked to join in the complaints and invectives of the Byzantine historian.[111] We have seen how the rising city was adorned by the vanity and despotism of the Imperial founder; in the ruins of paganism some gods and heroes were saved from the axe of superstition; and the forum and hippodrome were dignified with the relics of a better age. Several of these are described by Nicetas,[112] in a florid and affected style; and from his descriptions I shall select some interesting particulars. 1. The victorious charioteers were cast in bronze, at their own or the public charge, and fitly placed in the hippodrome; they stood aloft in their chariots, wheeling round the goal; the spectators could admire their attitude, and judge of the resemblance; and of these figures the most perfect might have been transported from the Olympic stadium. 2. The sphynx, river-horse, and crocodile denote the climate and manufacture of Egypt and the spoils of that ancient province. 3. The she-wolf suckling Romulus and Remus: a subject alike pleasing to the *old* and the *new* Romans, but which could rarely be treated before the decline of the Greek sculpture. 4. An eagle holding and tearing a serpent in his talons: a domestic monument of the Byzantines, which they ascribed, not to a human artist,

---

[110] Nicetas uses very harsh expressions, παρ' ἀγραμμάτοις βαρβάροις, καὶ τέλεον ἀναλφαβήτοις (Fragment. apud Fabric. Bibliot. Græc. tom. vi. p. 414). This reproach, it is true, applies most strongly to their ignorance of Greek, and of Homer. In their own language, the Latins of the xiith and xiiith centuries were not destitute of literature. See Harris's Philological Inquiries, p. iii. c. 9, 10, 11.

[111] Nicetas was of Chonæ in Phrygia ([near] the old Colossæ of St. Paul); he raised himself to the honours of senator, judge of the veil, and great logothete; beheld the fall of the empire, retired to Nice, and composed an elaborate history, from the death of Alexius Comnenus to the reign of Henry. [See above, vol. 5, Appendix, p. 538.]

[112] A manuscript of Nicetas, in the Bodleian library, contains this curious fragment on the statues of Constantinople, which fraud, or shame, or rather carelessness, has dropt in the common editions. It is published by Fabricius (Bibliot. Græc. tom. vi. p. 405-416), and immoderately praised by the late ingenious Mr. Harris of Salisbury (Philological Inquiries, p. iii. c. 5, p. 301-312).

but the magic power of the philosopher Apollonius, who, by his talisman, delivered the city from such venomous reptiles. 5. An ass and his driver, which were erected by Augustus in his colony of Nicopolis, to commemorate a verbal omen of the victory of Actium. 6. An equestrian statue, which passed, in the vulgar opinion, for Joshua, the Jewish conqueror, stretching out his hand to stop the course of the descending sun. A more classical tradition recognised the figures of Bellerophon and Pegasus; and the free attitude of the steed seemed to mark that he trod on air rather than on the earth. 7. A square and lofty obelisk of brass: the sides were embossed with a variety or picturesque and rural scenes: birds singing; rustics labouring of playing on their pipes; sheep bleating; lambs skipping; the sea, and a scene of fish and fishing; little naked Cupids laughing, playing, and pelting each other with apples; and, on the summit, a female figure turning with the slightest breath, and thence denominated *the wind's attendant*. 8. The Phrygian shepherd presenting to Venus the prize of beauty, the apple of discord. 9. The incomparable statue of Helen, which is delineated by Nicetas in the words of admiration and love : her well-turned feet, snowy arms, rosy lips, bewitching smiles, swimming eyes, arched eye-brows, the harmony of her shape, the lightness of her drapery, and her flowing locks that waved in the wind : a beauty that might have moved her barbarian destroyers to pity and remorse. 10. The manly or divine form of Hercules,[113] as he was restored to life by the master-hand of Lysippus, of such magnitude that his thumb was equal to the waist, his leg to the stature, of a common man; [114] his chest ample, his shoulders broad, his limbs strong and muscular, his hair curled, his aspect commanding. Without his bow, or quiver, or club, his lion's skin thrown carelessly over him, he was seated on an osier basket, his right leg and arm stretched to the utmost, his left knee bent, and supporting his elbow, his head reclining on his left hand, his countenance indignant and pensive. 11. A colossal statue of Juno, which had once adorned

[Anemo-dulion]

---

[113] To illustrate the statue of Hercules, Mr. Harris quotes a Greek epigram, and engraves a beautiful gem, which does not however copy the attitude of the statue. In the latter, Hercules had not his club, and his right leg and arm were extended.

[114] I transcribe these proportions, which appear to me inconsistent with each other, and may possibly show that the boasted taste of Nicetas was no more than affectation and vanity.

her temple of Samos; the enormous head by four yoke of oxen was laboriously drawn to the palace. 12. Another colossus, of Pallas or Minerva, thirty feet in height, and representing, with admirable spirit, the attributes and character of the martial maid. Before we accuse the Latins, it is just to remark that this Pallas was destroyed after the first siege by the fear and superstition of the Greeks themselves.[115] The other statues of brass which I have enumerated were broken and melted by the unfeeling avarice of the crusaders; the cost and labour were consumed in a moment; the soul of genius evaporated in smoke ; and the remnant of base metal was coined into money for the payment of the troops. Bronze is not the most durable of monuments: from the marble form of Phidias and Praxiteles the Latins might turn aside with stupid contempt;[116] but, unless they were crushed by some accidental injury, those useless stones stood secure on their pedestals.[117] The most enlightened of the strangers, above the gross and sensual pursuits of their countrymen, more piously exercised the right of conquest in the search and seizure of the relics of the saints.[118] Immense was the supply of heads and bones, crosses and images, that were scattered by this revolution over the churches of Europe ; and such was the increase of pilgrimage and oblation that no branch, perhaps, of more lucrative plunder was imported from the East.[119] Of the writings of antiquity many that still existed in the twelfth century are now lost. But the pilgrims were not solicitous to save or transport the volumes of an unknown tongue ; the perishable substance of paper or parchment can only be preserved by the multiplicity of copies ; the literature of the Greeks had almost centred in the metropolis ; and, without computing the extent of our loss, we may

[115] Nicetas, in Isaaco Angelo et Alexio, c. 3, p. 359. The Latin editor very properly observes that the historian, in his bombast style, produces ex pulice elephantem.

[116] In two passages of Nicetas (edit. Paris, p. 360. Fabric. p. 408), the Latins are branded with the lively reproach of οἱ τοῦ καλοῦ ἀνέραστοι βάρβαροι, and their avarice of brass is clearly expressed. Yet the Venetians had the merit of removing four bronze horses from Constantinople to the place of St. Mark (Sanuto, Vite de' Dogi, in Muratori, Script. Rerum Italicarum, tom. xxii. p. 534).

[117] Winckelman, Hist. de l'Art, tom. iii. p. 269, 270.

[118] See the pious robbery of the abbot Martin, who transferred a rich cargo to his monastery of Paris, diocese of Basil (Gunther, Hist. C. P. c. 19, 23, 24). Yet in secreting this booty the saint incurred an excommunication, and perhaps broke his oath.

[119] Fleury, Hist. Ecclés. tom. xvi. p. 139-145.

drop a tear over the libraries that have perished in the triple fire of Constantinople. [120]

[120] I shall conclude this chapter with the notice of a modern history, which illustrates the taking of Constantinople by the Latins ; but which has fallen somewhat late into my hands.   Paolo Ramusio, the son of the compiler of Voyages, was directed by the senate of Venice to write the history of the conquest ; and this order, which he received in his youth, he executed in a mature age, by an elegant Latin work, de Bello Constantinopolitano et Imperatoribus Comnenis per Gallos et Venetos restitutis [Libri vi. ; older edition, 1604] (Venet. 1635, in folio).   Ramusio [Rannusio], or Rhamnusus, transcribes and translates, sequitur ad unguem, a Ms. of Villehardouin, which he possessed ; but he enriches his narrative with Greek and Latin materials, and we are indebted to him for a correct state of the fleet, the names of the fifty Venetian nobles who commanded the galleys of the republic, and the patriot opposition of Pantaleon Barbus to the choice of the doge for emperor.

CHAPTER LXI

Partition of the Empire by the French and Venetians—Five Latin Emperors of the Houses of Flanders and Courtenay —Their Wars against the Bulgarians and Greeks—Weakness and Poverty of the Latin Empire—Recovery of Constantinople by the Greeks—General Consequences of the Crusades

AFTER the death of the lawful princes, the French and Venetians, confident of justice and victory, agreed to divide and regulate their future possessions.[1] It was stipulated by treaty, that twelve electors, six of either nation, should be nominated ; that a majority should choose the emperor of the East; and that, if the votes were equal, the decision of chance should ascertain the successful candidate. To him, with all the titles and prerogatives of the Byzantine throne, they assigned the two palaces of Boucoleon and Blachernæ, with a fourth part of the Greek monarchy. It was defined that the three remaining portions should be equally shared between the republic of Venice and the barons of France ; that each feudatory, with an honourable exception for the doge, should acknowledge and perform the duties of homage and military service to the supreme head of the empire; that the nation which gave an emperor should resign to their brethren the choice of a patriarch ; and that the pilgrims, whatever might be their impatience to visit the Holy Land, should devote another year to the conquest and defence of the Greek provinces. After the conquest of Constantinople by the Latins, the treaty was confirmed and executed ; and the first and most important

Election of the emperor Baldwin I. A.D. 1204, May 9-16 [Partition treaty]

[from March 31, 1204]

---

[1] See the original treaty of partition, in the Venetian Chronicle of Andrew Dandolo, p. 326-330 [Tafel und Thomas, Urkunden zur ältern Handels- und Staatsgeschichte der Republik Venedig, i. 454. The treaty was concluded and drawn up before the city was taken], and the subsequent election in Villehardouin, No. 136-140, with Ducange in his Observations, and the 1st book of his Histoire de Constantinople sous l'Empire des François.

step was the creation of an emperor. The six electors of the
French nation were all ecclesiastics, the abbot of Loces, the
archbishop elect of Acre in Palestine, and the bishops of Troyes,
Soissons, Halberstadt, and Bethlehem, the last of whom exercised
in the camp the office of pope's legate; their profession and
knowledge were respectable; and, as *they* could not be the
objects, they were best qualified to be authors, of the choice.
The six Venetians were the principal servants of the state, and
in this list the noble families of Querini and Contarini are still
proud to discover their ancestors. The twelve assembled in
the chapel of the palace ; and, after the solemn invocation of
the Holy Ghost, they proceeded to deliberate and vote. A just
impulse of respect and gratitude prompted them to crown the
virtues of the doge ; his wisdom had inspired their enterprise ;
and the most youthful knights might envy and applaud the
exploits of blindness and age. But the patriot Dandolo was
devoid of all personal ambition, and fully satisfied that he had
been judged worthy to reign. His nomination was overruled
by the Venetians themselves ; his countrymen, and perhaps
his friends,[2] represented, with the eloquence of truth, the
mischiefs that might arise to national freedom and the common
cause from the union of two incompatible characters, of the first
magistrate of a republic and the emperor of the East. The
exclusion of the doge left room for the more equal merits
of Boniface and Baldwin; and at their names all meaner
candidates respectfully withdrew. The marquis of Montferrat
was recommended by his mature age and fair reputation, by
the choice of the adventurers and the wishes of the Greeks;
nor can I believe that Venice, the mistress of the sea, could be
seriously apprehensive of a petty lord at the foot of the Alps.[3]
But the count of Flanders was the chief of a wealthy and
warlike people; he was valiant, pious, and chaste; in the
prime of life, since he was only thirty-two years of age; a
descendant of Charlemagne, a cousin of the king of France,

[2] After mentioning the nomination of the doge by a French elector, his kinsman Andrew Dandolo approves his exclusion, quidam Venetorum fidelis et nobilis senex, usus oratione satis probabili, &c., which has been embroidered by modern writers from Blondus to Le Beau.

[3] Nicetas (p. 384), with the vain ignorance of a Greek, describes the marquis of Montferrat as a *maritime* power. Λαμπαρδίαν δὲ οἰκεῖσθαι παράλιον. Was he deceived by the Byzantine theme of Lombardy, which extended along the coast of Calabria ?

and a compeer of the prelates and barons who had yielded
with reluctance to the command of a foreigner. Without the
chapel, these barons, with the doge and marquis at their head,
expected the decision of the twelve electors. It was announced
by the bishop of Soissons, in the name of his colleagues : " Ye
have sworn to obey the prince whom we should choose : by
our unanimous suffrage, Baldwin, count of Flanders and Hai-
nault, is now your sovereign, and the emperor of the East ".
He was saluted with loud applause, and the proclamation
was re-echoed throughout the city by the joy of the Latins
and the trembling adulation of the Greeks. Boniface was the
first to kiss the hand of his rival, and to raise him on the buckler ; and Baldwin was transported to the cathedral and solemnly
invested with the purple buskins. At the end of three weeks
he was crowned by the legate, in the vacancy of a patriarch ;
but the Venetian clergy soon filled the chapter of St. Sophia,
seated Thomas Morosini on the ecclesiastical throne, and
employed every art to perpetuate, in their own nation, the
honours and benefices of the Greek church.[4] Without delay,
the successor of Constantine instructed Palestine, France, and
Rome of this memorable revolution. To Palestine he sent, as
a trophy, the gates of Constantinople and the chain of the
harbour ;[5] and adopted from the Assise of Jerusalem the laws
or customs best adapted to a French colony and conquest in
the East.[6] In his epistles, the natives of France are encouraged
to swell that colony and to secure that conquest, to people a
magnificent city and a fertile land, which will reward the
labours both of the priest and the soldier. He congratulates
the Roman pontiff on the restoration of his authority in the
East ; invites him to extinguish the Greek schism by his presence
in a general council ; and implores his blessing and forgiveness
for the disobedient pilgrims. Prudence and dignity are blended
in the answer of Innocent.[7] In the subversion of the Byzantine

[4] They exacted an oath from Thomas Morosini to appoint no canons of St.
Sophia, the lawful electors, except Venetians who had lived ten years at Venice, &c.
But the foreign clergy were envious, the pope disapproved this national monopoly, and
of the six Latin patriarchs of Constantinople only the first and last were Venetians.
[5] Nicetas, p. 383.
[6] [The Assises of Jerusalem, at least the Assise of the Haute Cour, was probably
not codified so early as 1204. But it had been introduced into the Peloponnesus
before 1275.]
[7] The Epistles of Innocent III. are a rich fund for the ecclesiastical and civil
institution of the Latin empire of Constantinople ; and the most important of these

empire, he arraigns the vices of man and adores the providence of God; the conquerors will be absolved or condemned by their future conduct; the validity of their treaty depends on the judgment of St. Peter; but he inculcates their most sacred duty of establishing a just subordination of obedience and tribute, from the Greeks to the Latins, from the magistrate to the clergy, and from the clergy to the pope.

Division of the Greek empire   In the division of the Greek provinces,[8] the share of the Venetians was more ample than that of the Latin emperor. No more than one fourth was appropriated to his domain; a clear moiety of the remainder was reserved for Venice; and the other moiety was distributed among the adventurers of France and Lombardy. The venerable Dandolo was proclaimed despot of Romania, and invested, after the Greek fashion, with the purple buskins. He ended, at Constantinople, his long and glorious life; and, if the prerogative was personal, the title was used by his successors till the middle of the fourteenth century, with the singular though true addition of lords of one fourth and a half of the Roman empire.[9] The doge, a slave of the state, was seldom permitted to depart from the helm of the republic; but his place was supplied by the *bail*, or regent, who exercised a supreme jurisdiction over the colony of Venetians; they possessed three of the eight quarters of the city; and his independent tribunal was composed of six judges, four counsellors, two chamberlains, two fiscal advocates, and a constable. Their long experience of the Eastern trade enabled them to select their portion with discernment; they had rashly accepted the dominion and defence of Hadrianople; but it was the more reasonable aim of their policy to form a chain of factories and cities and islands along the maritime coast, from the neighbourhood of Ragusa to the Hellespont and the Bosphorus. The labour and cost of such extensive conquests exhausted their

epistles (of which the collection in 2 vols. in folio, is published by Stephen Baluze) are inserted in his Gesta, in Muratori, Script. Rerum Italicarum, tom. iii. p. 1, c. 94-105. [Migne, Patrol. Lat., vols. 214, 215, 216.]

[8] In the treaty of partition, most of the names are corrupted by the scribes; they might be restored, and a good map, suited to the last age of the Byzantine empire, would be an improvement of geography; but, alas! d'Anville is no more! [The act of partition annexed to the treaty with geographical notes was edited by Tafel in his Symbolæ criticæ geographiam Byzantinam spectantes, part 2.]

[9] Their style was Dominus quartæ partis et dimidiæ imperii Romani, till Giovanni Dolfino, who was elected Doge in the year 1356 (Sanuto, p. 530, 641). For the government of Constantinople, see Ducange, Histoire de C. P. p. 37.

treasury; they abandoned their maxims of government, adopted a feudal system, and contented themselves with the homage of their nobles,[10] for the possessions which these private vassals undertook to reduce and maintain. And thus it was that the family of Sanut acquired the duchy of Naxos, which involved the greatest part of the Archipelago. For the price of ten thousand marks the republic purchased of the marquis of Montferrat the fertile island of Crete, or Candia, with the ruins of an hundred cities;[11] but its improvement was stinted by the proud and narrow spirit of an aristocracy;[12] and the wisest senators would confess that the sea, not the land, was the treasury of St. Mark. In the moiety of the adventurers, the marquis Boniface might claim the most liberal reward; and, besides the isle of Crete, his exclusion from the throne was compensated by the royal title and the provinces beyond the Hellespont. But he prudently exchanged that distant and difficult conquest for the kingdom of Thessalonica, or Macedonia, twelve days' journey from the capital, where he might be supported by the neighbouring powers of his brother-in-law the king of Hungary.[13] His progress was hailed by the voluntary or reluctant acclamations of the natives; and Greece, the proper and ancient Greece, again received a Latin conqueror,[14] who trod with indifference

[10] Ducange (Hist. de C. P. ii. 6) has marked the conquests made by the state or nobles of Venice of the islands of Candia, Corfu, Cephalonia, Zante, Naxos, Paros, Melos, Andros, Myconè, Scyro, Cea, and Lemnos. [See Appendix 18.]

[11] Boniface sold the isle of Candia, Aug. 12, A.D. 1204. See the acts in Sanuto, p. 533; but I cannot understand how it could be his mother's portion, or how she could be the daughter of an emperor Alexius. [Boniface's *Refutatio Cretis* is printed in Tafel und Thomas, Urkunden, 512, and in Buchon, Recherches et Matériaux, i. 10. Crete had been formally promised him by the young Alexius. He seems to have claimed Thessalonica on the ground that his brother had been created king of Thessalonica by Manuel, see above, p. 388. The erection of the kingdom of Thessalonica was by no means agreeable to Baldwin; it threatened, weakened, and perhaps ruined the Empire of Romania. War was imminent between Baldwin and Boniface, but the Doge persuaded Baldwin to yield.]

[12] In the year 1212, the doge Peter Zani sent a colony to Candia, drawn from every quarter of Venice. But, in their savage manners and frequent rebellions, the Candiots may be compared to the Corsicans under the yoke of Genoa; and, when I compare the accounts of Belon and Tournefort, I cannot discern much difference between the Venetian and the Turkish island.

[13] [He married Margaret, widow of Isaac Angelus.]

[14] Villehardouin (No. 159, 160, 173-177) and Nicetas (p. 387-394) describe the expedition into Greece of the marquis Boniface. The Choniate might derive his information from his brother Michael, archbishop of Athens, whom he paints as an orator, a statesman, and a saint. His encomium of Athens, and the description of Tempe, should be published from the Bodleian Ms. of Nicetas (Fabric. Bibliot. Græc. tom. vi. p. 405), and would have deserved Mr. Harris's inquiries. [The works of Michael Akominatos have been published in a full edition by S. Lampros

that classic ground.   He viewed with a careless eye the beauties of the valley of Tempe; traversed with a cautious step the
straits of Thermopylæ; occupied the unknown cities of Thebes,
Athens, and Argos ;[15] and assaulted the fortifications of Corinth
and Napoli,[16] which resisted his arms.   The lots of the Latin
pilgrims were regulated by chance, or choice, or subsequent
exchange; and they abused, with intemperate joy, the triumph
over the lives and fortunes of a great people.   After a minute
survey of the provinces, they weighed in the scales of avarice
the revenue of each district, the advantage of the situation, and
the ample or scanty supplies for the maintenance of soldiers
and horses.   Their presumption claimed and divided the long-
lost dependencies of the Roman sceptre; the Nile and Euphrates
rolled through their imaginary realms; and happy was the
warrior who drew for his prize the palace of the Turkish sultan
of Iconium.[17]   I shall not descend to the pedigree of families and
the rent-rolls of estates, but I wish to specify that the counts
of Blois and St. Pol were invested with the duchy of Nice and
the lordship of Demotica;[18] the principal fiefs were held by the
service of constable, chamberlain, cup-bearer, butler, and chief
cook; and our historian, Jeffrey of Villehardouin, obtained a

(1879-80, 2 vols.).   The dirge on Athens had been already published by Boissonade
in Anecdota Græca, 5, p. 373 *sqq.* (1833).   Gregorovius in his Geschichte der
Stadt Athen im Mittelalter (where he draws a most interesting sketch of Akominatos in caps. 7 and 8) gives specimens of a German translation of the dirge, p.
243-4.]
    [15] [Leo Sguros of Nauplia made himself master of Nauplia, Argos, Corinth, and
Thebes.   He besieged Athens (see below, p. 505, note 71) ; and the Acropolis, defended
by the archbishop Akominatos, defied him.   From Thebes he went to Thessaly, and
meeting the Emperor Alexius at Larissa married his daughter and received from him
the title of *Sebastohypertatos*.   When Boniface and his knights approached, father-
in-law and son-in-law retreated to Thermopylæ, but did not await the approach of
the enemy.   Bodonitza close to the pass was granted by Boniface, as a fief to Guy
Pallavicini.   Before he proceeded against Thebes, Amphissa, which about this
time assumes the name Salona (or Sula), was taken, and given with the neighbouring districts including Delphi and the port of Galaxidi to Thomas of Stromon-
court.   For Thebes and Athens see below, p. 505.]
    [16] Napoli di Romania, or Nauplia, the ancient sea-port of Argos, is still a place
of strength and consideration, situate on a rocky peninsula, with a good harbour
(Chandler's Travels into Greece, p. 227).   [It narrowly escaped becoming the
capital of the modern kingdom of Greece.]
    [17] I have softened the expression of Nicetas, who strives to expose the presump-
tion of the Franks.   See de Rebus post C. P. expugnatam, p. 375-384.
    [18] A city surrounded by the river Hebrus, and six leagues to the south of Ha-
drianople, received from its double wall the Greek name of Didymoteichos, insensibly corrupted into Demotica and Dimot.   I have preferred the more convenient
and modern appellation of Demotica.   This place was the last Turkish residence of
Charles XII.

fair establishment on the banks of the Hebrus, and united the double office of marshal of Champagne and Romania. At the head of his knights and archers each baron mounted on horseback to secure the possession of his share, and their first efforts were generally successful. But the public force was weakened by their dispersion; and a thousand quarrels must arise under a law, and among men, whose sole umpire was the sword. Within three months after the conquest of Constantinople, the emperor and the king of Thessalonica drew their hostile followers into the field; they were reconciled by the authority of the doge, the advice of the marshal, and the firm freedom of their peers.[19]

Two fugitives, who had reigned at Constantinople, still asserted the title of emperor; and the subjects of their fallen throne might be moved to pity by the misfortunes of the elder Alexius, or excited to revenge by the spirit of Mourzoufle. A domestic alliance, a common interest, a similar guilt, and a merit of extinguishing his enemies, a brother and a nephew, induced the more recent usurper to unite with the former the relics of his power. Mourzoufle was received with smiles and honours in the camp of his father Alexius; but the wicked can never love, and should rarely trust, their fellow-criminals: he was seized in the bath, deprived of his eyes, stripped of his troops and treasures, and turned out to wander an object of horror and contempt to those who with more propriety could hate, and with more justice could punish, the assassin of the emperor Isaac and his son. As the tyrant, pursued by fear or remorse, was stealing over to Asia, he was seized by the Latins of Constantinople, and condemned, after an open trial, to an ignominious death. His judges debated the mode of his execution, the axe, the wheel, or the stake; and it was resolved that Mourzoufle[20] should ascend the Theodosian column, a pillar of white marble of one hundred and forty-seven feet in height.[21]

Revolt of the Greeks. A.D. 1204, &c.

---

[19] Their quarrel is told by Villehardouin (No. 146-158) with the spirit of freedom. The merit and reputation of the marshal are acknowledged by the Greek historian (p. 387), μέγα παρὰ τοῖς Λατίνων δυναμένου στρατεύμασι : unlike some modern heroes, whose exploits are only visible in their own memoirs.

[20] See the fate of Mourzoufle in Nicetas (p. 393), Villehardouin (No. 141-145, 163), and Guntherus (c. 20, 21). Neither the marshal nor the monk afford a grain of pity for a tyrant or rebel, whose punishment, however, was more unexampled than his crime.

[21] The column of Arcadius, which represents in basso-relievo his victories, or those of his father Theodosius, is still extant at Constantinople. It is described

From the summit he was cast down headlong, and dashed in pieces on the pavement, in the presence of innumerable spectators, who filled the forum of Taurus, and admired the accomplishment of an old prediction, which was explained by this singular event.[22] The fate of Alexius is less tragical: he was sent by the marquis a captive to Italy, and a gift to the king of the Romans; but he had not much to applaud his fortune, if the sentence of imprisonment and exile were changed from a fortress in the Alps to a monastery in Asia. But his daughter, before the national calamity, had been given in marriage to a young hero, who continued the succession, and restored the throne, of the Greek princes.[23] The valour of Theodore Lascaris was signalised in the two sieges of Constantinople. After the flight of Mourzoufle, when the Latins were already in the city, he offered himself as their emperor to the soldiers and people; and his ambition, which might be virtuous, was undoubtedly brave. Could he have infused a soul into the multitude, they might have crushed the strangers under their feet; their abject despair refused his aid; and Theodore retired to breathe the air of freedom in Anatolia, beyond the immediate view and pursuit of the conquerors. Under the title, at first of despot, and afterwards of emperor, he drew to his standard the bolder spirits, who were fortified against slavery by the contempt of life; and, as every means was lawful for the public safety, implored without scruple the alliance of the Turkish sultan. Nice, where Theodore established his residence, Prusa and Philadelphia, Smyrna and Ephesus, opened their gates to their deliverer; he derived strength and reputation from his victories, and even from his defeats; and the successor of Constantine preserved a fragment of the empire from the banks of the Mæander to the suburbs of Nicomedia, and at length of Constantinople. Another portion, distant and obscure, was possessed by the lineal heir

Theodore Lascaris, Emperor of Nice. A.D. 1204-1222

The dukes and emperors of Trebizond

and measured, Gyllius (Topograph. iv. 7), Banduri (ad l. i. Antiquit. C. P. p. 507, &c.), and Tournefort (Voyage du Levant, tom. ii. lettre xii. p. 231). [Nothing of the column remains now except its base.]

[22] The nonsense of Gunther and the modern Greeks concerning this *columna fatidica* is unworthy of notice; but it is singular enough that, fifty years before the Latin conquest, the poet Tzetzes (Chiliad, ix. 277) relates the dream of a matron, who saw an army in the forum, and a man sitting on the column, clapping his hands and uttering a loud exclamation.

[23] The dynasties of Nice, Trebizond, and Epirus (of which Nicetas saw the origin without much pleasure or hope) are learnedly explored, and clearly represented, in the Familiæ Byzantinæ of Ducange.

of the Comneni, a son of the virtuous Manuel, a grandson of the tyrant Andronicus. His name was Alexius; and the epithet of *great* was applied perhaps to his stature, rather than to his exploits. By the indulgence of the Angeli,[24] he was appointed governor or duke of Trebizond :[25] his birth gave him ambition, the revolution independence; and, without changing his title, he reigned in peace from Sinope to the Phasis, along the coast of the Black Sea. His nameless son and successor[26] is described as the vassal of the sultan, whom he served with two hundred lances; that Comnenian prince was no more than duke of Trebizond, and the title of emperor was first assumed by the pride and envy of the grandson of Alexius. In the West, a third fragment was saved from the common shipwreck by Michael, a bastard of the house of Angeli,[27] who, before the

The despots of Epirus

[24] [Rather, by the help of his aunt, queen Thamar of Iberia. On the death of Andronicus in 1185 his two grandsons, Alexius and David, escaped to Iberia. Their aunt helped Alexius to found the independent state of Trapezus in 1204 : and there he assumed the title of Grand-Komnenos. His brother David seized Paphlagonia. The Comneni never made common cause with the Emperors of Nicæa against the common enemies, either Turks or Latins. On the contrary, Theodore Lascaris defeated David and wrested his kingdom from him, leaving him only a small region about Sinope (1212), and in 1214 the Turks captured Sinope and David fell fighting. On the other hand, Alexius maintained himself at Trebizond, and the Empire of Trebizond survived the Turkish conquest of Constantinople by eight years.]

[25] Except some facts in Pachymer and Nicephorus Gregoras, which will hereafter be used, the Byzantine writers disdain to speak of the empire of Trebizond, or principality of the *Lazi*; and among the Latins, it is conspicuous only in the romances of the xivth or xvth centuries. Yet the indefatigable Ducange has dug out (Fam. Byz. p. 192) two authentic passages in Vincent of Beauvais (l. xxxi. c. 144), and the protonotary Ogerius (apud Wading, A.D. 1279, No. 4). [The short history of the Emperors of Trebizond from 1204-1426, by Michael Panaretos of Trebizond (lived in first half of 15th century) was published by Tafel at the end of his edition of Eustathius (p. 362 *sqq*.), 1833. It was translated in St. Martin's ed. of Lebeau's Hist. du bas-empire, vol. xx. p. 482 *sqq*. The first, who went thoroughly into the history of Trebizond, was Fallmerayer, and he published more material. See the Abhandlungen of the Bavarian Academy, 3 cl., vol. 3, 1843 ; and Geschichte des Kaiserthums von Trapezunt, 1827. The story is told at length by Finlay in History of Greece, vol. iv. p. 307 *sqq*. But there is much more material, and A. Papadopulos-Kerameus issued in 1897, vol. i. of Fontes Historiæ Imperii Trapezuntini. A new history of Trapezus, from the earliest times to the present day, has appeared in modern Greek : Ἱστορία τῆς Τραπεζοῦντος (Odessa), 1898, by T. E. Evangelides.]

[26] [His stepson Andronicus Gidos succeeded him in 1222, and was succeeded in 1235, by John, the eldest son of Alexius, who reigned only three years. Then came Manuel ; and then John, who assumed the title "Emperor of the East, Iberia and Peratea," avoiding the title of Roman Emperor, in order to keep the peace with the Palaeologi of Constantinople. Peratea was a part of the Crimea which acknowledged his sway.]

[27] [Michael was natural son of Constantine Angelus, uncle of the Emperors Isaac and Alexius III. He and his successors assumed the name *Comnenus Angelus Ducas*. Michael was murdered in 1214 and succeeded by his brother Theodore.]

revolution, had been known as an hostage, a soldier, and a rebel. His flight from the camp of the marquis Boniface secured his freedom; by his marriage with the governor's daughter he commanded the important place of Durazzo, assumed the title of despot, and founded a strong and conspicuous principality in Epirus, Ætolia, and Thessaly, which have ever been peopled by a warlike race. The Greeks, who had offered their service to their new sovereigns, were excluded by the haughty Latins [28] from all civil and military honours, as a nation born to tremble and obey. Their resentment prompted them to show that they might have been useful friends, since they could be dangerous enemies; their nerves were braced by adversity; whatever was learned or holy, whatever was noble or valiant, rolled away into the independent states of Trebizond, Epirus, and Nice; and a single patrician is marked by the ambiguous praise of attachment and loyalty to the Franks. The vulgar herd of the cities and the country would have gladly submitted to a mild and regular servitude; and the transient disorders of war would have been obliterated by some years of industry and peace. But peace was banished, and industry was crushed, in the disorders of the feudal system. The *Roman* emperors of Constantinople, if they were endowed with abilities, were armed with power for the protection of their subjects; their laws were wise and their administration was simple. The Latin throne was filled by a titular prince, the chief, and often the servant, of his licentious confederates: the fiefs of the empire, from a kingdom to a castle, were held and ruled by the sword of the barons; and their discord, poverty, and ignorance extended their ramifications of tyranny to the most sequestered villages. The Greeks were oppressed by the double weight of the priest, who was invested with temporal power, and of the soldier, who was inflamed by fanatic hatred: and the insuperable bar of religion and language for ever separated the stranger and the native. As long as the crusaders were united at Constantinople, the memory of their conquest and the terror of their arms imposed silence on the captive land; their dispersion

---

[28] The portrait of the French Latins is drawn in Nicetas by the hand of prejudice and resentment: οὐδὲν τῶν ἄλλων ἐθνῶν εἰς Ἄρεος ἔργα παρασυμβεβλῆσθαι ἠνείχοντο, ἀλλ᾽ οὐδέ τις τῶν χαρίτων ἢ τῶν μουσῶν παρὰ τοῖς βαρβάροις τούτοις ἐπεξενίζετο, καὶ παρὰ τοῦτο οἶμαι τὴν φύσιν ἦσαν ἀνήμεροι, καὶ τὸν χόλον εἶχον τοῦ λόγου προτρέχοντα.

A BULGARIAN RULER: THE TSAR JOHN ALEXANDER WITH HIS WIFE
THEODORA AND TWO SONS; FROM A BULGARIAN GOSPEL OF A.D. 1355-6
BELONGING TO LORD ZOUCHE

betrayed the smallness of their numbers and the defects of their discipline; and some failures and mischances revealed the secret that they were not invincible. As the fear of the Greeks abated, their hatred increased. They murmured; they conspired; and, before a year of slavery had elapsed, they implored or accepted the succour of a barbarian, whose power they had felt, and whose gratitude they trusted.[29]

The Latin conquerors had been saluted with a solemn and early embassy from John, or Joannice, or Calo-John, the revolted chief of the Bulgarians and Walachians. He deemed himself their brother, as the votary of the Roman pontiff, from whom he had received the regal title and an holy banner; and in the subversion of the Greek monarchy he might aspire to the name of their friend and accomplice. But Calo-John was astonished to find that the count of Flanders had assumed the pomp and pride of the successors of Constantine; and his ambassadors were dismissed with an haughty message, that the rebel must deserve a pardon by touching with his forehead the footstool of the Imperial throne. His resentment [30] would have exhaled in acts of violence and blood; his cooler policy watched the rising discontent of the Greeks; affected a tender concern for their sufferings; and promised that their first struggles for freedom should be supported by his person and kingdom. The conspiracy was propagated by national hatred, the firmest band of association and secrecy: the Greeks were impatient to sheathe their daggers in the breasts of the victorious strangers; but the execution was prudently delayed, till Henry, the emperor's brother, had transported the flower of his troops beyond the Hellespont. Most of the towns and villages of Thrace were true to the moment and the signal: and the Latins, without arms or suspicion, were slaughtered by the vile and merciless revenge of their slaves. From Demotica, the first scene of the massacre, the surviving vassals of the count of St. Pol escaped

The Bulgarian war.
A.D. 1205

---

[29] I here begin to use with freedom and confidence, the eight books of the Histoire de C. P. sous l'Empire des François, which Ducange has given as a supplement to Villehardouin; and which, in a barbarous style, deserves the praise of an original and classic work.

[30] In Calo-John's answer to the Pope, we may find his claims and complaints (Gesta Innocent. III. c. 108, 109); he was cherished at Rome as the prodigal son. [The name Kalo-John was also used of John Vatatzes, and of the young John Lascaris, son of Theodore II.; see Mêliarakês, 'Ιστορία τοῦ βασιλείου τῆς Νικαίας, p. 541, note.]

to Hadrianople; but the French and Venetians who occupied that city were slain or expelled by the furious multitude; the garrisons that could effect their retreat fell back on each other towards the metropolis; and the fortresses that separately stood against the rebels were ignorant of each other's and of their sovereign's fate.   The voice of fame and fear announced the revolt of the Greeks and the rapid approach of their Bulgarian ally; and Calo-John, not depending on the forces of his own kingdom, had drawn from the Scythian wilderness a body of fourteen thousand Comans, who drank, as it was said, the blood of their captives, and sacrificed the Christians on the altars of their gods.[31]

Alarmed by this sudden and growing danger, the emperor dispatched a swift messenger to recall count Henry and his troops; and, had Baldwin expected the return of his gallant brother, with a supply of twenty thousand Armenians, he might have encountered the invader with equal numbers and a decisive superiority of arms and discipline.   But the spirit of chivalry could seldom discriminate caution from cowardice; and the Emperor took the field with an hundred and forty knights, and their train of archers and serjeants.   The marshal, who dissuaded and obeyed, led the vanguard in their march to Hadrianople; the main body was commanded by the count of Blois; the aged doge of Venice followed with the rear; and their scanty numbers were increased on all sides by the fugitive Latins.   They undertook to besiege the rebels of Hadrianople; and such was the pious tendency of the crusades that they employed the holy week in pillaging the country for their subsistence, and in framing engines for the destruction of their fellow-Christians.   But the Latins were soon interrupted and alarmed by the light calvary of the Comans, who boldly skirmished to the edge of their imperfect lines; and a proclamation was issued by the marshal of Romania, that on the trumpet's sound the cavalry should mount and form, but that none, under pain of death, should abandon themselves to a desultory and dangerous pursuit.   This wise injunction was

March

---

[31] The Comans were a Tartar or Turkman horde, which encamped in the xiith and xiiith centuries on the verge of Moldavia.   The greater part were Pagans, but some were Mahometans, and the whole horde was converted to Christianity (A.D. 1370) by Lewis, king of Hungary.   [See above, p. 153, n. 52, and p. 248, n. 36.]

first disobeyed by the count of Blois, who involved the emperor
in his rashness and ruin. The Comans, of the Parthian or
Tartar school, fled before their first charge ; but, after a career of
two leagues, when the knights and their horses were almost
breathless, they suddenly turned, rallied, and encompassed the
heavy squadrons of the Franks. The count was slain on the Defeat and captivity of Baldwin.
field ; the emperor was made prisoner ; and, if the one disdained
to fly, if the other refused to yield, their personal bravery made A.D. 1205, April 15
a poor atonement for their ignorance or neglect of the duties of
a general.[32]

Proud of his victory and his royal prize, the Bulgarian advanced to relieve Hadrianople and achieve the destruction of
the Latins. They must inevitably have been destroyed, if the
marshal of Romania had not displayed a cool courage and consummate skill, uncommon in all ages, but most uncommon in
those times, when war was a passion rather than a science.
His grief and fears were poured into the firm and faithful Retreat of the Latins
bosom of the doge ; but in the camp he diffused an assurance
of safety, which could only be realised by the general belief.
All day he maintained his perilous station between the city
and the barbarians : Villehardouin decamped in silence at the
dead of night; and his masterly retreat of three days would
have deserved the praise of Xenophon and the ten thousand.
In the rear the Marshal supported the weight of the pursuit ;
in the front he moderated the impatience of the fugitives ; and,
wherever the Comans approached, they were repelled by a line
of impenetrable spears. On the third day, the weary troops
beheld the sea, the solitary town of Rodosto,[33] and their friends,
who had landed from the Asiatic shore. They embraced, they
wept; but they united their arms and counsels; and, in his
brother's absence, count Henry assumed the regency of the
empire, at once in a state of childhood and caducity.[34] If

[32] Nicetas, from ignorance or malice, imputes the defeat to the cowardice of
Dandolo (p. 383) ; but Villehardouin shares his own glory with his venerable friend,
qui viels home ére et gote ne veoit, mais mult ére sages et preus et vigueros (No.
193).

[33] The truth of geography and the original text of Villehardouin (No. 194 [366])
place Rodosto [Rhædestus] three days' journey (trois jornées) from Hadrianople ;
but Vigenère, in his version, has most absurdly substituted *trois heures ;* and this
error, which is not corrected by Ducange, has entrapped several moderns, whose
names I shall spare.

[34] The reign and end of Baldwin are related by Villehardouin and Nicetas (p.
386-416) ; and their omissions are supplied by Ducange, in his Observations, and
to the end of his first book.

the Comans withdrew from the summer-heats, seven thousand Latins, in the hour of danger, deserted Constantinople, their brethren, and their vows. Some partial success was overbalanced by the loss of one hundred and twenty knights in the field of Rusium; and of the Imperial domain no more was left than the capital, with two or three adjacent fortresses on the shores of Europe and Asia. The king of Bulgaria was resistless and inexorable; and Calo-John respectfully eluded the demands of the pope, who conjured his new proselyte to restore peace and the emperor to the afflicted Latins. The deliverance of Baldwin was no longer, he said, in the power of

Death of the Emperor

man: that prince had died in prison; and the manner of his death is variously related by ignorance and credulity. The lovers of a tragic legend will be pleased to hear that the royal captive was tempted by the amorous queen of the Bulgarians; that his chaste refusal exposed him to the falsehood of a woman and the jealousy of a savage ; that his hands and feet were severed from his body; that his bleeding trunk was cast among the carcases of dogs and horses; and that he breathed three days before he was devoured by the birds of prey.[35] About twenty years afterwards, in a wood of the Netherlands, an hermit announced himself as the true Baldwin, the emperor of Constantinople, and the lawful sovereign of Flanders. He related the wonders of his escape, his adventures, and his penance, among a people prone to believe and to rebel: and, in the first transport, Flanders acknowledged her long-lost sovereign. A short examination before the French court detected the impostor, who was punished with an ignominious death; but the Flemings still adhered to the pleasing error; and the countess Jane is accused by the gravest historians of sacrificing to her ambition the life of an unfortunate father.[36]

Reign and character of Henry. A.D. 1206, Aug. 20— A.D. 1216, June 11

In all civilised hostility a treaty is established for the exchange or ransom of prisoners; and, if their captivity be prolonged, their condition is known, and they are treated ac-

---

[35] After brushing away all doubtful and improbable circumstances, we may prove the death of Baldwin: 1. By the firm belief of the French barons (Villehardouin, No. 230). 2. By the declaration by Calo-John himself, who excuses his not releasing the captive emperor, quia debitum carnis exsolverat cum carcere teneretur (Gesta Innocent. III., c. 109).

[36] See the story of this impostor from the French and Flemish writers in Ducange, Hist. de C. P. iii. 9; and the ridiculous fables that were believed by the monks of St. Alban's in Matthew Paris, Hist. Major, p. 271-272.

cording to their rank with humanity or honour. But the savage Bulgarian was a stranger to the laws of war; his prisons were involved in darkness and silence; and above a year elapsed before the Latins could be assured of the death of Baldwin, before his brother, the regent Henry, would consent to assume the title of emperor. His moderation was applauded by the Greeks as an act of rare and inimitable virtue. Their light and perfidious ambition was eager to seize or anticipate the moment of a vacancy, while a law of succession, the guardian both of the prince and people, was gradually defined and confirmed in the hereditary monarchies of Europe. In the support of the Eastern empire Henry was gradually left without an associate, as the heroes of the crusade retired from the world or from the war. The doge of Venice, the venerable [June 1] Dandolo, in the fulness of years and glory, sunk into the grave The marquis of Montferrat was slowly recalled from the Peloponnesian war to the revenge of Baldwin and the defence of Thessalonica. Some nice disputes of feudal homage and service were reconciled in a personal interview between the emperor and the king; they were firmly united by mutual esteem and the common danger; and their alliance was sealed by the nuptial of Henry with the daughter of the Italian prince. He [Agnes] soon deplored the loss of his friend and father. At the persuasion of some faithful Greeks, Boniface made a bold and successful inroad among the hills of Rhodope: the Bulgarians fled on his approach; they assembled to harass his retreat. On the intelligence that his rear was attacked, without waiting for any defensive armour, he leaped on horseback, couched his lance, and drove the enemies before him; but in the rash pursuit he was pierced with a mortal wound; and the head of the king of [near Mosynopolis] Thessalonica was presented to Calo-John, who enjoyed the honours, without the merit, of victory. It is here, at this melancholy event, that the pen or the voice of Jeffrey of Villehardouin seems to drop or to expire; [37] and, if he still exercised his military office of marshal of Romania, his subsequent exploits

---

[37] Villehardouin, No. 257. I quote, with regret, this lamentable conclusion, where we lose at once the original history, and the rich illustrations of Ducange. The last pages may derive some light from Henry's two epistles to Innocent III. (Gesta, c. 106, 107). [Villehardouin's story is poorly continued by Henry of Valenciennes, whose chronicle is printed along with Villehardouin in Wailly's edition (ed. 3, 1882).]

are buried in oblivion.[38]   The character of Henry was not unequal to his arduous situation: in the siege of Constantinople,
and beyond the Hellespont, he had deserved the fame of a
valiant knight and a skilful commander; and his courage was
tempered with a degree of prudence and mildness unknown to
his impetuous brother.   In the double war against the Greeks
of Asia and the Bulgarians of Europe, he was ever the foremost
on shipboard or on horseback; and, though he cautiously provided for the success of his arms, the drooping Latins were
often roused by his example to save and to second their fearless emperor.   But such efforts, and some supplies of men and
money from France, were of less avail than the errors, the
cruelty, and the death of their most formidable adversary.   When
the despair of the Greek subjects invited Calo-John as their deliverer, they hoped that he would protect their liberty and adopt
their laws; they were soon taught to compare the degrees of
national ferocity, and to execrate the savage conqueror, who no
longer dissembled his intention of dispeopling Thrace, of demolishing the cities, and of transplanting the inhabitants beyond
the Danube.   Many towns and villages of Thrace were already
evacuated; an heap of ruins marked the place of Philippopolis, and a similar calamity was expected at Demotica and
Hadrianople by the first authors of the revolt.   They raised a
cry of grief and repentance to the throne of Henry; the emperor alone had the magnanimity to forgive and trust them.
No more than four hundred knights, with their serjeants and
archers, could be assembled under his banner; and with this
slender force he fought and repulsed the Bulgarian, who, besides
his infantry, was at the head of forty thousand horse.   In this
expedition, Henry felt the difference between an hostile and a
friendly country; the remaining cities were preserved by his
arms; and the savage, with shame and loss, was compelled to
relinquish his prey.   The siege of Thessalonica was the last of
the evils which Calo-John inflicted or suffered; he was stabbed
in the night in his tent; and the general, perhaps the assassin,
who found him weltering in his blood, ascribed the blow, with

---

[38] The marshal was alive in 1212, but he probably died soon afterwards, without returning to France (Ducange, Observations sur Villehardouin, p. 238).   His
fief of Messinople, the gift of Boniface, was the ancient Maximianopolis, which
flourished in the time of Ammianus Marcellinus, among the cities of Thrace (No.
141).   [Messinopolis is the Mosynopolis of Greek historians.]

general applause, to the lance of St. Demetrius.[39] After several victories the prudence of Henry concluded an honourable peace with the successor of the tyrant, and with the Greek princes of Nice and Epirus. If he ceded some doubtful limits, an ample kingdom was reserved for himself and his feudatories; and his reign, which lasted only ten years, afforded a short interval of prosperity and peace. Far above the narrow policy of Baldwin and Boniface, he freely entrusted to the Greeks the most important offices of the state and army; and this liberality of sentiment and practice was the more seasonable, as the princes of Nice and Epirus had already learned to seduce and employ the mercenary valour of the Latins. It was the aim of Henry to unite and reward his deserving subjects of every nation and language; but he appeared less solicitous to accomplish the impracticable union of the two churches. Pelagius, the Pope's legate, who acted as the sovereign of Constantinople, had interdicted the worship of the Greeks, and sternly imposed the payment of tithes, the double procession of the Holy Ghost, and a blind obedience to the Roman pontiff. As the weaker party, they pleaded the duties of conscience, and implored the rights of toleration: "Our bodies," they said, "are Cæsar's, but our souls belong only to God". The persecution was checked by the firmness of the emperor;[40] and, if we can believe that the same prince was poisoned by the Greeks themselves, we must entertain a contemptible idea of the sense and gratitude of mankind. His valour was a vulgar attribute which he shared with ten thousand knights; but Henry possessed the superior courage to oppose, in a superstitious age, the pride and avarice of the clergy. In the cathedral of St. Sophia, he presumed to place his throne on the right hand of the patriarch; and this presumption excited the sharpest censure of pope Innocent the Third.[41] By a salutary edict, one of the first examples of the laws of mortmain, he prohibited the alienation of fiefs; many of the Latins, desirous of returning to Europe, resigned their estates to the church

---

[39] The church of this patron of Thessalonica was served by the canons of the holy sepulchre, and contained a divine ointment which distilled daily and stupendous miracles (Ducange, Hist. de C. P. ii. 4).

[40] Acropolita (c. 17) observes the persecution of the legate, and the toleration of Henry ('Ερη, ['Ερρῆ gen.; 'Ερρῆς nom.] as he calls him) κλυδῶνα κατεστόρεσε.

[41] [The dispute with Innocent was compromised at a parliament which Henry held at Ravennika in northern Greece (near Zeituni ?) on May 2, 1210.]

for a spiritual or temporal reward; these holy lands were immediately discharged from military service; and a colony of soldiers would have been gradually transformed into a college of priests.[42]

Peter of Courtenay emperor of Constantinople. A.D. 1217, April 9 The virtuous Henry died at Thessalonica, in the defence of that kingdom, and of an infant, the son of his friend Boniface. In the two first emperors of Constantinople, the male line of the counts of Flanders was extinct. But their sister Yolande was the wife of a French prince, the mother of a numerous progeny; and one of her daughters had married Andrew, king of Hungary, a brave and pious champion of the cross. By seating him on the Byzantine throne, the barons of Romania would have acquired the forces of a neighbouring and warlike kingdom; but the prudent Andrew revered the laws of succession; and the princess Yolande, with her husband, Peter of Courtenay, count of Auxerre, was invited by the Latins to assume the empire of the East. The royal birth of his father, the noble origin of his mother, recommended to the barons of France the first-cousin of their king. His reputation was fair, his possessions were ample, and in the bloody crusade against the Albigeois the soldiers and the priests had been abundantly satisfied of his zeal and valour. Vanity might applaud the elevation of a French emperor of Constantinople; but prudence must pity, rather than envy, his treacherous and imaginary greatness. To assert and adorn his title, he was reduced to sell or mortgage the best of his patrimony. By these expedients, the liberality of his royal kinsman, Philip Augustus, and the national spirit of chivalry, he was enabled to pass the Alps at the head of one hundred and forty knights and five thousand five hundred serjeants and archers. After some hesitation, pope Honorius the Third was persuaded to crown the successor of Constantine; but he performed the ceremony in a church without the walls, lest he should seem to imply, or to bestow, any right of sovereignty over the ancient capital of the empire. The Venetians had engaged to transport Peter and his forces beyond the Adriatic, and the empress, with her four children, to the Byzantine

---

[42] See the reign of Henry, in Ducange (Hist. de C. P. l. i. c. 35-41, l. ii. c. 1-22), who is much indebted to the Epistles of the Popes. Le Beau (Hist. du Bas Empire, tom. xxi. p. 120-122) has found, perhaps in Doutreman, some laws of Henry, which determined the service of fiefs and the prerogatives of the emperor.

palace ; but they required, as the price of their service, that he should recover Durazzo from the despot of Epirus. Michael Angelus, or Comnenus, the first of his dynasty, had bequeathed [A.D. 1214] the succession of his power and ambition to Theodore, his legitimate brother, who already threatened and invaded the establishments of the Latins. After discharging his debt by a fruitless assault, the emperor raised the siege to prosecute a long and perilous journey over land from Durazzo to Thessalonica. He was soon lost in the mountains of Epirus ; the passes were fortified ; his provisions exhausted ; he was delayed and deceived His captivity and by a treacherous negotiàtion ; and, after Peter of Courtenay and death. A.D. the Roman legate had been arrested in a banquet, the French 1217-1219 troops, without leaders or hopes, were eager to exchange their arms for the delusive promise of mercy and bread. The Vatican thundered ; and the impious Theodore was threatened with the vengeance of earth and heaven ; but the captive emperor and his soldiers were forgotten, and the reproaches of the pope are confined to the imprisonment of his legate. No sooner was he satisfied by the deliverance of the priest and a promise of spiritual obedience, than he pardoned and protected the despot of Epirus. His peremptory commands suspended the ardour of the Venetians and the king of Hungary ; and it was only by a natural or untimely death [43] that Peter of Courtenay was released from his hopeless captivity.[44]

The long ignorance of his fate, and the presence of the law- Robert, ful sovereign, of Yolande, his wife or widow, delayed the pro- Emperor of Constantinople. A.D. clamation of a new emperor. Before her death, and in the 1221-1228 midst of her grief, she was delivered of a son, who was named Baldwin, the last and most unfortunate of the Latin princes of Constantinople. His birth endeared him to the barons of Romania ; but his childhood would have prolonged the troubles of a minority, and his claims were superseded by the elder claims of his brethren. The first of these, Philip of Courtenay, who derived from his mother the inheritance of Namur, had the

---

[43] Acropolita (c. 14) affirms that Peter of Courtenay died by the sword (ἔργον μαχαίρας γενέσθαι) ; but from his dark expressions, I should conclude a previous captivity, ὡς πάντας ἄρδην δεσμώτας ποιῆσαι σὺν πᾶσι σκεύεσι. The Chronicle of Auxerre delays the emperor's death till the year 1219 ; and Auxerre is in the neighbourhood of Courtenay.

[44] See the reign and death of Peter of Courtenay in Ducange (Hist. de C. P. l. ii. c. 22-28), who feebly strives to excuse the neglect of the emperor by Honorius III.

wisdom to prefer the substance of a marquisate to the shadow of an empire; and on his refusal, Robert, the second of the sons of Peter and Yolande, was called to the throne of Constantinople. Warned by his father's mischance, he pursued his slow and secure journey through Germany and along the Danube; a passage was opened by his sister's marriage with the king of Hungary; and the emperor Robert was crowned by the patriarch in the cathedral of St. Sophia. But his reign was an æra of calamity and disgrace; and the colony, as it was styled, of NEW FRANCE yielded on all sides to the Greeks of Nice and Epirus.

[A.D. 1222] After a victory, which he owed to his perfidy rather than his courage, Theodore Angelus entered the kingdom of Thessalonica, expelled the feeble Demetrius, the son of the marquis Boniface, erected his standard on the walls of Hadrianople, and added, by his vanity, a third or fourth name to the list of rival emperors. The relics of the Asiatic province were swept away by John Vataces, the son-in-law and successor of Theodore Lascaris, and who, in a triumphant reign of thirty-three years, displayed [A.D. 1222-54] the virtues both of peace and war. Under his discipline, the swords of the French mercenaries were the most effectual instrument of his conquests, and their desertion from the service of their country was at once a symptom and a cause of the rising ascendant of the Greeks. By the construction of a fleet he obtained the command of the Hellespont, reduced the islands of Lesbos and Rhodes,[45] attacked the Venetians of Candia, and intercepted the rare and parsimonious succours of the West. Once, and once only, the Latin emperor sent an army against [Battle of Poimanenos. A.D. 1224] Vataces; and, in the defeat of that army, the veteran knights, the last of the original conquerors, were left on the field of battle. But the success of a foreign enemy was less painful to the pusillanimous Robert than the insolence of his Latin subjects, who confounded the weakness of the emperor and of the empire. His personal misfortunes will prove the anarchy of the government and the ferociousness of the times. The amorous youth had neglected his Greek bride, the daughter of Vataces, to introduce into the palace a beautiful maid, of a private, though

[45] [When the empire was overthrown by the crusaders, Leo Gabalas made himself master of Rhodes. In 1233 John Vatatzes compelled him to acknowledge his supremacy, but left him in possession. The island was conquered by the knights of St. John in 1310.]

noble, family of Artois; and her mother had been tempted by
the lustre of the purple to forfeit her engagements with a
gentleman of Burgundy. His love was converted into rage;
he assembled his friends, forced the palace gates, threw the
mother into the sea, and inhumanly cut off the nose and lips
of the wife or concubine of the emperor. Instead of punishing
the offender, the barons avowed and applauded the savage deed,[46]
which, as a prince and as a man, it was impossible that Robert
should forgive. He escaped from the guilty city to implore the
justice or compassion of the pope; the emperor was coolly exhorted to return to his station; before he could obey, he sunk
under the weight of grief, shame, and impotent resentment.[47]

It was only in the age of chivalry that valour could ascend
from a private station to the thrones of Jerusalem and Constantinople. The titular kingdom of Jerusalem had devolved to
Mary, the daughter of Isabella and Conrad of Montferrat, and
the grand-daughter of Almeric or Amaury. She was given to
John of Brienne, of a noble family in Champagne, by the public
voice, and the judgment of Philip Augustus, who named him as
the most worthy champion of the Holy Land.[48] In the fifth
crusade, he led an hundred thousand Latins to the conquest of
Egypt; by him the siege of Damietta was achieved; and the
subsequent failure was justly ascribed to the pride and avarice
of the legate. After the marriage of his daughter with Frederic
the Second,[49] he was provoked by the emperor's ingratitude to
accept the command of the army of the church; and, though
advanced in life, and despoiled of royalty, the sword and spirit
of John of Brienne were still ready for the service of Christendom. In the seven years of his brother's reign Baldwin of
Courtenay had not emerged from a state of childhood, and the

Baldwin II.
and John
of Brienne,
Emperors
of Constan-
tinople.
A.D. 1228-
1237

---

[46] Marinus Sanutus (Secreta Fidelium Crucis, l. ii. p. 4, c. 18, p. 73) is so much
delighted with this bloody deed that he has transcribed it in his margin as a bonum
exemplum. Yet he acknowledges the damsel for the lawful wife of Robert.
[47] See the reign of Robert in Ducange (Hist. de C. P. l. iii. c. 1-12). [Finlay
thinks that Robert should have "seized the culprit immediately, and hung him in
his armour before the palace gates, with his shield round his neck" (iv. p. 114).]
[48] Rex igitur Franciæ, deliberatione habitâ, respondit nuntiis, se daturum homi-
nem Syriæ partibus aptum, in armis probum (preux), in bellis securum, in agendis
providum, Johannem comitem Brennensem. Sanut. Secret. Fidelium, l. iii. p. xi.
c. 4, p. 205. Matthew Paris, p. 159.
[49] Giannone (Istoria Civile, tom. ii. l. xvi. p. 380-385) discusses the marriage of
Frederic II. with the daughter of John of Brienne, and the double union of the
crowns of Naples and Jerusalem.

barons of Romania felt the strong necessity of placing the sceptre in the hands of a man and a hero. The veteran king of Jerusalem might have disdained the name and office of regent; they agreed to invest him for his life with the title and prerogatives of emperor, on the sole condition that Baldwin should marry his second daughter and succeed at a mature age to the throne of Constantinople.[50] The expectation, both of the Greeks and Latins, was kindled by the renown, the choice, and the presence of John of Brienne ; and they admired his martial aspect, his green and vigorous age of more than fourscore years, and his size and stature, which surpassed the common measure of mankind.[51] But avarice and the love of ease appear to have chilled the ardour of enterprise; his troops were disbanded, and two years rolled away without action or honour, till he was awakened [52] by the dangerous alliance of Vataces, emperor of Nice, and of Azan, king of Bulgaria.[53] They besieged Constantinople by sea and land, with an army of one hundred thousand men, and a fleet of three hundred ships of war ; while the entire force of the Latin emperor was reduced to one hundred and sixty knights and a small addition of serjeants and archers. I tremble to relate that, instead of defending the city, the hero made a sally at the head of his cavalry; and that, of forty-eight squadrons of the enemy, no more than three escaped from the edge of his invincible sword. Fired by his example, the infantry

[margin note: [A.D. 1229]]
[margin note: [Mary]]
[margin note: [A.D. 1235]]

[50] [For the act see Buchon, Recherches et Matériaux, p. 21-23.]

[51] Acropolita, c. 27. The historian was at that time a boy, and educated at Constantinople. In 1233, when he was eleven years old, his father broke the Latin chain, left a splendid fortune, and escaped to the Greek court of Nice, where his son was raised to the highest honours.

[52] [He did not arrive at Constantinople till 1231.]

[53] [For this able and humane prince, see Jireček, Geschichte der Bulgaren, chap. xvi. He defeated the forces of Thessalonica and Epirus in the battle of Klokotnitza (near the Strymon), 1230, and extended his power over the greater part of Thrace, Macedonia and Albania. His empire touched three seas and included the cities of Belgrade and Hadrianople. An inscription in the cathedral of Trnovo, which he built, records his deeds as follows : " In the year 6738 [= 1230] Indiction 3, I, Joannes Asēn, the Tsar, faithful servant of God in Christ, sovereign of the Bulgarians, son of the old Asēn, have built this magnificent church and adorned it with paintings, in honour of the Forty Martyrs, with whose help, in the 12th year of my reign, when the church was painted, I made an expedition to Romania and defeated the Greek army and took the Tsar, Kyr Thodor Komnin, prisoner, with all his bolyars. I conquered all the countries from Odrin [Hadrianople] to Dratz [Durazzo],—Greek, Albanian and Servian. The Franks have only retained the towns about Tzarigrad [Constantinople] and that city itself; but even they submitted to my empire when they had no other Emperor but me, and I permitted them to continue, as God so willed. For without him neither work nor word is accomplished. Glory to him for ever, Amen." (Jireček, p. 251-2.)]

and citizens boarded the vessels that anchored close to the walls ; and twenty-five were dragged in triumph into the harbour of Constantinople.   At the summons of the emperor, the vassals [A.D. 1236] and allies armed in her defence ; broke through every obstacle that opposed their passage; and, in the succeeding year, obtained a second victory over the same enemies.   By the rude poets of the age, John of Brienne is compared to Hector, Roland, and Judas Maccabæus;[54] but their credit and his glory receives some abatement from the silence of the Greeks.[55]   The empire was soon deprived of the last of her champions; and the dying [A.D. 1237] monarch was ambitious to enter paradise in the habit of a Franciscan friar.[56]

In the double victory of John of Brienne, I cannot discover Baldwin II. the name or exploits of his pupil Baldwin, who had attained March 23– the age of military service, and who succeeded to the Imperial July 25 dignity on the decease of his adopted father.[57]   The royal youth was employed on a commission more suitable to his temper ; he was sent to visit the Western courts, of the pope more especially, and of the king of France ; to excite their pity by the view of his innocence and distress ; and to obtain some supplies of men or money for the relief of the sinking empire.   He thrice repeated these mendicant visits, in which he seemed to prolong his stay and postpone his return ; of the five-and-twenty years of his reign, a greater number were spent

A.D. 1237,
A.D. 1261,

---

[54] Philip Mouskes, bishop of Tournay (A.D. 1274-1282), has composed a poem, or rather a string of verses, in bad old Flemish French, on the Latin emperors of Constantinople, which Ducange has published at the end of Villehardouin. [What Ducange published was an extract from the Chronique rimée of Mouskès, which began with the Trojan war.   The whole work was first published by De Reiffenberg in 1836.   Gibbon identifies Mouskès with Philip of Ghent, who became bishop of Tournay in 1274.   This is an error.   Mouskès was a native of Tournay and died in 1244.]   See p. 224, for the prowess of John of Brienne.

N'Aie, Ector, Roll' ne Ogiers
Ne Judas Machabeus li fiers
Tant ne fit d'armes en estors
Com fist li Rois Jehans cel jors,
Et il defors et il dedans
La paru sa force et ses sens
Et li hardiment qu'il avoit.

[55] [John Asēn, threatened by the approach of Zenghis Khan (see below, chap. lxiv.), gave up the war and made a separate peace and alliance with the Eastern Emperors.   But the alliance was soon abandoned, and Asēn returned to his friendship with Nicæa.]

[56] See the reign of John de Brienne, in Ducange, Hist. de C. P. l. iii. c. 13-26.

[57] See the reign of Baldwin II. till his expulsion from Constantinople, in Ducange (Hist. de C. P. l. iv. c. 1-34, the end l. v. c. 1-33).

abroad than at home ; and in no place did the emperor deem himself less free and secure than in his native country and his capital. On some public occasions, his vanity might be soothed by the title of Augustus and by the honours of the purple ; and at the general council of Lyons, when Frederic the Second was excommunicated and deposed, his Oriental colleague was enthroned on the right hand of the pope. But how often was the exile, the vagrant, the Imperial beggar humbled with scorn, insulted with pity, and degraded in his own eyes and those of the nations ! In his first visit to England he was stopt at Dover by a severe reprimand that he should presume, without leave, to enter an independent kingdom. After some delay, Baldwin, however, was permitted to pursue his journey, was entertained with cold civility, and thankfully departed with a present of seven hundred marks.[58] From the avarice of Rome he could only obtain the proclamation of a crusade, and a treasure of indulgences : a coin whose currency was depreciated by too frequent and indiscriminate abuse. His birth and misfortunes recommended him to the generosity of his cousin, Lewis the Ninth ; but the martial zeal of the saint was diverted from Constantinople to Egypt and Palestine ; and the public and private poverty of Baldwin was alleviated, for a moment, by the alienation of the marquisate of Namur and the lordship of Courtenay, the last remains of his inheritance.[59] By such shameful or ruinous expedients he once more returned to Romania, with an army of thirty thousand soldiers, whose numbers were doubled in the apprehension of the Greeks. His first dispatches to France and England announced his victories and his hopes ; he had reduced the country round the capital to the distance of three days' journey ; and, if he succeeded against an important though nameless city (most probably Chiorli),[60] the frontier would be safe and the passage accessible. But

[A.D. 1239]

[A.D. 1240]

---

[58] Matthew Paris relates the two visits of Baldwin II. to the English court, p. 396, 637 ; his return to Greece armatâ manu, p. 407, his letters of his nomen formidabile, &c., p. 481 (a passage which had escaped Ducange), his expulsion, p. 850.

[59] Louis IX. disapproved and stopped the alienation of Courtenay (Ducange, l. iv. c. 23). It is now annexed to the royal demesne, but granted for a term (*engage*) to the family of Boulanvilliers. Courtenay, in the election of Nemours in the Isle de France, is a town of 900 inhabitants, with the remains of a castle (Mélanges tirés d'une grande Bibliothèque, tom. xiv. p. 74-77).

[60] [Tzurulon, Chorlu, on the Chorlu-Su, a tributary of the Erginus, to the northwest of Heraclea (Erekli).]

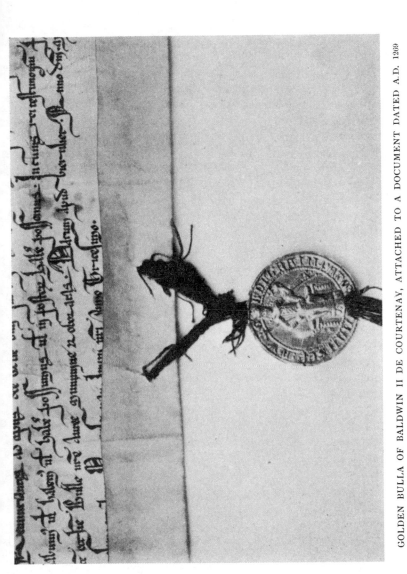

GOLDEN BULLA OF BALDWIN II DE COURTENAY, ATTACHED TO A DOCUMENT DATED A.D. 1269

BRITISH MUSEUM

these expectations (if Baldwin was sincere) quickly vanished like a dream ; the troops and treasures of France melted away in his unskilful hands ; and the throne of the Latin emperor was protected by a dishonourable alliance with the Turks and Comans. To secure the former, he consented to bestow his niece on the unbelieving sultan of Cogni ; to please the latter, he complied with their Pagan rites : a dog was sacrificed between the two armies ; and the contracting parties tasted each other's blood, as a pledge of their fidelity.[61] In the palace or prison of Constantinople, the successor of Augustus demolished the vacant houses for winter-fuel, and stripped the lead from the churches for the daily expenses of his family. Some usurious loans were dealt with a scanty hand by the merchants of Italy ; and Philip, his son and heir, was pawned at Venice as the security for a debt.[62] Thirst, hunger, and nakedness are positive evils ; but wealth is relative ; and a prince, who would be rich in a private station, may be exposed by the increase of his wants to all the anxiety and bitterness of poverty.

But in this abject distress the emperor and empire were still possessed of an ideal treasure, which drew its fantastic value from the superstition of the Christian world. The merit of the true cross was somewhat impaired by its frequent division ; and a long captivity among the infidels might shed some suspicion on the fragments that were produced in the East and West. But another relic of the Passion was preserved in the Imperial chapel of Constantinople ; and the crown of thorns, which had been placed on the head of Christ, was equally precious and authentic. It had formerly been the practice of the Egyptian debtors to deposit, as a security, the mummies of their parents ; and both their honour and religion were bound for the redemption of the pledge. In the same manner, and in the absence of the emperor, the barons of Romania borrowed the sum of thirteen thousand one hundred and thirty-four pieces of gold,[63] on the credit of the holy crown ; they failed

The holy crown of thorns

---

[61] Joinville, p. 104, édit. du Louvre. A Coman prince, who died without baptism, was buried at the gates of Constantinople with a live retinue of slaves and horses.

[62] Sanut. Secret. Fidel. Crucis, l. ii. p. iv. c. 18, p. 73.

[63] Under the words *Perparus, Perpera, Hyperperum*, Ducange is short and vague : Monetæ genus. From a corrupt passage of Guntherus (Hist. C. P. c. 8, p.

in the performance of their contract; and a rich Venetian, Nicholas Querini, undertook to satisfy their impatient creditors, on condition that the relic should be lodged at Venice, to become his absolute property if it were not redeemed within a short and definite term. The barons apprised their sovereign of the hard treaty and impending loss; and, as the empire could not afford a ransom of seven thousand pounds sterling, Baldwin was anxious to snatch the prize from the Venetians, and to vest it with more honour and emolument in the hands of the most Christian king.[64] Yet the negotiation was attended with some delicacy. In the purchase of relics, the saint would have started at the guilt of simony; but, if the mode of expression were changed, he might lawfully repay the debt, accept the gift, and acknowledge the obligation. His ambassadors, two Dominicans, were dispatched to Venice, to redeem and receive the holy crown, which had escaped the dangers of the sea and the galleys of Vataces. On opening a wooden box, they recognised the seals of the doge and barons, which were applied on a shrine of silver; and within this shrine the monument of the Passion was enclosed in a golden vase. The reluctant Venetians yielded to justice and power; the emperor Frederic granted a free and honourable passage; the court of France advanced as far as Troyes in Champagne, to meet with devotion this inestimable relic; it was borne in triumph through Paris by the king himself, barefoot, and in his shirt; and a free gift of ten thousand marks of silver reconciled Baldwin to his loss. The success of this transaction tempted the Latin emperor to offer with the same generosity the remaining furniture of his chapel:[65] a large and authentic portion of the true cross; the baby-linen of the Son of God; the lance, the spunge, and the chain, of his Passion; the rod of Moses; and part of the scull of St. John the Baptist. For the reception of these

---

10), I guess that the Perpera was the nummus aureus, the fourth part of a mark of silver, or about ten shillings sterling in value. In lead it would be too contemptible.

[64] For the translation of the holy crown, &c. from Constantinople to Paris, see Ducange (Hist. de C. P. l. iv. c. 11-14, 24, 35), and Fleury (Hist. Ecclés. tom. xvii. p. 201-204).

[65] Mélanges tirés d'une grande Bibliothèque, tom. xliii. p. 201-205. The Lutrin of Boileau exhibits the inside, the soul and manners of the *Sainte Chapelle;* and many facts relative to the institution are collected and explained by the commentators, Brossette and de St. Marc.

spiritual treasures, twenty thousand marks were expended by St. Louis on a stately foundation, the holy chapel of Paris, on which the muse of Boileau has bestowed a comic immortality. The truth of such remote and ancient relics, which cannot be proved by any human testimony, must be admitted by those who believe in the miracles which they have performed. About the middle of the last age, an inveterate ulcer was touched and cured by an holy prickle of the holy crown: [66] the prodigy is attested by the most pious and enlightened Christians of France; nor will the fact be easily disproved, except by those who are armed with a general antidote against religious credulity.[67]

The Latins of Constantinople [68] were on all sides encompassed and pressed: their sole hope, the last delay of their ruin, was in the division of their Greek and Bulgarian enemies; and of this hope they were deprived by the superior arms and policy of Vataces, emperor of Nice. From the Propontis to the rocky coast of Pamphylia, Asia was peaceful and prosperous under his reign; and the events of every campaign extended his influence in Europe. The strong cities of the hills of Macedonia and Thrace were rescued from the Bulgarians; and their kingdom was circumscribed by its present and proper limits, along the southern banks of the Danube. The sole emperor of the Romans could no longer brook that a lord of Epirus, a Comnenian prince of the West, should presume to dispute or share the honours of the purple; and the humble Demetrius changed [A.D. 1243] the colour of his buskins, and accepted with gratitude the appellation of despot. His own subjects were exasperated by his baseness and incapacity: they implored the protection of their supreme lord. After some resistance, the kingdom of Thessa-

Progress of the Greeks. A.D. 1237-1261

---

[66] It was performed A.D. 1656, March 24, on the niece of Pascal'; and that superior genius, with Arnauld, Nicole, &c. were on the spot to believe and attest a miracle which confounded the Jesuits, and saved Port Royal (Oeuvres de Racine, tom. vi. p. 176-187, in his eloquent History of Port Royal).

[67] Voltaire (Siècle de Louis XIV. c. 37; Oeuvres, tom. ix. p. 178, 179) strives to invalidate the fact; but Hume (Essays, vol. ii. p. 483, 484), with more skill and success, seizes the battery, and turns the cannon against his enemies.

[68] The gradual losses of the Latins may be traced in the third, fourth, and fifth books of the compilation of Ducange; but of the Greek conquests he has dropped many circumstances, which may be recovered from the large History of George Acropolita, and the three first books of Nicephorus Gregoras, two writers of the Byzantine series, who have had the good fortune to meet with learned editors, Leo Allatius at Rome, and John Boivin in the Academy of Inscriptions of Paris.

lonica was united to the empire of Nice ;[69] and Vataces reigned without a competitor from the Turkish borders to the Adriatic gulf. The princes of Europe revered his merit and power; and, had he subscribed an orthodox creed, it should seem that the pope would have abandoned without reluctance the Latin throne of Constantinople. But the death of Vataces, the short

[Theodore II. A.D. 1254-8] and busy reign of Theodore his son, and the helpless infancy of his grandson John, suspended the restoration of the Greeks. In the next, chapter I shall explain their domestic revolutions ; in this place it will be sufficient to observe that the young prince was oppressed by the ambition of his guardian and colleague,

[Michael Palæologus, the Greek Emperor. A.D. 1259, Dec. 1 [Jan. 1260]] Michael Palæologus, who displayed the virtues and vices that belong to the founder of a new dynasty. The emperor Baldwin had flattered himself that he might recover some provinces or cities by an impotent negotiation. His ambassadors were dismissed from Nice with mockery and contempt. At every place which they named, Palæologus alleged some special reason which rendered it dear and valuable in his eyes: in the one he was born ; in another he had been first promoted to military command ; and in a third he had enjoyed, and hoped long to enjoy, the pleasures of the chase. " And what, then, do you propose to give us ? " said the astonished deputies. " Nothing," replied the Greek, " not a foot of land. If your master be desirous of peace, let him pay me, as an annual tribute, the sum which he receives from the trade and customs of Constantinople. On these terms I may allow him to reign. If he refuses, it is war. I am not ignorant of the art of war, and I trust the event to God and my sword." [70] An expedition

[Michael II.] against the despot of Epirus was the first prelude of his arms. If a victory was followed by a defeat; if the race of the Com-

[69] [The conquest of Thessalonica, from the young Demetrius, son of Boniface, by Theodore Angelus, despot of Epirus, and Theodore's assumption of the Imperial title A.D. 1222, have been briefly mentioned above, p. 450. His brother Manuel, and then his son John, succeeded to the Empire of Salonica. It was a matter of political importance for Vatatzes to bring this rival Empire into subjection; he marched against Thessalonica, but raised the siege (A.D. 1243) on condition that John should lay down the title of Emperor and assume that of despot. John died in the following year and was succeeded by his brother Demetrius ; but in 1246 Demetrius was removed by Vatatzes, and Thessalonica became definitely part of the empire of Nicæa. Thus the Thessalonian empire lasted 1222-1243. Meanwhile Epirus had split off from the empire of Salonica, in 1236-7, under Michael II. (a bastard son of Michael I.), whose Despotate survived that Empire. See below, note 71.]

[70] George Acropolita, c. lxxviii. p. 89, 90, edit. Paris.

neni or Angeli survived in those mountains his efforts and his reign; the captivity of Villehardouin, prince of Achaia, deprived the Latins of the most active and powerful vassal of their expiring monarchy.[71]   The republics of Venice and Genoa disputed, in the first of their naval wars, the command of the sea and the commerce of the East.   Pride and interest attached the Venetians to the defence of Constantinople : their rivals were tempted to promote the designs of her enemies, and the alliance of the Genoese with the schismatic conqueror provoked the indignation of the Latin church.[72]   [Battle of Pelagonia. Autumn, A.D. 1259]

Intent on his great object, the emperor Michael visited in person and strengthened the troops and fortifications of Thrace.   The remains of the Latins were driven from their last possessions; he assaulted without success the suburbs of Galata ;[73] and corresponded with a perfidious baron,[74] who proved unwilling, or unable, to open the gates of the metropolis.   The next spring,[75] his favourite general, Alexius Strategopulus, whom he had decorated with the title of Cæsar, passed the Hellespont with eight hundred horse and some infantry,[76] on   [Constantinople recovered by the Greeks, A.D. 1261, June [July] 25]

[71] [This victory was won by John Palæologus, brother of Michael, in the plain of Pelagonia near Kastoria, in Macedonia.   The despot of Epirus, Michael II. (bastard of Michael I.), had extended his sway to the Vardar, and threatened Salonica. He was supported by Manfred, king of Sicily, who sent four hundred knights to his aid, as well as William Villehardouin, prince of Achaia.   Finlay places the coronation of Michael Palæologus in Jan. 1259—*before* the battle of Pelagonia (iii. 339) ; but it seems to have been subsequent, in Jan. 1260 ; see Mêliarakês, Ἱστορία τοῦ βασιλείου τῆς Νικαίας κ.τ.λ. (1898), p. 536-543.]

[72] The Greeks, ashamed of any foreign aid, disguise the alliance and succour of the Genoese ; but the fact is proved by the testimony of J. Villani (Chron. l. vi. c. 71, in Muratori, Script. Rerum Italicarum, tom. xiii. p. 202, 203) and William de Nangis (Annales de St. Louis, p. 248, in the Louvre Joinville), two impartial foreigners ; and Urban IV. threatened to deprive Genoa of her archbishop.   [For the treaty of Michael with Genoa in March, 1261, see Buchon, Recherches et matériaux, p. 462 *sqq.* (in French), or Zachariä v. Lingenthal, Jus. Græco-Rom., iii. p. 574 *sqq.* (in Latin).   The Genoese undertook to furnish a fleet ; but when these ships arrived Michael was already in possession of the city.]

[73] [Spring, 1260.]

[74] [Anseau de Cayeux (if that is the name), who was married to a sister-in-law of John Vatatzes.   Cp. Mêliarakês, *op. cit.*, p. 551-2.]

[75] [Michael himself in this spring passed and repassed repeatedly from Asia to Europe.   He first took Selymbria, which was a valuable basis for further operations (Pachymeres, p. 110).   Ecclesiastical business then recalled him to Asia ; and having settled this he recrossed the Hellespont and for the second time besieged Galata (Pachymeres, p. 118 *sqq.*).   He raised the siege and returned to Nymphæum, where he concluded the treaty with the Genoese.]

[76] Some precautions must be used in reconciling the discordant numbers : the 800 soldiers of Nicetas ; the 25,000 of Spandugino (apud Ducange, l. v. c. 24) ; the Greeks and Scythians of Acropolita ; and the numerous army of Michael, in the Epistles of pope Urban IV. (i. 129).

a secret expedition. His instructions enjoined him to approach, to listen, to watch, but not to risk any doubtful or dangerous enterprise against the city. The adjacent territory between the Propontis and the Black Sea was cultivated by an hardy race of peasants and outlaws, exercised in arms, uncertain in their allegiance, but inclined by language, religion, and present advantage, to the party of the Greeks. They were styled the *volunteers*,[77] and by their free service the army of `Alexius, with the regulars of Thrace and the Coman auxiliaries,[78] was augmented to the number of five and twenty thousand men. By the ardour of the volunteers, and by his own ambition, the Cæsar was stimulated to disobey the precise orders of his master, in the just confidence that success would plead his pardon and reward. The weakness of Constantinople, and the distress and terror of the Latins, were familiar to the observation of the volunteers; and they represented the present moment as the most propitious to surprise and conquest. A [Marco Gradenigo] rash youth, the new governor of the Venetian colony, had sailed away with thirty galleys and the best of the French knights, on a wild expedition to Daphnusia, a town on the Black Sea, at a distance of forty leagues;[79] and the remaining Latins were without strength or suspicion. They were informed that Alexius had passed the Hellespont; but their apprehensions were lulled by the smallness of his original numbers, and their imprudence had not watched the subsequent increase of his army. If he left his main body to second and support his operations, he might advance unperceived in the night with a chosen detachment. While some applied scaling ladders to the lowest part of the walls, they were secure of an old Greek, who would introduce their companions through a subterranean passage into his house;[80] they could soon on

---

[77] Θελημάταριοι. They are described and named by Pachymer (l. ii. c. 14). [The chief of these, who was very active in the capture of the city, was named Kutritzakês.]

[78] It is needless to seek these Comans in the deserts of Tartary, or even of Moldavia. A part of the horde had submitted to John Vataces and was probably settled as a nursery of soldiers on some waste lands of Thrace (Cantacuzen. l. i. c. 2).

[79] [Daphnusia, a town on a little island (now desert and named Kefken Adassi) off the coast of Bithynia, about 70 miles east of the mouth of the Bosphorus. *Thynias* was another name. Cp. Ramsay, Hist. Geography of Asia Minor, p. 182.]

[80] [Near the Gate of Selymbria or Pegæ (see above, vol. ii., plan opp. p. 159); and it was through this gate that the entrance was to be broken.]

the inside break an entrance through the golden gate, which had been long obstructed; and the conqueror would be in the heart of the city, before the Latins were conscious of their danger. After some debate, the Cæsar resigned himself to the faith of the volunteers; they were trusty, bold, and successful; and in describing the plan I have already related the execution and success.[81] But no sooner had Alexius passed the threshold of the golden gate than he trembled at his own rashness; he paused, he deliberated, till the desperate volunteers urged him forwards by the assurance that in retreat lay the greatest and most inevitable danger. Whilst the Cæsar kept his regulars in firm array, the Comans dispersed themselves on all sides; an alarm was sounded, and the threats of fire and pillage compelled the citizens to a decisive resolution. The Greeks of Constantinople remembered their native sovereigns; the Genoese merchants, their recent alliance and Venetian foes; every quarter was in arms; and the air resounded with a general acclamation of " Long life and victory to Michael and John, the august emperors of the Romans!" Their rival Baldwin was awakened by the sound; but the most pressing danger could not prompt him to draw his sword in the defence of a city which he deserted, perhaps, with more pleasure than regret: he fled from the palace to the sea-shore, where he descried the welcome sails of the fleet returning from the vain and fruitless attempt on Daphnusia. Constantinople was irrecoverably lost; but the Latin emperor and the principal families embarked on board the Venetian galleys, and steered for the isle of Eubœa, and afterwards for Italy, where the royal fugitive was entertained by the pope and Sicilian king with a mixture of contempt and pity. From the loss of Constantinople to his death, he consumed [A.D. 1272] thirteen years, soliciting the Catholic powers to join in his restoration: the lesson had been familiar to his youth; nor was his last exile more indigent or shameful than his three former pilgrimages to the courts of Europe. His son Philip was the heir of an ideal empire; and the pretensions of *his* daughter

---

[81] The loss of Constantinople is briefly told by the Latins; the conquest is described with more satisfaction by the Greeks: by Acropolita (c. 85), Pachymer (l. ii. c. 26, 27), Nicephorus Gregoras (l. iv. c. 1, 2). See Ducange, Hist. de C. P. l. v. c. 19-27. [It is also described by Phrantzes, p. 17-20, ed. Bonn; and in an anonymous poem on the Loss (1204) and Recovery (1261) of Constantinople, composed in A.D. 1392 (published by Buchon, Recherches historiques, 2, p. 335 *sqq.*, 1845).]

Catherine were transported by her marriage to Charles of Valois, the brother of Philip the Fair, king of France. The house of Courtenay was represented in the female line by successive alliances, till the title of emperor of Constantinople, too bulky and sonorous for a private name, modestly expired in silence and oblivion.[82]

General consequences of the crusades   After this narrative of the expeditions of the Latins to Palestine and Constantinople, I cannot dismiss the subject without revolving the general consequences on the countries that were the scene, and on the nations that were the actors, of these memorable crusades.[83]   As soon as the arms of the Franks were withdrawn, the impression, though not the memory, was erased in the Mahometan realms of Egypt and Syria.   The faithful disciples of the prophet were never tempted by a profane desire to study the laws or language of the idolaters; nor did the simplicity of their primitive manners receive the slightest alteration from their intercourse in peace and war with the unknown strangers of the West.   The Greeks, who thought themselves proud, but who were only vain, shewed a disposition somewhat less inflexible.   In the efforts for the recovery of their empire they emulated the valour, discipline, and tactics of their antagonists.   The modern literature of the West they might justly despise ; but its free spirit would instruct them in the rights of man; and some institutions of public and private life were adopted from the French.   The correspondence of Constantinople and Italy diffused the knowledge of the Latin tongue ; and several of the fathers and classics were at length honoured with a Greek version.[84]   But the national and re-

---

[82] See the three last books (l. v. viii.), and the genealogical tables of Ducange. In the year 1382, the titular emperor of Constantinople was James de Baux [titular Emperor, 1373-1383], duke of Andria in the kingdom of Naples, the son of Margaret, daughter of Catherine de Valois [married to Philip of Tarentum], daughter of Catherine [married to Charles of Valois], daughter of Philip, son of Baldwin II. (Ducange, l. viii. c. 37, 38).   It is uncertain whether he left any posterity.

[83] Abulfeda, who saw the conclusion of the crusades, speaks of the kingdom of the Franks, and those of the negroes, as equally unknown (Prolegom. ad Geograph.). Had he not disdained the Latin language, how easily might the Syrian prince have found books and interpreters !

[84] A short and superficial account of these versions from Latin into Greek is given by Huet (de Interpretatione et de claris Interpretibus, p. 131-135).   Maximus Planudes, a monk of Constantinople (A.D. 1327-1353 [born c. 1260, died 1310]) has translated Cæsar's Commentaries, the Somnium Scipionis, the Metamorphoses and Heroides of Ovid [the proverbial philosophy of the elder Cato, Boethius' De Consolatione], &c.   (Fabric. Bib. Græc. tom. x. p. 533 [ed. Harl. xi. 682 *sqq.* ; Krumbacher, Gesch. der byz. Litt., 543 *sqq.* The Letters of Planudes have been

ligious prejudices of the Orientals were inflamed by persecution; and the reign of the Latins confirmed the separation of the two churches.

If we compare, at the æra of the crusades, the Latins of Europe with the Greeks and Arabians, their respective degrees of knowledge, industry and art, our rude ancestors must be content with the third rank in the scale of nations. Their successive improvement and present superiority may be ascribed to a peculiar energy of character, to an active and imitative spirit, unknown to their more polished rivals, who at that time were in a stationary or retrograde state. With such a disposition, the Latins should have derived the most early and essential benefits from a series of events which opened to their eyes the prospect of the world, and introduced them to a long and frequent intercourse with the more cultivated regions of the East. The first and most obvious progress was in trade and manufactures, in the arts which are strongly prompted by the thirst of wealth, the calls of necessity, and the gratification of the sense or vanity. Among the crowd of unthinking fanatics, a captive or a pilgrim might sometimes observe the superior refinements of Cairo and Constantinople: the first importer of windmills [85] was the benefactor of nations; and, if such blessings are enjoyed without any grateful remembrance, history has condescended to notice the more apparent luxuries of silk and sugar, which were transported into Italy from Greece and Egypt. But the intellectual wants of the Latins were more slowly felt and supplied; the ardour of studious curiosity was awakened in Europe by different causes and more recent events; and, in the age of the crusades, they viewed with careless indifference the literature of the Greeks and Arabians. Some rudiments of mathematical and medicinal knowledge might be imparted in practice and in figures; necessity might produce some interpreters for the grosser business of merchants and soldiers; but the commerce of the Orientals had not diffused the study and knowledge of their languages in the schools of Europe.[86]

edited by M. Treu (1890), who has established the chronology of his life (Zur Gesch. der Ueberlieferung von Plutarchs Moralia, 1877)].)

[85] Windmills, first invented in the dry country of Asia Minor, were used in Normandy as early as the year 1105 (Vie privée des François, tom. i. p. 42, 43; Ducange, Gloss. Latin. tom. iv. p. 474).

[86] See the complaints of Roger Bacon (Biographia Britannica, vol. i. p. 418, Kippis's edition). If Bacon himself, or Gerbert, understood *some* Greek they were prodigies, and owed nothing to the commerce of the East.

If a similar principle of religion repulsed the idiom of the
Koran, it should have excited their patience and curiosity to
understand the original text of the gospel; and the same
grammar would have unfolded the sense of Plato and the
beauties of Homer. Yet in a reign of sixty years, the Latins
of Constantinople disdained the speech and learning of
their subjects; and the manuscripts were the only treasures
which the natives might enjoy without rapine or envy. Aristotle was indeed the oracle of the Western universities; but it
was a barbarous Aristotle; and, instead of ascending to the
fountain-head, his Latin votaries humbly accepted a corrupt
and remote version from the Jews and Moors of Andalusia.
The principle of the crusades was a savage fanaticism; and the
most important effects were analogous to the cause. Each
pilgrim was ambitious to return with his sacred spoils, the
relics of Greece and Palestine;[87] and each relic was preceded
and followed by a train of miracles and visions. The belief
of the Catholics was corrupted by new legends, their practice
by new superstitions; and the establishment of the inquisition,
the mendicant orders of monks and friars, the last abuse of indulgences, and the final progress of idolatry, flowed from the
baleful fountain of the holy war. The active spirit of the
Latins preyed on the vitals of their reason and religion; and,
if the ninth and tenth centuries were the times of darkness,
the thirteenth and fourteenth were the age of absurdity and
fable.

In the profession of Christianity, in the cultivation of a
fertile land, the northern conquerors of the Roman empire insensibly mingled with the provincials and rekindled the embers
of the arts of antiquity. Their settlements about the age of
Charlemagne had acquired some degree of order and stability,
when they were overwhelmed by new swarms of invaders, the
Normans, Saracens,[88] and Hungarians, who replunged the
western countries of Europe into their former state of anarchy
and barbarism. About the eleventh century, the second tempest

[87] Such was the opinion of the great Leibnitz (Oeuvres de Fontenelle, tom. v.
p. 458), a master of the history of the middle ages. I shall only instance the pedigree of the Carmelites, and the flight of the house of Loretto, which were both derived from Palestine.
[88] If I rank the Saracens with the barbarians, it is only relative to their wars,
or rather inroads, in Italy and France, where their sole purpose was to plunder and
destroy.

had subsided by the expulsion or conversion of the enemies of
Christendom : the tide of civilisation, which had so long ebbed,
began to flow with a steady and accelerated course ; and a
fairer prospect was opened to the hopes and efforts of the rising
generations. Great was the success, and rapid the progress,
during the two hundred years of the crusades ; and some philosophers have applauded the propitious influence of these holy
wars, which appear to me to have checked, rather than for-
warded, the maturity of Europe.[89] The lives and labours of
millions, which were buried in the East, would have been more
profitably employed in the improvement of their native country :
the accumulated stock of industry and wealth would have overflowed in navigation and trade ; and the Latins would have
been enriched and enlightened by a pure and friendly correspondence with the climates of the East. In one respect I can
indeed perceive the accidental operation of the crusades, not so
much in producing a benefit, as in removing an evil. The larger
portion of the inhabitants of Europe was chained to the soil,
without freedom, or property, or knowledge ; and the two orders
of ecclesiastics and nobles, whose numbers were comparatively
small, alone deserved the name of citizens and men. This
oppressive system was supported by the arts of the clergy and
the swords of the barons. The authority of the priests operated
in the darker ages as a salutary antidote : they prevented the
total extinction of letters, mitigated the fierceness of the times,
sheltered the poor and defenceless, and preserved or revived
the peace and order of civil society. But the independence,
rapine, and discord of the feudal lords were unmixed with any
semblance of good ; and every hope of industry and improvement was crushed by the iron weight of the martial aristocracy.
Among the causes that undermined the Gothic edifice, a conspicuous place must be allowed to the crusades. The estates
of the barons were dissipated, and their race was often extinguished, in these costly and perilous expeditions. Their poverty
extorted from their pride those charters of freedom which unlocked the fetters of the slave, secured the farm of the peasant
and the shop of the artificer, and gradually restored a substance

[89] On this interesting subject, the progress of society in Europe, a strong ray of
philosophic light has broke from Scotland in our own times ; and it is with private
as well as public regard that I repeat the names of Hume, Robertson, and Adam
Smith.

and a soul to the most numerous and useful part of the community.   The conflagration which destroyed the tall and barren trees of the forest gave air and scope to the vegetation of the smaller and nutritive plants of the soil.

DIGRESSION ON THE FAMILY OF COURTENAY.

The purple of three emperors who have reigned at Constantinople will authorise or excuse a digression on the origin and singular fortunes of the house of COURTENAY,[90] in the three principal branches: I. Of Edessa; II. Of France; and III. Of England; of which the last only has survived the revolutions of eight hundred years.

Origin of the family of Courtenay. A.D. 1020

I. Before the introduction of trade, which scatters riches, and of knowledge, which dispels prejudice, the prerogative of birth is most strongly felt and most humbly acknowledged.   In every age the laws and manners of the Germans have discriminated the ranks of society: the dukes and counts, who shared the empire of Charlemagne, converted their office to an inheritance; and to his children each feudal lord bequeathed his honour and his sword.   The proudest families are content to lose, in the darkness of the middle ages, the tree of their pedigree, which, however deep and lofty, must ultimately rise from a plebeian root; and their historians must descend ten centuries below the Christian æra, before they can ascertain any lineal succession by the evidence of surnames, of arms, and of authentic records. With the first rays of light[91] we discern the nobility and opulence of Atho, a French knight: his nobility, in the rank and title of a nameless father; his opulence, in the foundation of the castle of Courtenay, in the district of Gatinois, about fifty-six miles to the south of Paris.   From the reign of Robert, the son of Hugh Capet, the barons of Courtenay are conspicuous among

----

[90] I have applied, but not confined, myself to *A Genealogical History of the Noble and Illustrious Family of Courtenay, by Ezra Cleaveland, Tutor to Sir William Courtenay, and Rector of Honiton; Exon.* 1735, *in folio.*   The first part is extracted from William of Tyre; the second from Bouchet's French history; and the third from various memorials, public, provincial, and private, of the Courtenays of Devonshire.   The rector of Honiton has more gratitude than industry, and more industry than criticism.

[91] The primitive record of the family is a passage of the Continuator of Aimoin, a monk of Fleury, who wrote in the xiith century.   See his Chronicle, in the Historians of France (tom. xi. p. 176).

the immediate vassals of the crown ; and Joscelin, the grandson
of Atho and a noble dame, is enrolled among the heroes of the
first crusade.   A domestic alliance (their mothers were sisters)
attached him to the standard of Baldwin of Bruges, the second I. The
count of Edessa : a princely fief, which he was worthy to receive, Edessa.
and able to maintain, announces the number of his martial fol- 1152
lowers; and, after the departure of his cousin, Joscelin himself
was invested with the county of Edessa on both sides of the
Euphrates.   By economy in peace his territories were replenished with Latin and Syrian subjects; his magazines with
corn, wine, and oil; his castles with gold and silver, with arms
and horses.   In a holy warfare of thirty years he was alternately
a conqueror and a captive; but he died like a soldier, in an
horse-litter at the head of his troops; and his last glance beheld
the flight of the Turkish invaders who had presumed on his age
and infirmities.   His son and successor, of the same name, was
less deficient in valour than in vigilance; but he sometimes
forgot that dominion is acquired and maintained by the same
arts.   He challenged the hostility of the Turks, without securing
the friendship of the prince of Antioch ; and, amidst the peaceful luxury of Turbessel, in Syria,[92] Joscelin neglected the defence
of the Christian frontier beyond the Euphrates.   In his absence,
Zenghi, the first of the Atabeks, besieged and stormed his capital,
Edessa, which was feebly defended by a timorous and disloyal
crowd of Orientals ; the Franks were oppressed in a bold attempt
for its recovery, and Courtenay ended his days in the prison of
Aleppo.   He still left a fair and ample patrimony.   But the
victorious Turks oppressed on all sides the weakness of a widow
and orphan; and, for the equivalent of an annual pension, they
resigned to the Greek emperor the charge of defending, and the
shame of losing, the last relics of the Latin conquest.   The
countess-dowager of Edessa retired to Jerusalem with her two
children : the daughter, Agnes, became the wife and mother of
a king; the son, Joscelin the Third, accepted the office of seneschal, the first of the kingdom, and held his new estates in Palestine by the service of fifty knights.   His name appears with
honour in all the transactions of peace and war; but he finally

---

[92] Turbessel, or as it is now styled Telbesher, is fixed by d'Anville four and
twenty miles from the great passage over the Euphrates at Zeugma. [Tell Bāsher,
now Sāleri Kaleh, "a large mound with ruins near the village of Tulbashar," two
days' journey north of Aleppo (Sir C. Wilson, note to Bahā ad-Din, p. 58).]

vanishes in the fall of Jerusalem; and the name of Courtenay, in this branch of Edessa, was lost by the marriage of his two daughters with a French and a German baron.[93]

II. The Courtenays of France

II. While Joscelin reigned beyond the Euphrates, his elder brother, Milo, the son of Joscelin, the son of Atho, continued, near the Seine, to possess the castle of their fathers, which was at length inherited by Rainaud, or Reginald, the youngest of his three sons. Examples of genius or virtue must be rare in the annals of the oldest families; and, in a remote age, their pride will embrace a deed of rapine and violence; such, however, as could not be perpetrated without some superiority of courage, or at least of power. A descendant of Reginald of Courtenay may blush for the public robber who stripped and imprisoned several merchants, after they had satisfied the king's duties at Sens and Orleans. He will glory in the offence, since the bold offender could not be compelled to obedience and restitution, till the regent and the count of Champagne prepared to march against him at the head of an army.[94] Reginald bestowed his estates

Their alliance with the royal family. A.D. 1150

on his eldest daughter, and his daughter on the seventh son of king Louis the Fat; and their marriage was crowned with a numerous offspring. We might expect that a private should have merged in a royal name; and that the descendants of Peter of France and Elizabeth of Courtenay would have enjoyed the title and honours of princes of the blood. But this legitimate claim was long neglected and finally denied; and the causes of their disgrace will represent the story of this second branch. 1. Of all the families now extant, the most ancient, doubtless, and the most illustrious is the house of France, which has occupied the same throne above eight hundred years, and descends, in a clear and lineal series of males, from the middle of the ninth century.[95] In the age of the crusades it was already revered

---

[93] His possessions are distinguished in the Assises of Jerusalem (c. 326) among the feudal tenures of the kingdom, which must therefore have been collected between the years 1153 and 1187. His pedigree may be found in the Lignages d'Outremer, c. 16.

[94] The rapine and satisfaction of Reginald de Courtenay are preposterously arranged in the epistles of the abbot and regent Suger (cxiv. cxvi.), the best memorials of the age (Duchesne, Scriptores Hist. Franc. tom. iv. p. 530).

[95] In the beginning of the xith century, after naming the father and grandfather of Hugh Capet, the monk Glaber is obliged to add, cujus genus valde in-ante reperitur obscurum. Yet we are assured that the great-grandfather of Hugh Capet was Robert the Strong, count of Anjou (A.D. 863-873), a noble Frank of Neustria, Neustricus . . . generosæ stirpis, who was slain in the defence of his country

both in the East and West. But from Hugh Capet to the marriage of Peter no more than five reigns or generations had elapsed ; and so precarious was their title that the eldest sons, as a necessary precaution, were previously crowned during the lifetime of their fathers. The peers of France have long maintained their precedency before the younger branches of the royal line ; nor had the princes of the blood, in the twelfth century, acquired that hereditary lustre which is now diffused over the most remote candidates for the succession. 2. The barons of Courtenay must have stood high in their own estimation, and in that of the world, since they could impose on the son of a king the obligation of adopting for himself and all his descendants the name and arms of their daughter and his wife. In the marriage of an heiress with her inferior or her equal, such exchange was often required and allowed ; but, as they continued to diverge from the regal stem, the sons of Louis the Fat were insensibly confounded with their maternal ancestors ; and the new Courtenays might deserve to forfeit the honours of their birth, which a motive of interest had tempted them to renounce. 3. The shame was far more permanent than the reward, and a momentary blaze was followed by a long darkness. The eldest son of these nuptials, Peter of Courtenay, had married, as I have already mentioned, the sister of the counts of Flanders, the two first emperors of Constantinople ; he rashly accepted the invitation of the barons of Romania ; his two sons, Robert and Baldwin, successively held and lost the remains of the Latin empire in the East, and the grand-daughter of Baldwin the Second again mingled her blood with the blood of France and of Valois. To support the expenses of a troubled and transitory reign, their patrimonial estates were mortgaged or sold ; and the last emperors of Constantinople depended on the annual charity of Rome and Naples.

While the elder brothers dissipated their wealth in romantic

against the Normans, dum patriæ fines tuebatur. Beyond Robert, all is conjecture or fable. It is a probable conjecture that the third race descended from the second by Childebrand, the brother of Charles Martel. It is an absurd fable that the second was allied to the first by the marriage of Ansbert, a Roman senator and the ancestor of St. Arnoul, with Blitilde, a daughter of Clotaire I. The Saxon origin of the house of France is an ancient but incredible opinion. See a judicious memoir of M. de Foncemagne (Mémoires de l'Académie des Inscriptions, tom. xx. p. 548-579). He had promised to declare his own opinion in a second memoir, which has never appeared.

adventures, and the castle of Courtenay was profaned by a plebeian owner, the younger branches of that adopted name were
propagated and multiplied. But their splendour was clouded by
poverty and time: after the decease of Robert, great butler of
France, they descended from princes to barons; the next generations were confounded with the simple gentry; the descendants
of Hugh Capet could no longer be visible in the rural lords of
Tanlay and of Champignelles. The more adventurous embraced,
without dishonour, the profession of a soldier; the least active
and opulent might sink, like their cousins of the branch of
Dreux, into the condition of peasants. Their royal descent,
in a dark period of four hundred years, became each day more
obsolete and ambiguous; and their pedigree, instead of being enrolled in the annals of the kingdom, must be painfully searched
by the minute diligence of heralds and genealogists. It was not
till the end of the sixteenth century, on the accession of a family
almost as remote as their own, that the princely spirit of the
Courtenays again revived; and the question of the nobility provoked them to assert the royalty of their blood. They appealed
to the justice and compassion of Henry the Fourth; obtained a
favourable opinion from twenty lawyers of Italy and Germany,
and modestly compared themselves to the descendants of king
David, whose prerogatives were not impaired by the lapse of
ages, or the trade of a carpenter.[96] But every ear was deaf, and
every circumstance was adverse, to their lawful claims. The
Bourbon kings were justified by the neglect of the Valois; the
princes of the blood, more recent and lofty, disdained the alliance
of this humble kindred; the parliament, without denying their
proofs, eluded a dangerous precedent by an arbitrary distinction
and established St. Louis as the first father of the royal line.[97]

---

[96] Of the various petitions, apologies, &c., published by the *princes* of Courtenay,
I have seen the three following all in octavo: 1. De Stirpe et Origine Domus de
Courtenay; addita sunt Responsa celeberrimorum Europæ Jurisconsultorum, Paris,
1607. 2. Représentation du Procédé tenu a l'instance faicte devant le Roi, par
Messieurs de Courtenay, pour la conversation de l'Honneur et Dignité de leur
Maison, Branch de la Royalle Maison de France, a Paris, 1613. 3. Représentation
du subject qui a porté Messieurs de Salles et de Fraville, de la Maison de Courte-
nays, à se retirer hors du Royaume, 1614. It was an homicide, for which the
Courtenays expected to be pardoned, or tried, as princes of the blood.

[97] The sense of the parliaments is thus expressed by Thuanus: Principis nomen
nusquam in Galliâ tributum, nisi iis qui per matres e regibus nostris originem re-
petunt: qui nunc tantum a Ludovico Nono beatæ memoriæ numerantur: nam
Cortinaei et Drooensces, a Ludovico crasso genus ducentes, hodie inter eos minime
recensentur:—a distinction of expediency rather than justice. The sanctity of

A repetition of complaints and protests was repeatedly disregarded : and the hopeless pursuit was terminated in the present century by the death of the last male of the family.[98] Their painful and anxious situation was alleviated by the pride of conscious virtue; they sternly rejected the temptations of fortune and favour; and a dying Courtenay would have sacrificed his son, if the youth could have renounced, for any temporal interest, the right and title of a legitimate prince of the blood of France.[99]

III. According to the old register of Ford Abbey, the Courtenays of Devonshire are descended from Prince *Florus*, the second son of Peter, and the grandson of Louis the Fat.[100] This fable of the grateful or venal monks was too respectfully entertained by our antiquaries, Camden [101] and Dugdale ; [102] but it is so clearly repugnant to truth and time, that the rational pride of the family now refuses to accept this imaginary founder. Their most faithful historians believe that, after giving his daughter to the king's son, Reginald of Courtenay abandoned his possessions in France, and obtained from the English monarch a second wife and a new inheritance. It is certain, at least, that Henry the Second distinguished in his camps and councils *a* Reginald, of the name, arms, and, as it may be fairly presumed, of the genuine race of the Courtenays of France. The right of wardship enabled a feudal lord to reward his vassal with the marriage and estate of a noble heiress; and Reginald of Courtenay acquired a fair establishment in Devonshire, where his

III. The Courtenays of England.

Louis IX. could not invest him with any special prerogative, and all the decendants of Hugh Capet must be included in his original compact with the French nation.

[98] The last male of the Courtenays was Charles Roger, who died in the year 1730, without leaving any sons. The last female was Helen de Courtenay, who married Louis de Beaufremont. Her title of Princesse du Sang Royal de France was suppressed (February 7, 1737) by an *arrêt* of the parliament of Paris.

[99] The singular anecdote to which I allude, is related in the Recueil des Pièces intéressantes et peu connues (Maestricht, 1786, in four vols. 12mo) ; and the unknown editor [M. de la Place, of Calais] quotes his author, who had received it from Helen de Courtenay, Marquise de Beaufremont.

[100] Dugdale, Monasticon Anglicanum, vol. i. p. 786. Yet this fable must have been invented before the reign of Edward III. The profuse devotion of the three first generations to Ford Abbey was followed by oppression on one side and ingratitude on the other; and in the sixth generation the monks ceased to register the births, actions, and deaths of their patrons.

[101] In his Britannia, in the list of the earls of Devonshire. His expression, e regio sanguine ortos credunt, betrays, however, some doubt or suspicion.

[102] In his Baronage, p. i. p. 634, he refers to his own Monasticon. Should he not have corrected the register of Ford Abbey, and annihilated the phantom Florus, by the unquestionable evidence of the French historians ?

posterity has been seated above six hundred years.[103]   From a
Norman baron, Baldwin de Brioniis, who had been invested
by the Conqueror, Hawise, the wife of Reginald, derived the
honour of Okehampton, which was held by the service of ninety-
three knights; and a female might claim the manly offices of
hereditary viscount or sheriff, and of captain of the royal castle
of Exeter.   Their son Robert married the sister of the earl of
Devon; at the end of a century, on the failure of the family
of Rivers,[104] his great-grandson, Hugh the Second, succeeded to
a title which was still considered as a territorial dignity; and

The Earls
of Devon-
shire

twelve earls of Devonshire, of the name of Courtenay, have
flourished in a period of two hundred and twenty years.   They
were ranked among the chief of the barons of the realm; nor
was it till after a strenuous dispute that they yielded to the fief
of Arundel the first place in the parliament of England; their
alliances were contracted with the noblest families, the Veres,
Despensers, St. Johns, Talbots, Bohuns, and even the Plantagenets themselves; and in a contest with John of Lancaster, a
Courtenay, bishop of London, and afterwards archbishop of
Canterbury, might be accused of profane confidence in the
strength and number of his kindred.   In peace, the earls of
Devon resided in their numerous castles and manors of the
west; their ample revenue was appropriated to devotion and
hospitality; and the epitaph of Edward, surnamed, from his
misfortunes, the *blind*, from his virtues, the *good*, Earl, inculcates with much ingenuity a moral sentence, which may,
however, be abused by thoughtless generosity.   After a grateful
commemoration of the fifty-five years of union and happiness,
which he enjoyed with Mabel his wife, the good Earl, thus
speaks from the tomb:

> What we gave, we have;
> What we spent, we had;
> What we left, we lost.[105]

[103] Besides the third and most valuable book of Cleaveland's History, I have
consulted Dugdale, the father of our genealogical science (Baronage, p. i. p. 634-
643).

[104] This great family, de Ripuariis, de Redvers, de Rivers, ended, in Edward
the First's time, in Isabella de Fortibus, a famous and potent dowager, who long
survived her brother and husband (Dugdale, Baronage, p. i. p. 254-257).

[105] Cleaveland, p. 142. By some it is assigned to a Rivers, earl of Devon;
but the English denotes the xvth rather than the xiiith century.

But their *losses*, in this sense, were far superior to their gifts
and expenses; and their heirs, not less than the poor, were
the objects of their paternal care.   The sums which they paid
for livery and seisin attest the greatness of their possessions ;
and several estates have remained in their family since the
thirteenth and fourteenth centuries.   In war, the Courtenays
of England fulfilled the duties, and deserved the honours, of
chivalry.   They were often entrusted to levy and command
the militia of Devonshire and Cornwall; they often attended
their supreme lord to the borders of Scotland; and in foreign
service, for a stipulated price, they sometimes maintained fourscore men at arms and as many archers.   By sea and land
they fought under the standard of the Edwards and Henries;
their names are conspicuous in battles, in tournaments, and in
the original list of the order of the Garter; three brothers
shared the Spanish victory of the Black Prince; and in the
lapse of six generations the English Courtenays had learned to
despise the nation and country from which they derived their
origin.   In the quarrel of the two Roses, the earls of Devon
adhered to the house of Lancaster, and three brothers successively died either in the field or on the scaffold.   Their
honours and estates were restored by Henry the Seventh ; a
daughter of Edward the Fourth was not disgraced by the nuptials of a Courtenay; their son, who was created marquis of
Exeter, enjoyed the favour of his cousin, Henry the Eighth;
and in the camp of Cloth of Gold he broke a lance against the
French monarch.   But the favour of Henry was the prelude
of disgrace; his disgrace was the signal of death; and of the
victims of the jealous tyrant, the marquis of Exeter is one of
the most noble and guiltless.   His son Edward lived a prisoner
in the Tower, and died an exile at Padua; and the secret love
of Queen Mary, whom he slighted, perhaps for the princess
Elizabeth, has shed a romantic colour on the story of this
beautiful youth.   The relics of his patrimony were conveyed
into strange families by the marriages of his four aunts; and
his personal honours, as if they had been legally extinct, were
revived by the patents of succeeding princes.   But there still
survived a lineal descendant of Hugh, the first earl of Devon, a
younger branch of the Courtenays, who have been seated at
Powderham Castle above four hundred years, from the reign of

Edward the Third to the present hour. Their estates have been increased by the grant and improvement of lands in Ireland, and they have been recently restored to the honours of the peerage. Yet the Courtenays still retain the plaintive motto, which asserts the innocence, and deplores the fall, of their ancient house.[106] While they sigh for past greatness, they are doubtless sensible of present blessings; in the long series of the Courtenay annals, the most splendid æra is likewise the most unfortunate; nor can an opulent peer of Britain be inclined to envy the emperors of Constantinople, who wandered over Europe to solicit alms for the support of their dignity and the defence of their capital.

[106] *Ubi lapsus! Quid feci?* a motto which was probably adopted by the Powderham branch, after the loss of the earldom of Devonshire, &c. The primitive arms of the Courtenays were, *or, three torteaux, gules*, which seem to denote their affinity with Godfrey of Bouillon and the ancient counts of Boulogne.

[Some further information on the family of the Courtneys will be found in a short note in the Gentleman's Magazine for July, 1839, p. 39. Cp. Smith's note in his ed. of Gibbon, vol. vii. p. 354.]

CHAPTER LXII

The Greek Emperors of Nice and Constantinople—Elevation and Reign of Michael Palæologus—His false Union with the Pope and the Latin Church—Hostile Designs of Charles of Anjou—Revolt of Sicily—War of the Catalans in Asia and Greece—Revolutions and Present State of Athens

THE loss of Constantinople restored a momentary vigour to the Greeks. From their palaces the princes and nobles were driven into the field; and the fragments of the falling monarchy were grasped by the hands of the most vigorous or the most skilful candidates. In the long and barren pages of the Byzantine annals,[1] it would not be an easy task to equal the two characters of Theodore Lascaris and John Ducas Vataces,[2] who replanted and upheld the Roman standard at Nice in Bithynia. The difference of their virtues was happily suited to the diversity of their situation. In his first efforts the fugitive Lascaris commanded only three cities and two thousand soldiers; his reign was the season of generous and active despair; in every military operation he staked his life and crown; and his enemies, of the Hellespont and the

Restoration of the Greek Empire

Theodore Lascaris. A.D. 1204-1222

---

[1] For the reigns of the Nicene emperors, more especially of John Vataces and his son, their minister, George Acropolita, is the only genuine contemporary; but George Pachymer returned to Constantinople with the Greeks, at the age of nineteen (Hanckius, de Script. Byzant. c. 33, 34, p. 564-578; Fabric. Bibliot. Græc. tom. vi. p. 448-460). Yet the history of Nicephorus Gregoras, though of the xivth century, is a valuable narrative from the taking of Constantinople by the Latins. [We have subsidiary contemporary sources, such as the autobiography of Nicephorus Blemmydes (edited by A. Heisenberg, 1896), who was an important person at the courts of Vatatzes and Theodore II. See Appendix 1. The Empire of Nicæa and Despotate of Epirus have been treated in the histories of Finlay and Hopf, but more fully in a more recent special work in modern Greek by Antonios Mêliarakês: Ἱστορία τοῦ βασιλείου τῆς Νικαίας καὶ τοῦ δεσποτάτου τῆς Ἠπείρου, 1898. See also Heisenberg, Kaiser Johannes Batatzes der Barmhergige, Byzantinische Zeitschrift, xiv. 160 *sqq.* (1905), where a legendary life or encomium of John, composed in the fourteenth century, is printed.]

[2] Nicephorus Gregoras (l. ii. c. 1) distinguishes between the ὀξεῖα ὁρμή of Lascaris, and the εὐστάθεια of Vataces. The two portraits are in a very good style.

John
Ducas
Vataces.
A.D. 1222-
1255 [1254].
Oct. 30

Mæander, were surprised by his celerity and subdued by his boldness. A victorious reign of eighteen years expanded the principality of Nice to the magnitude of an empire. The throne of his successor and son-in-law, Vataces, was founded on a more solid basis, a larger scope, and more plentiful resources; and it was the temper as well as the interest of Vataces to calculate the risk, to expect the moment, and to ensure the success of his ambitious designs. In the decline of the Latins I have briefly exposed the progress of the Greeks: the prudent and gradual advances of a conqueror, who, in a reign of thirty-three years, rescued the provinces from national and foreign usurpers, till he pressed on all sides the Imperial city, a leafless and sapless trunk, which must fall at the first stroke of the axe. But his interior and peaceful administration is still more deserving of notice and praise.[3] The calamities of the times had wasted the numbers and the substance of the Greeks; the motives and the means of agriculture were extirpated; and the most fertile lands were left without cultivation or inhabitants. A portion of this vacant property was occupied and improved by the command, and for the benefit, of the emperor; a powerful hand and a vigilant eye supplied and surpassed, by a skilful management, the minute diligence of a private farmer; the royal domain became the garden and granary of Asia; and without impoverishing the people the sovereign acquired a fund of innocent and productive wealth. According to the nature of the soil, his lands were sown with corn or planted with vines; the pastures were filled with horses and oxen, with sheep and hogs; and, when Vataces presented to the empress a crown of diamonds and pearls, he informed her with a smile that this precious ornament arose from the sale of the eggs of his innumerable poultry. The produce of his domain was applied to the maintenance of his palace and hospitals, the calls of dignity and benevolence; the lesson was still more useful than the revenue; the plough was restored to its ancient security and honour; and the nobles were taught to seek a sure and independent revenue from their estates, instead of adorning their splendid beggary by the oppression of the people, or (what is almost the same) by the favours of the court. The superfluous

---

[3] Pachymer, l. i. c. 23, 24; Nic. Greg. l. ii. c. 6. The reader of the Byzantines must observe how rarely we are indulged with such precious details.

stock of corn and cattle was eagerly purchased by the Turks, with whom Vataces preserved a strict and sincere alliance; but he discouraged the importation of foreign manufactures, the costly silks of the East and the curious labours of the Italian looms. " The demands of nature and necessity," was he accustomed to say, "are indispensable; but the influence of fashion may rise and sink at the breath of a monarch"; and both his precept and example recommended simplicity of manners and the use of domestic industry. The education of youth and the revival of learning were the most serious objects of his care; and, without deciding the precedency, he pronounced with truth that a prince and a philosopher [4] are the two most eminent characters of human society. His first wife was Irene, the daughter of Theodore Lascaris, a woman more illustrious by her personal merit, the milder virtues of her sex, than by the blood of the Angeli and Comneni, that flowed in her veins and transmitted the inheritance of the empire. After her death, he was contracted to Anne, or Constance, a natural [A.D. 1244] daughter of the emperor Frederic the Second; [5] but, as the bride had not attained the years of puberty, Vataces placed in his solitary bed an Italian damsel of her train; [6] and his amorous weakness bestowed on the concubine the honours, though not the title, of lawful empress. His frailty was censured as a flagitious and damnable sin by the monks; and their rude invectives exercised and displayed the patience of the royal lover. A philosophic age may excuse a single vice, which was redeemed by a crowd of virtues; and, in the review of his faults, and the more intemperate passions of Lascaris, the judg-

---

[4] Μόνοι γὰρ ἀπάντων ἀνθρώπων ὀνομαστότατοι βασιλεὺς καὶ φιλόσοφος (Georg. Acropol. c. 32). The emperor, in a familiar conversation, examined and encouraged the studies of his future logothete.

[5] [Her mother was Bianca Lancia of Piedmont. Frederick seems to have married her ultimately (towards the close of his life) and legitimised her children (Matthew Paris, ed. Lond., vol. 7, p. 216). The lady's true name was Constance (as western writers called her); only Greek writers name her Anna, so that she was probably baptized under this name into the Greek church.]

[6] [The Greek writers call her the Μαρκεζίνα—Marchioness. Her liaison with the Emperor caused an incident which produced a quarrel between him and Nicephorus Blemmydes. She entered the Monastery of St. Gregory in grand costume. Blemmydes, when he observed her presence, ordered the communion service to be discontinued. Vatatzes refused to punish a just man, as the Marchioness demanded, but showed his resentment by breaking off all relations with him. Besides Nicephorus Gregoras, i. p. 45, 46, we have a description of the incident from the pen of Blemmydes himself in his autobiography, c. 41 (ed. Heisenberg).]

ment of their contemporaries was softened by gratitude to the second founders of the empire.[7] The slaves of the Latins, without law or peace, applauded the happiness of their brethren who had resumed their national freedom; and Vataces employed the laudable policy of convincing the Greeks of every dominion that it was their interest to be enrolled in the number of his subjects.

Theodore
Lascaris II.
A.D. 1255,
October 30
—A.D. 1259
[1258], August

A strong shade of degeneracy is visible between John Vataces and his son Theodore; between the founder who sustained the weight, and the heir who enjoyed the splendour, of the Imperial crown.[8] Yet the character of Theodore was not devoid of energy; he had been educated in the school of his father, in the exercise of war and hunting: Constantinople was yet spared; but in the three years of a short reign he thrice led

[A.D. 1256, 1257]

his armies into the heart of Bulgaria.[9] His virtues were sullied by a choleric and suspicious temper: the first of these may be ascribed to the ignorance of control; and the second might naturally arise from a dark and imperfect view of the corruption of mankind.

[1257]

On a march in Bulgaria he consulted on a question of policy his principal ministers; and the Greek logothete, George Acropolita, presumed to offend him by the declaration of a free and honest opinion. The emperor half unsheathed his scymetar; but his more deliberate rage reserved Acropolita for a baser punishment. One of the first officers of the empire was ordered to dismount, stripped of his robes, and extended on the ground in the presence of the prince and army. In this posture he was chastised with so many and such heavy blows from the clubs of two guards or executioners that, when Theodore commanded them to cease, the great logothete was scarcely able to rise and crawl away to his tent. After a se-

---

[7] Compare Acropolita (c. 18, 52) and the two first books of Nicephorus Gregoras.

[8] A Persian saying, that Cyrus was the *father*, and Darius the *master*, of his subjects, was applied to Vataces and his son. But Pachymer (l. i. c. 23) has mistaken the mild Darius for the cruel Cambyses, despot or tyrant of his people. By the institution of taxes, Darius had incurred the less odious, but more contemptible, name of Κάπηλος, *merchant* or *broker* (Herodotus, iii. 89).

[9] [Theodore led two expeditions in person against the Bulgarians, in 1256 and 1257. At the end of the second expedition he had a meeting with Theodora Petraleipha, the wife of Michael II., Despot of Epirus, at Thessalonica, where a marriage was both arranged and celebrated between his daughter Maria and her son Nicephorus. The third expedition, to which Gibbon refers, was that of 1258 against Michael II., which however was conducted not by Theodore but by Michael Palæologus, the future emperor.]

clusion of some days, he was recalled by a peremptory mandate
to his seat in council; and so dead were the Greeks to the
sense of honour and shame that it is from the narrative of the
sufferer himself that we acquire the knowledge of his disgrace.[10]
The cruelty of the emperor was exasperated by the pangs of
sickness, the approach of a premature end, and the suspicion of
poison and magic.[11]   The lives and fortunes, the eyes and limbs,
of his kinsmen and nobles were sacrificed to each sally of passion; and, before he died, the son of Vataces might deserve
from the people, or at least from the Court, the appellation of
tyrant.   A matron of the family of the Palæologi[12] had provoked his anger by refusing to bestow her beauteous daughter
on the vile plebeian who was recommended by his caprice.
Without regard to her birth or age, her body, as high as the
neck, was inclosed in a sack with several cats, who were pricked
with pins to irritate their fury against their unfortunate fellow-
captive.   In his last hours the emperor testified a wish to forgive and be forgiven, a just anxiety for the fate of John, his
son and successor, who, at the age of eight years, was condemned to the dangers of a long minority.   His last choice Minority of
entrusted the office of guardian to the sanctity of the patriarch caris. A.D.
Arsenius, and to the courage of George Muzalon, the great August
domestic, who was equally distinguished by the royal favour and
the public hatred.   Since their connection with the Latins, the
names and privileges of hereditary rank had insinuated themselves into the Greek monarchy; and the noble families[13] were

---

[10] Acropolita (c. 63) seems to admire his own firmness in sustaining a beating,
and not returning to council till he was called.   He relates the exploits of Theodore, and his own services, from c. 53 to c. 74 of his History.   See the third book
of Nicephorus Gregoras. [Among some unpublished works of this remarkable
monarch, Theodore Lascaris, is an encomium on George Acropolites. He also wrote
a rhetorical estimate of his contemporary Frederick II.   George Acropolites made
a collection of his letters.   Professor Krumbacher has designated Theodore II.
"as statesman, writer, and man, one of the most interesting figures of Byzantium,
a sort of oriental parallel to his great contemporary Frederick II.; a degenerate,
no doubt; intellectually highly gifted, bodily weak, without moral force, with
a nervous system fatally preponderant" (op. cit., p. 478).   On his theological
productions cp. J. Dräseke, Byz. Zeitschrift, iii. p. 498 sqq.   The correspondence of
Theodore Lascaris has been edited by N. Festa, Theodori Ducæ Lascaris Epistolæ
ccxvii, Florence, 1898.]
[11] [He seems to have suffered from a cerebral disease, and to have been subject to fits of epilepsy.   Cp. Méliarakês, op. cit., p. 479.]
[12] [A sister of Michael Palæologus.]
[13] Pachymer (l. i. c. 21) names and discriminates fifteen or twenty Greek families,
καὶ ὅσοι ἄλλοι, οἷς ἡ μεγαλογενὴς σεῖρα καὶ χρυσῆ συγκεκρότητο.   Does he mean, by this
decoration, a figurative or a real golden chain?   Perhaps both.

provoked by the elevation of a worthless favourite, to whose
influence they imputed the errors and calamities of the late
reign.   In the first council after the emperor's death, Muzalon,
from a lofty throne, pronounced a laboured apology of his conduct and intentions: his modesty was subdued by an unanimous
assurance of esteem and fidelity; and his most inveterate enemies were the loudest to salute him as the guardian and saviour
of the Romans.   Eight days were sufficient to prepare the execution of the conspiracy.   On the ninth, the obsequies of the
deceased monarch were solemnised in the cathedral of Magnesia,[14] an Asiatic city, where he expired, on the banks of the
Hermus and at the foot of Mount Sipylus.   The holy rites were
interrupted by a sedition of the guards: Muzalon, his brothers,
and his adherents were massacred at the foot of the altar ; and
the absent patriarch was associated with a new colleague, with
Michael Palæologus, the most illustrious, in birth and merit, of
the Greek nobles.[15]

Family and
character
of Michael
Palæologus

Of those who are proud of their ancestors, the far greater
part must be content with local or domestic renown: and few
there are who dare trust the memorials of their family to the
public annals of their country.   As early as the middle of the
eleventh century, the noble race of the Palæologi[16] stands high
and conspicuous in the Byzantine history: it was the valiant
George Palæologus who placed the father of the Comneni on
the throne; and his kinsmen or descendants continue, in each
generation, to lead the armies and councils of the state.   The
purple was not dishonoured by their alliance ; and, had the law
of succession, and female succession, been strictly observed, the
wife of Theodore Lascaris must have yielded to her elder sister,
the mother of Michael Palæologus, who afterwards raised his
family to the throne.   In his person, the splendour of birth was

---

[14] The old geographers, with Cellarius and d'Anville, and our travellers, particularly Pocock and Chandler, will teach us to distinguish the two Magnesias of
Asia Minor, of the Mæander and of Sipylus.   The latter, our present object, is
still flourishing for a Turkish city, and lies eight hours, or leagues, to the north-
east of Smyrna (Tournefort, Voyage du Levant, tom. iii. lettre xxiii. p. 365-370.
Chandler's Travels into Asia Minor, p. 267).

[15] See Acropolita (c. 75, 76, &c.), who lived too near the times ; Pachymer (l. i.
c. 13-25) ; Gregoras (l. iii. c. 3-5).

[16] The pedigree of Palæologus is explained by Ducange (Famil. Byzant. p. 230,
&c.) ; the events of his private life are related by Pachymer (l. i. c. 7-12), and
Gregoras (l. ii. 8, l. iii. 2, 4, l. iv. 1), with visible favour to the father of the reigning dynasty.

A GREEK MONASTERY: COURT AND FOUNTAIN OF LAVRA ON MOUNT
ATHOS

dignified by the merit of the soldier and statesman: in his early youth he was promoted to the office of *Constable* or commander [κοντό σταυλος] of the French mercenaries; the private expense of a day never exceeded three pieces of gold; but his ambition was rapacious and profuse; and his gifts were doubled by the graces of his conversation and manners. The love of the soldiers and people excited the jealousy of the court; and Michael thrice escaped from the dangers in which he was involved by his own imprudence or that of his friends. I. Under the reign of Justice and Vataces, a dispute arose [17] between two officers, one of whom accused the other of maintaining the hereditary right of the Palæologi. The cause was decided, according to the new jurisprudence of the Latins, by single combat: the defendant was overthrown; but he persisted in declaring that himself alone was guilty; and that he had uttered these rash or treasonable speeches without the approbation or knowledge of his patron. Yet a cloud of suspicion hung over the innocence of the constable; he was still pursued by the whispers of malevolence; and a subtile courtier, the archbishop of Philadelphia, urged him to accept the judgment of God in the fiery proof of the ordeal.[18] Three days before the trial, the patient's arm was inclosed in a bag and secured by the royal signet; and it was incumbent on him to bear a red-hot ball of iron three times from the altar to the rails of the sanctuary, without artifice and without injury. Palæologus eluded the dangerous experiment with sense and pleasantry. "I am a soldier," said he, "and will boldly enter the lists with my accusers; but a layman, a sinner like myself, is not endowed with the gift of miracles. *Your* piety, most holy prelate, may deserve the interposition of Heaven, and from your hands I will receive the fiery globe, the pledge of my innocence." The archbishop started; the emperor smiled; and the absolution or pardon of Michael was approved by new rewards and new services. II. In the succeeding reign, as he held the government of Nice, he was secretly informed that the mind of the absent prince was pois-

---

[17] Acropolita (c. 50) relates the circumstances of this curious adventure, which seems to have escaped the more recent writers.

[18] Pachymer (l. i. c. 12), who speaks with proper contempt of this barbarous trial, affirms that he had seen in his youth many persons who had sustained, without injury, the fiery ordeal. As a Greek, he is credulous; but the ingenuity of the Greeks might furnish some remedies of art or fraud against their own superstition or that of their tyrant.

oned with jealousy; and that death or blindness would be his
final reward. Instead of awaiting the return and sentence of
Theodore, the constable, with some followers, escaped from the
city and the empire; and, though he was plundered by the
Turkmans of the desert, he found an hospitable refuge in the
court of the sultan. In the ambiguous state of an exile, Michael
reconciled the duties of gratitude and loyalty; drawing his
sword against the Tartars; admonishing the garrisons of the
Roman limit; and promoting, by his influence, the restoration
of peace, in which his pardon and recall were honourably included. III. While he guarded the West against the despot
of Epirus, Michael was again suspected and condemned in the
palace; and such was his loyalty or weakness that he submitted
to be led in chains above six hundred miles from Durazzo to
Nice. The civility of the messenger alleviated his disgrace;
the emperor's sickness dispelled his danger; and the last breath
of Theodore, which recommended his infant son, at once acknowledged the innocence and the power of Palæologus.

His eleva-
tion to the
throne   But his innocence had been too unworthily treated, and his
power was too strongly felt, to curb an aspiring subject in the
fair field that was offered to his ambition.[19] In the council after
the death of Theodore, he was the first to pronounce, and the
first to violate, the oath of allegiance to Muzalon; and so dexterous was his conduct that he reaped the benefit, without incur-
ring the guilt, or at least the reproach, of the subsequent massacre.
In the choice of a regent, he balanced the interests and passions
of the candidates; turned their envy and hatred from himself
against each other, and forced every competitor to own that,
after his own claims, those of Palæologus were best entitled to
the preference. Under the title of Great Duke, he accepted or
assumed, during a long minority, the active powers of government; the patriarch was a venerable name; and the factious
nobles were seduced, or oppressed, by the ascendant of his genius.
The fruits of the economy of Vataces were deposited in a strong
castle on the banks of the Hermus,[20] in the custody of the faith-

[19] Without comparing Pachymer to Thucydides or Tacitus, I will praise his
narrative (l. i. c. 13-32, l. iii. c. 1-9), which pursues the ascent of Palæologus with
eloquence, perspicuity, and tolerable freedom. Acropolita is more cautious, and
Gregoras more concise.
[20] [In Astytzion on the Scamander. The treasures here were deposited by
Theodore II.]

ful Varangians ; the constable retained his command or influence over the foreign troops ; he employed the guards to possess the treasure, and the treasure to corrupt the guards ; and, whatsoever might be the abuse of the public money, his character was above the suspicion of private avarice.   By himself, or by his emissaries, he strove to persuade every rank of subjects that their own prosperity would rise in just proportion to the establishment of his authority.   The weight of taxes was suspended, the perpetual theme of popular complaint ; and he prohibited the trials by the ordeal and judicial combat.   These barbaric institutions were already abolished or undermined in France [21] and England ; [22] and the appeal to the sword offended the sense of a civilised, [23] and the temper of an unwarlike, people.   For the future maintenance of their wives and children the veterans were grateful ; the priest and the philosopher applauded his ardent zeal for the advancement of religion and learning ; and his vague promise of rewarding merit was applied by every candidate to his own hopes. Conscious of the influence of the clergy, Michael successfully laboured to secure the suffrage of that powerful order.   Their expensive journey from Nice to Magnesia afforded a decent and ample pretence ; the leading prelates were tempted by the liberality of his nocturnal visits ; and the incorruptible patriarch was flattered by the homage of his new colleague, who led his mule by the bridle into the town, and removed to a respectful distance the importunity of the crowd.   Without renouncing his title by royal descent, Palæologus encouraged a free discussion into the advantages of elective monarchy ; and his adherents asked, with the insolence of triumph, What patient would trust his health, or what merchant would abandon his vessel, to the *hereditary*

[21] The judicial combat was abolished by St. Louis in his own territories ; and his example and authority were at length prevalent in France (Esprit des Loix, l. xxviii. c. 29).

[22] In civil cases, Henry II. gave an option to the defendant ; Glanville prefers the proof by evidence, and that by judicial combat is reprobated in the Fleta.   Yet the trial by battle has never been abrogated in the English law, and it was ordered by the judges as late as the beginning of the last century.

[23] Yet an ingenious friend has urged to me, in mitigation of this practice, 1. *That*, in nations emerging from barbarism, it moderates the licence of private war and arbitrary revenge. 2. *That* it is less absurd than the trials by the ordeal, or boiling water, or the cross, which it has contributed to abolish. 3. *That* it served at least as a test of personal courage : a quality so seldom united with a base disposition that the danger of the trial might be some check to a malicious prosecutor, and an useful barrier against injustice supported by power.   The gallant and unfortunate earl of Surrey might probably have escaped his unmerited fate, had not his demand of the combat against his accuser been over-ruled.

skill of a physician or a pilot? The youth of the emperor and the impending dangers of a minority required the support of a mature and experienced guardian; of an associate raised above the envy of his equals, and invested with the name and prerogatives of royalty. For the interest of the prince and people, without any views for himself or his family, the Great Duke consented to guard and instruct the son of Theodore; but he sighed for the happy moment when he might restore to his firmer hands the administration of his patrimony, and enjoy the blessings of a private station. He was first invested with the title and prerogatives of *despot*, which bestowed the purple ornaments, and the second place in the Roman monarchy. It was afterwards agreed that John and Michael should be proclaimed as joint emperors, and raised on the buckler, but that the pre-eminence should be reserved for the birth-right of the former. A mutual league of amity was pledged between the royal partners; and, in case of a rupture, the subjects were bound, by their oath of allegiance, to declare themselves against the aggressor: an ambiguous name, the seed of discord and civil war. Palæologus was content; but on the day of his coronation, and in the

[Jan., A.D. 1260]

cathedral of Nice, his zealous adherents most vehemently urged the just priority of his age and merit. The unseasonable dispute was eluded by postponing to a more convenient opportunity the coronation of John Lascaris; and he walked with a slight diadem in the train of his guardian, who alone received the Imperial

Michael Palæologus Emperor. A.D. 1260, Jan. 1

crown from the hands of the patriarch. It was not without extreme reluctance that Arsenius abandoned the cause of his pupil; but the Varangians brandished their battle-axes; a sign of assent was extorted from the trembling youth; and some voices were heard, that the life of a child should no longer impede the settlement of the nation. A full harvest of honours and employments was distributed among his friends by the grateful Palæologus. In his own family he created a despot and two sebastocrators; Alexius Strategopulus was decorated with the title of Cæsar; and that veteran commander soon repaid the obligation, by restoring Constantinople to the Greek emperor.

Recovery of Constantinople. A.D. 1261, July 25

It was in the second year of his reign, while he resided in the palace and gardens of Nymphæum,[24] near Smyrna, that the

[24] The site of Nymphæum is not clearly defined in ancient or modern geography. [Turkish Nif; it lay on the road from Smyrna to Sardis. Cp. Ramsay, Asia

first messenger arrived at the dead of night; and the stupendous intelligence was imparted to Michael, after he had been gently waked by the tender precaution of his sister Eulogia. The man was unknown or obscure; he produced no letters from the victorious Cæsar; nor could it easily be credited, after the defeat of Vataces and the recent failure of Palæologus himself, that the capital had been surprised by a detachment of eight hundred soldiers. As an hostage, the doubtful author was confined, with the assurance of death or an ample recompense; and the court was left some hours in the anxiety of hope and fear, till the messengers of Alexius arrived with the authentic intelligence, and displayed the trophies of the conquest, the sword and sceptre,[25] the buskins and bonnet,[26] of the usurper Baldwin, which he had dropt in his precipitate flight. A general assembly of the bishops, senators, and nobles was immediately convened, and never perhaps was an event received with more heartfelt and universal joy. In a studied oration, the new sovereign of Constantinople congratulated his own and the public fortune. "There was a time," said he, "a far distant time, when the Roman empire extended to the Adriatic, the Tigris, and the confines of Ethiopia. After the loss of the provinces, our capital itself, in these last and calamitous days, has been wrested from our hands by the barbarians of the West. From the lowest ebb, the tide of prosperity has again returned in our favour; but our prosperity was that of fugitives and exiles; and, when we were asked, Which was the country of the Romans? we indicated with a blush the climate of the globe and the quarter of the heavens. The Divine Providence has now restored to our arms the city of Constantine, the

Minor, p. 108.] But from the last hours of Vataces (Acropolita, c. 52) it is evident the palace and gardens of his favourite residence were in the neighbourhood of Smyrna. Nymphæum might be loosely placed in Lydia (Gregoras, l. vi. 6). [Pachymeres says that Michael was at Nymphæum when he received the glad tidings; but Gregoras says Nicaea, and Acropolites says Meteorion. As Acropolites was with Michael at the time, we must follow him (so Méliarakês, p. 509). Meteorion "must have been in the Hermos valley, and may possibly be the purely Byzantine fortress Gurduk Kalesi, a few miles north of Thyateira, near the site of Attaleia " (Ramsay, *op. cit.*, p. 131).]
   [25] This sceptre, the emblem of justice and power, was a long staff, such as was used by the heroes in Homer. By the latter Greeks it was named *Dicanice*, and the Imperial sceptre was distinguished as usual by the red or purple colour.
   [26] Acropolita affirms (c. 87) that this bonnet was after the French fashion; but from the ruby at the point or summit Ducange (Hist. de C. P. l. v. c. 28, 29) believes that it was the high-crowned hat of the Greeks. Could Acropolita mistake the dress of his own court?

sacred seat of religion and empire; and it will depend on our valour and conduct to render this important acquisition the pledge and omen of future victories." So eager was the impatience of the prince and people that Michael made his triumphal entry into Constantinople only twenty days after the expulsion of the Latins. The golden gate was thrown open at his approach; the devout conqueror dismounted from his horse; and a miraculous image of Mary, the Conductress, was borne before him, that the divine Virgin in person might appear to conduct him to the temple of her Son, the cathedral of St. Sophia. But, after the first transport of devotion and pride, he sighed at the dreary prospect of solitude and ruin. The palace was defiled with smoke and dirt, and the gross intemperance of the Franks; whole streets had been consumed by fire, or were decayed by the injuries of time; the sacred and profane edifices were stripped of their ornaments; and, as if they were conscious of their approaching exile, the industry of the Latins had been confined to the work of pillage and destruction. Trade had expired under the pressure of anarchy and distress; and the number of inhabitants had decreased with the opulence of the city. It was the first care of the Greek monarch to reinstate the nobles in the palaces of their fathers; and the houses or the ground which they occupied were restored to the families that could exhibit a legal right of inheritance. But the far greater part was extinct or lost; the vacant property had devolved to the lord; he repeopled Constantinople by a liberal invitation to the provinces; and the brave *volunteers* were seated in the capital which had been recovered by their arms. The French barons and the principal families had retired with their emperor; but the patient and humble crowd of Latins was attached to the country, and indifferent to the change of masters. Instead of banishing the factories of the Pisans, Venetians, and Genoese, the prudent conqueror accepted their oaths of allegiance, encouraged their industry, confirmed their privileges, and allowed them to live under the jurisdiction of their proper magistrates. Of these nations, the Pisans and Venetians preserved their respective quarters in the city; but the services and powers of the Genoese deserved at the same time the gratitude [27] and the jealousy of the Greeks. Their independent

Return of the Greek Emperor. A.D. 1261, Aug. 14

---

[27] [The Genoese had sent ships, in accordance with the treaty of Nymphæum; but these had not arrived in time to be of actual service.]

colony was first planted at the sea-port town of Heraclea in
Thrace. They were speedily recalled, and settled in the exclusive possession of the suburb of Galata, an advantageous
post, in which they revived the commerce, and insulted the
majesty, of the Byzantine empire.[28]

The recovery of Constantinople was celebrated as the æra
of a new empire: the conqueror, alone, and by the right of
the sword, renewed his coronation in the church of St. Sophia;
and the name and honours of John Lascaris, his pupil and lawful sovereign, were insensibly abolished. But his claims still
lived in the minds of the people; and the royal youth must
speedily attain the years, of manhood and ambition. By fear
or conscience, Palæologus was restrained from dipping his
hands in innocent and royal blood ; but the anxiety of an
usurper and a parent urged him to secure his throne by one of
those imperfect crimes so familiar to the modern Greeks. The
loss of sight incapacitated the young prince for the active business of the world: instead of the brutal violence of tearing out
his eyes, the visual nerve was destroyed by the intense glare of
a red-hot bason,[29] and John Lascaris was removed to a distant
castle, where he spent many years in privacy and oblivion.
Such cool and deliberate guilt may seem incompatible with remorse; but, if Michael could trust the mercy of Heaven, he
was not inaccessible to the reproaches and vengeance of mankind, which he had provoked by cruelty and treason. His
cruelty imposed on a servile court the duties of applause or
silence; but the clergy had a right to speak in the name of
their invisible master; and their holy legions were led by a
prelate, whose character was above the temptations of hope or
fear. After a short abdication of his dignity, Arsenius[30] had

*Palæolo-
gus blinds
and
banishes
the young
Emperor.
A.D. 1261,
Dec. 25*

---

[28] See Pachymer (l. 2, c. 28-33), Acropolita (c. 88), Nicephorus Gregoras (l. iv.
7), and for the treatment of the subject Latins, Ducange (l. v. c. 30, 31).

[29] This milder invention for extinguishing the sight was tried by the philosopher
Democritus on himself, when he sought to withdraw his mind from the visible
world: a foolish story! The word *abacinare*, in Latin and Italian, has furnished
Ducange (Gloss. Latin.) with an opportunity to review the various modes of
blinding: the more violent were, scooping, burning with an iron or hot vinegar,
and binding the head with a strong cord till the eyes burst from their sockets.
Ingenious tyrants !

[30] See the first retreat and restoration of Arsenius, in Pachymer (l. ii. c. 15, 1.
iii. c. 1, 2), and Nicephorus Gregoras (l. iii. c. 1, l. iv. c. 1). Posterity justly accused
the ἀφέλεια and ῥᾳθυμία of Arsenius, the virtues of an hermit, the vices of a minister
(l. xii. c. 2).

consented to ascend the ecclesiastical throne of Constantinople, and to preside in the restoration of the church. His pious simplicity was long deceived by the arts of Palæologus; and his patience and submission might soothe the usurper, and protect the safety of the young prince. On the news of his inhuman treatment, the patriarch unsheathed the spiritual sword; and superstition, on this occasion, was enlisted in the cause of humanity and justice. In a synod of bishops, who were stimulated by the example of his zeal, the patriarch pronounced a

sentence of excommunication; though his prudence still repeated the name of Michael in the public prayers. The eastern prelates had not adopted the dangerous maxims of ancient Rome; nor did they presume to enforce their censures, by deposing princes, or absolving nations from their oaths of allegiance. But the Christian who had been separated from God and the church became an object of horror; and, in a turbulent and fanatic capital, that horror might arm the hand of an assassin or inflame a sedition of the people. Palæologus felt his danger, confessed his guilt, and deprecated his judge: the act was irretrievable; the prize was obtained; and the most rigorous penance, which he solicited, would have raised the sinner to the reputation of a saint. The unrelenting patriarch refused to announce any means of atonement or any hopes of mercy; and condescended only to pronounce that, for so great a crime, great indeed must be the satisfaction. "Do you require," said Michael, "that I should abdicate the empire?" And at these words he offered, or seemed to offer, the sword of state. Arsenius eagerly grasped this pledge of sovereignty; but, when he perceived that the emperor was unwilling to purchase absolution at so dear a rate, he indignantly escaped to his cell, and left the royal sinner kneeling and weeping before the door.[31]

The danger and scandal of this excommunication subsisted above three years, till the popular clamour was assuaged by time and repentance; till the brethren of Arsenius condemned his inflexible spirit, so repugnant to the unbounded forgiveness of the gospel. The emperor had artfully insinuated that, if he were still rejected at home, he might seek, in the Roman

[31] The crime and excommunication of Michael are fairly told by Pachymer (l. iii. c. 10, 14, 19, &c.), and Gregoras (l. iv. c. 4). His confession and penance restored their freedom.

pontiff, a more indulgent judge; but it was far more easy and
effectual to find or to place that judge at the head of the
Byzantine church. Arsenius was involved in a vague rumour
of conspiracy and disaffection; some irregular steps in his ordination and government were liable to censure; a synod deposed
him from the episcopal office; and he was transported under a
guard of soldiers to a small island of the Propontis. Before his
exile, he sullenly requested that a strict account might be
taken of the treasures of the church; boasted that his whole
riches, three pieces of gold, had been earned by transcribing
the Psalms; continued to assert the freedom of his mind; and
denied, with his last breath, the pardon which was implored
by the royal sinner.[32] After some delay, Gregory, bishop of
Hadrianople, was translated to the Byzantine throne; but his
authority was found insufficient to support the absolution of
the emperor; and Joseph, a reverend monk, was substituted to
that important function. This edifying scene was represented
in the presence of the senate and people; at the end of six
years, the humble penitent was restored to the communion of
the faithful; and humanity will rejoice that a milder treatment
of the captive Lascaris was stipulated as a proof of his remorse.
But the spirit of Arsenius still survived in a powerful faction
of the monks and clergy, who persevered above forty-eight
years in an obstinate schism. Their scruples were treated
with tenderness and respect by Michael and his son; and the
reconciliation of the Arsenites was the serious labour of the
church and state. In the confidence of fanaticism, they had
proposed to try their cause by a miracle; and, when the two
papers that contained their own and the adverse cause were
cast into a fiery brazier, they expected that the Catholic verity
would be respected by the flames. Alas! the two papers were
indiscriminately consumed, and this unforeseen accident produced the union of a day, and renewed the quarrel of an age.[33]

[32] Pachymer relates the exile of Arsenius (l. v. c. 1-16); he was one of the
commissaries who visited him in the desert island. The last testament of the
unforgiving patriarch is still extant (Dupin, Bibliothèque Ecclésiastique, tom. x.
p. 95).
[33] Pachymer (l. vii. c. 22) relates this miraculous trial like a philosopher, and
treats with similar contempt a plot of the Arsenites, to hide a revelation in the
coffin of some old saint (l. vii. c. 13). He compensates this incredulity by an image that weeps, another that bleeds (l. vii. c. 30), and the miraculous cures of a
deaf and a mute patient (l. xi. c. 32).

The final treaty displayed the victory of the Arsenites; the clergy abstained during forty days from all ecclesiastical functions; a slight penance was imposed on the laity; the body of Arsenius was deposited in the sanctuary; and in the name of the departed saint the prince and people were released from the sins of their fathers.[34]

Reign of Michael Palæologus. A.D. 1259, Dec. 1—A.D. 1282, Dec. 11 The establishment of his family was the motive, or at least the pretence, of the crime of Palæologus; and he was impatient to confirm the succession, by sharing with his eldest son the honours of the purple. Andronicus, afterwards surnamed the Reign of Andronicus the Elder. A.D. 1273, Nov. 8—A.D. 1332, Feb. 13 Elder, was proclaimed and crowned emperor of the Romans, in the fifteenth year of his age; and, from the first æra of a prolix and inglorious reign, he held that august title nine years as the colleague, and fifty as the successor, of his father. Michael himself, had he died in a private station, would have been thought more worthy of the empire; and the assaults of his temporal and spiritual enemies left him few moments to labour for his own fame or the happiness of his subjects. He wrested from the Franks several of the noblest islands of the Archipelago, Lesbos, Chios, and Rhodes;[35] his brother Constantine was sent to command in Malvasia and Sparta; and the eastern side of the Morea, from Argos and Napoli to Cape Tænarus, was repossessed by the Greeks.[36] This effusion of Christian blood was loudly condemned by the patriarch; and the insolent priest presumed to interpose his fears and scruples between the arms of princes. But, in the prosecution of these Western conquests, the countries beyond the Hellespont were left naked to the Turks; and their depredations verified the prophecy of a dying senator, that the recovery of Constantinople would be the ruin of Asia. The victories of Michael were achieved by his lieutenants; his sword rusted in the palace; and, in the transactions of the emperor with the popes and the

---

[34] The story of the Arsenites is spread through the thirteen books of Pachymer. Their union and triumph are reserved for Nicephorus Gregoras (l. vii. c. 9), who neither loves nor esteems these sectaries.

[35] [These islands were subject to Michael, but not conquered by him; see Appendix 18.]

[36] [Michael released William Villehardouin, prince of Achaia, who had been taken prisoner at the battle of Pelagonia (see above, p. 459). For his liberty William undertook to become a vassal of the Empire, and to hand over to Michael the fortresses of Misithra, Maina and Monembasia. See (besides Pachymeres, Gibbon's source) the Chronicle of Morea, ed. by John Schmitt, London, 1904.]

king of Naples, his political arts were stained with cruelty and
fraud.[37]

I. The Vatican was the most natural refuge of a Latin em- His union
with the
peror, who had been driven from his throne; and pope Urban Latin
church.
the Fourth appeared to pity the misfortunes, and vindicate the A.D. 1274-
1277
cause, of the fugitive, Baldwin. A crusade, with plenary indulgence, was preached by his command against the schismatic
Greeks; he excommunicated their allies and adherents; solicited Louis the Ninth in favour of his kinsman; and demanded
a tenth of the ecclesiastic revenues of France and England for
the service of the holy war.[38] The subtile Greek, who watched
the rising tempest of the West, attempted to suspend or soothe
the hostility of the pope, by suppliant embassies and respectful
letters; but he insinuated that the establishment of peace must
prepare the reconciliation and obedience of the Eastern church.
The Roman court could not be deceived by so gross an artifice;
and Michael was admonished that the repentance of the son
should precede the forgiveness of the father; and that *faith* (an
ambiguous word) was the only basis of friendship and alliance.
After a long and affected delay, the approach of danger and
the importunity of Gregory the Tenth compelled him to enter
on a more serious negotiation; he alleged the example of the
great Vataces; and the Greek clergy, who understood the intentions of their prince, were not alarmed by the first steps of
reconciliation and respect. But, when he pressed the conclusion of the treaty, they strenuously declared that the Latins,
though not in name, were heretics in fact, and that they despised those strangers as the vilest and most despicable portion
of the human race.[39] It was the task of the emperor to persuade, to corrupt, to intimidate, the most popular ecclesiastics,
to gain the vote of each individual, and alternately to urge the
arguments of Christian charity and the public welfare. The

---

[37] Of the xiii books of Pachymer, the first six (as the ivth and vth of Nicephorus Gregoras) contain the reign of Michael, at the time of whose death he
was forty years of age. Instead of breaking, like his editor the Père Poussin,
his history into two parts, I follow Ducange and Cousin, who number the xiii books
in one series.

[38] Ducange, Hist. de C. P. l. v. c. 33, &c. from the Epistles of Urban IV.

[39] From their mercantile intercourse with the Venetians and Genoese, they
branded the Latins as κάπηλοι and βάναυσοι (Pachymer, l. v. c. 10). "Some are
heretics in name; others, like the Latins, in fact," said the learned Veccus (l. v. c.
12), who soon afterwards became a convert (c. 15, 16), and a patriarch (c. 24).

texts of the fathers and the arms of the Franks were balanced
in the theological and political scale; and, without approving
the addition to the Nicene creed, the most moderate were
taught to confess that the two hostile propositions of proceeding from the Father BY the Son, and of proceeding from the
Father AND the Son, might be reduced to a safe and catholic
sense.[40] The supremacy of the pope was a doctrine more easy
to conceive, but more painful to acknowledge ; yet Michael represented to his monks and prelates that they might submit
to name the Roman bishop as the first of the patriarchs, and
that their distance and discretion would guard the liberties of
the Eastern church from the mischievous consequences of the
right of appeal. He protested that he would sacrifice his life
and empire rather than yield the smallest point of orthodox
faith or national independence ; and this declaration was sealed
and ratified by a golden bull. The patriarch Joseph withdrew
to a monastery, to resign or resume his throne, according to
the event of the treaty; the letters of union and obedience
were subscribed by the emperor, his son Andronicus, and thirty-
five archbishops and metropolitans, with their respective synods;
and the episcopal list was multiplied by many dioceses which
were annihilated under the yoke of the infidels. An embassy
was composed of some trusty ministers and prelates; they embarked for Italy, with rich ornaments and rare perfumes for the
altar of St. Peter; and their secret orders authorised and recommended a boundless compliance. They were received in
[A.D. 1274] the general council of Lyons, by pope Gregory the Tenth, at
the head of five hundred bishops.[41] He embraced with tears
his long-lost and repentant children; accepted the oath of the
ambassadors, who abjured the schism in the name of the two
emperors; adorned the prelates with the ring and mitre;
chaunted in Greek and Latin the Nicene creed, with the
addition of *filioque ;* and rejoiced in the union of the East and
West, which had been reserved for his reign. To consummate

[40] In this class we may place Pachymer himself, whose copious and candid narrative occupies the vth and vith books of his history. Yet the Greek is silent on the council of Lyons, and seems to believe that the popes always resided in Rome and Italy.
[41] See the Acts of the Council of Lyons in the year 1274. Fleury, Hist. Ecclésiastique, tom. xviii. p. 181-199. Dupin, Bibliot. Eccles. tom. x. p. 135. [George Acropolites was the chief ambassador of Michael.]

this pious work, the Byzantine deputies were speedily followed by the pope's nuncios; and their instruction discloses the policy of the Vatican, which could not be satisfied with the vain title of supremacy. After viewing the temper of the prince and people, they were enjoined to absolve the schismatic clergy who should subscribe and swear their abjuration and obedience; to establish in all the churches the use of the perfect creed; to prepare the entrance of a cardinal legate, with the full powers and dignity of his office; and to instruct the emperor in the advantages which he might derive from the temporal protection of the Roman pontiff.[42]

But they found a country without a friend, a nation in which the names of Rome and Union were pronounced with abhorrence. The patriarch Joseph was indeed removed; his place was filled by Veccus,[43] an ecclesiastic of learning and moderation; and the emperor was still urged by the same motives, to persevere in the same professions. But, in his private language, Palæologus affected to deplore the pride, and to blame the innovations, of the Latins; and, while he debased his character by this double hypocrisy, he justified and punished the opposition of his subjects. By the joint suffrage of the new and the ancient Rome, a sentence of excommunication was pronounced against the obstinate schismatics : the censures of the church were executed by the sword of Michael; on the failure of persuasion, he tried the arguments of prison and exile, of whipping and mutilation: those touchstones, says an historian, of cowards and the brave. Two Greeks still reigned in Ætolia, Epirus, and Thessaly, with the appellation of despots; they had yielded to the sovereign of Constantinople; but they rejected the chains of the Roman pontiff, and supported their refusal by successful arms. Under their protection, the fugitive monks and bishops assembled in hostile synods, and retorted the name of heretic with the galling addition of apostate; the prince of Trebizond was tempted to

His persecution of the Greeks. A.D. 1277-1282

---

[42] This curious instruction, which has been drawn with more or less honesty by Wading and Leo Allatius from the archives of the Vatican, is given in an abstract or version by Fleury (tom. xviii. p. 252-258).

[43] [Johannes Veccus (Patriarch, 1275) was the chief theologian who supported the Union. His work, On the Union and Peace of the Churches of Old and New Rome, and others on the same subject, were published in the Græcia Orthodoxa of Leo Allatius (vol. i., 1652) and will be found in Migne, P. G. vol. 141. His most formidable controversial opponent, Gregory of Cyprus (for whose works see Migne, vol. 142), became Patriarch in 1283.]

assume the forfeit title of emperor; and even the Latins of Negropont, Thebes, Athens, and the Morea forgot the merits of the convert, to join, with open or clandestine aid, the enemies of Palæologus. His favourite generals, of his own blood and family, successively deserted or betrayed the sacrilegious trust. His sister Eulogia, a niece, and two female cousins, conspired against him; another niece, Mary queen of Bulgaria, negotiated his ruin with the sultan of Egypt; and in the public eye their treason was consecrated as the most sublime virtue.[44]   To the pope's nuncios, who urged the consummation of the work, Palæologus exposed a naked recital of all that he had done and suffered for their sake. They were assured that the guilty sectaries, of both sexes and every rank, had been deprived of their honours, their fortunes, and their liberty: a spreading list of confiscation and punishment, which involved many persons, the dearest to the emperor, or the best deserving of his favour. They were conducted to the prison, to behold four princes of the royal blood chained in the four corners, and shaking their fetters in an agony of grief and rage. Two of these captives were afterwards released, the one by submission, the other by death; but the obstinacy of their two companions was chastised by the loss of their eyes; and the Greeks, the least adverse to the union, deplore that cruel and inauspicious tragedy.[45]   Persecutors must expect the hatred of those whom they oppress; but they commonly find some consolation in the testimony of their conscience, the applause of their party, and, perhaps, the success of their undertaking. But the hypocrisy of Michael, which was prompted only by political motives, must have forced him to hate himself, to despise his followers, and to esteem and envy the rebel champions, by whom he was detested and despised.[46]   While his violence was abhorred at

---

[44] This frank and authentic confession of Michael's distress is exhibited in barbarous Latin by Ogerius, who signs himself Protonotarius Interpretum, and transcribed by Wading from the Mss. of the Vatican (A.D. 1278, No. 3). His Annals of the Franciscan order, the Fratres Minores, in xvii volumes in folio (Rome, 1741), I have now accidentally seen among the waste paper of a bookseller.

[45] See the vith book of Pachymer, particularly the chapters 1, 11, 16, 18, 24-27. He is the more credible, as he speaks of this persecution with less anger than sorrow.

[46] [Finlay shows no mercy to Michael. "He was a type of the empire he reestablished and transmitted to his descendants. He was selfish, hypocritical, able and accomplished, an inborn liar, vain, meddling, ambitious, cruel and rapacious. He has gained renown in history as the restorer of the Eastern Empire; he ought

Constantinople, at Rome his slowness was arraigned and his sincerity suspected; till at length pope Martin the Fourth [A.D. 1280] excluded the Greek emperor from the pale of a church into which he was striving to reduce a schismatic people.   No sooner had the tyrant expired than the union was dissolved and ab- The union jured by unanimous consent; the churches were purified; the A.D. 1283 penitents were reconciled; and his son Andronicus, after weeping the sins and errors of his youth, most piously denied his father the burial of a prince and a Christian.[47]

II. In the distress of the Latins, the walls and towers of Charles of Constantinople had fallen to decay; they were restored and dues fortified by the policy of Michael, who deposited a plenteous Sicily. A.D. store of corn and salt provisions, to sustain the siege which he 26 might hourly expect from the resentment of the Western powers. Of these, the sovereign of the Two Sicilies was the most formidable neighbour; but, as long as they were possessed by Mainfroy, the bastard of Frederic the Second, his monarchy [Manfred] was the bulwark rather than the annoyance of the Eastern empire.   The usurper, though a brave and active prince, was sufficiently employed in the defence of his throne; his proscription by successive popes had separated Mainfroy from the common cause of the Latins; and the forces that might have besieged Constantinople were detained in a crusade against the domestic enemy of Rome.   The prize of her avenger, the crown of the Two Sicilies, was won and worn by the brother of St. Louis, by Charles, count of Anjou and Provence, who led the chivalry of France on this holy expedition.[48]   The disaffection of his Christian subjects compelled Mainfroy to enlist a colony of Saracens, whom his father had planted in Apulia; and this

to be execrated as the corrupter of the Greek race, for his reign affords a signal example of the extent to which a nation may be degraded by the misconduct of its sovereign when he is entrusted with despotic power " (vol. 3, p. 372).]

[47] Pachymer, l. vii. c. 1-11, 17.   The speech of Andronicus the Elder (lib. xii. c. 2) is a curious record, which proves that, if the Greeks were the slaves of the emperor, the emperor was not less the slave of superstition and the clergy.

[48] The best accounts, the nearest the time, the most full and entertaining, of the conquest of Naples by Charles of Anjou, may be found in the Florentine Chronicles of Ricordano Malespina [leg. Malespini] (c. 175-193) and Giovanni Villani (l. vii. c. 1-10, 25-30), which are published by Muratori in the viiith and xiiith volumes of the historians of Italy.   In his Annals (tom. xi. p. 56-72), he has abridged these great events, which are likewise described in the Istoria Civile of Giannone (tom. ii. l. xix. ; tom. iii. l. xx.).   [The chronicle attributed to Malespini has been proved not to be original but to depend on Villani.   See Scheffer-Boichorst, in Sybels Historische Zeitschrift, 24, p. 274 sqq. (1870).]

odious succour will explain the defiance of the Catholic hero,
who rejected all terms of accommodation: "Bear this message,"
said Charles, "to the sultan of Nocera, that God and the sword
are umpire between us; and that he shall either send me to
paradise, or I will send him to the pit of hell". The armies
met, and, though I am ignorant of Mainfroy's doom in the other
world, in this he lost his friends, his kingdom, and his life, in
the bloody battle of Benevento. Naples and Sicily were immediately peopled with a warlike race of French nobles; and
their aspiring leader embraced the future conquest of Africa,
Greece, and Palestine. The most specious reasons might point
his first arms against the Byzantine empire; and Palæologus,
diffident of his own strength, repeatedly appealed from the ambition of Charles to the humanity of St. Louis, who still preserved a just ascendant over the mind of his ferocious brother.
For a while the attention of that brother was confined at home
by the invasion of Conradin, the last heir of the Imperial house
of Swabia; but the hapless boy sunk in the unequal conflict;
and his execution on a public scaffold taught the rivals of Charles
to tremble for their heads as well as their dominions. A second
respite was obtained by the last crusade of St. Louis to the
African coast; and the double motive of interest and duty
urged the king of Naples to assist, with his powers and his
presence, the holy enterprise. The death of St. Louis released
him from the importunity of a virtuous censor; the king of
Tunis confessed himself the tributary and vassal of the crown
of Sicily; and the boldest of the French knights were free to
enlist under his banner against the Greek empire. A treaty
and a marriage united his interest with the house of Courtenay;
his daughter, Beatrice, was promised to Philip, son and heir of
the emperor Baldwin; a pension of six hundred ounces of gold
was allowed for his maintenance; and his generous father distributed among his allies the kingdoms and provinces of the
East, reserving only Constantinople, and one day's journey
round the city, for the Imperial domain.[49] In this perilous
moment, Palæologus was the most eager to subscribe the creed,
and implore the protection, of the Roman pontiff, who assumed,
with propriety and weight, the character of an angel of peace,

Threatens the Greek empire. A.D. 1270, &c.

---

[49] Ducange, Hist. de C. P. l. v. c. 49-56, l. vi. c. 1-13. See Pachymer, l. iv. c.
29, l. v. c. 7-10, 25, l. vi. c. 30, 32, 33, and Nicephorus Gregoras, l. iv. 5, l. v. 1, 6.

the common father of the Christians. By his voice the sword of Charles was chained in the scabbard ; and the Greek ambassadors beheld him, in the pope's antichamber, biting his ivory sceptre in a transport of fury, and deeply resenting the refusal to enfranchise and consecrate his arms. He appears to have respected the disinterested mediation of Gregory the Tenth ; but Charles was insensibly disgusted by the pride and partiality of Nicholas the Third ; and his attachment to his kindred, the Ursini family, alienated the most strenuous champion from the service of the church. The hostile league against the Greeks, of Philip the Latin emperor, the king of the Two Sicilies, and the republic of Venice, was ripened into execution ; and the election of Martin the Fourth, a French pope, gave a sanction [A.D. 1280] to the cause. Of the allies, Philip supplied his name, Martin, a bull of excommunication, the Venetians, a squadron of forty galleys ; and the formidable powers of Charles consisted of forty counts, ten thousand men at arms, a numerous body of infantry, and a fleet of more than three hundred ships and transports. A distant day was appointed for assembling this mighty force in the harbour of Brindisi; and a previous attempt was risked with a detachment of three hundred knights, who invaded Albania and besieged the fortress of Belgrade. Their defeat might amuse with a triumph the vanity of Constantinople; but the more sagacious Michael, despairing of his arms, depended on the effects of a conspiracy; on the secret workings of a rat, who gnawed the bow-string [50] of the Sicilian tyrant.

Among the proscribed adherents of the house of Swabia, Palæologus instigates the revolt of Sicily. A.D. 1280 John of Procida forfeited a small island of that name in the bay of Naples. His birth was noble, but his education was learned ; and, in the poverty of exile, he was relieved by the practice of physic, which he had studied in the school of Salerno. Fortune had left him nothing to lose except life ; and to despise life is the first qualification of a rebel. Procida was endowed with the art of negotiation, to enforce his reasons and disguise his motives ; and, in his various transactions with nations and men, he could persuade each party that he laboured solely for *their* interest. The new kingdoms of Charles were

---

[50] The reader of Herodotus will recollect how miraculously the Assyrian host of Sennacherib was disarmed and destroyed (l. ii. c. 141).

afflicted by every species of fiscal and military oppression;[51] and
the lives and fortunes of his Italian subjects were sacrificed to
the greatness of their master and the licentiousness of his followers.   The hatred of Naples was repressed by his presence;
but the looser government of his vicegerents excited the contempt, as well as the aversion, of the Sicilians; the island was
roused to a sense of freedom by the eloquence of Procida; and
he displayed to every baron his private interest in the common
cause.   In the confidence of foreign aid, he successively visited
[Peter III.] the courts of the Greek emperor and of Peter, king of Arragon,[52] who possessed the maritime countries of Valentia and
Catalonia.   To the ambitious Peter a crown was presented,
[leg. which he might justly claim by his marriage with the sister of
daughter] Mainfroy, and by the dying voice of Conradin, who from the
scaffold had cast a ring to his heir and avenger.   Palæologus
was easily persuaded to divert his enemy from a foreign war by
a rebellion at home; and a Greek subsidy of twenty-five thousand ounces of gold was most profitably applied to arm a Catalan fleet, which sailed under an holy banner to the specious
attack of the Saracens of Africa.   In the disguise of a monk
or beggar, the indefatigable missionary of revolt flew from Constantinople to Rome, and from Sicily to Saragossa; the treaty
was sealed with the signet of pope Nicholas himself, the enemy
of Charles; and his deed of gift transferred the fiefs of St.
Peter from the house of Anjou to that of Arragon.   So widely
diffused and so freely circulated, the secret was preserved above
two years with impenetrable discretion; and each of the conspirators imbibed the maxim of Peter, who declared that he
would cut off his left hand, if it were conscious of the intentions
of his right.   The mine was prepared with deep and dangerous
artifice; but it may be questioned whether the instant explosion of Palermo were the effect of accident or design.

On the vigil of Easter, a procession of the disarmed citizens
visited a church without the walls; and a noble damsel was

---

[51] According to Sabas Malaspina (Hist. Sicula, l. iii. c. 16, in Muratori, tom.
viii. p. 832), a zealous Guelph, the subjects of Charles, who had reviled Mainfroy
as a wolf, began to regret him as a lamb; and he justifies their discontent by the
oppressions of the French government (l. vi. c. 2, 7).   See the Sicilian manifesto
in Nicholas Specialis (l. i. c. 11, in Muratori, tom. x. p. 930).

[52] See the character and counsels of Peter of Arragon, in Mariana (Hist. Hispan.
l. xiv. c. 6, tom. ii. p. 133).   The reader forgives the Jesuit's defects, in favour
always of his style, and often of his sense.

rudely insulted by a French soldier.[53] The ravisher was instantly punished with death; and, if the people was at first scattered by a military force, their numbers and fury prevailed: the conspirators seized the opportunity; the flame spread over the island; and eight thousand French were exterminated in a promiscuous massacre, which has obtained the name of the Sicilian Vespers.[54] From every city the banners of freedom and the church were displayed; the revolt was inspired by the presence or the soul of Procida; and Peter of Arragon, who sailed from the African coast to Palermo, was saluted as the king and saviour of the isle. By the rebellion of a people on whom he had so long trampled with impunity, Charles was astonished and confounded; and in the first agony of grief and devotion he was heard to exclaim, "O God! if thou hast decreed to humble me, grant me at least a gentle and gradual descent from the pinnacle of greatness". His fleet and army, which already filled the sea-ports of Italy, were hastily recalled from the service of the Grecian war; and the situation of Messina exposed that town to the first storm of his revenge. Feeble in themselves, and yet hopeless of foreign succour, the citizens would have repented and submitted, on the assurance of full pardon and their ancient privileges. But the pride of the monarch was already rekindled; and the most fervent intreaties of the legate could extort no more than a promise, that he would forgive the remainder, after a chosen list of eight hundred rebels had been yielded to his discretion. The despair of the Messinese renewed their courage; Peter of Arragon approached to their relief;[55] and his rival was driven back

The Sicilian Vespers. A.D. 1282, March 30

---

[53] After enumerating the sufferings of his country, Nicholas Specialis adds, in the true spirit of Italian jealousy, Quæ omnia et graviora quidem, ut arbitror, patienti animo Siculi tolerassent, nisi (quod primum cunctis dominantibus cavendum est) alienas fœminas invasissent (l. i. c. 2, p. 924).

[54] The French were long taught to remember this bloody lesson: "If I am provoked," said Henry the Fourth, "I will breakfast at Milan, and dine at Naples". "Your Majesty," replied the Spanish ambassador, "may perhaps arrive in Sicily for vespers."

[55] This revolt, with the subsequent victory, are related by two national writers, Bartholemy a Neocastro (in Muratori, tom. xiii. [and in Del Re, Cronisti e scrittori, vol. 2]) and Nicholas Specialis (in Muratori, tom. x.), the one a contemporary, the other of the next century. The patriot Specialis disclaims the name of rebellion and all previous correspondence with Peter of Arragon (nullo communicato consilio), who *happened* to be with a fleet and army on the African coast (l. i. c. 4, 9). [For the Sicilian vespers and the sequel, see also the contemporary chronicle of Bernard d'Esclot (an obscure figure), which is published by Buchon in his Chroniques

by the failure of provision, and the terrors of the equinox, to the Calabrian shore.   At the same moment, the Catalan admiral, the famous Roger de Loria, swept the channel with an invincible squadron: the French fleet, more numerous in transports than in galleys, was either burnt or destroyed; and the same blow assured the independence of Sicily and the safety of the Greek empire.   A few days before his death, the emperor Michael rejoiced in the fall of an enemy whom he hated and esteemed; and perhaps he might be content with the popular judgment that, had they not been matched with each other, Constantinople and Italy must speedily have obeyed the same master.[56]   From this disastrous moment, the life of Charles was a series of misfortunes; his capital was insulted, his son was made prisoner, and he sunk into the grave without recovering the isle of Sicily, which, after a war of twenty years, was finally severed from the throne of Naples, and transferred, as an independent kingdom, to a younger branch of the house of Arragon.[57]

Defeat of Charles. Oct. 2

I shall not, I trust, be accused of superstition; but I must remark that, even in this world, the natural order of events will sometimes afford the strong appearances of moral retribution.   The first Palæologus had saved his empire by involving the kingdoms of the West in rebellion and blood; and from these seeds of discord uprose a generation of iron men, who assaulted and endangered the empire of his son.   In modern times our debts and taxes are the secret poison, which still corrodes the bosom of peace; but in the weak and disorderly government of the middle ages it was agitated by the present evil of the disbanded armies.   Too idle to work, too proud to beg, the mercenaries were accustomed to a life of rapine: they could rob with more dignity and effect under a banner and a chief; and the sovereign, to whom their service was useless and their presence importunate, endeavoured to discharge the torrent on some neighbouring countries.   After the peace

The service and war of the Cata- lans in the Greek em- pire. A.D. 1303-1307

Etrangères (1860), c. 81 *sqq.*; and also an anonymous contemporary relation of the conspiracy of John Prochyta, in the Sicilian idiom; of which Buchon (*ib.* p. 736 *sqq.*) has given a French translation.]

[56] Nicephorus Gregoras (l. v. c. 6) admires the wisdom of Providence in this equal balance of states and princes.   For the honour of Palæologus, I had rather this balance had been observed by an Italian writer.

[57] See the Chronicle of Villani, the xith volume of the Annali d'Italia of Mura- tori, and the xxth and xxist books of the Istoria Civile of Giannone.

of Sicily, many thousands of Genoese, *Catalans*,[58] &c., who
had fought, by sea and land, under the standard of Anjou or
Arragon, were blended into one nation by the resemblance of
their manners and interest.   They heard that the Greek provinces of Asia were invaded by the Turks: they resolved to
share the harvest of pay and plunder; and Frederic, king of
Sicily, most liberally contributed the means of their departure.
In a warfare of twenty years, a ship, or a camp, was become
their country; arms were their sole profession and property;
valour was the only virtue which they knew; their women had
imbibed the fearless temper of their lovers and husbands; it
was reported that, with a stroke of their broad sword, the
Catalans could cleave a horseman and an horse; and the report
itself was a powerful weapon.   Roger de Flor was the most
popular of their chiefs; and his personal merit overshadowed
the dignity of his prouder rivals of Arragon.   The offspring of
a marriage between a German gentleman[59] of the court of
Frederic the Second and a damsel of Brindisi, Roger was successively a templar, an apostate, a pirate, and at length the
richest and most powerful admiral of the Mediterranean.   He
sailed from Messina to Constantinople, with eighteen galleys,
four great ships, and eight thousand adventurers; and his previous treaty was faithfully accomplished by Andronicus the
Elder, who accepted with joy and terror this formidable succour.[60]   A palace was allotted for his reception, and a niece of
the emperor was given in marriage to the valiant stranger, [Sept. 1303]
who was immediately created Great Duke or Admiral of Ro- [Megaduc]
mania.   After a decent repose, he transported his troops over
to Propontis, and boldly led them against the Turks; in two
bloody battles thirty thousand of the Moslems were slain;

[58] In this motley multitude, the Catalans and Spaniards, the bravest of the
soldiery, were styled by themselves and the Greeks *Amogavares* [Al-mugavari =
scouts].   Moncada derives their origin from the Goths, and Pachymer (l. xi. c.
22) from the Arabs ; and, in spite of national and religious pride, I am afraid the
latter is in the right.

[59] [A falconer (Ramon Muntaner, c. 194).   His name was Richard Blum.   It
was translated by an Italian equivalent.   See Buchon's note.]

[60] [Before he went himself, Roger sent envoys to make the terms.   The Emperor's niece, whom he married, was daughter of the Bulgarian Tsar, John Asēn
IV. (whom Muntaner calls the emperador Lantzaura, c. 199).   As to the numbers
of the expedition Muntaner says (c. 201) that there were about 36 sail; 1500
horsemen ; 4000 almogavars ; 1000 foot-soldiers; as well as the oarsmen and
sailors.]

he raised the siege of Philadelphia, and deserved the name of the deliverer of Asia. But, after a short season of prosperity, the cloud of slavery and ruin again burst on that unhappy province. The inhabitants escaped (says a Greek historian) from the smoke into the flames; and the hostility of the Turks was less pernicious than the friendship of the Catalans. The lives and fortunes which they had rescued, they considered as their own; the willing or reluctant maid was saved from the race of circumcision for the embraces of a Christian soldier; the exaction of fines and supplies was enforced by licentious rapine and arbitrary executions; and, on the resistance of Magnesia, the Great Duke besieged a city of the Roman empire.[61] These disorders he excused by the wrongs and passions of a victorious army; nor would his own authority or person have been safe, had he dared to punish his faithful followers, who were defrauded of the just and convenanted price of their services. The threats and complaints of Andronicus disclosed the nakedness of the empire. His golden bull had invited no more than five hundred horse and a thousand foot soldiers; yet the crowd of volunteers, who migrated to the East, had been enlisted and fed by his spontaneous bounty. While his bravest allies were content with three Byzants, or pieces of gold, for their monthly pay, an ounce or even two ounces of gold were assigned to the Catalans, whose annual pension would thus amount to near an hundred pounds sterling; one of their chiefs had modestly rated at three hundred thousand crowns the value of his *future* merits; and above a million had been issued from the treasury for the maintenance of these costly mercenaries. A cruel tax had been imposed on the corn of the husbandman: one third was retrenched from the salaries of the public officers; and the standard of the coin was so shamefully debased that of the four-and-twenty parts only five were of pure gold.[62] At the summons of the emperor, Roger evacuated a

---

[61] Some idea may be formed of the population of these cities, from the 36,000 inhabitants of Tralles, which, in the preceding reign, was rebuilt by the emperor, and ruined by the Turks (Pachymer, l. vi. c. 20, 21).

[62] I have collected these pecuniary circumstances from Pachymer (l. xi. c. 21; l. xii. c. 4, 5, 8, 14, 19), who describes the progressive degradation of the gold coin. Even in the prosperous times of John Ducas Vataces, the byzants were composed in equal proportions of the pure and the baser metal. The poverty of Michael Palæologus compelled him to strike a new coin, with nine parts, or carats, of gold, and fifteen of copper alloy. After his death the standard rose to ten carats, till in

province which no longer supplied the materials of rapine; but
he refused to disperse his troops; and, while his style was respectful, his conduct was independent and hostile. He protested that, if the emperor should march against him, he would
advance forty paces to kiss the ground before him; but, in
rising from this prostrate attitude, Roger had a life and sword
at the service of his friends. The Great Duke of Romania
condescended to accept the title and ornaments of Cæsar; but
he rejected the new proposal of the government of Asia, with
a subsidy of corn and money, on condition that he should reduce his troops to the harmless number of three thousand men.
Assassination is the last resource of cowards. The Cæsar was
tempted to visit the royal residence of Hadrianople: in the apartment, and before the eyes, of the empress, he was stabbed by [March 28,
the Alani [62a] guards; [63] and, though the deed was imputed to their A.D. 1305]
private revenge, his countrymen, who dwelt at Constantinople
in the security of peace, were involved in the same proscription
by the prince or people. The loss of their leader intimidated
the crowd of adventurers, who hoisted the sails of flight, and
were soon scattered round the coasts of the Mediterranean. But
a veteran band of fifteen hundred Catalans or French stood firm
in the strong fortress of Gallipoli on the Hellespont, displayed
the banners of Arragon, and offered to revenge and justify their
chief by an equal combat of ten or an hundred warriors. Instead of accepting this bold defiance, the emperor Michael, the
son and colleague of Andronicus, resolved to oppress them with
the weight of multitudes: every nerve was strained to form an
army of thirteen thousand horse and thirty thousand foot; and
the Propontis was covered with the ships of the Greeks and
Genoese. In two battles by sea and land, these mighty forces
were encountered and overthrown by the despair and discipline
of the Catalans; the young emperor fled to the palace; and an

---

the public distress it was reduced to the moiety. The Prince was relieved for a
moment, while credit and commerce were for ever blasted. In France, the gold
coin is of twenty-two carats (one-twelfth alloy), and the standard of England and
Holland is still higher.

[62a] [Is this a misprint for Alanic or Alan?]

[63] [Roger had crossed to Europe to help the Emperor Andronicus against the
Bulgarians. Before returning he wished to take leave of the young Emperor " Kyr
Michael " who was at Hadrianople, though it was known that Michael bore him a
grudge. Roger's wife and others tried to dissuade him, in vain (Muntaner, c.
213, 215).]

insufficient guard of light horse was left for the protection of the open country. Victory renewed the hopes and numbers of the adventurers: every nation was blended under the name and standard of the *great company*; and three thousand Turkish proselytes deserted from the Imperial service to join this military association. In the possession of Gallipoli,[64] the Catalans intercepted the trade of Constantinople and the Black Sea, while they spread their devastations on either side of the Hellespont over the confines of Europe and Asia. To prevent their approach, the greatest part of the Byzantine territory was laid waste by the Greeks themselves: the peasants and their cattle retired into the city; and myriads of sheep and oxen, for which neither place nor food could be procured, were unprofitably slaughtered on the same day. Four times the emperor Andronicus sued for peace, and four times he was inflexibly repulsed, till the want of provisions, and the discord of the chiefs, compelled the Catalans to evacuate the banks of the Hellespont and the neighbourhood of the capital. After their separation from the Turks, the remains of the great company pursued their march through Macedonia and Thessaly, to seek a new establishment in the heart of Greece.[65]

Revolutions of Athens. A.D. 1204-1456   After some ages of oblivion, Greece was awakened to new misfortunes by the arms of the Latins. In the two hundred and fifty years between the first and the last conquest of Constantinople, that venerable land was disputed by a multitude of petty tyrants; without the comforts of freedom and genius, her ancient cities were again plunged in foreign and intestine war; and, if servitude be preferable to anarchy, they might repose with joy under the Turkish yoke. I shall not pursue the obscure and various dynasties that rose and fell on the continent or in

---

[64] [Ramon Muntaner, the historian of the expedition, was for a long time captain of Gallipoli, and he describes (c. 225) the good time he had.]

[65] The Catalan war is most copiously related by Pachymer, in the xith, xiith, and xiiith books, till he breaks off in the year 1308. Nicephorus Gregoras (l. vii. 3-6) is more concise and complete. Ducange, who adopts these adventurers as French, has hunted their footsteps with his usual diligence (Hist. de C. P. l. vi. c. 22-46). He quotes an Arragonese history, which I have read with pleasure, and which the Spaniards extol as a model of style and composition (Expedicion de los Catalanes y Arragoneses contra Turcos y Griegos; Barcelona, 1623, in quarto; Madrid, 1777, in octavo). Don Francisco de Moncada, Conde de Osona, may imitate Cæsar or Sallust; he may transcribe the Greek or Italian contemporaries; but he never quotes his authorities, and I cannot discern any national records of the exploits of his countrymen. [See Appendix 1.]

the isles;[66] but our silence on the fate of ATHENS [67] would argue a strange ingratitude to the first and purest school of liberal science and amusement. In the partition of the empire, the principality of Athens and Thebes was assigned to Otho de la [A.D. 1205-1225] Roche, a noble warrior of Burgundy,[68] with the title of Great Duke,[69] which the Latins understood in their own sense, and the Greeks more foolishly derived from the age of Constantine.[70] Otho followed the standard of the marquis of Montferrat; the ample state, which he acquired by a miracle of conduct or fortune,[71] was peaceably inherited by his son and two grandsons,[72] till the family, though not the nation, was changed, by the marriage of an heiress, into the elder branch of the house of Brienne. The son of that marriage, Walter de Brienne, succeeded to the duchy [A.D. 1308] of Athens; and, with the aid of some Catalan mercenaries, whom he invested with fiefs, reduced above thirty castles of the vassal or neighbouring lords. But, when he was informed of the approach and ambition of the great company, he collected a force of seven hundred knights, six thousand four hundred horse, and

---

[66] [For a summary of the island dynasties see Appendix 18.]

[67] See the laborious history of Ducange, whose accurate table of the French dynasties recapitulates the thirty-five passages in which he mentions the dukes of Athens. [Gregorovius, Geschichte der Stadt Athen im Mittelalter, 1889; W. Miller, The Latins in the Levant, 1908.]

[68] He is twice mentioned by Villehardouin with honour (No. 151, 235); and under the first passage Ducange observes all that can be known of his person and family.

[69] From these Latin princes of the xivth century, Boccace, Chaucer, and Shakespeare have borrowed their Theseus *Duke* of Athens. [And Dante, Inferno, 12, 17.] An ignorant age transfers its own language and manners to the most distant times. [Otto de la Roche had not the ducal title. He called himself *sire* (not *grand sire*) or *dominus* Athenarum. The title is μέγας κύρ in the Chronicle of Morea. The ducal title was first assumed by Guy I. in 1260 with permission of Louis IX. of France. Megara went along with Athens as a *pertinence* (cum pertinentia Megaron, in the Act of Partition).]

[70] The same Constantine gave to Sicily a king, to Russia the *magnus dapifer* of the empire, to Thebes the *primicerius*: and these absurd fables are properly lashed by Ducange (ad Nicephor. Greg. l. vii. c. 5). By the Latins, the lord of Thebes was styled, by corruption, the Megas Kurios, or Grand Sire! [See last note. He took his title from Athens, not from Thebes.]

[71] *Quodam miraculo*, says Alberic. He was probably received by Michael Choniates, the archbishop who had defended Athens against the tyrant Leo Sgurus [A.D. 1204] (Nicetas in Baldwino [p. 805, ed. Bonn]). Michael was the brother of the historian Nicetas; and his encomium of Athens is still extant in Ms. in the Bodleian Library (Fabric. Bibliot. Græc. tom. vi. p. 405). [See above, p. 436, note 15. It is supposed that Archbishop Akominatos made conditions of surrender with Boniface. The Western soldiers sacrilegiously pillaged the Parthenon church. Akominatos left Athens after its occupation by De la Roche.]

[72] [This should be: nephew, two grand-nephews, and a great-grand-nephew, Guy II. A.D. 1287-1308. Guy II.'s aunt Isabella had married Hugh de Brienne; Walter de Brienne was their son.]

[Battle of
the Cephi-
sus or
Orcho-
menos.
A.D. 1310,
March] eight thousand foot, and boldly met them on the banks of the river Cephisus in Bœotia.[73] The Catalans amounted to no more than three thousand five hundred horse and four thousand foot; but the deficiency of numbers was compensated by stratagem and order.   They formed round their camp an artificial inundation: the duke and his knights advanced without fear or precaution on the verdant meadow; their horses plunged into the bog; and he was cut in pieces, with the greatest part of the French cavalry.   His family and nation were expelled; and his son, Walter de Brienne, the titular duke of Athens, the tyrant of Florence, and the constable of France, lost his life in the field of Poitiers.   Attica and Bœotia were the rewards of the victorious Catalans; they married the widows and daughters of the

[A.D. 1311-
1326] slain; and during fourteen years the great company was the terror of the Grecian states.   Their factions drove them to acknowledge the sovereignty of the house of Arragon;[74] and, during the remainder of the fourteenth century, Athens, as a government or an appanage, was successively bestowed by the kings of Sicily.   After the French and Catalans, the third

[A.D. 1386] dynasty was that of the Accaioli, a family, plebeian at Florence, potent at Naples, and sovereign in Greece.   Athens, which they embellished with new buildings, became the capital of a state that extended over Thebes, Argos, Corinth, Delphi, and a part

[A.D. 1456] of Thessaly; and their reign was finally determined by Mahomet the Second, who strangled the last duke, and educated his sons in the discipline and religion of the seraglio.[75]

Present
state of
Athens Athens,[76] though no more than the shadow of her former self, still contains about eight or ten thousand inhabitants: of these, three-fourths are Greeks in religion and language; and the Turks, who compose the remainder, have relaxed, in their intercourse with the citizens, somewhat of the pride and gravity

[73] [See Ramon Muntaner, chap. 240.]
[74] [They also held Neopatras in Thessaly; their title was Duke of Athens and Neopatras; and the kings of Spain retained the title.]
[75] [For the Acciajoli see Appendix 17.]
[76] The modern account of Athens, and the Athenians, is extracted from Spon (Voyage en Grèce, tom. ii. p. 79-199) and Wheler (Travels into Greece, p. 337-414), Stuart (Antiquities of Athens, *passim*), and Chandler (Travels into Greece, p. 23-172). The first of these travellers visited Greece in the year 1676, the last 1765; and ninety years had not produced much difference in the tranquil scene. [At the end of the 12th century Michael Akominatos deplores the decline of Athens (for his dirge see above, p. 436, note 14). He says that he has become a barbarian by living so long in Athens (ed. Lampros, vol. 2, p. 44).]

of their national character. The olive-tree, the gift of Minerva, flourishes in Attica; nor has the honey of Mount Hymettus lost any part of its exquisite flavour;[77] but the languid trade is monopolized by strangers; and the agriculture of a barren land is abandoned to the vagrant Walachians. The Athenians are still distinguished by the subtlety and acuteness of their understandings; but these qualities, unless ennobled by freedom and enlightened by study, will degenerate into a low and selfish cunning; and it is a proverbial saying of the country, " From the Jews of Thessalonica, the Turks of Negropont, and the Greeks of Athens, good Lord, deliver us! " This artful people has eluded the tyranny of the Turkish bashaws by an expedient which alleviates their servitude and aggravates their shame. About the middle of the last century, the Athenians chose for their protector the Kislar Aga, or chief black eunuch of the seraglio. This Æthiopian slave, who possesses the Sultan's ear, condescends to accept the tribute of thirty thousand crowns; his lieutenant, the Waywode, whom he annually confirms, may reserve for his own about five or six thousand more; and such is the policy of the citizens that they seldom fail to remove and punish an oppressive governor. Their private differences are decided by the archbishop, one of the richest prelates of the Greek church, since he possesses a revenue of one thousand pounds sterling; and by a tribunal of the eight *geronti* or elders, chosen in the eight quarters of the city. The noble families cannot trace their pedigree above three hundred years; but their principal members are distinguished by a grave demeanour, a fur cap, and the lofty appellation of *archon*. By some, who delight in the contrast, the modern language of Athens is represented as the most corrupt and barbarous of the seventy dialects of the vulgar Greek:[78] this picture is too darkly coloured; but it would not be easy, in the country of Plato and Demosthenes, to find a reader, or a copy, of their works. The

---

[77] The ancients, or at least the Athenians, believed that all the bees in the world had been propagated from Mount Hymettus. They taught that health might be preserved, and life prolonged, by the external use of oil and the internal use of honey (Geoponica, l. xv. c. 7, p. 1089-1094, edit. Niclas).

[78] Ducange, Glossar. Græc. Præfat. p. 8, who quotes for his author Theodosius Zygomalas, a modern grammarian [of the 16th cent.]. Yet Spon (tom. ii. p. 194), and Wheler (p. 355), no incompetent judges, entertain a more favourable opinion of the Attic dialect.

Athenians walk with supine indifference among the glorious ruins of antiquity; and such is the debasement of their character that they are incapable of admiring the genius of their predecessors.[79]

[79] Yet we must not accuse them of corrupting the name of Athens, which they still call Athini.   From the εἰς τὴν 'Αθήνην we have formed our own barbarism of *Setines*.   [*Setines* comes from (στὰ)ς 'Αθήνας.]

BYZANTINE HOUSES AT MISTRA, PROBABLY 14TH CENTURY

CHAPTER LXIII

Civil Wars, and Ruin of the Greek Empire — Reigns of Andronicus, the Elder and Younger, and John Palæologus—Regency, Revolt, Reign, and Abdication, of John Cantacuzene—Establishment of a Genoese Colony at Pera or Galata—Their Wars with the Empire and City of Constantinople

THE long reign of Andronicus[1] the Elder is chiefly memorable by the disputes of the Greek church, the invasion of the Catalans, and the rise of the Ottoman power. He is celebrated as the most learned and virtuous prince of the age; but such virtue and such learning contributed neither to the perfection of the individual nor to the happiness of society. A slave of the most abject superstition, he was surrounded on all sides by visible and invisible enemies; nor were the flames of hell less dreadful to his fancy than those of a Catalan or Turkish war. Under the reign of the Palæologi, the choice of the patriarch was the most important business of the state; the heads of the Greek church were ambitious and fanatic monks; and their vices or virtues, their learning or ignorance, were equally mischievous or contemptible. By his intemperate discipline, the patriarch Athanasius[2] excited the hatred of the clergy and people: he was heard to declare that the sinner should swallow the last dregs of the cup of penance; and the foolish tale was propagated of his punishing a sacrilegious ass that had tasted the lettuce of a convent-garden. Driven from [A.D. 1294] the throne by the universal clamour, Athanasius composed, before

Supersti-tion of An-dronicus and the times. A.D. 1282-1320

---

[1] Andronicus himself will justify our freedom in the invective (Nicephorus Gregoras, l. i. c. 1) which he pronounced against historic falsehood. It is true that his censure is more pointedly urged against calumny than against adulation.

[2] For the anathema in the pigeon's nest, see Pachymer (l. ix. c. 24), who relates the general history of Athanasius (l. viii. c. 13-16, 20-24; l. x. c. 27-29, 31-36; l. xi. c. 1-3, 5, 6; l. xiii. c. 8, 10, 23, 35), and is followed by Nicephorus Gregoras (l. vi. c. 5, 7; l. vii. c. 1, 9), who includes the second retreat of this second Chrysostom.

his retreat, two papers of a very opposite cast. His public testament was in the tone of charity and resignation; the private codicil breathed the direst anathemas against the authors of his disgrace, whom he excluded for ever from the communion of the Holy Trinity, the angels, and the saints. This last paper he enclosed in an earthen pot, which was placed, by his order, on the top of one of the pillars in the dome of St. Sophia, in the distant hope of discovery and revenge. At the end of four years, some youths, climbing by a ladder in search of pigeons' nests, detected the fatal secret; and, as Andronicus felt himself touched and bound by the excommunication, he trembled on the brink of the abyss which had been so treacherously dug under his feet. A synod of bishops was instantly convened to debate this important question; the rashness of these clandestine anathemas was generally condemned; but, as the knot could be untied only by the same hand, as that hand was now deprived of the crosier, it appeared that this posthumous decree was irrevocable by any earthly power. Some faint testimonies of repentance and pardon were extorted from the author of the mischief; but the conscience of the emperor was still wounded, and he desired, with no less ardour than Athanasius himself, the restoration of a patriarch by whom alone he could be healed. At the dead of night a monk rudely knocked at the door of the royal bed-chamber, announcing a revelation of plague and famine, of inundations and earthquakes. Andronicus started from his bed, and spent the night in prayer, till he felt, or thought that he felt, a slight motion of the earth. The emperor, on foot, led the bishops and monks to the cell of Athanasius; and, after a proper resistance, the saint, from whom this message had been sent, consented to absolve the prince and [A.D. 1309] govern the church of Constantinople. Untamed by disgrace and hardened by solitude, the shepherd was again odious to the flock; and his enemies contrived a singular and, as it proved, a successful mode of revenge. In the night they stole away the foot-stool or foot-cloth of his throne, which they secretly replaced with the decoration of a satirical picture. The emperor was painted with a bridle in his mouth, and Athanasius leading the tractable beast to the feet of Christ. The authors of the libel were detected and punished; but, as their lives had [A.D. 1311] been spared, the Christian priest in sullen indignation retired to his cell; and the eyes of Andronicus, which had been opened for a moment, were again closed by his successor.

If this transaction be one of the most curious and important of a reign of fifty years, I cannot at least accuse the brevity of my materials, since I reduce into some few pages the enormous folios of Pachymer,[3] Cantacuzene,[4] and Nicephorus Gregoras,[5] who have composed the prolix and languid story of the times. The name and situation of the emperor John Cantacuzene might inspire the most lively curiosity. His memorials of forty years extend from the revolt of the younger Andronicus to his own abdication of the empire; and it is observed that, like Moses and Cæsar, he was the principal actor in the scenes which he describes. But in this eloquent work we should vainly seek the sincerity of an hero or a penitent. Retired in a cloister from the vices and passions of the world, he presents not a confession, but an apology, of the life of an ambitious statesman. Instead of unfolding the true counsels and characters of men, he displays the smooth and specious surface of events, highly varnished with his own praises and those of his friends. Their motives are always pure; their ends always legitimate; they conspire and rebel without any views of interest; and the violence which they inflict or suffer is celebrated as a spontaneous effect of reason and virtue.

After the example of the first of the Palæologi, the elder Andronicus associated his son Michael to the honours of the purple; and, from the age of eighteen to his premature death, that prince was acknowledged, above twenty-five years, as the second emperor of the Greeks.[6] At the head of an army, he

First disputes between the elder and younger Andronicus. A.D. 1320

---

[3] Pachymer, in seven books, 377 folio pages, describes the first twenty-six years of Andronicus the Elder; and marks the date of his composition by the current news or lie of the day (A.D. 1308). Either death or disgust prevented him from resuming the pen.

[4] After an interval of twelve years from the conclusion of Pachymer, Cantacuzenus takes up the pen; and his first book (c. 1-59, p. 9-150) relates the civil war and the eight last years of the elder Andronicus. The ingenious comparison of Moses and Cæsar is fancied by his French translator, the president Cousin.

[5] Nicephorus Gregoras more briefly includes the entire life and reign of Andronicus the Elder (l. vi. c. i.; l. x. c. 1, p. 96-291). This is the part of which Cantacuzene complains as a false and malicious representation of his conduct.

[6] He was crowned May 21, 1295, and died October 12, 1320 (Ducange, Fam. Byz. p. 239). His brother, Theodore, by a second marriage, inherited the marquisate of Montferrat, apostatized to the religion and manners of the Latins (ὅτι καὶ γνώμῃ καὶ πίστει καὶ σχήματι, καὶ γενείων κουρᾷ καὶ πᾶσιν ἔθεσιν Λατῖνος ἦν ἀκραιφνής, Nic. Greg. l. ix. c. 1), and founded a dynasty of Italian princes, which was extinguished A.D. 1533 (Ducange, Fam. Byz. p. 249-253).

excited neither the fears of the enemy nor the jealousy of the court; his modesty and patience were never tempted to compute the years of his father; nor was that father compelled to repent of his liberality either by the virtues or vices of his son. The son of Michael was named Andronicus from his grandfather, to whose early favour he was introduced by that nominal resemblance. The blossoms of wit and beauty increased the fondness of the elder Andronicus ; and, with the common vanity of the age, he expected to realise in the second, the hope which had been disappointed in the first, generation. The boy was educated in the palace as an heir and a favourite ; and, in the oaths and acclamations of the people, the *august triad* was formed by the names of the father, the son, and the grandson. But the younger Andronicus was speedily corrupted by his infant greatness, while he beheld, with puerile impatience, the double obstacle that hung, and might long hang, over his rising ambition. It was not to acquire fame, or to diffuse happiness, that he so eagerly aspired; wealth and impunity were in his eyes the most precious attributes of a monarch; and his first indiscreet demand was the sovereignty of some rich and fertile island, where he might lead a life of independence and pleasure. The emperor was offended by the loud and frequent intemperance which disturbed his capital; the sums which his parsimony denied were supplied by the Genoese usurers of Pera; and the oppressive debt, which consolidated the interest of a faction, could be discharged only by a revolution. A beautiful female, a matron in rank, a prostitute in manners, had instructed the younger Andronicus in the rudiments of love; but he had reason to suspect the nocturnal visits of a rival ; and a stranger passing through the street was pierced by the arrows of his guards, who were placed in ambush at her door. That stranger was his brother, prince Manuel, who languished and died of his wound; and the emperor Michael, their common father, whose health was in a declining state, expired on the eighth day, lamenting the loss of both his children.[7] However guiltless in his intention, the younger Andronicus might impute a brother's and a father's death to the consequence of his own

[A.D. 1320]

---

[7] We are indebted to Nicephorus Gregoras (l. viii. c. 1) for the knowledge of this tragic adventure; while Cantacuzene more discreetly conceals the vices of Andronicus the Younger, of which he was the witness and perhaps the associate (l. i. c. 1, &c.).

vices; and deep was the sigh of thinking and feeling men, when they perceived, instead of sorrow and repentance, his ill-dissembled joy on the removal of two odious competitors. By these melancholy events, and the increase of his disorders, the mind of the elder emperor was gradually alienated; and, after many fruitless reproofs, he transferred on another grandson [8] his hopes and affection. The change was announced by the new oath of allegiance to the reigning sovereign and the *person* whom he should appoint for his successor; and the acknowledged heir, after a repetition of insults and complaints, was exposed to the indignity of a public trial. Before the sentence, which would probably have condemned him to a dungeon or a cell, the emperor was informed that the palace courts were filled with the armed followers of his grandson; the judgment was softened to a treaty of reconciliation; and the triumphant escape of the prince encouraged the ardour of the younger faction.

Yet the capital, the clergy, and the senate adhered to the person, or at least to the government, of the old emperor; and it was only in the provinces, by flight, and revolt, and foreign succour, that the malcontents could hope to vindicate their cause and subvert his throne. The soul of the enterprise was the great domestic, John Cantacuzene; the sally from Constantinople is the first date of his actions and memorials; and, if his own pen be most descriptive of his patriotism, an unfriendly historian has not refused to celebrate the zeal and ability which he displayed in the service of the young emperor. That prince escaped from the capital under the pretence of hunting; erected his standard at Hadrianople; and, in a few days, assembled fifty thousand horse and foot, whom neither honour nor duty could have armed against the barbarians. Such a force might have saved or commanded the empire; but their counsels were discordant, their motions were slow and doubtful, and their progress was checked by intrigue and negotiation. The quarrel of the two Andronici was protracted, and suspended, and renewed, during a ruinous period of seven years. In the first treaty the relics of the Greek empire were divided: Constantinople, Thessalonica, and the islands, were

Three civil wars between the two emperors. A.D. 1321, April 20—A.D. 1328, May 23

---

[8] His destined heir was Michael Catharus, the bastard of Constantine his second son. In this project of excluding his grandson Andronicus, Nicephorus Gregoras (l. viii. c. 3 [p. 295-6, ed. Bonn]) agrees with Cantacuzene (l. i. c. 1, 2).

left to the elder, while the younger acquired the sovereignty of the greatest part of Thrace, from Philippi to the Byzantine limit. By the second treaty he stipulated the payment of his troops, his immediate coronation, and an adequate share of the power and revenue of the state. The third civil war was terminated by the surprise of Constantinople, the final retreat of the old emperor, and the sole reign of his victorious grandson. The reasons of this delay may be found in the characters of the men and of the times. When the heir of the monarchy first pleaded his wrongs and his apprehensions, he was heard with pity and applause; and his adherents repeated on all sides the inconsistent promise that he would increase the pay of the soldiers and alleviate the burdens of the people. The grievances of forty years were mingled in his revolt; and the rising generation was fatigued by the endless prospect of a reign whose favourites and maxims were of other times. The youth of Andronicus had been without spirit, his age was without reverence; his taxes produced an annual revenue of five hundred thousand pounds; yet the richest of the sovereigns of Christendom was incapable of maintaining three thousand horse and twenty galleys, to resist the destructive progress of the Turks.[9] " How different," said the younger Andronicus, "is my situation from that of the son of Philip! Alexander might complain that his father would leave him nothing to conquer; alas! my grandsire will leave me nothing to lose." But the Greeks were soon admonished that the public disorders could not be healed by a civil war; and their young favourite was not destined to be the saviour of a falling empire. On the first repulse, his party was broken by his own levity, their intestine discord, and the intrigues of the ancient court, which tempted each malcontent to desert or betray the cause of rebellion. Andronicus the Younger was touched with remorse, or fatigued with business, or deceived by negotiation; pleasure rather than power was his aim; and the licence of maintaining a thousand hounds, a thousand hawks, and a thousand huntsmen, was sufficient to sully his fame and disarm his ambition.

Corona-
tion of the
younger
Androni-
cus. A.D.
1325, Feb. 2

[9] See Nicephorus Gregoras, l. viii. c. 6. The younger Andronicus complained that in four years and four months a sum of 350,000 byzants of gold was due to him for the expenses of his household (Cantacuzen. l. i. c. 48). Yet he would have remitted the debt, if he might have been allowed to squeeze the farmers of the revenue.

Let us now survey the catastrophe of this busy plot and the final situation of the principal actors.[10] The age of Andronicus was consumed in civil discord; and, amidst the events of war and treaty, his power and reputation continually decayed, till the fatal night in which the gates of the city and palace were opened without resistance to his grandson. His principal commander scorned the repeated warnings of danger; and retiring to rest in the vain security of ignorance, abandoned the feeble monarch, with some priests and pages, to the terrors of a sleepless night. These terrors were quickly realised by the hostile shouts which proclaimed the titles and victory of Andronicus the Younger; and the aged emperor, falling prostrate before an image of the Virgin, dispatched a suppliant message to resign the sceptre and to obtain his life at the hands of the conqueror. The answer of his grandson was decent and pious; at the prayer of his friends, the younger Andronicus assumed the sole administration; but the elder still enjoyed the name and pre-eminence of the first emperor, the use of the great palace, and a pension of twenty-four thousand pieces of gold, one half of which was assigned on the royal treasure, and the other on the fishery of Constantinople. But his impotence was soon exposed to contempt and oblivion; the vast silence of the palace was disturbed only by the cattle and poultry of the neighbourhood, which roved with impunity through the solitary courts; and a reduced allowance of ten thousand pieces of gold [11] was all that he could ask and more than he could hope. His calamities were embittered by the gradual extinction of sight: his confinement was rendered each day more rigorous; and during the absence and sickness of his grandson, his inhuman keepers, by the threats of instant death, compelled him to exchange the purple for the monastic habit and profession. The [A.D. 1330] monk *Antony* had renounced the pomp of the world: yet he had occasion for a coarse fur in the winter-season; and, as wine was forbidden by his confessor, and water by his physician, the

Marginal notes: The elder Andronicus abdicates the government. A.D. 1328, May 24

---

[10] I follow the Chronology of Nicephorus Gregoras, who is remarkably exact. It is proved that Cantacuzene has mistaken the dates of his own actions, or rather that his text has been corrupted by ignorant transcribers.

[11] I have endeavoured to reconcile the 24,000 [*leg.* 12,000] pieces of Cantacuzene (l. ii. c. i. [vol. i. p. 311, ed. Bonn]) with the 10,000 of Nicephorus Gregoras (l. ix. c. 2); the one of whom wished to soften, the other to magnify, the hardships of the old emperor.

sherbet of Egypt was his common drink.   It was not without difficulty that the late emperor could procure three or four pieces to satisfy these simple wants; and, if he bestowed the gold to relieve the more painful distress of a friend, the sacrifice is of some weight in the scale of humanity and religion.   Four

His death.
A.D. 1332,
Feb. 13

years after his abdication, Andronicus, or Antony, expired in a cell, in the seventy-fourth year of his age; and the last strain of adulation could only promise a more splendid crown of glory in heaven than he had enjoyed upon earth.[12]

Reign of
Androni-
cus the
younger.
A.D. 1328,
May 24—
A.D. 1341,
June 15

Nor was the reign of the younger, more glorious or fortunate than that of the elder, Andronicus.[13]   He gathered the fruits of ambition: but the taste was transient and bitter; in the supreme station he lost the remains of his early popularity; and the defects of his character became still more conspicuous to the world.   The public reproach urged him to march in person against the Turks; nor did his courage fail in the hour of trial; but a defeat and wound were the only trophies of his expedition in Asia, which confirmed the establishment of the Ottoman monarchy.   The abuses of the civil government attained their full maturity and perfection; his neglect of forms, and the confusion of national dresses, are deplored by the Greeks as the fatal symptoms of the decay of the empire.   Andronicus was old before his time; the intemperance of youth had accelerated the infirmities of age; and, after being rescued from a dangerous malady by nature, or physic, or the Virgin, he was snatched away before he had accomplished his forty-fifth year.

His two
wives

He was twice married; and, as the progress of the Latins in arms and arts had softened the prejudices of the Byzantine court, his two wives were chosen in the princely houses of Germany and Italy.   The first, Agnes at home, Irene in Greece, was daughter of the duke of Brunswick.   Her father[14] was a petty

---

[12] See Nicephorus Gregoras (l. ix. 6-8, 10, 14 ; l. x. c. 1).   The historian had tasted of the prosperity, and shared the retreat, of his benefactor; and that friendship, which "waits or to the scaffold or the cell," should not lightly be accused as " a hireling, a prostitute to praise ".

[13] The sole reign of Andronicus the younger is described by Cantacuzene (l. ii. c. 1-40, p. 191-339) and Nicephorus Gregoras (l. ix. c. 7—l. xi. c. 11, p. 262-361).

[14] Agnes, or Irene, was the daughter of duke Henry the Wonderful, the chief of the house of Brunswick, and the fourth in descent from the famous Henry the Lion, duke of Saxony and Bavaria, and conqueror of the Salvi on the Baltic coast. Her brother Henry was surnamed the *Greek*, from his two journeys into the East; but these journeys were subsequent to his sister's marriage; and I am ignorant

lord [15] in the poor and savage regions of the north of Germany; [16] yet he derived some revenue from his silver mines; [17] and his family is celebrated by the Greeks as the most ancient and noble of the Teutonic name.[18] After the death of this childless princess, Andronicus sought in marriage, Jane, the sister of the count of Savoy; [19] and his suit was preferred to that of the French king.[20] The count respected in his sister the superior majesty of a Roman empress; her retinue was composed of knights and ladies; she was regenerated and crowned in St. Sophia, under the more orthodox appellation of Anne; and, at the nuptial feast, the Greeks and Italians vied with each other in the martial exercises of tilts and tournaments.

The empress Anne of Savoy survived her husband. Their son, John Palæologus, was left an orphan and an emperor, in the ninth year of his age; and his weakness was protected by the first and most deserving of the Greeks. The long and

Reign of John Palæolo-gus. A.D. 1341, June 15—A.D. 1391

how Agnes was discovered in the heart of Germany, and recommended to the Byzantine court (Rimius, Memoirs of the House of Brunswick, p. 126-137).

[15] Henry the Wonderful was the founder of the branch of Grubenhagen, extinct in the year 1596 (Rimius, p. 287). He resided in the Castle of Wolfenbüttel, and possessed no more than a sixth part of the allodial estates of Brunswick and Lune-burg, which the Guelph family had saved from the confiscation of their great fiefs. The frequent partitions among brothers had almost ruined the princely houses of Germany, till that just but pernicious law was slowly superseded by the right of primogeniture. The principality of Grubenhagen, one of the last remains of the Hercynian forest, is a woody, mountainous, and barren tract (Busching's Geography, vol. vi. p. 270-286; English translation).

[16] The royal author of the Memoirs of Brandenburg will teach us how justly, in a much later period, the north of Germany deserved the epithets of poor and barbarous (Essai sur les Mœurs, &c.). In the year 1306, in the woods of Lune-burg, some wild people, of the Vened race, were allowed to bury alive their infirm and useless parents (Rimius, p. 136).

[17] The assertion of Tacitus that Germany was destitute of the precious metals must be taken, even in his own time, with some limitation (Germania, c. 5, Annal. xi. 20). According to Spener (Hist. Germaniæ Pragmatica, tom. i. p. 351), Argentifodinae in Hercyniis montibus, imperante Othone magno (A.D. 968), pri-mum apertæ, largam etiam opes augendi dederunt copiam; but Rimius (p. 258, 259) defers till the year 1016 the discovery of the silver mines of Grubenhagen, or the Upper Hartz, which were productive in the beginning of the xivth century, and which still yield a considerable revenue to the house of Brunswick.

[18] Cantacuzene has given a most honourable testimony, ἦν δ' ἐκ Γερμανῶν αὕτη θυγατὴρ δουκὸς ντὶ μπρουζουὶκ (the modern Greeks employ the ντ for the δ, and the μπ for the β, and the whole will read, in the Italian idiom, di Brunzuic), τοῦ παρ' αὐτοῖς ἐπιφανεστάτου, καὶ λαμπρότητι πάντας τοὺς ὁμοφύλους ὑπερβάλλοντος τοῦ γένους. The praise is just in itself, and pleasing to an English ear.

[19] Anne, or Jane, was one of the four daughters of Amédée the Great, by a second marriage, and half-sister of his successor, Edward count of Savoy (Anderson's Tables, p. 650). See Cantacuzene (l. i. c. 40-42).

[20] That king, if the fact be true, must have been Charles the Fair, who, in five years (1321-1326), was married to three wives (Anderson, p. 628). Anne of Savoy arrived at Constantinople in February, 1326.

cordial friendship of his father for John Cantacuzene is alike honourable to the prince and the subject. It had been formed amidst the pleasures of their youth ; their families were almost equally noble ;[21] and the recent lustre of the purple was amply compensated by the energy of a private education. We have seen that the young emperor was saved by Cantacuzene from the power of his grandfather; and, after six years of civil war, the same favourite brought him back in triumph to the palace of Constantinople. Under the reign of Andronicus the Younger, the great domestic ruled the emperor and the empire; and it was by his valour and conduct that the isle of Lesbos and the principality of Ætolia were restored to their ancient allegiance. His enemies confess that, among the public robbers, Cantacuzene alone was moderate and abstemious ; and the free and voluntary account which he produces of his own wealth [22] may sustain the presumption that it was devolved by inheritance, and not accumulated by rapine. He does not indeed specify the value of his money, plate, and jewels; yet, after a voluntary gift of two hundred vases of silver, after much had been secreted by his friends and plundered by his foes, his forfeit treasures were sufficient for the equipment of a fleet of seventy galleys. He does not measure the size and number of his estates ; but his granaries were heaped with an incredible store of wheat and barley; and the labour of a thousand yoke of oxen might cultivate, according to the practice of antiquity, about sixty-two thousand five hundred acres of arable land.[23] His pastures were stocked with two thousand five hundred brood mares, two hundred camels, three hundred mules, five hundred asses, five thousand horned cattle, fifty thousand hogs, and seventy thousand sheep:[24] a precious record of rural opulence,

---

[21] The noble race of the Cantacuzeni (illustrious from the xith century in the Byzantine annals) was drawn from the Paladins of France, the heroes of those romances which, in the xiiith century, were translated and read by the Greeks (Ducange, Fam. Byzant. p. 258). [Monograph on Cantacuzene: V. Parisot, Cantacuzène, Homme d'état et historien, 1845.]

[22] See Cantacuzene (l. iii. c. 24, 30, 36).

[23] Saserna, in Gaul, and Columella, in Italy or Spain, allow two yoke of oxen, two drivers, and six labourers, for two hundred jugera (125 English acres) of arable land ; and three more men must be added if there be much underwood (Columella de Re Rustica, l. ii. c. 13, p. 441, edit. Gesner).

[24] In this enumeration (l. iii. c. 30), the French translation of the President Cousin is blotted with three palpable and essential errors. 1. He omits the 1000 yoke of working oxen. 2. He interprets the πεντακόσιαι πρὸς δισχιλίαις, by the

in the last period of the empire, and in a land, most probably in Thrace, so repeatedly wasted by foreign and domestic hostility. The favour of Cantacuzene was above his fortune. In the moments of familiarity, in the hour of sickness, the emperor was desirous to level the distance between them, and pressed his friend to accept the diadem and purple. The virtue of the great domestic, which is attested by his own pen, resisted the dangerous proposal; but the last testament of Andronicus the Younger named him the guardian of his son and the regent of the empire. ^{He is left regent of the empire}

Had the regent found a suitable return of obedience and gratitude, perhaps he would have acted with pure and zealous fidelity in the service of his pupil.[25] A guard of five hundred soldiers watched over his person and the palace; the funeral of the late emperor was decently performed; the capital was silent and submissive; and five hundred letters, which Cantacuzene dispatched in the first month, informed the provinces of their loss and their duty. The prospect of a tranquil minority was blasted by the Great Duke or Admiral Apocaucus; and, to exaggerate *his* perfidy, the Imperial historian is pleased to magnify his own imprudence in raising him to that office against the advice of his more sagacious sovereign. Bold and subtle, rapacious and profuse, the avarice and ambition of Apocaucus were by turns subservient to each other; and his talents were applied to the ruin of his country. His arrogance was heightened by the command of a naval force and an impregnable castle, and, under the mask of oaths and flattery, he secretly conspired against his benefactor. The female court of the empress was bribed and directed; he encouraged Anne of Savoy to assert, by the law of nature, the tutelage of her son; the love of power was disguised by the anxiety of maternal tenderness; and the founder of the Palæologi had instructed his posterity to dread the example of a perfidious guardian. The patriarch John of Apri was a proud and feeble old man, encompassed by a numerous and hungry kindred. He produced an

^{His regency is attacked, A.D. 1341} ^{by Apocaucus} ^{by the empress Anne of Savoy} ^{by the patriarch}

number of fifteen hundred. [The mistake has not been corrected in the Bonn edition, vol. ii. p. 185.] 3. He confounds myriads with chiliads, and gives Cantacuzene no more than 5000 hogs. Put not your trust in translations!

[25] See the regency and reign of John Cantacuzenus, and the whole progress of the civil war, in his own history (l. iii. c. 1-100, p. 348-700), and in that of Nicephorus Gregoras (l. xii. c. 1—l. xv. c. 9, p. 353-492).

obsolete epistle of Andronicus, which bequeathed the prince and people to his pious care: the fate of his predecessor Arsenius prompted him to prevent, rather than punish, the crimes of an usurper; and Apocaucus smiled at the success of his own flattery, when he beheld the Byzantine priest assuming the state and temporal claims of the Roman pontiff.[26] Between three persons so different in their situation and character, a private league was concluded: a shadow of authority was restored to the senate; and the people was tempted by the name of freedom. By this powerful confederacy, the great domestic was assaulted at first with clandestine, at length with open, arms. His prerogatives were disputed; his opinions slighted; his friends persecuted; and his safety was threatened both in the camp and city. In his absence on the public service, he was accused of treason; proscribed as an enemy of the church and state; and delivered, with all his adherents, to the sword of justice, the vengeance of the people, and the power of the devil: his fortunes were confiscated; his aged mother was cast into prison; all his past services were buried in oblivion; and he was driven by injustice to perpetrate the crime of which he was accused.[27] From the review of his preceding conduct, Cantacuzene appears to have been guiltless of any treasonable designs; and the only suspicion of his innocence must arise from the vehemence of his protestations, and the sublime purity which he ascribes to his own virtue. While the empress and the patriarch still affected the appearance of harmony, he repeatedly solicited the permission of retiring to a private, and even a monastic, life. After he had been declared a public enemy, it was his fervent wish to throw himself at the feet of the young emperor, and to receive without a murmur the stroke of the executioner: it was not without reluctance that he listened to the voice of reason, which inculcated the sacred duty of saving his family and friends, and proved that he could only save them by drawing the sword and assuming the Imperial title.

[26] He assumed the royal privilege of red shoes or buskins; placed on his head a mitre of silk and gold; subscribed his epistles with hyacinth or green ink; and claimed for the new, whatever Constantine had given to the ancient, Rome (Cantacuzen. l. iii. c. 36; Nic. Gregoras, l. xiv. c. 3).

[27] Nic. Gregoras (l. xii. c. 5) confesses the innocence and virtues of Cantacuzenus, the guilt and flagitious vices of Apocaucus; nor does he dissemble the motive of his personal and religious enmity to the former; νῦν δὲ διὰ κακίαν ἄλλων, αἴτιος ὁ πρᾳότατος τῆς τῶν ὅλων ἔδοξεν εἶναι φθορᾶς.

In the strong city of Demotica, his peculiar domain, the em- Cantacu-
zene as-
sumes the
purple.
A.D. 1341,
Oct. 26 peror John Cantacuzenus was invested with the purple buskins; his right leg was clothed by his noble kinsmen, the left by the Latin chiefs, on whom he conferred the order of knighthood. But even in this act of revolt he was still studious of loyalty; and the titles of John Palæologus and Anne of Savoy were proclaimed before his own name and that of his wife Irene. Such vain ceremony is a thin disguise of rebellion, nor are there perhaps any *personal* wrongs that can authorise a subject to take arms against his sovereign; but the want of preparation and success may confirm the assurance of the usurper that this decisive step was the effect of necessity rather than of choice. Constantinople adhered to the young emperor; the king of Bulgaria was invited to the relief of Hadrianople; the principal cities of Thrace and Macedonia, after some hesitation, renounced their obedience to the great domestic; and the leaders of the troops and provinces were induced, by their private interest, to prefer the loose dominion of a woman and a priest.[28] The army of Cantacuzene, in sixteen divisions, was stationed on the banks of the Melas, to tempt or intimidate the capital; it was dispersed by treachery or fear; and the officers, more especially the mercenary Latins, accepted the bribes, and embraced the service, of the Byzantine court. After this loss, the rebel emperor (he fluctuated between the two characters) took the road of Thessalonica with a chosen remnant; but he failed in his enterprise on that important place; and he was closely pursued by the Great Duke, his enemy Apocaucus, at the head of a superior power by sea and land. Driven from the coast, in his march, or rather flight, into the mountains of Servia, Cantacuzene assembled his troops to scrutinise those who were worthy and willing to accompany his broken fortunes. A base majority bowed and retired; and his trusty band was diminished to two thousand, and at last to five hundred, volunteers. The *cral*,[29] or despot of the Ser- [Stephen
Dushan]

---

[28] [The people seem to have clung to the legitimate heir; the officials to have supported Cantacuzene.]

[29] The princes of Servia (Ducange, Famil. Dalmaticæ, &c., c. 2-4, 9) were styled Despots in Greek, and Cral in their native idiom (Ducange, Gloss. Græc. p. 751). That title, the equivalent of king, appears to be of Sclavonic origin, from whence it has been borrowed by the Hungarians, the modern Greeks, and even by the Turks (Leunclavius, Pandect. Turc. p. 422), who reserve the name of Padishah for the Emperor. To obtain the latter instead of the former is the ambition of the French at Constantinople (Avertissement á l'Histoire de Timur Bec, p. 39). [The

vians, received him with generous hospitality; but the ally was insensibly degraded to a suppliant, an hostage, a captive; and, in this miserable dependence, he waited at the door of the barbarian, who could dispose of the life and liberty of a Roman emperor. The most tempting offers could not persuade the cral to violate his trust; but he soon inclined to the stronger side; and his friend was dismissed without injury to a new vicissitude of hopes and perils. Near six years the flame of discord burnt with various success and unabated rage: the cities were distracted by the faction of the nobles and the plebeians—the Cantacuzeni and Palæologi; and the Bulgarians, the Servians, and the Turks were invoked on both sides as the instruments of private ambition and the common ruin. The regent deplored the calamities of which he was the author and victim; and his own experience might dictate a just and lively remark on the different nature of foreign and civil war. "The former," said he, "is the external warmth of summer, always tolerable, and often beneficial; the latter is the deadly heat of a fever, which consumes without a remedy the vitals of the constitution."[30]

The introduction of barbarians and savages into the contests of civilised nations is a measure pregnant with shame and mischief; which the interest of the moment may compel, but which is reprobated by the best principles of humanity and reason. It is the practice of both sides to accuse their enemies of the guilt of the first alliances; and those who fail in their negotiations are loudest in their censure of the example which they envy and would gladly imitate. The Turks of Asia were less barbarous, perhaps, than the shepherds of Bulgaria and Servia;[31] but their religion rendered them the implacable foes

The civil war. A.D. 1341-1347

Victory of Cantacuzene

Servian and Bulgarian *Kral*, "king," from which the Hungarian *Király*, "king," is borrowed, seems to be derived from *Karl* the Great; just as the German and Slavonic word for Emperor is from the name of Cæsar. We find Κράλ in a Greek diploma of King (and saint) Stephen of Hungary : ἐγὼ Στέφανος Χριστιανὸς ὁ καὶ κρὰλ πάσης Οὑγγρίας. It is cited in Hunfalvy's Magyarország Ethnographiája, p. 322.]

[30] Nic. Gregoras, l. xii. c. 14. It is surprising that Cantacuzene has not inserted this just and lively image in his own writings.

[31] [The author does not seem to realise, he certainly has not brought out, the dominant position of Servia at this time under its king Stephen Dushan, a name which deserves a place in the history of the Fall of the Roman Empire. Servia was the strongest power in the peninsula under Stephen (1331-1355), and its boundaries extended from the Danube to the gulf of Arta. "He was a man of great ambition and was celebrated for his gigantic stature and personal courage. His subjects boasted of his liberality and success in war; his enemies reproached him with faithlessness and cruelty. He had driven his father Stephen VII. [Urosh

of Rome and Christianity.   To acquire the friendship of their
emirs, the two factions vied with each other in baseness and
profusion ; the dexterity of Cantacuzene obtained the preference ;
but the succour and victory were dearly purchased by the marriage of his daughter with an infidel, the captivity of many
thousand Christians, and the passage of the Ottomans into Europe, the last and fatal stroke in the fall of the Roman empire.
The inclining scale was decided in his favour by the death of [A.D. 1345,
Apocaucus, the just, though singular, retribution of his crimes. June 11]
A crowd of nobles or plebeians, whom he feared or hated, had
been seized by his orders in the capital and the provinces ; and
the old palace of Constantine was assigned for the place of their
confinement.   Some alterations in raising the walls and narrowing the cells had been ingeniously contrived to prevent their
escape and aggravate their misery ; and the work was incessantly
pressed by the daily visits of the tyrant.   His guards watched
at the gate, and, as he stood in the inner court to overlook the
architects, without fear or suspicion, he was assaulted and laid
breathless on the ground, by two resolute prisoners of the
Palæologian race,[32] who were armed with sticks and animated
by despair.   On the rumour of revenge and liberty, the captive

III.] from the throne, and the old man had been murdered in prison by the rebellious
nobles of Servia, who feared lest a reconciliation should take place with his son.
Stephen Dushan passed seven years of his youth at Constantinople, where he became acquainted with all the defects of the Byzantine government and with all the
vices of Greek society.   The circumstances in which the rival Emperors were placed
during the year 1345 were extremely favourable to his ambitious projects, and he
seized the opportunity to extend his conquests in every direction.   To the east he
rendered himself master of the whole valley of the Strymon, took the large and
flourishing city of Serres and garrisoned all the fortresses as far as the wall that
defended the pass of Christopolis.   He extended his dominions along the shores of
the Adriatic, and to the south he carried his arms to the gulf of Ambracia.   He
subdued the Vallachians of Thessaly, and placed strong garrisons in Achrida,
Kastoria, and Joannina.   Flushed with victory he at last formed the ambitious
scheme of depriving the Greeks of their political and ecclesiastical supremacy in
the Eastern Empire and transferring them to the Servians " (Finlay, iv. p. 441-2).
In 1346 he was crowned at Skopia as " Tsar of the Serbs and Greeks," and gave
his son the title of Kral ; and he raised his archbishop to the rank of Patriarch.
The prosperity of his reign is better shown by the growth of trade in the Servian
towns than by the increase of Servian territory.   Moreover Stephen did for Servia
what Yaroslav did for Russia ; he drew up a code of laws, which might be quoted
to modify Gibbon's contemptuous references to the Servians as barbarians.   This
Zakonik has been repeatedly edited, by Schafarik, Miklosich, Novakovich and
Zigel.]
    [32] The two avengers were both Palæologi, who might resent, with royal in-
dignation, the shame of their chains.   The tragedy of Apocaucus may deserve a
peculiar reference to Cantacuzene (l. iii. c. 86 [leg. 87-8]) and Nic. Gregoras (l. xiv.
c. 10).

multitude broke their fetters, fortified their prison, and exposed from the battlements the tyrant's head, presuming on the favour of the people and the clemency of the empress. Anne of Savoy might rejoice in the fall of an haughty and ambitious minister; but, while she delayed to resolve or to act, the populace, more especially the mariners, were excited by the widow of the Great Duke to a sedition, an assault, and a massacre. The prisoners (of whom the far greater part were guiltless or inglorious of the deed) escaped to a neighbouring church; they were slaughtered at the foot of the altar; and in his death the monster was not less bloody and venomous than in his life. Yet his talents alone upheld the cause of the young emperor; and his surviving associates, suspicious of each other, abandoned the conduct of the war, and rejected the fairest terms of accommodation. In the beginning of the dispute, the empress felt and complained that she was deceived by the enemies of Cantacuzene; the patriarch was employed to preach against the forgiveness of injuries; and her promise of immortal hatred was sealed by an oath under the penalty of excommunication.[33] But Anne soon learned to hate without a teacher: she beheld the misfortunes of the empire with the indifference of a stranger: her jealousy was exasperated by the competition of a rival empress; and, on the first symptoms of a more yielding temper, she threatened the patriarch to convene a synod and degrade him from his office. Their incapacity and discord would have afforded the most decisive advantage; but the civil war was protracted by the weakness of both parties; and the moderation of Cantacuzene has not escaped the reproach of timidity and indolence. He successively recovered the provinces and cities;[34]

[33] Cantacuzene accuses the patriarch, and spares the empress, the mother of his sovereign (l. iii. 33, 34), against whom Nic. Gregoras expresses a particular animosity (l. xiv. 10, 11; xv. 5). It is true that they do not speak exactly of the same time.

[34] [" The Greek Empire consisted of several detached provinces when Cantacuzenos seated himself on the throne; and the inhabitants of these different parts could only communicate freely by sea. The direct intercourse by land, even between Constantinople and Thessalonica, by the Egnatian Way, was interrupted, for the Servian Emperor possessed Amphipolis, and all the country about the mouth of the Strymon from Philippi to the lake Bolbe. The nucleus of the imperial power consisted of the city of Constantinople and the greater part of Thrace. On the Asiatic side of the Bosphorus, the Greek possessions were confined to the suburb of Skutari, a few forts and a narrow strip of coast extending from Chalcedon to the Black Sea. In Thrace the frontier extended from Sozopolis along the mountains to the south-west, passing about a day's journey to the north of Adria-

and the realm of his pupil was measured by the walls of Constantinople; but the metropolis alone counterbalanced the rest of the empire; nor could he attempt that important conquest, till he had secured in his favour the public voice and a private correspondence. An Italian, of the name of Facciolati,[35] had succeeded to the office of Great Duke: the ships, the guards, and the golden gate were subject to his command; but his humble ambition was bribed to become the instrument of treachery; and the revolution was accomplished without danger or bloodshed. Destitute of the powers of resistance or the hope of relief, the inflexible Anne would have still defended the palace, and have smiled to behold the capital in flames, rather than in the possession of a rival. She yielded to the prayers of her friends and enemies; and the treaty was dictated by the conqueror, who professed a loyal and zealous attachment to the son of his benefactor. The marriage of his daughter with John Palæologus was at length consummated: the hereditary right of the pupil was acknowledged; but the sole administration during ten years was vested in the guardian. Two emperors and three empresses were seated on the Byzantine throne; and a general amnesty quieted the apprehensions, and confirmed the property, of the most guilty subjects. The festival of the coronation and nuptials was celebrated with the appearance of concord and magnificence, and both were equally fallacious.

He re-enters Constantinople. A.D. 1347, January [February] 8

nople, and descending to the Aegean Sea at the pass and fortress of Christopolis. It included the districts of Morrha and the Thracian Chalkidike [of which Gratianopolis was the chief town]. The second portion of the Empire in importance consisted of the rich and populous city of Thessalonica, with the western part of the Macedonian Chalkidike and its three peninsulas of Cassandra, Longos and Agionoros ["Αγιον "Ορος]. By land it was entirely enclosed in the Servian empire. The third detached portion of the empire consisted of a part of Vallachian Thessaly and of Albanian Epirus, which formed a small imperial province interposed between the Servian empire and the Catalan duchy of Athens and Neopatras. The fourth consisted of the Greek province in the Peloponnesus, which obtained the name of the Despotat of Misithra, and embraced about one third of the peninsula. Cantacuzenos conferred the government on his second son, Manuel, who preserved his place by force of arms after his father was driven from the throne. The remaining fragments of the empire consisted of a few islands in the Aegean Sea which had escaped the domination of the Venetians, the Genoese, and the Knights of St. John; and of the cities of Philadelphia and Phocaea, which still recognised the suzerainty of Constantinople, though surrounded by the territories of the emirs of Aidin and Saroukhan. Such were the relics of the Byzantine empire." Finlay, iii. p. 447-8.]

[35] The traitor and treason are revealed by Nic. Gregoras (l. xv. c. 8), but the name is more discreetly suppressed by his great accomplice (Cantacuzen. l. iii. c. 99).

During the late troubles, the treasures of the state, and even the palace, had been alienated or embezzled : the royal banquet was served in pewter or earthenware ; and such was the proud poverty of the times that the absence of gold and jewels was supplied by the paltry artifices of glass and gilt leather.[36]

I hasten to conclude the personal history of John Cantacuzene.[37] He triumphed and reigned ; but his reign and triumph were clouded by the discontent of his own and the adverse faction. His followers might style the general amnesty an act of pardon for his enemies and of oblivion for his friends : [38] in his cause their estates had been forfeited or plundered ; and, as they wandered naked and hungry through the streets, they cursed the selfish generosity of a leader who, on the throne of the empire, might relinquish without merit his private inheritance. The adherents of the empress blushed to hold their lives and fortunes by the precarious favour of an usurper ; and the thirst of revenge was concealed by a tender concern for the succession, and even the safety, of her son. They were justly alarmed by a petition of the friends of Cantacuzene, that they might be released from their oath of allegiance to the Palæologi and entrusted with the defence of some cautionary towns : a measure supported with argument and eloquence ; and which was rejected (says the Imperial historian) " by *my* sublime and almost incredible virtue ". His repose was disturbed by the sound of plots and seditions ; and he trembled lest the lawful prince should be stolen away by some foreign or domestic enemy, who would inscribe his name and his wrongs in the banners of rebellion. As the son of Andronicus advanced in the years of manhood, he began to feel and to act for himself ; and his rising ambition was rather stimulated than checked by the imitation of his father's vices. If we may trust his own professions, Cantacuzene laboured with honest industry to correct these sordid and

---

[36] Nic. Greg. l. xv. 11. There were, however, some pearls, but very thinly sprinkled. The rest of the stones had only παντοδαπὴν χροιὰν πρὸς τὸ διαυγές.

[37] From his return to Constantinople, Cantacuzene continues his history, and that of the empire, one year beyond the abdication of his son Matthew, A.D. 1357 (l. iv. c. 1-50, p. 705-911). Nicephorus Gregoras ends with the synod of Constantinople, in the year 1351 (l. xxii. c. 3, p. 660, the rest, to the conclusion of the xxivth book, p. 717, is all controversy) ; and his fourteen last books are still Mss. in the king of France's library. [See Appendix 1.]

[38] The emperor (Cantacuzen. l. iv. c. 1) represents his own virtues, and Nic. Gregoras (l. xv. c. 11) the complaints of his friends, who suffered by its effects. I have lent them the words of our poor cavaliers after the Restoration.

sensual appetites, and to raise the mind of the young prince to a level with his fortune. In the Servian expedition [39] the two emperors showed themselves in cordial harmony to the troops and provinces; and the younger colleague was initiated by the elder in the mysteries of war and government. After the conclusion of the peace, Palæologus was left at Thessalonica, a royal residence and a frontier station, to secure by his absence the peace of Constantinople, and to withdraw his youth from the temptations of a luxurious capital. But the distance weakened the powers of control, and the son of Andronicus was surrounded with artful or unthinking companions, who taught him to hate his guardian, to deplore his exile, and to vindicate his rights. A private treaty with the cral or despot of Servia was soon followed by an open revolt; and Cantacuzene, on the throne of the elder Andronicus, defended the cause of age and prerogative, which in his youth he had so vigorously attacked. At his request, the empress-mother undertook the voyage of Thessalonica, and the office of mediation: she returned without success; and unless Anne of Savoy was instructed by adversity, we may doubt the sincerity, or at least the fervour, of her zeal. While the regent grasped the sceptre with a firm and vigorous hand, she had been instructed to declare that the ten years of his legal administration would soon elapse; and that, after a full trial of the vanity of the world, the emperor Cantacuzene sighed for the repose of a cloister, and was ambitious only of an heavenly crown. Had these sentiments been genuine, his voluntary abdication would have restored the peace of the empire, and his conscience would have been relieved by an act of justice. Palæologus alone was responsible for his future government; and, whatever might be his vices, they were surely less formidable than the calamities of a civil war, in which the barbarians and infidels were again

John Palæologus takes up arms against him. A.D. 1353

---

[39] [One important consequence of the Servian conquests, and the wars connected therewith, may be noticed here,—the Albanian invasion of Greece. The highlanders of northern Epirus, descendants of the ancient Illyrians, and speaking an idiom which represents the old Illyrian language, descended into Thessaly, laid it waste, and were a terror to the Catalan adventurers themselves. They settled in the Thessalian mountains and spread over Greece, where they formed a new element in the population. The Albanian settlers speak their own language, amid the surrounding Greeks, to the present day, therein differing remarkably from the Slavonic settlers, who adopted the Greek tongue. For the Albanians, see Hahn, Albanesische Studien, 1853; G. Meyer, Albanesische Studien, in Sitzungsberichte of Vienna Academy, vols. 104, 107, 125, 132, 134 (1883-1896), and his Essays und Studien, p. 49 sqq.]

invited to assist the Greeks in their mutual destruction. By the arms of the Turks, who now struck a deep and everlasting root in Europe, Cantacuzene prevailed in the third conquest in which he had been involved; and the young emperor, driven from the sea and land, was compelled to take shelter among the Latins of the isle of Tenedos. His insolence and obstinacy provoked the victor to a step which must render the quarrel irreconcileable; and the association of his son Matthew, whom he invested with the purple, established the succession in the family of the Cantacuzeni. But Constantinople was still attached to the blood of her ancient princes; and this last injury accelerated the restoration of the rightful heir. A noble Genoese espoused the cause of Palæologus, obtained a promise of his sister, and achieved the revolution with two galleys and two thousand five hundred auxiliaries. Under the pretence of distress they were admitted into the lesser port; a gate was opened, and the Latin shout of "Long life and victory to the emperor John Palæologus!" was answered by a general rising in his favour. A numerous and loyal party yet adhered to the standard of Cantacuzene; but he asserts in his history (does he hope for belief?) that his tender conscience rejected the assurance of conquest: that, in free obedience to the voice of religion and philosophy, he descended from the throne and embraced with pleasure the monastic habit and profession.[40] So soon as he ceased to be a prince, his successor was not unwilling that he should be a saint; the remainder of his life was devoted to piety and learning; in the cells of Constantinople and mount Athos, the monk Joasaph was respected as the temporal and spiritual father of the emperor; and, if he issued from his retreat, it was as the minister of peace, to subdue the obstinacy, and solicit the pardon, of his rebellious son.[41]

Yet in the cloister, the mind of Cantacuzene was still exer-

Abdication of Cantacuzene. A.D. 1355, January

---

[40] The awkward apology of Cantacuzene (l. iv. c. 39-42), who relates, with visible confusion, his own downfall, may be supplied by the less accurate but more honest narratives of Matthew Villani (l. iv. c. 46, in the Script. Rerum Ital. tom. xiv. p. 268) and Ducas (c. 10, 11).

[41] Cantacuzene, in the year 1375, was honoured with a letter from the pope (Fleury, Hist. Ecclés. tom. xx. p. 250). His death is placed, by a respectable authority, on the 20th of November, 1411 (Ducange, Fam. Byzant. p. 260). But, if he were of the age of his companion Andronicus the Younger, he must have lived 116 years: a rare instance of longevity, which in so illustrious a person would have attracted universal notice. [Date of death: A.D. 1383.]

cised by theological war. He sharpened a controversial pen Dispute concerning the light of mount Thabor. A.D. 1341-1351 against the Jews and Mahometans;[42] and in every state he defended with equal zeal the divine light of mount Thabor, a memorable question which consummates the religious follies of the Greeks. The fakirs of India[43] and the monks of the Oriental church were alike persuaded that in total abstraction of the faculties of the mind and body the purer spirit may ascend to the enjoyment and vision of the Deity. The opinion and practice of the monasteries of mount Athos[44] will be best represented in the words of an abbot who flourished in the eleventh century. "When thou art alone in thy cell," says the ascetic teacher, "shut thy door, and seat thyself in a corner; raise thy mind above all things vain and transitory; recline thy beard and chin on thy breast; turn thy eyes and thy thoughts towards the middle of thy belly, the region of the navel; and search the place of the heart, the seat of the soul. At first, all will be dark and comfortless; but, if you persevere day and night, you will feel an ineffable joy; and no sooner has the soul discovered the place of the heart than it is involved in a mystic and etherial light." This light, the production of a distempered fancy, the creature of an empty stomach and an empty brain, was adored by the Quietists as the pure and perfect essence of God [Ἡσυχά-σται] himself; and, as long as the folly was confined to mount Athos, the simple solitaries were not inquisitive how the divine essence could be a *material* substance, or how an *immaterial* substance could be perceived by the eyes of the body. But in the reign of the younger Andronicus these monasteries were visited by Barlaam,[45] a Calabrian monk, who was equally skilled in philosophy and theology; who possessed the languages of the Greeks

---

[42] His four discourses, or books, were printed at Basil, 1543 (Fabric. Bibliot. Græc. tom. vi. p. 473) [reprinted in Migne, Patr. Gr. vol. 154, p. 372 *sqq.*]. He composed them to satisfy a proselyte who was assaulted with letters from his friends of Ispahan. Cantacuzene had read the Koran; but I understand from Maracci that he adopts the vulgar prejudices and fables against Mahomet and his religion.

[43] See the Voyages de Bernier, tom. i. p. 127.

[44] Mosheim, Institut. Hist. Eccles. p. 522, 523. Fleury, Hist. Ecclés. tom. xx. p. 22, 24, 107-114, &c. The former unfolds the causes with the judgment of a philosopher, the latter transcribes and translates with the prejudices of a Catholic priest.

[45] Basnage (in Canisii Antiq. Lectiones, tom. iv. p. 363-368) has investigated the character and story of Barlaam. The duplicity of his opinions had inspired some doubts of the identity of his person. See likewise Fabricius (Bibliot. Græc. tom. x. p. 427-432). [G. Mandolori, Fra Barlaamo Calabrese, maestro del Petrarca, 1888.]

and Latins; and whose versatile genius could maintain their opposite creeds, according to the interest of the moment. The indiscretion of an ascetic revealed to the curious traveller the secrets of mental prayer; and Barlaam embraced the opportunity of ridiculing the Quietists, who placed the soul in the navel; of accusing the monks of mount Athos of heresy and blasphemy. His attack compelled the more learned to renounce or dissemble the simple devotion of their brethren; and Gregory Palamas introduced a scholastic distinction between the essence and operation of God.[46] His inaccessible essence dwells in the midst of an uncreated and eternal light; and this beatific vision of the saints had been manifested to the disciples on mount Thabor, in the transfiguration of Christ. Yet this distinction could not escape the reproach of polytheism; the eternity of the light of Thabor was fiercely denied; and Barlaam still charged the Palamites with holding two eternal substances, a visible and an invisible God. From the rage of the monks of mount Athos, who threatened his life, the Calabrian retired to Constantinople, where his smooth and specious manners introduced him to the favour of the great domestic and the emperor.

[Barlaam condemned. Synod of 1341] The court and the city were involved in this theological dispute, which flamed amidst the civil war; but the doctrine of Barlaam was disgraced by his flight and apostacy; the Palamites triumphed; and their adversary, the patriarch John of Apri, was deposed by the consent of the adverse factions of the state. In the character of emperor and theologian, Cantacuzene presided in the synod of the Greek church, which established, as an article of faith, the uncreated light of mount Thabor; and, after so many insults, the reason of mankind was slightly wounded by the addition of a single absurdity. Many rolls of paper or parchment have been blotted; and the impenitent sectaries, who refused to subscribe the orthodox creed, were deprived of the honours of Christian burial; but in the next age the question was forgotten; nor can I learn that the axe or the

[46] [The chief upholders of Barlaam were Gregory Akindynos (for whose works see Migne, P. G. vol. 151) and Nicephorus Gregoras, whose Φλωρέντιος ἢ περὶ σοφίας (in Jahns Archiv, 10, p. 485 sqq., 1844) is founded on a dispute with Barlaam. The chief opponent was Gregory Palamas, who had lived at Athos, and came forward as defender of the Hesychasts, to whose doctrine he gave a dogmatic basis (cp. Ehrhard, ap. Krumbacher, p. 103). Some of his works are printed in Migne, P. G. vols. 150, 151; a large number are happily buried in Mss.]

AN ORIENTAL MONASTERY: CHILIANDARI, ON MOUNT ATHOS

faggot were employed for the extirpation of the Barlaamite heresy.[47]

For the conclusion of this chapter I have reserved the Geno- Establishese war, which shook the throne of Cantacuzene and betrayed ment of the debility of the Greek empire. The Genoese, who, after the recovery of Constantinople, were seated in the suburb of Pera or Galata, received that honourable fief from the bounty of the emperor. They were indulged in the use of their laws and magistrates; but they submitted to the duties of vassals and subjects: the forcible word of *liegemen*[48] was borrowed from the Latin jurisprudence; and their *podestà*, or chief, before he entered on his office, saluted the Emperor with loyal acclamations and vows of fidelity. Genoa sealed a firm alliance with the Greeks; and, in case of a defensive war, a supply of fifty empty galleys, and a succour of fifty galleys completely armed and manned, was promised by the republic to the empire. In the revival of a naval force it was the aim of Michael Palæologus to deliver himself from a foreign aid; and his vigorous government contained the Genoese of Galata within those limits which the insolence of wealth and freedom provoked them to exceed. A sailor threatened that they should soon be masters of Constantinople, and slew the Greek who resented this national affront; and an armed vessel, after refusing to salute the palace, was guilty of some acts of piracy in the Black Sea. Their countrymen threatened to support their cause; but the long and open village of Galata was instantly surrounded by the Imperial troops; till, in the moment of the assault, the prostrate Genoese implored the clemency of their sovereign. The defenceless situation which secured their obedience exposed them to the attack of their Venetian rivals, who, in the reign of the elder Andronicus, presumed to violate the majesty of the throne. On the approach of their fleets, the Genoese, with

the Genoese at Pera or Galata. A.D. 1261-1347

---

[47] See Cantacuzene (l. ii. c. 39, 40; l. iv. c. 3, 23-25) and Nic. Gregoras (l. xi. c. 10; l. xv. 3, 7, &c.), whose last books, from the 19th to the 24th, are almost confined to a subject so interesting to the authors. Boivin (in Vit. Nic. Gregoræ), from the unpublished books, and Fabricius (Bibliot. Græc. tom. x. p. 462-473), or rather Montfaucon, from the Mss. of the Coislin Library, have added some facts and documents. [Sauli, Colonia dei Genovesi in Galata.]

[48] Pachymer (l. v. c. 10) very properly explains λιζίους (*ligios*) by ἰδίους. The use of these words, in the Greek and Latin of the feudal times, may be amply understood from the Glossaries of Ducange (Græc. p. 811, 812, Latin. tom. iv. p. 109-111).

their families and effects, retired into the city ; their empty
habitations were reduced to ashes ; and the feeble prince, who
had viewed the destruction of his suburb, expressed his resentment, not by arms, but by ambassadors. This misfortune,
however, was advantageous to the Genoese, who obtained, and
imperceptibly abused, the dangerous licence of surrounding
Galata with a strong wall; of introducing into the ditch the
waters of the sea ; of erecting lofty turrets; and of mounting
a train of military engines on the rampart. The narrow bounds
in which they had been circumscribed were insufficient for the
growing colony ; each day they acquired some addition of
landed property ; and the adjacent hills were covered with their
villas and castles, which they joined and protected by new
fortifications.[49] The navigation and trade of the Euxine was
the patrimony of the Greek emperors, who commanded the
narrow entrance, the gates, as it were, of that inland sea.   In
the reign of Michael Palæologus, their prerogative was acknowledged by the sultan of Egypt, who solicited and obtained the
liberty of sending an annual ship for the purchase of slaves in
Circassia and the Lesser Tartary : a liberty pregnant with
mischief to the Christian cause, since these youths were transformed by education and discipline into the formidable Mamalukes.[50] From the colony of Pera the Genoese engaged with
superior advantage in the lucrative trade of the Black Sea ;
and their industry supplied the Greeks with fish and corn, two
articles of food almost equally important to a superstitious people.
The spontaneous bounty of nature appears to have bestowed
the harvests of the Ukraine, the produce of a rude and savage
husbandry ; and the endless exportation of salt fish and caviar
is annually renewed by the enormous sturgeons that are caught
at the mouth of the Don, or Tanais, in their last station of

Their trade
and inso-
lence

[49] The establishment and progress of the Genoese at Pera, or Galata, is described by Ducange (C. P. Christiana, l. i. p. 68, 69), from the Byzantine historians
Pachymer (l. ii. c. 35, l. v. 10, 30, l. ix. 15, l. xii. 6, 9), Nicephorus Gregoras (l.
v. c. 4, l. vi. c. 11, l. ix. c. 5, l. xi. c. 1, l. xv. c. 1, 6), and Cantacuzene (l. i. c. 12,
l. ii. c. 29, &c.). [The golden Bulls of Michael VIII. (A.D. 1261) and Andronicus
the Elder (A.D. 1304) granting privileges to the Genoese will be found in Zachariä
von Lingenthal, Jus Græco-Romanum, iii. p. 574 sqq., p. 623 sqq.]

[50] Both Pachymer (l. iii. c. 3-5) and Nic. Gregoras (l. iv. c. 7) understand and
deplore the effects of this dangerous indulgence. Bibars, sultan of Egypt, himself a Tartar, but a devote Musulman, obtained from the children of Zingis the
permission to build a stately mosque in the capital of Crimea (De Guignes, Hist.
des Huns, tom. iii. p. 343).

the rich mud and shallow water of the Mæotis.[51]   The waters
of the Oxus, the Caspian, the Volga, and the Don opened
a rare and laborious passage for the gems and spices of India;
and, after three months' march, the caravans of Carizme met
the Italian vessels in the harbours of Crimea.[52]   These various
branches of trade were monopolized by the diligence and the
power of the Genoese.   Their rivals of Venice and Pisa were
forcibly expelled; the natives were awed by the castles and
cities, which arose on the foundations of their humble factories;
and their principal establishment of Caffa[53] was besieged without effect by the Tartar powers.   Destitute of a navy, the
Greeks were oppressed by these haughty merchants, who fed
or famished Constantinople, according to their interest.   They
proceeded to usurp the customs, the fishery, and even the toll,
of the Bosphorus; and, while they derived from these objects
a revenue of two hundred thousand pieces of gold, a remnant
of thirty thousand was reluctantly allowed to the emperor.[54]
The colony of Pera or Galata acted, in peace and war, as an
independent state; and, as it will happen in distant settlements, the Genoese podestà too often forgot that he was the
servant of his own masters.

These usurpations were encouraged by the weakness of the
elder Andronicus, and by the civil wars that afflicted his age
and the minority of his grandson.   The talents of Cantacuzene
were employed to the ruin, rather than the restoration, of the
empire; and after his domestic victory he was condemned to
an ignominious trial, whether the Greeks or the Genoese should
reign in Constantinople.   The merchants of Pera were offended
by his refusal of some contiguous lands, some commanding
heights, which they proposed to cover with new fortifications;

Their war with the emperor Cantacu- zene. A.D. 1348

[51] Chardin (Voyages en Perse, tom. i. p. 48) was assured at Caffa that these
fishes were sometimes twenty-four or twenty-six feet long, weighed eight or nine
hundred pounds, and yielded three or four quintals of caviar.   The corn of the
Bosphorus had supplied the Athenians in [and long before] the time of Demosthenes.
[52] De Guignes, Hist. des Huns, tom. iii. p. 343, 344.   Viaggi di Ramusio, tom.
i. fol. 400.   But this land or water carriage could only be practicable when Tartary was united under a wise and powerful monarch.
[53] Nic. Gregoras (l. xiii. c. 12) is judicious and well-informed on the trade and
colonies of the Black Sea.   Chardin describes the present ruins of Caffa, where,
in forty days, he saw above 400 sail employed in the corn and fish trade (Voyages
en Perse, tom. i. p. 46-48).
[54] See Nic. Gregoras, l. xvii. c. 1.

and in the absence of the emperor, who was detained at Demotica by sickness, they ventured to brave the debility of a
female reign. A Byzantine vessel, which had presumed to fish
at the mouth of the harbour, was sunk by these audacious
strangers; the fishermen were murdered. Instead of suing
for pardon, the Genoese demanded satisfaction; required, in
an haughty strain, that the Greeks should renounce the exercise
of navigation; and encountered, with regular arms, the first
sallies of the popular indignation. They instantly occupied the
debateable land; and by the labour of a whole people, of either
sex and of every age, the wall was raised, and the ditch was
sunk, with incredible speed. At the same time they attacked
and burnt two Byzantine galleys; while the three others, the
remainder of the Imperial navy, escaped from their hand; the
habitations without the gates, or along the shore, were pillaged
and destroyed; and the care of the regent, of the empress
Irene, was confined to the preservation of the city. The return
of Cantacuzene dispelled the public consternation: the emperor inclined to peaceful counsels; but he yielded to the
obstinacy of his enemies, who rejected all reasonable terms,
and to the ardour of his subjects, who threatened, in the style
of scripture, to break them in pieces like a potter's vessel. Yet
they reluctantly paid the taxes that he imposed for the construction of ships and the expenses of the war; and, as the
two nations were masters, the one of the land, the other of the
sea, Constantinople and Pera were pressed by the evils of a
mutual siege. The merchants of the colony, who had believed
that a few days would terminate the war, already murmured
at their losses; the succours from their mother-country were
delayed by the factions of Genoa; and the most cautious embraced the opportunity of a Rhodian vessel to remove their
families and effects from the scene of hostility. In the spring,
the Byzantine fleet, seven galleys and a train of smaller vessels,
issued from the mouth of the harbour and steered in a single
line along the shore of Pera; unskilfully presenting their sides
to the beaks of the adverse squadron. The crews were composed of peasants and mechanics; nor was their ignorance
compensated by the native courage of barbarians. The wind
was strong, the waves were rough; and no sooner did the
Greeks perceive a distant and inactive enemy, than they leaped

Destruc-
tion of his
fleet. A.D.
1349

headlong into the sea, from a doubtful to an inevitable peril. The troops that marched to the attack of the lines of Pera were struck at the same moment with a similar panic; and the Genoese were astonished, and almost ashamed, at their double victory. Their triumphant vessels, crowned with flowers, and dragging after them the captive galleys, repeatedly passed and repassed before the palace. The only virtue of the emperor was patience, and the hope of revenge his sole consolation. Yet the distress of both parties interposed a temporary agreement; and the shame of the empire was disguised by a thin veil of dignity and power. Summoning the chiefs of the colony, Cantacuzene affected to despise the trivial object of the debate; and, after a mild reproof, most liberally granted the lands, which had been previously resigned to the seeming custody of his officers.[55]

But the emperor was soon solicited to violate the treaty, and to join his arms with the Venetians, the perpetual enemies of Genoa and her colonies. While he compared the reasons of peace and war, his moderation was provoked by a wanton insult of the inhabitants of Pera, who discharged from their rampart a large stone that fell in the midst of Constantinople. On his just complaint, they coldly blamed the imprudence of their engineer; but the next day the insult was repeated, and they exulted in a second proof that the royal city was not beyond the reach of their artillery. Cantacuzene instantly signed his treaty with the Venetians; but the weight of the Roman empire was scarcely felt in the balance of these opulent and powerful republics.[56] From the straits of Gibraltar to the mouth of the Tanais, their fleets encountered each other with various success; and a memorable battle was fought in the narrow sea, under the walls of Constantinople. It would not be an easy task to reconcile the accounts of the Greeks, the Venetians, and the Genoese;[57] and,

Victory of the Genoese over the Venetians and Greeks. A.D. 1352, Feb. 13

---

[55] The events of this war are related by Cantacuzene (l. iv. c. 11) with obscurity and confusion, and by Nic. Gregoras (l. xvii. c. 1-7) in a clear and honest narrative. The priest was less responsible than the prince for the defeat of the fleet.

[56] The second war is darkly told by Cantacuzene (l. iv. c. 18, p. 24, 25, 28-32), who wishes to disguise what he dares not deny. I regret this part of Nic. Gregoras, which is still in Ms. at Paris. [It has since been edited, see Appendix 1.]

[57] Muratori (Annali d'Italia, tom. xii. p. 144) refers to the most ancient Chronicles of Venice (Caresinus [Raffaino Carasini; ob. 1390], the continuator of Andrew Dandolus, tom. xii. p. 421, 422), and Genoa (George Stella [ob. 1420], Annales Genuenses, tom. xvii. p. 1091, 1092); both which I have diligently consulted in his great Collection of the Historians of Italy.

while I depend on the narrative of an impartial historian,[58] I shall borrow from each nation the facts that redound to their own disgrace and the honour of their foes.   The Venetians, with their allies, the Catalans, had the advantage of number; and their fleet, with the poor addition of eight Byzantine galleys, amounted to seventy-five sail; the Genoese did not exceed sixty-four; but in those times their ships of war were distinguished by the superiority of their size and strength.   The names and families of their naval commanders, Pisani and Doria, are illustrious in the annals of their country; but the personal merit of the former was eclipsed by the fame and abilities of his rival.

[Battle of Bracho-
phagos or
Prote] They engaged in tempestuous weather; and the tumultuary conflict was continued from the dawn to the extinction of light. The enemies of the Genoese applaud their prowess; the friends of the Venetians are dissatisfied with their behaviour; but all parties agree in praising the skill and boldness of the Catalans, who, with many wounds, sustained the brunt of the action. On the separation of the fleets, the event might appear doubtful; but the thirteen Genoese galleys, that had been sunk or taken, were compensated by a double loss of the allies: of fourteen Venetians, ten Catalans, and two Greeks; and even the grief of the conquerors expressed the assurance and habit of more decisive victories.   Pisani confessed his defeat by retiring into a fortified harbour, from whence, under the pretext of the orders of the senate, he steered with a broken and flying squadron for the isle of Candia, and abandoned to his rivals the sovereignty of the sea.   In a public epistle,[59] addressed to the doge and senate, Petrarch employs his eloquence to reconcile the maritime powers, the two luminaries of Italy.   The orator celebrates the valour and victory of the Genoese, the first of men in the exercise of naval war; he drops a tear on the misfortunes of their Venetian brethren; but he exhorts them to pursue with fire and sword the base and perfidious Greeks; to purge the metropolis of the East from the heresy with which it was in-

---

[58] See the Chronicle of Matteo Villani of Florence, l. ii. c. 59, 60, p. 145-147, c. 74, 75, p. 156, 157, in Muratori's Collection, tom. xiv.

[59] The Abbé de Sade (Mémoires sur la Vie de Pétrarque, tom. iii. p. 257-263) translates this letter, which he had copied from a Ms. in the king of France's library.   Though a servant of the Duke of Milan, Petrarch pours forth his astonishment and grief at the defeat and despair of the Genoese in the following year (p. 323-332).

fected.   Deserted by their friends, the Greeks were incapable Their treaty with the empire. May 6
of resistance; and, three months after the battle, the emperor
Cantacuzene solicited and subscribed a treaty, which for ever
banished the Venetians and Catalans, and granted to the
Genoese a monopoly of trade and almost a right of dominion.[60]
The Roman empire (I smile in transcribing the name) might
soon have sunk into a province of Genoa, if the ambition of the
republic had not been checked by the ruin of her freedom and
naval power.   A long contest of one hundred and thirty years
was determined by the triumph of Venice; and the factions of
the Genoese compelled them to seek for domestic peace under
the protection of a foreign lord, the duke of Milan, or the French
king.   Yet the spirit of commerce survived that of conquest;
and the colony of Pera still awed the capital, and navigated the
Euxine, till it was involved by the Turks in the final servitude
of Constantinople itself.

[60] [Text (the Latin copy) in Sauli, Colonia dei Genovesi in Galata, ii. 216; and
in Zachariä von Lingenthal, Jus Graeco-Romanum, iii. 706.]

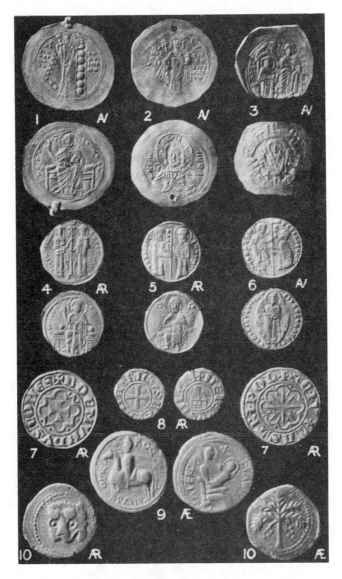

COINS, FROM ALEXIUS I TO ANDRONICUS III; COINS OF
DOGES, KINGS OF JERUSALEM AND SICILY

BRITISH MUSEUM. (SEE LIST OF ILLUSTRATIONS)

APPENDIX

ADDITIONAL NOTES BY THE EDITOR

1. AUTHORITIES

GREEK SOURCES

PHOTIUS was born at Constantinople about the beginning of the ninth century. He was related by blood to the Patriarch Tarasius, and his uncle was a brother-in-law of the Empress Theodora (wife of Theophilus). He had enjoyed an excellent training in grammar and philology, and devoted his early years to teaching, a congenial employment which he did not abandon after he had been promoted to the Patriarchate (A.D. 858). " His house was still a salon of culture, the resort of the curious who desired instruction. Books were read aloud and the master of the house criticized their style and their matter." [1] He was an indefatigable collector of books, and his learning probably surpassed that of any of the mediæval Greeks (not excepting Psellus). For his historical importance and public career, see above, p. 384-5.

Of his profane works the most famous—which Gibbon singles out—was his *Myriobiblon* or *Bibliotheca*, written (before A.D. 858) for his brother Tarasius, who desired information about the books which during his absence had been read and discussed in the circle of Photius. It contains most valuable extracts from writers whose works are no longer extant, and the criticisms of Photius are marked by acuteness and independence. The *Lexicon*, compiled doubtless by a secretary or pupil, is a later work.[2] There are about 300 extant letters (260 in Migne, P. G. vol. 102, and in the edition of Valettas, 1864 ; others edited by Papadopulos—Kerameus, Petersburg, 1896).

A recent critic has said that the importance of Photius as a theologian has been often exaggerated.[3] Of his theological writings only those pertaining to the controversy of the day need be mentioned here. In the treatise On the Mystagogia of the Holy Ghost he has put together all the evidence from scripture and the Fathers in favour of the Greek doctrine, but assigns more weight to theological argument than to authority. This is characteristic of the man. It is also to be observed (as Ehrhard remarks) that he does not attack the Roman church directly ; but he appeals to previous Popes as supporters of the true view, in opposition to Jerome, Augustine, &c.

Two of the homilies of Photius have historical importance as sources for the Russian invasion of A.D. 860. They were edited by P. Uspenski in 1864, and with improved text by A. Nauck in Lexicon Vindobonense, p. 201-232 (1867) ; reprinted in Müller's Frag. Hist. Gr. 5, p. 162 *sqq.*, and included in the complete edition of Aristarchos, Λόγοι καὶ ὁμιλίαι, 2 vols., 1900.

Most of the works of Photius are collected in Migne's Patr. Gr. vols. 101-104. The chief work on Photius is that of J. Hergenröther, in 3 volumes : Photius,

---

[1] Krumbacher, Gesch. der Byz. Litt. p. 516.
[2] Ed. S. A. Naber, 1864-5.
[3] Ehrhard, in Krumbacher's Byz. Litt. p. 74.

539

Patriarch von Konstantinopel, sein Leben, seine Schriften, und das griechische Schisma (1867-9), a learned, and valuable work.

The *Tactica* of the Emperor Leo VI. contains a great deal that is merely a re-edition of the Strategicon ascribed to the Emperor Maurice. The general organisation, the drill, the rules for marching and camping, the arms, are still the same as in the 6th century. But there is a great deal that is new. A good account and criticism of the work will be found in Oman's History of the Art of War, vol. 2, p. 184 *sqq.* " The reader is distinctly prepossessed in favour of Leo by the frank and handsome acknowledgment which he makes of the merits and services of his general, Nicephorus Phocas, whose successful tactics and new military devices are cited again and again with admiration. The best parts of his book are the chapters on organisation, recruiting, the services of transport and supply, and the methods required for dealing with the various barbarian neighbours of the empire. . . . The weakest point, on the other hand,—as is perhaps natural,—is that which deals with strategy. . . . Characteristic, too, of the author's want of aggressive energy, and of the defensive system which he made his policy is the lack of directions for campaigns of invasion in an enemy's country. Leo contemplates raids on hostile soil, but not permanent conquests. . . . Another weak point is his neglect to support precept by example; his directions would be much the clearer if he would supplement them by definite historical cases in which they had led to success " (*ib.*, p. 184-5).

Zachariä von Lingenthal propounded [4] the theory that the Leo to whom the title of the Tactics ascribes the authorship was not Leo VI. but Leo III., and that consequently the work belongs to the first half of the eighth century. But internal evidence is inconsistent with this theory. Besides the references to Nicephorus Phocas mentioned above, the author speaks of "our father the Emperor Basil," and describes his dealings with the Slavs, 18, § 101; the Bulgarians who were still heathen in the reign of Leo the Iconoclast appear as Christians in this treatise, 18, § 42, 44, and 61; the capture of Theodosiopolis from the Saracens (under Leo VI., cp. Const. Porph., de Adm. Imp. c. 45, p. 199-200, ed. Bonn) is mentioned.

The most interesting chapters of the work are c. 18, which contains an account of the military customs of the nations with which the empire was brought into hostile contact (Saracens, Bulgarians, Hungarians, Slavs, Franks), and c. 19, on naval warfare (see below, Appendix 5). [The edition of Meursius used by Gibbon is reprinted in Migne's Patr. Gr. 107, p. 671 *sqq.*]

Only a part of the two Books De Cerimoniis aulae Byzantinae which pass under the name of Constantine Porphyrogennetos is really due to that Emperor.

The first 83 chapters of Bk. I. represent the treatise on the *Court Ceremonies* which he compiled by putting together existing documents which prescribed the order of the various ceremonies. The work is arranged as follows : Chaps. 1-37, religious ceremonies (thus chap. 1 gives the order of processions to the Great Church —St. Sophia; chap. 2, the ceremonies on Christmas Day; chap. 3, those on the Epiphany, &c., in the order of the calendar); chaps. 38-44, the ceremonies on great secular occasions, such as the coronation of the Emperor and the Empress; chaps. 45-59, ceremonies on the promotions of ministers and palace functionaries; chaps. 60-64, an Emperor's funeral, and other solemnities; chaps. 65-83, palace banquets, public games, and other ceremonies.[5]

The remaining chapters of Bk. I. are an excrescence and were added at a later date. Chaps. 84-95 are an extract from the work of Peter the Patrician who wrote under Justinian I. (cp. headings to chaps. 84 and 95). Chap. 96 contains an account of the inauguration of Nicephorus Phocas, and chap. 97 perhaps dates from the reign of Tzimisces.

The matter printed in the Bonn ed. as an Appendix to Book I. is a totally

---

[4] In Byz. Zeitschrift, ii. 606 *sqq.* ; iii. 437 *sqq.*
[5] C. 83 contains the famous Γοτθικόν or Gothic Weihnachtspiel which has given rise to much discussion, German antiquarians vainly trying to find in the acclamations old German words.

distinct work, dealing with military expeditions against the Saracens led by the Emperor in person, as I have shown in Eng. Hist. Review, July, 1907, where I propose to call it περὶ τῶν βασιλικῶν ταξειδίων.

The second Book, as it stands, contains many documents which did not originally form part of Constantine's treatise. Thus chaps. 44 and 45 contain the returns of the expenses, &c., of naval armaments against Crete in A.D. 902 and 949; chap. 50 contains a list of themes which belongs to the reign of Leo VI.; chap. 52-4, a separate treatise on the order of precedence at Imperial banquets composed by PHILOTHEUS protospatharius in A.D. 899-900.

The work of Philotheus (entitled Klêtorologion), which is a highly important source for the official organization of the Empire in the 9th and 10th centuries, has been edited separately by Bury, Imperial Administrative System in the Ninth Century (Supplemental Papers of British Academy, i., 1911).

The Ceremonies are included in the Bonn ed. of the Byzantine writers (1829), with Reiske's notes in a separate volume. The composition of the work has been analysed by Bury, the Ceremonial Book of Constantine Porphyrogennetos, Eng. Hist. Review, April and July, 1907; for the elucidation of the ceremonies, &c., see D. Bieliaiev, Byzantina, vol. 2 (1893), vol. 3 (1907). See also Ebersolt, Le grand Palais de Constantinople et le livre des cérémonies, 1910.

The work on the *Themes* (in 2 Books, see above, p. 70 *sqq.*) was composed while Romanus I. was still alive, and after, probably not very long after, A.D. 934 (see Rambaud, L'empire grec au dixième siècle, p. 165). For an Armenian general Melias is mentioned, who was alive in 934, as recently dead; and the theme of Seleucia is noticed, which seems to have been formed after 934. For the contents of the book, cp. below, Appendix 3.

The treatise on the *Administration of the Empire* is dealt with in a separate note below, Appendix 4.

GEORGE CODINUS (probably 15th century) is merely a name, associated with three works: a short, worthless chronicle (ed. Bonn, 1843); an account of the offices of the Imperial Court and of St. Sophia, generally quoted as *De Officiis* (ed. Bonn, 1839); the *Patria* of Constantinople (ed. Bonn, 1843). But it is only with the third of these works that Codinus, whoever he was, can have any connexion. The Chronicle is anonymous in the Mss., and there is no reason for ascribing it to Codinus. The *De Officiis* is likewise anonymous, and the attribution of it to Codinus was due to the blunder of an editor; it is a composition of the end of the 14th and beginning of the 15th century. As for the Πάτρια Κωνσταντινοπόλεως, see above, vol. ii., Appendix 8, p. 574.

EUSTATHIUS, educated at Constantinople, became Archbishop of Thessalonica in 1175; he died c. 1193. Besides his famous commentaries on Homer, his commentary on Pindar, and his paraphrase of the geographical poem of Dionysius, he composed an account of the Norman siege of Thessalonica in A.D. 1185. ιThis original work was published by L. F. Tafel in A.D. 1832 (Eustathii Opuscula, i. p. 267-307) and reprinted by Bekker at the end of the Bonn ed. of Leo Grammaticus. There are also extant various speeches (*e.g.* a funeral oration by the Emperor Manuel) which have been published by Tafel in his edition of the lesser works of Eustathius and in his treatise De Thessalonica ejusque agro (1839). A collection of letters (some not by Eustathius but by Psellus) is also published by Tafel (Eustathii Op. p. 507 *sqq.*) and some others by Regel, Fontes rerum Byzantinarum, i. (1892).

GEORGE ACROPOLITES, born in 1217 at Constantinople, migrated to Nicæa at the age of eighteen, and studied there under the learned Nicephorus Blemmydes. He was appointed (1244) to the office of Grand Logothete, and instructed the young prince Theodore Lascaris who afterwards became emperor. Unsuccessful as a general in the war with the Despot of Epirus (1257), he was made prisoner, and after his release he was employed by Michael Palæologus as a diplomatist. He represented the Greek Emperor at the Council of Lyons, for the purpose of bringing about a reunion of the Greek and Latin Churches. He died in 1282. His history embraces the period from 1203 to the recovery of Constantinople in 1261, and is thus a continuation of Nicetas. For the second half of the period treated it is not only a contemporary work, but the work of one who was in a good position for observing political events. [The Χρονικὴ συγγραφή in its original form was published by Leo Allatius in 1651, and is reprinted in the Venice and Bonn collections. These editions have been superseded by that of A. Heisenberg, 2 vols., 1903. An abridgment was published by Dousa in 1614. There is also, in a Ms. at Milan, a copy of the work with interpolations (designated as such) by a contemporary of Acropolites (see Krumbacher, Gesch. der byz. Litt., p. 287 ; A. Heisenberg, Studien zur Textgeschichte des Georgios Akropolites, 1894).]

GEORGE PACHYMERES (A.D. 1242-1310) carries us on from the point where Acropolites deserts us. He is the chief literary figure of the first fifty years of the restored Empire. His work in 13 Books begins at A.D. 1255 and comes down to 1308. His chief interest was in the theological controversies of the day, and there is far too much theology and disputation about dogma in his history; but this was what absorbed the attention of the men of his time. " Pachymeres, by his culture and literary activity, overtops his contemporaries, and may be designated as the greatest Byzantine Polyhistor of the 13th century. We see in him the lights and shadows of the age of the Palæologi. He is not wanting in learning, originality, and wit. But he does not achieve the independence of view and expression, which distinguishes a Photius or a Psellus." Other works of Pachymeres are extant, but only his autobiography in hexameter verses need be mentioned here (it was suggested by Gregory Nazianzen's περὶ ἑαυτοῦ). It is worthy of note—as a symptom of the approaching renaissance—that Pachymeres adopted the *Attic*, instead of the Roman, *names* of the months. [The edition of Possinus, used by Gibbon, was reprinted in the Bonn collection, 1835.]

NICEPHORUS GREGORAS (1295-c. 1359) of Heraclea in Pontus was educated at Constantinople, and enjoyed the teaching of Theodore Metochites, who was distinguished not only as a trusted councillor of the Emperor Andronicus, but as a man of encyclopædic learning.[6] Nicephorus won the favour of Andronicus, but on that Emperor's deposition in 1328 his property was confiscated and he had to live in retirement. He came forth from his retreat to do theological battle with the pugnacious Barlaam of Calabria, who was forming a sort of school in Constantinople (see above, c. lxiii. p. 530) ; and his victory in this controversy was rewarded by reinstatement in his property and offices. Subsequently he played a prominent part in the renewed attempts at reuniting the eastern and western churches. He fell into disfavour with Cantacuzenus and was banished to a monastery. His Roman History in 37 Books begins with the Latin capture of Constantinople in 1204, and reaches to 1359. But the greater part of this period, 1204-1320, is treated briefly in the first 7 Books, which may be regarded as an introduction to the main subject of his work, namely his own times (1320-1359). This history, like that of Pachymeres, is disproportionately occupied with theological disputation, and is, as Krumbacher says, " eine memoirenhafte Parteischrift im vollsten Sinne des Wortes ". In style, Gregoras essays to imitate Plato ; for such base uses has Platonic prose been exploited. [Only Books 1-24 were accessible to Gibbon, as he complains (ed. Boivin, 1702). The remaining Books 25-37 (numbered 23-36) were first edited by Bekker in the Bonn ed., vol. 3, 1855. Among other works of Gregoras may be mentioned his funeral oration on Theodore Metochites, ed. by Meursius, 1618 (Th. Metochitae hist. Rom., liber singularis).]

For the Emperor CANTACUZENUS and his history, see above, cap. lxiii. and cp. p. 518, n. 21. Cp. also J. Dräseke, Zu Johannes Kantakuzenos, in Byzantinische Zeitschrift, 9, 72 *sqq.*, 1900. [In the Bonn series, ed. by Schopen in 3 vols., 1828-32.]

---

[6] His chief literary remains are a collection of Miscellaneous Essays, which has been edited by C. G. Müller and T. Kiessling, 1821 ; and a large number of rhetorical exercises and astronomical and scientific treatises. His occasional poems have not yet been completely published.

NICEPHORUS BLEMMYDES was, beside George Acropolites, the most important literary figure at the court of the Emperor of Nicæa. He was born at Constantinople (c. 1198), and soon after the Latin Conquest migrated to Asia; and in Prusa, Nicæa, Smyrna, and Scamander he received a liberal education under the best masters of the day. He became proficient in logic, rhetoric and mathematics, and studied medicine. He finally embraced a clerical career; he took an active part in the controversies with the Latins in the reign of John Vatatzes, and was a teacher of the young prince THEODORE LASCARIS. The extant correspondence of Theodore and Blemmydes testifies their friendly intimacy. But Blemmydes was an opinionated man; he was constantly offending and taking offence; and he finally became a monk and retired to a monastery at Ephesus which he built himself. He had the refusal of the Patriarchate in 1255, and he died c. 1272. His autobiography and his letters (monuments of pedantry and conceit) have importance for the history of his time. Besides theological, scientific, and other works, he composed an icon basilike (βασιλικός ἀνδριάς) for his royal pupil.[7] [The autobiography (in two parts) has been edited by A. Heisenberg, 1896. An edition of the Letters is a desideratum. The Letters of the Emperor Theodore Lascaris II. were published by N. Festa (Epistulæ ccxvii) in 1898.]

In the first quarter of the 14th century, a native of the Morea, certainly half a Frank, and possibly half a Greek, by birth, composed a versified chronicle of the Latin conquest of the Peloponnesus and its history during the 13th century. This work is generally known as the CHRONICLE OF MOREA.[8] The author is thoroughly Grecized, so far as language is concerned; he writes the vulgar tongue as a native; but feels towards the Greeks the dislike and contempt of a ruling stranger for the conquered population. He may have been a Gasmul (Γασμοῦλος, supposed to be derived from gas (garçon) and mulus), as the offspring of a Frank father by a Greek mother was called. It is a thoroughly prosaic work, thrown into the form of wooden political verses; and what it loses in literary interest through its author's lack of talent, it gains in historical objectivity. A long prologue relates the events of the first and the fourth crusades; the main part of the work embraces the history of the Principality of Achaea from 1205 to 1292. The book appealed to the Franks, not to the Greeks, of the Peloponnesus; and shows how Greek had become the language of the conquerors. It was freely translated into French soon after its composition; and this version (with a continuation down to 1304), which was made before the year 1341, is preserved (under the title "The Book of the Conquest of Constantinople and the Empire of Roumania and the country of the Principality of Morea"). J. A. Buchon was the first to edit both the Greek and the French; but he sought to show that the French was the original and the Greek the version. The true relation of the two texts has been established by the researches of the late John Schmitt (Die Chronik von Morea, 1889).

[Of the Greek original there are two widely different redactions, of which one, preserved in a Paris Ms., was published by Buchon in his Chroniques étrangères relatives aux expeditions françaises pendant le xiii. siècle, in 1840; the other, preserved in a Copenhagen Ms., was published in the second volume of his Recherches historiques sur la principauté française de Morée et ses hautes baronies (1845), while in the first vol. of this latter work he edited the French text. A final edition, with the Paris and Copenhagen texts on opposite pages, and a collation of the Turin Ms., by John Schmitt, appeared in 1904 (London).][9]

SLAVONIC SOURCES

The old Russian chronicle, which goes by the name of NESTOR and comprises the history of Russia and the neighbouring countries from the middle of the ninth

---

[7] It will be found in Migne, P. G., vol. 142, p. 611 sqq.

[8] It is sometimes referred to as Βιβλίον τῆς κουγκέστας, a title which the first editor Buchon gave it without authority.

[9] There are also versions in Aragonese and in Italian.

century to the year 1110, has come down in two redactions : (1) the Laurentian Ms., written by Laurence of Souzdal in 1377, and (2) the Hypatian, written in the monastery of St. Hypatius at Kostroma in the 15th century. All other Mss. can be traced back to either of these two. In neither of them does the old chronicle stand alone ; it is augmented by continuations which are independent.

The work was compiled apparently in the year 1114-1115,[10] and it can be divided into two parts.[11] (1) Caps. 1-12, without chronological arrangement. It is to this part alone that the title refers : " History of old times by the monk of the monastery of Theodosius Peshtcherski, of the making of Russia, and who reigned first at Kiev (cp. c. 6), and of the origin of the Russian land ". (2) The rest of the works, chaps. 13-89, is arranged in the form of annals. It falls into three parts, indicated by the compiler in cap. 13. (a) Caps. 14-36, from the year 852 to death of Sviatoslav, 972 ; (b) caps. 37-58, to the death of Jaroslav, 1054 ; (c) caps. 59-89, to the death of Sviatopolk, 1114.[12]

Sources of the chronicle : [13] (1) George the monk, in an old Bulgarian translation of 10th century (cp. chap. 11 ; see also chaps. 24, 65). (2) A work ascribed to Methodius of Patara (3rd cent.) : " On the things which happened from the creation and the things which will happen in the future "—also doubtless through a Slavonic translation.[14] (3) Lives of the apostles of the Slavs, Cyril and Methodius. (4) The Bible. (5) The Palaia (collection of Bible-stories), in Slavonic form. (6) The Symbolum Fidei of Michael Syncellus in Slavonic version (c. 42). (7) Oral information indicated by the chronicler ; communications of (a) the monk Jeremiah who was old enough to remember the conversion of the Russians, c. 68 ; (b) Gurata Rogovich of Novgorod, c. 80 ; (c) John, an old man of ninety, from whose mouth the chronicler received many notices. (8) A relation of the murder of Boris and Gleb by their brother Sviatopolk ; an account which does not agree with the biography of these saints by the monk Nestor, but does agree with the relation of the monk Jacob.[15] (9) A Paschal calendar in which there were a few notices entered opposite to some of the years. (10) Written and dated notices preserved at Kiev, beginning with A.D. 882, the year in which the centre of the Russian realm was transferred from Novgorod to Kiev. Srkulj conjectures that these notices were drawn up in the Norse language by a Norman who had learned to write in England or Gaul, and perhaps in Runic characters. (11) Local chronicles, cp. a chronicle of Novgorod, of the existence of which we are otherwise certified. (12) Possibly a relation of the story of Vasilko, c. 82.

The traditional view that the monk Nestor, who wrote the biography of Boris and Gleb, and a life of Theodosius of Peshtcherski (see above, p. 173), was the author of the chronicle is generally rejected. Nestor lived in the latter part of the 11th century, and, as we do not know the date of his death, so far as chronology is concerned, he *might* have compiled the chronicle in 1115. But not only does the account of Boris and Gleb (as noticed above) not agree with Nestor's biography of those sainted princes, but there are striking discrepancies between the chronicler's and Nestor's accounts of Theodosius. And, while the chronicler expressly says that he was an eye-witness, Nestor expressly says that he derived his information from others. It is very hard to get over this. There are two other candidates for the authorship : (1) Sylvester, abbot of St. Michael, who states, at the end of the Chronicle in the Laurentian Ms., that he " wrote these books of annals " in

---

[10] Sreznevski, Drevnije pamjatniky russk. pisima i jazyka, p. 47.

[11] Cp. Bestuzhev-Riumin, O sostavie russkich Lietopisei (in the Lietopisi zaniatii archeogr. Kommissii 1865-6), p. 19-35.

[12] There is a question as to the end of the chronicle. M. Leger thinks it reached down to 1113 ; but in the Laurentian Ms. it stops in 1110.

[13] See a good Summary in Stjepan Srkulj, Die Entstehung der ältesten russischen sogenannten Nestorchronik (1896), p. 7 *sqq.* ; Leger, Introduction to his translation, p. xiv.-xvii. ; Pogodin, Nestor, ein. nist.-crit. Untersuchung, tr, Loewe (1844) ; Bestuzhev-Riumin, *op. cit.*

[14] Suhomlinov ascribes the work to the Patriarch Methodius of the 9th century. See Srkulj, *op. cit.*, p. 10.

[15] Sreznevski, Skazanie o sv. Borisie i Gliebie, 1860, Some think that Jacob used the account in the Chronicle, c. 47.

A.D. 1116; as long as Nestor was regarded as the author, the word for *wrote* was interpreted as *copied* (though a different compound is usually employed in that sense), but Golubinski and Kostomarov have proposed to regard the abbot as the author and not a mere copyist; (2) the monk Basil who is mentioned in the story of Vasilko (c. 82), and speaks there in the first person: "I went to find Vasilko". But this may be explained by supposing that the compiler of the chronicle has mechanically copied, without making the necessary change of person, a relation of the episode of Vasilko written by this Basil. The authorship of the chronicle is not solved; we can only say that the compiler was a monk of the Peshtcherski monastery of Kiev.

[For a minute study of Nestor the editions of the Laurentian (1846 and 1872) and the Hypatian (1846 and 1871) Mss. published by the Archæographical Commission must be used. For ordinary purposes the text of Miklosich (1860) is still convenient. Excellent French translation by L. Leger, Chronique dite de Nestor, 1884, with an index [16] which is half a commentary.]

LATIN AND OTHER WESTERN SOURCES

AMATUS of Salerno, monk of Monte Cassino and bishop of an unknown see, wrote about A.D. 1080 a history of the Norman conquest of southern Italy, taking as a model the Historia Langobardorum of Paul the Deacon. We do not possess the work in its original shape, but only in a faulty French translation, made perhaps c. 1300 A.D., which has survived in a single Ms. It was edited for the first time, and not well, by Champollion-Figeac in 1835 (L'Ystoire de li Normant et la Chronique de Robert Viscart, par Aimé, moine de Mont-Cassin), but has been recently edited by O. Delarc, 1892. The work is divided into 8 Books, and embraces the history of the Normans, from their first appearance in Italy to A.D. 1078. "It is," says Giesebrecht, "no dry monosyllabic annalistic account, but a full narrative of the conquest with most attractive details, told with charming *naïveté*. Yet Amatus does not overlook the significance of the events which he relates, in their ecumenical context. His view grasps the contemporary Norman conquest of England, the valiant feats of the French knights against the Saracens of Spain, and the influence of Norman mercenaries in the Byzantine empire. In beginning his work (which he dedicates to the Abbot Desiderius, Robert Guiscard's intimate friend) he is conscious that a red thread runs through all these undertakings of the knight-errants and that God has some special purpose in His dealings with this victorious race." [For criticism of the work, see F. Hirsch in Forschungen zur deutschen Geschichte, 8, p. 205 *sqq.* (1868).]

Amatus was unknown to Gibbon, but he was a source of the most important works which Gibbon used. He was one of the sources of the poem of WILLIAM OF APULIA (begun c. A.D. 1099, finished by A.D. 1111), who also utilised the Annals of Bari. Now that we have Amatus (as well as the Annals of Bari) the value of William lies in the circumstance that he used also a lost biography of Robert Guiscard. [New ed. by Wilmans, in Pertz, Mon. ix. p. 239 *sqq.*]

Amatus was also a source of GEOFFREY MALATERRA, who wrote the history of the Normans in Sicily (up to 1099) at the instance of Count Roger (see above, Gibbon's notes in chap. lvi.). [For the relation of this to the Anonymi Vaticani Historia Sicula, see A. Heskel, Die Hist. Sic. des Anon. Vat. und des Gaufredus Malaterra, 1891.]

LEO, monk and librarian of Monte Cassino, afterwards Cardinal-bishop of Ostia (died 1115), wrote a chronicle of his monastery, which he carried down to A.D. 1075. It is a laudable work, for which ample material (discreetly used by Leo) lay in the library of the monastery. [Ed. by Wattenbach in Pertz, Mon. vii. p. 574 *sqq.* Cp. Balzani, Le cronache Italiane nel medio evo, p. 150 *sqq.* (1884).] The work was continued (c. 1140) by the Deacon PETER, who belonged to the family of the Counts of Tusculum, as far as the year 1137. [Ed. Wattenbach, *ib.* p. 727 *sqq.*]

[16] There are unfortunately many mistakes in the references to the numbers of the chapters.

Other sources (Annales Barenses, Chron. breve Nortmannicum, &c.) are mentioned in the notes of chap. lvi. It should be observed that there is no good authority for the name "Lupus protospatharius," under which name one of the Bari chronicles is always cited. Contemporary Beneventane annals are preserved in (1 Annales Beneventani, in Pertz, Mon. iii. p. 173 *sqq.*, and (2) the incomplete Chronicon of the Beneventane Falco (in Del Re's Cronisti, vol. i. p. 161 *sqq.*); both of which up to 1112 have a common origin. Cp. Giesebrecht, Gesch. der deutschen Kaiserzeit, iii. 1069.

The credibility of the history of HUGO FALCANDUS has been exhibited in some detail by F. Hillger (Das Verhältniss des Hugo Falcandus zu Romuald von Salerno, 1878), and Gibbon's high estimate seems to be justified. Gibbon is also right in rejecting the guess of Clément the Benedictine that the historian is to be identified with Hugo Foucault, Abbot of St. Denis (from 1186-1197). In the first place Foucault would never be Latinised as Falcandus. In the second place, the only plausible evidence for the identification does not bear examination. It is a letter of Peter of Blois to an abbot H. of St. Denys (Opera, ed. Giles, ep. 116, i. p. 178), in which Peter asks his correspondent to send him a *tractatus quem de statu aut potius de casu vestro in Sicilia descripsistis*. But this description does not apply to the Historia Sicula of Falcandus; and it has been shown by Schröter that the correspondent of Peter is probably not Hugo Foucault, but his successor in the abbacy, Hugo of Mediolanum. Schröter has fully refuted this particular identification, and has also refuted the view (held by Amari, Freeman, and others) that Falcandus was a Norman or Frank. On the contrary Falcandus was probably born in Sicily, which he knew well, especially Palermo, and when he wrote his history, he was living not north of the Alps (for he speaks of the Franks, &c., as *transalpini, transmontani*) but in southern Italy. He wrote his Historia Sicula, which reaches from 1154 to 1169, later than 1169, probably (in part at least) after 1181, for he speaks (p. 272, ed. Muratori) of Alexander III. as *qui tunc Romanae praesidebat ecclesiae*, and Alexander died in 1181 (F. Schröter, Uber die Heimath des Hugo Falcandus, 1880). The letter to Peter of Palermo which is prefixed to the History as a sort of dedication seems to have been a perfectly independent composition, written immediately after the death of William the Good in November, 1189, and before the election of Tancred two months later. [Opera cit. of Schröter and Hillger; Freeman, Historical Essays, 3rd ser.; and cp. Holzach, *op. cit.* above, p. 228, note 145; Del Re, preface to his edition (cp. above, p. 228, note 145).]

Compared with Falcandus, ROMUALD, Archbishop of Salerno, is by no means so ingenuous. Although he does not directly falsify facts, his deliberate omissions have the effect of falsifying history; and these omissions were due to the desire of placing the Sicilian court in a favourable light. He is in fact a court historian, and his Annals clearly betray it. The tendency is shown in his cautious reserve touching the deeds and policy of the cruel and ambitious Chancellor Majo. Romuald was related to the royal family and was often entrusted with confidential and important missions. He was a strong supporter of the papacy, but it has been remarked that he entertained "national" ideas—Italy for the Italians, not for the trans-Alpines. He was a learned man and skilled in medicine. [Cp. above, p. 216, n. 111; p. 217, n. 116.]

On the diplomatic documents of the Norman kings, see K. A. Kehr, Die Urkunden der normannisch-Sizilischen Könige, 1902.

The name of the author of the GESTA FRANCORUM was unknown even to those contemporary writers who made use of the work. Whatever his name was, he seems to have been a native of Southern Italy; he accompanied the Norman crusaders who were led by Boemund, across the Illyric peninsula, and shared their fortunes till the end of 1098, when he separated from them at Antioch and attached himself to the Provençals, with whom he went on to Jerusalem. He was not an ecclesiastic like most authors of the age, but a knight. He wrote his history from time to time, during the crusade, according as he had leisure. It falls into eight divisions, each concluded by *Amen;* and these divisions seem to mark the various stages of the composition; they do not correspond to any artistic or logical distribution of the work. Having finished his book at Jerusalem, the author deposited it there—perhaps in the Church of the Holy Sepulchre—where it could be, and was, consulted or copied by pilgrims of an inquiring turn of mind. The author was a pious and enthusiastic crusader, genuinely interested in the religious object of the enterprise; he entirely sinks his own individuality, and identifies himself with the whole company of his fellows. Up to the autumn of 1098 he is devoted to his own leader Boemund; but after c. 29 it has been noticed that the laudatory epithets which have hitherto attended Boemund's name disappear, and, although no criticism is passed, the author thus, almost unintentionally, shows his dissatisfaction with the selfish quarrels between Boemund and Raymond, and has clearly ceased to regard Boemund as a disinterested leader. No written sources were used by the author of the *Gesta* except the Bible and Sibylline Oracles. [See the edition by H. Hagenmeyer, 1889, with full introduction and exegetical notes.]

TUDEBOD of Sivrai, who himself took part in the First Crusade, incorporated (before A.D. 1111) almost the whole of the *Gesta* in his Historia de Hierosolymitano itinere; and it used to be thought that the Gesta was merely an abridged copy of his work. The true relation of the two works was shown by H. von Sybel.

The HISTORIA BELLI SACRI, an anonymous work, was compiled after A.D. 1131, from the Gesta and Tudebod. The works of Raymond of Agiles and Radulf of Caen were also used. [Ed. in the Recueil, iii. p. 169 *sqq.*] The EXPEDITIO CONTRA TURCOS, c. 1094, is also for the most part an excerpt from the Gesta.

RAYMOND of Agiles, in his Historia Francorum qui ceperunt Jerusalem, gives the history of the First Crusade from the Provençal side. It has been shown by Hagenmeyer (Gesta Francorum, p. 50 *sqq.*) that he made use of the Gesta; and Sybel, who held that the two works were entirely independent, remarks on the harmony of the narratives. Raymond is impulsive and gushing, he is superstitious in the most vulgar sense; but his good faith is undoubted, and he reproduces truly his impressions of events. In details he seems to be very accurate. (See the criticism of Sybel, Gesch. des ersten Kreuzzuges, ed. 2, p. 15 *sqq.*; C. Klein, Raimund von Aguilers, 1892.)

FULCHER of Chartres accompanied the host of Robert of Normandy and Stephen of Blois through Apulia and Bulgaria to Nicæa. At Marash he went off with Baldwin against Edessa, and for events in Edessa he is the only eye-witness among the western historians; but from the moment when he begins to be of unique value for Edessa, he becomes of minor importance for the general course of the Crusade. After Godfrey's death he accompanied Baldwin, the new king, to Jerusalem, and remained at his court. His work, which seems to have been written down as a sort of diary, from day to day or month to month, is of the highest importance for the kingdom of Jerusalem from the accession of Baldwin down to 1127 where it ends. Fulcher consulted the Gesta for the events of the First Crusade, of which he was not an eye-witness. (Cp. Sybel, *op. cit.* p. 46 *sqq.* Hagenmeyer, *op. cit.* p. 58 *sqq.*)

GUIBERT (born A.D. 1153), of good family, became abbot of Nogent in 1104. In his Historia quae dicitur Gesta per Francos, he has thrown the Gesta Francorum into a literary form and added a good deal from other sources. The history of the First Crusade ceases with Bk. 6, and in Bk. 7 he has cast together a variety of notices connected with the kingdom of Jerusalem up to 1104. He had been present at the Council of Clermont, he was personally acquainted with Count Robert of Flanders, from whom he derived some pieces of information, and he had various connexions throughout France which were useful to him in the composition of his book. He is conscious of his own importance, and proud of his literary style; he writes with the air of a well-read dignitary of the Church. (Cp. Sybel, *op. cit.* p. 33-4.)

BALDRIC, who became Archbishop of Dol in 1107, was of a very different character and temper from Guibert, and has been taken under the special protection of Sybel, who is pleased "to meet such a pure, peaceful, and cheerful nature in times so stern and warlike". Baldric was opposed to the fashionable asceticism; he lived in literary retirement, enjoying his books and garden, taking as little a part as he could in the ecclesiastical strife which raged around, and exercising as mildly as possible his archiepiscopal powers. He died in 1130. His Historia Jerusalem, composed in 1108, is entirely founded on the Gesta,—the work, as he says, of *nescio quis compilator* (in the Prologue). See Sybel, *op. cit.* p. 35 *sqq.*

Of little value is the compilation of ROBERT the Monk of Reims, who (sometime in the first two decades of the 12th century) undertook the task of translating the Gesta into a better Latin style and adding a notice on the Council of Clermont. It has been shown by Sybel that there is no foundation for the opinion that Robert took part in the Crusade or visited the Holy Land; had he done so, he would certainly have stated the circumstance in his Prologue. (Sybel, *op. cit.* p. 44-6.)

Of FULCO, who wrote an account in hexameters of the events of the First Crusade up to the siege of Nicæa, we know nothing more than that he was a contemporary and was acquainted with Gilo who continued the work. His account has no historical value; he used the Gesta, but did not rifle that source in such a wholesale manner as GILO of Toucy, his collaborator, who took up the subject at the siege of Nicæa. Gilo, who calls himself:

o nomine Parisiensis
incola Tuciaci non inficiandus alumnus,

was appointed in 1121 bishop of Tusculum, and composed his Libellus de via Hierosolymitana between 1118 and 1121. For the first four Books he used Robert the Monk and Albert of Aachen as well as the Gesta; for Bks. 5 and 6 he simply paraphrased the Gesta. (Cp. Hagenmeyer, *op. cit.* p. 74-6.) [Complete ed. in Migne, P. L. vol. 155.]

RADULF of Caen took no part in the Crusade, but he went to Palestine soon afterwards and stood in intimate relations with Tancred. After Tancred's death he determined to write an account of that leader's exploits, Gesta Tancredi in expeditione Hierosolymitana, which he dedicated to Arnulf, Patriarch of Jerusalem. For all that concerns Tancred personally his statements are of great value, but otherwise he has the position merely of a second-hand writer in regard to the general history of the First Crusade. The importance of his information about the capture of Antioch has been pointed out by Sybel. Hagenmeyer has made it probable that he used the Gesta. [Ed. in Muratori, Scr. rer. It., vol. 5, p. 285 *sqq.*; Recueil, iii. p. 603 *sqq.*]

The chronicle of ALBERT of Aachen contains one of the most remarkable of the narratives of the First Crusade. From this book, says Sybel, we hear the voice not of a single person, but of regiments speaking with a thousand tongues; we get a picture of western Europe as it was shaken and affected by that ecumenical event. The story is told vividly, uninterrupted by any reflections on the part of the author; who is profoundly impressed by the marvellous character of the tale which he has to tell; has no scruple in reporting inconsistent statements; and does not trouble himself much about chronology and topography. But the canon of Aachen, who compiled the work as we have it, in the third decade of the 12th century, is not responsible for the swing of the story. He was little more than the copyist of the history of an unknown writer, who belonged to the Lotharingian crusaders and settled in the kingdom of Jerusalem after the First Crusade. Thus we have, in Albert of Aachen, the history of the Crusade from the Lotharingian side. The unknown author probably composed his history some time after the events; Hagenmeyer has shown that he has made use of the Gesta. [The most important contribution to the criticism of Albert is the monograph of Kugler, Albert von Aachen, 1885, which is to be supplemented by Kühn's article in the Neues Archiv, 12, p. 545 *sqq.*, 1887.]

The Hierosolymita (or Libellus de expugnatione Hierosolymitana) of EKKE-
HARD, of the Benedictine abbey of Aura near Kissingen, was published in the
Amplissima Collectio of Martene and Durand (vol. 5, p. 511 *sqq.*), where it might
have been consulted by Gibbon, but he does not seem to have known of it. Ekkehard went overland to Constantinople with a company of German pilgrims in 1101,
sailed from the Imperial city to Joppa, remained six weeks in Palestine, and started
on his return journey before the year was out. He became abbot of his monastery
and died in 1125. His Chronicon Universale is a famous work and is the chief
authority for German history from A.D. 1080 to the year of the author's death. The
Hierosolymita has the value of a contemporary work by one who had himself seen
the Holy Land and the Greek Empire. [Edited in Pertz, Mon. vi. p. 265 *sqq.*; and
by Riant in the Recueil, vol. 5, p. 1 *sqq.*; but most convenient is the separate edition
of Hagenmeyer, 1877.]

Another contemporary writer on the First Crusade, who had himself visited
Palestine, is CAFARO di Caschifelone, of Genoa. He went out with the Genoese
squadron which sailed to the help of the Crusaders in 1100. He was at Jerusalem
at Easter 1101 and took part in the sieges of Arsuf and Caesarea in the same year.
He became afterwards a great person in his native city, was five times consul, composed Annales Genuenses, and died in 1166. His work De Liberatione civitatum
Orientis was not accessible to Gibbon; for it was first published in 1859 by L.
Ansaldo (Cronaca della prima Crociata, in vol. i. of the Acts of the Società Ligure
di storia patria). It was then edited by Pertz, Mon. xviii. p. 40 *sqq.*; and in
vol. v. of the Recueil des historiens des croisades. Contents : chaps. 1-10 give the
events of the First Crusade before the author's arrival on the scene; c. 11 relates
the arrival of the Genoese fleet at Laodicea, and the defeat of the Lombard expedition in Asia Minor in 1101; chaps. 12-18 (in the edition of the Recueil) are an extract from the Annales Genuenses, inserted in this place by the editor Riant, and
describing the events of the year 1100-1101; chaps. 19-27 enumerate the towns of
Syria and their distances from one another; describe the capture of Margat in 1140
by the Crusaders; a naval battle between the Genoese and Greeks; and the
capture of Tortosa, Tripolis, and other places. The work seems never to have been
completed.

For the authorship of the Itinerarium Peregrinorum et Gesta regis Ricardi,
see above, p. 367, note 89. It remains to be added that in its Latin form the
work is not an original composition, but is a very free elaboration of a French
poem written by a Norman named AMBROSE, in rhyming verses of seven syllables.
In the prologue to the Latin work (p. 4, ed. Stubbs) the writer says *nos in castris
fuisse cum scripsimus ;* but we should expect him to mention the fact that he had
first written his account in Franco-Gallic. Nicholas Trivet (at the beginning ·of
the 14th cent.) distinctly ascribes the Itinerarium to Richard of London, Canon
of the Holy Trinity (qui itinerarium regis prosa et metro scripsit) ;[17] but the
contemporary Chronicon Terrae Sanctae (see below) states that the Prior of the
Holy Trinity of London caused it to be translated from French into Latin (ex
Gallica lingua in Latinum transferri fecit).[18] The natural inference is that
Richard the Canon transformed the rhymed French of Ambrose into a Latin prose
dress; but it is not evident why the name of Ambrose is suppressed. Nor is it quite
clear whether Trivet, when he says *prosa et metro*, meant the French verse and
the Latin prose, or whether *metro* refers to the Latin rhymes which are occasion-
ally introduced (chiefly in Bk. I.) in the Itinerarium. [Extracts from the Carmen
Ambrosii are edited by F. Liebermann (1885) in Pertz, Mon. 27, 532 *sqq.* See
Wattenbach, Deutschlands Geschichtsquellen, ed. 6, ii. p. 316.]

For the crusade of Richard I. RALPH OF COGGESHALL's Chronicon Anglicanum
(A.D. 1066-1223) is an important authority, and it was the source of the account in
Matthew Paris. Ralph, who was abbot of the Cistercian Monastery of Coggeshall, in
Essex, died about 1228, was not in the Holy Land himself, but he obtained his in-
formation from eye-witnesses (*e.g.* from Hugh de Neville, who described for him the

---

[17] Stubbs, Introduction, p. xli.   [18] *Ib.*, p. xii.

episode of Joppa in Aug. 1192, and from Anselm, the king's chaplain). [Edited in the Rolls series by J. Stevenson, 1875.]

Another contemporary account of the Third Crusade is contained in the CHRONICON TERRAE SANCTAE, ascribed without any reason to Ralph of Coggeshall, and printed along with his Chronicle in Martene and Durand, Ampl. Coll. vol. 5, and in the Rolls series (p. 209 sqq.). An independent narrative, derived apparently from a crusader's journal,[19] is incorporated in the Gesta Henrici II. et Ricardi I., which goes under the name of Benedict of Peterborough (who, though he did not compose the work, caused it to be compiled). [Edited by Stubbs in the Rolls series, 1867.] Material for Richard's Crusade will also be found in other contemporary English historians, such as Ralph de Diceto, William of Newburgh, &c.

WILLIAM OF TYRE is the greatest of the historians of the Crusades and one of the greatest historians of the Middle Ages. He was born in Palestine in 1127 and became archbishop of Tyre in 1174. A learned man, who had studied ancient Latin authors (whom he often cites), he had the advantage of being acquainted with Arabic, and he used Arabic books to compose a history of the Saracens from the time of Mohammad (see his Prologue to the History of the Crusades). He was always in close contact with the public affairs of the kingdom of Jerusalem, political as well as ecclesiastical. He was the tutor of Baldwin IV., and was made Chancellor of the kingdom by that king. His great work (Historia rerum in partibus transmarinis gestarum) falls into two parts: (1) Books 1-15, to A.D. 1144: so far his narrative depends on "the relation of others" (Bk. 16, c. 1), and he has used (though he does not say so) the works of earlier writers (such as Fulcher of Chartres, and Albert of Aachen), as well as the memories of older men with whom he was acquainted; but his judgment is throughout entirely independent. (2) Books 16-23, to A.D. 1184: here he writes as a contemporary eye-witness, but he is careful and conscientious in informing himself, from every possible source, concerning the events which he relates; and he is remarkably cautious in his statements of facts. The miraculous seldom plays a part in his story; he is unfeignedly pious, but he seeks an earthly explanation of every earthly event.[20] His history, along with the Book of the Assises, is the chief material for forming a picture of the Latin colonies in Palestine. Chronology, Sybel remarks, is the weak side of his work; and we may add that it is often spoiled by too much rhetoric. It was translated into French in the second quarter of the 13th century. [Included in the Recueil, Hist. Occ., vol. i. (1844).]

The work of William of Tyre was continued in French by ERNOUL (squire of Balian, lord of Ibelin; he had taken part in the battle of Hittin and the siege of Jerusalem) down to 1229; and by BERNARD (the Treasurer of St. Peter at Corbie) down to 1231. These continuations were continued by anonymous writers down to 1277; and the French translation of William along with the continuations was current as a single work under the title of the Chronique d'Outremer, or L'Estoire de Éracles.[21] [The Continuations were first critically examined and analysed by M. de Mas-Latrie,[22] who edited the works of Ernoul and Bernard (1871). Edition of Guillaume de Tyr et ses Continuateurs, by P. Paris, 2 vols., 1879-80.]

It may be added here that the charters and letters pertaining to the Kingdom of Jerusalem have been edited under the title Regesta Regni Hierosolymitani, by Röhricht, 1893. The documents bearing on the First Crusade have been collected by Hagenmeyer, Epistolæ et chartæ ad historiam primi belli sacri spectantes quæ supersunt aevo æquales et genuinæ, 1901. The numismatic material has been collected and studied by M. G. Schlumberger: Numismatique de l'Orient Latin, 1878.

Marshal VILLEHARDOUIN's Conquest of Constantinople is, along with Nicetas, the main guide of Gibbon in his account of the Fourth Crusade. Gibbon thought,

[19] Cp. Stubbs, Introd. to Itinerarium, p. xxxviii.
[20] Sybel, Gesch. des ersten Kreuzzuges, ed. 2, p. 120.
[21] An absurd title taken from the opening sentence of William of Tyre.
[22] Essai de classification, &c., in Bibl. de l'école des chartes, Sér. V. t. i. 38 sqq., 140 sqq. (1860); and in his ed. of Ernoul and Bernard, p. 473 sqq.

and it has been generally thought till late years, that this famous book, composed by one of the wisest and most moderate of the Crusaders, was a perfectly naïve and candid narrative, partial indeed to the conduct of the conquerors, but still—when allowance has been made for the point of view—a faithful relation of facts without an *arrière pensée*. But, if there are some who, like his editor M. de Wailly, still maintain the unblemished candour of Villehardouin as an author, recent criticism in the light of new evidence leaves hardly room for reasonable doubt that Villehardouin's work was deliberately intended to deceive the European public as to the actual facts of the Fourth Crusade. There can be no question that Villehardouin was behind the scenes; he represents the expedition against Constantinople as an accidental diversion, which was never intended when the Crusade was organized; and therefore his candour can be rescued only by proving that the episode of Constantinople was really nothing more than a diversion. But the facts do not admit of such an interpretation. During the year which elapsed between the consent of the Venetian Republic to transport the Crusaders and the time when the Crusaders assembled at Venice (A.D. 1201-2), the two most important forces concerned in the enterprise—Venice and Boniface of Montfrrat—had determined to divert the Crusade from its proper and original purpose. Venice had determined that, wherever the knights sailed, they should *not* sail to the place whither she had undertaken to transport them, namely to the shores of Egypt. For in the course of that eventful year she made a treaty with the Sultan of Egypt, pledging herself that Egypt should not be invaded. And on his part, Boniface of Montferrat had arranged with the Emperor Philip and Alexius that the swords of the Crusaders should be employed at Constantinople. (For all this see above, p. 400-1, n. 51 and 53, and p. 404, n. 63.) On these facts, which were of the first importance, Villehardouin says not a word; and one cannot hesitate to conclude that his silence is deliberate. In fact, his book is, as has been said, an " official " version of the disgraceful episode. The Fourth Crusade shocked public opinion in Europe; men asked how such a thing had befallen, how the men who had gone forth to do battle against the infidels had been drawn aside from their pious purpose to attack Christian states. The story of Villehardouin, a studied suppression of the truth, was the answer. [Mas-Latrie and Riant take practically this point of view, which has been presented well and moderately by E. Pears in his Fall of Constantinople (an excellent work), 1885. J. Tessier, La diversion sur Zara et Constantinople (1884), defends Villehardouin. Cp. also L. Streit's Venedig und die Wendung des vierten Kreuzzuges gegen Constantinopel; and W. Norden, Der vierte Kreuzzug im Rahmen der Beziehungen des Abendlandes zu Byzanz, 1898.—Editions: by N. de Wailly, 3rd ed., 1882 ; E. Bouchet, 2 vols., 1891.]

Besides Gunther's work, which Gibbon used (see p. 401, note 54), some new sources on the Fourth Crusade have been made accessible. The most important of these is the work of ROBERT DE CLARY, Li estoires de chiaus qui conquisent Constantinoble ; which, being " non-official," supplies us with a check on Villehardouin. [Printed by Riant in 1868 and again in 1871, but in so few copies that neither issue could be properly called an edition. Edited (1873) by Hopf in his Chroniques Gréco-romanes, p. 1 *sqq.*]

Another contemporary account is preserved, the DEVASTATIO CONSTANTINOPOLITANA, by an anonymous Frank, and is an official diary of the Crusade. [Pertz, Mon. xvi. p. 9 *sqq.* ; Hopf, Chron. Gréco-romanes, p. 86 *sqq.*]

The work of Moncada, which Ducange and Gibbon used for the history of the Catalan expedition, is merely a loose compilation of the original Chronicle of RAMON MUNTANER, who was not only a contemporary but one of the most prominent members of the Catalan Grand Company. A Catalonian of good family, born at Peralada, in 1255, he went to reside at Valencia in 1276, witnessed the French invasion of Philip the Bold in 1285, and in 1300 set sail for Sicily and attached himself to the fortunes of Roger de Flor, whom he accompanied to the east. He returned to the west in 1308; died and was buried at Valencia about 1336. The account of the doings of the Catalans in the east is of course written from their point of view; and the adventurer passes lightly over their pillage and oppression. It is one of the most interesting books of the period. [Most recent edition of the original Catalan, by J. Corolen, 1886 ; conveniently consulted in Buchon's French version, in Chroniques étrangères (1860). Monographs : A. Rubió y Lluch, La expedicion y dominacion de los Catalanes en oriente juzgedas por los Griegos, 1883, and Los Navarros en Grecia y el ducado Catalan de Atenas en la época de su invasion, 1886 (this deals with a later period) ; G. Schlumberger, Expédition des " Almugavares " ou routiers catalans en Orient, 1902.]

ORIENTAL SOURCES

[Extracts from the writers mentioned below, and others, will be found in vol. iv. of Michaud's Bibliothèque des Croisades (1829), translated and arranged by M. Reinaud.]

IMĀD AD-DĪN al-Kātib al-Ispahāni was born at Ispahan in A.D. 1125, and studied at Baghdad. He obtained civil service appointments, but fell into disfavour and was imprisoned; after which he went to Damascus, where Nūr ad-Dīn was ruling. He became the friend of prince Saladin, and was soon appointed secretary of state under Nūr ad-Dīn, but after this potentate's death his position was precarious, and he set out to return to Baghdad. But hearing of Saladin's successes in Egypt he went back to Damascus and attached himself to his old friend. After Saladin's death (A.D. 1193) he withdrew into private life. He wrote a history of the Crusades with the affected title : Historia Cossica [Coss was a contemporary of Mohammad] de expugnatione Codsica [that is, Hierosolymitana], of which extracts were published by Schultens; he also wrote a History of the Seljūks. See Wüstenfeld, Arabische Geschichtschreiber, no. 284.

BAHĀ AD-DĪN (the name is often corrupted to Bohadin) was born in 1145 at Mōsil, and became professor there in 1174 in the college founded by Kamāl ad-Dīn. In 1188 he made the pilgrimage to Mecca, and on his way back visited Damascus, where Saladin sent for him and offered him a professorship at Cairo. This he declined, but he afterwards took service under Saladin and was appointed judge of the army and to a high official post at Jerusalem. After Saladin's death he was made judge of Aleppo, where he founded a college and mosque, and a school for teaching the traditions of the Prophet. He died in 1234. His biography of Saladin is one of the most important sources for the Third Crusade, and the most important source for the life of Saladin. [Edited with French translation in vol. iii. of the Recueil des historiens des Croisades, Hist. Or. (Here too will be found a notice of the author's life by Ibn Khallikān.) Translation (unscholarly) published by the Palestine Exploration Fund, 1897.]

Abū l-Hasan Alī IBN AL-ATHIR was born A.D. 1160. He studied at Mōsil and was there when Saladin besieged it in 1186. He was in Syria about 1189, so that he saw something of the Third Crusade. But he was a man of letters and took little part in public affairs. He wrote (1) a history of the Atābegs of Mōsil and (2) a universal history from the creation of the world to A.D. 1231. The part of this second work bearing on the Crusades, from A.D. 1098 to 1190, will be found in the Recueil, Hist. Or. vol. i. p. 189 sqq.; and on the author's life see ib. p. 752 sqq. The history of the Atābegs is published in the 2nd part of vol. ii.

KAMĀL AD-DĪN ibn al-Adīm, born c. A.D. 1192, belonged to the family of the cadhis of Aleppo. Having studied at Baghdad and visited Damascus, Jerusalem, &c., he became judge of Aleppo himself, and afterwards vizier. When the Tartars destroyed the place in A.D. 1260, he fled to Egypt. He wrote a History of his native city, and part of this is the Récit de la première croisade et des quatorze années suivantes, published in Defrémery, Mémoires d'histoire orientale, 1854. [Recueil des hist. des Croisades, Hist. Or. vol. iii. p. 577 sqq.]

Abū-l-Kāsim ABD AR-RAHMĀN (called Abū Shāma, "father of moles") was born in Damascus A.D. 1202 and assassinated A.D. 1266. He wrote Liber duorum hortorum de historia duorum regnorum, a history of the reigns of Nūr ad-Dīn and Saladin, which is edited by Quatremère in vol. ii. of the Recueil des hist. des Croisades, Hist. Or.

JALĀL AD-DĪN (A.D. 1207-1298) was born at Hamāh in Syria and afterwards went to Egypt, where he was a witness of the invasion of Louis IX. He visited Italy (1260) as the ambassador of the Sultan Baybars to King Manfred. He was a teacher of Abū-l-Fidā, who lauds his wide knowledge. He wrote a history of the Ayyūbid lords of Egypt. The work which Reinaud used for Michaud's Bibliothèque des Croisades is either part of this history or a separate work.

ABU-L-FIDĀ, born at Damascus A.D. 1273, belonged to the family of the lords of Hamāh (a side branch of the Ayyūbids). He was present at the conquest of Tripolis in A.D. 1289 and at the siege of Acre (which fell A.D. 1291); and he joined in the military expeditions of his cousin Mahmūd II. of Hamāh. He took part also in the expeditions of the Egyptian Sultan, to whom he was always loyal. In A.D. 1310 he received himself the title of sultan, as lord of Hamāh. But in this new dignity, which he was reluctant to accept, he used to go every year to Cairo to present gifts to his liege lord. He died in A.D. 1332, having ruled Hamāh for eleven years. His great work, Compendium historiae generis humani, came down to A.D. 1329. (The first or pre-Mohammadan part has been edited with Lat. tr. by Fleischer in 1831; the second, or Life of Mohammad—ed. by Gagnier, 1723—was translated into French by M. des Vergers, 1837.) The post-Mohammadan part of this work was edited by Reiske in 5 vols. under the title Annales Moslemici, with Lat. transl. (1789-1794); Gibbon had access to extracts in the Auctarium to the Vita Saladini of Schultens (1732). A summary of Abū-l-Fidā's account of the Crusades will be found in vol. i. of the Recueil, Hist. Or. [F. Wilken, Commentatio de bellorum cura ex Abulf. hist., 1798.]

A large number of extracts from Armenian writers, bearing on the Crusades, are published with French translation by Dulaurier in the Recueil des historiens des Croisades, Doc. Arm. tome i. Among these is the Chronological Table (A.D. 1076-1307) of HAITUM (p. 469 sqq.), who belonged to the family of the princes of Lampron, and became Count of Courcy (Gorigos). He became a monk of the Praemonstratensian order in 1305 and went to Cyprus. He visited Clement V. at Avignon, and Gibbon refers to the History of the Tartars, which he dictated, at the Pope's request, in French to Nicolas Falconi, who immediately translated it into Latin. This work of "Haythonus" is extant in both forms. Among the other sources included in this collection of Dulaurier may be mentioned : a rhymed chronicle on the kings of Little Armenia, by Vahram of Edessa, of the 13th cent. (p. 493 sqq.); works of St. Narses of Lampron (born 1153); extracts from Cyriac (Guiragos) of Gantzac (born 1201-2), who wrote a history of Armenia[23] from the time of Gregory Illuminator to 1269-70. There are also extracts from the chronicle of SAMUEL of Ani, which reached from the beginning of the world to 1177-8 (p. 447 sqq.), and from its continuation up to 1339-40: this chronicle was published in a Latin translation by Mai and Zohrab, 1818, which is reprinted in Migne's Patr. Gr. 19, p. 599 sqq. But the best known of these Armenian authors is MATTHEW of Edessa, whose chronicle covers a century and three quarters (A.D. 963-1136). We know nothing of the author's life, except that he flourished in the first quarter of the 12th century. His work is interesting as well as valuable; his style simple, without elegance and art; for he was a man without much culture and had probably read little. He depended much on oral information (derived from "old men"); but he has preserved a couple of original documents (one of them is a letter of the Emperor Tzimisces to an Armenian king, c. 16). He is an ardent Armenian patriot;

[23] This has been translated (along with a tenth century historian, Uchtanes of Edessa) by Brosset, 1870-1.

he hates the Greeks as well as the Turks, and he is, not without good cause, bitter against the Frank conquerors. [French translation by Dulaurier (along with the Continuation by the priest Gregory to A.D. 1164), 1858, in the Bibliothèque hist. Arménienne. Extracts in the Recueil, p. 1 *sqq.*]

COINS. W. Wroth, Catalogue of the Coins [of the Vandals, Ostrogoths and Lombards, and] of the Empires of Thessalonica, Nicæa, and Trebizond, in the British Museum, 1911.

MODERN WORKS. Finlay, History of Greece, vols. ii.-iv.; Hopf, Griechische Geschichte (in Ersch und Gruber, Enzyklopädie, *sub* Griechenland); Gregorovius, Geschichte der Stadt Athen im Mittelalter, 1897 ; Ranke, Weltgeschichte, vol. 8. For military history : C. Oman, History of the Art of War, vol. 2, books iv. and v. For papal diplomacy from eleventh to fifteenth century : W. Norden, Das Papsttum und Byzanz, 1903.

For the ecclesiastical schism in the eleventh century : L. Bréhier, Le schisme orientale du xie siècle, 1899 ; J. Dräseke, Psellos und seine Anklageschrift gegen den Patriarchen Michael Kerularios, in Zeitschrift für wissenschaftliche Theologie, 48, 194 *sqq.*, 362 *sqq.* (1905).

For the Normans : G. de Blasiis, La insurrezione pugliese e la conquista Normanna nel secolo xi., 1864 ; J. W. Barlow, The Normans in Southern Italy, 1886 ; O. Delarc, Les Normands en Italie, 1883 ; L. von Heinemann, Geschichte der Normannen in Unter-Italien und Sizilien, vol. i., 1893 ; F. Chalandon, Histoire de la Normandie en Italie et en Sicile, 2 vols., 1907. See also J. Gay, L'Italie méridionale et l'empire byzantin, 1904 ; E. Caspar, Roger II. (1101-1154) und die Gründung der normannisch-sizilischen Monarchie, 1904.

For the Crusades : F. Wilken, Gesch. der Kreuzzüge, 7 vols., 1807-32 ; Michaud, Histoire des Croisades (in 6 vols.), 1825 (Eng. tr. in 3 vols., by W. Robson, 1852) ; H. von Sybel, Geschichte des ersten Kreuzzuges, 1881 (ed. 2) ; B. von Kugler, Geschichte der Kreuzzüge, 1880, and Studien zur Gesch. des 2ten Kreuzzuges, 1866 ; Röhricht, Geschichte des Königreichs Jerusalem, 1898 ; Geschichte des ersten Kreuzzuges, 1901 ; H. Prutz, Kulturgeschichte der Kreuzzüge, 1883 ; Archer and Kingsford, The Crusades ; G. Le Strange, Palestine under the Muslims, 1890 ; W. B. Stevenson, The Crusades in the East, 1907 (in this work the Crusades are treated as part of *eastern* history, and there are valuable corrections of the chronology) ; L. Bréhier, L'Eglise et l'Orient au moyen âge : Les Croisades, 1907. See also Chalandon's monograph on Alexius Comnenus, referred to above, vol. v. p. 242, n. 71. For Frederick Barbarossa : K. Zimmert, Der Friede zu Adrianopel (Februar 1190) in Byzantinische Zeitschrift, 11, 303 *sqq.*, 1902, and Der deutsch-byzantinische Konflikt vom Juli 1189 bis Februar 1190, *ib.* 12, 42 *sqq.*, 1903. For the crusade of Louis IX.: Davis, The Invasion of Egypt in 1249, by Louis IX., 1898. For the Knights of St. John : I. Delaville le Roulx, Les Hospitaliers en Terre Sainte et à Chypre (1100-1310), 1904. For the institutions and organisation of the Kingdom : G. Dodu, Hist. des institutions monarchiques dans le royaume latin de Jér., 1894.

For the Latin Empire of Romania : E. Gerland, Geschichte des lateinischen Kaiserreiches von Konstantinopel, Iter Teil, 1905. For the Latin States founded in Greeklands after 1204 : Sir Rennell Rodd, The Princes of Achaia and the Chronicles of Morea, A Study of Greece in the Middle Ages, 2 vols., 1907 ; W. Miller, The Latins in the Levant, A History of Frankish Greece (1204-1566), 1908. See also G. Caro, Genua und die Mächte am Mittelmeer (1257-1311), 2 vols., 1895, 1899. For smaller monographs, see below, Appendix 18.

For the Empire of Nicæa : A. Mêliarakês, Ἱστορία τοῦ Βασιλείου τῆς Νικαίας καὶ τοῦ Δεσποτάτου τῆς Ἠπείρου (1204-1261), 1898 ; I. B. Pappadopoulos, Théodore II. Lascaris, Empereur de Nicée, 1908 ; A. Heisenberg, Kaiser Johannes Batatzes der Barmherzige, Eine mittelgriechische Legende, in Byzantinische Zeitschrift, 14, 160 *sqq.*, 1905. The general history of the Greek Empire in the 13th and 14th centuries is reviewed in the first chapters of E. Pears, The Destruction of the Greek Empire, 1903.

2. SARACEN COINAGE—(P. 5)

The following account of the introduction of a separate coinage by the Omay-yads is taken from Mr. Stanley Lane-Poole's Coins and Medals, p. 164 *sqq*.

" It took the Arabs half a century to discover the need of a separate coinage of their own. At first they were content to borrow their gold and copper currency from the Byzantine Empire, which they had driven out of Syria, and their silver coins from the Sassanian kings of Persia, whom they had overthrown at the battles of Kadisia and Nehavend. The Byzantine gold served them till the seventy-sixth year of the Flight, when a new, but theologically unsound and consequently evanescent, type was invented, bearing the effigy of the reigning Khalif instead of that of Heraclius, and Arabic instead of Greek inscriptions. So, too, the Sassanian silver pieces were left unaltered, save for the addition of a governor's name in Pehlvi letters. The Khalif 'Aly or one of his lieutenants seems to have attempted to inaugurate a purely Muslim coinage, exactly resembling that which was after-wards adopted ; but only one example of this issue is known to exist, in the Paris collection, together with three other silver coins struck at Damascus and Merv be-tween A.H. 60 and 70, of a precisely similar type. These four coins are clearly early and ephemeral attempts at the introduction of a distinctive Mohammadan coinage, and their recent discovery in no way upsets the received Muslim tradition that it was the Khalif 'Abd-El-Melik who, in the year of the Flight 76 (or, on the evidence of the coins themselves, 77), inaugurated the regular Muslim coinage which was thenceforward issued from all the mints of the empire, so long as the dynasty endured, and which gave its general character to the whole currency of the kingdoms of Islam. The copper coinage founded on the Byzantine passed through more and earlier phases than the gold and silver, but it always held [an] insignificant place in the Muslim currency. . . ."

The gold and silver coins of 'Abd-El-Melik " both bear the same formulæ of faith : on the obverse, in the area, ' There is no god but God alone, He hath no partner ' ; around which is arranged a marginal inscription, ' Mohammad is the apostle of God, who sent him with the guidance and religion of truth, that he might make it triumph over all other religions in spite of the idolaters,' the gold stopping at ' other religions '. This inscription occurs on the reverse of the silver instead of the obverse, while the date inscription, which is found on the reverse of the gold, appears on the obverse of the silver. The reverse area declares that ' God is One, God is the Eternal : He begetteth not, nor is begotten ' ; here the gold ends, but the silver continues, ' and there is none like unto Him '. The margin of the gold runs, ' In the name of God : the Dînâr was struck in the year seven and seventy ' ; the silver substituting ' Dirhem ' for ' Dînâr,' and inserting the place of issue immediately after the word Dirhem, *e.g.*, ' El-Andalus (*i.e.* Andalusia) in the year 116 '. The mint is not given on the early gold coins, probably because they were usually struck at the Khalif's capital, Damascus.

" These original dînârs (a name formed from the Roman denarius) and dirhems (drachma) of the Khalif of Damascus formed the model of all Muslim coinages for many centuries ; and their respective weights—65 and 43 grains—served as the standard of all subsequent issues up to comparatively recent times. The finest was about ·979 gold in the dînârs, and ·960 to ·970 silver in the dirhem. The Moham-madan coinage was generally very pure. . . . At first ten dirhems went to the dînâr, but the relation varied from age to age."

Thus the dînâr of the Omayyad Caliphs, weighing on the average 65·3 grains of almost pure gold, was worth about 11s. 6d. In later times there were double dînârs, and under the Omayyads there were thirds of a dînâr, which weighed less than half a dirhem.

As to a coin which Gibbon supposes (p. 5, note 9) to be preserved in the Bod-leian Library, Mr. S. Lane-Poole kindly informed me that no such coin exists there. " The Wâsit coins there preserved were acquired long after Gibbon's time and none has the date 88 A.H. There is a dirhem of that year in the British Museum weighing 44·6 grains. [S. Lane-Poole, Catalogue of Mohammadan Coins in the Bodleian Library, 1888 ; Catalogue of Oriental Coins in the British Museum, vol. i. no. 174 (1875).] "

3. THE THEMES OF THE ROMAN EMPIRE—(P. 65, 70 *sqq.*)

[Modern investigations : Rambaud, L'empire grec au dixième siècle, p. 175 *sqq.*; Bury, Later Roman Empire, vol. ii., p. 339 *sqq.*; Diehl, L'origine du régime des thèmes dans l'empire byzantin (in Etudes d'histoire du moyen âge dédiées à Gabriel Monod, 1896); Schlumberger, Sigillographie byzantine, passim, 1884 ; Gelzer, Die Genesis der byzantinischen Themenverfassung, Abhandlungen der kön. Gesellschaft der Wissenschaften, phil.-hist. Cl. xviii., 1899 ; Brooks, Arabic Lists of the Byzantine Themes, Journal of Hellenic Studies, xxi. p. 67 *sqq.*, 1901 ; Kulakovski, K voprosu o themakh vizantiiskoi imperii, Izbornik Kievskii, 25, No. xi., 1904.]

In the eighth century we find the Empire divided into a number of *themes*, each of which is governed by a *stratêgos*. Not only the title of the governor, but the word theme (θέμα, a regiment) shows their military origin. These themes originated in the seventh century. In the latter part of that century we find the empire consisting of a number of large military provinces, not yet called themes, but probably known as στρατηγίαι. We have no official list of them; but from literary notices we can reconstruct an approximate list of the provinces c. 700 A.D. :—[1]

1. The Armeniacs.	6. The Helladics.
2. The Anatolics.	7. Italy.
3. The Opsikion.	8. Sicily.
4. The Marines.	9. Africa.
5. Thrace.	

We have to consider first how this system originated, and secondly how it developed into the system of themes which we find two centuries later. The origin and development up to the end of the eighth century have been worked out most fully by Gelzer in the admirable work named above.

The identification of the stratêgoi of the seventh century with the magistri militum of the sixth century gives the clue to the origin of the thematic system. (This was pointed out in Bury's Later Roman Empire, ii. 346-8.) The stratêgos of the Armeniacs is the magister militum of Armenia, instituted by Justinian ; the stratêgos of the Anatolics is the magister militum per Orientem ; the "count" of the Opsikians corresponds to the mag. mil. praesentalis ;[2] the stratêgos of Thrace is the mag. mil. per Thraciam ; the stratêgos of the Helladics is probably the representative of the mag. mil. per Illyricum. The magistri militum of Africa and Italy remain under the title of exarchs. The maritime provinces arose probably, as Diehl attractively suggests, from the province of Caria, Cyprus, Rhodes, the Cyclades and Scythia, instituted by Justinian, and placed by him under a quaestor Justinianus.

Thus, what happened was this. In the seventh century the old system of dioceses and provinces was swept away. Its place was taken by the already existing division of the Empire into military provinces—the spheres of the magistri militum ; and a new Greek nomenclature was introduced. The cause of the change was the extreme peril of the Empire from the Saracens. The needs of defence suggested a military organization ; when the frontier was reduced and every province was exposed to the attacks of the enemy, there was a natural tendency to unite civil and military power. In the west, the exarch of Africa and the exarch of Italy are the magistri militum who have got into their hands the power of the Praetorian prefects of Africa and Italy respectively ; and in the same way in the east, the stratêgoi of Thrace, the Anatolics, the Armeniacs and the Opsikians, have each a parcel of the prerogatives of the Praetorian Prefect of the East.

During the eighth and ninth centuries the provinces came to be generally called themes, and the list was modified in several ways. (1) It was reduced by losses of territory ; thus Africa was lost. (2) Some of the large provinces were broken up into a number of smaller. (3) Some small frontier districts, which were called

---

[1] Diehl, L'origine des Thèmes, p. 9 ; Bury, Later Roman Empire, ii. p. 345.
[2] Diehl, *ib.* p. 15. Diehl has developed this explanation more fully.

clisurarchies (κλεισοίρα, a mountain pass), and had been dependent on one of the larger districts, were raised to the dignity of independent themes. For example, the Marine theme ultimately became three : the Cibyrrhaeot,[3] the theme of Samos, and the Aegean Sea.

We can trace in the chronicles some changes of this kind which were carried out between the seventh and the tenth centuries. But it is not till the middle of the ninth century that we get any official list to give us a general view of the divisions of the Empire. The treatise on the themes by the Emperor Constantine (see above, p. 70 *sqq.*), composed about A.D. 934, is generally taken as the basis of investigation, and, when historians feel themselves called upon to give a list of the Byzantine themes, they always quote his. In my opinion this is a mistake. We possess better lists than Constantine's, of a somewhat earlier date. Emperor though Constantine was, his list is not official; it is a concoction, in which actual facts are blended with unmethodical antiquarian research. His treatise is valuable indeed ; but it should be criticised in the light of the *official* lists which we possess.

(1) The earliest list is the Taktikon, published by Uspenski in the Izviestiia russkago arkheol. Instituta v. Konstantinopolie, iii., 100 *sqq.*, 1808. It was drawn up in the reign of Michael III. and Theodora (A.D. 842-856), probably soon after A.D. 842. It was unknown to Gelzer, but has been utilised by Bury, The Imperial Administrative System in the Ninth Century, 1910, and by the same writer in his History of the Eastern Roman Empire, Chapter VII., 1912.

Belonging to the same period we have a list of themes, preserved in Arabic writers (Ibn Khurdadhbah, etc.), utilised by Gelzer and examined more fully by Brooks (article cited above).

From these data, combined with various incidental notices in Byzantine writers, we are able to conclude that at the very beginning of the ninth century there were *five* large Asiatic Themes : Anatolic, Armeniac, Opsikian, Thracesian, and Bucellarian; that in A.D. 842 there were *seven*, Paphlagonia and Chaldia having been added (while Cappadocia, Charsianon, and Coloneia formed minor provinces) ; that in A.D. 863 there were *nine*, Cappadocia and Coloneia having been elevated to the rank of strategiai (while Charsianon and Seleucia were clisurarchies). At the last date, there were two naval Themes, Cibyrrhaeot and the Aegean ; and nine European Themes, Thrace, Macedonia, Hellas, Peloponnesus [created before A.D. 813, probably by Nicephorus I.], Thessalonica, Dyrrhachium, Cephalonia, Sicily, and the Klimata (Cherson) ; while Calabria was under a *dux*, and Dalmatia and Cyprus under archons. See Bury, History of the Eastern Roman Empire, Chap. VII., § 2.

(2) The next list is one included in the Kletorologion of Philotheus (see above, p. 541) : Const. Porph. De Cer., Bk. ii. c. 52, p. 713-14 and 727-8. The stratēgoi of the themes are enumerated with other officials in their order of precedence. The list of Philotheus represents the system of the early years of Leo VI.

(3) A table of the salaries of the governors of themes and clisurae, in the reign of Leo VI., included in c. 50 of the Second Book of the De Cerimoniis. But its editor lived in the reign of Romanus I. For he speaks of the governors of Sebastea, Lycandos, Seleucia, Leontocomis, as having been *at that time*, that is in Leo's reign, clisurarchs (ὡς ἂν τότε κλεισουράρχης). In other words, a list was used in which these four districts appeared as clisurarchies. Subsequently they were made themes (stretegiai) and the editor brought them up to date.

(4) The Treatise on the Themes. We must criticise Constantine for including Sicily and Cyprus, which did not belong to the Empire, and at the same time omitting Dalmatia, where there was the semblance of a province. Constantine raises the Optimaton to the dignity of a theme, but apologizes for doing so ; it is only a quasi-theme. In this he was justified ; for, though the Optimaton was not governed by a stratêgos but by a domesticus, and was not in a line with the other themes, it was a geographical province. But the most serious matter that calls for

---

[3] The Cibyrrhaeot Theme was not promoted to thematic dignity till the latter part of the eighth century. This is proved by the seal of "Theophilus, Imperial spathar and turmarch of the Cibyrrhaeots," see Schlumberger, Sigillographie byzantine, p. 261.

criticism is Constantine's inconsistency in stating definitely that Charsianon and Cappadocia are themes, and yet not enumerating them in his list. He discusses them under the heading of the Armeniac theme, but they should have headings of their own. This unaccountable procedure has led to the supposition that these two themes were temporarily merged in the Armeniac, out of which they had originally been evolved.

(5) A number of notices in the treatise de Administratione supply material for reconstructing a list of the themes c. A.D. 950-2.

(6) To these sources must be added, the seals of the various military and civil officers of the themes. M. Gustave Schlumberger's important work, Sigillographie byzantine (1884), illustrates the lists.

Sardinia passed away from the empire in the 9th century, but it seems to have never formed a regular theme. We have however traces of its East-Roman governors in the 9th cent. A seal of Theodotus, who was " hypatos and dux of Sardinia," has been preserved; and also seals of archons of Cagliari, with the curious style ΑΡΧΟΝΤΙ ΜΕΡΕΙΑΣ ΚΑΛΑΡΕΟΣ.

4. CONSTANTINE PORPHYROGENNETOS ON THE ADMINISTRATION OF THE EMPIRE—(P. 66-96)

The treatise of Constantine Porphyrogennetos on the Administration of the Roman Empire is one of the most interesting books of the Middle Ages, and one of the most precious for the early mediæval history of south-eastern Europe. The author wrote it as a handbook for the guidance of his son Romanus. Internal evidence allows us to infer the exact date of its composition : A.D. 948-952. See Bury, The Treatise De administrando imperio, in Byzantinische Zeitschrift, 15, 517 *sqq.*, where the work is analysed, the dates of a number of the chapters determined, and the sources investigated.

In his preface[1] Constantine promises his son instruction on four subjects. He will explain (1) which of the neighbouring nations may be a source of danger to the Empire, and what nations may be played off against those formidable neighbours; (2) how the unreasonable demands of neighbouring peoples may be eluded. (3) He will give a geographical and ethnographical description of the various nations and an account of their relations with the Empire ; and (4) enumerate recent changes and innovations in the condition and administration of the Empire. This programme is followed. A summary of the contents of the book will probably interest readers of Gibbon, and it may be divided under these four heads.

I. (Chaps. 1-12)

Chap. 1. Concerning the Patzinaks, and the importance of being at peace with them.

c. 2.   The relations of the Patzinaks with the Russians ('Ρῶs).

c. 3.   The relations of the Patzinaks with the Hungarians (Τοῦρκοι).

c. 4.   Conclusion, drawn from c. 3 and c. 4, that, if the Empire is on good terms with the Patzinaks, it need not fear Russian or Hungarian invasions, since the Russians and Hungarians cannot leave their countries exposed to the depredations of the Patzinaks.

c. 5.   Relations of the Patzinaks with the Bulgarians.

c. 6.   Relations of the Patzinaks with the Chersonites.

c. 7.   The sending of Imperial ambassadors to the Patzinaks via Cherson.

c. 8.   The route of Imperial ambassadors to the Patzinaks via the Danube and the Dnieper.

c. 9.   The route of Russians coming by water from Russia to Constantinople. An account of the Dnieper waterfalls (cp. below, Appendix 15).

c. 10.   Concerning Chazaria. War can be made on the Chazars with the help of their neighbours the Uzes, or of the Alans.

c. 11.   Concerning the forts of Cherson and Bosporus, and how the Alans can attack the Chazars.

[1] P. 66, ed. Bonn.

c. 12. Black Bulgaria (*i.e.* Bulgaria on the Volga) can also attack the Chazars. [Thus there are three checks on the Chazars : the Uzes, the Alans, and the Eastern Bulgarians.]

c. 13*a*. The nations which march on the Hungarians.

II. (c. 13) [2]

c. 13*b*. Showing how unreasonable requests on the part of barbarian nations are to be met. Three such requests, which an Emperor must never grant, are dealt with : (1) for Imperial robes and crowns (of the kind called καμελαύκια) ; (2) for Greek fire ; (3) for a bride of the Imperial family. The authority of Constantine the Great is in all cases to be quoted as a reason for refusal. For the exceptions to (3) see above, p. 91.

III. (c. 14-46)

c. 14. The genealogy of Mohammad.
c. 15. The race of the Fātimids.
c. 16. The date of the Hijra (ἔξοδος of the Saracens).
c. 17. An extract from the Chronicle of Theophanes on the death of Mohammad and his doctrine.
c. 18. Abū Bekr.
c. 19. Omar (at Jerusalem).
c. 20. Othmān.
c. 21, c. 22. Extracts from the Chronicle of Theophanes on the caliphates of Muāwia and some of his successors.
c. 23, c. 24. Iberia and Spain. (Quotations from old geographers.)
c. 25*a*. Extract from Theophanes on Aetius and Boniface (in the reign of Valentinian III.).
c. 25*b*. On the divisions of the Caliphate.[3]
c. 26. The genealogy of King Hugo of Burgundy (whose daughter married Romanus II.). [A.D. 949-50.]
c. 27. The theme of Lombardy, its principates, and governments. (An account of Italy, containing strange mistakes and curious transliterations.) [A.D. 948-9.]
c. 28. The founding of Venice.
c. 29. Dalmatia and the adjacent peoples. Gives an account of the Croats and Serbs; enumerates the coast cities of Dalmatia, names the islands off the coast, &c., &c.
c. 30. Account of the themes of Dalmatia. Historical and geographical information about the Croatian and Servian settlements. [A.D. 951-2.]
c. 31. More about the Croatians (Χρωβάτοι). ⎫
c. 32. More about the Serbs (Σέρβλοι). ⎪
c. 33. The Zachlums. ⎪
c. 34. The Terbuniates and Kanalites. ⎬ [A.D. 948-9.]
c. 35. The people of Dioclea. ⎪
c. 36. The Paganoi or Arentans. ⎭
c. 37. The Patzinaks, their country, history, and social organization. [A.D. 952 or 951.]
c. 38. The Hungarians, their migrations.
c. 39. The Kabars (a tribe of the Khazars).
c. 40. The tribes of the Kabars and Hungarians. More about the Hungarians and their later history.
c. 41. Moravia and its prince Sphendoplok.

[2] The first two paragraphs of c. 13, with the title of the chapter (p. 81, ed. B.), really belong to part i., and should be separated from the rest of c. 13 (which ought to be entitled περὶ τῶν ἀκαίρων αἰτήσεων τῶν ἐθνῶν).
[3] P. 113, l. 6 to end ; this piece ought to be a separate chapter.

5. THE BYZANTINE NAVY—(P. 95 sqq.)

The history of the Byzantine sea-power has still to be written. The chief sources (up to the tenth century) are Leo's *Tactics*, c. 19 (περὶ ναυμαχίας); the official returns of two expeditions to Crete in the tenth century, included in "Constantine's " *de Cerimoniis*, ii. c. 44 and 45; and (on naval commands under Basil I. and Leo VI.) Constantine, *De Adm. Imp.* c. 51. The chief modern studies that treat the subject are: Gfrörer, Das byzantinische Seewesen (c. 22 in his Byzantinische Geschichten, Bd. ii. p. 401 sqq.); C. de la Roncière, Charlemagne et la civilisation maritime au ixᵉ siècle (in Moyen Age, 2ᵉ sér. t. i. p. 201 sqq., 1897); C. Neumann, Die byzantinisch Marine; Ihre Verfassung und ihr Verfall. Studien zur Geschichte des 10 bis 12 Jahrhunderts (in Hist. Zeitschrift, B. 45, p. 1 sqq., 1898); Bury, The Naval Policy of the Roman Empire, in the Centenario della nascita di Michele Amari, vol. ii., 21 sqq. (Palermo), 1910. Add G. Schlumberger, Nicéphore Phocas, p. 52-66.

In the 6th century, after the fall of the Vandal kingdom, the Empire had no sea-foes to fear, and there was therefore no reason to maintain a powerful navy. The Mediterranean, though all its coasts were not part of the Empire, was practically once more an Imperial lake. This circumstance is a sufficient defence against the indictment which Gfrörer[1] brought against Justinian for neglecting the navy.

---

[4] See Finlay, ii. 354 sqq., and R. Garnett, the Story of Gycia in the Eng. Hist. Review, vol. xii. p. 100 sqq. (1897), where it is made probable that this episode belongs not to the Byzantine, but to an earlier period of the history of Cherson, probably to 36-16 B.C.

[1] *Op. cit.* p. 402-4.

The scene changed in the second half of the seventh century, when the Saracens took to the sea. The Emperors had to defend their coasts and islands against a hostile maritime power. Consequently a new naval organization was planned and carried out; and we must impute the merit of this achievement to the successors of Heraclius. We have indeed no notices, in any of our authorities, of the creation of the Imperial navies, but it is clear that the new system had been established before the days of Anastasius III. and Leo III. Under Theophilus and Michael III. the naval organization was remodelled and improved; the settlement of the Saracens in Crete, and their incursions in the Aegean, were facts which urgently forced the Emperors to look to their ships. From this time till the latter part of the eleventh century, the fleets of the Empire were the strongest in the Mediterranean.

There were two fleets, the Imperial and the Provincial (Thematic).[2] The several contingents of the provincial fleet supplied by the themes of the Cibyrrhaeots, the Aegean, and Samos,[3] were always ready for action, like the thematic armies. A standing Imperial fleet existed in the 9th century under the Amorian Emperors and was commanded by the Imperial Admiral ($\delta\rho o\nu\gamma\gamma\acute{a}\rho\iota os$ $\tau\hat{\omega}\nu$ $\pi\lambda o\hat{\iota}\mu\omega\nu$).[4] This admiral, the great Drungarios, was strictly commander of the Imperial fleet, but on occasions when the Imperial and Provincial fleets acted together he would naturally be the commander in chief. The admirals of the divisions of the Provincial fleet had the title of drungarios, when they were first instituted.[5] But they were afterwards promoted to the title of *stratēgos*.

The Imperial fleet in the tenth century was larger than the Provincial. Thus in the Cretan expedition of A.D. 902—for which Gibbon gives the total figures (p. 98)—the contingents of the fleets were as follows :—

Imperial Fleet		{ 60 dromonds. { 40 pamphylians.
Provincial Fleet	Cibyrrh. Theme	{ 15 dromonds. { 16 pamphylians.
	Samos ,,	{ 10 dromonds. { 12 pamphylians.
	Aegean ,,	{ 10 dromonds. { 7 pamphylians.
	Total	{ 35 dromonds. { 35 pamphylians.

(Helladic Theme, 10 dromonds.)

But, though the provincial squadrons formed a smaller armament, they had the advantage of being always prepared for war.

The causes of the decay of the Byzantine navy in the eleventh century have been studied by C. Neumann, in the essay cited above. He shows that the anti-military policy of the emperors in the third quarter of that century affected the navy as well as the army (cp. above, vol. 5, p. 222, n. 67). But the main cause was the Seljūk conquest. It completely disorganized the themes which furnished the contingents of the Provincial fleet. In the 12th century the Emperors depended on the navy of Venice, which they paid by commercial privileges.

The dromonds or biremes were of different sizes and builds. Thus the largest size might be manned by a crew of 300 to 290. Those of a medium size might hold, like the old Greek triremes, about 200 men. There were still smaller ones, which, besides a hundred oarsmen who propelled them, contained only a few

[2] A system seems to have been established whereby, in case Constantinople itself were threatened, a squadron of vessels could be got together for its defence without much delay. This was managed by an arrangement with the shipowners of the capital; but as to the nature of this arrangement (it seems to have been a sort of "indenture" system) we have only some obscure hints. Theophanes, *sub.* A.M. 6302, p. 487, ed. de Boor.

[3] Hellas also supplied naval contingents sometimes (as in the Cretan expedition, A.D. 902), but was not one of the fleet themes proper.

[4] Cp. Cedrenus, ii. p. 219, p. 227 ; Gfrörer, *op. cit.* p. 433.

[5] Cp. Leo, Tactics, 19, § 23, 24.

officers, steersmen, &c. (perhaps twenty in all). Then there was a special kind of biremes, distinguished by build, not by size, called Pamphylians, and probably remarkable for their swiftness. The Emperor Leo in his Tactics directs that the admiral's ship should be very large and swift and of Pamphylian build.[6] The pamphylians in the Cretan expedition of A.D. 902 were of two sizes: the larger manned by 160 men, the smaller by 130. The importance of these Pamphylian vessels ought, I think, to be taken in connexion with the importance of the Cibyrrhaeot theme (see above, App. 3), which received its name from Pamphylian Cibyra. We may suspect that Cibyra was a centre of shipbuilding.

Besides the biremes, ships with single banks of oars were used, especially for scouting purposes. They were called galleys.[7] The name dromond or " runner " was a general name for a warship and could be applied to the galleys [8] as well as to the biremes; but in common use it was probably restricted to biremes, and even to those biremes which were not of Pamphylian build.

Gibbon describes the ξυλόκαστρον, an erection which was built above the middle deck of the largest warships, to protect the soldiers who cast stones and darts against the enemy. There was another wooden erection at the prow, which was also manned by soldiers, but it served the special purpose of protecting the fire-tube which was placed at the prow.

The combustible substances on which the Byzantines relied so much, and apparently with good reason, in their naval warfare, were of various kinds and were used in various ways; and the confusion of them under the common name of Greek or marine fire (of which the chief ingredient was naphtha) has led to some mis-apprehensions. The simplest fire weapon was probably the " hand-tube " (χειρο-σίφων),[9] a tube full of combustibles, which was flung by the hand like a " squib " and exploded on board the enemy's vessel. The marines who cast these weapons were the " grenadiers " of the Middle Ages.[10] " Artificial fire "—probably in a liquid state—was also kept in pots (χύτραι), which may have been cast upon the hostile ships by engines. Such pots are represented in pictures of warships in an old Arabic Ms. preserved in the Bibliothèque Nationale, and reproduced by M. Schlumberger in his work on Nicephorus Phocas.[11] But there was another method of hurling " artificial fire ". Combustibles which exploded when they reached the enemy's ships were propelled through tubes, which were managed by a gunner (siphonator).

6. THE PAULICIAN HERESY—(C. LIV.)

In Gibbon's day the material for the origin, early history, and tenets of the Paulicians consisted of Bk. i. of the work of Photius on the Manichaeans, and the History of the Manichaeans by Petros Sikeliotes. The work of Photius was edited by J. C. Wolf in his Anecdota Graeca, i., ii. (1722);[1] but Gibbon did not consult it (above, chap. liv. note 1). There was further the account of the Bogomils in the *Panoplia* of Euthymius Zigabenus, a monk who lived under Alexius Comnenus and is celebrated in the Alexiad of Anna. A Latin translation was published by P. F. Zinos in 1555; the Greek text edited by a Greek monk (Metrophanes) in 1710. It may be read in Migne, P. G., vol. 130. The section on the Bogomils was edited separately by Gieseler in 1841-2.

[6] 19, § 37, τὸ δὴ λεγόμενον πάμφυλον. Gfrörer attempted to prove that the pamphylians were manned by chosen crews, and derived their name from πάμφυλος (" belonging to all nations "), not from the country. But the passage in the Tactics does not support this view. The admiral's ship is to be manned by ἐξ ἅπαντος τοῦ στρατοῦ ἐπιλέκτους; but this proves nothing for other pamphylians. But the large number of pamphylians in both the Imperial and Provincial fleet (cp. the numbers in the Cretan expedition, given above) disproves Gfrörer's hypothesis.

[7] Tactics, 19, § 10, γαλαίας ἢ μονήρεις.
[8] *Ibid.*   [9] Tactics, 19, § 57.
[10] Some Arab grenades (first explained by de Saulcy) still exist.   Cp. illustration in Schlumberger, Nicéphore Phocas, p. 59.
[11] P. 55, 57.
[1] Reprinted in Migne, P. G., vol. 102.

The documents which have come to light since are closely connected with the accounts of Photius and Peter ; they bring few new facts or fictions, but they bring material for criticizing the facts and fictions already known. (1) In 1849 Gieseler published a tract [2] of a certain Abbot Peter, containing an account of the Paulicians similar to that of Photius and Peter Sikeliotes (with whom Gieseler identified the author). (2) The publication of the chronicle of George Monachus by Muralt in 1859 showed that this chronicle had incorporated a similar account in his work.

We have then four documents, which presume one original account whereon all depend, directly or indirectly, if indeed one of them is not itself the original source. The problem of determining their relations to one another and the common original is complicated by (1) the nature of Photius, Bk. i., and (2) the variations in the Mss. of George Monachus.

The " First Book " of Photius falls into two parts : I. chaps. 1-15, which contains (a) a history of the Paulicians, chaps. 1-10 ; and (b) an account of earlier Manichaean movements, chaps. 11-14 ; II. chaps. 15-27, a history of the Paulicians, going over the same ground, but differently, and adding a brief notice of the revolt of Chrysocheir. Part I. (a) corresponds closely to the accounts of Abbot Peter, Peter Sik.,[3] and George Mon. ; and its Photian authorship seems assured by the testimony of Euthymius Zigabenus. Part II. was a distinct composition originally, and was tacked on to the Photian work. Thus " Photius " resolves itself into two documents, one Photian, the other Pseudo-Photian.

The credit of having made this clear belongs to Karapet Ter-Mkrttschian, who published in 1893 a treatise entitled " Die Paulikianer im byzantinischen Kaiserreiche und verwandte ketzerische Erscheinungen in Armenien ". This investigation, although it is ill arranged and leads to no satisfactory conclusion, has yet been of great use in opening up the whole question, as well as by publishing out-of-the-way evidence on various obscure Armenian sects. While Gieseler held that the treatise of the " Abbot Peter " was simply an extract from the work of Peter Sikeliotes, Ter-Mkrttschian tries to prove that the Abbot Peter is the oldest of our existing sources—the source of George Monachus, and Photius (Bk. 1 (a)). [The Armenian scholar further propounded (p. 122 sqq.) the impossible theory that Peter Sikeliotes wrote in the time of Alexius Comnenus—when the Paulician and Bogomil question was engaging the attention of the court and the public. It is impossible, because the date of the Vatican Ms. of the treatise of Peter is earlier. As to the Pseudo-Photian account, Ter-Mkrttschian holds that its author utilised the work of Euthymius Zigabenus (p. 8-9).]

After Ter-Mkrttschian came J. Friedrich (Der ursprüngliche bei Georgios Monachos nur theilweise erhaltene Bericht über die Paulikianer, published in the Sitzungsberichte of the Bavarian Academy, 1896, p. 67 sqq.). Friedrich denied that the Abbot Peter's tract was the source used by George Monachus ; and he published (p. 70-81), as the original source of all the extant accounts, the passage of George Monachus as it appears in the Madrid Ms. of the chronicle. In this Ms. the passage is more than twice as long than in other Mss., the additional matter consisting chiefly of directions to Christians how they were to refute a Paulician heretic when they met one. According to Friedrich, the work of the Abbot Peter is an extract from this treatise, preserved in the Madrid Ms. ; and the accounts in the other Mss. of George Monachus are likewise extracts.

But the view of Friedrich has been upset conclusively by C. de Boor, the only scholar who is thoroughly master of the facts about the Mss. of George Monachus. In a short paper in the Byzantinische Zeitschrift, vii. p. 40 sqq. (1898), de Boor has shown that the additional matter in the Madrid Ms. comes from an interpolator. George seems to have made a second version of his chronicle, and in revising it he consulted his sources, or some of them, again. This seems to be the only hypothesis on which the peculiarities of one Ms., Coislin. 305, can be explained. In the case of the Paulician passage, de Boor points out that in the first form of his work (represented by Coislin. 305) he used an original source ;

---

[2] Title: Πέτρου ἐλαχίστου μοναχοῦ Ἡγουμένου περὶ Παυλικιανῶν τῶν καὶ Μανιχαίων.
[3] Peter Sik. reverses the order of (a) and (b).

from which he again drew at more length on a second revision (represented by the other Mss.). It is therefore the second revision which we must compare with the work of the Abbot Peter in order to determine whether the Abbot Peter is the original source. De Boor does not decide this ; but calls attention to two passages which might seem to show that the Abbot used the second revision of George the Monk, and one passage which rather points to the independence of the Abbot. On the whole, the second alternative seems more probable.

The present state of the question may be summed up as follows : The (1) original sketch of the Paulician heresy, its origin and history—whereon all our extant accounts ultimately depend—is lost. This original work was used by (2) George the Monk (in the 9th century) for his chronicle ; (a) in Coislin. 305 we have a shorter extract, (b) in the other Mss. (and Muralt's text) we have a fuller extract. (3) The tract of the Abbot Peter was either taken from the second edition of George the Monk, or was independently extracted from the original work ; but it was not the original work itself. (4) It is not quite certain whether the treatise of Photius was derived from the derivative work of the Abbot Peter (so Ter-Mkrttschian ; and this is also the opinion of Ehrhard, in Krumbacher's Byz. Litt. p. 76 ; but Friedrich argues against this view, op. cit. p. 85-6) ; perhaps it is more likely that Photius also used the original work. (5) The position of Peter Sikeliotes is quite uncertain (see below). (6) The interpolation in the Madrid Ms. of George the Monk (see above) was added not later than the 10th century, in which period the Ms. was written. Then come (7) Euthymius Zigabenus in the Panoplia, c. 1100 A.D., and (8) Pseudo-Photius.

The unsolved problem touching Peter Sikeliotes would have no historical importance, except for his statements about his own mission to Tephrice, and the intention of the Paulicians of the east to send missionaries to Bulgaria, and the dedication of his work to an Archbishop of Bulgaria. He says that he himself was sent to Tephrice by Michael III. for the ransom of captives. But the title of the treatise is curious : Πέτρου Σικελιώτου ἱστορία . . . προσωποποιηθεῖσα ὡς πρὸς τὸν Ἀρχιεπίσκοπον Βουλγαρίας. The word προσωποποιηθεῖσα suggests that the historical setting of the treatise is fictitious. In denying the historical value of this evidence as to the propagation of Paulicianism in Bulgaria at such an early date, Ter-Mkrttschian (p. 13 sqq.) and Friedrich (p. 101-2) are agreed. According to the life of St. Clement of Bulgaria (ed. Miklosich, p. 34) the heresy did not enter the country till after Clement's death in A.D. 916 (Friedrich, ib.).

Ter-Mkrttschian endeavours to prove that the Paulicians were simply Marcionites. Friedrich argues against this view, on the ground of some statements in the text which he published from the Madrid Ms., where the creator of the visible world is identified with the devil. But these statements may have been interpolated in the tenth century from a Bogomil source.

On the Armenian Paulicians and cognate sects, see Döllinger's Beiträge zur Sektengeschichte des Mittelalters ; Ter-Mkrttschian's work, already cited ; and Conybeare's Key of Truth (see below). The basis of Döllinger's study was the treatise " Against the Paulicians " of the Armenian Patriarch John Ozniensis (published in his works, 1834, ed. Archer). Cp. Conybeare, op. cit. infra, App. iv. Ter-Mkrttschian has rendered new evidence accessible.

In his History of the Bulgarians,[4] Jireček gives the result of the investigations of Rački and other Slavonic scholars into the original doctrines of the Bogomils. (1) They rejected the Old Testament, the Fathers, and ecclesiastical tradition. They accepted the New Testament, and laid weight on a number of old apocryphal works. (2) They held two principles, equal in age and power : one good (a triune being = God) ; the other bad (= Satan), who created the visible world, caused the Fall, governed the world during the period of the Old Testament. (3) The body of Christ the Redeemer was only an apparent, not a real body (for everything corporeal is the work of Satan) ; Mary was an angel. The sacraments are corporeal, and therefore Satanic, symbols. (4) They rejected the use of

---

[4] Geschichte der Bulgaren, p. 176 sqq.

crucifixes and icons, and regarded churches as the abodes of evil spirits. (5) Only adults were received into their church ; the ceremony consisted of fasting and prayer—not baptism, for water is created by Satan. (6) They had no hierarchy; but an executive, consisting of a senior or bishop, and two grades of Apostles. (7) Besides the ordinary Christians there was a special order of the Perfect or the Good, who renounced all earthly possessions, marriage, and the use of animal food. These chosen few dressed in black, lived like hermits, and were not allowed to speak to an unbeliever except for the purpose of converting him. (8) No Bogomil was allowed to drink wine. (9) The Bulgarian Bogomils prayed four times every day and four times every night ; the Greek seven times every day, five times every night. They prayed whenever they crossed a bridge or entered a village. They had no holy days. (10) They had a death-bed ceremony (called in the west *la convenensa*). Whoever died without the advantage of this ceremony went to hell, the ultimate abode of all unbelievers. They did not believe in a purgatory.

We cannot, however, feel certain that this is a fair presentation of the Bogomil doctrines. It is unfortunate that none of their books of ritual, &c., are known to exist.

As early as the tenth century a schism arose in the Bogomil church. A view was promulgated that Satan was not coeval with God, but only a later creation, a fallen angel. This view prevailed in the Bulgarian church, but the Dragoviči clung to the old dualism. The modified doctrine was adopted for the most part by the Bogomils of the west (Albigenses, &c.) except at Toulouse and Albano on Lake Garda (Jireček, *op. cit.* p. 213).

The kinship of the Bogomil doctrines to the Paulician is obvious. But it has not been proved that they are historically derived from the Paulician ; though there are historical reasons for supposing Paulician influence.

Since the above was written, F. C. Conybeare published (1898) the Armenian text and an English translation of the book of the Paulicians of Thonrak in Armenia. This book is entitled the Key of Truth and seems to have been drawn up by the beginning of the ninth century. This liturgy considerably modifies our views touching the nature of Paulicianism, which appears to have had nothing to do with Marcionism, but to have been a revival of the old doctrine of Adoptionism according to which Jesus was a man and nothing more until in his thirtieth year he was baptized by John and the Spirit of God came down and entered into him ; then and thereby he became the Son of God. Of this Adoptionist view we have two ancient monuments, the *Shepherd of Hermas* and the *Acts of Archelaus*. The doctrine survived in Spain until the 8th and 9th centuries ; and this fact suggests the conjecture that it also lingered on in southern France, so that the heresy of the Cathars and Albigenses would not have been a mere imported Bogomilism, but an ancient local survival. Conybeare thinks that it lived on from early times in the Balkan peninsula, "where it was probably the basis of Bogomilism ".

There can be no doubt that Conybeare's discovery brings us nearer to the true nature of Paulicianism. In this book the Paulicians speak for themselves, and free themselves from the charges of Manichaeism and dualism which have been always brought against them. Conybeare thinks that *Paulician*, the Armenian form of *Paulian*, is derived from Paul of Samosata, whose followers were known to the Greeks of the 4th century as Pauliani. Gregory Magistros [5] (who in the 11th century was commissioned by the Emperor Constantine IX. to drive the Paulicians or Thonraki out of Imperial Armenia) states that the Paulicians " got their poison from Paul of Samosata," the last great representative of the Adoptionist doctrine. Conybeare suggests that, the aim of the Imperial government having been to drive the Adoptionist Church outside the Empire, the Paulians "took refuge in Mesopotamia and later in the Mohammedan dominions generally, where they were tolerated and where their own type of belief, as we see from the *Acts of Archelaus*,

[5] Conybeare publishes a translation of Letters of Gregory which bear on Paulicianism, in Appendix iii.

had never ceased to be accounted orthodox. They were thus lost sight of almost for centuries by the Greek theologians of Constantinople and other great centres. When at last they again made themselves felt as the extreme left wing of the iconoclasts—the great party of revolt against the revived Greek paganism of the eighth century—it was the orthodox or Grecised Armenians that, as it were, introduced them afresh to the notice of the Greeks" (Introduction, p. cvi.).

7. THE SLAVS IN THE PELOPONNESUS—(P. 73)

All unprejudiced investigators now admit the cogency of the evidence which shows that by the middle of the eighth century there was a very large Slavonic element in the population of the Peloponnesus.[1] The Slavonic settlements began in the latter half of the sixth century, and in the middle of the eighth century the depopulation caused by the great plague invited the intrusion of large masses. The general complexion of the peninsula was so Slavonic that it was called Sclavonia. The only question to be determined is, how were these strangers distributed, and what parts of the Peloponnesus were Slavized? For answering these questions, the names of places are our chief evidence. Here, as in the Slavonic districts which became part of Germany, the Slavs ultimately gave up their own language and exerted hardly any sensible influence on the language which they adopted ; but they introduced new local names which survived. It was just the reverse, as has been well remarked by Philippson, in the case of the Albanese settlers, who in the fourteenth century brought a new ethnical element into the Peloponnesus. The Albanians preserved their own language, but the old local names were not altered.

Now we find Slavonic names scattered about in all parts of the Peloponnesus ; but they are comparatively few on the Eastern side, in Argolis and Eastern Laconia. They are numerous in Arcadia and Achaia, in Elis, Messenia and Western Laconia. But the existence of Slavonic settlements does not prove that the old Hellenic inhabitants were abolished in these districts. In fact we can only say that a large part of Elis, the slopes of Taygetus, and a district in the south of Laconia, were exclusively given over to the Slavs. Between Megalopolis and Sparta there was an important town, which has completely disappeared, called Veligosti ; and this region was probably a centre of Slavonic settlers.

See the impartial investigation of A. Philippson, Zur Ethnographie des Peloponnes, in Petermann's Mittheilungen, vol. 36, p. 1 *sqq.* and 33 *sqq.*, 1890.

The conversion and Hellenization of the Slavs went on together from the ninth century, and, with the exception of the settlements in Taygetus and the Arcadian mountains, were completed by the twelfth century. At the time of the conquest of the Peloponnesus by Villehardouin, four ethnical elements are distinguished by Philippson : (1) Remains of the old Hellenes, mixed with Slavs, in Maina and Tzakonia (Kynuria), (2) Byzantine Greeks (*i.e.*, Byzantinized Hellenes, and settlers from other parts of the Empire) in the towns. (3) Greek-speaking Slavo-Greeks (sprung from unions of Slavs and Greeks). (4) Almost pure Slavs in Arcadia and Taygetus. The 2nd and 3rd classes tend to coalesce and ultimately become indistinguishable (except in physiognomy).

The old Greek element lived on purest perhaps in the district of north-eastern Laconia. The inhabitants came to be called Tzakones and the district Tzakonia ; and they developed a remarkable dialect of their own. They were long supposed to be Slavs. See A. Thumb, Die ethnographische Stellung der Zakonen (Indogerm. Forschungen, iv. 195 *sqq.*, 1894).

Fallmerayer, in harmony with his Slavonic theory, proposed to derive the name *Morea* from the Slavonic *more*, sea. This etymology defied the linguistic

---

[1] The thesis of Fallmerayer, who denied that there were any descendants of the ancient Hellenes in Greece, was refuted by Hopf (and Hertzberg and others) ; but all Hopf's arguments are not convincing. Fallmerayer's brilliant book stimulated the investigation of the subject (Geschichte der Halbinsel Morea im Mittelalter, 2 vols., 1830-6).

laws of Slavonic word-formation. Other unacceptable derivations have been suggested, but we have at last got back to the old mulberry, but in a new sense. ὁ Μορέας is formed from μορέα, "mulberry tree," with the meaning "plantation or region of mulberry trees" (= μορεών). We find the name first applied to Elis, whence it spread to the whole Peloponnesus; and it is a memorial of the extensive cultivation of mulberries for the manufacture of silk. This explanation is due to the learned and scientific Greek philologist, G. N. Hatzidakês (Byz. Zeitsch., 2, p. 283 sqq. and 5, p. 341 sqq.).

8. EARLY HISTORY OF THE BULGARIANS—(P. 136 sqq.)

Bulgaria and Russia are Slavonic countries, Bulgarian and Russian are Slavonic languages; but it is an important historical fact that the true Bulgarians and the true Russians, who created these Slavonic states, were not Slavs themselves and did not speak Slavonic tongues. The Russian invader was a Teuton (Scandinavian); he belonged, at all events, to the same Indo-European family as the Slavs whom he conquered. But the Bulgarian invader was a Tartar, of wholly different ethnic affinities from the people whom he subdued. It both cases the conqueror was assimilated, gradually forgot his own tongue, and learned the language of his subjects; in both cases he gave the name of his own race to the state which he founded. And both cases point to the same truth touching the Slavs: their strong power of assimilation, and their lack of the political instinct and force which are necessary for creating and organizing a political union. Both Bulgaria and Russia were made by strangers.

(1) We first met Bulgarians in the fifth century, after the break-up of the Empire of Attila. We then saw them settled somewhere north of the Danube— it is best to say roughly between the Danube and the Dnieper—and sometimes appearing south of the Danube. (2) We saw them next, a century later, as subjects of the Avar empire. We saw also (above, vol. 4, App. 15) that they were closely connected with the Utigurs and Kotrigurs. (3) The next important event in the history of the Bulgarians is the break-up of the Avar empire. In this break-up they themselves assisted. In the reign of Heraclius, the Bulgarian king Kur't revolts against the chagan of the Avars and makes an alliance with Heraclius, towards the close of that emperor's reign (c. 635-6).[1] At this time the Bulgarians (Onogundurs) and their fellows the Utigurs seem to have been united under a common king; Kur't is designated as lord of the Utigurs. (4) Soon afterwards under Kur't's second successor Esperikh, the Bulgarians crossed the Danube and made a settlement on the right bank near the mouth, at Oglos, marked by earth fortifications at S. Nikolitsel (near the ancient Noviodunum). This town was probably that which is mentioned in later times under the name of Little Preslav. The date of this movement to the south of the Danube appears from a native document (the Regnal List, see next Appendix) to be A.D. 659-60 (not as was usually supposed from a confused notice in Theophanes, c. A.D. 679).

The Bulgarians on the Danube had kinsfolk far to the east, who in the tenth century lived between the Volga and the Kama. They are generally known as the Bulgarians of the Volga, also as the Outer Bulgarians; their country was distinguished as Black Bulgaria[2] from White Bulgaria on the Danube. The city of these Bulgarians was destroyed by Timour, but their name is still preserved in the village of Bolgary in the province of Kasan. Towards the end of the ninth century the Mohammadan religion began to take root among the Bulgarians of the Volga, and the conversion was completed in the year A.D. 922. We have a good account of their country and their customs from the Arabic traveller Ibn Fozlan.[3]

[1] Nicephorus, p. 24, ed. de Boor. Nicephorus calls him Kuvrat "lord of the Unogundurs"; he is clearly the same as Kuvrat (or Κοβρᾶτος) lord of the "Huns and Bulgarians" mentioned below, p. 36; the Krovat of Theophanes and the Kur't of the old Bulgarian list (see next Appendix).

[2] Constantine Porph., De Adm. Imp. c. 12, ἡ μαύρη Βουλγαρία. Cp. Βελοχρωβατία (white Croatia), Μαυροβλαχία, &c.

[3] See C. M. Frahn, Aelteste Nachrichten über die Wolga-Bulgharen, in Memoirs of the Academy of St. Petersburg (series vi.), i. p. 550 (1832). Cp. Roesler, Romänische Studien, p. 242 sqq.

The Outer Bulgarians are to be distinguished from the Inner Bulgarians, who are identical with the Utigurs, in the neighbourhood of the Lake of Azov.

Roesler, Hunfalvy and others have sustained that the Bulgarians were not of Turkish, but of Finnish race. But they have not proved their case.[4]

For the customs of the Danubian Bulgarians which point to their Tartar origin, see the Responses of Pope Nicholas (in the ninth century) to the matters on which they consulted him.[5]

[For the Inner and Outer Bulgarians, cp. F. Westberg, Beiträge zur Klärung orientalischer Quellen über Osteuropa, i. and ii., in Izviestiia imp. Akad. Nauk. xi. 4, Nov. and Dec. 1899 ; and K analizu vostochnikh istochnikov o vostochnoi Evropie, 2 parts, in Zhurnal min. nar. prosvieshcheniia (N.S.) xiii. and xiv., 1908.]

9. LIST OF ANCIENT BULGARIAN PRINCES—(P. 139)

A curious fragment of an old list of Bulgarian princes from the earliest times up to A.D. 765, was edited by A. Popov in 1866 (Obzor Chronographov russkoi redaktsii, i. 25, 866). It is reproduced by Jireček (Geschichte der Bulgaren, p. 127). The list is drawn up in the language of the Slavs of Bulgaria, but contains non-Slavonic words, belonging to the tongue of the Bulgarian conquerors. Various attempts were made to explain the Bulgarian words (by Hilferding, Kunik, Radlov, Kuun), but none of them was satisfactory. A Greek inscription discovered some years ago at Chatalar, near the ancient Preslav, in Bulgaria, supplied a clue. The inscription records the foundation of Preslav by Omurtag, and dates it to the 15th indiction of the Greeks and the year σιγοραλεμ of the Bulgarians. The only 15th indiction in Omurtag's reign was A.D. 821-2. Now σιγοραλεμ is identical with *šegor alem* in our document. With this clue, the Bulgarian numerals in the List can be interpreted, and the List (which has evidently suffered considerable corruption) can be largely revised and reconstructed, as I have shown in my article : The Chronological Cycle of the Bulgarians, in Byzantinische Zeitschrift, xix. 127 *sqq.*, 1910. I believe I have demonstrated that the Bulgarians reckoned by a chronological cycle of 60 lunar years, of which the era was the year of the crossing of the Danube by Esperikh (A.D. 659-60, see last Appendix). *Šegor alem* is, for instance, year 58 of this cycle (*alem* = 50, *šegor* = 8). The other numerals are : 1 *vereni*, 2 *dvanš*, 3 *tokh*, 4 *somor*, 5 *dilom*, 6 *dokhs*, 9 *tek* (?), 10 *ekhtem*, 20 *al'tom*, 30 *tvirem*, 40 *vechem*, 60 *tutom*.

The translation of the document according to my revised text is as follows :—

[A.D. 159-450.] " Avitochol lived 300 years ; he belonged to the race of Dulo ; and his year was *dilom tvirem*.

[A.D. 450-554.] " Irnik lived 100 years and 8 ; he belonged to the race of Dulo ; and his year was *dilom tvirem*.

[A.D. 554-567.] " Gostun ruled as viceroy [for 13 years ; he belonged to the race of ; and his year was *tokh al'tem*.

[A.D. 567-579.] " (Anon.) ruled as viceroy] for 12 years ; he was of the race of Ermi ; and his year was *dokhs tvirem*.

[A.D. 579-637.] " Kur't reigned for 60 years ; he was of the race of Dulo ; but his year was *šegor věčem*.

[A.D. 637-640.] " Bezmêr 3 years ; he was of the race of Dulo ; and his year was *šegor věčem*.

" These 5 princes (k'nęz) held the principality on the other side of the Danube for 515 years, with shorn heads.

[A.D. 659.] " And then Esperikh, prince, came to (this) side of the Danube, where they are till this day.

[A.D. 640-660.] " Esperikh, prince 21 years ; he was of the race of Dulo; his year was *vereni alem*. ['Ασπαρουχ.]

[A.D. 660-687.] " (Anon.) reigned for 28 years ; he was of the race of Dulo ; and his year was *dvanš echtem*.

---

[4] For the Turkish side see Vámbéry, A magyarok eredete, cap. iv. p. 48 *sqq.*

[5] They will be found in any collection of Acta Conciliorum, *e.g.* in Mansi, vol. xv. p. 401 *sqq.*

[A.D. 687-696.] " [(*Anon.*) reigned for 9 years; he was of the race of Dulo; and his year was] *tvirem.*

[A.D. 696-719.] " Tervel 24 years; he was of the race of Dulo; his year was *tek vechem.* [Τερβέλης.]

[A.D. 719-729.] " [(*Anon.*) 10 years; he was of the race of Dulo; his year was *tokh ekhtem.*]

[A.D. 729-744.] " Sevar 15 years; he was of the race of Dulo; his year was *tokh al'tom.*

[A.D. 744-760.] " Kormisoš 17 years; he was of the race of Vokil; his year was *šegor tvirem.* [Κορμέσιος.]

" This prince changed the race of Dulo—that is to say Vichtun (?).

[A.D. 760-763.] " Telets 3 years; he was of the race of Ugain; and his year was *somor alem.* He too was of another race. [Τελέτζης.]

[A.D. 763-770.] " Vinech 7 years; he was of the race of Ukil; his year was *šegor alem.*

[A.D. 770 ?] " Umor 40 days; he was of the race of Ugil; his [year] was *dilom tatom.*" [Οὔμαρος.]

It is to be observed that Vinech is obviously identical with Sabinos (son-in-law of Kormisoš) whose elevation and deposition are recorded by Theophanes and Nicephorus. Baian (Paganos) was raised to the throne in his place. Nicephorus relates that Umar was set up by Sabinos as a rival of Baian, who is not recognised at all by the compiler of the Regnal List.

[My results are described and developed by V. N. Zlatarski, Imali si sŭ Blgaritie svoe lietobroenie, in Spisanie na Blgarskata akademiia na naukitie, I. 1, 1911.]

10. OLD BULGARIAN INSCRIPTIONS—(P. 140)

Stone records of Bulgarian khans of the ninth century, with Greek inscriptions, have been found in various parts of Bulgaria, and throw light upon obscure corners of Bulgarian history. Some of these memorials were found at Pliska, which is now known to be the name of the early Bulgarian capital. Pliska lay to the northeast of Shumla, close to the modern village of Aboba. The fortified town and the palatial residence within it were excavated some twelve years ago under the direction of Th. Uspenski and K. Shkorpil. The archæological results have been published as the xth volume of the Izviestiia of the Russian Archæological Institute at Constantinople, and in this publication most (not all) of the Greek Bulgarian inscriptions are collected. An account of Pliska will be found in Bury, History of the Eastern Roman Empire, chap. viii. § 1.

The most important inscriptions are records of Omurtag and his successor Malamir. One of them, mentioned above in Appendix 9, records the foundation of Preslav, the town which was to supersede Pliska, by Omurtag. Another, on a pillar of red marble preserved in a church at Trnovo, states that the same khan built a new house on the Danube, and a tomb halfway between this house and the old palace (at Pliska). The new house was probably at Kadykei, near Tutrakan (the ancient Transmarisea), an important point on the Danube, and the tomb has been identified with a mound at Mumdzhilar. The text of the inscription is given in a defective form by Jireček, Geschichte der Bulgaren, p. 148; it has been revised by Uspenski in his paper O drevnostiakh goroda Trnova in the Izviestiia of the Russian Archæological Institute at Constantinople, vii. 1. *sqq.*, 1902.

Another valuable inscription is one found at Suleiman-Keui, which records, as I have shown, the terms of the Thirty Years' Treaty which Omurtag concluded with the Emperor Leo V. in A.D. 815-6. The text will be found in Izviestiia, x. 220 *sq.*, and (with English translation) in Bury, The Bulgarian Treaty of A.D. 814, in English Historical Review, April, 1910.

11. THE NORTHERN LIMITS OF THE FIRST BULGARIAN KINGDOM —(P. 139)

There is evidence to show that the kingdom over which Esperikh and Crum ruled was not confined to the Lower Moesia, the country between the Danube and the Balkan range. There is no doubt that Bulgaria included Walachia and Bessarabia, and it is probable that it extended to the Dnieper, which was in the 8th and 9th centuries the western limit of the loose empire of the Khazars, until about the middle of the 9th century the Patzinaks pressed forward to the Dnieper, while the Hungarians occupied the lands farther west towards the Danube and curtailed the Bulgarian dominion. We have certain evidence for the extension of Bulgaria as far as the Dnieper in an inscription of the Khan Omurtag (cp. Bury, History of the Eastern Roman Empire, 366).

The extension of Bulgaria north of the Danube in the time of Crum is proved by a passage in the Anonymous writer of the ninth century, of whose work a fragment on the reign of Leo V. is preserved (p. 345 in the Bonn ed. of Leo Grammaticus). There we find " Bulgaria beyond the Danube " (ἐκεῖθεν τοῦ ῞Ιστρου ποταμοῦ) ; Crum transported a multitude of prisoners thither. This is borne out by the Bavarian geographer of the ninth century, who mentions the country of the Bulgarians as one of the countries *north* of the Danube.[1]

There is also reason to suppose that the Bulgarians exercised a loose supremacy in Transylvania. The chief evidence is the enumeration of a number of Dacian towns as belonging to the regions occupied by the Bulgarians, in the Ravennate Geographer ;[2] and the circumstance that the Bulgarians used to sell salt to the Moravians[3] (there being salt mines in Transylvania, and none in Bulgaria south of the Danube).

To an unbiassed inquirer the evidence certainly renders it probable that during the 8th century when the Avar monarchy was weak and soon about to yield to the arms of Charles the Great, the Bulgarians extended their power over the Slavs and Vlachs of Siebenbürgen. This was certainly what under the circumstances was likely to happen ; and the scanty evidence seems to point to the conclusion that it did happen. There is no reason to suppose that a part of the Bulgarian people settled in Siebenbürgen ; only that Siebenbürgen was more or less subject to the princes of Bulgaria during the ninth century until the Magyar invasion. Unfortunately, this question is mixed up with the burning Roumanian question ; and the Hungarians firmly reject the idea of a Bulgarian period in Siebenbürgen. The first active promulgator of the view seems to have been Engel,[4] and Hunfalvy devotes several pages to the task of demolishing the "képzelt tiszai Bolgárság," as he calls it, "the imaginary Bulgaria on the Theiss ".[5] The Roumanians welcome the notion of a northern Bulgaria, because it would explain the existence of the Bulgarian rite in the Roumanian church, and deprive the Hungarians of an argument for *their* doctrine, that the Roumanians are late intruders in Transylvania and carried the Bulgarian rite with them from the country south of the Danube.

For the temporary dominion of the Bulgarians in the regions of the Drave and Save, including the towns of Sirmium and Singidunum (Belgrade), in the ninth century, see Bury, *op. cit.* 365.

12. THE CONVERSION OF THE SLAVS—(P. 140)

It is remarkable that Gibbon has given no account of the Apostles of the Slavs, the brothers Constantine and Methodius ; whose work was far more important for the conversion of the Slavonic world to the Christian faith than that of Ulfilas for the conversion of the Germans. Little enough is known of the lives of these men, and their names were soon surrounded with discrepant traditions and legends in various countries—in Moravia and Bohemia, Pannonia and Bulgaria.

---

[1] Ad septentrionalem plagam Danubii. . . . Vulgarii, regio est immensa et populus multus habens civitates V. The others mentioned are Bohemia and Moravia ; and the three countries are described as regions " que terminant in finibus nostris ". See Schafarik, Slawische Altertümer, ed. Wuttke, ii. p. 673.

[2] Ed. Pinder and Parthey, p. 185.

[3] Annals of Fulda in Pertz, Mon. i. 408. Cp. Xénopol, Histoire des Roumains, i. p. 134.

[4] In his Geschichte des alten Pannoniens und der Bulgarei (1767).

[5] Magyarország Ethnographiája, p. 167 *sqq.*

There seems no reason to doubt that they were born in Thessalonica, and the date of the birth of Constantine, the elder of the two, probably falls about A.D. 827. In Thessalonica they were in the midst of Slavonic districts and had opportunities of becoming acquainted with the Slavonic language in their youth. Constantine went to Constantinople and became a priest. His learning won him the title of Philosopher and the friendship of Photius ; [1] but, when Photius started the doctrine of two souls in man, Constantine opposed him. It was probably soon after the elevation of Photius to the Patriarchate (Dec. A.D. 858) that Constantine, who had a gift for languages, went as a missionary to the Chazars (perhaps A.D. 860-1), who are said to have begged the Emperor to send them a teacher. While he was at Cherson, learning the Chazaric language, he " discovered " the remains of the martyr Pope Clement I., which he afterwards brought to Rome.[2] On his return from Chazaria he undertook a new mission. Christianity had already made some way among the Slavs of Moravia, through the missionary activity of the bishops of Passau. Thus Moravia seemed annexed to the Latin Church. But the Moravian king Rostislav quarrelled with his German and Bulgarian neighbours, and sought the political support of the Eastern Emperor. He sent ambassadors to Michael III., and asked, according to the legend, for a man who would be able to teach his flock the Christian faith in their own tongue. Constantine, by his knowledge of Slavonic and his missionary experience, was marked out as the suitable apostle ; and he went to Moravia, taking with him his brother Methodius (A.D. 864). They worked among the Moravians for about three and a half years, having apparently obtained the reluctant recognition of the bishop of Passau. Pope Nicholas summoned the two brothers (A.D. 867) to Rome, but died before their arrival ; and his successor Hadrian II. ordained Methodius a priest (A.D. 868). A premature death carried Constantine away at Rome (Feb. 14, A.D. 869) ; he assumed *Cyril* as a monastic name before his death. Methodius returned to Moravia. He was afterwards made bishop of Pannonia and died in 885.

The great achievement of Constantine or Cyril was the invention of a Slavonic alphabet. His immediate missionary work was in Moravia ; but by framing an alphabet and translating the gospels into Slavonic he affected, as no other single man has ever done, every Slavonic people. He did what Ulfilas did for the Goths, what Mesrob did for the Armenians, but his work was destined to have incomparably greater ecumenical importance than that of either. The alphabet which he invented (doubtless before A.D. 863) is known as the *glagolitic ;* and we have a good many early documents written in this character in various parts of the Slavonic world. But ultimately the use of it became confined to Istria and the Croatian coast ; for it was superseded by another alphabet, clearer and more practical. This later alphabet is known as the *cyrillic ;* and has been supposed—and is still supposed—by many to be the alphabet which Cyril invented. The cyrillic alphabet is undisguisedly Greek ; the letters are Greek uncials (capitals) with a few additional signs. The glagolitic, on the other hand, has deliberately disguised its origin from Greek cursive letters. This disguise doubtless facilitated and was intended to facilitate its reception by the Slavs. It is probable that Constantine, in his literary work, had his eye on Bulgaria ; for his translations, composed in Macedonian Slavonic, were unsuited for the Moravians, who spoke a different form of Slavonic (Slovák). Cp. Bury, History of the Eastern Roman Empire, 397 *sqq.*

Directly neither Cyril nor Methodius had anything to do with the conversion of Bulgaria. But the conversion of Bulgaria took place in their days ; the invention of the alphabet facilitated the conversion. The fact seems to be that, fearing that Boris, who had made an alliance with King Lewis the German in A.D. 862, would embrace Latin Christianity—a serious political danger for the Eastern Empire— Michael III. made a military demonstration in Bulgaria in the summer of A.D. 863, and induced Boris to consent to receive Christianity from Constantinople. In return

[1] Cp. the Preface of Anastasius to the Council of A.D. 869 ; Mansi, Conc. 16, 6.
[2] This is the subject of the Translatio S. Clementis (in Acta Sanctorum, March 9), possibly composed under the direction of the contemporary Gauderic, bishop of Velletri. It is an important source, and new light has been thrown on it by a letter of Anastasius to Gauderic, published by J. Friedrich in the Sitzungsberichte of the Bavarian Academy, Heft 3, 1892.

for this submission, a small district in Thrace was conceded to Bulgaria. (See Bury, *op. cit.*, 383 *sq.*) Boris was baptised ; the Emperor stood sponsor ; and he too the name of Michael. He then introduced Christianity forcibly among his people, executing fifty-two persons who resisted. The date of the conversion is A.D. 865. But it was not long before Boris turned away from Constantinople and sought to connect the Bulgarian Church with Rome. He sent envoys (A.D. 866) to Pope Nicholas I., with 106 questions, and the answers of the Pope,[3] which are preserved, throw some interesting light on Bulgarian customs. If the successor of Nicholas had shown tact and discretion, Bulgaria might have been won for the Latin Church ; but Hadrian II. tried the patience of Boris, and in A.D. 870 Bulgaria received an archbishop from Constantinople and ten bishoprics were founded. Boris sent his son Simeon to be educated at New Rome. It was not long before Slavonic books and the Slavonic liturgy were introduced into Bulgaria.

[Only a few works out of the enormous literature on the apostles of the Slavs need be mentioned. J. A. Ginzel, Geschichte der Slawenapostel Cyrill und Method, und der Slawischen Liturgie (1857). V. Jagić, article in the Zapiski of the Imperial Acad. of St. Petersburg, vol. li. (1886). L. K. Goetz, Gesch. der Slavenapostel Konstantinus und Methodius (1897). F. Pastrnek, Dějiny slovanských Apoštolii Cyrilla a Methoda (Prague, 1902). F. Snopek, Konstantinus—Cyrillus und Methodius, die Slavenapostel (Kremsier, 1911). A. Brückner, Thesen zur cyrillo—methodianischen Frage, in Archiv für slavische Philologie, 28, 229 *sqq.*, 1906. V. Jagić, Zur Entstehungs-geschichte der kirchenslavischen Sprache, 2 parts, in Denkschriften der k. Akad. der Wissenchaften in Wien, phil.-hist. Cl., 47, 1900. Cp. also the account in Bretholz's Geschichte Mährens.]

13. THE HUNGARIANS—(P. 143 *sqq.*)

The chief sources for the history of the Hungarians, before they took up their abode in Hungary, are (1) Leo, Tactics, c. 18, § 45 *sqq.* ; and Constantine Porphyrogennetos, De Adm. Imp., c. 38, 39, 40 ; (2) the accounts of Ibn Rusta, who wrote A.D. 912-13 and other Arabic writers ; (3) some notices in western chronicles of the ninth century ; (4) traditions in the native chronicles of Hungary. It has been proved that the chronicle of the Anonymous Scribe of King Béla,[1] which used to be regarded as a trustworthy source for early Hungarian history, is a " Machwerk " of the 13th century ; [2] but the author as well as Simon de Kéza (for his Chronicon Hungaricum) had some old sources, from which they derived some genuine traditions, which criticism can detect and may use with discretion. A collection of the texts of all the documents relating to early Hungarian history, with Hungarian translations, will be found in the volume published by the Hungary Academy of Sciences, entitled A Magyar Honfoglalás Kútfői, 1900.

The main questions in dispute with regard to the Hungarians and their early antiquity are two : concerning their ethnical affinity, and concerning the course of their wanderings from the most primitive habitation, to which they can be traced, up to their appearance between the Dnieper and the Danube. It may be said, I think, that we have not sufficient data to justify dogmatism in regard to either of these questions.

As to their ethnical position, are the Hungarians Turkish or Finnic ? Their language shows both elements ; and the two rival theories appeal to it. Those who maintain that the Hungarians are Turkish explain the Finnic part of the vocabulary by a long sojourn in the neighbourhood of the Voguls and Ostjaks ; while those who hold that they were brethren of the Voguls, Ostjaks, and Finns, explain the Turkish element by borrowings in the course of their subsequent wanderings. For the latter theory it must be said that the most elementary portion of the Hungarian vocabulary is undoubtedly related to the Vogul, Ostjak, and their kindred languages. This comes out clearly in the numerals, and in a large number of common words.[3] If we set side by side lists of Hungarian words which are

---

[3] Included in Collections of Acta Conciliorum.
[1] Best ed. by C. Fejérpataky (1892).
[2] R. Roesler, Romänische Studien, p. 147 *sqq.* On the Hungarian sources, see H. Marczali, Ungarns Geschichtsquellen, 1882.
[3] As a specimen, for comparison of the Hungarian language with the Vogulic which

clearly Turkish or clearly Finnic, leaving out all the unconvincing etymologies which the rival theorists serve up, it is difficult to avoid concluding that the primitive element is the Finnic.[4]

It seems most probable that the Magyars at one time dwelled in Jugria, in the regions of the Irtish, where they were neighbours of the Voguls. They migrated southward and in the beginning of the 9th century they had taken up their abode within the empire of the Chazars, and they amalgamated with themselves a Chazaric tribe called the Kabars (Const. Porph. c. 39), who became part of the Hungarian nation. These Kabars, according to Constantine, taught the Hungarians the tongue of the Chazars. Hence the upholders of the Finnic origin of the Turks can explain the Turkish element in Hungarian by a known cause, the coalition with the Kabars. But it is probable that, before the incorporation of the Kabars, the Hungarians had been seriously affected by the influence of Turkish neighbours.

According to the text of Constantine, the Hungarians abode only three years in "*Lebedia* near Chazaria". This land of Lebedia was probably between the Don and the Dnieper; and it has been supposed that the date of their sojourn there was between A.D. 830 and 840. For it is in the reign of Theophilus, c. 837-39, that they first appear upon the horizon of the Eastern Empire (cp. the Continuation of George Mon. [*i.e.* Simeon Magister, p. 818, ed. Bonn], where they are called Οὔγγροι, Οὔννοι, and Τοῦρκοι). But "three years" in Constantine's text is certainly wrong. It may be an error for "thirty-three" or "thirty or some much higher figure"; in any case the sojourn in Lebedia was much longer than three years. Cp. Bury, History of the Eastern Roman Empire, 491. At some time in the ninth century, the Patzinaks drove the Hungarians westward, and they established themselves in Atelkuzu (probably meaning "between rivers"), as they called the land between the Dnieper and the Danube. The date of the migration has been recently assigned by Westberg to A.D. 825 or thereabouts (K analizu vostochnik istochnikov o vostochnoi Evropie, in Zhurnal min. nar. prosv., 49 *sqq.*, March, 1908); but I believe it to have been later, c. A.D. 860 (see Bury, *op. cit.* 489 *sq.*).

The same enemies, who had driven the Hungarians out of Lebedia, drove them again out of Atelkuzu. The Patzinaks were themselves subdued by a combined attack of the Khazars and the Uzes; they crossed the Dnieper, dislodged the Hungarians, who were thus driven farther west; and this was the cause of their settlement in the modern Hungary. The event happened fifty-five years before Constantine wrote c. 37 of his De Administratione; *i.e.*, probably in A.D. 896 or 897 (cp. Appendix 4). The notice in Regino's Chronicle under the year 889 anticipates subsequent events.[5]

is the most closely connected, I subjoin the names of the first seven numerals (the original numerical system seems to have been heptadic):—

1 : H. egy, V. äk, äkve.
2 : H. két, kettö, V. kit, kiti.
3 : H. harm, V. korm.
4 : H. négy, V. neljä.
5 : H. öt, V. ät.
6 : H. hat, V. kat.
7 : H. hét, V. sat.

(The Turkish words for these numbers are totally different.)

The word for 100 is the same in both languages : H. száz, V. sat (Finnish sata). But 10 is quite different : H. tiz, V. lau (and Finnish kymmen differs from both); 20 coincides : H. húsz, V. kus; and in the first part of the compound which signifies 8 (probably $10 - 2$) the same element occurs : H. *nyol*-cz, V. *n'ala*-lu; so for 80 : H. nyolcz-van, V. n'ol-sat (? $100 - 20$).

[4] For the Finnic origin, P. Hunfalvy, Magyarország Ethnographiája, 1876, and Die Ungern oder Magyaren, 1881. For the Turkish, A Vámbéry, A Magyarok eredete, 1882. For the "Ugrian" or Finnic or "Ugro-Finnic" languages, see Budenz in the 4th vol. of Bezzenberger's Beiträge zur kunde der Indogermanischen Sprachen (Die Verzweigung der Ugrischen Sprachen).

[5] On the chronology see E. Dümmler, Geschichte des ostfränkischen Reichs (ed. 2), iii. 438 *sqq.*—Count Géza Kuun in his Relationum Hungarorum—Hist. Antiquissima, vol. i. (1893) p. 136, tries to establish, instead of a three years' sojourn in Lebedia and a long (fifty years') sojourn in Atelkuzu, a long sojourn in Lebedia (up to A.D. 889) and a short (seven or eight years') sojourn in Atelkuzu.

It is to the Hungarians as they were when they lived in Atelkuzu, and not to the contemporary Hungarians who were already settled in their final home, that the description of Ibn Rusta (taken from some earlier writer) applies. He describes their land as between the Patzinaks and the Esegel tribe of the Bulgarians (clearly a tribe north of the Danube, in Walachia or Bessarabia). Ibn Rusta further mentions two rivers in the land of the Hungarians, one of them greater than the Oxus. Probably the Dnieper and the Bug are meant.[6] He says that *Kende* is the title of their king, but there is another dignitary whom all obey in matters connected with attack or defence, and he is entitled *jila*. The *kende* clearly corresponds to the prince or ἄρχων of Constantine Porphyrogennetos (c. 40) ; Arpad, for example, was a kende. The *jila* is also mentioned by Constantine, as γυλᾶς ; to whom, however, he ascribes the function of a judge.[7] It seems that the title kende was adopted by the Hungarians from the Chazars ; for the title of the Chazar viceroy was *kenderchagan*.

Ibn Rusta says that the Hungarians rule over the Slavs, whom they oppress with heavy burdens ; that they worship fire ; that they trade in the slaves whom they capture, with Greek merchants at Kerch.[8]

A word may be said about the name Magyar. It was doubtless the name of a single tribe before it became the name of the whole people ; and the third of the 8 tribes enumerated by Constantine (c. 40 *ad init.*) was that of Megerê (τοῦ Μεγέρη). In another place (c. 37) Constantine mentions the Μάζαροι as dwelling in the 9th century near the river Ural, where they were neighbours of the Patzinaks ; but without any suggestion that they are identical with the Hungarians, whom he always calls *Turks*. I suspect that the Bashkirs are really meant. Hungarian scholars find other traces of the Magyar name between the Black Sea and the Caspian : thus there are two villages called Mājār in the neighbourhood of Derbend ;[9] and K. Szabó wished to detect the word in Muager (Μουαγέρην), whom Theophanes mentions as the brother of Gordas, king of the Huns near the Cimmerian Bosporus. It has also been proposed to connect the name of a fortress, τὸ Ματζάρων (mentioned by Theophylactus Simocatta, ii. 18, 7). It was on the confines of the Roman and Persian dominions, but its exact position is unknown.

14. ORIGIN OF RUSSIA—(P. 154 *sqq.*)

No competent critic now doubts that the Russians, who founded states at Novgorod and Kiev, subdued the Slavonic tribes and organized them into a political power,—who, in short, made Russia,—were of Scandinavian or Norse origin. It is therefore unnecessary to treat this matter any longer as a disputed question ; it will be enough to state briefly the most important evidence. The evidence is indeed insuperable, except to insuperable prejudice.

(1) The early writers, who mention the Russians, attest their identity with the Scandinavians or Normans. The first notice is in the Annales Bertiniani *ad ann.* 839 (Pertz, Mon. i. 484), Rhos vocari dicebant . . . comperit eos gentis esse Sueonum. Liutprand (Antapodosis, v. 15) says that they were Normans (nos vero a positione loci nominamus Nordmannos). The chronicle of "Nestor" identifies them with the Varangians, or regards them as belonging to the Varangian stock ; and for the Scandinavian origin of the Varangians see above, p. 155, note 58. The Continuation of George the Monk (Symeon Magister) states more generally and less accurately their German origin (= Theoph. Contin. p. 423, ed. B., ἐκ Φράγγων γένους)[1].

---

[6] Cp. Kuun, *op. cit.* vol. i. p. 184.

[7] Constantine mentions a third dignitary, inferior to the γυλᾶς, and entitled *karchas*.

[8] The notice of Ibn Rusta will be found in some shape in all recent works on the early Hungarians, *e.g.* in Kuun's work cited above, vol. i. p. 165-6, and in the Hungarian collection mentioned in the first paragraph of this Appendix. Ibn Rusta used to be called Ibn Dasta.

[9] Kuun, *op. cit.* p. 93.

[1] Yakūbi, writing before the end of the 9th cent., calls the heathen who attacked Seville in 844 *Rūs*.

(2) The Russians spoke Norse, not Slavonic. This is proved by the 9th chapter of Constantine's de Administratione, where the Russian and Slavonic languages are distinguished ('Ρωσιστί and Σκλαβινιστί), and the Russian names of the water-falls are unmistakably Scandinavian. See below, Appendix 15.

(3) The names of the first Russian princes and the names of the signatories of the first Russian treaties are Norse. *Riurik* is the old Norse Hraerikr; *Oleg* is Helgi; *Olga*, Helga; *Igor* ('Ιγγωρ; Inger in Liutprand) is Ingvarr. The boyars who are named in the treaty of A.D. 912 (Nestor, c. 22) are Kary (Swedish, Kari), Ingeld (O. Norse, Ingialdr), Farlof (Swedish), Vermud (O. Norse, Vermunde), Rulaf (O. Norse, Hrodleifr), Ruald (O. Norse, Hroaldr), Goud (cp. Runic Kudi), Karn (Scandinavian), Frelal (O. N., Fridleifr), Rouar (O. N., Hroarr), Trouan (O. N., Droandr), Lidouf (O. N., Lidufr ?), Fost (Swedish). There remain two uncertain names, Aktevou and Stemid. Similarly the large proportion of the names in the treaty of 945 (c. 27) are Scandinavian.

(4) The Finnish name for Sweden is *Ruotsi*, the Esthonian is *Rôts;* and we can hardly hesitate to identify this with the name of Russia; Old Slavonic Rous', Greek 'Ρώs.[2] The name (neither Finnish nor Slavonic) is derived by Thomsen from the Scandinavian *rods* (rods-menn=rowers, oarsmen) ; the difficulty is the dropping out of the dental in Rous, 'Ρώs.

Thus the current opinion which prevailed when the Russians first appeared on the stage of history ; the evidence of their language ; the evidence of their names ; and the survival of the ancient meaning of the Russian name in Finnic, concur in establishing the Scandinavian origin of the Russians.

For a development of these arguments and other minor evidence see V. Thomsen's work, The Relations between Ancient Russia and Scandinavia, and the Origin of the Russian State (Ilchester Lectures), 1877 ; E. Kunik, Die Berufung der Schwedischen Rodsen durch die Finnen und Slaven, 1844 ; and see Mémoires of the Imperial Academy of Russia, vii. sér. 22, p. 279 *sqq.* and 409 *sqq.*; Bestuzhev-Riumin, Russkaia Istoriia (vol. i.), 1872 ; Pogodin, O proizkhozhdenii Rusi, 1825, Drevniaia Russkaia Istoriia, 1871, and other works. The two most eminent op-position advocates were: Ilovaiski, Razyskaniia o nachalie Rusi, 1876, and Istoriia Rossii (Part 1, Kiev period), 1876 ; and Gedeonov, Izsliedovaniia o variazhskom voprosie, 1862, Variagi i Rus', 1876.

15. THE WATERFALLS OF THE DNIEPER—(P. 159)

In the 9th chapter of his Treatise on the Administration of the Empire, Con-stantine Porphyrogennetos gives a most interesting description of the route of Russian merchants from Novgorod (Νεβογαρδάs) to Constantinople, by way of Kiev and the Dnieper, and enumerates the rapids of this river, giving in each case both its Russian and its Slavonic name. This passage is of high importance, for it shows that the language which Constantine meant by Russian ('Ρωσιστί) was Scandi-navian and not Slavonic. Vilhelm Thomsen of Copenhagen in his Ilchester lectures on "Relations between Ancient Russia and Scandinavia, and the Origin of the Russian State" (1877) has supplied an excellent commentary.

1st waterfall is called Essupê ('Εσσουπῆ) in both languages, with the meaning *sleepless* (μὴ κοιμᾶσθαι). It follows that the two names sounded nearly alike to Constantine. The Slavonic for "do not sleep" would be *ne spi* (and perhaps 'Εσσουπῆ in an error for Νεσσουπῆ) ; and Professor Thomsen says that the corresponding phrase in Old Norse would be *sofeigi* or *sofattu*. This is not quite satisfactory.

2nd waterfall is (*a*) in Russian, Ulvorsi (Οὐλβορσί), and (*b*) in Slavonic, Ostro-vuniprach ('Οστροθουνίπραχ), with the meaning, the islet of the fall ; (*a*) =holm-fors ; (*b*) =ostrov' nii prag (islet-fall).

3rd waterfall is called Gelandri (Γελανδρί), which in Slavonic means noise of the fall. Only one name is given, and it is said to be Slavonic. But it

---

[2] 'Ρώs is the exact equivalent of Nestor's Rous', which is a collective tribe name = "the Russians". 'Ρωσία, Russia, was formed from 'Ρώs, and the Russian name Rossiia was a later formation on Greek analogy.

obviously represents the Norse participle *gellandi*, "the echoing"; so that the Slavonic name (probably nearly the same as the modern name *zvonets* with the same meaning) is omitted. Constantine's usual formula is Ῥωσιστίμὲν . . . Σκλαβανιστὶ δὲ; but in this place he changes it: τὸν λεγόμενον Γελανδρί, ὃ ἑρμηνεύεται Σκλαβινιστὶ ἦχος φραγμοῦ. I would suggest that ζβινιτς or σβινιτς or something of the kind fell out after Σκλαβινιστί.

4th waterfall is Aeifor (᾽Αειφόρ, so in Paris Ms. 2009) in Russian, and Neasit (Νεασήτ) in Slavonic,—so called, Constantine says, because pelicans make their nests in the stones. The old Slavonic for pelican closely resembles Νεασήτ, but the fall cannot have been called pelican; this must have been a misinterpretation. Thomsen very ingeniously suggests that the true name corresponded to the modern *Nenasytets* and meant insatiable (a name appropriate to the nature of this rapid); while Aeifor (eiforr) meant ever-forward, ever-precipitate.

5th waterfall is Varuforos (βαρουφόρος) in Russian, Vulne prach (βουλνηπράχ) in Slavonic; "because it forms a great lake," or, if we read δίνην for λίμνην, "because it forms a great vortex". Both words can be recognised at once as meaning "wave-fall".

6th waterfall is Leanti (Λεάντι) in Russian, Verutze (Βερούτζη) in Slavonic, meaning "the seething of water" (βράσμα νεροῦ). Verutze is obviously from *v'rieti*, to boil. Thomsen explains Leanti as the participle *hlaejandi*, laughing. In this case the meanings of the two names are not identical.

7th waterfall is Strukun (Στρούκουν, so in Paris Ms. 2009) in Russian, Napreze (Ναπρεζή) in Slavonic, meaning a small waterfall. Thomsen identifies Strukun with Norse *strok*, Swedish *struk*, a rapid current (especially where narrow—as in the case of this rapid); and suggests that the Slavonic name might be connected with *brz*, quick. I suspect that (Να-) πρεζή represents a diminutive of *porog*, *prag* (waterfall).

16. THE ASSISES OF JERUSALEM—(P. 330)

It is agreed by most competent critics of the present century that Godfrey of Bouillon neither drew up the Assises of Jerusalem as they have come down to us nor put into writing any code of law whatever. This is the opinion of such special students of the Crusades as Wilken, Sybel, Stubbs, Kugler, and Prutz; and it has been very forcibly put by Gaston Dodu in his Histoire des Institutions monarchiques dans le royaume Latin de Jérusalem 1099-1291 (1894). In the first place, we find no mention of such a code in contemporary sources; the earliest authorities who mention it are Ibelin and Philip of Novara in the 13th century. Then, supposing such a code had been compiled, it is hard to understand why it should have been placed in the Holy Sepulchre and why the presence of nine persons should have been necessary to consult it. For the purpose of a code is that it should be referred to without difficulty. Thirdly, the remark of William of Tyre as to the experience of Baldwin III. in judicial matters makes distinctly against the existence of a code. He says: juris consuetudinarii quo regnum regebatur Orientale, plenam habens experientiam: ita ut in rebus dubiis etiam seniores regni principes eius consulerent experientiam et consulti pectoris eruditionem mirarentur (xvi. 2, cp. on Amalric i. xix. 2). The expression "the customary law by which the kingdom was governed" suggests that no code existed.

Fourthly, if the code existed, what became of it? Ibelin and Philip of Novara say that it was lost when Jerusalem was taken by Saladin in 1187. But the circumstances of that capture are inconsistent with the probability of such a loss. There were no military excesses and Saladin allowed the inhabitants a delay of forty days to sell or save their property before he entered the city (Ernoul, c. 18; cp. Dodu, p. 45). It is highly unlikely that the Christians would have failed to rescue a possession so valuable and portable as their Code. The Patriarch could not have overlooked it when he carried forth the treasures of the churches (as

Ibn al-Athīr mentions). And, if it were unaccountably forgotten, we should have to suppose that Saladin caused it to be destroyed afterwards when it was found. And had he done so, it is highly unlikely that the act would not have been mentioned by some of the Frank chroniclers.

The conclusion is that the kings of Jerusalem in the twelfth century did not give decisions according to a code drawn up at the time of the foundation of the kingdom, but themselves helped to build up a structure of Customary Law, which in the following century was collected and compiled in the book of the Assises by John Ibelin, A.D. 1255.

This book of Ibelin has not come down to us in its original form. There were two redactions : (1) at Nicosia in Cyprus in 1368 under the direction of an assembly of Cypriote lords, and (2) in the same place in 1531, by a commission appointed by the Venetian government. Both these rehandlings introduced a number of corrections into the *Assise de la haute cour*.

The *Assises de la cour des bourgeois* stands on a different footing. This work seems to have existed perhaps from the end of the twelfth century. It was not *supposed* to have been destroyed in 1187; it was not, so far as we know, edited by Ibelin ; nor was it revised at Nicosia in 1368. (Cp. Dodu, p. 54, 55.)

The study of the Assises of Jerusalem may now be supplemented by the Assises of Antioch, preserved in an Armenian version, which has been translated into French (published by the Mekhitarist Society, Venice, 1876).

How far is the policy of Godfrey of Bouillon represented in the Assises? In answer to this question, the observations of Stubbs may be quoted :—[1]

" We trace his hand in the prescribing constant military service (not definite or merely for a certain period of each year), in the non-recognition of representation in inheritance, in the rules designed to prevent the accumulation of fiefs in a single hand, in the stringent regulations for the marriages of widows and heiresses. These features all belonged to an earlier age, to a time when every knight represented a knight's fee, and when no fee could be suffered to neglect its duty ; when the maintenance of the conquered country was deemed more important than the inheritances of minors or the will of widows and heiresses. That these provisions were wise is proved by the fact that it was in these very points that the hazard of the Frank kingdom lay. . . . Other portions of the Assises are to be ascribed to the necessities of the state of things that followed the recovery of Palestine by the Saracens ; such, for instance, as the decision how far deforcement by the Turks defeats seisin ; and were of importance only in the event of a reconquest."

17. THE ACCIAJOLI—(P. 506)

If Gibbon had been more fully acquainted with the history of the family of the Acciajoli, he would have probably devoted some pages to the rise of their fortunes. They rose to such power and influence in Greece in the 14th century that the subjoined account, taken from Finlay (vol. iv. p. 157 *sqq.*)—with a few additions in square brackets—will not be out of place.

" Several members of the family of Acciajoli, which formed a distinguished commercial company at Florence in the thirteenth century, settled in the Peloponnesus about the middle of the fourteenth, under the protection of Robert, king of Naples. Nicholas Acciajoli was invested, in the year 334, with the administration of the lands which the company had acquired in payment or in security of the loans it had made to the royal House of Anjou ; and he acquired additional possessions in the principality of Achaia, both by purchase and grant, from Catherine of Valois, titular empress of Romania and regent of Achaia for her son prince Robert. [It is disputed whether he was her lover.] The encroachments of the mercantile spirit on the feudal system are displayed in the concessions obtained by Nicholas Acciajoli in the grants he received from Catherine of Valois. He was invested with the power of mortgaging, exchanging, and selling his fiefs,

[1] Itinerarium Regis Ricardi (Rolls series), Introduction, p. xc., xci.

without any previous authorisation from his suzerain. Nicholas acted as principal minister of Catherine during a residence of three years in the Morea ; and he made use of his position, like a prudent banker, to obtain considerable grants of territory. He returned to Italy in 1341 and never again visited Greece; but his estates in Achaia were administered by his relations and other members of the banking house at Florence, many of whom obtained considerable fiefs for themselves through his influence.

"Nicholas Acciajoli was appointed hereditary grand seneschal of the kingdom of Naples by queen Jeanne, whom he accompanied in her flight to Provence when she was driven from her kingdom by Louis of Hungary. On her return he received the rich country of Amalfi, as a reward for his fidelity, and subsequently Malta was added to his possessions. He was an able statesman and a keen political intriguer ; and he was almost the first example of the superior position the purse of the moneyed citizen was destined to assume over the sword of the feudal baron and the learning of the politic churchman. Nicholas Acciajoli was the first of that banking aristocracy which has since held an important position in European history. He was the type of a class destined at times to decide the fate of kingdoms and at times to arrest the progress of armies. He certainly deserved to have his life written by a man of genius, but his superciliousness and assumption of princely state, even in his intercourse with the friends of his youth, disgusted Boccaccio, who alone of Florentine contemporaries could have left a vivid sketch of the career which raised him from the partner of a banking-house to the rank of a great feudal baron and to live in the companionship of kings. Boccaccio, offended by his insolence, seems not to have appreciated his true importance as the type of a coming age and a new state of society ; and the indignant and satirical record he has left of the pride and presumption of the mercantile noble is by no means a correct portrait of the Neapolitan minister. Yet even Boccaccio records in his usual truthful manner that Nicholas had dispersed powerful armies, though he unjustly depreciates the merit of the success, because the victory was gained by combinations effected by gold, and not by the headlong charge of a line of lances. [Boccaccio dedicated his *Donne illustri* to Niccolo's sister Andrea, the countess of Monte Oderisio.]

"Nicholas Acciajoli obtained a grant of the barony and hereditary governorship of the fortress of Corinth in the year 1358. He was already in possession of the castles of Vulcano [at Ithome], Piadha near Epidauros, and large estates in other parts of the Peloponnesus. He died in 1365 ; [1] and his sons Angelo and Robert succeeded in turn to the barony and government of Corinth. Angelo mortgaged Corinth to his relative [second cousin], Nerio Acciajoli, who already possessed fiefs in Achaia, and who took up his residence at Corinth on account of the political and military importance of the fortress as well as to enable him to administer the revenues of the barony in the most profitable manner.

"Nerio Acciajoli, though he held the governorship of Corinth only as the deputy of his relation, and the barony only in security of a debt, was nevertheless, from his ability, enterprising character, great wealth, and extensive connexions, one of the most influential barons of Achaia ; and, from the disorderly state of the principality he was enabled to act as an independent prince."

"The Catalans were the constant rivals of the Franks of Achaia, and Nerio Acciajoli, as governor of Corinth, was the guardian of the principality against their hostile projects. The marriage of the young countess of Salona [whose father Count Lewis died 1382] involved the two parties in war. The mother of the bride was a Greek lady ; she betrothed her daughter to Simeon [Stephen Ducas], son of the prince of Vallachian Thessaly ; and the Catalans, with the two Laurias at their head, supported this arrangement. But the barons of Achaia, headed by Nerio Acciajoli, pretended that the Prince of Achaia as feudal suzerain of Athens was entitled to dispose of the hand of the countess. Nerio was determined to bestow

---

[1] [There is great memorial of Niccolo at Florence, the Gothic Certosa San Lorenzo. Gregorovius calls it "the first monument of historical relations between Florence and Greece"; for just as Pisa used her revenue from Constantinople to build her cathedral, Niccolo devoted moneys from Greece to build San Lorenzo. His tomb is to be seen in a subterranean chapel.]

the young countess, with all her immense possessions, on a relative of the Acciajoli family, named Peter Sarrasin.[1] The war concerning the countess of Salona and her heritage appears to have commenced about the year 1386 [1385]. The Catalans were defeated ; and Nerio gained possession of Athens, Thebes, and Livadea."

" About the commencement of the year 1394 Ladislas, king of Naples conferred on him by patent the title of Duke of Athens—Athens forming, as the king pretended, part of the principality of Achaia."

Nerio died in 1394. His illegitimate son Antonio inherited Thebes and Livadia, and wrested to himself the government of Athens, which Nerio's will had placed under the protection of Venice on behalf of his daughter (the wife of Count Tocco of Cephalonia). Under Antonio "Athens enjoyed uninterrupted tranquillity for forty years. The republic of Florence deemed it an object worthy of its especial attention to obtain a commercial treaty with the duchy, for the purpose of securing to the citizens of the republic all the privileges enjoyed by the Venetians, Catalans, and Genoese." The conclusion of this treaty is almost the only event recorded concerning the external relations of Athens during the long reign of Antonio. The Athenians appear to have lived happily under his government : and he himself seems to have spent his time in a joyous manner, inviting his Florentine relations to Greece, and entertaining them with festivals and hunting parties. Yet he was neither a spendthrift nor a tyrant ; for Chalcocondylas, whose father lived at his court, records that, while he accumulated great wealth with prudent economy, he at the same time adorned the city of Athens with many new buildings. He died in 1435, and was succeeded by Nerio II., grandson of Donato, the brother of Nerio I.

[Buchon, Nouvelles Recherches, vols. i. and ii. : L. Tanfani, Niccolo Acciajoli, 1863 ; Hopf, De Historiæ Ducatus Atheniensis Fontibus ; Gregorovius, Geschichte der Stadt Athen im Mittelalter, vol. ii.]

18. THE ISLAND DYNASTIES AFTER THE LATIN CONQUEST—(P. 505)

The facts about the history of the Greek islands during the 13th, 14th and 15th centuries were enveloped in obscurity, and fictions and false hypotheses were current, until the industry of C. Hopf drew the material from the archives of Vienna and Venice. His publications rendered the work of Buchon and Finlay obsolete so far as the islands are concerned. He won the right of referring with contempt to Buchon's schönrednerische Fabeleien und Finlays geistreich-unkritischer Hypothesenwust. The following list of the island-lordships is taken from his Urkunden und Zusätze zur Geschichte der Insel Andros und ihrer Beherrscher in dem Zeitraume von 1207 to 1566, published in the Sitzungsberichte of the Vienna Academy, 1856, vol. 21, p. 221 sqq.

Corfu.	Venetian 1207-c. 1214; to Despotate of Epirus c. 1214-1259 ; King Manfred and Filippo Chinardo 1259-1267 ; Neapolitan 1267-1386 ; Venetian 1386-1797.
Cefalonia, Zante, Ithaca.	Despotate of Epirus 1205-1337 ; Greek Empire 1337-1357 ; the Tocchi 1357-1482.
Santa Maura.	Despotate of Epirus 1205-1331 ; Giorgi 1331-1362 ; the Tocchi 1362-1482.
Paxo.	With Cefalonia 1205-1357 ; St. Ippolyto 1357-1484 ; Ugoth (Gotti) 1484-1527. With Cerigotto 1527-1797.
Cerigo (Cythera).	The Venieri 1207-1269; the Monojanni 1267-1309 ; the Venieri 1309-1797.

[1] [His own brother-in-law ; for he was married to Agnes Saraceno.]

Cerigotto.	The Viari 1207-1655; the Foscarini and Giustiniani 1655-1797.
Salamis.	With Athens.
Aegina.	With Carystos 1205-1317; Aragonese 1317-c. 1400; Cavopena c. 1400-1451; Venetian 1451-1537.
Delos, Gyaros, Cythnos, (Patmos).	With Naxos. [Sanudo allowed Patmos, the apostle's island, to preserve its independence.]
Tinos and Miconos.	The Ghisi 1207-1390; Venetian 1390-1718. (Held in fief by Venetian counts belonging to the houses of Bembo, Quirini, and Fabieri 1407-1429.)
Andros.	The Dandoli 1207-1233; the Ghisi 1233-c. 1250; the Sanudi c. 1250-1384; the Zeni 1384-1437; the Sommaripa 1437-1566.
Syra.	With Naxos.
Zia (Ceos).[1]	$\frac{1}{4}$: The Giustiniani 1207-1366; the da Coronia 1366-1464; the Gozzadini 1464-1537.
	$\frac{1}{4}$: The Michieli 1207-1355; the Premarini 1355 forward.
	$\frac{1}{2}$: The Ghisi 1207-1328; the Premarini 1328-1375.
	$\frac{9}{16}$: The Premarini 1375-1537.
	$\frac{3}{16}$: The Sanudi 1375-1405; the Gozzadini 1405-1537.
Serfene (Seriphos).[1]	$\frac{1}{4}$: the Michieli 1207-1537.
	$\frac{1}{4}$: the Giustiniani 1207-c. 1412; the Adoldi 1412 forward.
	$\frac{1}{2}$: the Ghisi 1207-1334; the Bragadini 1334-1354; the Minotti 1354-1373; the Adoldi 1373-1432; the Michieli 1432-1537.
Thermia (Cythnos).	The Sanudi 1207-c. 1320; the Castelli c. 1322-1331; the Gozzadini 1331-1537.
Sifanto (Siphnos), Sikino, Polycandro (Pholegandros).	The Sanudi 1207-1269 (titular 1341; the Grimani titular 1341-1537); Greek Empire 1269-1307; the da Coronia 1307-1464; the Gozzadini 1464-1617.
Milos and Cimolos.	The Sanudi 1207-1376; the Crispi 1376-1566.
Santorin (Thera) and Therasia.	The Barozzi 1207-1335; with Naxos 1335-1477; the Pisani 1477-1487; with Naxos 1487-1537.
Namfio (Anaphe).	The Foscoli 1207-1269; Greek Empire 1269-1307; the Gozzadini 1307-1420; the Crispi 1420-1469; the Barbari 1469-1528; the Pisani 1528-1537.
Nio (Anaea).	The Sanudi 1207-1269; Greek Empire 1269-1292; the Schiavi 1292-c. 1320; with Naxos c. 1320-1420; collateral branch of the Crispi 1420-1508; the Pisani 1508-1537.
Paros and Nausa.	With Naxos 1207-1389; the Sommaripa 1389-1516; the Venieri 1516-1531; the Sagredi 1531-1537.
Antiparos.	With Paros 1207-1439; the Loredani 1439-c. 1490; the Pisani 1490-1537.

[1] Ceos and Seriphos were under the Greek Empire from 1269 to 1296.

Naxos.	The Sanudi 1207-1362; the Dalle Carceri 1362-1383; the Crispi 1383-1566.
Scyros, Sciathos, ⎱ Chelidromi. ⎰	The Ghisi 1207-1269; Greek Empire 1269-1455; Venetian 1455-1537.
Scopelos.	The Ghisi 1207-1262; the Tiepoli 1262-1310; the Greek Empire 1310-1454; Venetian 1454-1538.
Negroponte.	$\frac{1}{3}$: the dalle Carceri 1205-1254; the Da Verona 1254-1383; the Sommaripa 1383-1470.
	$\frac{1}{3}$: the Peccorari 1205-1214; the dalle Carceri 1214-c. 1300; the Ghisi c. 1300-1390; Venetian 1390-1470.
	$\frac{1}{3}$: The da Verona 1205-1383; the da Noyer 1383-1470.
Carystos (in Negroponte).	The dalle Carceri 1205-c. 1254; the Cicons c. 1254-1292; the da Verona, 1292-1317; Aragonese 1317-1365; Venetian 1365-1386; the Giustiniani 1386-1404; Venetian 1404-1406; the Giorgi 1406-1470.
Lemnos.	The Navigajosi (with these, subsequently, the Gradenighi and Foscari) 1207-1269; Greek Empire 1269-1453; the Gattilusj 1453-1462.
Lesbos.	The Greek Empire 1205-1355; the Gattilusj 1355-1462.
Chios, Samos.	With Constantinople (Empire of Romania) 1205-1247; with Lesbos 1247-1303; the Zaccaria 1303-1333; Greek Empire 1333-1346; the joint stock company of the Giustiniani, in 14 and more branches, 1346-1566.
Nikaria (Icaria).	The Beazzani 1205-1333; with Chios 1333-1481; the Knights of St. John 1309-1521.
Stampali (Astypalaea).	The Quirini 1207-1269; Greek Empire 1269-1310; the Quirini and Grimani 1310-1537.
Amorgos.	The Ghisi 1207-1267; Greek Empire 1269-1296 [? 1303]; the Ghisi 1296-1368; $\frac{1}{2}$: the Quirini 1368-1537; $\frac{1}{2}$: the Grimani 1368-1446; the Quirini 1446-1537.
Nisyros, Piscopia, Calchi.	With Rhodes 1205-1306; the Assanti 1306-1385; with Rhodes 1385-1521.
Rhodes.	Gavalas 1204-1246; Greek Empire 1246-1283; the Aidonoghlii 1283-1309; the Knights of St. John 1309-1521.
Scarpanto (Carpathos).	With Rhodes 1204-1306; the Moreschi 1306-1309; the Cornari 1309-1522.
Candia.	Montferrat 1203-1204; Venetian 1204-1669.

[See further Hopf's Chroniques gréco-romanes inédites on peu connues (1873), genealogical tables at the end, and his Griechische Geschichte (cited above, App. 1, *ad fin.*); on Carystos, his art. in the Sitzungsber. of the Vienna Acad., 11, p. 555 *sqq.* (1853); on Andros, *ib.*, 16, p. 23 *sqq.* (1855); on Chios, his article on the Giustiniani in Ersch and Gruber's Enzyklopädie, vol. 68, p. 290 *sqq.*, 1859 (cp. T. Bent, The Lords of Chios, Eng. Hist. Rev., 4, p. 467 *sqq.* (1889), and W. Miller, The Zaccaria of Phocaea and Chios (1275-1329), Journal of Hellenic Studies, 31, 1911 ; on the Archipelago Hopf's Veneto-byzantinische Analekten, 1860, and his article on the Ghisi in Ersch and Gruber, vol. 64, p. 336 *sqq.*, 1857 ; on Negroponte, see J. B. Bury, The Lombards and Venetians in Euboea, in Journal of Hellenic Studies, 7, p. 309 *sqq.*, 8, p. 194 *sqq.*, 9, p. 91 *sqq.* (1886-8) ; L. de Mas-Latrie in the Rev. de l'Orient Latin, 1, p. 413 *sqq.* (1893).]

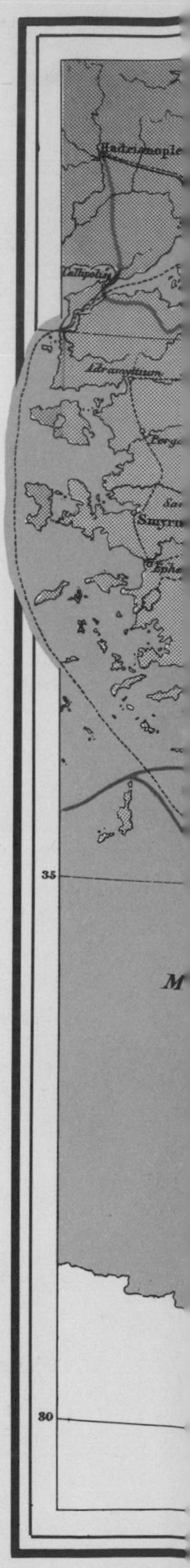

Hadrianople

Gallipoli

Abrundium

Pergamus

Smyrna

Ephesus

35

30

M

MAP ILLUSTRATING
THE CRUSADES
———— Route of Godfrey and 1st Crusaders
·······Route of Conrad III, Lewis VII, and
2nd Crusaders
———— Route of Emperor Frederick, Richard I,
Philip II, and 3rd Crusaders